Children's Well-Being: Indicators and Research

Volume 25

Series Editor

Asher Ben-Arieh, Paul Baerwald School of Social Work & Social Welfare, The Hebrew University of Jerusalem, Jerusalem, Israel

Editorial Board Members

J. Lawrence Aber, New York University, New York, USA
Johnathan Bradshaw, University of York, York, UK
Ferran Casas, University of Girona, Girona, Spain
Ick-Joong Chung, Duksung Women's University, Seoul, Korea (Republic of)
Howard Dubowitz, University of Maryland, Baltimore, USA
Ivar Frønes, University of Oslo, Oslo, Norway
Frank Furstenberg, University of Pennsylvania, Philadelphia, USA
Robbie Gilligan, Trinity College Dublin, Dublin, Ireland
Robert M. George, University of Chicago, Chicago, USA
Ian Gough, University of Bath, Bath, UK
An-Magritt Jensen, Norwegian University of Science and Technology, Trondheim, Norway
Sheila B. Kamerman, Columbia University, New York, USA
Jill. E Korbin, Case Western Reserve University, Cleaveland, USA
Dagmar Kutsar, University of Tartu, Tartu, Estonia
Kenneth C. Land, Duke University, Durham, USA
Bong Joo Lee, Seoul National University, Seoul, Korea (Republic of)
Jan Mason, University of Western Sydney, Sydney, Australia
Kristin A. Moore, Child Trends, Maryland, USA
Bernhard Nauck, Chemnitz University of Technology, Chemnitz, Germany
Usha S. Nayar, Tata Institute of Social Sciences, Mumbai, India
Shelley Phipps, Dalhousie University, Halifax, NS, Canada
Jackie Sanders, Massey University, Palmerston North, New Zealand
Giovanni Sgritta, University of Rome, Rome, Italy
Thomas S. Weisner, University of California, Los Angeles, USA
Helmut Wintersberger, University of Vienna, Vienna, Austria

This series focuses on the subject of measurements and indicators of children's well being and their usage, within multiple domains and in diverse cultures. More specifically, the series seeks to present measures and data resources, analysis of data, exploration of theoretical issues, and information about the status of children, as well as the implementation of this information in policy and practice. By doing so it aims to explore how child indicators can be used to improve the development and the well being of children.

With an international perspective the series will provide a unique applied perspective, by bringing in a variety of analytical models, varied perspectives, and a variety of social policy regimes.

Children's Well-Being: Indicators and Research will be unique and exclusive in the field of measures and indicators of children's lives and will be a source of high quality, policy impact and rigorous scientific papers.

More information about this series at http://www.springer.com/series/8162

Ziba Vaghri • Jean Zermatten •
Gerison Lansdown • Roberta Ruggiero
Editors

Monitoring State Compliance with the UN Convention on the Rights of the Child

An Analysis of Attributes

Editors
Ziba Vaghri
University of New Brunswick
Saint John, Canada

Jean Zermatten
Centre for Children's Rights Studies
University of Geneva
Geneva, Switzerland

Gerison Lansdown
Carleton University
Ottawa, Canada

Roberta Ruggiero
Centre for Children's Rights Studies
University of Geneva
Geneva, Switzerland

ISSN 1879-5196 ISSN 1879-520X (electronic)
Children's Well-Being: Indicators and Research
ISBN 978-3-030-84646-6 ISBN 978-3-030-84647-3 (eBook)
https://doi.org/10.1007/978-3-030-84647-3

© The Editor(s) (if applicable) and The Author(s) 2022. This book is an open access publication.
Open Access This book is licensed under the terms of the Creative Commons Attribution 4.0 International License (http://creativecommons.org/licenses/by/4.0/), which permits use, sharing, adaptation, distribution and reproduction in any medium or format, as long as you give appropriate credit to the original author(s) and the source, provide a link to the Creative Commons license and indicate if changes were made.
The images or other third party material in this book are included in the book's Creative Commons license, unless indicated otherwise in a credit line to the material. If material is not included in the book's Creative Commons license and your intended use is not permitted by statutory regulation or exceeds the permitted use, you will need to obtain permission directly from the copyright holder.
The use of general descriptive names, registered names, trademarks, service marks, etc. in this publication does not imply, even in the absence of a specific statement, that such names are exempt from the relevant protective laws and regulations and therefore free for general use.
The publisher, the authors, and the editors are safe to assume that the advice and information in this book are believed to be true and accurate at the date of publication. Neither the publisher nor the authors or the editors give a warranty, expressed or implied, with respect to the material contained herein or for any errors or omissions that may have been made. The publisher remains neutral with regard to jurisdictional claims in published maps and institutional affiliations.

This Springer imprint is published by the registered company Springer Nature Switzerland AG.
The registered company address is: Gewerbestrasse 11, 6330 Cham, Switzerland

Foreword

This book is part of a long-standing period of the work of an international team of experts that has been encouraged and supported by the United Nations Committee of the Rights of the Child and it successive chairpersons since its inception. This period has commenced with the *Indicators of General Comment 7* (also known as the Early Childhood Rights Indicators) and resulted in the development of the *GlobalChild Platform*, a comprehensive child rights monitoring platform. During our tenure as the chairs of the UN CRC Committee, we have worked with this team and supported and guided their work.

As the past and present Chairs of the CRC, we have borne witness to the fact that—in spite of the progress in many areas—there is still insufficient understanding about what the rights of children entail and how to interpret and implement them. Thirty years after the adoption of the CRC by the UN General Assembly, children's rights continue to be violated routinely and repeatedly in countries throughout the world. There is an urgent and pressing need for tools that can facilitate a better understanding of legislative and policy development in support of different rights of children and the implementation and monitoring of these structures vis-à-vis the child outcomes. This publication has been produced to contribute to better understanding in that process.

Additionally, by identifying the key constituent attributes of each article and providing a succinct overview of the relevant jurisprudence, this book will contribute to the Committee's scrutiny of States Parties and provide a framework for the implementation and monitoring of those rights at the national level. As a result, we believe that the information presented in this book will benefit children and all stakeholders of children's rights, in all 196 countries that are States Parties to the Convention on the Rights of the Child.

Chairpersons of the Committee on the Rights of the Child (2006-2021)
Egbert Doek 2001–2007
Yanghee Lee 2007–2011
Kristen Sandberg, 2013–2015
Benyam Dawit Mezmur, 2015–2017
Renate Winter, 2017–2019
Luis Ernesto Pedernera Reyna 2019-2021

Foreword

The United Nations Convention on the Rights of the Child—the most widely ratified human rights treaty in the world—entered into force in 1990. This was a major milestone, but only the beginning of the long journey toward greater respect for the rights of children and young people. Three decades of reporting from the States Parties to the Committee on the Rights of the Child have revealed many gaps between the promise of the convention and the reality on the ground for children. As with other human rights treaties, the full realization of children's rights under the convention remains a challenge.

This book is an article-by-article analysis of almost all substantive, organizational, and procedural provisions of the Convention. These analyses have identified the main attributes to be considered when measuring a State's progressive implementation of the convention. As a global advocate for children's right to freedom from violence, this will be a valuable resource for my mandate, as it will be for other child rights advocates. Providing clarity on what child rights obligations mean in practice is an essential part of effective advocacy with States Parties.

I acknowledge the significant contribution of many child rights experts and advocates to creating this book. While it is a stand-alone publication, it will also serve as an important compendium and reference tool for people working with the *GlobalChild* platform—the first comprehensive child rights monitoring platform to collect data and track change in securing children's rights using the human rights-based approach to indicators. I believe both the platform and this textbook will contribute to a better interpretation as well as enforcement of all rights under the convention, including children's rights to protection from violence, neglect, exploitation, and abuse.

Najat Maalla M'jid
Special Representative of UN Secretary-General on Violence against Children

Contents

1 **Introduction** 1
  Gerison Lansdown, Roberta Ruggiero, Ziba Vaghri,
  and Jean Zermatten

Part I General Principles

2 **Article 2: The Right to Non-discrimination** 11
  Gerison Lansdown

3 **Article 3: The Best Interest of the Child** 21
  Roberta Ruggiero

4 **Article 6: The Rights to Life, Survival, and Development** 31
  Ziba Vaghri

5 **Article 12: The Right to Be Heard** 41
  Gerison Lansdown

Part II Civil and Political Rights

6 **Article 7: The Right to a Name, Nationality, and to Know
  and Be Cared for by Parents** 51
  Adem Arkadas-Thibert and Gerison Lansdown

7 **Article 8: The Right to Preservation of Identity** 59
  Adem Arkadas-Thibert

8 **Article 13: The Right to Freedom of Expression** 65
  Gerison Lansdown and Ziba Vaghri

9 **Article 14: The Right to Freedom of Thought, Conscience,
  and Religion** 75
  Roberta Ruggiero

10 Article 15: The Right to Freedom of Association and Assembly . . .   85
    Gerison Lansdown

11 Article 16: The Right to Protection of Privacy   93
    Christian Whalen

12 Article 17: The Right to Access to Diverse Sources
    of Information 103
    Gerison Lansdown

Part III Family Environment and Alternative Care Rights

13 Article 5: The Right to Parental Guidance Consistent with the
    Evolving Capacity of the Child 117
    Gerison Lansdown

14 Article 9: The Right Not to Be Separated from Parents 125
    Christian Whalen

15 Article 10: The Right to Family Reunification 135
    Christian Whalen

16 Article 11: The Right to Protection from Illicit Transfer
    and Non-return of Children Abroad 145
    Ziba Vaghri and Gavin Kotze

17 Article 18: Rights Concerning Parental Responsibility 153
    Roberta Ruggiero

18 Article 20: Rights Concerning Children Deprived of Their
    Family Environment 163
    Adem Arkadas-Thibert and Gerison Lansdown

19 Chapter 7: Article 21—Adoption 171
    Gerison Lansdown

20 Article 25: The Right to Periodic Review of Treatment
    and All Other Circumstances of Placement 183
    Gerison Lansdown and Ziba Vaghri

Part IV Disability, Health, and Welfare Rights

21 Article 23: The Rights of Children with Disabilities 193
    Gerison Lansdown

22 Article 24: The Right to Health 205
    Christian Whalen

23	**Article 26: The Right to Benefit from Social Security** . . . . Roberta Ruggiero	217
24	**Article 27: The Right to a Standard of Living Adequate for Physical, Mental, Spiritual, Moral, and Social Development** . . . Adem Arkadas-Thibert and Gerison Lansdown	227
25	**Article 33: The Right to Protection from Illicit Use of Narcotic Drugs and Psychotropic Substances** . . . . Damon Barrett and Ziba Vaghri	237

Part V Education, Leisure, and Cultural Activities Rights

26	**Article 28: The Right to Education** . . . . Gerison Lansdown and Ziba Vaghri	247
27	**Article 29: The Aims of Education** . . . . Gerison Lansdown, Katherine Covell, and Ziba Vaghri	261
28	**Article 30: Cultural, Religious, and Linguistic Rights of Minority or Indigenous Children** . . . . Adem Arkadas-Thibert and Roberta Ruggiero	271
29	**Article 31: The Rights to Rest, Play, Recreation, and Cultural and Artistic Activities** . . . . Gerison Lansdown	281

Part VI Protection Measures from Violence

30	**Article 19: The Right to Protection from All Forms of Violence** . . . Christian Whalen	293
31	**Article 37: Prohibition of Torture, Capital Punishment, and Arbitrary Deprivation of Liberty** . . . . Christian Whalen	303
32	**Article 39: The Right to Physical and Psychological Recovery of Child Victims** . . . . Ziba Vaghri, Katherine Covell, and Gerison Lansdown	313

Part VII Protection Measures from Exploitation

33	**Article 32: The Right to Protection from Economic Exploitation and Hazardous Activities** . . . . Gerison Lansdown	327
34	**Article 34: The Right to Protection from All Forms of Sexual Exploitation and Sexual Abuse** . . . . Adem Arkadas-Thibert	339

Part VIII Protection Measures for Children in Vulnerable Situations

35 **Article 36: The Right to Protection from Other Forms of Exploitation** 349
   Adem Arkadas-Thibert

36 **Article 22: The Right to Protection for Refugee and Asylum-Seeking Children** 357
   Christian Whalen

37 **Article 35: Prevention of Abduction, Sale, and Trafficking** 369
   Adem Arkadas-Thibert and Gerison Lansdown

38 **Article 38: The Right to Protection from Armed Conflict** 379
   Gerison Lansdown

39 **Article 40: The Rights in the Juvenile Justice Setting** 391
   Roberta Ruggiero

Part IX General Measures of Implementation

40 **Article 1: Definition of a Child** 407
   Gerison Lansdown and Ziba Vaghri

41 **Article 4: States Parties' Obligations** 413
   Roberta Ruggiero

42 **Articles 42 and 44(6): Making the Convention and States Parties' Compliance Widely Known** 425
   Christian Whalen and Gerison Lansdown

Appendix 431

Chapter 1
Introduction

Gerison Lansdown, Roberta Ruggiero, Ziba Vaghri, and Jean Zermatten

This publication is one of the outcomes of over a decade of work, under the auspices of the United Nations Committee on the Rights of the Child, to explore how to monitor and evaluate States Parties' compliance with the obligations they undertook when they ratified the UN Convention on the Rights of the Child (the Convention). A full account of the project work to date has been provided in Vaghri, Krappmann, and Doek's article 'From the Indicators of General Comment No. 7 to GlobalChild' (2019). Grounded in that foundational work, this book relies on that project work to provide a conceptual framing of the Convention, through the identification of the attributes of each right that provides the basis for the development of indicators against which to measure progress.

Although there are multiple sets of benchmarks and indicators already developed to measure many aspects of children's well-being, for example, in the fields of health and education, less investment has been made in understanding how to assess implementation of children's rights.[1] There is a dearth of widely recognised indicators, for example, in respect of children's civil and political rights or rights to protection from violence or exploitation. It is perhaps helpful to elaborate why this matters.

---

[1] See, for example, Bradshaw et al. (2007).

G. Lansdown (✉)
Carleton University, Ottawa, ON, Canada

R. Ruggiero (✉) · J. Zermatten (✉)
Centre for Children's Rights Studies, University of Geneva, Geneva, Switzerland
e-mail: roberta.ruggiero@unige.ch; jean.zermatten@childsrights.org

Z. Vaghri (✉)
University of New Brunswick Saint John, Saint John, NB, Canada
e-mail: ziba.vaghri@unb.ca

Well-being is a description of a sense of physical, social, intellectual, and emotional health in relation to self, others, and the environment. It is a concept which has its roots in understanding the level of life quality and happiness (Ben-Arieh & Frønes, 2011, p. 461). Child well-being can be measured through a focus on the child's material well-being, their housing and social environment, their educational status and quality of school life, their susceptibility to risk behaviours, and their health and safety. Ben-Arieh argues that indicators relevant to human well-being must encompass aspects of life from the biological, psychological, and social perspectives. However, well-being is an end in itself and offers no prescription on how it should be achieved: its focus is on the outcomes in children's lives. A well-being perspective can be understood as reaching beyond the confines of a human rights treaty that is ultimately a legal document. It demands a stronger focus on the internal child than is often articulated within the rights framework.

By contrast, children's rights are a set of universal standards or norms rooted in formal entitlement to their fulfilment and corresponding obligations on those providing that guarantee. They can be measured both in terms of actions undertaken by duty bearers on behalf of children and the consequent impact of those actions in ensuring the realisation of the rights in the Convention. Rights impose accountability, necessitate a commitment to the rights of every child, demand recognition that rights are indivisible, and require a commitment to participation of the child in the approaches adopted to implement their rights. In other words, the realisation of rights requires a holistic analysis of measures undertaken by States Parties in respect of every right, taking into account the Convention's four General Principles:

- Non-discrimination
- Best interests
- Optimal development
- Being heard.

The realisation of rights involves scrutiny not only of outcomes, but also the structures and processes that States Parties have put in place to achieve those outcomes. Of course, the child rights based approach to monitoring is not inconsistent with a commitment to child well-being. Indeed, well-being is integrally embedded throughout the framework of the Convention. It is present in articles relating to best interests, optimum development, aims of education to develop personality, talents, and mental and physical abilities to fullest potential, commitment to children's physical, mental, spiritual, moral and social development, and freedom from harm, violence and exploitation. It is also present in the preamble, which notes the role of the family in promoting children's well-being, and the need for love, happiness and understanding.

The importance of further work on the development of child rights indicators was highlighted after the Committee on the Rights of the Child produced *General Comment 7 (GC7): Implementing child rights in early childhood* (2006). While, in theory, General Comment no. 7 provided authoritative guidance to States Parties in fulfilling their obligations to young children, it lacked practical application and concrete direction. In response, in 2006, The Human Early Learning Partnership,

Canada, led by the late Clyde Hertzman, together with other child rights and child development scholars, approached the Committee to explore possible approaches to increase the utility of General Comment no. 7 as a child rights instrument and as a tool for promoting early childhood development.

The result was a proposal to develop monitoring, data collection, and indicator systems for comprehensive analyses of early child development. The subsequent work, undertaken by the GC7 Indicators Group,[2] led to the development of a set of seventeen indicators, each addressing a specific right for young children, following the Structure, Process, and Outcome model later published by the Office of the High Commissioner on Human Rights (United Nations OHCHR, 2012). Subsequent pilots in Tanzania (Vaghri et al., 2011), Chile (Vaghri et al., 2013), and British Colombia, Canada (Vaghri, 2018), demonstrated that the indicators could work as a method for national, inter-sectoral self-study to identify policies, programmes, and outcomes in early childhood, and proved valuable as a tool to assess the degree to which the conditions conducive to fulfilling child rights for young children were in place (Vaghri & De Souza, 2021).

Building on this work, the next step was to develop indicator sets to apply to every article of the Convention on the Rights of the Child, that would be available on an electronic monitoring platform. This platform, named GlobalChild, was envisaged to act as a rigorous child rights reporting system, resulting in reports that were evidence-based and focused, yet comprehensive, and with the capacity to track positive or negative changes in States Parties' compliance over time. As countries continued reporting data into GlobalChild, the platform would become a global repository of data on child rights and child development from all signatories to the Convention. The data sets could then facilitate research on a variety of child rights and public policy issues.

With this vision in mind, in 2016, with the generous support of the Canadian Institutes for Health Research and with an international team of researchers, child rights advocates, and child development experts, a 5-year plan started to develop the GlobalChild platform. An Indicator Development Team researched and developed indicators for the monitoring platform in two phases (United Nations OHCHR, 2012). Phase I defined the human rights-based attributes of each Convention article. This was necessary to help inform the nature and range of indicators necessary to ensure full implementation. Phase II then identified Structural, Process, and Outcome indicators, using the identified attributes as the framework. Once in use by States Parties, the GlobalChild platform, through its standardisation and streamlining of monitoring and reporting systems, will promote States Parties' accountability to children and strengthen the oversight role of the Committee on the Rights of the Child.

This publication comprises the compilation of the work of Phase 1 of the GlobalChild initiative to identify the core attributes of the Convention rights. It

---

[2]To view the names and biographies of the GC7 Indicators Team members, please visit: https://crcindicators.uvic.ca/index.php/content/about

has been developed to provide a succinct legal analysis of all the substantive, organizational and procedural provisions of the Convention. It articulates the human rights-based attributes of each article and interprets the legal international standards of the right through the lens of these characteristics, thus ensuring that no aspect of the right is overlooked. An attribute is a key dimension of a human right. For example, in relation to the right to non-discrimination, the attributes are:

- Non-discrimination in the realisation of all rights for all children within the jurisdiction
- Non-discrimination on the basis of status, actions, or beliefs, of parents, guardians, or family members
- Special measures to address discrimination.

These three attributes collectively reflect the essence of the normative content of the right. Accordingly, the aim was to identify those attributes for each article. They needed to be mutually exclusive but comprehensive, and together provide a well-articulated and complete analysis of the focus and scope of that right. This analysis assisted developing a high quality, policy impact evaluation of States Parties' interventions for the enhancement of children's well-being and the fulfilment of children's rights. Overall, the book provides a comprehensive interpretation for States Parties to consider when fulfilling their obligations towards progressive implementation of the Convention and affords a framework and guidance to the Committee on the Rights of the Child in monitoring that progress. In addition, the book provides a summative overview that should prove invaluable for both advocates for and students of children's human rights.

The process of developing the attributes for each article of the Convention was undertaken through a rigorous process, building on the methodology developed by the OHCHR (United Nations OHCHR, 2012). For each article, an exhaustive desk review of the relevant legal standards was undertaken, drawing on the *Travaux Préparatoires*, interpretations by the Committee on the Rights of the Child and other relevant treaty bodies through their General Comments and Concluding Observations, applicable international instruments and standards, and recent legal commentaries.

The attributes identified are presented following a common format, which includes:

- An overview introducing the background and overall scope of the article.
- An explanation of the implications of the four General Principles (Articles 2, 3, 6 and 12) in understanding the subject article.
- A list of the articles in the Convention where the subject article has significant relevance. While recognising the universality of human rights, this list highlights where the article specifically impacts or needs to be understood in the light of other rights. Where a right has application to every article, for example, Article 4 on general measures or Article 1 on the definition of a child, it is not included in this section.

- A list of other relevant international instruments that have a bearing on either the history or the implementation of the article. In some cases, where they are relevant, regional instruments are included. The level of detail provided in these lists varies in accordance with the implications for the subject article. For example, in Articles 26 and 30, a greater degree of explanatory information on the relevant instruments is provided.
- A short legal analysis of each attribute with a view to providing a comprehensive understanding of its meaning and implications.

The articles have been placed in nine thematic clusters, broadly aligned with those established by the Committee on the Rights of the Child in its reporting guidelines to States Parties. Where the publication differs from the clustering of the Committee guidelines, this is done to simplify understanding of each section of the book. For example, we have placed Article 1 together with Articles 4, 42 and 44.6, as they are all concerned with the scope and implementation of the Convention, rather than being substantive rights of the child. We also separated out rights relating to exploitation from those linked with protection of children in vulnerable settings.

It is important to note this book is not intended as a thorough analytical commentary of the rights in the Convention. Many other authors have undertaken more comprehensive critical analyses of children's rights both in theory and practice. Rather, it is designed to provide a policy instrument, in which, for each article, after an introduction to the origins, the reader will find the condensation of the core elements of each legal provision springing from interpretation by the relevant UN treaty bodies and other human rights authorities. Each right is located within a framework that facilitates an understanding of the background to and locus of the right, the essential characteristics or attributes of each right, the framework of action necessary for the implementation of the right and its related policy development, and a referral system to monitor the States Parties' compliance.

The attributes identified were subjected to several reviews and feedback-seeking processes to avoid subjectivity in their selection. First, the draft papers were reviewed internally by each of the five members of the Indicator Development Team[3] and revised accordingly. Three major external reviews further strengthened the attributes identification process.

A high-level review of the attribute papers for each set of attributes was undertaken by global experts[4] on the theme of the cluster. Following the consequent revisions, the attributes were reviewed by the Reference Group, consisting of internationally renowned experts,[5] at a face-to-face meeting in Geneva.

---

[3] To view the names and biographies of the Global Child Project Indicators Development Team members, please visit: https://www.unb.ca/globalchild/projects/globalchild/team.html

[4] To view the names and affiliations of experts consulted during the GlobalChild project, please visit: https://www.unb.ca/globalchild/projects/globalchild/expertreviewers.html

[5] To view the names and biographies of the members of the Global Child Project Reference Group, please visit: https://www.unb.ca/globalchild/projects/globalchild/reference-group.html

Finally, to further ensure the quality and pertinence of the attributes to the living reality of children, an international child consultative review component was undertaken through the Global Child Rights Dialog (GCRD). The GCRD was conducted in collaboration with Queen's University; Belfast's Centre for Children's Rights (CCR), in collaboration with Professor Laura Lundy; and other partners including Save the Children Canada and the Initiative for Article 12 (InArt12) from Greece. Child-friendly versions of the papers for each article were prepared. The GCRD undertook workshops with children from all five regions of the globe (Africa, Americas, Asia, Europe, and Oceania) to discuss and hear their thoughts about the attributes for each Convention article and to share their input. Almost two thousand children between the ages of 11 and 17 years participated from 52 sites in 35 countries, including Argentina, Canada, Greece, India, Japan, Russia, and Sierra Leone.[6] The Indicator Development Team used this information to understand how children viewed their rights and the actions they felt necessary for enhanced compliance. Quotes from the children highlighting the priorities they identified are included with each article in the book and were used to help inform the subsequent drawing up of child rights indicators.

Once all these external review processes had been completed, a final internal review and redrafting was undertaken by the Indicator Development Team to ensure consistency and coherence, and to bring the papers up to date in order to reflect any recent and relevant developments and research.

References

Ben-Arieh, A., & Frønes, I. (2011). Taxonomy for child well-being indicators: A framework for the analysis of the well-being of children. *Childhood, 18*(4), 460–476. https://doi.org/10.1177/0907568211398159

Bradshaw, J., Hoelscher, P., & Richardson, D. (2007). An index of child well-being in the European Union. *Social Indicators Research, 80*(1), 133–177. https://doi.org/10.1007/s11205-006-9024-z

UN Committee on the Rights of the Child. (2006, September 20). *General comment no. 7 (2005) Implementing child rights in early childhood, CRC/C/GC/7/Rev.1*. Accessed October 12, 2020, from https://digitallibrary.un.org/record/584854?ln=en.

United Nations OHCHR. (2012). *Human rights indicators: A guide to measurement and implementation, HR/PUB/12/5*. United Nations. https://www.ohchr.org/Documents/Publications/Human_rights_indicators_en.pdf

Vaghri, Z. (2018). *Piloting early childhood rights indicators in British Columbia: Protection against violence*. Global Child.

---

[6]To view the full list of the participating countries of the GCRD, please visit: https://www.unb.ca/globalchild/projects/gcrd/countries.html

Vaghri, Z., & De Souza, L. (2021). Child protection in British Columbia: Moving toward primary prevention. *Journal of Canadian Public Administration, 64*(3). https://doi.org/10.1111/capa.12430

Vaghri, Z., Krappmann, L., Arkadas, A., Hertzman, C., & Fenn, C. (2011). *Piloting the indicators of general comment (GC7): Implementing child rights in early childhood.* Final report submitted to UNICEF (Tanzania) and the Government of the United Republic of Tanzania.

Vaghri, Z., Krappmann, L., Arkadas, A., Hertzman, C., Fenn, C., & Diaz, C. (2013). *Piloting the indicators of general comment (GC7): Implementing child rights in early childhood.* Final report submitted to UNICEF (Chile) and the Government of Chile.

Vaghri, Z., Krappmann, L., & Doek, J. (2019). From the indicators of general comment no. 7 to GlobalChild: A decade of work to enhance State Parties' accountability to children. *The International Journal of Children's Rights, 27*(4), 821–851. https://doi.org/10.1163/15718182-02704009

Open Access This chapter is licensed under the terms of the Creative Commons Attribution 4.0 International License (http://creativecommons.org/licenses/by/4.0/), which permits use, sharing, adaptation, distribution and reproduction in any medium or format, as long as you give appropriate credit to the original author(s) and the source, provide a link to the Creative Commons license and indicate if changes were made.

The images or other third party material in this chapter are included in the chapter's Creative Commons license, unless indicated otherwise in a credit line to the material. If material is not included in the chapter's Creative Commons license and your intended use is not permitted by statutory regulation or exceeds the permitted use, you will need to obtain permission directly from the copyright holder.

Part I
General Principles

Articles 2, 3, 6, and 12

Introduction

This part addresses four rights embodied in the Convention on the Rights of the Child (the Convention) that have been identified, by the Committee on the Rights of the Child (the Committee), as General Principles that must inform the realisation of all other rights. These rights are expressed in four articles:

- Article 2: the right to non-discrimination
- Article 3: the best interests of the child
- Article 6: the right to life and optimum development
- Article 12: the right to be heard.

The General Principles constitute a thread that encompasses and influences the implementation of the Convention. For example, in consideration of Article 28, the right to education, legislative and policy measures, backed up by appropriate training and support of teachers, must be introduced to guarantee that no child is discriminated against in their right to access education, within the school environment itself, or within the educational system as a whole. The educational system, including teaching methods, curriculum, school design and timetable, and behaviour policies, must be developed to promote explicitly the best interests and optimum development of every child. Finally, children of all ages must be afforded the opportunity to be heard in relation to their education, in the way their schools are run, and in relation to the development of education legislation, policy, and budgeting.

A rights-based approach needs to be founded on a transparent, participatory, inclusive, and accountable process. Together, the four General Principles contribute to such a process. They clarify not only the desired outcomes from the implementation of each right in the Convention, but also the approach that must be adopted in their realisation.

Chapter 2
Article 2: The Right to Non-discrimination

Gerison Lansdown

1. States Parties shall respect and ensure the rights set forth in the present Convention to each child within their jurisdiction without discrimination of any kind, irrespective of the child's or his or her parent's or legal guardian's race, colour, sex, language, religion, political or other opinion, national, ethnic or social origin, property, disability, birth or other status.
2. States Parties shall take all appropriate measures to ensure that the child is protected against all forms of discrimination or punishment on the basis of the status, activities, expressed opinions, or beliefs of the child's parents, legal guardians, or family members.

What Did Children Say?
'This kind of activities, like the one that we are doing right now, should happen more in our schools. To make us overcome stereotypes. To be closer to each other and become better friends.' *(Western Europe/Other)*

'Campaigns through social media should help everyone understand, identify and avoid discrimination.' *(Western Europe/Other)*

'Opportunities should be given in school for familiarisation with diversity. Meetings should be organised with students from different counties. We should learn about cultures of other countries and learn to live together and not to be racist.' *(Western Europe/Other)*

G. Lansdown (✉)
Carleton University, Ottawa, ON, Canada

Overview

Non-discrimination, and its positive corollary, equality, are cross-cutting human rights invoked in all international human rights instruments (United Nations OHCHR, 2012, p. 81). While equality means the absence of discrimination, upholding the principle of non-discrimination between groups will produce equality (Bayefsky, 1990, p. 5). Non-discrimination is both a substantive and a procedural right that must be applied in the realisation of all other rights (Abramson, 2008, p. 4).

Discrimination has been defined by the Human Rights Committee as

> any distinction, exclusion, restriction or preference which is based on any ground such as race, colour, sex, language, religion, political or other opinion, national or social origin, property, birth or other status, and which has the purpose or effect of nullifying or impairing the recognition, enjoyment or exercise by all persons, on equal footing, of all rights and freedoms (UN Human Rights Committee, 1989, para. 7).

It is important to note that the provision of 'or other status' makes clear that this list is non-exhaustive. Non-discrimination is an absolute right, subject to no conditionality or qualifications such as progressive realisation, appropriateness or feasibility, or public welfare overrides (Abramson, 2008, pp. 40–42). The Committee on the Rights of Persons with Disabilities, for example, has affirmed that non-discrimination in respect of inclusive education is a core obligation that must be implemented with immediate effect (2016, para. 40(a)). However, the goal of equality sometimes requires States Parties to take affirmative action to diminish or eliminate conditions that cause or help to perpetuate discrimination. Such action is legitimate differentiation (UN Human Rights Committee, 1989, para. 8).

Within the Convention, Article 2 is worded in broadly comparable language with the Article 2 provisions on non-discrimination embodied in previous core human rights instruments, such as the Universal Declaration of Human Rights, the International Covenant on Civil and Political Rights (ICCPR), and the International Covenant on Economic, Social and Cultural Rights. However, it does contain significant differences. It includes two additional grounds for protection from discrimination, namely ethnic origin and disability. It also potentially strengthens the jurisdictional accountability of States Parties by removing the provision contained in the ICCPR that individuals must be living within the territory and subject to the state jurisdiction and requires only that they are within the jurisdiction of the state. Accordingly, the protection it affords extends to migrant, undocumented, refugee and asylum-seeking children living within the jurisdiction of the state. The Convention provision further, uniquely, protects children from discrimination based not only upon their personal traits and protected characteristics, but also from discrimination based upon their parents' or guardians' association with a class of persons protected from discrimination. In addition, in paragraph 2, this protection is reinforced by a new provision in international human rights law, whereby States Parties must take all appropriate measures to protect the child from all forms of discrimination or punishment on the basis of the actions, beliefs, or status of the parents, family members, or other guardians. In these ways, Article 2 affords children entitlement to the same protections from discrimination as adults, while considering their special status as children dependent on the adults who care for them (Besson & Kleber, 2019).

General Principles

Article 3 The principle of non-discrimination underpins the determination of the best interests of the child. States Parties must undertake appropriate proactive measures to guarantee effective equal opportunities for all children to ensure their best interests are addressed and realised (UN Committee on the Rights of the Child, 2013, para. 41).

Article 6 Discrimination impedes the optimum development of the child, whether it takes the form of denial of services, on the basis of equality of opportunity, prejudice, or social exclusion, or physical and psychological abuse. Compliance with Article 2 is therefore integral to the meaningful implementation of Article 6.

Article 12 The views of the child, wherever appropriate, must be sought in any consideration of discrimination. In addition, when a child experiences discrimination on any grounds, they must be provided with the opportunity to register a complaint and be provided with safe and accessible means of seeking redress.

Articles Related or Linked to Article 2

The Committee has identified Article 2 as one of four General Principles, and as such it must be applied as a constant reference for the implementation of all other rights (Pais, 1997). However, its implications need to be understood in relation to the following articles:

- **Article 1** provides an explanation as to who is a child in the context of the Convention. Article 2 then affirms that the rights in the Convention must be respected and ensured for every such child.
- **Article 4** elaborates the means by which the obligations to respect rights as described in Article 2 must be fulfilled.

In addition, the following articles highlight constituencies of children for whom additional attention is needed to ensure that their right to non-discrimination is equally protected on the same basis as other children:

- **Article 20**, children in need of alternative care
- **Article 21**, children being placed with adoptive families
- **Article 22**, children who are refugees or asylum seekers
- **Article 23**, children with disabilities
- **Article 30**, children from minority or indigenous communities

- **Article 37,** children deprived of liberty
- **Article 38,** children affected by armed conflict
- **Article 40,** children in conflict with the law

Relevant Instruments

The principle of non-discrimination originates in the 1945 United Nations Charter, which in Article 1 (3) provides an equality guarantee, and establishes the foundation for all subsequent human rights treaty development:

> To achieve international cooperation in solving international problems of an economic, social, cultural, or humanitarian character, and in promoting and encouraging respect for human rights and for fundamental freedoms for all without distinction as to race, sex, language, or religion.

Non-discrimination is therefore integral to all human rights treaties. Thus, the following list is indicative rather than exhaustive:

Common Article 2s are embodied in the following treaties:

- UN Universal Declaration of Human Rights (1948)
- International Covenant on Civil and Political Rights (1966)
- International Covenant on Economic, Social and Cultural Rights (1966).

In addition, there are specific non-discrimination treaties, which do not establish rights but elaborate the obligations on States Parties to uphold rights contained in other treaties, in respect of groups of individuals, for example:

- UN Convention against Discrimination in Education (1960)
- ILO Convention 111, Discrimination (Employment and Occupation) (1958)
- International Convention on the Elimination of all forms of Racial Discrimination (1966)
- UN Convention on the Elimination of All Forms of Discrimination against Women (1979)
- UN Convention on the Rights of Persons with Disabilities (2006).

Regional treaties including non-discrimination provisions, for example:

- European Convention on Human Rights (1950)
- American Convention on Human Rights 'Pact of San Jose, Costa Rica' (B-32) (1978)
- African Charter on the Rights and Welfare of the Child (1990).

Attributes

Attribute One: Non-discrimination in the Realisation of all Rights for All Children Within the Jurisdiction

The first critical contribution of Article 2 is to define the scope of the obligations of States Parties regarding children. It does so in two ways. First, it introduces the obligation on States Parties to 'respect and ensure' the rights in the Convention, thus requiring them to refrain from actions that violate the rights of the child and to take all necessary actions to enable the child to enjoy their rights (Alston, 1992, p. 5). In this regard, it is closely linked with Article 4. Where Article 2 constitutes an obligation of result, Article 4 elaborates the measures necessary to achieve that result (Pais, 1997). Second, it extends those obligations to every child 'within the jurisdiction,' regardless of status, including visitors, children of migrant workers, and undocumented immigrants (UN Committee on the Rights of the Child, 2003a, para. 18).

In other words, States Parties must secure rights for all children under their authority and responsibility living within any territory over which the state has power (Abramson, 2008, pp. 127–28; Pais, 1997, p. 417). In this regard, the Committee has stressed the imperative, in federal states, of ensuring equal protection for all children (2003b, para. 19).

The concept of discrimination comprises three key dimensions (Abramson, 2008, p. 29):

- Treating a child differently
- When doing so has either the purpose or the effect of impairing or harming them
- The differentiation is based on a prohibited ground in relation to a right contained in the Convention.

The Committee has stressed the requirement for States Parties to adopt a proactive commitment to the elimination of discrimination through legislation which reflects all the prohibited grounds (1993, para. 14). The scope of such legislation must address governmental and private or non-governmental actors, given that violations are often perpetrated by private action or private individuals (Weiwei, 2004, p. 22). The prohibited grounds include the child's or their parents' or legal guardians' race, colour, sex, language, religion, political or other opinion, national, ethnic or social origin, property, disability, and birth or other status.

Existing legislation must also be reviewed to ensure it does not include provisions that discriminate (UN Committee on the Rights of the Child, 2002a, paras. 27–28). In its General Comments and its Concluding Observations, the Committee consistently highlights many different groups of children who are particularly vulnerable to discrimination, including girls, children with disabilities, Roma children, and indigenous children.[1] In this regard, it is important to recognise intersectionality and multiple forms of discrimination that impact groups of children, for example, girls with disabilities.

The Committee has also elaborated on the provision 'or other status' to identify additional grounds for discrimination, including, for example, sexual orientation and transgender or intersex status (2016, para. 33), HIV status (2001, para. 3), and children in street situations (2017, para. 25). It has argued that both early childhood and adolescence can be a source of discrimination (2016, para. 21). For example, young children are particularly at risk of being denied their right to express their views and have them given due weight (UN Committee on the Rights of the Child, 2006, para. 11(b)), whereas adolescents can face hostile treatment directly as a consequence of their age and status (UN Committee on the Rights of the Child, 2016, para. 21).

Attribute Two: Non-discrimination on the Basis of Status, Actions, or Beliefs, of Parents, Guardians, or Family Members

Paragraph 2 introduces an obligation on States Parties to take all appropriate measures to ensure that the child is protected against all forms of discrimination or punishment on the basis of the status, actions, or beliefs of parents, guardians, or family members. Unlike paragraph 1, this is a qualified and not an absolute obligation, requiring only that appropriate measures are undertaken (Abramson, 2008, p. 132). In other words, it establishes an obligation of conduct rather than result, as is the case with paragraph 1. However, interestingly, it also differs from paragraph 1 in that its scope is not limited to discrimination in respect of the rights in the Convention.

The text comprises two distinct elements. First, States Parties must not *discriminate* against a child because of family members' status, actions, or beliefs. For example, affording differential legal status to a child born to unmarried rather than married parents would constitute a violation of Article 2 (UN Committee on the Rights of the Child, 1995b, para. 21), an issue highlighted repeatedly as of particular concern during the drafting of the Convention (Office of the United Nations High Commissioner for Human Rights & Rädda Barnen (Society: Sweden), 2007, pp. 315, 325–327). Second, a child must not be *punished* as a consequence of family members' status, actions, or beliefs. For example, one sibling should not be excluded from school because of the behaviour of another sibling. Implementation of paragraph 2 requires that States Parties take measures to ensure that any existing

---

[1] See, for example, the Committee report on the eighth session (1995a, p. 3); General Comment no. 9, Children with Disabilities (2007, paras. 8–10); Concluding Observations: Spain (2018, paras. 14–15).

constitution, legislation, court decisions, or administrative policy comply with both these elements.

Attribute Three: Special Measures to Address Discrimination

Beyond legislation, the Committee has identified measures required by States Parties to implement Article 2. It emphasises the importance of collecting disaggregated data to identify children experiencing discrimination (2003a, para. 12). It also recommends that States Parties[2]:

- Develop comprehensive strategies
- Undertake research into discrimination
- Introduce information and awareness raising campaigns
- Involve religious, community, and political leaders to influence attitudes and discourage discrimination
- Enact special measures or positive discrimination to eliminate barriers to the attainment of equality for a particular group of children.

Importance is also attached to the need for education systems to address issues such as gender discrimination in the curriculum and exclusion of children with disabilities, and to affirm the role of education in promoting respect for difference (UN Committee on the Rights of the Child, 2001, para. 10).

References

Abramson, B. (2008). *A commentary on the United Nations Convention on the Rights of the Child, article 2: The right of non-discrimination*. Brill Nijhoff. Accessed May 16, 2020, from https://brill.com/view/title/11624.

Alston, P. (1992). The legal framework of the Convention on the Rights of the Child. *Bulletin of Human Rights, 91*(2), 1–15.

Bayefsky, A. F. (1990). The principle of equality or non-discrimination in international law. *Human Rights Law Journal, 11*(1), 1–34.

Besson, S., & Kleber, E. (2019). Article 2: The right to non-discrimination. In J. Tobin (Ed.), *The UN Convention on the Rights of the Child: A commentary*. Oxford University Press.

Office of the United Nations High Commissioner for Human Rights & Rädda Barnen (Society: Sweden). (2007). *Legislative history of the Convention on the Rights of the Child*. United Nations. https://digitallibrary.un.org/record/602462?ln=en

Pais, M. S. (1997). The Convention on the Rights of the Child. In *Manual on human rights reporting under six major international human rights instruments HR/PUB/91/1 (Rev.1)* (pp. 393–505). OHCHR. Accessed May 16, 2020, from https://www.refworld.org/docid/428085252.html.

---

[2] See, for example, Concluding observations for Niger (2002b, para. 28), Bangladesh (1997, paras. 15, 35), and India (2000, para. 31).

UN Committee on the Rights of Persons with Disabilities. (2016, September 2). *General comment No. 4 (2016), Article 24: Right to inclusive education, CRPD/C/GC/4*. Accessed October 12, 2020, from https://digitallibrary.un.org/record/1313836?ln=en.
UN Committee on the Rights of the Child. (1993, February 18). *Concluding observations: Bolivia, CRC/C/15/Add.1*. Accessed October 11, 2020, from https://digitallibrary.un.org/record/197306?ln=en.
UN Committee on the Rights of the Child. (1995a, January 9–27). *Report on the 8th session, Geneva, CRC/C/38*. https://digitallibrary.un.org/record/182587?ln=en
UN Committee on the Rights of the Child. (1995b, June 20). *Concluding observations: Nicaragua, CRC/C/15/Add.36*. Accessed October 11, 2020, from https://digitallibrary.un.org/record/191818?ln=en.
UN Committee on the Rights of the Child. (1997, June 18). *Concluding observations: Bangladesh, CRC/C/15/Add.74*. Accessed October 10, 2020, from https://digitallibrary.un.org/record/241624?ln=en.
UN Committee on the Rights of the Child. (2000, February 23). *Concluding observations: India, CRC/C/15/Add.115*. Accessed October 11, 2020, from https://digitallibrary.un.org/record/412551?ln=en.
UN Committee on the Rights of the Child. (2001, April 17). *General comment no. 1 (2001) Article 29 (1): The Aims of Education, CRC/GC/2001/1*. Accessed October 10, 2020, from https://digitallibrary.un.org/record/447223?ln=en.
UN Committee on the Rights of the Child. (2002a, March 21). *Concluding observations: Lebanon, CRC/C/15/Add.169*. Accessed October 11, 2020, from https://digitallibrary.un.org/record/467259?ln=en.
UN Committee on the Rights of the Child. (2002b, June 13). *Concluding observations: Niger, CRC/C/15/Add.179*. Accessed October 11, 2020, from https://digitallibrary.un.org/record/473482?ln=en.
UN Committee on the Rights of the Child. (2003a, November 27). *General comment no. 5 (2003) General measures of implementation of the Convention on the Rights of the Child (arts. 4, 42 and 44, para. 6), CRC/GC/2003/5*. Accessed October 12, 2020, from https://digitallibrary.un.org/record/513415?ln=en.
UN Committee on the Rights of the Child. (2003b, October 27). *Concluding observations: Canada, CRC/C/15/Add.215*. Accessed October 11, 2020, from https://digitallibrary.un.org/record/513561?ln=en.
UN Committee on the Rights of the Child. (2006, September 20). *General comment no. 7 (2005) Implementing child rights in early childhood, CRC/C/GC/7/Rev.1*. Accessed October 12, 2020, from https://digitallibrary.un.org/record/584854?ln=en.
UN Committee on the Rights of the Child. (2007, November 13). *General comment no. 9 (2006) The rights of children with disabilities, CRC/C/GC/9*. Accessed October 12, 2020, from https://digitallibrary.un.org/record/593891?ln=en.
UN Committee on the Rights of the Child. (2013, May 29). *General comment no. 14 (2013) On the right of the child to have his or her best interests taken as a primary consideration (art. 3, para. 1), CRC/C/GC/14*. Accessed October 12, 2020, from https://digitallibrary.un.org/record/778523?ln=en.
UN Committee on the Rights of the Child. (2016, December 6). *General comment no. 20 (2016) on the implementation of the rights of the child during adolescence, CRC/C/GC/20*. Accessed October 12, 2020, from https://digitallibrary.un.org/record/855544?ln=en.
UN Committee on the Rights of the Child. (2017, June 21). *General comment no. 21 (2017) on children in street situations, CRC/C/GC/21*. Accessed October 12, 2020, from https://digitallibrary.un.org/record/1304490?ln=en.

UN Committee on the Rights of the Child. (2018, March 5). *Concluding observations: Spain, CRC/C/ESP/CO/5-6*. Accessed October 11, 2020, from https://digitallibrary.un.org/record/1476613?ln=en.

UN Human Rights Committee. (1989, November 21). *CCPR general comment no. 18 (1989) Non-discrimination, CCPR/C/21/Rev.1/Add.1*. https://digitallibrary.un.org/record/84170?ln=en

United Nations OHCHR. (2012). *Human rights indicators: A guide to measurement and implementation, HR/PUB/12/5*. United Nations. https://www.ohchr.org/Documents/Publications/Human_rights_indicators_en.pdf

Weiwei, L. (2004). *Equality and non-discrimination under international human rights law*. The Norwegian Centre for Human Rights. https://www.jus.uio.no/smr/english/about/programmes/china/Publications/articles_and_books/Article_LWW_2004.pdf

Open Access This chapter is licensed under the terms of the Creative Commons Attribution 4.0 International License (http://creativecommons.org/licenses/by/4.0/), which permits use, sharing, adaptation, distribution and reproduction in any medium or format, as long as you give appropriate credit to the original author(s) and the source, provide a link to the Creative Commons license and indicate if changes were made.

The images or other third party material in this chapter are included in the chapter's Creative Commons license, unless indicated otherwise in a credit line to the material. If material is not included in the chapter's Creative Commons license and your intended use is not permitted by statutory regulation or exceeds the permitted use, you will need to obtain permission directly from the copyright holder.

Chapter 3
Article 3: The Best Interest of the Child

Roberta Ruggiero

1. In all actions concerning children, whether undertaken by public or private social welfare institutions, courts of law, administrative authorities or legislative bodies, the best interests of the child shall be a primary consideration.
2. States Parties undertake to ensure the child such protection and care as is necessary for his or her well-being, taking into account the rights and duties of his or her parents, legal guardians, or other individuals legally responsible for him or her, and, to this end, shall take all appropriate legislative and administrative measures.
3. States Parties shall ensure that the institutions, services and facilities responsible for the care or protection of children shall conform with the standards established by competent authorities, particularly in the areas of safety, health, in the number and suitability of their staff, as well as competent supervision.

What Did Children Say?
'When parents make decisions or something related to their children, they should discuss with their children and make decisions based on best interests of their children.' *(Eastern Europe)*

(continued)

R. Ruggiero (✉)
Centre for Children's Rights Studies, University of Geneva, Geneva, Switzerland
e-mail: roberta.ruggiero@unige.ch

> 'An independent inspector can visit schools, hospitals and institutions, ask questions and observe the situation there.' *(Eastern Europe)*
> 'Specialised psychologists in schools, institutions and courts should help to understand what the best interest for children in every case.' *(Eastern Europe)*

Overview

Article 3(1) introduces a fundamental principle into international human rights treaties' provisions. It attributes to the child 'the right to have his or her best interests assessed and taken into account as a primary consideration in all actions or decisions that concern him or her, both in the public and private sphere' (UN Committee on the Rights of the Child, 2013, para. 1).

At the international level, this principle made its first appearance in the 1959 Declaration of the Rights of the Child (Principle 2), but its inclusion in national legislation pre-dates the adoption of the Declaration. However, in the 1959 Declaration, the child's best interests are to be *'the paramount* consideration,' so they are determinant in the decision process, whereas in Article 3(1) they are only *'a primary* consideration,' so one of the possible determinant factors (Freeman, 2007, pp. 25–26).

The first draft of this article reproduced the same wording as Principle 2 of the 1959 Declaration, but some delegations were uncomfortable about it and an alternative draft was submitted in 1980. In it, *the* was replaced with *a* in qualifying the *primary consideration*. However, considering the complexity of the concept of best interests, it did not give rise to lengthy debate at the drafting stage and only in 1988 a second and last amendment was agreed to integrate a reference to 'legislative bodies' after 'administrative authorities.' This intervention broadened the scope of the article implying that legislative measures should also be 'accompanied by "child impact" statements' (Freeman, 2007, p. 26).

It has been argued that Article 3 underpins all the other provisions of the Convention (UN Committee on the Rights of the Child, 2003, para. 12, 2009, para. 2). Best interests is one of the most complicated concepts to pin down, and the Committee defines it as 'a dynamic concept that requires an assessment appropriate to the specific context.' What is encompassed by best interests depends on how the concept is understood. For example, different cultural approaches will inevitably outline different understandings of what is in a child's best interests (Freeman, 2007, p. 1). However, the Committee has frequently addressed such structural problems by maintaining that the obligation to consider the children's best interest requires the assessment of the impact of the decision on the child and that its implementation should always lead to the respect of other Convention rights. The 'adult's judgment of a child's best interests cannot override the obligation to respect all the child's rights under the Convention' (UN Committee on the Rights of the Child, 2011, para. 61). In other words, 'the rights of the child precede the best interests standard' and the implementation cannot be done without reference to the rights of the child (Freeman, 2007, p. 5). Furthermore, as clarified by the Committee in General Comment no. 14 in 2013, 'no right could be compromised by a negative interpretation of the child's best interests' (2013, para. 4).

The other two paragraphs of Article 3 ensure the child's best interests and well-being within their daily ecosystem. Article 3(2) pertains to the well-being of the child in all circumstances while respecting the rights and duties of parents. Article 3 (3) concerns the obligation of States Parties to ensure that institutions, services, and facilities for children 'comply with the established standards,' and that mechanisms are in place to ensure that the standards are respected.

General Principles

Article 2 The 'right to non-discrimination is not a passive obligation' (Besson & Kleber, 2019, p. 51) Therefore, the simple prohibition of all forms of discrimination is not enough for the article's full implementation. It also requires 'appropriate proactive measures' to ensure effective equal opportunities for all children to enjoy their rights under the Convention. These passive and active measures need to be undertaken in compliance with Article 3 (UN Committee on the Rights of the Child, 2013, para. 41).

Article 6 'In the assessment and determination of the child's best interests, the State must ensure full respect for his or her inherent right to life, survival, and development' (UN Committee on the Rights of the Child, 2013, para. 42).

Article 12 There is an inextricable link between Article 3(1) and Article 12. They have complementary roles: Article 3 is meant to realise the child's best interests, and Article 12 provides the methodology for hearing the views of the child in the assessment of their best interests. Article 3, paragraph 1, cannot be correctly applied if the requirements of Article 12 are not met (UN Committee on the Rights of the Child, 2009, paras. 70–74, 2013, para. 43).

Articles Related or Linked to Article 3

Article 3 is a General Principle. Its application needs to be considered in relation to the implementation of all the other Convention rights. However, rights that require specific consideration of the child's best interests are:

- **Article 9(1) and (3)**, separation from parents
- **Article 18(1)**, parental responsibilities for their children
- **Article 20**, deprivation of family environment
- **Article 21**, adoption

- **Article 37(c)**, separation from adults in detention
- **Article 40(2)(b)(iii)**, presence of parents at court hearings of penal matters involving a juvenile.

Relevant Instruments

UN Declaration of the Rights of the Child (1959), Principle 2, 'In the enactment of laws for this purpose, the best interests of the child shall be the paramount consideration.'

UN Convention on the Elimination of All Forms of Discrimination against Women (1979), Article 5(b), on the exercise of parental responsibility and Article 16(1)(d) in relation to marriage and family responsibility.

UN Convention on the Rights of Persons with Disabilities (2006), Article 7(2), requires that in all actions concerning children with disabilities, the best interests of the child shall be a primary consideration.

European Convention on Recognition and Enforcement of Decisions concerning Custody of Children and on Restoration of Custody of Children (1980), Article 10(1)(b), refers to the 'welfare of the child' in the decision-making process.

African Charter on the Rights and Welfare of the Child (1990), Article 4(1), 'the best interests of the child shall be the primary consideration' in all actions 'by any person,' so parents are included.

Hague Convention on Protection of Children and Co-operation in Respect of Intercountry Adoption (1993), Article 1(a), 'to ensure that intercountry adoptions take place in the best interests of the child.'

European Convention on the Exercise of Children's Rights (1996), Article 2(1) states that the 'object of the present Convention is, in the best interests of children, to promote their rights, to grant them procedural rights and to facilitate the exercise of these rights.'

Attributes

Attribute One: The Best Interests of the Child as a Primary Consideration

Interpretation of the best interests of the child has been elaborated by the Committee in its concluding observations to States Parties' reports and in General Comment no. 14. In the latter, the Committee underlines that the 'child's best interests' is a threefold concept:

- **A substantive right:** It is an individual and collective right, which guarantees that the 'best interests' of the child/children involved is 'assessed and taken as a

primary consideration...in order to reach a decision on the issue at stake', and the guarantee that the Convention rights will be implemented
- **A fundamental, interpretative legal principle:** 'If a legal provision is open to more than one interpretation, the interpretation which most effectively serves the child's best interests should be chosen'
- **A rule of procedure:** Whenever a decision is to be made, 'the decision-making process must include an evaluation of the possible impact, positive or negative, of the decision on the child or children concerned.' The assessment and determination of the best interests of the child require procedural guarantees (2013, para. 6).

General Comment no. 14 also provides a legal analysis of Article 3(1): 'In all actions concerning children, whether undertaken by public or private social welfare institutions, courts of law, administrative authorities or legislative bodies.'

With the word action, the Committee includes all the 'decisions, but also all acts, conduct, proposals, services, procedures and other measures' undertaken by public and private bodies and which directly or indirectly impact children as a group or a single child (2006, para. 13(b)). Therefore, Article 3(1) sets a very wide obligation on States Parties to 'duly consider the child's best interests.' 'It is a comprehensive obligation encompassing all public and private social welfare institutions, courts of law, administrative authorities, and legislative bodies involving or concerning children' (UN Committee on the Rights of the Child, 2013, para. 25).

Assessing the child's best interests is a unique activity that should be undertaken in each individual case, in the light of the specific circumstances of each child or group of children or children in general, including individual characteristics, as well as the social and cultural context in which the child or children find themselves. General Comment no. 14, in order to provide concrete guidance on how to assess the best interests of the child, draws up 'a non-exhaustive and non-hierarchical list of elements that could be included in a best interests assessment by any decision-maker having to determine a child's best interests' (UN Committee on the Rights of the Child, 2013, paras. 48–84). Furthermore, the Committee recommends that the assessment of the best interests of the child or of a group of children must comprise both short and long-term considerations for the child involved (2007, para. 26). This demands a continuous process of child rights impact assessment to foresee the impact that any proposed law, policy, or budgetary allocation may have on children, and child rights impact evaluation, to evaluate the actual impact of implementation (UN Committee on the Rights of the Child, 2013, para. 35).

The Best Interests of the Child There is no clear definition of best interests, but in its General Comment no. 14, the Committee sets out a detailed explanation of this principle. It is a complex and adaptable concept, which needs to be determined on a case-by-case basis. The judge, administrative, social, or educational authority 'will be able to clarify the concept and make concrete use thereof', only if the assessment is done on an individual basis, according to the specific situation of the child or children concerned, and taking into consideration their personal context, situation and needs (Freeman, 2007, pp. 50–60; UN Committee on the Rights of the Child, 2013, paras. 32–34).

Furthermore, the assessment of a child's best interests must include respect for the child's right to express their views freely, and due weight given to said views in all matters affecting the child (UN Committee on the Rights of the Child, 2009). Article 3(1), 'cannot be correctly applied if the requirements of Article 12 are not met' (UN Committee on the Rights of the Child, 2009, paras. 70–74, 2013, paras. 43–45).

A Primary Consideration States Parties need to incorporate a full and formal process of assessing and determining the best interests of the child in all cases in which a decision will have a major impact on a child or children. In these cases, a greater level of protection and detailed procedures to consider their best interests is appropriate (UN Committee on the Rights of the Child, 2002, para. 10, 2005, paras. 19–21, 2013, para. 20). The expression 'primary consideration' attributes to the children's best interests a stronger position in comparison with other considerations. This is justified on the basis of the 'special situation of the child: dependency, maturity, legal status and, often, voicelessness' and the fact that if the interests of children 'are not highlighted, they tend to be overlooked' (UN Committee on the Rights of the Child, 2013, para. 37).

However, since Article 3(1) covers a wide range of situations, the Committee acknowledges the need for flexibility in its implementation. Once assessed, the best interests of the child might conflict with other interests or rights, for example, that of other children, public authorities, parents, caregivers, etc. For the Committee, the balancing of the contrasting interests can be operated only on a case-by-case basis evaluation. In the search for suitable compromise, authorities and decision-makers must weigh the rights of all those concerned, bearing in mind that the best interests of the child have high priority and are not just one of several considerations (Freeman, 2007, pp. 60–64). This cannot be overruled 'when an action has an undeniable impact on the children concerned (UN Committee on the Rights of the Child, 2013, paras. 39–40).'

Conversely, in the case of adoption, this balancing of contrasting interests is not needed. In Article 21, the principle of 'best interests' is further strengthened. 'It is not simply to be a primary consideration' but 'the paramount consideration.' Thus, it is the 'determining factor' (UN Committee on the Rights of the Child, 2013, para. 38).

Attribute Two: Care and Protection—Safety Net

Article 3(2) focuses on the States Parties' obligation to ensure necessary protection and care for the child, considering the rights and duties of parents and others legally responsible for the child. It reiterates a general obligation of the States Parties, which is linked to their obligations under the other General Principles (Articles 2, 6, and 12) and to other Convention specific obligations, for example:

- Provide 'appropriate assistance to parents and legal guardians' in their child-rearing responsibilities (Article 18(2))

- Provide 'special protection and assistance' to children deprived of their family environment (Article 20(1))
- Recognise the rights of children to benefit from social security (Article 26)
- Provide an adequate standard of living (Articles 27)
- Protect children from all forms of violence and exploitation (Articles 19, 32, 33, 34, 35, 36 and 37) (Hodgkin et al., 2007, p. 41).

However, Article 3(2) also states a backstop or umbrella provision, which fills eventual lacunae present in the Convention, by imposing on States Parties the responsibility to take 'all appropriate legislative and administrative measures' necessary for the child's well-being. Therefore, this article imposes on States Parties the responsibility of last resort to ensure the well-being of all those most vulnerable children that are neglected by its provisions (Freeman, 2007, pp. 66–67; Hodgkin et al., 2007, p. 40). The appropriate legislative and administrative measures to be undertaken must comply with Article 3(1) and Article 4 of the Convention.

Attribute Three: Adequate Standards for Institutions, Services, and Facilities Dedicated to the Care and Protection of the Child

Article 3(3) requires the establishment of appropriate standards for institutions, services, and facilities responsible for the care or protection of children. Other provisions of the Convention deal with particular services that the States Parties should create, for example:

- 'Those dedicated to the care of children' (Article 18(2) and (3))
- Alternative care for children out of their family environment (Article 20)
- Care for children with disabilities (Article 23)
- Rehabilitative care (Article 39)
- Institutional and other care related to the juvenile justice system (Article 40).

Article 3(3) provides no exhaustive list of the areas in which standards must be established, but it does mention 'particularly in the areas of safety, health, in the number and suitability of their staff, as well as competent supervision.' Therefore, it is correct to affirm that it requires the determination of appropriate standards for all services already identified in the Convention and for all of those not specifically mentioned in it. This is in line with the increasing range of alternative care services that States Parties are requested to set up to ensure childcare and protection (Freeman, 2007, pp. 71–72; Hodgkin et al., 2007, p. 41).

Article 3(3) equally applies to state institutions and non-state institutions. For its implementation, it requires the reviewing of the national legal framework dedicated to these institutions and services, the adoption of appropriate standards, and the creation of adequate inspection institutions with the mandate of monitoring of the respect of those quality standards, which applies not only to the quality of the service provided but also to the staff involved (Hodgkin et al., 2007, pp. 41–42; UN Committee on the Rights of the Child, 2006, paras. 23, 32).

References

Besson, S., & Kleber, E. (2019). Article 2: The right to non-discrimination. In J. Tobin (Ed.), *The UN Convention on the Rights of the Child: A commentary*. Oxford University Press.

Freeman, M. (2007). *A commentary on the United Nations Convention on the Rights of the Child, Article 3: The best interests of the child*. Brill Nijhoff.

Hodgkin, R., Newell, P., & UNICEF. (2007). *Implementation handbook for the Convention on the Rights of the Child* (3rd ed.). UNICEF. Accessed September 21, 2020, from https://digitallibrary.un.org/record/620060?ln=en

UN Committee on the Rights of the Child. (2002, November 15). *General comment no. 2 (2002) The role of independent national human rights institutions in the promotion and protection of the rights of the child, CRC/GC/2002/2*. Accessed October 12, 2020, from https://digitallibrary.un.org/record/490983?ln=en.

UN Committee on the Rights of the Child. (2003, November 27). *General comment no. 5 (2003) General measures of implementation of the Convention on the Rights of the Child (arts. 4, 42 and 44, para. 6), CRC/GC/2003/5*. Accessed October 12, 2020, from https://digitallibrary.un.org/record/513415?ln=en.

UN Committee on the Rights of the Child. (2005, September 1). *General comment no. 6 (2005) Treatment of unaccompanied and separated children outside their country of origin, CRC/GC/2005/6*. Accessed October 12, 2020, from https://digitallibrary.un.org/record/566055?ln=en.

UN Committee on the Rights of the Child. (2006, September 20). *General comment no. 7 (2005) Implementing child rights in early childhood, CRC/C/GC/7/Rev.1*. Accessed October 12, 2020, from https://digitallibrary.un.org/record/584854?ln=en.

UN Committee on the Rights of the Child. (2007, March 2). *General comment no. 8 (2006) The right of the child to protection from corporal punishment and other cruel or degrading forms of punishment (arts. 19; 28, para. 2; and 37, inter alia), CRC/C/GC/8*. Accessed October 12, 2020, from https://digitallibrary.un.org/record/583961?ln=en.

UN Committee on the Rights of the Child. (2009, February 12). *General comment no. 11 (2009), Indigenous children and their rights under the Convention, CRC/C/GC/11*. Accessed October 24, 2020, from https://digitallibrary.un.org/record/648790?ln=en.

UN Committee on the Rights of the Child. (2011, April 18). *General comment no. 13 (2011) The right of the child to freedom from all forms of violence, CRC/C/GC/13*. Accessed October 12, 2020, from https://digitallibrary.un.org/record/711722?ln=en.

UN Committee on the Rights of the Child. (2013, May 29). *General comment no. 14 (2013) On the right of the child to have his or her best interests taken as a primary consideration (art. 3, para. 1), CRC/C/GC/14*. Accessed October 12, 2020, from https://digitallibrary.un.org/record/778523?ln=en.

Open Access This chapter is licensed under the terms of the Creative Commons Attribution 4.0 International License (http://creativecommons.org/licenses/by/4.0/), which permits use, sharing, adaptation, distribution and reproduction in any medium or format, as long as you give appropriate credit to the original author(s) and the source, provide a link to the Creative Commons license and indicate if changes were made.

The images or other third party material in this chapter are included in the chapter's Creative Commons license, unless indicated otherwise in a credit line to the material. If material is not included in the chapter's Creative Commons license and your intended use is not permitted by statutory regulation or exceeds the permitted use, you will need to obtain permission directly from the copyright holder.

Chapter 4
Article 6: The Rights to Life, Survival, and Development

Ziba Vaghri

1. States Parties recognise that every child has the inherent right to life.
2. States Parties shall ensure to the maximum extent possible the survival and development of the child.

What Did Children Say?
'A minimum income for every family with children should be secured by the government and reports should be available about its provision.' *(Eastern Europe)*

'Children must have a health insurance for making sure that they will grow up without health challenges make their growth difficult.' *(Asia-Pacific)*

'All government departments should do everything they can to ensure the survival and development of children. For example, government should set up more schools so that we children have opportunities to continue their schoolwork.' *(Asia-Pacific)*

Z. Vaghri (✉)
University of New Brunswick Saint John, Saint John, NB, Canada
e-mail: ziba.vaghri@unb.ca

Overview

Article 6 guarantees the child's inherent right to life, and, for the first time in an international human rights treaty, introduces the right to survival and development.[1] The right to life is the only right defined as inherent in the Convention. It extends beyond a negative obligation of non-interference, imposing a proactive obligation to take all comprehensive legislative, administrative, and other positive measures to ensure the inherent and indivisible right to life and survival of the child (Nowak, 2005, pp. 17–18). Although the right to life is not absolute, the standard to justify any failure to protect the life of a child is exceptionally high (Peleg & Tobin, 2019). States Parties are required to provide explicit protections in law which include strict circumscribing of measures that arbitrarily and non-arbitrarily deprive a child's life (Nowak, 2005, p. 2). Consistent with Article 37, Article 6 must be interpreted as imposing a prohibition on the death penalty (UN Committee on the Rights of the Child, 2010, paras. 32–33, 2012a, paras. 37–38). In addition, in line with Article 1, which avoids taking a position on the commencement of life, Article 6 does not adopt a view with regard to whether life begins at the point of conception or a live birth. States Parties are therefore able to determine this issue themselves (Peleg & Tobin, 2019; UN Committee on the Rights of the Child, 2005a, para. 64 (c)). The Working Group drafting the Convention noted that staying silent on such matters was intentional so as 'not to prejudice the interpretation of Article 1 or any other provisions of the Convention by State Parties' (UN Commission on Human Rights, 1989, pp. 8–15).

Paragraph 2 of Article 6 introduces the obligation on States Parties to ensure the survival and development of the child to the maximum extent possible.[2] The development of the child has been interpreted by the Committee as needing to be understood 'in its broadest sense as a holistic concept embracing the child's physical, mental, spiritual moral and psychological development' (2003, para. 12, 2013a, para. 18). It imposes an obligation on States Parties to introduce all appropriate measures, both positive and negative, to promote the survival and development of the child. Its implementation is integrally linked to the Convention in its entirety, and in particular the principle of the best interests of the child in Article 3, as well as the rights to health and an adequate standard of living and education in Articles 24, 27,

---

[1] See General Guidelines for Initial Reports (UN Committee on the Rights of the Child, 1991, para. 13), and General Guidelines for Periodic Reports (UN Committee on the Rights of the Child, 1996, para. 40), where it defined Article 6: 'specific measures taken to guarantee the child's right to life and to create an environment conducive to ensuring to the maximum extent possible the survival and development of the child, including physical, mental, spiritual, moral, psychological and social development, in a manner compatible with human dignity, and to prepare the child for an individual life in a free society.'

[2] As defined in the Convention on the Rights of the Child Article 27, General Comment No. 5 (UN Committee on the Rights of the Child, 2003), a report on implementation in the context of migration (UN Office of the High Commissioner for Human Rights (OHCHR), 2010), and the Implementation handbook (Hodgkin et al., 2007)

28 and 29 (Nowak, 2005, p. 14). General Comment no. 7 illustrates this point by drawing the links to 'health, adequate nutrition, social security and adequate standard of living, a healthy safe environment, education and play, along with the respect for parental responsibility and the provision of assistance and quality services' (UN Committee on the Rights of the Child, 2006, para. 10).

General Principles

Article 2 Measures such as access to information, services, and supports that promote life and development must be undertaken to prevent discrimination of children, including those with disabilities and survivors of gender-based violence.

Article 3 Innately linked to child's right to life, survival, and development, Article 3 obliges States to 'create an environment that respects human dignity and ensures the holistic development of every child. In the assessment and determination of the child's best interests, the State must ensure full respect for his or her inherent right to life, survival and, development' (UN Committee on the Rights of the Child, 2013b, para. 42).

Article 12 The views of children must be listened to and given due weight in all matters that affect their life, survival, and development.

Articles Related or Linked to Article 6

As a General Principle, Article 3 needs to be considered in relation to the implementation of all the other Convention rights. However, rights that require specific consideration of the child's right to life and optimum survival and development include those below.

Article 19, protection from all forms of violence that are detrimental to the child's life and development.

Article 32 offers protections from economic exploitation and hazardous work.

Article 33 protects children from the use of illicit narcotics and psychotropic substances, as well as being protected from involvement in the trade, production, and trafficking of illicit drugs.

Article 34 protects from sexual exploitation and abuse, including inducement and coercion to engage in unlawful activity, exploitation through prostitution and other unlawful practices as well as exploitative use in pornographic materials and production.

Article 35, protections to prevent abduction, sale, or trafficking of children for any purpose or in any form.

Article 36 protects from all other forms of exploitation prejudicial to any aspect of a child's welfare.

Article 37(a) prohibits torture and cruel, inhumane, and degrading treatment and punishment. Securing the right to life is therefore conceived as right to personal liberty and security. This includes the prohibition of capital punishment of children. Article 6 of both the Convention and the ICCPR reinforce the abolishment of the death penalty for children. It is not enough to not apply the death penalty, but rather legislation must be explicit in the prohibition of its use. Children's optimum development must also be protected from the potential harm that might be imposed by excessive use of force by law enforcement or others in power.

Article 38 relates to the protection of the child in armed conflict. The risk to life is considerable for the child in these circumstances. Apart from the risk of death, children living in a conflict zone can be vulnerable to displacement, recruitment, malnutrition, poor health and sanitation, and related illnesses. These children are also at potential risk of torture, disappearance, extrajudicial killings and social cleansing (UN Committee on the Rights of the Child, 2000a, paras. 30–31, 2000b, paras. 34–35). In zones of conflict, landmines have been responsible for the deaths of children and other members of the community. Importantly, ICCPR declares there is no derogation permitted even in times of emergency (United Nations, 2006, p. 166).

Relevant Instruments

The UN Universal Declaration of Human Rights (1948), Article 3, affirms 'the right to life, liberty, and security of person.'

The International Covenant on Civil and Political Rights (1966), Article 6, while asserting the right to life, declares it be protected by law and that a person must not be arbitrarily deprived of life (United Nations, 2006, p. 166).

The UN Convention on the Rights of Persons with Disabilities (2006), Article 10, asserts States Parties affirm the inherent right to life, and the employment of all measures to ensure people with disabilities the enjoyment of that right on the equal basis as other persons. This would include equal access to systems of health and care available to other members of society. Children with disabilities, particularly infants, are highlighted as being vulnerable to exclusion or discrimination as a result of impoverished systems of care and limited access to health. States Parties are urged to outlaw harmful practices that impinge on the right to life of children with disabilities. States Parties are also required to raise public awareness, enact legislation, and review and revise laws that directly or indirectly violate the right to life, survival, and development of children with disabilities (UN Committee on the Rights of the Child, 2007, para. 31).

Attributes

Attribute One: Respect for and Protection of Inherent Right to Life of the Child

The right to life has been referred to as 'the supreme right,' as without it all other human rights would be devoid of meaning (UN Human Rights Committee, 2019, paras. 2–3). Furthermore, its recognition by the Committee as a General Principle affirms the imperative to take it into account in the implementation of all other rights (Doek, 2015).

Unlike other human rights treaties, the States Parties' obligation for the respect for inherent right to life in Article 6 does not come with a limitation clause of arbitrary deprivation of life. It therefore prohibits any act that is detrimental to the child's inherent dignity and right to life, including death penalty, corporal punishment, torture or other cruel, inhuman, or degrading treatment or punishment (Nowak, 2005, pp. 18–24). The Committee has argued that the right to life requires more than refraining from imposition of the death penalty, and places positive obligations to prohibit children from receiving life sentences. The right to life means more than simply being alive—the quality of life is as relevant as its preservation (UN Committee on the Rights of the Child, 2011a, para. 38).

Likewise, obligations to protect the child's inherent right to life go beyond traditional understanding of the state protecting the child from undue interference of right to life by the state itself or private parties. It requires States Parties to set up comprehensive legislative measures, including in the fields of criminal law, family law, and police and labour law, as well as due diligence through effective implementation and enforcement of these laws (Nowak, 2005, pp. 24–36). For example, action is needed to protect children from loss of life, investigate and prosecute where necessary in cases of loss of life, and provide compensation and reparation as appropriate (Peleg & Tobin, 2019). Furthermore, the right to life is inextricably linked to the right to survival, requiring measures to increase life expectancy as well as those that protect against and mitigate the consequences of climate change, including, for example[3]:

- Lowering preventable causes of death and infant mortality
- Promoting universal sanitation
- Accessibility to clean water and pre-natal care
- Eliminating malnutrition and epidemics
- Increasing safety to reduce traffic and other forms of accident such as drowning.

Measures to protect children from violence are fundamental to the preservation of the right to life. The Committee has identified, for example, gang-related violence

---

[3] See, for example: Concluding Observations: Portugal (2014a, para. 29), Concluding Observations: Mozambique (2009a, paras. 33–34), the Implementation Handbook (Hodgkin et al., 2007, p. 84), and the declaration of the World Summit for Children (World Summit for Children, 1990).

and the vulnerability of children in street situations to violent threats to life as violations of Article 6, and called on States Parties to adopt a coordinated and structured approach to addressing these issues and ensuring the right to life of these children (2014b, paras. 3–5).[4] In line with Article 2, the Committee has also called attention to the obligation of States Parties to undertake measures that address discriminatory harmful practices that can threaten the right to life, including gender-based violence, forced marriages, gender selection, matters related to affected LGBTQ and intersex children, early marriage, 'honour killings,' and ritualistic killing of children with albinism, those accused of witchcraft, or children with disabilities (2007, para. 31, 2013c, para. 28).

In addition, the Committee has highlighted concerns over the issue of child suicide, particularly among those held in detention, and urged States Parties to take measures that address factors that render children vulnerable to suicide and self-harm, and to seek to minimise all possible risk (Peleg & Tobin, 2019). Finally, the Committee has expressed repeated concern over the impact of armed conflict on the child's right to life.[5] Protection of the right to life in these contexts is complex and requires an understanding of the interface between international humanitarian law and human rights law (addressed more fully under Article 38). However, it has urged States Parties to strengthen protection of children in respect of conflicts in which the state itself and non-state actors are responsible for breaching the right to life.[6]

Attribute Two: Ensuring the Development and the Survival of the Child to the Maximum Extent Possible

The inclusion of the obligation to ensure to the maximum extent possible the survival and development of the child reflects a commitment to translate into international human rights law the provisions in the 1959 Declaration of the Rights of the Child to provide special protection and 'to grow and develop in health.' Thus, paragraph 2 of Article 6 needs to be understood as providing the umbrella protection for survival and development of the child.

The obligations to ensure the survival of the child are elaborated in multiple articles in the Convention, including (Nowak, 2005, pp. 43–48):

---

[4] See, for example, concluding observations for Venezuela (2014b, para. 32) and Jamaica (2015, paras. 24–25).

[5] See, for example, concluding observations for Iraq (2000c, para. 23) and the Philippines (1995, para. 32).

[6] See, for example, concluding observations for Israel (2013d, paras. 25–26) and the Democratic Republic of Congo (2009b, para. 33).

- The right to health and adequate nutrition (Article 24)
- The right to an adequate standard of living, eradication of poverty and provision of basic material needs (Article 27)
- The right to recovery and rehabilitation (Articles 19 and 39)
- The right to preventive measures from harm such as provisions of information to children and parent for optimal development of the child (Articles 24, 5, 12, 17)
- Protection from exploitation and abuse in general and in times of forced displacement by natural and/or man-made causes. (Articles 19, 32–36).

In general, the factors most critical to a child's survival are more appropriately dealt with under the relevant articles. However, the Committee has used Article 6 to highlight a range of issues related to the survival of children, including acute respiratory infections and diarrhoea, anaemia, measles, pneumonia, HIV/AIDS, poor pre- and post-natal care, and low immunisation rates.[7]

The right to development must be understood in terms of the personal development of the child, rather than wider collective social and economic development. The concept is referenced throughout the Convention, including:

- Education including development of the child's talents, personality, respect for human rights, environment (Articles 28–29)
- Supportive measures to parents so that they can provide the best possible parenting (Articles 18 and 27 para 3) (UN Committee on the Rights of the Child, 2016, para. 50; UN Human Rights Council, 2016)
- Provision for children with disabilities including cultural and spiritual development (Article 23)
- An adequate standard of living for children's physical, mental, spiritual, moral and social development (Article 27)
- Protection for children against work that is harmful to their health or physical, mental, spiritual moral or social development.

The breadth of the implications of the right to survival and development can therefore be seen to provide a clear underpinning for the Committee's decision to identify Article 6 as a General Principle. Although most of the Committee's relevant recommendations could be applied to other specific rights, it has nevertheless used Article 6 to press States Parties to undertake all appropriate legislative, administrative, social, and educational measures to ensure the survival and development of the child, including:

- The needs of children in street situations (2017, paras. 31–32)
- Household food insecurity (2008a, para. 30)
- Access to sanitation (2008b, para. 30)
- Outreach of health, nutrition and birth registration services (2011b, para. 35(b))

---

[7]See, for example, concluding observations for Nepal (2005b, para. 60) and Côte d'Ivoire (2001, para. 38).

- Access to early years care (2004, para. 35)
- Support for pregnant adolescents (2012b, para. 32).

However, while the text in paragraph 2 demands that States Parties 'ensure' the survival and development of the child, the consequent obligations are qualified by the phrase 'to the maximum extent possible.' The factors that can be used to justify limitations on efforts on the part of the state include availability of resources, and acts or omission by parents, other actors, or the child themself (Peleg & Tobin, 2019).

References

Doek, J. E. (2015). Article 6 CRC and the views of the CRC Committee. *Stellenbosch Law Review, 26*(2), 254–271.

Hodgkin, R., Newell, P., & UNICEF. (2007). *Implementation handbook for the Convention on the Rights of the Child* (3rd ed.). UNICEF. Accessed September 21, 2020, from https://digitallibrary.un.org/record/620060?ln=en

Nowak, M. (2005). *A commentary on the United Nations Convention on the Rights of the Child, Article 6: The right to life, survival and development*. Brill Nijhoff. Accessed September 22, 2020, from https://brill.com/view/title/11606.

Peleg, N., & Tobin, J. (2019). Article 6: The rights to life, survival and development. In J. Tobin (Ed.), *The UN Convention on the Rights of the Child: A commentary* (pp. 186–236). Oxford University Press.

UN Commission on Human Rights. (1989). *Report of the Working Group on a Draft Convention on the Rights of the Child, 1989, E/CN.4/1989/48*. Accessed October 12, 2020, from https://digitallibrary.un.org/record/57437?ln=en.

UN Committee on the Rights of the Child. (1991, October 30). *General guidelines regarding the form and content of initial reports to be submitted by States Parties under article 44, paragraph 1(a), of the Convention, CRC/C/5*. Accessed October 12, 2020, from https://digitallibrary.un.org/record/137523?ln=en.

UN Committee on the Rights of the Child. (1995, June 20). *Concluding observations: Nicaragua, CRC/C/15/Add.36*. Accessed October 11, 2020, from https://digitallibrary.un.org/record/191818?ln=en.

UN Committee on the Rights of the Child. (1996, November 20). *General guidelines regarding the form and contents of periodic reports to be submitted by states parties under article 44, paragraph 1 (b) of the Convention, CRC/C/58*. Accessed October 12, 2020, from https://digitallibrary.un.org/record/230051?ln=en.

UN Committee on the Rights of the Child. (2000a, October 16). *Concluding observations: Burundi, CRC/C/15/Add.133*. Accessed October 11, 2020, from https://digitallibrary.un.org/record/429241?ln=en.

UN Committee on the Rights of the Child. (2000b, October 16). *Concluding observations: Colombia, CRC/C/15/Add.137*. Accessed October 11, 2020, from https://digitallibrary.un.org/record/429246?ln=en.

UN Committee on the Rights of the Child. (2000c, June 28). *Concluding observations: Iran, CRC/C/15/Add.123*. Accessed October 12 2020, from https://digitallibrary.un.org/record/422916?ln=en.

UN Committee on the Rights of the Child. (2001, July 9). *Concluding observations: Côte d'Ivoire, CRC/C/15/Add.155*. https://digitallibrary.un.org/record/451939?ln=en

UN Committee on the Rights of the Child. (2003, November 27). *General comment no. 5 (2003) General measures of implementation of the Convention on the Rights of the Child (arts. 4, 42 and 44, para. 6), CRC/GC/2003/5*. Accessed October 12, 2020, from https://digitallibrary.un.org/record/513415?ln=en.

UN Committee on the Rights of the Child. (2004, February 26). *Concluding observations: Slovenia, CRC/C/15/Add.230*. Accessed October 12, 2020, from https://digitallibrary.un.org/record/530811?ln=en.

UN Committee on the Rights of the Child. (2005a, September 21). *Concluding observations: Costa Rica, CRC/C/15/Add.266*. Accessed October 11, 2020, from https://digitallibrary.un.org/record/570468?ln=en.

UN Committee on the Rights of the Child. (2005b, September 1). *Concluding observations: Nepal, CRC/C/15/Add.261*. Accessed October 11, 2020, https://digitallibrary.un.org/record/569886?ln=en.

UN Committee on the Rights of the Child. (2006, September 20). *General comment no. 7 (2005) Implementing child rights in early childhood, CRC/C/GC/7/Rev.1*. Accessed October 12, 2020, from https://digitallibrary.un.org/record/584854?ln=en.

UN Committee on the Rights of the Child. (2007, November 13). *General comment no. 9 (2006) The rights of children with disabilities, CRC/C/GC/9*. Accessed October 12, 2020, from https://digitallibrary.un.org/record/593891?ln=en.

UN Committee on the Rights of the Child. (2008a, June 20). *Concluding observations: Sierra Leone, CRC/C/SLE/CO/2*. Accessed October 12, 2020, from https://digitallibrary.un.org/record/630782?ln=en.

UN Committee on the Rights of the Child. (2008b, October 7). *Concluding observations: Djibouti, CRC/C/DJI/CO/2*. Accessed October 12, 2020, from https://digitallibrary.un.org/record/639146?ln=en.

UN Committee on the Rights of the Child. (2009a, November 4). *Concluding observations: Mozambique, CRC/C/MOZ/CO/2*. Accessed October 11, 2020, from https://digitallibrary.un.org/record/671008?ln=en.

UN Committee on the Rights of the Child. (2009b, February 10). *Concluding observations: Democratic Republic of the Congo, CRC/C/COD/CO/2*. Accessed October 12, 2020, from https://digitallibrary.un.org/record/648538?ln=en.

UN Committee on the Rights of the Child. (2010, June 21). *Concluding observations: Nigeria, CRC/C/NGA/CO/3-4*. Accessed October 11, 2020, from https://digitallibrary.un.org/record/685180?ln=en.

UN Committee on the Rights of the Child. (2011a, July 15). *Concluding observations: Egypt, CRC/C/EGY/CO/3-4*. Accessed October 11, 2020, from https://digitallibrary.un.org/record/707466?ln=en.

UN Committee on the Rights of the Child. (2011b, August 3). *Concluding observations: Bahrain, CRC/C/BHR/CO/2-3*. https://digitallibrary.un.org/record/708488?ln=en

UN Committee on the Rights of the Child. (2012a, December 13). *Concluding observations: Liberia, CRC/C/LBR/CO/2-4*. Accessed October 11, 2020, from https://digitallibrary.un.org/record/739973?ln=en.

UN Committee on the Rights of the Child. (2012b, October 16). *Concluding observations: Namibia, CRC/C/NAM/CO/2-3*. Accessed October 12, 2020, from https://digitallibrary.un.org/record/736633?ln=en.

UN Committee on the Rights of the Child. (2013a, April 17). *General comment no. 16 (2013) on State obligations regarding the impact of the business sector on children's rights, CRC/C/GC/16*. Accessed October 12, 2020, from https://digitallibrary.un.org/record/778525?ln=en.

UN Committee on the Rights of the Child. (2013b, May 29). *General comment no. 14 (2013) On the right of the child to have his or her best interests taken as a primary consideration (art. 3, para. 1), CRC/C/GC/14*. Accessed October 12, 2020, from https://digitallibrary.un.org/record/778523?ln=en.

UN Committee on the Rights of the Child. (2013c, July 8). *Concluding observations: Guinea-Bissau, CRC/C/GNB/CO/2-4*. Accessed October 12, 2020, from https://digitallibrary.un.org/record/756269?ln=en.

UN Committee on the Rights of the Child. (2013d, July 4). *Concluding observations: Israel, CRC/C/ISR/CO/2-4*. Accessed October 12, 2020, from https://digitallibrary.un.org/record/756274?ln=en.

UN Committee on the Rights of the Child. (2014a, February 25). *Concluding observations: Portugal, CRC/C/PRT/CO/3-4*. Accessed October 11, 2020, from https://digitallibrary.un.org/record/778846?ln=en.

UN Committee on the Rights of the Child. (2014b, October 13). *Concluding observations: Venezuela, CRC/C/VEN/CO/3-5*. Accessed October 12, 2020, from https://digitallibrary.un.org/record/785293?ln=en.

UN Committee on the Rights of the Child. (2015, March 10). *Concluding observations: Jamaica, CRC/C/JAM/CO/3-4*. Accessed October 12, 2020, from https://digitallibrary.un.org/record/789759?ln=en.

UN Committee on the Rights of the Child. (2016, December 6). *General comment no. 20 (2016) on the implementation of the rights of the child during adolescence, CRC/C/GC/20*. Accessed October 12, 2020, from https://digitallibrary.un.org/record/855544?ln=en.

UN Committee on the Rights of the Child. (2017, June 21). *General comment no. 21 (2017) on children in street situations, CRC/C/GC/21*. Accessed October 12, 2020, from https://digitallibrary.un.org/record/1304490?ln=en.

UN Human Rights Committee. (2019, September 3). *CCPR general comment no. 36 (2019) Article 6, Right to life, CCPR/C/GC/36*. https://digitallibrary.un.org/record/3884724?ln=en

UN Human Rights Council. (2016). *Report of the Special Rapporteur on the right of everyone to the enjoyment of the highest attainable standard of physical and mental health A/HRC/32/32*. http://digitallibrary.un.org/record/842322

United Nations. (2006). *Compilation of general comments and general recommendations adopted by human rights treaty bodies, HRI/GEN/1/Rev. 8*. UN. Accessed April 19, 2020, from http://digitallibrary.un.org/record/576098.

UN Office of the High Commissioner for Human Rights (OHCHR). (2010). *Report of the Office of the United Nations High Commissioner for Human Rights on challenges and best practices in the implementation of the international framework for the protection of the rights of the child in the context of migration, 2010, A/HRC/15/29*. https://documents-dds-ny.un.org/doc/UNDOC/GEN/G10/151/41/pdf/G1015141.pdf?OpenElement

World Summit for Children. (1990). *World declaration on survival, protection and development of children*. https://ec.europa.eu/anti-trafficking/sites/antitrafficking/files/world_declaration_on_children_1990_en_1.pdf

Open Access This chapter is licensed under the terms of the Creative Commons Attribution 4.0 International License (http://creativecommons.org/licenses/by/4.0/), which permits use, sharing, adaptation, distribution and reproduction in any medium or format, as long as you give appropriate credit to the original author(s) and the source, provide a link to the Creative Commons license and indicate if changes were made.

The images or other third party material in this chapter are included in the chapter's Creative Commons license, unless indicated otherwise in a credit line to the material. If material is not included in the chapter's Creative Commons license and your intended use is not permitted by statutory regulation or exceeds the permitted use, you will need to obtain permission directly from the copyright holder.

Chapter 5
Article 12: The Right to Be Heard

Gerison Lansdown

> 1. States Parties shall assure to the child who is capable of forming his or her own views the right to express those views freely in all matters affecting the child, the views of the child being given due weight in accordance with the age and maturity of the child.
> 2. For this purpose, the child shall in particular be provided the opportunity to be heard in any judicial and administrative proceedings affecting the child, either directly, or through a representative or an appropriate body, in a manner consistent with the procedural rules of national law.

> **What Did Children Say?**
> 'Youth parliament or similar institutions representing all groups of children of the society and different ages should operate throughout the year and express their opinion to Ministers on all relevant draft laws. The same should happen with local authorities and all public agencies.' *(Eastern Europe)*
>
> 'Everyone working with children should be well educated and trained how to listen to children. Professionals should be trained to understand children also through their drawings.' *(Eastern Europe)*
>
> 'There would be social workers specifically trained and designated to support disabled youth, since those youth need more care in order to comfortably share their voice.' *(Western Europe/Other)*

G. Lansdown (✉)
Carleton University, Ottawa, ON, Canada

© The Author(s) 2022
Z. Vaghri et al. (eds.), *Monitoring State Compliance with the UN Convention on the Rights of the Child*, Children's Well-Being: Indicators and Research 25, https://doi.org/10.1007/978-3-030-84647-3_5

Overview

Article 12 introduces a fundamentally new right into international human rights law. In recognition of children's lack of legal autonomy in decision-making, it provides that every child capable of forming a view must be assured the right to express that view and have it given due weight in accordance with age and maturity, including in judicial and administrative proceedings (UN Committee on the Rights of the Child, 2009, para. 1). In place of a traditional focus on children's lack of competence, it establishes an obligation to consider how to enable them to engage (van Bueren, 1998, p. 136). In other words, it transforms the status of the child from one of passive recipient of adult care and protection to one of active participation and agency.

This provision was introduced into the drafting process in 1981, and although it underwent multiple revisions relating to its scope and linkages with other provisions such as best interests and rights and responsibilities of parents, the final text was adopted with relatively little dispute (Office of the United Nations High Commissioner for Human Rights and Rädda Barnen (Society: Sweden), 2007, pp. 437–444). Importantly, the qualification relating to age and maturity applies only to the weight afforded the views expressed, and not the actual expression of views. Furthermore, while imposing an obligation on States Parties to consider the child's view, it does not pose any corresponding obligation on children to express one. It has been commonly conceptualised as participation and represents one of the fundamental values of the Convention, while posing one of its major challenges to prevailing attitudes towards children (Pais, 1997, p. 426).[1] The Committee has emphasised its significance as a means of political and civil engagement through which children can advocate for their rights and hold states accountable (2016, para. 24). Opportunities for accountability and redress have been further strengthened through the adoption of the third protocol to the Convention on a complaints procedure.[2]

The requirement that States Parties must 'assure to the child' the right to express views is a powerful formulation, placing a strong and unequivocal obligation to undertake the measures necessary to realise this right. This requires that the views of the child are solicited and that they are given due weight (UN Committee on the Rights of the Child, 2009, para. 19). The Committee has interpreted Article 12 as a substantive and a procedural right. Accordingly, it is both a free-standing right of the child and integral to the realisation of all rights (2006a, para. 2). Thus, to ensure implementation of the Convention, States Parties must ensure that children are enabled to express their views and that these views inform the actions undertaken by the state to give effect to child rights.

---

[1] Also see Kay Tisdall's *Children and Young People's Participation* (2015, p. 196).

[2] Optional Protocol to the Convention on the Rights of the Child on a communications procedure, adopted and opened for signature, ratification, and accession by General Assembly resolution A/RES/66/138 of 19 December 2011 and entered into force on 14 April 2014 (UN General Assembly, 2011).

Article 12, while closely aligned to Article 13, freedom of expression, is restricted to matters affecting the child, albeit this has been interpreted widely by the Committee. However, it goes further in imposing an obligation on States Parties to introduce the legal framework and mechanisms necessary to facilitate opportunities to express views, both individually and collectively, and thereby support the active involvement of the child in all actions affecting them, and to give due weight to those views once expressed.

Article 12 also needs to be understood alongside the other civil rights in the Convention, including Article 15, the right to freedom of association and assembly and Article 17, the right to information.

General Principles

Article 2 Article 12 asserts that every child capable of forming a view has the right to express that view. Accordingly, the Committee has emphasised the obligations of States to address discrimination to ensure the right of every child to be heard and participate in all matters affecting them on an equal basis with others. It has highlighted that customary attitudes and practices can serve to undermine and place limitations on the exercise of the right to be heard. It therefore encourages States Parties to undertake appropriate measures to raise awareness and educate communities as to the negative impact of such attitudes in order to achieve full implementation of the rights of every child (2009, paras. 75–76).

Article 3 The determination of the best interests of the child needs to be informed by the views of the child. Thus, whereas the best interests of the child is the objective to be achieved, the participation of the child is a means through which those interests can be assessed and understood.

Article 6 Child participation serves as a process that promotes the full development of the child's personality and evolving capacities consistent with Article 6.

Articles Related or Linked to Article 12

As Article 12 has been identified by the Committee on the Rights of the Child as a General Principle, as well as a human right, its application needs to be considered in the realisation of all other rights. However, the concept of participation as exemplified in Article 12 is closely linked with:

- **Article 13**, freedom of expression
- **Article 14**, freedom of thought, conscience, and religion
- **Article 15**, freedom of association and assembly
- **Article 16**, right to privacy

- **Article 17**, access to information
- **Article 40**, fair trial guarantees of Article 40(2)b)
- **Optional Protocol to the Convention on the Rights of the Child on a communications procedure**

Relevant Instruments

International Covenant on Civil and Political Rights (1966), Article 19

UN Convention on the Rights of Persons with Disabilities (2006), Articles 4 (3) and 7

African Charter on the Rights and Welfare of the Child (1990), Article 4 (2)

Guidelines of the Committee of Ministers of the Council of Europe on child friendly justice (2010)

Recommendation of the Committee of Ministers of the Council of Europe on the participation of children and young people under the age of 18 (2012).

Attributes

Attribute One: The Right to Be Heard

Interpretation of the right to express views has been elaborated by the Committee in its Day of General Discussion on Article 12, and in General Comment no. 12:

Every Child Capable of Forming His or Her Own Views The Committee emphasises that this formulation must not be interpreted as a limitation on children but represents an obligation for States Parties to assess the capacity of a child to form an autonomous opinion to the greatest extent possible (2009, para. 20). States Parties should presume capacity rather than require the child to demonstrate it. The Committee discourages States Parties from introducing age limits on the exercise of this right, underlining that very young children can form views even if unable to articulate them verbally (2006b, para. 14).

The onus rests with States Parties to facilitate the expression of views, including for children with disabilities and minority, indigenous, and migrant children (UN Committee on the Rights of the Child, 2009, para. 21). Furthermore, children have the right to express views affecting them as individuals, for example, in health care, family life, education, or child protection and also at a broader level on issues affecting them as a group or constituency.

Express Those Views Freely Children must be aware of their right under Article 12 to express their views, and therefore States Parties must adopt measures to provide them with this information (UN Committee on the Rights of the Child, 2003, para. 26, 2004, para. 22). Furthermore, to ensure the free expression of views, children must be enabled to participate without coercion or pressure and in environments in which they feel safe and respected (UN Committee on the Rights of the Child, 2009, paras. 22–25).

In All Matters Affecting the Child During the drafting process, proposals to restrict the expression of views to specific issues were rejected in favour of a formulation entitling children to express view on all matters affecting them (Office of the United Nations High Commissioner for Human Rights and Rädda Barnen (Society: Sweden), 2007, pp. 437–444). In practice, the Committee supports a broad interpretation of matters, including issues not directly addressed in the Convention. For example, it highlights the importance of children's participation in respect of child protection, emergency situations, national, and international settings, and in the development of prevention strategies, and play and recreational activities, as well as all settings in which children are based.

Due Weight Given to Views in Accordance with Age and Maturity It is not sufficient to facilitate the expression of views; it is also necessary to give them serious consideration (UN Committee on the Rights of the Child, 2009, para. 28). While there is no restriction on the right to express views other than the capacity to form them, the weight afforded to those views must take account of the age and maturity of the child. Significantly, this provision recognises that it is not appropriate to use age alone as a determinant of levels of understanding, with multiple factors influencing capacity in this regard, including cultural expectations, levels of support, individual factors, experience, and provision of information (Lansdown, 2005, p. 41; UN Committee on the Rights of the Child, 2009, para. 29). The Committee emphasises that recognition must be afforded to children's increasing levels of responsibility for matters affecting them as they acquire capacities (UN Committee on the Rights of the Child, 2012, para. 85).

Attribute Two: Right to Be Heard in All Judicial and Administrative Proceedings Directly or Through a Representative

Paragraph 2 must be implemented for all relevant judicial and administrative proceedings affecting the child without limitations. It extends to proceedings initiated by the child, such as complaints against ill-treatment and school exclusion appeals, and those initiated by others which affect the child, such as parental separation or adoption, child protection or criminal proceedings, and immigration hearings (UN Committee on the Rights of the Child, 2009, paras. 32–33). States Parties must introduce legislative measures to require all such proceedings to explain how children's views have been taken into consideration.

Paragraph 2 also makes clear that the child's views must be heard within any proceeding, whether directly, or through a representative on behalf of the child. This principle should not be confused with the obligation in Article 3 to ensure that the best interests of the child are a primary consideration in all matters affecting the child. A representative for the child must transmit the child's views correctly (UN Committee on the Rights of the Child, 2009, para. 36). The final section of paragraph 2, requiring that systems for hearing the child's voice must be in accordance with procedural rules of national law, was included to stress the need for national law to include specific references to allow for the implementation of this right. It should not be interpreted as a means of allowing weak national laws to undermine full enjoyment of the child's right to be heard. Such an interpretation would be contrary to Article 4 of the Convention (Pais, 1997, p. 429).

Attribute Three: Access to Redress and Complaints Procedures

Integral to the right to express views is the right to access complaints procedures and mechanisms for redress when rights are violated. They must be accessible, safe, and effective in providing remedies for rights violations, and children must be assured that using them will not expose them to risk of violence or punishment. States Parties should establish national human rights institutions for children with a broad mandate and, in particular, powers to consider individual complaints and investigations, including those submitted directly or on behalf of children (UN Committee on the Rights of the Child, 2002). Where a child has exhausted all avenues of complaint without successful resolution, a complaint can be made by an individual child, a group of children, or someone acting on their behalf, to the Committee on the Right of the Child under the 3rd Optional Protocol (UN General Assembly, 2011).

Attribute Four: Legislative and Administrative Measures to Implement Article 12

The Committee urges States Parties take action through education, training, and public campaigns to address traditional and paternalistic attitudes that mitigate against the realisation of Article 12, with particular attention to the situation of girls (UN Committee on the Rights of the Child, 2006c, para. 28, 2017, para. 17). It encourages States Parties to support initiatives to create forums where children can elaborate their views including school councils, child clubs, and children's parliaments.[3]

Action is also needed, including through legislation and regulations, to establish the right to be heard in all settings, and to ensure the right to be heard in the development, implementation, and monitoring of all laws, policies, and programmes

---

[3] See, for example, Concluding Observations: Spain (2018, para. 17(f)).

relating to children and implemented at all levels, from the family to schools and community, and in all institutions involving children (UN Committee on the Rights of the Child, 2006d, para. 25, 2009, para. 27). Furthermore, the Convention on the Rights of Persons with Disabilities (Article 4 (3)) explicitly demands that children with disabilities, through their representative organisations, must be consulted in the development and implementation of all legislation and policies affecting them.

References

Lansdown, G. (2005). *The evolving capacities of the child*. UNICEF Innocenti Research Centre.

Office of the United Nations High Commissioner for Human Rights & Rädda Barnen (Society: Sweden). (2007). *Legislative history of the Convention on the Rights of the Child*. United Nations. https://digitallibrary.un.org/record/602462?ln=en

Pais, M. S. (1997). The Convention on the Rights of the Child. In *Manual on human rights reporting under six major international human rights instruments HR/PUB/91/1 (Rev.1)* (pp. 393–505). OHCHR. Accessed May 16, 2020, from https://www.refworld.org/docid/428085252.html.

UN Committee on the Rights of the Child. (2002, November 15). *General comment no. 2 (2002) The role of independent national human rights institutions in the promotion and protection of the rights of the child, CRC/GC/2002/2*. Accessed October 12, 2020, from https://digitallibrary.un.org/record/490983?ln=en.

UN Committee on the Rights of the Child. (2003, January 31). *Concluding observations: Iceland, CRC/C/15/Add.203*. Accessed October 12, 2020, from https://digitallibrary.un.org/record/497804?ln=en.

UN Committee on the Rights of the Child. (2004, June 30). *Concluding observations: France, CRC/C/15/Add.240*. Accessed October 12, 2020, from https://digitallibrary.un.org/record/536574?ln=en.

UN Committee on the Rights of the Child. (2006a). *Day of general discussion: The right of the child to be heard*. Accessed October 12, 2020, from https://www.ohchr.org/EN/HRBodies/CRC/Pages/DiscussionDays.aspx.

UN Committee on the Rights of the Child. (2006b, September 20). *General comment no. 7 (2005) Implementing child rights in early childhood, CRC/C/GC/7/Rev.1*. Accessed October 12, 2020, from https://digitallibrary.un.org/record/584854?ln=en.

UN Committee on the Rights of the Child. (2006c, June 8). *Concluding observations: Mexico, CRC/C/MEX/CO/3*. https://digitallibrary.un.org/record/582289?ln=en

UN Committee on the Rights of the Child. (2006d, March 17). *Concluding observations: Hungary, CRC/C/HUN/CO/2*. Accessed October 11, 2020, from https://digitallibrary.un.org/record/575773?ln=en.

UN Committee on the Rights of the Child. (2009, February 12). *General comment no. 11 (2009), Indigenous children and their rights under the Convention, CRC/C/GC/11*. Accessed October 24, 2020, from https://digitallibrary.un.org/record/648790?ln=en.

UN Committee on the Rights of the Child. (2012, October 16). *Concluding observations: Namibia, CRC/C/NAM/CO/2-3*. Accessed October 12, 2020, from https://digitallibrary.un.org/record/736633?ln=en.

UN Committee on the Rights of the Child. (2016, December 6). *General comment no. 20 (2016) on the implementation of the rights of the child during adolescence, CRC/C/GC/20*. Accessed October 12, 2020, from https://digitallibrary.un.org/record/855544?ln=en.

UN Committee on the Rights of the Child. (2017, February 28). *Concluding observations: Guatemala, CRC/C/GTM/5-6*. Accessed October 12, 2020, from https://digitallibrary.un.org/record/536574?ln=en.

UN Committee on the Rights of the Child. (2018, March 5). *Concluding observations: Spain, CRC/C/ESP/CO/5-6*. Accessed October 11, 2020, from https://digitallibrary.un.org/record/1476613?ln=en.

UN General Assembly. (2011, December 19). *Optional protocol to the Convention on the Rights of the Child on a communications procedure, A/RES/66/138*. Accessed October 12, 2020, from https://digitallibrary.un.org/record/720587?ln=en.

van Bueren, G. (1998). *The international law on the rights of the child*. Brill Nijhoff. Accessed September 22, 2020, from https://brill.com/view/title/10563.

Open Access This chapter is licensed under the terms of the Creative Commons Attribution 4.0 International License (http://creativecommons.org/licenses/by/4.0/), which permits use, sharing, adaptation, distribution and reproduction in any medium or format, as long as you give appropriate credit to the original author(s) and the source, provide a link to the Creative Commons license and indicate if changes were made.

The images or other third party material in this chapter are included in the chapter's Creative Commons license, unless indicated otherwise in a credit line to the material. If material is not included in the chapter's Creative Commons license and your intended use is not permitted by statutory regulation or exceeds the permitted use, you will need to obtain permission directly from the copyright holder.

Part II
Civil and Political Rights

Articles 7, 8, 13, 14, 15, 16, and 17

Introduction

The Convention on the Rights of the Child (the Convention) was a breakthrough in international human rights law, as it gave explicit recognition to children as subjects of civil and political rights. Although the International Covenant on Civil and Political Rights (ICCPR) extended to all people by virtue of their humanity, little explicit attention had previously been given to the specific implications of those rights in respect of children. Both Declarations on the Rights of the Child, in 1924 and 1959, emphasised the vulnerability of children and their consequent entitlement to protection but gave scant recognition to their status as active subjects with agency and incremental capacity to exercise rights on their own behalf.

The Convention transformed the landscape in terms of children's status as rights holders. In Articles 13, 14, 15, and 16, it asserts that existing rights to freedom of expression, thought, conscience, religion, association, and assembly, and to privacy, apply explicitly and equally to children. In so doing, the Convention affirms recognition of the child as a person, with views independent of parents or family, and entitled to recognition of their dignity and uniqueness as an individual. Article 7 builds on the ICCPR, not only establishing entitlement to name and nationality, but adding in the right to know and be cared for by parents. Article 8, a new provision, recognised the imperative for preservation of a child's identity, reflecting the concern at the time of drafting that children born to parents who disappeared under military dictatorships were denied knowledge of their identity. More recently, this provision has played an important role in establishing the rights to identity for children born, for example, through assisted reproductive techniques. Finally, the Convention added a new right in Article 17, establishing the right to information from the mass media, recognising its crucial role in the lives of children and its importance in enabling them to exercise their rights.

The Committee on the Rights of the Child (the Committee), in its Concluding Observations and General Comments, has helped elaborate how those rights must be interpreted, considering the role for parental guidance in line with children's evolving capacities. Critically, it has argued that while parents play a key role in helping provide direction to their children, it must always be remembered that 'the more a child knows and understands, the more their parents will have to transform direction and guidance into reminders and gradually to an exchange on an equal footing' (UN Committee on the Rights of the Child 2016, para. 18). Furthermore, 'it is the child who exercises the right to freedom of religion, not the parent, and the parental role necessarily diminishes as the child acquires an increasingly active role in exercising choice throughout adolescence' (UN Committee on the Rights of the Child 2016, para. 43) This part examines the civil and political rights contained in the Convention and their implications for the status of the child.

Reference

UN Committee on the Rights of the Child. (2016). General Comment No. 20 (2016) on the implementation of the rights of the child during adolescence, December 6, 2016, CRC/C/GC/20. https://digitallibrary.un.org/record/855544?ln=en. Accessed 12 October 2020

Chapter 6
Article 7: The Right to a Name, Nationality, and to Know and Be Cared for by Parents

Adem Arkadas-Thibert and Gerison Lansdown

1. The child shall be registered immediately after birth and shall have the right from birth to a name, the right to acquire a nationality and, as far as possible, the right to know and be cared for by his or her parents.
2. States Parties shall ensure the implementation of these rights in accordance with their national law and their obligations under the relevant international instruments in this field, in particular where the child would otherwise be stateless.

What Did Children Say?
'Government should provide birth certificates and medical reports to let the children know where they came from.' *(Asia-Pacific)*

'Government should aware every parent on the process and importance of childbirth registration.' *(Asia-Pacific)*

'Government should simplify the process of registration.' *(Asia-Pacific)*

'Hospitals should not release newborns before ensuring that they are registered.' *(Eastern Europe)*

A. Arkadas-Thibert (✉)
Marseille, France

G. Lansdown
Carleton University, Ottawa, ON, Canada

Overview

The rights to a name, birth registration, and nationality are well-established rights in international and national laws. All non-discrimination clauses of all international and regional human rights treaties include birth as a prohibited ground for discrimination. The Convention built on these treaties and introduced a new component asserting the right of the child to know and be cared for by their parents, in recognition that parental care is as important for the child's psychological stability and development as a name and nationality (Office of the United Nations High Commissioner for Human Rights and Rädda Barnen (Society: Sweden), 2007, pp. 379–80; Scruton, 2007, p. 92). Although Article 7 does not explicitly grant citizenship, international law does not make a distinction between citizenship and nationality. Rather, it regards the former as completely determined by the latter (Scruton, 2007).

The wording of Article 7 creates a strong presumption in support of the child's right to nationality and citizenship but not an absolute guarantee against statelessness (Tobin & Seow, 2019, p. 241). Proposals during the drafting of Article 7 were put forward to introduce a right to be granted nationality based on where the child was born. However, this was rejected in favour of a provision that enabled a child to acquire nationality either through the nationality of their parents or their place of birth, subject to the national law of the country (Office of the United Nations High Commissioner for Human Rights and Rädda Barnen (Society: Sweden), 2007, para. 103).

Overall, Article 7 aims to facilitate recognition of the legal personality of the child as an independent human being having agency to exercise their rights everywhere from birth, through the right to a name, through provision of full citizenship rights, through nationality, and through preventing statelessness (Hodgkin et al., 2007, pp. 97–109). In addition, in recognition of the importance of the child's parentage to their identity and optimum development, the article introduces an additional element as foundational to the best interest of the child: the right of the child to know their parents and to be cared for by their parents.

General Principles

Article 2 Birth is included as one of the prohibited grounds of discrimination in Article 2 of the Convention. Accordingly, all children must be registered without delay at birth and granted a nationality without discrimination. The Committee has highlighted concerns[1] relating to many groups of children at risk of discrimination with regard to birth registration and/or nationality including refugees, children of

---

[1] For example, see Concluding observations: Estonia (UN Committee on the Rights of the Child, 2003) and Concluding observations: Jordan (UN Committee on the Rights of the Child, 1994a).

unmarried couples, children who were born after their parents divorced, children born out of surrogacy agreements, adopted children, children born during flight from a conflict/refugee children, children of migrant parents, children of nomadic tribes, children of indigenous groups, and children of ethnic minorities (UN Office of the High Commissioner for Human Rights (OHCHR), 2010, paras. 57–61).

Article 3 In certain countries, the right of an adopted child or a child born through assisted reproductive technologies to know their birth parents is overridden in favour of the right of parents to privacy and confidentiality. Although such approaches are sometimes defended as promoting the best interests of the child (Odievre v. France, 2003), the Committee has argued that Article 7 creates strong presumption in favour of full disclosure of a child's genetic parentage. In other words, the child's best interests are served by access to information relating to their birth and birth parents (UN Committee on the Rights of the Child, 2004, para. 23, 2005a, paras. 28–29, 2005b, para. 38 et al., 2009, para. 16). In addition, the right to be cared for by one's parents is qualified by the phrase 'as far as possible.' The imperative to secure the best interests of the child would be a potential factor in determining whether it was possible to for a child to be cared for by their parents.

Article 6 Many services that are imperative for a child's development, as well as lifesaving services provided by public administration, require birth registration of the child or introduce limitations on nationality grounds. Therefore, the right to a name and nationality can be understood as an enabling right and indispensable for life and development of the child. However, lack of registration should not be used as an excuse to discriminate against those children whose birth registration is marred by inadequate or latent discriminatory laws and policies.

Article 12 Children's civil and political participation as citizens of a given country is dependent on their registration as a national in that country. Any restriction of birth registration hampers the child from exercising and enjoying their rights to participation. For example, restricting right to peaceful assembly only to those who are citizens infringes the right to fully participate in public life.

Articles Related or Linked to Article 7

Article 8, preservation of identity, including nationality, name, and family relations, relies on the name and nationality of the child being afforded from the birth of the child

Article 9, separation from parents constitutes a greater risk for children lacking birth registration

Article 10, family reunification is highly dependent on children having access to documentation relating to their birth registration

Article 18, parents have joint responsibility for their children and should be named on the birth certificate wherever possible

Article 20, children deprived of their family environment are entitled to access their original birth registration documents in order to provide them with knowledge of their birth family and to provide continuity

Article 21, adoption and inter-country adoption can result in children being provided with a new name and parents, but children should have access to their original birth registration wherever possible

Article 22, asylum seeking and refugee children are at greater risk of loss of identity and will often require birth documentation in order to apply for refugee status

Article 30, children of minorities or indigenous peoples will often be at risk of discrimination and loss of status if they are unable to provide birth registration documentation

Article 35, prevention of sale, trafficking and abduction necessitates that children have access to their birth registration documents.

Relevant Instruments

The UN Universal Declaration of Human Rights (1948), Article 15, provides for the right to a nationality.

The International Covenant on Civil and Political Rights (1966), Article 24, provides for rights to birth registration and to a nationality.

Some other human rights treaties also cover these rights:

- International Convention on the Elimination of all forms of Racial Discrimination (1966), Article 5
- UN Convention on the Elimination of All Forms of Discrimination against Women (1979), Article 9
- International Convention on the Protection of the Rights of All Migrant Workers and Members of Their Families (1990), Article 29
- UN Convention on the Rights of Persons with Disabilities (2006), Article 18
- UN International Convention for the Protection of All Persons from Enforced Disappearance (2007), Article 25
- American Convention on Human Rights 'Pact of San Jose, Costa Rica' (B-32) (1978), Article 20
- African Charter on the Rights and Welfare of the Child (1990), Article 6
- Protocol to the African Charter on Human and Peoples' Rights on the Rights of Women in Africa (2003), Article 6.

Attributes

Attribute One: Free, Compulsory, and Accessible Birth Registration Immediately After Birth of All Children

A central tenet of Article 7 is free, compulsory, and accessible birth registration, immediately after the child's birth. Information on implementation of this right constitutes part of the common core document that all treaty bodies require from States Parties in their constructive dialogues with them (United Nations, 2009). As the Human Rights Committee pointed out in their General Comment no. 17 on the Rights of the Child (ICCPR 2011), birth registration is an enabling right, and must therefore be free, compulsory, and accessible for all, including hard to reach populations, through mobile units, public information campaigns, and as part of pre-natal and post-natal health care services (United Nations, 2006, p. 183).

Birth registration is a vital passport to accessing health services, social security, and education. It can be facilitated using digital and mobile birth registration systems. There also need to be opportunities for non-registered children to have their birth registration easily completed later through health care, educational, and social services (United Nations, 2006, p. 183).

Attribute Two: Acquiring a Name, Nationality, and Prevention of Statelessness of a Child

The right to a name from birth is widely recognised in international law and affords the child both legal status and an identity and sense of self. Although the naming of a child at birth is, inevitably, a right exercised by the parents on behalf of the child, the Committee makes clear that there are limits to the scope of parental discretion. In line with Article 12, a child of sufficient age and maturity has the right to change, or refuse to change, their name.[2] Such a circumstance might arise, for example, in the context of parental divorce, separation, or marriage, or adoption.

Closely linked to the right to a name is the right to acquisition of nationality, a provision which, as with birth registration, States Parties are required to provide information on for all treaty bodies. It is an enabling right and included in non-discrimination clauses, as a necessary pathway to non-discriminatory service provision for children (United Nations, 2009). The Committee has emphasised that States Parties must adopt all possible measures to ensure that every child has a nationality from birth. This requirement effectively imposes an obligation on States Parties to ensure that no child is left stateless (UN Committee on the Protection of the

---

[2] See, for example, Concluding observations for Niue Islands (UN Committee on the Rights of the Child, 2013a, paras. 30–31) and Federal republic of Yugoslavia, (Serbia and Montenegro) (UN Committee on the Rights of the Child, 1996, para. 31).

Rights of All Migrant Workers and Members of Their Families and UN Committee on the Rights of the Child, 2017, paras. 20–26). To this end, it has recommended to States Parties that they collect data on stateless children, collaborate with relevant international agencies, legislate to protect against arbitrary deprivation of nationality, and become party to relevant international instruments that protect against statelessness (Tobin & Seow, 2019, p. 256).

In accordance with Article 2, States Parties should not discriminate in respect of acquisition of nationality, on the basis of the nationality of a child being different to the country in which they live, or because of the lack of nationality (UN Committee on the Protection of the Rights of All Migrant Workers and Members of Their Families and UN Committee on the Rights of the Child, 2017, para. 25). States Parties must provide options for children to acquire citizenship without discrimination within their jurisdiction (UN Committee on the Rights of the Child, 2005c, paras. 11, 12). Consideration should also be given to both parents equally being able to pass their nationality to their children, in accordance with Article 9 of the Convention on the Elimination of All Forms of Discrimination against Women.

Attribute Three: Knowing and Being Cared for by Their Parents

All children have a right to know their origins and their parents. The right of the child to know and be cared for by their parents, as far as possible, provides a baseline for interpretation of other rights relating to the child's right to family life, including the presumption against separation from parents (Article 9), family reunification (Article 10), responsibilities for both parents to care for their children (Articles 18 and 27), and the rights of children in alternative care and to adoption (Articles 20 and 21) (Tobin & Seow, 2019, p. 239). The Convention does not define parents, but the Committee has stressed the need to understand the term in its broadest sense to include 'biological, adoptive, or foster parents or members of the extended family or community as provided for by local custom' (UN Committee on the Rights of the Child, 2013b, para. 59). Furthermore, taken in conjunction with Article 8, the right to preserve identity, the term can also be understood to include knowing the identity of any person with whom they have a gestational or biological link, for example, as a result of assisted reproductive technologies or surrogacy (Gaskin v. The United Kingdom, 1989, para. 39).

The qualification that this right must be exercised 'as far as possible' allows that in some circumstances it may not be possible for the child to know their parents: the parentage may not be known, disclosure may run counter to the child's best interests, or it may lead to a conflict of other interests such as the privacy of a biological parent.

However, the presumption is very strongly in favour of the child's right to know.[3] In cases where the child is placed in protective custody of another family in the form of foster care, adoption, or institutional care, the child should be provided with option to know their parents and origins (UN Committee on the Rights of the Child, 2004, para. 23, 2005a, paras. 28, 29, 2005b, para. 38 et al.). This option should consider the best interests of the child, providing the child with enough information to make an informed decision.

References

Gaskin v. The United Kingdom. (1989). European Court of Human Rights. Accessed October 22, 2020, from http://hudoc.echr.coe.int/eng?i=001-57491.

Hodgkin, R., Newell, P., & UNICEF. (2007). *Implementation handbook for the Convention on the Rights of the Child* (3rd ed.). UNICEF. Accessed September 21, 2020, from https://digitallibrary.un.org/record/620060?ln=en.

Odievre v. France. (2003). European Court of Human Rights. Accessed October 13, 2020, from http://hudoc.echr.coe.int/eng?i=001-60935.

Office of the United Nations High Commissioner for Human Rights & Rädda Barnen (Society: Sweden). (2007). *Legislative history of the Convention on the Rights of the Child*. United Nations. https://digitallibrary.un.org/record/602462?ln=en

Scruton, R. (2007). *The Palgrave Macmillan dictionary of political thought* (3rd ed.). Palgrave Macmillan. https://doi.org/10.1057/9780230625099

Tobin, J., & Seow, F. S. (2019). Article 7: The rights to birth registration, a name, nationality and to know and be cared for by parents. In J. Tobin (Ed.), *The UN Convention on the Rights of the Child: A commentary* (pp. 237–280). Oxford University Press.

UN Committee on the Protection of the Rights of All Migrant Workers and Members of Their Families & UN Committee on the Rights of the Child. (2017, November 16). *Joint general comment no. 23 (2017) on State obligations regarding the human rights of children in the context of international migration in countries of origin, transit, destination and return, CMW/C/GC/4, CRC/C/GC/23*. Accessed October 12, 2020, from https://digitallibrary.un.org/record/1323015?ln=en.

UN Committee on the Rights of the Child. (1994a, April 25). *Concluding observations: Jordan, CRC/C/15/Add.21*. Accessed October 12, 2020, from https://digitallibrary.un.org/record/161440?ln=en.

UN Committee on the Rights of the Child. (1994b, April 25). *Concluding observations: Norway, CRC/C/15/Add.23*. Accessed October 23, 2020, from https://digitallibrary.un.org/record/197744?ln=en.

UN Committee on the Rights of the Child. (1995, February 15). *Concluding observations: Denmark, CRC/C/15/Add.33*. Accessed October 23, 2020, from https://digitallibrary.un.org/record/198497?ln=en.

UN Committee on the Rights of the Child. (1996, February 13). *Concluding observations: Yugoslavia (Serbia and Montenegro), CRC/C/15/Add.49*. Accessed October 11, 2020, from https://digitallibrary.un.org/record/210143?ln=en.

---

[3] See, for example, concluding observations of the Committee on Norway (1994b, para. 10), Denmark (1995, para. 11), Morocco (2014, para. 33), Luxembourg (2005a, paras. 28, 29), France (2004, para. 23), and Armenia (2005b, para. 38 et al.) CRC/C/15/Add.225, para. 38 et al.

UN Committee on the Rights of the Child. (2003, March 17). *Concluding observations: Estonia, CRC/C/15/Add.196*. Accessed October 12, 2020, from https://digitallibrary.un.org/record/497792?ln=en.

UN Committee on the Rights of the Child. (2004, June 30). *Concluding observations: France, CRC/C/15/Add.240*. Accessed October 12, 2020, from https://digitallibrary.un.org/record/536574?ln=en.

UN Committee on the Rights of the Child. (2005a, March 31). *Concluding observations: Luxembourg, CRC/C/15/Add.250*. Accessed October 11, 2020, from https://digitallibrary.un.org/record/557392?ln=en.

UN Committee on the Rights of the Child. (2005b, October 12). *Concluding observations: Algeria, CRC/C/15/Add.269*. Accessed October 24, 2020, from https://digitallibrary.un.org/record/570473?ln=en.

UN Committee on the Rights of the Child. (2005c, September 1). *General comment no. 6 (2005) treatment of unaccompanied and separated children outside their country of origin, CRC/GC/2005/6*. Accessed October 12, 2020, from https://digitallibrary.un.org/record/566055?ln=en.

UN Committee on the Rights of the Child. (2009, February 12). *General comment no. 11 (2009), Indigenous children and their rights under the Convention, CRC/C/GC/11*. Accessed October 24, 2020, from https://digitallibrary.un.org/record/648790?ln=en.

UN Committee on the Rights of the Child. (2013a, June 26). *Concluding observations: Niue, CRC/C/NIU/CO/1*. Accessed October 11, 2020, from https://digitallibrary.un.org/record/751626?ln=en.

UN Committee on the Rights of the Child. (2013b, May 29). *General comment no. 14 (2013) on the right of the child to have his or her best interests taken as a primary consideration (art. 3, para. 1), CRC/C/GC/14*. Accessed October 12, 2020, from https://digitallibrary.un.org/record/778523?ln=en.

UN Committee on the Rights of the Child. (2014, October 14). *Concluding observations: Morocco, CRC/C/MAR/CO/3-4*. Accessed October 23, 2020, from https://digitallibrary.un.org/record/793887?ln=en.

United Nations. (2006). *Compilation of general comments and general recommendations adopted by human rights treaty bodies, HRI/GEN/1/Rev. 8*. UN. Accessed April 19, 2020, from http://digitallibrary.un.org/record/576098.

United Nations. (2009). *Compilation of guidelines on the form and content of reports to be submitted by States parties to the international human rights treaties, HRI/GEN/2/Rev. 6*. UN. Accessed October 13, 2020, from https://digitallibrary.un.org/record/658873?ln=en.

UN Office of the High Commissioner for Human Rights (OHCHR). (2010). *Report of the Office of the United Nations High Commissioner for Human Rights on challenges and best practices in the implementation of the international framework for the protection of the rights of the child in the context of migration, 2010, A/HRC/15/29*. https://documents-dds-ny.un.org/doc/UNDOC/GEN/G10/151/41/pdf/G1015141.pdf?OpenElement

Open Access This chapter is licensed under the terms of the Creative Commons Attribution 4.0 International License (http://creativecommons.org/licenses/by/4.0/), which permits use, sharing, adaptation, distribution and reproduction in any medium or format, as long as you give appropriate credit to the original author(s) and the source, provide a link to the Creative Commons license and indicate if changes were made.

The images or other third party material in this chapter are included in the chapter's Creative Commons license, unless indicated otherwise in a credit line to the material. If material is not included in the chapter's Creative Commons license and your intended use is not permitted by statutory regulation or exceeds the permitted use, you will need to obtain permission directly from the copyright holder.

Chapter 7
Article 8: The Right to Preservation of Identity

Adem Arkadas-Thibert

1. States Parties undertake to respect the right of the child to preserve his or her identity, including nationality, name and family relations as recognized by law without unlawful interference.
2. Where a child is illegally deprived of some or all of the elements of his or her identity, States Parties shall provide appropriate assistance and protection, with a view to re-establishing speedily his or her identity.

What Did Children Say?
'Children are allowed to take passports as a right to their names, family and nationality.' (Africa)

'Countries should make birth certificates free', one individual saying it is 'ridiculous that some individuals have to pay for birth certificates.' (Western Europe/Other)

'It's important that the government does not make the process to get the documents too complicated.' (Western Europe/Other)

'Children should not be migrated from their home to anywhere without the presence of their parents.' (Asia-Pacific)

A. Arkadas-Thibert (✉)
Marseille, France

Overview

Article 8 provides for preservation of the identity of the child in general, and in particular preservation of their nationality, name, and family relations. As Tobin explains using the words of Geraldine Van Bueren, Article 8 is the vehicle through which a biological entity transforms into a legal being, confirming the 'existence of a specific legal personality capable of bearing rights and duties' (Tobin & Todres, 2019, p. 279; van Bueren, 1998, p. 117). Therefore, it is a prerequisite for the exercise of all human rights for children.

The unique quality of Article 8 relies upon it being the first human rights law provision recognising the right to preservation of the child's identity explicitly. Previous human rights treaties had only provided protection for specific elements of a person's identity, such as nationality, freedom of thought, conscience and religion, freedom of expression, respect for private life, and the right to participate in cultural life (Tobin & Todres, 2019, p. 280).

Article 8 was introduced by Argentina, which was then dealing with cases of enforced disappearances during the junta regime (Hodgkin et al., 2007, pp. 97–109). Many countries raised questions about its relevance, as preservation of identity had already been protected in other articles of the Convention (UN Commission on Human Rights, 1985, paras. 1–3). However, it was argued that children of parents who were subject to enforced disappearance were at greater risk of being discriminated against. In addition, cases arise where the nationality of a child, as part of their identity, cannot be preserved due to gender-based discrimination (denial of passing parental identity from mothers), civil status-based discrimination (children born out of wedlock), or migration-based discrimination (children of migrant parents, born or lived in the country for most of their life) (UN Human Rights Council. Working Group on Enforced or Involuntary Disappearances, 2013, para. 8). Furthermore, enforced disappearances of children or related cases of irregular adoptions may directly violate the right to preservation of identity by concealing the identity of the children and preventing re-establishment of the bond between the disappeared children and their families, their heritage, culture, and their identity (Pais, 1997, pp. 433–34).

In 2010, with the adoption of the International Convention for the Protection of All Persons from Enforced Disappearance (CED), another international human rights treaty recognised the right to one's identity. Articles 4 and 25 of the CED contribute to further define Article 8 of the Convention by:

- Criminalising abductions and enforced disappearance of children and punishing the perpetrators as a measure of countering impunity in such cases or times where state officials are involved in abductions
- Preventing and punishing enforced disappearances of children, their parents, and babies born during the captivity of pregnant mothers subjected to enforced disappearance
- Criminalising the falsification, concealment or destruction of documents attesting to the true identity of children

- Searching for or cooperating with others in the search for disappeared children and the return of children to their families of origin
- Having legal procedures in place to review adoption and, where appropriate, to annul any adoption or placement of children that originated in an enforced disappearance
- Preserving or reinstating the identity of the child with their nationality, name, and family relations.

Because CED is not a widely ratified human rights treaty, it is imperative for the best interests of the child that Article 8 of the Convention is interpreted along with CED to fill possible legal protection gaps for children.

More recently, references to Article 8 and the child's right to identity are recurrent in contexts including the 'children's right to know their genetic identity in the cases of assisted reproductive technology; their cultural and biological identity in cases of adoption and surrogacy; their gender identity in cases of gender reassignment; and the preservation of their disability identity in debates about genetic manipulation' (Tobin & Todres, 2019, p. 280). This illustrates the pivotal importance of the Article 8 in the attribution of the legal personality, and the breadth of issues impacting the preservation of a child's right to identity, beyond those that originally led to the inclusion of Article 8 in the Convention.

General Principles

Article 2 Children of parents who were subject to enforced disappearance themselves are at a greater risk of being discriminated against (Hodgkin et al., 2007, p. 113). Therefore, States Parties should have anti-discrimination legislation as a preventive measure for children from parents of minority groups, or certain ethnic, political, or social backgrounds (UN Human Rights Council. Working Group on Enforced or Involuntary Disappearances, 2013, para. 7). States Parties should introduce preventive and protective legal and policy measures to address discrimination against children affected by enforced disappearances and related cases of irregular adoptions.

Article 3 Article 8 is based on the best interests of the child, linking human rights law with international and national criminal law in situations of enforced disappearances and related cases of irregular adoptions (Doek, 2006, pp. 7–14). It provides legal guarantees for the right to preservation of recognition as a person before the law after irregular adoptions, along with protection of the right to liberty and security of the person from enforced disappearance (Office of the United Nations High Commissioner for Human Rights and Rädda Barnen (Society: Sweden), 2007, pp. 133–34).

Article 6 The right to preservation of identity of the child, including their nationality, name, and family relationships, is intertwined with their individuality and private life. Therefore, it is necessary for the development of the child (Pais, 1997, p. 433; UN Human Rights Council. Working Group on Enforced or Involuntary Disappearances, 2013, paras. 19–23). Enforced disappearances of children or related cases of irregular adoptions directly violate the right to preservation of identity by concealing the identity of the children and preventing re-establishment of the bond between the disappeared children and their families, their heritage, culture, and their identity (Pais, 1997, pp. 433–4).

Article 12 The right to participation is directly linked to the preservation of identity, as it relates to the child's right to be heard in decisions of administrative proceedings in situations of enforced disappearance, related cases of irregular adoptions, and other administrative procedures (UN Human Rights Council. Working Group on Enforced or Involuntary Disappearances, 2013, paras. 1–8).

Articles Related or Linked to Article 8

Article 7, preservation of identity relies on the right to a name and nationality, the prevention of statelessness, and to know and be cared for by parents.

Article 9, separation from parents may be detrimental to identity preservation and family relations.

Article 10, entering or leaving countries for family reunification requires a particular attention in term of procedural regulation to ensure identity preservation.

Article 11, illicit transfer and non-return of children abroad expose the child to the risk of losing identity, including nationality, name and family relations.

Article 16, protection from arbitrary interference in privacy, family, and home also contribute to ensure the respect of the right of the identity of the child at the related family relations from unlawful interference.

Article 20, children deprived of their family environment have the right to know their origins and background.

Article 30, right to enjoy culture, religion, and language; protecting the child against interference in children's identity and have continuity of upbringing, particularly with regard to their ethnic, cultural, and linguistic background

Relevant Instruments

For the reasons explained above, with the exception of the Articles 4 and 25 of the UN International Convention for the Protection of All Persons from Enforced Disappearance (2007), there is no other international or regional human rights treaty that contains a provision similar to Article 8 of the Convention.

Attributes

Attribute One: Establishment of Criminal and Procedural Preventive Measures

States Parties are required to introduce preventive measures for children affected by enforced disappearance and/or related cases of irregular adoptions. They must clearly criminalise enforced disappearances and irregular adoptions and introduce punitive clauses for perpetrators in their criminal code. The law must be implemented to eliminate impunity, through effective investigations and punishments (UN Human Rights Council. Working Group on Enforced or Involuntary Disappearances, 2013, paras. 41–45).

The States Parties that have a history of grave human rights violations, including enforced disappearances and irregular adoptions, should set up independent criminal and administrative oversight mechanisms, DNA databases, and compensation mechanisms. This would allow children affected to obtain redress and remedy for their infringed identity rights, including

- Re-establishing their identity
- Speedy family reunification re-establishing their relationship with their family, and
- Rehabilitation to affected children (as per CED Articles 4 and 25).

Attribute Two: Establishment of Protective Legal and Administrative Procedures

Attribute two deals with the protective component for children affected by enforced disappearance or related cases of irregular adoptions as well as other cases of preservation of nationality component of identity.

States Parties should have laws to protect children who are affected with enforced disappearance or related cases of irregular adoptions; specifically, their identities, including nationality, name, and family relationship, must be preserved through facilitating procedures for them to re-establish their identities and relationships without time limitation in bringing such cases to before a court of law (as per CED Article 24).

Laws should also provide compensation for any damages or loss of rights during time affected with enforced disappearance or related cases of irregular adoptions (Pais, 1997, pp. 433–4).

In addition, legislation should be introduced to protect children from discrimination by preserving their nationality-based identity through provision of options for acquiring nationality from both parents, regardless of the parents' civil status, and from having lived in the state for a significant period of time (UN Human Rights

Council. Working Group on Enforced or Involuntary Disappearances, 2013, paras. 30–36).

References

Doek, J. (2006). *A commentary on the United Nations Convention on the Rights of the Child, Articles 8-9: The right to preservation of identity and the right not to be separated from his or her parents*. Brill Nijhoff. Accessed October 23, 2020, from https://brill.com/view/title/11611.

Hodgkin, R., Newell, P., & UNICEF. (2007). *Implementation handbook for the Convention on the Rights of the Child* (3rd ed.). UNICEF. Accessed September 21, 2020, from https://digitallibrary.un.org/record/620060?ln=en

Office of the United Nations High Commissioner for Human Rights & Rädda Barnen (Society: Sweden). (2007). *Legislative history of the Convention on the Rights of the Child*. United Nations. https://digitallibrary.un.org/record/602462?ln=en

Pais, M. S. (1997). The Convention on the Rights of the Child. In *Manual on human rights reporting under six major international human rights instruments HR/PUB/91/1 (Rev.1)* (pp. 393–505). OHCHR. Accessed May 16, 2020, from https://www.refworld.org/docid/428085252.html.

Tobin, J., & Todres, J. (2019). Article 8: The right to preservation of a child's identity. In J. Tobin (Ed.), *The UN Convention on the Rights of the Child: A commentary* (pp. 281–306). Oxford University Press.

UN Commission on Human Rights. (1985, March 13). *Summary record of the 54th meeting, held at the Palais des Nations, Geneva, on Wednesday: Commission on Human Rights, 41st session. E/CN.4/1985/SR.54*. Accessed October 11, 2020, from https://digitallibrary.un.org/record/83533?ln=en.

UN Human Rights Council. Working Group on Enforced or Involuntary Disappearances. (2013). *General comment on children and enforced disappearances / adopted by the Working Group on Enforced or Involuntary Disappearances at its 98th session, 31 October–9 November 2012, A/HRC/WGEID/98/1*. Accessed October 23, 2020, from https://digitallibrary.un.org/record/768004?ln=en.

van Bueren, G. (1998). *The international law on the rights of the child*. Brill Nijhoff. Accessed September 22, 2020, from https://brill.com/view/title/10563.

Open Access This chapter is licensed under the terms of the Creative Commons Attribution 4.0 International License (http://creativecommons.org/licenses/by/4.0/), which permits use, sharing, adaptation, distribution and reproduction in any medium or format, as long as you give appropriate credit to the original author(s) and the source, provide a link to the Creative Commons license and indicate if changes were made.

The images or other third party material in this chapter are included in the chapter's Creative Commons license, unless indicated otherwise in a credit line to the material. If material is not included in the chapter's Creative Commons license and your intended use is not permitted by statutory regulation or exceeds the permitted use, you will need to obtain permission directly from the copyright holder.

Chapter 8
Article 13: The Right to Freedom of Expression

Gerison Lansdown and Ziba Vaghri

1. The child shall have the right to freedom of expression; this right shall include freedom to seek, receive and impart information and ideas of all kinds, regardless of frontiers, either orally, in writing or in print, in the form of art, or through any other media of the child's choice.
2. The exercise of this right may be subject to certain restrictions, but these shall only be such as are provided by law and are necessary:
   (a) For respect of the rights or reputations of others; or
   (b) For the protection of national security or of public order (ordre public), or of public health or morals.

What Did Children Say?
Government should create guidelines in schools to teach the students about the boundaries of their freedom of speech to prevent racist/sexist/harmful comments. *(Asia-Pacific)*

We have to make sure that children enjoy freedom of expression at home, in the street, in the school, in the courts and in public spaces. *(Africa)*

(continued)

G. Lansdown
Carleton University, Ottawa, ON, Canada

Z. Vaghri (✉)
University of New Brunswick Saint John, Saint John, NB, Canada
e-mail: ziba.vaghri@unb.ca

> Parents should tell us that there is harmful negative information, like naked picture, human trafficking, pornography, criticising others, learning about drugs, learning about beating. *(Africa)*
>
> The opportunity to have access to information, libraries, schools, websites in order to, we quote, 'be smart and know what to say.' *(Eastern Europe)*

Overview

The right to freedom of expression represents the foundation of a free society and constitutes a central dimension of human dignity and autonomy. Its inclusion in earlier human rights treaties has always been recognised, in principle, as extending to children as well as adults, but in practice this right has not been fully acknowledged, as exemplified by the failure to include such a provision in the 1924 and 1959 Declarations on the Rights of the Child (Tobin & Parkes, 2019, p. 437). Its explicit inclusion through Article 13 of the Convention provides affirmation of its equal relevance to the lives of children, and their equal entitlement to enjoy the freedom it affords. Its aim is to assure that a child, in all spheres of their public and private life, is able to express themself, and to seek, obtain, and share information and ideas without interference or being hampered by cultural, political, religious, or other barriers. Both dimensions are vital and mutually reinforcing. The freedom to seek and receive information provides the foundation for the child's development and understanding of their world and, in turn, contributes towards their consequent capacity to contribute, engage and express themselves (Thorgeirsdóttir, 2006).

Article 13 of the Convention differs from Article 19(1) of the ICCPR, in that it fails to include an explicit reference to children's rights to freedom of opinion. During the drafting of Article 13, there was a proposal to include a provision stating: 'the child shall have the right to hold opinions without interference' (Office of the United Nations High Commissioner for Human Rights and Rädda Barnen (Society: Sweden), 2007, p. 449). It was not included in the final text and the records of the drafting history offer no explanation for its deletion. However, the Committee has taken the view that the holding of an opinion is a precondition of the expression of views (UN Committee on the Rights of the Child, 2009, para. 81). The right to hold an opinion is therefore implicit in the right to freedom of expression.

Article 13 is not absolute and can be limited for the protection of the rights of others or for purposes of national security, public health, or morals. These restrictions broadly replicate those in the ICCPR, except that Article 13 does not include a reference to the fact that the exercise of the right itself imposes certain responsibilities on the individual. This can perhaps be explained in terms of the evolving capacities of the child and the role of parents to provide direction and guidance until such time as the child is able to exercise that responsibility for themselves.

General Principles

Article 2 Every child must be treated equally with regard to their right to free expression and inquiry, and access to information and ideas in accessible formats. However, many children can experience discrimination in exercising this right, including girls, minority and indigenous groups, children living in rural or remote areas, children with disabilities, migrants, refugees and asylum seekers, LGBTQ children, victims of sexual exploitation, and those in extreme poverty or living in institutions or alternative care. Such discrimination may be indirect, for example, through exclusion from or disadvantage in accessing opportunities to seek or impart information, in particular, and increasingly, in relation to their access to digital technologies. They may also experience direct discrimination in the form of abusive, hateful, or discriminatory communication or treatment, or hostility, threats, or punishment. In order to address potential discrimination, States Parties need to adopt measures to promote access to information, lower the cost of connectivity, provide free access to children in safe dedicated public spaces, and to invest in policies and programmes that support all children's use of digital technologies at school, home, and in their community (UNICEF Policy Lab, 2018). They should also adopt measures to prevent discriminatory harassment and harm.

Article 3 The best interests of the child are realised through the fullest possible implementation of the rights in the Convention (UN Committee on the Rights of the Child, 2013, para. 4). Accordingly, it can be understood that it is in the child's best interests to have their right to access and impart information freely fully respected. The best interests principle must also be taken into account in determining whether certain forms of information or expression might be harmful to them, bearing in mind their evolving capacities and development.

Article 6 The right to freedom of expression contributes to the fulfilment of Article 6, the right to life, survival and development, as neurobiology literature has clearly established the positive impact of expression and stimulation (giving and taking information) on the developing brain and overall development (Shonkoff, 2009). Analogies have been drawn between the necessity of freedom of expression for children's development and that of 'air and light for physical existence.' (Thorgeirsdóttir, 2006, p. 3). Additionally, the exercise of the right to access information could facilitate acquisition of information relevant to children's health and well-being consistent with Article 6 (Shonkoff, 2009).

Article 12 The right to freedom of expression is closely linked with Article 12 but differs in several significant ways. First, it is unlimited in scope, unlike Article 12 which is limited to 'all matters affecting the child.' Second, it is not limited to children capable of forming a view, as required in Article 12. Third, it includes a right to seek and receive information. Article 12 does not explicitly address the right to information, although in practice the expression of views does necessitate its provision. Finally, Article 13 imposes no obligation on adults to hear or to establish mechanisms through which to hear the views or opinions of children, a provision which is central to the obligations under Article 12 (UN Committee on the Rights of the Child, 2009, para. 81). Together, Article 12 and 13 are mutually reinforcing. Whereas Article 13 is a right that applies equally to adults and children, Article 12 adds strengthened protection for children to express their views in recognition of their lack of autonomy in decision-making in most arenas of their lives.

Articles Related or Linked to Article 13

Article 5, the responsibilities and duties of parents to provide appropriate guidance to children must take account of their evolving capacities in exercising their Article 13 rights.

Article 14, freedom of thought, conscience, and religion is closely linked to the right to freedom of expression.

Article 15, which provides for the child's right to freedom of association and peaceful assembly, represents a means of exercising their right to freedom of expression.

Article 16 requires that children are entitled to protection of privacy when exercising their right to freedom of expression.

Article 17, together with Article 13, provide for the right to access to information.

Articles 28 and 29, rights to and aims of education require both that children are able to learn about their rights to freedom of expression and also to exercise that right within the school environment.

Article 30 addresses the rights of indigenous children and children of minorities to enjoy own culture, religion, and language, and as such is closely linked with the right to freedom of expression.

Article 31, the right to play, and cultural activities, constitutes a central aspect of children's lives where they are able and entitled to exercise freedom of expression.

Relevant Instruments

UN Universal Declaration of Human Rights (1948), Article 19, also declares the right to expression and opinion a right of every human being.

International Covenant on Civil and Political Rights (1966), Article 19(1)

International Convention on the Elimination of all forms of Racial Discrimination (1966), Article 5

UN Convention on the Rights of Persons with Disabilities (2006), Article 21 (freedom of expression and opinion, and access to information) and Article 29 (freedom of participation in public and political life).

Attributes

Attribute One: Access to Information

Children are entitled to seek and receive information. Article 13 affirms that the child is an active agent in exploring information and not merely a recipient of ideas or information provided by others. This provision extends to the widest possible interpretation of information (Pais, 1997, p. 434). Children have the right to seek out information relating to the public domain, for example, on any issue or topic in which they have an interest or which can contribute to their education or health and development, or expression of their identity. Article 13 also extends the right to government information relating to their personal history or identity, for example, access to records or original birth certificates for children who have been placed in care, adopted, or born as a result of assisted reproductive techniques (Hussain and UN Commission on Human Rights, 1998, para. 14).

The right to information encompasses oral, written, and print forms, online and offline, and from a diversity of sources including newspapers, books, magazines, radio, television, Internet, social media, and the arts. Article 13 also entitles children to information regardless of frontiers and therefore must encompass the right to access information from different cultural, linguistic, social, political, and geographic arenas. In light of the growing significance of the digital environment as a source of information for children, and the obligation to protect children from harmful material, States Parties should ensure that digital providers introduce and enforce appropriate human content moderation to meet their child users' needs for both access and protection (Council of Europe, 2018, para. 20). Where content controls, including parental control tools and school filtering systems are used to protect children from harmful information, they must balance protection against children's right to access information, consistent with children's evolving capacities.

Attribute Two: Freedom of Imparting Information (from Children to Adults)

Every child is entitled to express and impart views without restriction in respect of age or capacity to any audience or indeed, to none, and on whatever issue they choose. The Committee has elaborated that the mode of expression can include 'spoken written and sign language, non-verbal expression such as images or objects of art, and the means of expression extend to books, newspapers, pamphlets, posters, banners, digital and audio-visual media, as well as dress and personal style' (UN Committee on the Rights of the Child, 2016, para. 42). Depending on the age of the child, it might also include clothing, hairstyles, role modelling, and different forms of sexual expression and identity, as well as more typical adult agendas such political or human rights discourse, personal commentary, cultural and artistic expression, or commercial advertising. It can also encompass content or forms that may be regarded as offensive, provided they do not breach the restrictions elaborated in paragraph 2 (UN Human Rights Committee, 2011, para. 11).

As with the right to seek and receive information, children are entitled to express their views across national, social, political, and cultural boundaries, including through the online world of the Internet and social media (LaRue & UN Human Rights Committee, 2011, paras. 20–21). Filters and other barriers, including safety measures, should not restrict children's freedom of expression. The Committee has expressed concern that where children express political or other views and identities in the digital environment, this can attract criticism, hostility, threats, or punishment and stressed that States Parties should take steps necessary to overcome these challenges, including actions to prevent the occurrence of harassment, threats, misinformation, censorship, data breaches, and digital surveillance (Cho et al., 2020).

Children's right to expression can only be restricted for reasons delineated in Article 13, paragraph 2, or where parents consider that limits are required in the best interests of the child, in relation to their evolving capacities and to protect them from harm.

Attribute Three: State Obligations

States Parties have an obligation to respect, protect, and fulfil the right to freedom of expression and, accordingly, must take all reasonable measures:

- To respect the right by ensuring that the state does not violate the right
- To protect the right by ensuring that non-state actors do not violate the right
- To fulfil the right by ensuring its effective realisation.

The Committee has consistently recommended that States Parties act with regard to meeting these obligations in respect of Article 13. Such action should include:

- Explicit recognition in law to safeguard the right of every child to freedom of expression, including guidance on the nature of any restrictions that can be imposed to avoid arbitrary interpretations of state laws and the Convention.[1]
- Effective mechanisms for protection of rights, and remedies when rights are violated (UN Human Rights Committee, 2011, para. 21). Such remedies must be safe and accessible to children.
- Education and awareness raising to enable children to understand, and therefore be able to exercise, the right to freedom of expression, and to acquire the necessary skills with which to do so. Such measures should address attitudes

---

[1] See, for example, Concluding Observations for Cuba (UN Committee on the Rights of the Child, 2011a, para. 33), Ukraine (UN Committee on the Rights of the Child, 2011b, para. 39), and Georgia (UN Committee on the Rights of the Child, 2000, para. 28).

among parents, communities, and schools that might restrict or undermine children's freedom of expression (UN Committee on the Rights of the Child, 2001, paras. 33–34).
- Measures to ensure that children have access to the information sources necessary to enable them to exercise the right to freedom of expression. The Committee has emphasised the importance of access for children to information from a diversity of national and international sources (UN Committee on the Rights of the Child, 2011c, para. 47(a)). There is also increasing recognition of the necessity for children to have access to the Internet and social media given the extent to which global communications, including the development and exchange of ideas and opinions, now function within this environment (UN Human Rights Committee, 2011, para. 15).

Attribute Four: Restrictions and Limitations

Like many rights, Article 13 is not absolute and can be subject to restrictions for the respect of the rights and reputation of others and for the protection of national security or of public order, or of public health or morals. Interestingly, unlike Article 19 of the ICCPR, it does not include reference to special duties and responsibilities of individuals in the exercise of the right to freedom of expression, and there is no reference in the drafting history of the Convention to explain this omission (Office of the United Nations High Commissioner for Human Rights and Rädda Barnen (Society: Sweden), 2007, pp. 445–52). However, the restrictions themselves are identical to those in the ICCPR and it can therefore be understood that the burden of that responsibility is undertaken on behalf of the child by their parents in accordance with the child's evolving capacities (Tobin & Parkes, 2019, p. 456).

The limitations imposed by the state on the exercise of Article 13 are subject to clear guidance. They must be provided for in law and establish clear criteria. They must be in pursuit of a legitimate aim and be proportionate to the attainment of that aim. In other words, they must be reasonable and necessary (UN Human Rights Committee, 2011, para. 2). Many of the restrictions imposed on children arise in the context of school, for example, in respect of school uniforms, dress and jewellery or political views. One notable case in the United States arose when children demanded the right to wear black armbands in protest of the Vietnam war, and in breach of a school policy forbidding such behaviour. The Supreme Court ruled in the children's favour, arguing that they do not 'shed their constitutional rights to freedom of speech or expression at the schoolhouse gate' (Tinker v. Des Moines Independent Community School District, 393 U.S. 503, 1969, p. 506).

References

Cho, A., Byrne, J., & Pelter, Z. (2020). *Digital civic engagement by young people*. UNICEF Office of Global Insight and Policy. Accessed December 18, 2020, from https://www.unicef.org/globalinsight/media/706/file/UNICEF-Global-Insight-digital-civic-engagement-2020.pdf.

Council of Europe. (2018). *Guidelines to respect, protect and fulfil the rights of the child in the digital environment: Recommendation CM/Rec(2018)7 of the Committee of Ministers* (No. 101818GBR). Accessed October 23, 2020, from https://edoc.coe.int/en/children-and-the-internet/7921-guidelines-to-respect-protect-and-fulfil-the-rights-of-the-child-in-the-digital-environment-recommendation-cmrec20187-of-the-committee-of-ministers.html.

Hussain, A., & UN Commission on Human Rights. (1998). *Promotion and protection of the right to freedom of opinion and expression: Report of the Special Rapporteur, E/CN.4/1998/40*. Accessed October 11, 2020, from https://digitallibrary.un.org/record/250257?ln=en.

LaRue, F., & UN Human Rights Committee. (2011). *Report of the special rapporteur on the promotion and protection of the right to freedom of opinion and expression, Frank La Rue, A/HRC/17/27*. Accessed October 23, 2020, from https://digitallibrary.un.org/record/706331?ln=en.

Office of the United Nations High Commissioner for Human Rights & Rädda Barnen (Society: Sweden). (2007). *Legislative history of the Convention on the Rights of the Child*. United Nations. https://digitallibrary.un.org/record/602462?ln=en

Pais, M. S. (1997). The Convention on the Rights of the Child. In *Manual on human rights reporting under six major international human rights instruments HR/PUB/91/1 (Rev.1)* (pp. 393–505). OHCHR. Accessed May 16, 2020, from https://www.refworld.org/docid/428085252.html.

Shonkoff, J. P. (2009). Mobilizing science to revitalize early childhood policy. *Issues in Science and Technology, XXVI*(1), 79–85.

Thorgeirsdóttir, H. (2006). *A commentary on the United Nations Convention on the Rights of the Child, Article 13: The right to freedom of expression*. Brill Nijhoff. Accessed October 23, 2020, from https://brill.com/view/title/11630.

Tinker v. Des Moines Independent Community School District, 393 U.S. 503. (1969, February 24). US Supreme Court. Accessed October 23, 2020, from https://supreme.justia.com/cases/federal/us/393/503/.

Tobin, J., & Parkes, A. (2019). Article 13: The right to freedom of expression. In J. Tobin (Ed.), *The UN Convention on the Rights of the Child: A commentary* (pp. 435–474). Oxford University Press.

UN Committee on the Rights of the Child. (2000, June 28). *Concluding observations: Georgia, CRC/C/15/Add.124*. Accessed October 23, 2020, from https://digitallibrary.un.org/record/422917?ln=en.

UN Committee on the Rights of the Child. (2001, July 9). *Concluding observations: Turkey, CRC/C/15/Add.152*. Accessed October 23, 2020, from https://digitallibrary.un.org/record/451935?ln=en.

UN Committee on the Rights of the Child. (2009, February 12). *General comment no. 11 (2009), indigenous children and their rights under the Convention, CRC/C/GC/11*. Accessed October 24, 2020, from https://digitallibrary.un.org/record/648790?ln=en.

UN Committee on the Rights of the Child. (2011a, August 3). *Concluding observations: Cuba, CRC/C/CUB/CO/2*. Accessed October 11, 2020, from https://digitallibrary.un.org/record/708489?ln=en.

UN Committee on the Rights of the Child. (2011b, April 21). *Concluding observations: Ukraine, CRC/C/UKR/CO/3-4*. Accessed October 12, 2020, from https://digitallibrary.un.org/record/702364?ln=en.

UN Committee on the Rights of the Child. (2011c, July 15). *Concluding observations: Egypt, CRC/C/EGY/CO/3-4*. Accessed October 11, 2020, from https://digitallibrary.un.org/record/707466?ln=en.

UN Committee on the Rights of the Child. (2013, May 29). *General comment no. 14 (2013) on the right of the child to have his or her best interests taken as a primary consideration (art. 3, para. 1), CRC/C/GC/14*. Accessed October 12, 2020, from https://digitallibrary.un.org/record/778523?ln=en.

UN Committee on the Rights of the Child. (2016, December 6). *General comment no. 20 (2016) on the implementation of the rights of the child during adolescence, CRC/C/GC/20*. Accessed October 12, 2020, from https://digitallibrary.un.org/record/855544?ln=en.

UN Human Rights Committee. (2011, September 12). *CCPR general comment no. 34 (2011) Article 19, Freedoms of opinion and expression, CCPR/C/GC/34*. https://digitallibrary.un.org/record/715606?ln=en

UNICEF Policy Lab. (2018). *Policy guide on children and digital connectivity*. Accessed October 23, 2020, from https://www.unicef.org/esa/media/3141/file/PolicyLab-Guide-DigitalConnectivity-Nov.6.18-lowres.pdf.

Open Access This chapter is licensed under the terms of the Creative Commons Attribution 4.0 International License (http://creativecommons.org/licenses/by/4.0/), which permits use, sharing, adaptation, distribution and reproduction in any medium or format, as long as you give appropriate credit to the original author(s) and the source, provide a link to the Creative Commons license and indicate if changes were made.

The images or other third party material in this chapter are included in the chapter's Creative Commons license, unless indicated otherwise in a credit line to the material. If material is not included in the chapter's Creative Commons license and your intended use is not permitted by statutory regulation or exceeds the permitted use, you will need to obtain permission directly from the copyright holder.

Chapter 9
Article 14: The Right to Freedom of Thought, Conscience, and Religion

Roberta Ruggiero

---

1. States Parties shall respect the right of the child to freedom of thought, conscience and religion.
2. States Parties shall respect the rights and duties of the parents and, when applicable, legal guardians, to provide direction to the child in the exercise of his or her right in a manner consistent with the evolving capacities of the child.
3. Freedom to manifest one's religion or beliefs may be subject only to such limitations as are prescribed by law and are necessary to protect public safety, order, health or morals, or the fundamental rights and freedoms of others.

What Did Children Say?
'There would be places of worship and religious texts from a variety of religions in each municipality.' *(Western Europe/Other)*

'Libraries have child-friendly access to different religious texts.' *(Western Europe/Other)*

'We would know the right is being protected by 'there being available world religion classes in schools for students to inform themselves, but also

(continued)

R. Ruggiero (✉)
Centre for Children's Rights Studies, University of Geneva, Geneva, Switzerland
e-mail: roberta.ruggiero@unige.ch

> the possibility to opt out of any religion class (in schools).'' *(Western Europe/ Other)*
> 'Laws are developed to prevent/discourage imposing religion on someone, partner, parents.' *(Eastern Europe)*

Overview

Article 14 of the Convention attributes to children the fundamental civil right to freedom of thought, conscience, and religion. As is the case for other autonomy and participation rights in the Convention, namely Articles 12 through 17, it represents a significant evolution for the recognition of children as an autonomous subject of law (Brems, 2005, p. 1).

It recognises the rights and duties of the parents, but in addition, it attributes them a 'guiding role.' Article 14(2) echoes Article 5 and reiterates the paradigm shift of the Convention, based on the respect for the responsibilities, rights, and duties of parents,[1] to provide, in a consistent manner consistent with the evolving capacities of the child, 'appropriate direction and guidance in the exercise by the child's rights as recognized in the CRC' (Brems, 2005).

Eva Brems, in her commentary on Article 14, defines the parental right outlined in Article 14(2) as an 'accessory to the child's right, rather than an autonomous right on an equal footing.' The author justifies this assumption because, during the drafting of Article 14, the Working Group adopted at first reading a version including a fourth paragraph modelled on Article 18(4) of the ICCPR,[2] but adding the child's choice on equal basis with that of the parents.[3] That this fourth paragraph was dropped in the final version underlines the intent of the drafters to attribute to children an autonomous position in the exercise of their rights.

Although Article 14(1) and (3) are in line with the wording of Article 18 of the ICCPR, Article 14(2) has a different phrasing, in comparison with the other international treaties and conventions, and it fails to include explicitly the children's right to adopt or change their religion.

---

[1] Included members of the extended family or community as provided for by local custom, legal guardians or other persons legally responsible for the child.

[2] Which reads as follows: 'The States Parties to the present Covenant undertake to have respect for the liberty of parents and, when applicable, legal guardians to ensure the religious and moral education of their children in conformity with their own convictions'.

[3] 'The States Parties shall equally respect the liberty of the child and his parents and, where applicable, legal guardians, to ensure the religious and moral education of the child in conformity with convictions of their choice' (Detrick et al., 1992, p. 246).

General Principles

Article 2 All rights should be recognised for each child without discrimination on the grounds of religion or opinions (including conviction and thought). Some groups of children can face direct or indirect discrimination in the exercise of Article 14. These include children belonging to a minority religious group, children with a specific diet regime imposed by their religion or belief, children wearing headscarves or other religious clothing or symbols, or in the exercise of conscientious objection in relation to compulsory education.[4] Article 14, in combination with Article 2, requires action from States Parties to remove all these forms of discrimination (Brems, 2005, p. 9; UN Committee on the Rights of the Child, 2016, para. 43).[5]

Article 3 The best interests of the child should be a primary consideration in all actions concerning children. In relation to Article 14, the preservation of the identity of the child (Article 8) plays a key role and must be respected and taken into consideration in the assessment of the child's best interests. For example, when considering a foster home or placement for a child, 'due regard shall be paid to the desirability of continuity in a child's upbringing and to the child's ethnic, religious, cultural and linguistic background (Article 20) and the decision-maker must take into consideration this specific context when assessing and determining the child's best interests' (UN Committee on the Rights of the Child, 2013, para. 55).

Article 6 Article 14 contributes to the preservation and growth of the identity of the child. Its full exercise allows the child to achieve his/her complete development.

Article 12 The child's views must be taken seriously. States Parties and parents should preserve the right of all children to express their views freely 'in all matters affecting the child', which includes in matters of freedom of thought, conscience, and religion, in terms of choice and manifestation (in particular in relation to conscience and religion). In addition, it introduces the obligation to provide opportunities to be heard in any judicial or administrative proceedings affecting the child.

Articles Related or Linked to Article 14

Articles 5 and 18 are echoed by Article 14 (2) and require respect for the role of the parents' direction to the child 'in a manner consistent with the evolving capacities of the child' (Brems, 2005, p. 25).

---

[4] For more details, see the *Report of the Special Rapporteur on freedom of religion or belief* (Bielefeldt, 2012, paras. 51–59) and the *Implementation handbook for the convention on the rights of the child* (Hodgkin et al., 2007, pp. 186–87, 191–92).

[5] See, for example, Concluding Observations for Poland (UN Committee on the Rights of the Child, 2002a, paras. 32, 33) and Tunisia (UN Committee on the Rights of the Child, 2002b, paras. 29, 30).

Article 8 protects the child's rights to preserve his or her identity, including religious identity.

Article 12 protects the rights to form and express views, to which is linked the concept of freedom of thought (Hodgkin et al., 2007, p. 178).

Article 13 protects freedom of expression, which extends to expression in the religious sphere (Detrick et al., 1992, p. 247; UN Commission on Human Rights, 1989, para. 284).

Article 15 protects freedom of association and of peaceful assembly, which extends to the context of religion.

Article 16 protects the child's privacy right, which in the religious sphere implies that children cannot be forced to reveal their thoughts (Brems, 2005, p. 8).

Article 17 applies to adequate information about religious matters.

Article 19 protects the child from all forms of physical or mental violence, including those perpetrated by States Parties and parents in exercising their guiding role under Article 14(2).

Article 20(3) provides that alternative care arrangements must pay due regard to the child's religious background and give continuity to this and the child's cultural identity (Brems, 2005, p. 8; Hodgkin et al., 2007, pp. 179, 182).

Article 23 for its emphasis on the right to specialised supports for the disabled child's spiritual development and fullest possible individual development.

Article 27 also contextualises Article 14 rights in relation to the right to a standard of living 'adequate for the child's physical, mental, spiritual, moral and social development.'

Articles 28 and 29, and in particular Article 29(1)(d): The latter stipulates that education shall be directed to the 'preparation of the child for responsible life in a free society, in the spirit of understanding, peace, tolerance, equality of sexes, and friendship among all peoples, ethnic, national and religious groups and persons of indigenous origin' (Brems, 2005, pp. 8, 9; Hodgkin et al., 2007, pp. 176, 177).[6]

Article 30 protects the right of children belonging to religious minorities to profess and practice their own religion (Brems, 2005, p. 8; Hodgkin et al., 2007, pp. 179, 182; UN Committee on the Rights of the Child, 2009, para. 16).

Article 38 and Optional Protocol to the Convention on the Rights of the Child on the involvement of children in armed conflict have some relevance for the protection of religious freedom and freedom of conscience:

- Article 38 and the Optional Protocol both refer to the international humanitarian law, which includes some provisions in respect of the 'religious freedom of prisoners of war, civilian internees, protected persons and population of occupied territories' (Brems, 2005, pp. 8, 9)

---

[6]The Article 29 (2) provision requires specific mention here since it is the UNCRC echo to ICCPR Article 18(4) and ICESCR Article 13(3) expressed not as a right of parents but as the right of individuals and bodies to establish separate educational institutions, for instance vocational or denominational schools.

- With reference to the freedom of conscience, an important aspect is the 'conscientious objection' to military service. In particular, for those countries that include some form of military training within the education system, when compulsory this could be in conflict with Article 14 (Hodgkin et al., 2007, pp. 177, 178).

Relevant Instruments

The civil right to freedom of thought, conscience, and religion is upheld for everyone in the following international documents:

- UN Universal Declaration of Human Rights (1948), Article 18
- UN Convention Against Discrimination in Education (1960)
- International Covenant on Civil and Political Rights (1966), Article 18
- International Covenant on Economic, Social and Cultural Rights (1966), Article 13(3)[7]
- International Convention on the Elimination of all forms of Racial Discrimination (1966), Article 5
- International Convention on the Protection of the Rights of All Migrant Workers and Members of Their Families (1990), Article 12
- European Convention on Human Rights (1950), Article 9
- Charter of Fundamental Rights of the European Union (2000), Article 10
- American Convention on Human Rights 'Pact of San Jose, Costa Rica' (B-32) (1978), Article 12
- African Charter on Human and Peoples' Rights (1981), Article 8
- African Charter on the Rights and Welfare of the Child (1990), Article 9. It mentions only a parental duty and not a right.

Attributes

Attribute One: The Scope of Children's Freedom of Thought, Conscience, and Religion

Due to the similar wording of Article 14(1) and (3) of the Convention to Article 18(1) and (3) of the ICCPR, in most situations the Committee provides interpretation

---

[7] Article 13(3) CESCR: 'The States Parties to the present Covenant undertake to have respect for the liberty of parents and, when applicable, legal guardians to choose for their children schools, other than those established by the public authorities, which conform to such minimum educational standards as may be laid down or approved by the State and to ensure the religious and moral education of their children in conformity with their own convictions'.

and recommendations quoting international instruments and recommendations issued by other treaty bodies in relation to Article 18 of the ICCPR. With reference to state legal regulation of Article 14, the Committee refers to the Human Rights Committee General Comment no 22 on Article 18 ICCPR (1993).[8] In it, the Human Rights Committee states that, 'the freedom of thought and conscience or on the freedom to have or adopt a religion or belief of one's choice does not permit any limitations whatsoever.'[9] The use of this interpretative approach to Article 14 by the Committee clarifies the position of the States Parties, which hold not only an obligation to respect but also an obligation to fulfil and protect the exercise of the right of the child to freedom of thought, conscience, and religion (Hodgkin et al., 2007, p. 186; Nowak, 2005, p. 311).

Consequently, the issues that may affect the full enjoyment of Article 14 are aspects of major concern for the Committee. Based on its Concluding Observations, they focus on the necessity of:

- Enacting legislation 'guaranteeing the freedom of religion for those under 18 years' (UN Committee on the Rights of the Child, 2005a, paras. 44, 45)
- Taking effective measures 'to prevent and eliminate all forms of discrimination on the grounds of religion or belief' (UN Committee on the Rights of the Child, 2000a, paras. 35, 36, 2005b, paras. 37, 38, 2005c, paras. 41, 42)
- Promoting 'religious tolerance and dialogue in society' (UN Committee on the Rights of the Child, 2000a, paras. 35, 36, 2005b, paras. 37, 38, 2005c, paras. 41, 42, 2006, paras. 34, 35)
- Repealing any ban instituted 'by local authorities on children of any age form participating in religious activities' (UN Committee on the Rights of the Child, 2005a, paras. 44, 45)
- Preventing, prohibiting and punishing 'any violent attack against religious activities, including demolition of places of worship' (UN Committee on the Rights of the Child, 2006, paras. 34, 35).

Attribute Two: Protection Against State Indoctrination

The Committee dedicates particular attention to the risk of state indoctrination of moral and religious beliefs in school systems. The Committee issued

---

[8]To be integrated with the 1981 Declaration on the Elimination of All Forms of Intolerance and of Discrimination Based on Religion or Belief, General Assembly resolution 36/55, the Resolution Commission on Human Rights 2000/33, the Human Rights Committee's General Comment no. 22, and concurring with the findings of the Human Rights Committee, ICCPR /C/79/Add.25 and the Committee on Economic, Social and Cultural Rights, E/C.12/1993/7.

[9]This is assured by article 18 ICCPR (and Article 14 of the Convention) and by the right to privacy set out in article 17 of the ICCPR (child's right to privacy is echoed in article 16 of the Convention) (United Nations, 2006, p. 195).

recommendations about two specific situations: freedom of religion and conscientious objection in school systems.

In its first General Comment, issued in 2001, on the aims of education, the Committee emphasises that 'children do not lose their human rights by virtue of passing through the school gates,' and specific attention should be dedicated to children's views in this setting (2001, para. 8). As a consequence, it is necessary to take all required measures to ensure that 'children may choose whether to participate in classes on religion or atheism' (UN Committee on the Rights of the Child, 2005a, paras. 44, 45).[10] This should also apply to the content of moral education, as explained by the Human Rights Committee, which clarifies that Article 18-(4) 'permits public school instruction in subjects such as the general history of religions and ethics if it is given in a neutral and objective way.' Therefore, for the Human Rights Committee, 'public education that includes instruction in a particular religion or belief is inconsistent with Article 18(4) unless provision is made for non-discriminatory exemptions or alternatives that would accommodate the wishes of parents and guardians' (United Nations, 2006, p. 196). Moreover, a provision offering stronger protection against state indoctrination is included in Article 5(1)(b) of the UN Convention against Discrimination in Education (1960). It refers to procedures in domestic legislation that must ensure 'the religious and moral education of the children in conformity with their own convictions; and no person or group of persons should be compelled to receive religious instruction inconsistent with his or their conviction.'[11]

With reference to the freedom of conscience, an important aspect is the conscientious objection to military service when it is not based on religion, but rather on other personal convictions such as pacifism. For those countries that include some form of military training within the education system, when this is compulsory, it could be in conflict with Article 14 (Brems, 2005, pp. 14–15).

Attribute Three: Protection Against Religious and Moral Instruction Imposed by Parents

Article 14 of the Convention is the object of the largest number of reservations or declarations made by States Parties. Some of these reservations or declaration are

---

[10] This applies also when the compulsory school curriculum does not provide for children's freedom of religion (UN Committee on the Rights of the Child, 2004, paras. 31, 32, 2005d, paras. 25, 26), or religious education in schools is not compulsory or there are arrangements for exemption but the choosing process is not adequate to achieve freedom of religion (UN Committee on the Rights of the Child, 2000b, paras. 26, 27, 2002a, paras. 32, 33, 2003, paras. 29, 30, 2005e, para. 20) For a larger analysis, see *Implementation handbook for the convention on the rights of the child* (Hodgkin et al., 2007, pp. 189–191).

[11] Article 5(1)(b) of the UN Convention against Discrimination in Education (1960) adopted by the General Conference of the United Nations Educational, Scientific and Cultural Organization on 14 December 1960.

meant to uphold parental rights and authority in relation to the civil rights of children (including Articles 13 and 15). Indeed, the most difficult issues are those in which children's freedom of thought, conscience, and religion are opposed to the rights and interests of their parents or legal guardians. This situation is addressed by Article 14 (2). Unfortunately, little support for the interpretation of this provision can be found in the international treaties.

With reference to the role of parents, in General Comment no. 20 the Committee urges States Parties to withdraw any reservations to Article 14 of the Convention and clarifies that 'it is the child who exercises the right to freedom of religion, not the parent, and the parental role necessarily diminishes as the child acquires an increasingly active role in exercising choice throughout adolescence' (2016, para. 43).

However, based on the wording of Article 14 of the Convention, Eva Brems notes the child's freedom of thought, conscience and religion 'can be restricted by their parents, and that States Parties may sometimes interfere in the parents' exercise of their duties in this respect' in order to determine the child's best interest, and allow the child to receive a religious and moral education better in line with their own convictions.[12]

In these specific cases, the States Parties have the responsibility to ensure that the child is not compelled to receive religious or moral instruction inconsistent with their convictions and to protect the child from all forms of physical or mental violence, including those perpetrated by parents in providing directions under Article 14(2).

References

Bielefeldt, H. (2012). *Elimination of all forms of religious intolerance, A/71/269*. UN. Accessed October 24, 2020, from http://digitallibrary.un.org/record/839421.

Brems, E. (2005). *A commentary on the United Nations Convention on the Rights of the Child, Article 14: The right to freedom of thought, conscience and religion*. Brill Nijhoff. Accessed October 23, 2020, from https://brill.com/view/title/11608.

Detrick, S., Doek, J. E., & Cantwell, N. (1992). *The United Nations Convention on the Rights of the Child: A guide to the "Travaux Préparatoires."* Martinus Nijhoff.

Hodgkin, R., Newell, P., & UNICEF. (2007). *Implementation handbook for the Convention on the Rights of the Child* (3rd ed.). UNICEF. Accessed September 21, 2020, from https://digitallibrary.un.org/record/620060?ln=en

Nowak, M. (2005). *U.N. Covenant on Civil and Political Rights: CCPR commentary*. N.P. Engel.

UN Commission on Human Rights. (1989). *Report of the Working Group on a Draft Convention on the Rights of the Child, E/CN.4/1989/48*. Accessed October 12, 2020, from https://digitallibrary.un.org/record/57437?ln=en.

UN Committee on the Rights of the Child. (2000a, June 28). *Concluding observations: Iran, CRC/C/15/Add.123*. Accessed October 12, 2020, from https://digitallibrary.un.org/record/422916?ln=en.

---

[12] Convention against Discrimination in Education Adopted by the General Conference at its eleventh session, adopted on 14 December 1960 and entered into force on 22 May 1962.

UN Committee on the Rights of the Child. (2000b, June 28). *Concluding observations: Norway, CRC/C/15/Add.126*. Accessed October 23, 2020, from https://digitallibrary.un.org/record/422919?ln=en.

UN Committee on the Rights of the Child. (2001, April 17). *General comment no. 1 (2001) Article 29 (1): The aims of education, CRC/GC/2001/1*. Accessed October 10, 2020, from https://digitallibrary.un.org/record/447223?ln=en.

UN Committee on the Rights of the Child. (2002a, October 30). *Concluding observations: Poland, CRC/C/15/Add.194*. Accessed October 24, 2020, from https://digitallibrary.un.org/record/481017?ln=en.

UN Committee on the Rights of the Child. (2002b, June 13). *Concluding observations: Tunisia, CRC/C/15/Add.181*. Accessed October 23, 2020, from https://digitallibrary.un.org/record/473484?ln=en.

UN Committee on the Rights of the Child. (2003, March 18). *Concluding observations: Italy, CRC/C/15/Add.198*. Accessed October 12, 2020, from https://digitallibrary.un.org/record/497795?ln=en.

UN Committee on the Rights of the Child. (2004, February 26). *Concluding observations: Armenia, CRC/C/15/Add.225*. Accessed October 11, 2020, from https://digitallibrary.un.org/record/530794?ln=en.

UN Committee on the Rights of the Child. (2005a, November 24). *Concluding observations: China, CRC/C/CHN/CO/2*. Accessed October 24, 2020, from https://digitallibrary.un.org/record/575653?ln=en.

UN Committee on the Rights of the Child. (2005b, October 12). *Concluding observations: Algeria, CRC/C/15/Add.269*. Accessed October 24, 2020, from https://digitallibrary.un.org/record/570473?ln=en.

UN Committee on the Rights of the Child. (2005c, March 31). *Concluding observations: Iran, CRC/C/15/Add.254*. Accessed October 12, 2020, from https://digitallibrary.un.org/record/557400?ln=en.

UN Committee on the Rights of the Child. (2005d, September 21). *Concluding observations: Costa Rica, CRC/C/15/Add.266*. Accessed October 11, 2020, from https://digitallibrary.un.org/record/570468?ln=en.

UN Committee on the Rights of the Child. (2005e, September 21). *Concluding observations: Norway, CRC/C/15/Add.263*. Accessed October 23, 2020, from https://digitallibrary.un.org/record/569887?ln=en.

UN Committee on the Rights of the Child. (2006, June 2). *Concluding observations: Turkmenistan, CRC/C/TKM/CO/1*. Accessed October 23, 2020, from https://digitallibrary.un.org/record/580376?ln=en.

UN Committee on the Rights of the Child. (2009, February 12). *General comment no. 11 (2009), Indigenous children and their rights under the Convention, CRC/C/GC/11*. Accessed October 24, 2020, from https://digitallibrary.un.org/record/648790?ln=en.

UN Committee on the Rights of the Child. (2013, May 29). *General comment no. 14 (2013) on the right of the child to have his or her best interests taken as a primary consideration (art. 3, para. 1), CRC/C/GC/14*. Accessed October 12, 2020, from https://digitallibrary.un.org/record/778523?ln=en.

UN Committee on the Rights of the Child. (2016, December 6). *General comment no. 20 (2016) on the implementation of the rights of the child during adolescence, CRC/C/GC/20*. Accessed October 12, 2020, from https://digitallibrary.un.org/record/855544?ln=en.

United Nations. (2006). *Compilation of general comments and general recommendations adopted by human rights treaty bodies, HRI/GEN/1/Rev. 8*. UN. Accessed April 19, 2020, from http://digitallibrary.un.org/record/576098.

Open Access This chapter is licensed under the terms of the Creative Commons Attribution 4.0 International License (http://creativecommons.org/licenses/by/4.0/), which permits use, sharing, adaptation, distribution and reproduction in any medium or format, as long as you give appropriate credit to the original author(s) and the source, provide a link to the Creative Commons license and indicate if changes were made.

The images or other third party material in this chapter are included in the chapter's Creative Commons license, unless indicated otherwise in a credit line to the material. If material is not included in the chapter's Creative Commons license and your intended use is not permitted by statutory regulation or exceeds the permitted use, you will need to obtain permission directly from the copyright holder.

Chapter 10
Article 15: The Right to Freedom of Association and Assembly

Gerison Lansdown

1. States Parties recognize the rights of the child to freedom of association and to freedom of peaceful assembly.
2. No restrictions may be placed on the exercise of these rights other than those imposed in conformity with the law and which are necessary in a democratic society in the interests of national security or public safety, public order (ordre public), the protection of public health or morals or the protection of the rights and freedoms of others.

What Did Children Say?
'What are the laws put forth by the government for those stopping us to peacefully associate ourselves in public and community places?' *(Africa)*

'Provide transportation to (events/meetings).' *(Western Europe/Other)*

'Schools should offer opportunities to develop activities as a group and should provide with information that students are able to organise and form groups based on topics of mutual interest 'example basketball club.'' *(Eastern Europe)*

'Have other children represent us; child conferences.' *(Africa)*

G. Lansdown (✉)
Carleton University, Ottawa, ON, Canada

Overview

Article 15 asserts that the right to freedom of association and peaceful assembly, first established in the Universal Declaration of Human Rights and subsequently included in the International Covenant on Civil and Political Rights and many other international and regional human rights treaties, applies equally to children.[1] Association and assembly are closely related and mutually reinforcing, but they constitute separate rights and need to be treated accordingly (Kiai & UN Human Rights Council, 2012, para. 4). Although there is a lack of jurisprudence differentiating association and assembly (Daly, 2016), it can be understood that the aim of association is to protect ongoing and continuing connections with others, whereas assembly tends to be more episodic (Lawyers Committee for Human Rights (U.S.) and Whittome, 1997, p. 61). Article 15 rights apply to children in the context of their engagement in political and social activities with others, including political demonstrations, and associations such youth groups, sports clubs, child-led groups, political parties, and working children's organisations and movements, as well as informal association and assembly through family, friendships, and social networks, on and offline. It also covers the right to access public spaces (UN Committee on the Rights of the Child, 2017, para. 36). Article 15 is one of the core civil and political rights in the Convention that, together with Article 12, combine to create the concept of participation. It is a qualified right: paragraph 2 outlines the restrictions on its exercise where deemed necessary for public safety and security.

The use of the term recognise, consistent with the wording in Article 21 of ICCPR, affirms that the right to association and peaceful assembly is a fundamental human right rather than a provision that the state can grant (Daly, 2016, p. 29). It is, accordingly, a strong formulation and implies positive obligations on States Parties to take reasonable steps to protect this right. Moreover, children's lack of autonomy and different legal status from adults requires additional measures by States Parties to facilitate and protect freedom of association and assembly (Daly, 2016, pp. 28–30). Where Article 15 differs from the ICCPR is in its failure to include an explicit articulation that freedom of association extends to the right to join a trade union, although none of the limitations outlined in paragraph 2 would justify a prohibition on children so doing.

General Principles

Article 2 Children should not be discriminated against on the basis of their age, for example, through blanket bans on membership or establishment of associations, or in the organisation of or participation in peaceful protests, applicable to persons under the age of 18 years old (Kiai & UN Human Rights Council, 2014, paras.

---

[1] UDHR, Article 2, CCPR Articles 21 &22.

23–24; UN Committee on the Rights of the Child, 2000, paras. 30–31). Groups of children can face direct or indirect discrimination in the exercise of Article 15 rights, including, school children, street children, children in detention, indigenous children, children with disabilities, LGBTQ children and girls. Article 2 necessitates action from States Parties to eliminate these discriminations.[2]

Article 3 Consideration of best interests in respect of Article 15 should be applied with a view to ensuring the full and effective enjoyment of all rights. Article 15 rights should not be compromised by a negative interpretation of best interests (UN Committee on the Rights of the Child, 2013a, para. 4). While Article 3 recognises a duty to consider the appropriate protection of children, best interests should be never used as an overarching principle to outweigh Article 15 rights, either for children as individuals or as a group (UN Committee on the Rights of the Child, 2013a, para. 19). Furthermore, States Parties could promote children's best interests in the exercise of their Article 15 rights, by, for example providing police with appropriate training.

Article 6 Children cannot be expected to mature into full members of society if they lack the experience of participation in public life.[3] Their development is enhanced by active engagement and participation in their communities. Any measures to deny them rights to association and assembly for their own safety must be fully justifiable. As with Article 3, the vulnerability of children should not be used as a general excuse to exclude them from accessing their freedom rights (Kiai & UN Human Rights Council, 2014, para. 10).

Article 12 Freedom of association and assembly provide important opportunities for children to exercise their right to express their views in accordance with Article 12, including through the development of their own associations and initiatives, and increasingly through the digital environment (UN Committee on the Rights of the Child, 2009, para. 128). When children can organise and participate in civic action, for example, it enhances their understanding of democratic processes and develops capacity for future engagement. It also strengthens their opportunity to lobby for economic, social and political change (Breen, 2019). However, Article 12 represents a right to express views, not an obligation to do so, and therefore care must be taken to avoid manipulated or coerced participation in such activities.

---

[2] See, for example, General Comment No. 21 on Children in Street Situations (UN Committee on the Rights of the Child, 2017), and Concluding Observations: Japan (UN Committee on the Rights of the Child, 2004, paras. 29–30).

[3] See, for example, Consideration of Reports of States Parties: Korea (UN Committee on the Rights of the Child, 1996, para. 50).

Articles Related or Linked to Article 15

Article 13 protects freedom of expression that is a key dimension of the freedom of association and assembly.

Article 14 protects the right to freedom of thought, conscience and religion that may be a reason for association or assembly.

Article 16 protects the right to arbitrary interference into children's membership of a particular association or to associate with certain others.

Article 29 elaborates the aims of education which include recognition that children must be prepared for life in a free society, including rights to freedom of association and assembly.

Article 31 protects the right to play, recreation, and participation in cultural life which cannot be achieved without freedom of association and assembly.

Article 32 protects children from harmful or exploitative work and, although not made explicit in Article 15, the right to freedom of association can be understood to extend to the right to form or join a trades union.

Article 37 protects children against arbitrary restriction of liberty or degrading treatment or punishment, including when exercising their right to freedom of assembly or association.

Relevant Instruments

The rights to freedom of association and assembly, or associated rights, are also included in the following international documents:

- UN Universal Declaration of Human Rights (1948), Article 20
- International Covenant on Civil and Political Rights (1966), Article 21
- UN Convention on the Elimination of All Forms of Discrimination against Women (1979), Article 7
- UN Convention on the Rights of Persons with Disabilities (2006), Article 29
- UN European Convention on Human Rights (1950), Article 11
- ILO Convention 87, Freedom of Association and Protection of the Right to Organise Convention (1948), Article 2
- ILO Convention 98, Right to Organise and Collective Bargaining Convention (1949) Article 2
- American Convention on Human Rights 'Pact of San Jose, Costa Rica' (B-32) (1978), Article 15
- African Charter on the Rights and Welfare of the Child (1990), Article 8

Attributes

Attribute One: Freedom of Association

It can be argued that freedom of association is fundamental to both the child's development and the realisation of other rights. It applies to the right to form or join organisations, clubs, and other forums, and covers associations which are formal and informal, one-off or continuing, face-to face or online, and for any purpose, including social, cultural, religious, educational, economic, and political (Daly, 2016, p. 36). The Committee has consistently argued that States Parties have obligations to facilitate and support the establishment by children of their own organisations (2009, paras. 128, 130, 2013b, para. 21, 2016, 2017, paras. 44–45), including opportunities for networking and collective advocacy (UN Committee on the Rights of the Child, 2014). States Parties have particular obligations to promote and protect this right, including in the digital environment, in view of the lack of traditional spaces where children can meet independently. Many social, civic, political, religious and cultural activities and organisations operate partially or exclusively in the digital environment (Kaye & UN Human Rights Council, 2018). Accordingly, States Parties should consider guaranteeing this right in law, ensuring that legislation aligns equally to digital settings. They should also actively remove the barriers that prevent children establishing their own organisations, for example, onerous registration requirements, or restrictions on opening bank accounts or receiving funding. In no circumstances should States Parties impose compulsory membership or control over the nature of children's participation (UN Committee on the Rights of the Child, 2013b, para. 21).

Although Article 15 does not expressly elaborate the right to join a trade union, the restrictions outlined in paragraph 2 do not justify any prohibition on children from either forming their own or joining existing unions (UN Commission on Human Rights, 1985). ILO Conventions 87 and 98 emphasise that these rights extend to all workers, without exception. Furthermore, Article 41, which stipulates that the standards of other international instruments should not be lowered by any provision in the Convention, lends further weight to the argument that Article 15 should be interpreted to include the right of working children to trade union rights to the same standard as that provided by the ICCPR (Daly, 2016, p. 35). The Committee has emphasised the imperative for children to have access to such organisations, and in particular, that children, including those under the legal age of work, must have access to mechanisms through which to negotiate for protection of their rights at work (UN Committee on the Rights of the Child, 2009, paras. 116–117).

Attribute Two: Freedom of Assembly

The right to freedom of assembly represents a means of public expression and is a foundation of a democratic society (Liberty, 2020). It extends to activities on and offline, both indoors and outdoors, in private or public settings, in one location or moving, with invited participants or open gatherings to political activities and meetings with peers (Nowak, 2005). It includes any peaceful protest marches, public and private meetings, or press conferences. It has particular significance for children as they commonly utilise public spaces because of a lack of dedicated child-friendly spaces where they can meet. Furthermore, children commonly lack political space to speak out or organise to influence the political or social structures around them.

Freedom of assembly has additional relevance during adolescence, when the need for opportunities to meet with peers in public spaces and independently of family takes on added significance as a major building block in children's social and emotional development (UN Committee on the Rights of the Child, 2016, para. 44). Children themselves have highlighted that the public visibility and networking opportunities in the digital environment can support forms of child-led activism and empower them as advocates for their rights (UN Committee on the Rights of the Child, 2018). The Committee has expressed concern over the decreasing tolerance of children in public spaces, particularly street children, who are widely denied the right to meet in public spaces without threat, harassment or removal. It has also highlighted their vulnerability to exploitative measures requiring or manipulating them into participation in protests or gatherings (UN Committee on the Rights of the Child, 2017, para. 39). Article 15 explicitly extends to the right to choose not to take part in an assembly.

States Parties should take action to facilitate and empower all children to exercise their Article 15 rights positively, including by promoting the creation of channels for child-led activism online, and to be able to challenge co-option and manipulation by adults (UN Committee on the Rights of the Child, 2014). Action should also be taken to establish the right to freedom of assembly in law and to remove barriers, such as age limits for participation in public demonstrations. In addition, in view of the vulnerabilities of children associated with their age, States Parties should guarantee children appropriate protection when exercising their right to peaceful assembly (Daly, 2016, pp. 28–30; UN Committee on the Rights of the Child, 2012, paras. 38–39).

Attribute Three: Restrictions Limited to Compliance with Democratic Interests

The restrictions on the exercise of Article 15 rights imposed in paragraph 2 are identical to those in equivalent international treaties. In other words, they can only be imposed in the interests of security, safety, public health or moral or the rights or freedoms of others. During the drafting process, it was determined that a provision limiting Article 15 rights to children's evolving capacities should not be included in Article 15, but rather, be included in a separate article, thereby applying to all rights equally. In other words, civil and political rights should not be marked out as subject to particular parental scrutiny, and States Parties should not seek to impose additional limitations on children in the exercise of Article 15 rights (Daly, 2016).

Measures introduced by States Parties to employ the best interests principle to limit Article 15 rights, or to impose status offences, blanket bans, anti-social behaviour orders, or curfews have been strongly criticised as violations (Kiai & UN Human Rights Council, 2014, paras. 23–24; UN Committee on the Rights of the Child, 2007, para. 8, 2008, paras. 34–35). Furthermore, any restrictions imposed must be necessary for a legitimate purpose, not be overbroad, be the least intrusive instrument possible for achieving their protective function, be proportionate to the interest to be protected and entail individual rather than collective assessment (UN Committee on the Rights of the Child, 2017, para. 39; UN Human Rights Committee, 2011, paras. 33–34).

References

Breen, C. (2019). Article 15: The rights to freedom of association and peaceful assembly. In J. Tobin (Ed.), *The UN Convention on the Rights of the Child: A commentary* (pp. 517–550). Oxford University Press.

Daly, A. (2016). *A commentary on the United Nations Convention on the Rights of the Child, Article 15: The right to freedom of association and to freedom of peaceful assembly*. Brill Nijhoff. Accessed October 24, 2020, from https://brill.com/view/title/11631.

Kaye, D., & UN Human Rights Council. (2018). *Promotion and protection of the right to freedom of opinion and expression: Report of the Special Rapporteur, A/73/348*. UN. Accessed October 24, 2020, from http://digitallibrary.un.org/record/1643488.

Kiai, M., & UN Human Rights Council. (2012). *Report of the special rapporteur on the rights to freedom of peaceful assembly and of association, A/HRC/20/27*. UN. Accessed October 24, 2020, from http://digitallibrary.un.org/record/730881.

Kiai, M., & UN Human Rights Council. (2014). *Report of the special rapporteur on the rights to freedom of peaceful assembly and of association, A/HRC/26/29*. UN. Accessed October 24, 2020, from https://digitallibrary.un.org/record/771816?ln=en.

Lawyers Committee for Human Rights (U.S.), & Whittome, C. (1997). *The neglected right: Freedom of association in international human rights law*. Lawyers Committee for Human Rights.

Liberty. (2020, December 23). Right to protest. Liberty. Accessed December 23, 2020, from https://www.libertyhumanrights.org.uk/right/right-to-protest/.

Nowak, M. (2005). *U.N. Covenant on Civil and Political Rights: CCPR commentary*. N.P. Engel.

UN Commission on Human Rights. (1985). *Report of the Working Group on a Draft Convention on the Rights of the Child, 1985, E/CN.4/1985/64*. UN. Accessed October 24, 2020, from http://digitallibrary.un.org/record/86526.

UN Committee on the Rights of the Child. (1996, January 19). *Summary record of the 277th meeting, held at the Palais des Nations, Geneva, on Friday: Consideration of the reports of states parties: Korea*. UN. Accessed October 24, 2020, from http://digitallibrary.un.org/record/210367.

UN Committee on the Rights of the Child. (2000, June 28). *Concluding observations: Georgia, CRC/C/15/Add.124*. Accessed October 23, 2020, from https://digitallibrary.un.org/record/422917?ln=en.

UN Committee on the Rights of the Child. (2004, February 26). *Concluding observations: Japan, CRC/C/15/Add.231*. Accessed October 24, 2020, from https://digitallibrary.un.org/record/530812?ln=en.

UN Committee on the Rights of the Child. (2007, April 25). *General comment no. 10 (2007) Children's rights in juvenile justice, CRC/C/GC/10*. Accessed October 12, 2020, from https://digitallibrary.un.org/record/599395?ln=en.

UN Committee on the Rights of the Child. (2008, October 20). *Concluding observations: United Kingdom, CRC/C/GBR/CO/4*. Accessed October 12, 2020, from https://digitallibrary.un.org/record/639907?ln=en.

UN Committee on the Rights of the Child. (2009, July 20). *General comment no. 12 (2009) The right of the child to be heard, CRC/C/GC/12*. Accessed October 12, 2020, from https://digitallibrary.un.org/record/671444?ln=en.

UN Committee on the Rights of the Child. (2012, July 20). *Concluding observations: Turkey, CRC/C/TUR/2-3*.

UN Committee on the Rights of the Child. (2013a, May 29). *General comment no. 14 (2013) On the right of the child to have his or her best interests taken as a primary consideration (art. 3, para. 1), CRC/C/GC/14*. Accessed October 12, 2020, from https://digitallibrary.un.org/record/778523?ln=en.

UN Committee on the Rights of the Child. (2013b, April 17). *General comment no. 17 (2013) on the right of the child to rest, leisure, play, recreational activities, cultural life and the arts (art. 31), CRC/C/GC/17*. Accessed October 12, 2020, from https://digitallibrary.un.org/record/778539?ln=en.

UN Committee on the Rights of the Child. (2014). *Day of general discussion: Digital media and children's rights*. UN. Accessed October 24, 2020, from https://www.ohchr.org/EN/HRBodies/CRC/Pages/Discussion2014.aspx.

UN Committee on the Rights of the Child. (2016, December 6). *General comment no. 20 (2016) on the implementation of the rights of the child during adolescence, CRC/C/GC/20*. Accessed October 12, 2020, from https://digitallibrary.un.org/record/855544?ln=en.

UN Committee on the Rights of the Child. (2017, June 21). *General comment no. 21 (2017) on children in street situations, CRC/C/GC/21*. Accessed October 12, 2020, from https://digitallibrary.un.org/record/1304490?ln=en.

UN Committee on the Rights of the Child. (2018). *Day of general discussion: Protecting and empowering children as human rights defenders*. Accessed December 18, 2020, from https://www.ohchr.org/Documents/HRBodies/CRC/Discussions/2018/crc_dgd_2018_outcomereport_en.pdf.

UN Human Rights Committee. (2011, September 12). *CCPR general comment no. 34 (2011) Article 19, Freedoms of opinion and expression, CCPR/C/GC/34*. https://digitallibrary.un.org/record/715606?ln=en

Open Access This chapter is licensed under the terms of the Creative Commons Attribution 4.0 International License (http://creativecommons.org/licenses/by/4.0/), which permits use, sharing, adaptation, distribution and reproduction in any medium or format, as long as you give appropriate credit to the original author(s) and the source, provide a link to the Creative Commons license and indicate if changes were made.

The images or other third party material in this chapter are included in the chapter's Creative Commons license, unless indicated otherwise in a credit line to the material. If material is not included in the chapter's Creative Commons license and your intended use is not permitted by statutory regulation or exceeds the permitted use, you will need to obtain permission directly from the copyright holder.

Chapter 11
Article 16: The Right to Protection of Privacy

Christian Whalen

> 1. No child shall be subjected to arbitrary or unlawful interference with his or her privacy, family, home or correspondence, nor to unlawful attacks on his or her honour and reputation.
> 2. The child has the right to the protection of the law against such interference or attacks.

What Did Children Say?
Parents and housemothers (in state care facilities) should ask if they can check your personal stuff because you sometimes don't want them to see the stuff. They should not read our diaries and not answer our phone calls. (*Africa*)

Government should pass a law banning unnecessary surveillance on the children. (*Asia-Pacific*)

The opportunity to be online and have a chat without fear of disclosure of chat and correspondence. (*Eastern Europe*)

Training for students as to how to protect their privacy in social media, and the impact of data mining. (*Eastern Europe*)

C. Whalen (✉)
Office of the Child, Youth and Seniors Advocate, Fredericton, NB, Canada
e-mail: Christian.Whalen@gnb.ca

Overview

Article 16 asserts the child's right to privacy in the exact terms of the International Covenant on Civil and Political Rights, but it innovates by juxtaposing this right to a new right in relation to the child's right to information in Article 17.[1] Protecting privacy in an information age requires a principled regulation of a child's right to access information that can promote their social, spiritual and moral development. The nexus between Articles 16 and 17 is therefore an important one. The *Travaux Préparatoires* reveal that the first drafts of the Convention included no provision on a right to privacy (Detrick et al., 1992, pp. 255–265). A draft provision was introduced by the United States 1982 stating: 'that the child and his parents are not subject to unlawful or arbitrary interference'. In 1983, the United States tried again to incorporate a right to privacy referencing only the child's right and not the parents' rights and in 1985, further recommended that the right to privacy be couched in a broader provision of civil and political rights generally. Eventually, it was agreed to include the right, as with other civil and political rights, following the text of the International Covenant on Civil and Political Rights as faithfully as possible.

Article 16 affirms the child's right to privacy, including informational privacy, personal and spatial privacy, and the right to solitude[2]; it also emphasises a right to protection against arbitrary or unlawful interference with the child's family, home or correspondence[3]; and a right to protect his or her honour and reputation.[4] Finally, the Article requires States Parties to protect children legally from interference or attacks on their privacy. Children's privacy can be particularly at risk within their parental home, within alternative care settings, and within institutional settings including schools and hospitals.[5] However, as for adults, children's privacy is increasingly at risk online (Innocenti, 2012). Threats to children's privacy may arise from the digital

---

[1] For a discussion in relation to the links between the right to privacy and the right to information more generally, see David Banisar's *The Right to Information and Privacy: Balancing Rights and Managing Conflicts* (2011).

[2] Prosser defined privacy as encompassing four basic rights of (1) a right to solitude; (2) protection from public disclosure of embarrassing facts; (3) protection from publicity placing one in a false light; and (4) protection from appropriation of one's name or likeness (1960). Cf Alan Westin, *Privacy and Freedom* (1967), who defined the four states of privacy as solitude, intimacy, anonymity and reserve.

[3] In reference to child privacy in institutional settings, see Niamh Joyce, *An Analysis of the Extent of the Juvenile Offender's Right to Privacy: Is the Child's Right to Privacy Circumvented by Public Interest?* (2011); regarding violations of a child's privacy at home and for the philosophical underpinnings of Article 16 see Joel Feinberg, 'The Child's Right to an Open Future' (1980).

[4] Libel and slander laws must protect children as well, and the Committee has expressed concern not merely about the application of these laws in individual cases but also to the treatment of children in general by the media (1996).

[5] The Committee interprets family, home and correspondence broadly, to encompass all relatives and significant persons living in familial contact with the child, every domicile or place of residence which a child may call home, and all forms of communication in which the child may have a privacy interest (Hodgkin et al., 2007, p. 210; UN Committee on the Rights of the Child, 2006, para. 15).

activities of others, whether peers, family, educators or strangers; from data collection and processing by public institutions, businesses and other organisations; and from criminal activities such as hacking and identity theft (Innocenti, 2017). The Committee has pointed out the significant rise in the range and incidence of privacy concerns related to the increase in mass collection of personal data and the multiplication of platforms for sharing of such data (UN Committee on the Rights of the Child, 2014 and 2021). While the text of the Convention directly reflects the formulation of the right to privacy in the ICCPR, the provision is also supple enough to defend children's privacy against the emergent threats of state surveillance and exploitative commerce.

General Principles

Article 2 The relationship between privacy rights and liberty interests, for instance those in Articles 6, 12, and 13 through to 17, is stronger than with equality interests and yet privacy rights of children intersect with the non-discrimination principle in Article 2 in important ways. For example, marginalised and vulnerable children, such as visible minorities, children with disabilities, LGBTQ children, and street or drug-endangered children may find themselves more often in institutional settings where their privacy rights may be infringed and may be particularly susceptible to privacy rights violations in those settings.

Article 3 The best interests of the child principle may at times be mistakenly invoked as a justification for breaching a child's privacy. Privacy interests are sometimes considered trivial,[6] a right that state officials may view as something to be overridden when the child's best interests require it. The Committee, however, has sought to dissuade governments from this view and has insisted that the best interests principle has to be applied in a manner consistent with the provisions of the Convention as a whole (2007, para. 26).

Article 6 The relationship between the child's right to life, survival, and maximum development, and the right to privacy, is a close one. The framers of the Convention were concerned that a strong right to privacy might infringe on parental authority, and accordingly, the provision initially included a limitation to safeguard parental authority. That limitation was eventually removed and recast as Article 5 (Detrick et al., 1992, pp. 258–259). The Convention balances the parents' role in nurturing

---

[6]The history of the evolution of privacy law as a common law tort both in the U.S. and in commonwealth jurisdictions shows how reluctant courts have been to engage in resolving privacy disputes. Lord Denning's flat denial of a tort of invasion of privacy in Re X a Minor, [1975] 1 All ER 697, is premised on the view that the law does not concern itself with trifles and that privacy violations are best regulated through norms and social conventions. Lawrence Lessig, like most American constitutional scholars, takes a different view and demonstrates how in an information age privacy must be protected as a foundational human rights norm (2006).

and guiding the child in the exercise of their rights, in a manner consistent with the child's evolving capacities, against the child's autonomy and liberty interests. The right to life, survival, and development are the kernel of the child's liberty interests in contributing to the child's development into an autonomous human being. Protecting the child's privacy is a critical factor in developing their autonomy, freedom, and agency.

Article 12 The child's right to express their views must be understood as a right, not an obligation (UN Committee on the Rights of the Child, 2009, para. 16). Children can choose not to express themselves, and in so doing are exercising a right to privacy. When children do express their opinions and views in decisions affecting them, they are entitled to a reasonable expectation of privacy.[7] For example, in health consultations, in decisions concerning placement in care, or concerning their experience as victims of abuse or neglect, there should be a presumption of confidentiality but with limits, linked to the child's right to protection, consideration of their best interests, and parental rights in relation to the upbringing of their children (Tobin & Field, 2019, pp. 570–571). Any decision to override the right to privacy or confidentiality must be informed by both evidence and the views of the child themselves. In court proceedings, the balancing of the child's right to privacy with the interests of fairness and due process in decision-making should always be carried out with regard for the child's best interests.[8]

Articles Related or Linked to Article 16

Article 5 provides that appropriate direction and guidance by parents and guardians must be consistent with the child's evolving capacities and, accordingly, must take account of their privacy rights in line with those capacities.

Article 7 which provides the right to a name, nationality and to know one's parents can, in certain circumstances, raise a conflict of interest between the privacy rights of the child and their parents.

Article 8, preservation of identity is integral to the child's protection of their privacy and sense of family and belonging.

Article 9, non-separation from parents unless in the child's best interests, but where such separation is necessary, it is imperative that in any proceedings, children's privacy is fully respected.

---

[7] In the context of criminal justice administration, confidentiality requirements are explicitly spelled out in the convention Article 40(2) (vii) and in the Committee's General Comments, for example General Comment no. 12, paragraph 61, but the nexus between Articles 12 and 16 is often in play in mental health and child protection proceedings as well (Hodgkin et al., 2007, p. 203).

[8] See, for example, A.B. v. Bragg Communications Inc. [2012] 2 S.C.R. 567, a case from the Supreme Court of Canada dealing with the balancing of a child's privacy interests with the demands of fairness in relation to the open court rule.

Article 13 provides for children's right to freedom of expression, but this is limited by the requirement that it is exercised in accordance with respect for the rights or reputations of others.

Article 17 provides for children's rights to information from the mass media, but such information must not violate child privacy rights.

Article 19 provides protection from violence but in any intervention to provide protection, the child's privacy rights must be respected.

Article 20, children in alternative forms of care must have their privacy rights respected.

Article 37 imposes a prohibition on cruel or unusual punishment and arbitrary deprivation of liberty, and where punishment or deprivation of liberty is imposed it must not violate children's privacy rights.

Article 40, children's privacy must be respected within the criminal justice system.

Relevant Instruments

UN Universal Declaration of Human Rights (1948), Article 12
   International Covenant on Civil and Political Rights (1966), Article 17
   European Convention on Human Rights (1950), Article 8
   American Convention on Human Rights 'Pact of San Jose, Costa Rica' (B-32) (1978), Article 11
   African Charter on the Rights and Welfare of the Child (1990), Article 10

Attributes

Attribute One: Interference with Privacy

Privacy is vital for children's agency, dignity and safety, and for the exercise of their rights (Innocenti, 2017; Kaye and UN Human Rights Council, 2018; UN General Assembly, 2019). One of the core values protected by the right to privacy is the right to be left alone, or the right to solitude. Janusz Korczak, for example, highlighted that even children in an orphanage, with dormitories and very limited privacy, needed a private space, be it a drawer or a suitcase to keep their more prized possessions, a place that would be only theirs (2009, p. 25).[9] Courts sometimes

---

[9] The Human Rights Committee also describes this right to solitude when it insists that 'competent public authorities should only be able to call for such information relating to an individual's private life the knowledge of which is essential in the interests of society': (United Nations, 2006, p. 18).

distinguish personal privacy from informational or spatial privacy.[10] The closer an intrusion comes to the biographical core of a child's privacy, the higher the onus against interference will be. National constitutional courts and regional human rights bodies have developed a clear jurisprudence in relation to privacy rights, placing strict limits on state intrusions on a child or any citizen's privacy. They insist that the law must protect against privacy infringements that are:

- not sanctioned by law
- arbitrary (in the sense that they must be carried out in the pursuit of legitimate state aims)
- unnecessary. It must be shown that the privacy infringement was not disproportionate to the legitimate aims sought and constituted the least intrusive means of securing those legitimate aims (Electronic Frontier Foundation, 2014).

The Convention also requires that States Parties take measures to protect children's privacy from intrusion by non-state actors. Violations of a child's intimacy, through relentless bullying, luring, and unwanted attention or touching infringe Article 16 (UN Committee on the Rights of the Child, 2014). Similarly, non-consensual collection of a child's biological data, through blood samples, voiceprints, and fingerprints may constitute infringements (Global Privacy Assembly, 2008). Consent-based schemes for the collection of such data may also infringe on privacy.[11] Threats to privacy are often online. Data mining and targeted marketing to children based upon their online web-surfing activities, and the use of embedded sensors in toys and clothes connected to automated systems, often lack transparency and may constitute violations of the child's right to be let alone (Milkaite & Verdoodt, 2017). School video surveillance also intrudes upon children's privacy and can only be justified if the interference is neither unlawful or arbitrary (Information and Privacy Commissioner of Ontario, 2015; Office of the Privacy Commissioner of Canada, 2012).

Attribute Two: Interference with Family, Home, or Correspondence

Article 16 also deals with spatial or territorial privacy and informational privacy which is given a very broad reading by the Committee, as it is in other constitutional law texts and human rights treaties (Hodgkin et al., 2007, pp. 210–211). The text is broad enough to encompass a trespass to property or to a family member, and

---

[10] For example, see R. v. Dyment [1988] 2 S.C.R. 417 (http://canlii.ca/t/1ftc6) and R. v. Plant [1993] 3 S.C.R. 281 (http://canlii.ca/t/1fs0w)

[11] As, for instance, when young internauts provide online consent to unscrupulous internet service providers or online game services through privacy policies that take unfair advantage or are couched in terms that children will not clearly understand (Lawford et al., 2008, p. 19).

although the Convention does not establish property rights for children, the privacy protections do afford children a certain right to exclusive enjoyment of their property and protection against the interference of others (Kilkelly, 2001, pp. 59–62). It also protects their relationships with family. For example, attempts at alienating a child from one of their parents or siblings could constitute a privacy rights violation (Kilkelly, 2001, pp. 50–54). In jurisdictions subject to the European Convention on Human Rights, the privacy rights of children are frequently invoked in child protection matters. However, most privacy infractions today are in relation to informational privacy, and increasingly in respect of the digital environment, for example, breaches of confidentiality, personal health information leaks, and surveillance. In many cases, intrusions into children's personal information that would be unacceptable for adults are justified for children in terms of their protection and best interests. However, any such intrusions must be valid and justified taking into account children's own views and their evolving capacities (Tobin & Field, 2019, p. 570).

Attribute Three: Unlawful Attacks on Honour and Reputation

Privacy experts maintain that we are moving from an information age to an economy founded on reputation (Lessig, 2010; Swallow, 2013). Article 16 rights protect children from traditional harms such as libel, slander, and misappropriation of their image. The Committee, for example has pointed to the vulnerability of street children to unlawful attacks on their honour and reputation (2017, paras. 27, 43, 60). The Committee has also argued that children's honour and reputation can also be abused as a group, for example, by the media denigrating them and their behaviour based merely on their age.[12] However, in the age of social media, where children are increasingly engaged in activities without parental supervision, children are particularly at risk of various online risks to the honour and reputation (Nyst, 2017). Increasingly the attacks on honour and reputation come in the form of distribution of sexts, cyber-bullying, child pornography and the unauthorised use of children's images online.

In order to constitute a violation, an attack must be intentional and contain untruthful statements (Tobin & Field, 2019, p. 594). The Human Rights Committee has argued that States Parties have to balance the rights embodied in Article 16 with the right to freedom of expression, but at the same time they also have an obligation to enable individuals to protect themselves from unlawful attacks and to have an effective remedy against those responsible (UN Human Rights Committee, 2011, para. 37; United Nations, 2006, p. 181).

---

[12] See, for example, Concluding Observations for Nicaragua (UN Committee on the Rights of the Child, 1995, paras. 17, 34).

Attribute Four: Protection of the Law Against Unlawful Interference or Attacks

Data monitoring and measurement of child privacy standards requires more than the simple proclamation of the rights to privacy. There must also be programmes to dissuade the public from these practices, to sanction them, and to provide recourses and remedies to victims of bullying and other privacy violation (United Nations, 2006, p. 182). Surveillance of children, together with any associated automated processing of personal data, must not be conducted routinely or indiscriminately, and not without children's knowledge (UN General Assembly, 2019). States Parties should review their own procedures regarding the collection and processing of children's personal data and correspondence to ensure they respect children's right to privacy, including in governmental decision-making and within the criminal justice system (UN General Assembly, 2019). Furthermore, any restrictions or intrusions on the child's right to privacy must be prescribed by law, necessary, and proportionate (UN Human Rights Council, 2017, para. 2; UN Office of the High Commissioner for Human Rights (OHCHR), 2014, para. 23). States Parties should also ensure the implementation of effective data protection legislation, and take other measures as necessary, to prevent arbitrary or unlawful interference with children's privacy, family, home or correspondence in relation to the digital environment (Albania et al., 2018; Nyst, 2017; UN General Assembly, 2019).

References

Albania, Argentina, Australia, Austria, Belgium, Bosnia and Herzegovina, et al. (2018). *The promotion, protection and enjoyment of human rights on the Internet: Draft resolution, 2018, A/HRC/38/L.10/Rev.1*. UN. Retrieved October 25, 2020, from http://digitallibrary.un.org/record/1639844

Banisar, D. (2011). *The right to information and privacy: Balancing rights and managing conflicts* (SSRN Scholarly Paper No. ID 1786473). Social Science Research Network. https://doi.org/10.2139/ssrn.1786473

Detrick, S., Doek, J. E., & Cantwell, N. (1992). *The United Nations convention on the rights of the child: A guide to the "Travaux Préparatoires."* Martinus Nijhoff Publishers.

Electronic Frontier Foundation. (2014). *Necessary & proportionate: International principles on the application of human rights to communications surveillance*. https://www.ohchr.org/Documents/Issues/Privacy/ElectronicFrontierFoundation.pdf

Feinberg, J. (1980). The child's right to an open future. In W. Aiken & H. Lafollette (Eds.), *Whose child? Children's rights, parental authority, and state power* (pp. 124–153). Littlefield Adams.

Global Privacy Assembly. (2008). *Resolution on children's online privacy—Adopted at the 30th international conference for data protection and privacy commissioners—Strasbourg, France 2008*. Retrieved October 25, 2020, from http://globalprivacyassembly.org/wp-content/uploads/2015/02/Resolution-on-Childrens-Online-Privacy-.pdf

Hodgkin, R., Newell, P., & UNICEF. (2007). *Implementation handbook for the convention on the rights of the child* (3rd ed.). UNICEF. Retrieved September 21, 2020, from https://digitallibrary.un.org/record/620060?ln=en

Information and Privacy Commissioner of Ontario. (2015). *Guidelines for the use of video surveillance*. Retrieved October 25, 2020, from https://www.ipc.on.ca/wp-content/uploads/Resources/2015_Guidelines_Surveillance.pdf

Joyce, N. (2011). An analysis of the extent of the juvenile offender's right to privacy: Is the child's right to privacy circumvented by public interest? *European Journal of Crime, Criminal Law and Criminal Justice, 19*(2), 113–124. https://doi.org/10.1163/157181711X566335

Kaye, D., & UN Human Rights Council. (2018). *Promotion and protection of the right to freedom of opinion and expression: Report of the Special Rapporteur, A/73/348*. UN. Retrieved October 24, 2020, from http://digitallibrary.un.org/record/1643488

Kilkelly, U. (2001). *The right to respect for private and family life: A guide to the implementation of Article 8 of the European Convention on Human Rights* (2003). : Council of Europe Publishing. Retrieved October 25, 2020, from https://rm.coe.int/090000168007ff47

Korczak, J. K. (2009). *Janusz Korczak: The child's right to respect—Lectures on today's challenges*. Council of Europe Publishing. https://rm.coe.int/09000016807ba985

Lawford, J., Taheri, M., & Public Interest Advocacy Centre (Canada). (2008). *All in the data family: Children's privacy online*. Retrieved October 25, 2020, from http://epe.lac-bac.gc.ca/100/200/300/public_interest_advocacy/children_final/children_final_small_fixed.pdf

Lessig, L. (2006). *Code: And other laws of cyberspace, version 2.0*. Basic Books.

Lessig, L. (2010, January 17). Sharing economies. *The Mindful Word*. Retrieved October 25, 2020, from https://www.themindfulword.org/2010/sharing-economies-lawrence-lessig

Milkaite, I., & Verdoodt, V. (2017). *The general data protection regulation and children's rights: Questions and answers for legislators, DPAs, industry, education, stakeholders and civil society*. Better Internet for Kids. Retrieved October 25, 2020, from https://www.betterinternetforkids.eu/documents/167024/2013511/GDPRRoundtable_June2017_FullReport.pdf

Nyst, C. (2017). *Privacy, protection of personal information and reputation rights*. UNICEF. https://www.unicef.org/csr/css/UNICEF_CRB_Digital_World_Series_PRIVACY.pdf

Office of the Privacy Commissioner of Canada. (2012). *Surveillance technologies and children*. Retrieved October 25, 2020, from https://www.priv.gc.ca/media/1751/opc_201210_e.pdf

Prosser, W. L. (1960). Privacy. *California Law Review, 48*(3), 383–423. https://doi.org/10.2307/3478805

Swallow, E. (2013, October 9). The rise of the reputation economy. *Forbes*. Retrieved October 25, 2020, from https://www.forbes.com/sites/ericaswallow/2013/10/09/reputation-economy/

Tobin, J., & Field, S. M. (2019). Article 16: The right to protection of privacy, family, home, correspondence, honour, and reputation. In J. Tobin (Ed.), *The UN convention on the rights of the child: A commentary* (pp. 551–599). Oxford University Press.

UN Committee on the Rights of the Child. (1995). *Concluding observations: Nicaragua, June 20, 1995, CRC/C/15/Add.36*. Retrieved October 11, 2020, from https://digitallibrary.un.org/record/191818?ln=en

UN Committee on the Rights of the Child. (1996). *Day of general discussion: The child and the media*. UN. Retrieved October 25, 2020, from https://www.ohchr.org/EN/HRBodies/CRC/Pages/DiscussionDays.aspx

UN Committee on the Rights of the Child. (2006). *General Comment No. 7 (2005) Implementing child rights in early childhood, September 20, 2006, CRC/C/GC/7/Rev.1*. Retrieved October 12, 2020, from https://digitallibrary.un.org/record/584854?ln=en

UN Committee on the Rights of the Child. (2007). *General Comment No. 8 (2006) The right of the child to protection from corporal punishment and other cruel or degrading forms of punishment (arts. 19; 28, para. 2; and 37, inter alia), March 2, 2007, CRC/C/GC/8*. Retrieved October 12, 2020, from https://digitallibrary.un.org/record/583961?ln=en

UN Committee on the Rights of the Child. (2009). *General Comment No. 12 (2009) The right of the child to be heard, July 20, 2009, CRC/C/GC/12*. Retrieved October 12, 2020, from https://digitallibrary.un.org/record/671444?ln=en

UN Committee on the Rights of the Child. (2014). *Day of general discussion: Digital media and children's rights*. UN. Retrieved October 24, 2020, from https://www.ohchr.org/EN/HRBodies/CRC/Pages/Discussion2014.aspx

UN Committee on the Rights of the Child. (2017). *General Comment No. 21 (2017) on children in street situations, June 21, 2017, CRC/C/GC/21*. Retrieved October 12, 2020, from https://digitallibrary.un.org/record/1304490?ln=en

UN Committee on the Rights of the Child. (2021). *General Comment No. 25 (2021) on children's rights in relation to the digital environment*. https://tbinternet.ohchr.org/_layouts/15/treatybodyexternal/Download.aspx?symbolno=CRC%2fC%2fGC%2f25&Lang=en

UN General Assembly. (2019). *The right to privacy in the digital age: Resolution adopted by the General Assembly, 2019, A/RES/73/179*. UN. Retrieved October 25, 2020, from http://digitallibrary.un.org/record/1661346

UN Human Rights Committee. (2011). *CCPR General Comment No. 34 (2011) Article 19, Freedoms of opinion and expression, September 12, 2011, CCPR/C/GC/34*. https://digitallibrary.un.org/record/715606?ln=en

UN Human Rights Council. (2017). *The right to privacy in the digital age: Resolution adopted by the Human Rights Council on 23 March 2017, A/HRC/RES/34/7*. UN. Retrieved October 25, 2020, from http://digitallibrary.un.org/record/1307661

UN Office of the High Commissioner for Human Rights (OHCHR). (2014). *The right to privacy in the digital age: Report of the Office of the United Nations High Commissioner for Human Rights, 2014, A/HRC/27/37*. UN. Retrieved October 25, 2020, from http://digitallibrary.un.org/record/777869

UNICEF Office of Research, Innocenti. (2012). *Child safety online: Global challenges and strategies*. Technical report. Retrieved October 25, 2020, from https://www.unicef-irc.org/publications/652-child-safety-online-global-challenges-and-strategies-technical-report.html

UNICEF Office of Research, Innocenti. (2017). *Child privacy in the age of web 2.0 and 3.0: Challenges and opportunities for policy*. Retrieved October 25, 2020, from https://www.unicef-irc.org/publications/926-child-privacy-in-the-age-of-web-20-and-30-challenges-and-opportunities-for-policy.html

United Nations. (2006). *Compilation of general comments and general recommendations adopted by human rights treaty bodies, HRI/GEN/1/Rev. 8*. UN. Retrieved April 19, 2020, from http://digitallibrary.un.org/record/576098

Westin, A. F. (1967). *Privacy and freedom*. Atheneum.

Open Access This chapter is licensed under the terms of the Creative Commons Attribution 4.0 International License (http://creativecommons.org/licenses/by/4.0/), which permits use, sharing, adaptation, distribution and reproduction in any medium or format, as long as you give appropriate credit to the original author(s) and the source, provide a link to the Creative Commons license and indicate if changes were made.

The images or other third party material in this chapter are included in the chapter's Creative Commons license, unless indicated otherwise in a credit line to the material. If material is not included in the chapter's Creative Commons license and your intended use is not permitted by statutory regulation or exceeds the permitted use, you will need to obtain permission directly from the copyright holder.

Chapter 12
Article 17: The Right to Access to Diverse Sources of Information

Gerison Lansdown

> States Parties recognize the important function performed by the mass media and shall ensure that the child has access to information and material from a diversity of national and international sources, especially those aimed at the promotion of his or her social, spiritual and moral well-being and physical and mental health. To this end, States Parties shall:
>
> (a) Encourage the mass media to disseminate information and material of social and cultural benefit to the child and in accordance with the spirit of article 29;
> (b) Encourage international co-operation in the production, exchange and dissemination of such information and material from a diversity of cultural, national and international sources;
> (c) Encourage the production and dissemination of children's books;
> (d) Encourage the mass media to have particular regard to the linguistic needs of the child who belongs to a minority group or who is indigenous;
> (e) Encourage the development of appropriate guidelines for the protection of the child from information and material injurious to his or her well-being, bearing in mind the provisions of articles 13 and 18.

G. Lansdown (✉)
Carleton University, Ottawa, ON, Canada

> **What Did Children Say?**
> 'Informing students of reliable sources/websites; and how to critique news.' (*Western Europe/Other*)
> 'The opportunity to have access to information, libraries, schools, websites in order to, we quote, "be smart and know what to say."' (*Eastern Europe*)
> If it is a big business, we will need our council representing government to provide us electricity or bigger generator with data service to be online always. (*Africa*)
> 'Website blocking'; 'safety settings'; 'Block harmful sites.' (*Western Europe/Other*)

Overview

Although linked closely with Article 13, the right to freedom of expression, Article 17 introduces a unique focus on the role of the mass media in relation to children's rights to information (Sacino, 2011). It places a duty on States Parties to ensure general access to information and material from a diversity of sources, rather than guaranteeing access to each individual child. The language employed in Article 17 obliges States Parties to encourage the media to fulfil this goal, and to adopt the necessary measures to support that process.

In its emphasis on the role of non-state actors in the provision of information, and the use of the term 'encourage,' the wording of Article 17 makes clear that it contains no coercive obligation on mass media to ensure access to material (Tobin & Handsley, 2019, p. 612). In particular, Article 17 encourages action to ensure that children, including those from minority or indigenous groups, have access to information from diverse national and international sources, which are of social and cultural benefit, consistent with the spirit of Article 29, the aims of education. It also places emphasis on sources of information aimed at promoting well-being, and physical and mental health.

Notably, Article 17 originated as a provision to protect children against harmful influences of media (Office of the United Nations High Commissioner for Human Rights and Rädda Barnen (Society: Sweden), 2007, p. 480). However, during the drafting process, it was observed that the media often did more good than harm, and that the article should be constructed positively (Office of the United Nations High Commissioner for Human Rights and Rädda Barnen (Society: Sweden), 2007, p. 481). Accordingly, only the final paragraph refers to the obligation to encourage guidelines to protect children from harmful or injurious material. It is important to note that the Committee has highlighted the degree to which the rapid development of the digital environment since Article 17 was first drafted has had significant impact on the nature of children's engagement with the mass media, regarding both access and protection (2006a, 2014a, 2016, para. 47).

General Principles

Article 2 Imposes three key obligations in respect of the mass media and Article 17:

- All children, without discrimination, should have access to mass media, in respect of outreach, language, age, and formats (Hodgkin et al., 2007; UN Committee on the Rights of the Child, 2007, para. 37; UN General Assembly, 1991, para. 62, 2006, Article 21)
- An obligation to ensure that mass media do not portray any groups of children in a discriminatory manner, inconsistent with their human rights[1]
- An obligation to challenge discriminatory or stigmatising stereotypes adverse to children's rights.[2]

Article 3 The balance in Article 17 between the right to access mass media and the right to protection from harm must be meditated by the best interests principle, consistent with Article 3 together with the child's own views and their evolving capacities.

Article 6 The overall focus of Article 17 is directed towards promotion of well-being and therefore in line with the obligation to ensure to the maximum extent possible the development of the child.

Article 12 Access to information, including through the mass media, is necessary is to enable children to express their views effectively (UN Committee on the Rights of the Child, 2009, paras. 82–83). In addition, Article 12 implies an obligation to provide children with opportunities to contribute to the development of media initiatives (UN Committee on the Rights of the Child, 1996).

Articles Related or Linked to Article 17

Article 13 protects freedom of expression that is contingent on the right to information through a diversity of sources.

Article 14 protects the right to freedom of thought, conscience and religion, the exercise of which requires access to information from a wide variety of sources.

Article 16 protects the right to privacy that can be threatened through the media, particularly in the context of the digital environment.

---

[1] See, for example, CRPD (UN General Assembly, 2006, para. 8) and General Recommendation No. 34 adopted by the Committee on Racial discrimination against people of African descent (UN Committee on the Elimination of Racial Discrimination, 2011, para. 30).

[2] See, for example, Day of General Discussion, The Children and the Media (UN Committee on the Rights of the Child, 1996) and General Comment no. 3 (UN Committee on the Rights of the Child, 2003, paras. 16–17).

Article 18 provides that parents have primary responsibility for the care of children. In so doing, they are key to ensuring that children have access to information and to protecting them from harmful exposure.

Article 19, together with Articles 34 and 36, provide the right to protection from exploitation including in the media.

Article 24 provides for the right to the best possible health. The mass media are a key source of potential information relating to health and well-being.

Article 29 elaborates the aims of education which include recognition that children must be prepared for life in a free society and plays a key part in enabling children to access information.

Article 30 protects the rights of minorities who are identified in Article 17 as being entitled to be given particular regard by the mass media.

Article 42 requires that States Parties make the provisions of the Convention widely known, including through mass media.

Relevant Instruments

No other human rights treaty has a directly comparable provision to Article 17, but the article has close linkages with the following:

UN Universal Declaration of Human Rights (1948), Article 19
International Covenant on Civil and Political Rights (1966), Article 19
UN Convention on the Rights of Persons with Disabilities (2006), Article 21
European Convention on Human Rights (1950), Article 11
American Convention on Human Rights 'Pact of San Jose, Costa Rica' (B-32) (1978), Article 13

Attributes

Attribute One: Diversity of Sources and Media

Article 17 implies that States Parties must ensure all children have access to communications from a diversity of mass media sources including from both public and private sectors. Diversity of sources is the means through which to achieve the goal of diversity of information (UN Committee on the Rights of the Child, 2014b, para. 28). It can include:

- breadth of ownership of media with multiple outlets for both production and dissemination of information
- the range of sources of information encompassing different cultures and perspectives and including media corporations, advertising agencies, publishers, journalists, editors, and producers

- different types of communication including news, culture, entertainment, literature, music, arts
- different media through which it is available including television, radio, the Internet, digital media including interactive media such as electronic games, social media platforms, newspapers, magazines, and books. (Sacino, 2011)

Article 17 does not impose duties on States Parties to provide information itself or to control the output of information or communications. Doing so would interfere with freedom of expression. Rather, it is to ensure an environment in which the diversity of mass media sources is made available. For example, this necessitates measures to avoid an over-concentration of private ownership of mass media. In the context of the obligation to ensure diversity from international as well as national sources, this also implies encouragement by joining or supporting organisations such as UNESCO or other regional bodies.

Attribute Two: Beneficial Information and Material

Whereas Attribute One focuses on the diversity of mass media, Attribute Two focuses on content. The Committee has observed that the mass media, including advertising and marketing industries, can have positive as well as negative impacts on children's rights (2013a, para. 58). Article 17 emphasises the role of mass media in ensuring the provision of information and material aimed at the promotion of social, spiritual, and moral well-being and physical and mental health.

This focus is reinforced in paragraph (a), which encourages dissemination of information and material of social and cultural social benefit to the child. The obligation with regard to content has been interpreted by the Committee to require States Parties to encourage mass media, both online and offline, to provide information necessary for the realisation of rights. This includes:

- promoting the values and aims of Article 29, including fostering understanding, peace and tolerance, and the optimum development of the child (UN Committee on the Rights of the Child, 2001, para. 21)
- promoting access to accurate and adequate information to support health and healthy lifestyles, including that relating to sexual and reproductive health (UN Committee on the Rights of Persons with Disabilities, 2016, para. 26)
- avoidance of promotion of material that violates children's rights through propagation of, for example, discrimination, racism, or misogyny.[3]

The Committee has also emphasised the role the mass media can play in raising awareness of the Convention, monitoring implementation of children's rights,

---

[3] See, for example, CRPD (UN General Assembly, 2006, Article 8, para 2) and General Comment no. 15 (UN Committee on the Rights of the Child, 2013b, para. 84).

producing programmes that are of educational and cultural value for children and facilitating access to and participation of children in the media (1996, 2014a).

Attribute Three: Access to Mass Media

Information through mass media needs to be available, relevant, and accessible for children, in all environments and settings, through language, outreach, age, and formats. Paragraph (c), for example, draws attention to the need for production and dissemination of children's books and paragraph (d) highlights the importance of having regard to the linguistic needs of minority groups of children. The Committee has highlighted that media, including through the Internet, must be accessible to children of all ages, those from rural and indigenous communities, children with different first languages, children in detention, and children with disabilities.[4] Availability of libraries is a key means of promoting access (UN Committee on the Rights of the Child, 2000, paras. 42–43).

In addition, States Parties should encourage opportunities for children to have direct access to the media as active participants and initiators, as a means of exercising their Article 12 rights, and to promote their optimum development. Children should not only be able to consume information material but also to have access to opportunities to participate themselves in the media (UN Committee on the Rights of the Child, 1996, 2006a, para. 36).

Attribute Four: Protection from Harmful Material

Article 17 paragraph (e) requires that States Parties encourage the development of guidelines for the protection of children from material harmful to their well-being. In this context, the nature or level of protection must be assessed with regard to the best interests of children, taking into account their evolving capacities and level of maturity (UN Committee on the Rights of the Child, 2013c). Notably, the language of encouragement implies not that States Parties themselves undertakes this task, but that they encourage others to do so. Furthermore, by referring to guidelines, it implies voluntary rather than legislative controls (Hodgkin et al., 2007). Importantly, it references Articles 13 and 18. In other words, it can be understood that any controls over censorship of the mass media would rely on the limitations imposed in Article 13 paragraph 2, rather than on Article 17.

The reference to Article 18 implies that it is primarily parents rather than the state who have responsibility for ensuring the protection of children from inappropriate or

---

[4]See, for example, Concluding Observations for Central African Republic (2000, paras. 42–43), Greece (2002, paras. 46–47), and Myanmar (2004, paras. 36–37).

harmful media. However, the Committee has repeatedly raised concerns about easy availability of inappropriate or offensive material and recommended that States Parties take all necessary measures to limit exposure of children, particularly in the digital environment, and protect them from such material (1996, 2006b, para. 35).[5] Providers of digital services should be encouraged to introduce measures such as parental controls, filtering systems, moderation and labelling of content, while ensuring that such provisions do not violate the child's freedom of expression and privacy.

It can be argued that, although recommendations seeking to impose obligations on States Parties appear to exceed the requirements embodied in Article 17, they are legitimate when taken in conjunction with Articles 3, 6, 19 and 24 (Tobin & Handsley, 2019, p. 633). The Committee has also argued that States Parties should facilitate the involvement of children themselves in the development of protective guidelines (2014a). States Parties should also adopt measures to support and empower children to understand the risks and adopt strategies to avoid harm.

References

Hodgkin, R., Newell, P., & UNICEF. (2007). *Implementation handbook for the convention on the rights of the child* (3rd ed.). UNICEF. Retrieved September 21, 2020, from https://digitallibrary.un.org/record/620060?ln=en

Office of the United Nations High Commissioner for Human Rights & Rädda barnen (Society: Sweden). (2007). *Legislative history of the convention on the rights of the child*. United Nations. https://digitallibrary.un.org/record/602462?ln=en

Sacino, S. (2011). *A commentary on the United Nations convention on the rights of the child, article 17: Access to a diversity of mass media sources*. Brill Nijhoff. Retrieved October 25, 2020, from https://brill.com/view/title/11633

Tobin, J., & Handsley, E. (2019). Article 17: The mass media and children: Diversity of sources, quality of content, and protection against harm. In J. Tobin (Ed.), *The UN convention on the rights of the child: A commentary* (pp. 600–645). Oxford University Press.

UN Committee on the Elimination of Racial Discrimination. (2011). *General recommendation no. 34 adopted by the Committee: Racial discrimination against people of African descent, 2011, CERD/C/GC/34*. UN. Retrieved October 26, 2020, from http://digitallibrary.un.org/record/714927

UN Committee on the Rights of Persons with Disabilities. (2016). *General Comment No. 4 (2016), Article 24: Right to inclusive education, September 2, 2016, CRPD/C/GC/4*. Retrieved October 12, 2020, from https://digitallibrary.un.org/record/1313836?ln=en

UN Committee on the Rights of the Child. (1996). *Day of general discussion: The child and the media*. UN. Retrieved October 25, 2020, from https://www.ohchr.org/EN/HRBodies/CRC/Pages/DiscussionDays.aspx

UN Committee on the Rights of the Child. (2000). *Concluding observations: Central African Republic, October 18, 2000, CRC/C/15/Add.138*. UN. Retrieved October 26, 2020, from http://digitallibrary.un.org/record/429820

---

[5] See also, for example, Concluding observations for Albania (2012, para. 38) and Australia (2005, para. 34).

UN Committee on the Rights of the Child. (2001). *General Comment No. 1 (2001) Article 29 (1): The Aims of Education, April 17, 2001, CRC/GC/2001/1*. Retrieved October 10, 2020, from https://digitallibrary.un.org/record/447223?ln=en

UN Committee on the Rights of the Child. (2002). *Concluding observations: Greece, April 2, 2002, CRC/C/15/Add.170*. UN. Retrieved October 26, 2020, from http://digitallibrary.un.org/record/473476

UN Committee on the Rights of the Child. (2003). *General Comment No. 3 (2003) HIV/AIDS and the rights of the child, March 17, 2003, CRC/GC/2003/3*. Retrieved October 12, 2020, from https://digitallibrary.un.org/record/501529?ln=en

UN Committee on the Rights of the Child. (2004). *Concluding observations: Myanmar, June 30, 2004, CRC/C/15/Add.237*. UN. Retrieved October 26, 2020, from http://digitallibrary.un.org/record/536569

UN Committee on the Rights of the Child. (2005). *Concluding observations: Australia, October 20, 2005, CRC/C/15/Add.268*. UN. Retrieved October 26, 2020, from http://digitallibrary.un.org/record/569889

UN Committee on the Rights of the Child. (2006a). *Day of general discussion: The right of the child to be heard*. Retrieved October 12, 2020, from https://www.ohchr.org/EN/HRBodies/CRC/Pages/DiscussionDays.aspx

UN Committee on the Rights of the Child. (2006b). *General Comment No. 7 (2005) Implementing child rights in early childhood, September 20, 2006, CRC/C/GC/7/Rev.1*. Retrieved October 12, 2020, from https://digitallibrary.un.org/record/584854?ln=en

UN Committee on the Rights of the Child. (2007). *General Comment No. 9 (2006) The rights of children with disabilities, November 13, 2007, CRC/C/GC/9*. Retrieved October 12, 2020, from https://digitallibrary.un.org/record/593891?ln=en

UN Committee on the Rights of the Child. (2009). *General Comment No. 12 (2009) The right of the child to be heard, July 20, 2009, CRC/C/GC/12*. Retrieved October 12, 2020, from https://digitallibrary.un.org/record/671444?ln=en

UN Committee on the Rights of the Child. (2012). *Concluding observations: Albania, December 7, 2012, CRC/C/ALB/CO/2-4*. UN. Retrieved October 26, 2020, from http://digitallibrary.un.org/record/739974

UN Committee on the Rights of the Child. (2013a). *General Comment No. 16 (2013) on State obligations regarding the impact of the business sector on children's rights, April 17, 2013, CRC/C/GC/16*. Retrieved October 12, 2020, from https://digitallibrary.un.org/record/778525?ln=en

UN Committee on the Rights of the Child. (2013b). *General Comment No. 15 (2013) on the right of the child to the enjoyment of the highest attainable standard of health (art. 24), April 17, 2013, CRC/C/GC/15*. UN. Retrieved October 26, 2020, from http://digitallibrary.un.org/record/778524

UN Committee on the Rights of the Child. (2013c). *General Comment No. 14 (2013) On the right of the child to have his or her best interests taken as a primary consideration (art. 3, para. 1), May 29, 2013, CRC/C/GC/14*. Retrieved October 12, 2020, from https://digitallibrary.un.org/record/778523?ln=en

UN Committee on the Rights of the Child. (2014a). *Day of general discussion: Digital media and children's rights*. UN. Retrieved October 24, 2020, from https://www.ohchr.org/EN/HRBodies/CRC/Pages/Discussion2014.aspx

UN Committee on the Rights of the Child. (2014b). *Concluding observations: Hungary, October 14, 2014, CRC/C/HUN/CO/3-5*. Retrieved October 11, 2020, from https://digitallibrary.un.org/record/793888?ln=en

UN Committee on the Rights of the Child. (2016). *General Comment No. 20 (2016) on the implementation of the rights of the child during adolescence, December 6, 2016, CRC/C/GC/20*. Retrieved October 12, 2020, from https://digitallibrary.un.org/record/855544?ln=en

UN General Assembly. (1991). *United Nations rules for the protection of juveniles deprived of their liberty, 1990, A/RES/45/113 (The Havana Rules)*. UN. Retrieved October 26, 2020, from http://digitallibrary.un.org/record/105555

UN General Assembly. (2006). *Convention on the rights of persons with disabilities, 2006, A/RES/61/106*. Retrieved May 3, 2020, from https://digitallibrary.un.org/record/588742?ln=en

Open Access This chapter is licensed under the terms of the Creative Commons Attribution 4.0 International License (http://creativecommons.org/licenses/by/4.0/), which permits use, sharing, adaptation, distribution and reproduction in any medium or format, as long as you give appropriate credit to the original author(s) and the source, provide a link to the Creative Commons license and indicate if changes were made.

The images or other third party material in this chapter are included in the chapter's Creative Commons license, unless indicated otherwise in a credit line to the material. If material is not included in the chapter's Creative Commons license and your intended use is not permitted by statutory regulation or exceeds the permitted use, you will need to obtain permission directly from the copyright holder.

Part III
Family Environment and Alternative Care Rights

Articles 5, 9, 10, 11, 18, 20, 21, and 25

Introduction

The Convention on the Rights of the Child (the Convention), in its recognition of the child as a subject of rights, has challenged many common assumptions about the status of the child within the family. At the time of its adoption and subsequently, concerns have been expressed by some that in recognising the child as an individual subject of rights, parental capacity to provide appropriate protection and care is diminished (Fagan 2001). However, although the Convention demands a culture of respect for the rights of children, within families as well as in the wider society, this does not undermine or diminish the role of parents. Indeed, the Committee on the Rights of the Child (the Committee) has argued consistently that the Convention actively strengthens family life (1994, p. 63). While its overall focus is clearly on the rights of the child, many of the rights it embodies elaborate a central role for parents as key players in the realisation of those rights. A close reading of the Convention, together with the concluding observations of the Committee, serve to highlight that, far from side-lining them, it acknowledges parents and other caregivers from four important and distinct perspectives.

First, families are fully recognised as playing a unique and vital role in the lives of children. The preambular statement includes reference to the family as the fundamental group of society and the natural environment for the growth and well-being of its members. It stresses that children should grow up in a family environment, in an atmosphere of happiness, love, and understanding. In other words, the family is the cornerstone for the realisation of children's rights and their optimum development.

Second, the Convention reaffirms the principle of respect for family autonomy already established in earlier human rights treaties.[1] In other words, it acknowledges the primacy of the family in respect of children. Parents are afforded rights and responsibilities in respect of their children, with a presumption of non-interference. This recognition is addressed in Article 5, respect for parental rights, duties, and responsibilities to provide direction and guidance to their children, although parental rights must be directed to the realisation of the rights of the child and reflect their evolving capacities. Respect for the family is also reflected in Article 7, the right of children, as far as possible, to know and be cared for by their parents, Article 8, preservation of identity, including the right to family relations without unlawful interference and Article 9, non-separation of children from parents unless in their best interests, and where separation is necessary, the right to maintain regular contact with the child.

Third, the Convention introduces explicit obligations on States Parties to provide the necessary institutions, services, support, and facilities to families to enable them to care adequately for their children. In other words, it recognises that although parents are the primary caregivers, they can only ensure the realisation of their children's rights, if the state provides the necessary environment. Thus, for example, Article 18 expressly recognises both parents as having the equal and primary responsibility for the upbringing of their child, but also requires the state to provide assistance to parents in their child-rearing responsibilities, and to make available institutions, facilities, and services for the care of children and childcare services for working parents.

Finally, the Convention introduces obligations on States Parties to take measures that proactively protect the rights of families, through measures that strengthen and support the inter-relationships between family members. This commitment is expressed in Article 9 (4), which requires that where a parent or child is separated from the family as a result of actions of the State Party, including detention, imprisonment or exile, the State Party must provide information about their whereabouts, and ensure that in so doing, no adverse consequences are entailed for the person concerned. It is also recognised in Article 10, which asserts that if a child or parents applies to enter or leave a state for the purposes of family reunification, States Parties must manage the request in a positive, humane and expeditious manner. Furthermore, where a child lives in a different state from his or her parents, states must allow the child or the parents to leave or enter the country in order to maintain contact.

The Convention also covers circumstances where families are unable or unwilling to care for their children, and the children's rights to alternative care and protection either temporarily or permanently. Articles 20, 21, and 25 address the obligations on States Parties to ensure appropriate and quality provision is made for these children, consistent with their best interests.

---

[1] See, for example, the International Covenant on Civil and Political Rights, article 17, and the European Convention on Human Rights, article 8.

Far from undermining the family, the Convention places the greatest importance on its centrality in the realisation of children's rights, and the need for a range of measures by States Parties to support family capacity to fulfil that function. However, although respectful of the family and its significance in children's lives, the Convention challenges the idea that the family is a private institution with complete autonomy in respect of children. Indeed, it elaborates a key role for the state to respect, protect, and fulfil children's rights within the family, requiring recognition that there is not always a coincidence of interests between the child and their parents, and that children must be acknowledged as individual rights holders (Pais 1997). This part explores these rights and responsibilities and how the Convention reconceptualises the relationship between the child, the family, and the state.

References

Fagan, P. (2001). *How U.N. Conventions on Women's and Children's Rights Undermine Family, Religion, and Sovereignty*. https://www.heritage.org/civil-rights/report/how-un-conventions-womens-and-childrens-rights-underminefamily-religion-and. Accessed 6 November 2020

Pais, M. S. (1997). The Convention on the Rights of the Child. In *Manual on Human Rights Reporting Under Six Major International Human Rights Instruments HR/PUB/91/1 (Rev.1)* (pp. 393–505). OHCHR. https://www.refworld.org/docid/428085252.html. Accessed 16 May 2020

UN Committee on the Rights of the Child. (1994). *Report on the 5th session, 10–28 January 1994, CRC/C/24*. https://digitallibrary.un.org/record/193291?ln=en. Accessed 12 October 2020

Chapter 13
Article 5: The Right to Parental Guidance Consistent with the Evolving Capacity of the Child

Gerison Lansdown

> States Parties shall respect the responsibilities, rights and duties of parents or, where applicable, the members of the extended family or community as provided for by local custom, legal guardians or other persons legally responsible for the child, to provide, in a manner consistent with the evolving capacities of the child, appropriate direction and guidance in the exercise by the child of the rights recognized in the present Convention.

> **What Did Children Say?**
> 'Governments can help, support families, plan visits by social workers. Have a closer follow-up. Children should participate in specific projects (with the presence of parents).' (*Western Europe/Other*)
>
> 'Parents' role is to provide food, affection, love, education, protection and clothing.' (*Western Europe/Other*)
>
> 'Does the government offer aid ("monetary or professional, for example social workers", to parents and children?' (*Western Europe/Other*)
>
> 'The State should intervene when children are in danger.' (*Western Europe/Other*)

G. Lansdown (✉)
Carleton University, Ottawa, ON, Canada

Overview

Article 5 is a unique provision in international human rights law, introducing a triangular relationship of responsibilities and accountabilities between the child, the child's parents or caregivers, and the state (Vučković-Šahović et al., 2012, pp. 155–164). It underwent radical transformation during the Convention drafting process. The original Polish draft contained no provision covering the issues addressed in Article 5 (Office of the United Nations High Commissioner for Human Rights and Rädda barnen (Society: Sweden), 2007, p. 357). Subsequent proposals were put forward to introduce a focus on the autonomy of the family and respect for their rights and responsibilities (Office of the United Nations High Commissioner for Human Rights and Rädda barnen (Society: Sweden), 2007, p. 358), reflecting existing provisions in other treaties.[1]

Further debate highlighted the imperative for a clearer focus on the rights of the child and led to the introduction of recognition that parents' rights and duties must reflect and be provided in accordance with the child's rights and their evolving capacities. In other words, the exercise of parental responsibilities must reflect the gradual capacity of the child to take increasing responsibilities for themself (UN Committee on the Rights of the Child, 2009, paras. 84, 85). Parental guidance, accordingly, must be appropriate, and directed towards the exercise by the child of the rights contained in the Convention. The inclusion of this provision, while maintaining recognition of the right of parents to protection from arbitrary interference from the state, also places boundaries on the exercise of arbitrary control over the child by their parents (Office of the United Nations High Commissioner for Human Rights and Rädda barnen (Society: Sweden), 2007, p. 359). It thereby affords the state a role in protecting the child in line with the rights embodied in the Convention.

The concept of evolving capacities introduces a framework for recognition that the Convention, in its entirety, obliges States Parties create an environment to ensure:

- Respect for the child's evolving capacities, recognising the child as a subject of rights, with gradual and increasing agency in exercising those rights for themself
- Protection of the child from exposure to risks inappropriate to their level of capacity
- Fulfilment of the child's optimum capacities (Lansdown, 2005, p. 15).

---

[1] See, for example, articles 18 and 23 of the International Covenant on Civil and Political Rights and article 10 of the International Covenant on Economic, Social and Cultural Rights.

General Principles

Article 2 The evolving capacities principle must be applied without discrimination. The Committee has consistently argued, for example, that there must be no discrimination in the setting of minimum age limits between boys and girls (2005, para. 19). It also highlights that children with disabilities can experience over-protection, leading to denial of both recognition of evolving capacities and opportunities to acquire increasing autonomy, and requires States Parties to adopt measures to address both direct and indirect discrimination in that regard (2007a).

Article 3 The rights and duties of parents derive from their responsibilities to act in the best interests of the child. This obligation is affirmed in Article 18, which states that the best interests of the child will be parents' basic concern, and necessitates that parents adjust the levels of guidance and support in accordance with the evolving capacities of the child. The evolving capacities of the child need to inform the determination of a child's best interests (UN Committee on the Rights of the Child, 2013).

Article 6 Article 5 affirms that appropriate parental guidance, consistent with respect for children's evolving capacities and directed to the exercise by the child of their rights, is necessary to promote the optimum development of the child. The Committee highlights obligations on States to contribute to the capacity of parents to fulfil this goal (2006).

Article 12 The right to express views and have them afforded due weight in accordance with age and maturity, as elaborated in Article 12, reaffirms the recognition of the importance of acknowledging the evolving capacities of the child. While all rights in the Convention apply to all children, Articles 5 and 12 testify to the importance of acknowledging that the nature of implementation, and that the active role of children in the realisation of rights, will vary in accordance with evolving capacities.

Articles Related to or Linked to Article 5

The concept of evolving capacities is relevant to the exercise of all rights but has particular relevance in respect of the following articles.

Article 1 defines a child as 'every human being below the age of eighteen years' and within that definition, Article 5 requires that legislation and practice must take account of the child's 'evolving capacities.'

Article 9 acknowledges the rights of parents not to be separated from a child unless in a child's best interests.

Article 14 requires that parents provide direction to the child in the exercise of his or her right in a manner consistent with the evolving capacities of the child.

Article 18 recognises the principle of parental responsibilities for bringing up their children.

Relevant Instruments

No other human rights treaty has a directly comparable provision to Article 5, but its origins derive from and are reflected in recognition of the role of the family as the natural and fundamental group unit of society, in the following treaties:

- UN Universal Declaration of Human Rights (1948), Article 16 (3)
- International Covenant on Civil and Political Rights (1966), Articles 18 & 23
- International Covenant on Economic, Social and Cultural Rights (1966), Articles 10
- UN Convention on the Elimination of All Forms of Discrimination against Women (1979), Article 16
- UN Convention on the Rights of Persons with Disabilities (2006), Article 23

Attributes

Attribute One: Respect for the Primacy of Parents and Comparable Care Givers

Article 5 reaffirms the general principle that States Parties must respect the primacy of parents in the upbringing of their children. In so doing, it recognises the responsibilities, rights, and duties of parents, and the consequent boundaries on the arbitrary intervention of the state into family life (Office of the United Nations High Commissioner for Human Rights and Rädda barnen (Society: Sweden), 2007, p. 359). This focus is consistent with the emphasis in the Convention of the family as the fundamental group of society, the natural environment for growth and well-being, and the need for necessary protection and assistance to enable families to assume their responsibilities (UN Committee on the Rights of the Child, 2003, para. 14; UN General Assembly, 1990, sec. preamble).

Article 5 extends responsibilities, rights and duties, where applicable, to other members of the extended family or community where they are recognised by local custom, as well as legal guardians and other persons legally responsible for the child, thereby acknowledging that children can be cared for through many different arrangements. This can include, for example, the nuclear family, extended family, and other traditional and modern community-based arrangements, all of which are valid 'provided they are consistent with children's rights and best interests' (UN Committee on the Rights of the Child, 2006, para. 15). This flexible definition of the family is emphasised in a General Comment of the Human Rights Committee as being 'interpreted broadly to include all persons composing it in the society of the State Party concerned' (United Nations, 2006, p. 184). Whatever form of family is recognised in a given society must be afforded the protections embodied in Article 23 of the International Covenant on Civil and Political Rights by the State Party (United Nations, 2006, p. 188).

Parental responsibilities, rights, and duties are not defined in either the International Covenant on Civil and Political Rights or the Convention on the Rights of the Child, but Article 5 makes clear that they are not absolute or inalienable. They derive from the obligation to act in the best interests of the child and to enable the exercise by the child of their rights.

Attribute Two: Appropriate Direction and Guidance

The direction and guidance that parents or other caregivers provide for children is qualified through three provisions. First, it must be appropriate. In this context, appropriate direction and guidance necessitates that it is provided in a manner consistent with the rights embodied in the Convention. Accordingly, parents cannot treat the child in ways that would serve to violate or neglect their rights, nor justify such behaviours on grounds of traditional cultures (UN Committee on the Rights of the Child, 1995, paras. 7, 13; UNICEF, 2007). The Committee has emphasised the importance of ensuring the balance between parental authority and the rights of the child (1994a, p. 63). States Parties must provide legislative and policy frameworks to ensure protection of the child from violations of their rights within the family.[2]

Second, direction and guidance must be provided in a manner consistent with the child's evolving capacities, and 'through dialogue, negotiation and participation' (UN Committee on the Rights of the Child, 1994b, para. 183 et seq, 2003, para. 7). Finally, it must be directed to the 'exercise by the child of (their) rights.' This provision highlights the child as a subject of rights. In other words, the role of parental guidance is to promote the agency of the child to claim their own rights, while providing the necessary protection in accordance with the child's evolving capacities. The Committee has encouraged States Parties to provide comprehensive support and education programmes to promote this understanding of parenthood (2006, paras. 20–21).

---

[2] See, for example, General Comment no. 13 (UN Committee on the Rights of the Child, 2011, paras. 38–44), and General Comment no. 8 (UN Committee on the Rights of the Child, 2007b, para. 22).

Attribute Three: Evolving Capacities of the Child

Although Article 5 has not been formally identified by Committee as one of the General Principles to be applied in the realisation of all other rights, the concept of the evolving capacities of the child is recognised as 'an enabling principle that addresses the process of maturation and learning through which children progressively acquire competencies, understanding and increasing levels of agency to take responsibility and exercise their rights' (UN Committee on the Rights of the Child, 2016). It recognises the child, irrespective of age, as an active participant in their own development, entitled to be afforded opportunities for the gradual acquisition of greater autonomy (UN Committee on the Rights of the Child, 2006, para. 14).

Article 5 can be understood to complement Article 12, the right of children to be heard in matters affecting them, by acknowledging the transfer of the exercise of rights from parents to children as they acquire sufficient maturity. It avoids the need for imposition of arbitrary universal age limits and acknowledges that the child must be respected to take increasing levels of responsibility consistent with their capacities. The exercise of parental rights and responsibilities must reflect children's evolving capacities in respect of the exercise of all rights in the Convention. Although, in addition to Article 5, the concept of evolving capacities is only specifically referenced in Article 14, it must be understood as having application in the realisation of all other rights.[3]

With regard to a number of Convention rights, the Committee recommends that States Parties consider the introduction of legal age limits, to protect children from premature exposure to the full responsibilities of adulthood (for example, child labour, marriage, use and sale of tobacco and alcohol) while ensuring appropriate respect for their emerging capacities (for example, consent to adoption, medical consent, access to sexual and reproductive health services) (2016, para. 20). At the wider policy level, the Committee also encourages recognition of the role of children themselves as active agents in both identification of risk and potential programmes to promote protection (2016, para. 19).

References

Lansdown, G. (2005). *The evolving capacities of the child*. UNICEF Innocenti Research Centre.
Office of the United Nations High Commissioner for Human Rights & Rädda barnen (Society: Sweden). (2007). *Legislative history of the convention on the rights of the child* (Vol. 1–2). United Nations. https://digitallibrary.un.org/record/602462?ln=en

---

[3] During discussion on Article 15, the right to freedom of association and assembly, the Working Group drafting the Convention argued against a reference to the evolving capacities of the child on the basis that a generic article would encompass the principle with application across all provisions of the Convention (Office of the United Nations High Commissioner for Human Rights and Rädda barnen (Society: Sweden), 2007, p. 467).

UN Committee on the Rights of the Child. (1994a). *Report on the 5th session, 10–28 January 1994, CRC/C/24*. Retrieved October 12, 2020, from https://digitallibrary.un.org/record/193291?ln=en

UN Committee on the Rights of the Child. (1994b). *Report on the 7th session, Geneva, 26 September-14 October 1994, CRC/C/34*. Retrieved October 12, 2020, from https://digitallibrary.un.org/record/183427?ln=en

UN Committee on the Rights of the Child. (1995). *Concluding observations: Holy See, Nov 27, 1995, CRC/C/15/Add.46*. Retrieved October 11, 2020, from https://digitallibrary.un.org/record/210287?ln=en

UN Committee on the Rights of the Child. (2003). *General Comment No. 4 (2003) Adolescent health and development in the context of the Convention on the Rights of the Child, July 1, 2003, CRC/GC/2003/4*. Retrieved October 12, 2020, from https://digitallibrary.un.org/record/503074?ln=en

UN Committee on the Rights of the Child. (2005). *General Guidelines regarding the form and content of periodic reports to be submitted by States parties under article 44, paragraph 1 (b) of the Convention, June 3, 2005, CRC/C/58/Rev.1*. Retrieved October 12, 2020, from https://digitallibrary.un.org/record/575788?ln=en

UN Committee on the Rights of the Child. (2006). *General Comment No. 7 (2005) Implementing child rights in early childhood, September 20, 2006, CRC/C/GC/7/Rev.1*. Retrieved October 12, 2020, from https://digitallibrary.un.org/record/584854?ln=en

UN Committee on the Rights of the Child. (2007a). *General Comment No. 9 (2006) The rights of children with disabilities, November 13, 2007, CRC/C/GC/9*. Retrieved October 12, 2020, from https://digitallibrary.un.org/record/593891?ln=en

UN Committee on the Rights of the Child. (2007b). *General Comment No. 8 (2006) The right of the child to protection from corporal punishment and other cruel or degrading forms of punishment (arts. 19; 28, para. 2; and 37, inter alia), March 2, 2007, CRC/C/GC/8*. Retrieved October 12, 2020, from https://digitallibrary.un.org/record/583961?ln=en

UN Committee on the Rights of the Child. (2009). *General Comment No. 12 (2009) The right of the child to be heard, July 20, 2009, CRC/C/GC/12*. Retrieved October 12, 2020, from https://digitallibrary.un.org/record/671444?ln=en

UN Committee on the Rights of the Child. (2011). *General Comment No. 13 (2011) The right of the child to freedom from all forms of violence, April 18, 2011, CRC/C/GC/13*. Retrieved October 12, 2020, from https://digitallibrary.un.org/record/711722?ln=en

UN Committee on the Rights of the Child. (2013). *General Comment No. 14 (2013) On the right of the child to have his or her best interests taken as a primary consideration (art. 3, para. 1), May 29, 2013, CRC/C/GC/14*. Retrieved October 12, 2020, from https://digitallibrary.un.org/record/778523?ln=en

UN Committee on the Rights of the Child. (2016). *General Comment No. 20 (2016) on the implementation of the rights of the child during adolescence, December 6, 2016, CRC/C/GC/20*. Retrieved October 12, 2020, from https://digitallibrary.un.org/record/855544?ln=en

UN General Assembly. (1990). *Convention on the rights of the child, 1990, A/RES/45/104*. Retrieved April 19, 2020, from https://digitallibrary.un.org/record/105613?ln=en

UNICEF. (2007). *Implementation Handbook for the Convention on the Rights of the Child* (3rd ed.). UNICEF. Retrieved April 19, 2020, from https://www.unicef.org/publications/index_43110.html

United Nations. (2006). *Compilation of general comments and general recommendations adopted by human rights treaty bodies, HRI/GEN/1/Rev. 8*. UN. Retrieved April 19, 2020, from http://digitallibrary.un.org/record/576098

Vučković-Šahović, N., Doek, J. E., & Zermatten, J. (2012). *The rights of the child in international law: Rights of the child in a nutshell and in context: All about children's rights*. Stämpfli.

Open Access This chapter is licensed under the terms of the Creative Commons Attribution 4.0 International License (http://creativecommons.org/licenses/by/4.0/), which permits use, sharing, adaptation, distribution and reproduction in any medium or format, as long as you give appropriate credit to the original author(s) and the source, provide a link to the Creative Commons license and indicate if changes were made.

The images or other third party material in this chapter are included in the chapter's Creative Commons license, unless indicated otherwise in a credit line to the material. If material is not included in the chapter's Creative Commons license and your intended use is not permitted by statutory regulation or exceeds the permitted use, you will need to obtain permission directly from the copyright holder.

Chapter 14
Article 9: The Right Not to Be Separated from Parents

Christian Whalen

1. States Parties shall ensure that a child shall not be separated from his or her parents against their will, except when competent authorities subject to judicial review determine, in accordance with applicable law and procedures, that such separation is necessary for the best interests of the child. Such determination may be necessary in a particular case such as one involving abuse or neglect of the child by the parents, or one where the parents are living separately and a decision must be made as to the child's place of residence.
2. In any proceedings pursuant to paragraph 1 of the present article, all interested parties shall be given an opportunity to participate in the proceedings and make their views known.
3. States Parties shall respect the right of the child who is separated from one or both parents to maintain personal relations and direct contact with both parents on a regular basis, except if it is contrary to the child's best interests.
4. Where such separation results from any action initiated by a State Party, such as the detention, imprisonment, exile, deportation or death (including death arising from any cause while the person is in the custody of the State) of one or both parents or of the child, that State Party shall, upon request, provide the parents, the child or, if appropriate, another member of the family with the essential information concerning the whereabouts of the absent member(s) of the family unless the provision of the information

(continued)

C. Whalen (✉)
Office of the Child, Youth and Seniors Advocate, Fredericton, NB, Canada
e-mail: Christian.Whalen@gnb.ca

would be detrimental to the well-being of the child. States Parties shall further ensure that the submission of such a request shall of itself entail no adverse consequences for the person(s) concerned.

What Did Children Say?
'Are children's voices being heard when separated from parents?' (*Latin America/Caribbean*)
'Government officials should personally take children to visit parents or give them the means of contact and communication with parent.' (*Africa*)
'When a child who lives with another person asides his parent is allowed to see/call them without any restrictions.' (*Africa*)
'The government should make and enforce rules and regulations that guide relatives/guardians in the care of their children.' (*Africa*)

Overview

Article 9 of the Convention is the first of a group of Articles, 9, 10, and 11, that are specific to children and which have no exact counterpart in general human rights treaties, outside of the regional child rights context in Africa.[1] The right not to be separated from parents, the right to leave and enter countries for family reunification, and the obligation on States Parties to take specific measures to combat the illicit transfer and non-return of children from abroad, work together to protect the child's right to secure family attachment and relationships. These rights therefore are to be read closely and in conjunction with one another and with other rights in the Convention that deal specifically with the child's family situation, including Articles 3, 5, 7, 16 18, 20, 21, and 27 (Tobin & Cashmore, 2019, pp. 308–310).

Article 9 serves as a gateway to these specific rights of children and sets out two main principles: children must not be separated from their parents unless the separation is necessary in their best interests, and the child and parents should not be separated without due process in any circumstance including child protection or child custody matters (Nowak, 2005, p. 121; UNICEF, 2007, p. 186). Article 9 also protects the child's right to maintain contact with both parents, unless their best interests indicate otherwise, and places an obligation on States Parties to keep parents and children informed of any state action that might impinge upon this right.

The *Travaux Préparatoires* show that Article 9 grew out of a proposal for an early draft of Article 10, and which focused on the child's right to a residence. Through the

---

[1] See Article 19 of the African Charter on the Rights and Welfare of the Child (African Union, 1981), adopted in 1990 with a provision on Parent Care and Protection which tracks the language of UNCRC Article 9 fairly closely.

several years of the Convention's drafting, the child's right to not be separated from their parents emerged as the central theme and this became Article 9 (Detrick et al., 1992). The focus of Article 9 is on separation from parents within the domestic context, while Articles 10 and 11 deal with the distinct elements of separation which can occur across international borders, respectively entering or leaving countries for family reunification and illicit transfer and non-return of children abroad (Detrick et al., 1992, p. 22).

General Principles

Article 2 Equality and non-discrimination rights are particularly relevant in applying Article 9 since minority and vulnerable child and youth populations, such as LBGTQ youth, disabled children, refugee children, street endangered children, children in poverty, drug-endangered youth, and children in situations of armed conflict are inherently at risk of being separated from their parents and without adequate due process (UN General Assembly, 2010, para. 9). The Committee has often warned against overrepresentation of indigenous children and minority children in systems of state care or juvenile detention (2012, paras. 53–58, 85–86).

Article 3 The child's best interests must be the determining consideration in all decisions affecting any separation from his or her parents. Article 9 takes the General Principle of Article 3 a step further, beyond the standard of primary consideration, and ensures that is upheld as the determining factor in decisions involving a separation, involving efforts to maintain contact with both parents, or with the child's extended family, or to be kept informed of state reasons requiring a separation of parent and child.

Article 6 The child's right to life, survival, and maximum development also relates closely to Article 9 rights, given the parents' primary role as caregivers. This principle emphasises the need to support parents in the assumption of their parental obligations, as the Committee has mentioned that children must not be removed from their parents merely because of the family's impoverished condition (UNICEF, 2007, p. 123; 2006a, paras. 37–38, 2006b, para. 30).[2]

Article 12 Paragraph 2 of Article 9 expressly reaffirms the Article 12 principle in relation to a child's right to express their views and have them considered in decisions relating to any matter arising from a separation from their parents, but the paragraph extends the same right to parents and indeed 'all interested parties.'

---

[2] Compare *Guidelines for Alternative Care* (UN General Assembly, 2010, para. 15)

Articles Related to or Linked to Article 9

Article 5 is a corresponding responsibility on parents to provide guidance and direction to their children.

Article 7 proclaims the child's right to know and to be cared for by their parents.

Article 8 protects the right to preservation of identity, including family relations and to be reconnected with family if these relations are disrupted.

Article 10 concerns the right to leave or enter one's country or one's parents for family reunification.

Article 11 recognises the child's right to be protected from international abduction.

Article 16 considers the child's right to privacy and the inviolability of his or her family life.

Article 18 recognises the common responsibilities of both parents with appropriate State supports for the upbringing and development of the child.

Article 20 concerns the child's right to alternative care if deprived of their family.

Article 21 covers the child's rights in relation to adoption.

Article 22 recognises the rights of refugee children and specifically their right to be reunited with family when separated.

Article 25 covers the child's right to periodic review of treatment when placed by the State away from their family.

Article 27 attributes the child's right to a decent standard of living, including the right to recover payment of alimony from parents abroad.

Article 35 affirms the child's right to be protected from abduction, sale, or trafficking.

Article 37 concerns the rights of children deprived of liberty to maintain contact with family.

Relevant Instruments

UN Universal Declaration of Human Rights (1948), Article 16, proclaims the right of men and women to marry and found a family, and establishes the family as the natural and fundamental element of society.

UN Declaration of the Rights of the Child (1959), Article 6, protects the child's right to 'grow up in the care and under the responsibility of his parents.'

International Covenant on Civil and Political Rights (1966), Articles 17, 23 and 24.

International Covenant on Economic, Social and Cultural Rights (1966), Article 10.

UN Convention on the Rights of Persons with Disabilities (2006), Article 23(4), protects the parent-child relationship in relation to both disabled parents and disabled children.

UN Guidelines for the Alternative Care of Children (2009)

European Convention on Human Rights (1950), Article 8, Right to Privacy and Family Life

American Convention on Human Rights 'Pact of San Jose, Costa Rica' (B-32) (1978), Article 11, privacy and family life, Article 12, freedom of conscience and right of parents to provide for the religious or moral education of their children in accordance with their own convictions, Articles 17–20 rights of the family, right to a name, rights of the child and right to a nationality.

African Charter on Human and Peoples' Rights (1981), Article 18, rights of the family, Article 27 and 29 Duty to family and society and duty to preserve harmonious development of the family.

African Charter on the Rights and Welfare of the Child (1990), Articles 18, 19, 25 and 30.

Attributes

Attribute One: No Separation from Parents Unless Necessary for the Child's Best Interests

The first attribute insists upon the child's right to be with their parents unless a separation is necessary in the child's best interest. The language of the provision speaks to the crucial importance of the bond between parent and child because the test is one of necessity and the determining criterion is the child's best interests. Governments may invoke many good reasons to detain a parent and force a separation between a parent and child, but the Convention requires States Parties to consider the child's best interests and determine whether separation is necessary on the basis of that criterion.

Article 9(1) gives two examples of when separation is necessary, in child protection matters and upon divorce or separation of the parents, but these are merely illustrative. Other examples of situations where separations occur and where the standards of necessity and best interests should be applied include situations where children are hospitalised for lengthy periods (UN Committee on the Rights of the Child, 2004a, paras. 51, 52), where parents are detained in prison,[3] where children are detained in prison (UN General Assembly, 1991, paras. 59–62), where parents work abroad (UN Committee on the Rights of the Child, 1994, paras. 16, 33, 2002a, paras. 30, 31), where children are affected by or involved in armed

---

[3]This includes the concern about detaining infants with their parents sentenced to serve time in prison: See Concluding Observations to Nepal (2005a, paras. 51–52); it also includes the creation of sentencing practices that allow sentences given to parents to be served in community and providing alternative care for children of detained adults while maintaining regular parent-child contact. See Concluding Observations to Mexico (2006c, para. 40) and UN Guidelines on Alternative Care of Children (UN General Assembly, 2010, para. 48).

conflict (UN Secretary General, 2016, paras. 9, 16, 18, 20), as a consequence of immigration, deportation and refugee matters (UN Committee on the Rights of the Child, 2005b, para. 50), or due to traditions or customs which force separation or child abandonment (such as unwed mothers, sex selection, intersex births, and birth deformities) (UNICEF, 2007, p. 127).

Attribute Two: No Separation from Parents Without Due Process Before Competent Authorities

Article 9 focusses on the due process requirements introduced by the words 'except when competent authorities subject to judicial review determine, in accordance with applicable law and procedure' in paragraph 1. The requirement in paragraph 2, that all interested parties be given the opportunity to participate and make their views known in these determinations, is a further aspect of this attribute of due process (UNICEF, 2007, p. 127). This includes, of course, the child's participation whose right to not be forcibly separated from his or her parents is conditioned by the terms 'against their will.' If the child is seeking emancipation or separation from one or both parents the entire proceedings may take a different course, which underscores the importance of the child's participation. The concluding observations provide guidance with respect to who is a competent authority (UN Committee on the Rights of the Child, 2002a, paras. 38, 39, 2004b, paras. 30, 31), how judicial review requires elements of fairness and due process (UNICEF, 2007, p. 128; UN Committee on the Rights of the Child, 2002b, paras. 36, 37, 2005c, para. 26, 2005d, para. 37), and how to elicit the views of the child (UN Committee on the Rights of the Child, 2003, paras. 38, 39, 2005e, paras. 23, 24). The Article also requires State Parties to enact clear laws and procedures to regulate such determinations. Guidance as to the fairness requirements of such laws can be found in the Beijing Rules as well as in the Guidelines for the Alternative Care of Children (UN General Assembly, 1985, Rule 3.2, 2010, paras. 9, 32, 48, 52). Any breach of these fairness requirements may be raised to question the legitimacy of a forced separation of child and parent and may constitute a violation of the child's rights under Article 9, which are both substantive and procedural.

Attribute Three: Right to Maintain Relations and Regular Contact with Both Parents, if Separated

The third attribute of Article 9 is set out in paragraph 3 and guarantees the child's right to maintain personal relations and direct contact with both parents on a regular basis if separated, unless doing so would be contrary to his or her best interests. States Parties laws should not privilege contact with one parent at the expense of the other, and contact and maintenance of relations with non-custodial parents is protected by the Convention (UN Committee on the Rights of the Child, 2004c, paras. 39, 40). Civil administrations should take special measures to promote relations and personal contact with parents by all appropriate means, including visitation, with or without supervision, and joint custody but also through telecommunications and social media. Children separated from their parents internationally also have a right to family reunification even when reunification cannot occur in the country of origin (UN Committee on the Rights of the Child, 2005f, paras. 81–90).

Attribute Four: Right to Be Informed of Whereabouts of Child or Parent if Detained

The fourth and final attribute of Article 9 is set out in paragraph 4 and elaborates the right of family members, including both children and parents, but also components of the extended family, to be informed of the whereabouts of a child or parent who is missing or detained as a result of some state action. Article 9 guards against the danger that children be kept unaware of life changing circumstances in their parents' lives no matter how harsh the truths (UN Committee on the Rights of the Child, 2004d, paras. 42, 43). Parents and children have a right to be informed of each other's situations even when they are apart. Article 9 only proposes minimum rules to guard against state impunity in the face of forced separations of parents and children (UNICEF, 2007, p. 131). Other international standards help complete State Party obligations in this regard. For instance, where children are detained, they have a right to be informed at the earliest possible time of any death or serious illness or injury of their family members (UN General Assembly, 1991, para. 58).

References

African Union. (1981). *African (Banjul) charter on human and peoples' rights* (No. CAB/LEG/67/3 rev.5, 21 ILM). https://www.achpr.org/legalinstruments/detail?id=49

Detrick, S., Doek, J. E., & Cantwell, N. (1992). *The United Nations Convention on the Rights of the Child: A guide to the "Travaux Préparatoires."* Martinus Nijhoff Publishers.

Nowak, M. (2005). *U.N. covenant on civil and political rights: CCPR commentary*. N.P. Engel.

Tobin, J., & Cashmore, J. (2019). Article 9: The rights not to be separated from parents. In J. Tobin (Ed.), *The UN Convention on the Rights of the Child: A commentary* (pp. 307–342). Oxford University Press.

UN Committee on the Rights of the Child. (1994). *Concluding observations: Sri Lanka, June 21, 1994, CRC/C/15/Add.40*. Retrieved November 6, 2020, from https://digitallibrary.un.org/record/191817?ln=en

UN Committee on the Rights of the Child. (2002a). *Concluding observations: St. Vincent and the Grenadines, June 13, 2002, CRC/C/15/Add.184*. Retrieved November 6, 2020, from https://digitallibrary.un.org/record/473488?ln=en

UN Committee on the Rights of the Child. (2002b). *Concluding observations: Lebanon, March 21, 2002, CRC/C/15/Add.169*. Retrieved October 11, 2020, from https://digitallibrary.un.org/record/467259?ln=en

UN Committee on the Rights of the Child. (2003). *Concluding observations: Haiti, March 18, 2003, CRC/C/15/Add.202*. Retrieved October 11, 2020, from https://digitallibrary.un.org/record/497803?ln=en

UN Committee on the Rights of the Child. (2004a). *Concluding observations: Croatia, November 3 2004, CRC/C/15/Add.243*. Retrieved October 11, 2020, from https://digitallibrary.un.org/record/557375?ln=en

UN Committee on the Rights of the Child. (2004b). *Concluding observations: Slovenia, February 26, 2004, CRC/C/15/Add.230*. Retrieved October 12, 2020, from https://digitallibrary.un.org/record/530811?ln=en

UN Committee on the Rights of the Child. (2004c). *Concluding observations: Antigua and Barbuda, November 3, 2004, CRC/C/15/Add.247*. UN. Retrieved November 6, 2020, from http://digitallibrary.un.org/record/557388

UN Committee on the Rights of the Child. (2004d). *Concluding observations: Korea, July 1, 2004, CRC/C/15/Add.239*. UN. Retrieved November 6, 2020, from http://digitallibrary.un.org/record/536573

UN Committee on the Rights of the Child. (2005a). *Concluding observations: Nepal, September 1, 2005, CRC/C/15/Add.261*. Retrieved October 11, 2020, from https://digitallibrary.un.org/record/569886?ln=en

UN Committee on the Rights of the Child. (2005b). *Concluding observations: China, November 24, 2005, CRC/C/CHN/CO/2*. Retrieved October 24, 2020, from https://digitallibrary.un.org/record/575653?ln=en

UN Committee on the Rights of the Child. (2005c). *Concluding observations: Finland, October 20, 2005, CRC/C/15/Add.272*. UN. Retrieved November 6, 2020, from http://digitallibrary.un.org/record/569953

UN Committee on the Rights of the Child. (2005d). *Concluding observations: Nicaragua, September 21, 2005, CRC/C/15/Add.265*. Retrieved October 11, 2020, from https://digitallibrary.un.org/record/570466?ln=en

UN Committee on the Rights of the Child. (2005e). *Concluding observations: Sweden, March 30, 2005, CRC/C/15/Add.248*. Retrieved October 11, 2020, from https://digitallibrary.un.org/record/557390?ln=en

UN Committee on the Rights of the Child. (2005f). *General Comment No. 6 (2005) Treatment of Unaccompanied and Separated Children Outside their Country of Origin, September 1, 2005, CRC/GC/2005/6*. Retrieved October 12, 2020, from https://digitallibrary.un.org/record/566055?ln=en

UN Committee on the Rights of the Child. (2006a). *Concluding observations: Azerbaijan, March 17, 2006, CRC/C/AZE/CO/2*. Retrieved October 11, 2020, https://digitallibrary.un.org/record/575654?ln=en

UN Committee on the Rights of the Child. (2006b). *Concluding observations: Hungary, March 17, 2006, CRC/C/HUN/CO/2*. Retrieved October 11, 2020, from https://digitallibrary.un.org/record/575773?ln=en

UN Committee on the Rights of the Child. (2006c). *Concluding observations: Mexico, June 8, 2006, CRC/C/MEX/CO/3*. https://digitallibrary.un.org/record/582289?ln=en

UN Committee on the Rights of the Child. (2012). *Concluding observations: Canada, December 6, 2012, CRC/C/CAN/CO/3-4*. Retrieved October 11, 2020, from https://digitallibrary.un.org/record/739319?ln=en

UN General Assembly. (1985). *United Nations standard minimum rules for the administration of juvenile justice ("The Beijing Rules"), 1985, A/RES/40/33*. Retrieved November 6, 2020, from http://digitallibrary.un.org/record/120958

UN General Assembly. (1991). *United Nations rules for the protection of juveniles deprived of their liberty, 1990, A/RES/45/113 (The Havana Rules)*. UN. Retrieved October 26, 2020, from http://digitallibrary.un.org/record/105555

UN General Assembly. (2010). *Guidelines for the alternative care of children, 2010, A/RES/64/142*. https://digitallibrary.un.org/record/673583?ln=en

UN Secretary General. (2016). *Children and armed conflict: Report of the Secretary-General, A/70/836 S/2016/360*. Retrieved November 6, 2020, from http://digitallibrary.un.org/record/830518

UNICEF. (2007). *Implementation handbook for the convention on the rights of the child* (3rd ed.) UNICEF. Retrieved April 19, 2020, from https://www.unicef.org/publications/index_43110.html

Open Access This chapter is licensed under the terms of the Creative Commons Attribution 4.0 International License (http://creativecommons.org/licenses/by/4.0/), which permits use, sharing, adaptation, distribution and reproduction in any medium or format, as long as you give appropriate credit to the original author(s) and the source, provide a link to the Creative Commons license and indicate if changes were made.

The images or other third party material in this chapter are included in the chapter's Creative Commons license, unless indicated otherwise in a credit line to the material. If material is not included in the chapter's Creative Commons license and your intended use is not permitted by statutory regulation or exceeds the permitted use, you will need to obtain permission directly from the copyright holder.

Chapter 15
Article 10: The Right to Family Reunification

Christian Whalen

1. In accordance with the obligation of States Parties under Article 9, paragraph 1, applications by a child or his or her parents to enter or leave a State Party for the purpose of family reunification shall be dealt with by States Parties in a positive, humane and expeditious manner. State Parties shall further ensure that the submission of such a request shall entail no adverse consequences for the applicants and for the members of their family.
2. A child whose parents reside in different States shall have the right to maintain on a regular basis, save in exceptional circumstances personal relations and direct contacts with both parents. Towards that end and in accordance with the obligation of States Parties under Article 9, paragraph 2, States Parties shall respect the right of the child and his or her parents to leave any country, including their own, and to enter their own country. The right to leave any country shall be subject only to such restrictions as are prescribed by law and which are necessary to protect the national security, public order (ordre public), public health or morals or the rights and freedoms of others and are consistent with the other rights recognized in the present Convention.

C. Whalen (✉)
Office of the Child, Youth and Seniors Advocate, Fredericton, NB, Canada
e-mail: Christian.Whalen@gnb.ca

What Did Children Say?
'The government should create a platform of contact when a child is being taken away from their parents' (*Africa*)

'Children [should] have a free phone line to contact parents abroad?' 'A phone line that would transfer the calls.' (*Western Europe/Other*)

'Can the children that are separated from one of their parents go see them at least once a year, even if the parents can't pay for it? One free plane ticket paid by the government.' (*Western Europe/Other*)

Best interests of the child must be a priority in the background checks to ensure children will be moved into a safe environment. (*Latin America/ Caribbean*)

Overview

Article 10 is a right closely related to Articles 9 and 11. Its inclusion in the Convention affirms the longstanding recognition that separation of a child from their parents can have long-term damaging effects on the child's development and well-being (UN Committee on the Rights of the Child, 2006, para. 18; UN General Assembly, 1948, Article 16(3), 1990, sec. preamble). The *Travaux Préparatoires* reveal that the framers of the Convention found it would be appropriate to deal with the right of the child not to be separated from their parents through these three separate provisions.

Article 10 addresses the right of children and their parents to enter or leave a state for the purpose of family reunification (UNICEF, 2007, pp. 135–136). It therefore constitutes a specialised application of the general right in Article 9 for parents and children not to be separated in domestic legal contexts, but it does not address the case of children who are abducted across international borders which is dealt with in Article 11. Article 10 was included as a separate provision to recognize the fact that keeping families united across international borders poses a challenge that requires separate treatment (Detrick et al., 1992, pp. 182–207). It is not, however, designed with the intention of affecting 'the general right of States to establish and regulate their respective immigration laws in accordance with their international obligations' (Detrick et al., 1992, p. 170).

There are many international treaties and agreements which have a bearing on the application of both Articles 10 and 11 and it was convenient to distinguish in two separate articles the rights of children who want to reunite with their parents across international borders with the consent of both parents from the separate case where one parent absconds with a child to a foreign country. Cases of child abduction, outside of the family context, as well as sale and trafficking, are dealt with even further and more generally in Article 35. For these reasons, Article 10 should be applied and interpreted in relation to the several rights which govern the child's family situation, including Articles 3, 5, 9, 18, 20, and 21. However, it also has to be interpreted and applied in relation to all the rights governing situations where children are on the move, such as Articles 6, 7, 8, 11, 16, 22, and 35, as well as the two first Optional Protocols to the Convention and those spelled out in other international conventions and agreements.

General Principles

Article 2 Most children affected by Article 10 are either economic migrants, refugees or children of separated parents living in different countries (UNICEF, 2007, p. 135). In every case, these children are already at a disadvantage in relation to their peers and that very status attracts the protection of Article 2's non-discrimination principle (UN Committee on the Rights of the Child, 2005a, para. 18). Additionally, other groups of children who are marginalised or discriminated against are at particular risk when in transit as unaccompanied or separated minors, for example, children with disabilities, children of minorities, indigenous children, LBGTQ youth, and current and former child soldiers. States Parties must remain vigilant to ensure equal access to the protection of Article 10 to all children within their borders, especially non-nationals (UN Committee on the Protection of the Rights of All Migrant Workers and Members of Their Families and UN Committee on the Rights of the Child, 2017, paras. 11, 19).

Article 3 The child's best interests must be a primary consideration in all decisions affecting any separation from their parents, including in relation to matters of family reunification across national borders (Vučković-Šahović et al., 2012, p. 170). Articles 10 and 3 must be considered together to ensure that the child's best interests are explicitly considered in decisions concerning the entry or return of children for the purpose of family reunification, whether in a temporary, recurring, or permanent basis. The Joint General Comment of the Committee on the protection of the Rights of All Migrant Workers and Members of Their Families and of the Committee on the Rights of the Child explicitly underscores the obligation of States Parties to the Convention to 'ensure that the best interests of the child are taken fully into consideration in immigration law, planning, implementation and assessment of migration policies and decisions on individual cases, including in granting or refusing applications on entry to or residence in a country, decisions regarding migration enforcement and restrictions on access to social rights by children and/or their parents or legal guardians, and decisions regarding family unity and child custody where the bests interests of the child shall be a primary consideration and thus have high priority' (2017, para. 29).[1]

---

[1] See also General Comment no. 14, paragraphs 30 through 33 and further (UN Committee on the Rights of the Child, 2013).

Article 6 The child's right to life, survival and maximum development relates closely to Article 10 rights, given the parents' primary role as caregivers. This principle emphasises the need to ensure that the child is brought up by their parents and to support parents in the assumption of their parental obligations. The protection of child rights in many states is at its weakest in immigration contexts (Harris et al., 2009; van Bueren, 2007, p. 123; Vučković-Šahović et al., 2012, pp. 165–170). In this specific context, the Committee is concerned about the 'lack of regular and safe channels for children and families to migrate,' which contributes to 'children taking life-threatening and extremely dangerous migration journeys. The same is true for border control and surveillance measures that focus on repression rather than facilitating, regulating and governing mobility, including detention and deportation practices, lack of timely family reunification opportunities and lack of avenues for regularization' (UN Committee on the Protection of the Rights of All Migrant Workers and Members of Their Families and UN Committee on the Rights of the Child, 2017, para. 41). International adoption procedures and surrogacy laws may also place children at risk in the context of international family reunification rights under Article 10.

Article 12 Article 10 can be supported through careful application of the Article 12 principle in relation to a child's right to express their views and have them considered in decisions relating to any application to enter or leave a country for the purpose of family reunification. Some experts have suggested that Article 10 is a weak right insofar as does not impose a clear obligation on States to allow entry, but only to treat such requests in a positive, humane and expeditious manner (UNICEF, 2007, p. 135; Vučković-Šahović et al., 2012, p. 168). Read in conjunction with Article 12 and the other General Principles, Article 10 takes on its full weight, beyond the guarantee that submissions of requests to leave or enter a country 'shall entail no adverse consequences for the applicants and for members of their families.' The Committee, in its Joint General Comment no. 22, strongly reinforces the States Parties obligation to ensure child participation in immigration matters affecting both children and their parents, as their best interests will be in play in both instances and children often have 'their own migration projects and migration-driving factors' (UN Committee on the Protection of the Rights of All Migrant Workers and Members of Their Families and UN Committee on the Rights of the Child, 2017, paras. 34–39).

Articles Related to or Linked to Article 10

Article 5 is a corresponding duty on parents to provide guidance and direction to their children.
  Article 7 proclaims the child's right to know and to be cared for by their parents.
  Article 8 protects the child's right to a named nationality, identity, and family relations and to be reconnected with family if these relations are disrupted.

Article 9 includes the right to not be separated from one's parents unless it is necessary in one's best interests as determined by competent authorities.
Article 11 is the child's right to be protected from international abduction.
Article 16 is the child's right to privacy and the inviolability of their family life.
Article 20 concerns the child's right to alternative care if deprived of their family.
Article 21 is the child's rights in relation to adoption.
Article 22 concerns the rights of refugee children and specifically their right to be reunited with family when separated.
Article 27 is the child's right to a decent standard of living, including the right to recover payment of alimony from parents abroad.
Article 35 is the child's right to be protected from abduction, sale, or trafficking.
Optional Protocol on the involvement of children in armed conflict.
Optional Protocol on the sale of children, child prostitution and child pornography.

Relevant Instruments

UN Convention Relating to the Status of Refugees (1951)
   UN Convention relating to the Status of Stateless Persons (1954)
   UN Declaration of the Rights of the Child (1959), Article 6, protects the child's right to 'grow up in the care and under the responsibility of his parents.'
   UN Convention on the Reduction of Statelessness (1961)
   International Covenant on Civil and Political Rights (1966), Articles 17, 23 and 24.
   International Covenant on Economic, Social and Cultural Rights (1966), Article 10.
   UN Protocol Relating to the Status of Refugees (1967)
   The Geneva convention for the amelioration of the condition of the wounded and sick in armed forces in the field (1949), and the Additional Protocols I and II
   Hague Convention on Protection of Children and Co-operation in Respect of Intercountry Adoption (1993)
   Hague Convention on Jurisdiction, Applicable Law, Recognition, Enforcement and Co-operation in Respect of Parental Responsibility and Measures for the Protection of Children (1996)
   European Convention on Human Rights (1950), Article 8, Right to Privacy and Family Life
   American Convention on Human Rights 'Pact of San Jose, Costa Rica' (B-32) (1978), Article 11, Privacy and Family Life, Articles 17–20 rights of the family, right to a name, rights of the child and right to nationality.
   African Charter on Human and Peoples' Rights (1981), Article 18, rights of the family, and Articles 27 and 29, Duty to family and society and duty to preserve harmonious development of the family.

Attributes

Attribute One: Requests to Enter or Leave a Country for Family Reunification Should Be Dealt with in a Positive, Humane, and Expeditious Manner

Article 10 comes as close to a guarantee of a right of entry for family reunification purposes as the consensus of nations would allow at the time of the Convention's drafting. The right applies to both the parents and the child: either can apply for reunification with the other. The choice of the word 'positive' was strategic with its ambiguity enabling a consensus to be built around the text. Accordingly, it provides a focus on strengthening procedures when reunification applications are made, rather than guaranteeing outcomes that are child friendly: it introduces a presumption in favour of reunification, not an entitlement (Pobjoy & Tobin, 2019, pp. 348, 351). Experts have opined that it means something less than favourable—in the sense that the outcome should not be pre-determined—but something more than objective (Detrick et al., 1992, p. 206; UNICEF, 2007, p. 136; UN Committee on the Rights of the Child, 2004a, para. 9). The Committee's jurisprudence reveals that the Committee expects States Parties to uphold the right to family reunification across national boundaries or to show reasons why the child's best interest might direct otherwise (UNICEF, 2007, pp. 136–137; UN Committee on the Rights of the Child, 1995a, paras. 7, 29, 2003a, para. 34, 2005b). Positive treatment of these rights claims would also include their application to decisions involving the deportation of children's parents (UN Committee on the Rights of the Child, 2000, paras. 30, 31, 2005c, para. 22). Humane treatment introduces a further criterion that can support decisions favouring family reunification to avoid discriminatory consequences as between categories of entrants (UN Committee on the Rights of the Child, 2005d, paras. 63, 64), to avoid detention of children for immigration purposes (UN Committee on the Rights of the Child, 2005a, paras. 61–63), or to avoid further endangerment of refugee children if reunification in the country of origin poses a reasonable risk of fundamental human rights violations (UN Committee on the Rights of the Child, 2005a, pp. 82, 83). Finally, entry and exit requests must be treated expeditiously, a topic frequently raised by the Committee in its concluding observations, as children perceive time in different ways than adults and time separated from one's parents can have lasting and cumulative impacts (1995b, paras. 13, 24, 2002, para. 34, 2003b, para. 46, p. 126, 2004b, para. 54, 2005e, para. 49).

Attribute Two: Requests to Enter or Leave a Country Should Entail no Adverse Consequences for the Child, the Parent, or Their Family Members

The second attribute is sobering testimony to the adversity faced by migrant children and their families. Applying for exit or entry to a country should never attract significant adverse consequences, but it may. States Parties representatives agreed on this consensus text to challenge the status quo in several countries, where immigration processes could attract consequences for one's relatives. The Committee has further contextualised this risk in its General Comment no. 6 (2005a, paras. 81–83), and experts warn against the risk that authorities in host countries might inadvertently trigger risks to a child's family by making incautious inquiries or breaching confidentiality (UNICEF, 2007, pp. 139, 316). Other international agreements further reinforce these standards (UN General Assembly, 1991, Articles 14, 22; United Nations, 2006, p. 191).

Attribute Three: Right to Maintain Relations and Regular Contact with Both Parents, if Separated and Residing in Different States

Finally, Article 10 speaks to another common situation outside the context of immigration, where the child's parents reside in separate countries following a separation. There are international conventions for the reciprocal enforcement of court orders for custody and access, but the Convention provides a broader child rights lens through which to apply these standards and to guide case resolution where those more detailed standards may not apply.[2] This may include measures taken to maintain personal relations and contacts through telecommunications technologies and social media, as well as through periodic visits by parents or children, or relatives. While granting of refugee status is sufficient grounds to refuse any option of family reunification within the country of origin, it does not always prevent temporary visits to the refugee's country of origin in order to maintain family contact, if safe temporary family visits are possible. This practice should not jeopardise the refugee child's immigration status in the host country (UNICEF, 2007, p. 139). In all situations, careful attention should be paid to preparation for reunification and monitoring post-reunification to ensure that children are fully protected (UN General Assembly, 2010, paras. 146–151).

---

[2] These include the Hague Convention on Civil Aspects of International Child Abduction (1980), the Hague Convention on Protection of Children and Cooperation in Respect of Inter-Country Adoption, and the Hague Convention on Jurisdiction, Applicable Law, Recognition, Enforcement and Cooperation in Respect of Parental Responsibility and Measures for the Protection of Children.

References

Detrick, S., Doek, J. E., & Cantwell, N. (1992). *The United Nations Convention on the Rights of the Child: A guide to the "Travaux Préparatoires."*. Martinus Nijhoff Publishers.

Harris, D., O'Boyle, M., Bates, E., & Buckley, C. (2009). *Harris, O'Boyle & Warbrick: Law of the European Convention on Human Rights* (2nd ed.). OUP Oxford.

Pobjoy, J. M., & Tobin, J. (2019). Article 10: The Right to family reunification. In J. Tobin (Ed.), *The UN Convention on the Rights of the Child: A commentary* (pp. 343–369). Oxford University Press.

UN Committee on the Protection of the Rights of All Migrant Workers and Members of Their Families, & UN Committee on the Rights of the Child. (2017). *Joint General Comment No. 3 (2017) of the Committee on the Protection of the Rights of All Migrant Workers and Members of Their Families and No. 22 (2017) of the Committee on the Rights of the Child on the general principles regarding the human rights of children in the context of international migration, CMW/C/GC/3, CRC/C/GC/22*. UN. Retrieved November 6, 2020, from http://digitallibrary.un.org/record/1323014

UN Committee on the Rights of the Child. (1995a). *Concluding observations: United Kingdom, February 15, 1995, CRC/C/15/Add.34*. UN. Retrieved November 6, 2020, from, http://digitallibrary.un.org/record/198509

UN Committee on the Rights of the Child. (1995b). *Concluding observations: Canada, June 20, 1994, CRC/C/15/Add.37*. UN. Retrieved November 6, 2020, from http://digitallibrary.un.org/record/200969

UN Committee on the Rights of the Child. (2000). *Concluding observations: Norway, June 28, 2000, CRC/C/15/Add.126*. Retrieved October 23, 2020, from https://digitallibrary.un.org/record/422919?ln=en

UN Committee on the Rights of the Child. (2002). *Concluding observations: Spain, June 13, 2002, CRC/C/15/Add.185*. UN. Retrieved November 6, 2020, from http://digitallibrary.un.org/record/473490

UN Committee on the Rights of the Child. (2003a). *Concluding observations: Estonia, March 17, 2003, CRC/C/15/Add.196*. Retrieved October 12, 2020, from https://digitallibrary.un.org/record/497792?ln=en

UN Committee on the Rights of the Child. (2003b). *Concluding observations: Canada, October 27, 2003, CRC/C/15/Add.215*. Retrieved October 11, 2020, from https://digitallibrary.un.org/record/513561?ln=en

UN Committee on the Rights of the Child. (2004a). *Concluding observations: Japan, February 26, 2004, CRC/C/15/Add.231*. Retrieved October 24, 2020, from https://digitallibrary.un.org/record/530812?ln=en

UN Committee on the Rights of the Child. (2004b). *Concluding observations: Germany, February 26, 2004, CRC/C/15/Add.226*. UN. Retrieved November 6, 2020, from http://digitallibrary.un.org/record/528932

UN Committee on the Rights of the Child. (2005a). *General Comment No. 6 (2005) Treatment of Unaccompanied and Separated Children Outside their Country of Origin, September 1, 2005, CRC/GC/2005/6*. Retrieved October 12, 2020, from https://digitallibrary.un.org/record/566055?ln=en

UN Committee on the Rights of the Child. (2005b). *Concluding observations: Austria, March 31, 2005, CRC/C/15/Add.251*. UN. Retrieved November 6, 2020, from http://digitallibrary.un.org/record/557397

UN Committee on the Rights of the Child. (2005c). *Concluding observations: Norway, September 21, 2005, CRC/C/15/Add.263*. Retrieved October 23, 2020, from https://digitallibrary.un.org/record/569887?ln=en

UN Committee on the Rights of the Child. (2005d). *Concluding observations: Australia, October 20, 2005, CRC/C/15/Add.268*. UN. Retrieved October 26, 2020, from http://digitallibrary.un.org/record/569889

UN Committee on the Rights of the Child. (2005e). *Concluding observations: Finland, October 20, 2005, CRC/C/15/Add.272*. UN. Retrieved November 6, 2020, from http://digitallibrary.un.org/record/569953

UN Committee on the Rights of the Child. (2006). *General Comment No. 7 (2005) Implementing child rights in early childhood, September 20, 2006, CRC/C/GC/7/Rev.1*. Retrieved October 12, 2020, from https://digitallibrary.un.org/record/584854?ln=en

UN Committee on the Rights of the Child. (2013). *General Comment No. 14 (2013) On the right of the child to have his or her best interests taken as a primary consideration (art. 3, para. 1), May 29, 2013, CRC/C/GC/14*. Retrieved October 12, 2020, from https://digitallibrary.un.org/record/778523?ln=en

UN General Assembly. (1948). *Universal Declaration of Human Rights, 1948, A/RES/217(III)[A]*. Retrieved October 12, 2020, from https://digitallibrary.un.org/record/666853?ln=en

UN General Assembly. (1990). *Convention on the Rights of the Child, 1990, A/RES/45/104*. Retrieved April 19, 2020, from https://digitallibrary.un.org/record/105613?ln=en

UN General Assembly. (1991). *International Convention on the Protection of the Rights of all Migrant Workers and Members of Their Families, 1990, A/RES/45/158*. UN. Retrieved November 6, 2020, from http://digitallibrary.un.org/record/105636

UN General Assembly. (2010). *Guidelines for the alternative care of children, 2010, A/RES/64/142*. https://digitallibrary.un.org/record/673583?ln=en

UNICEF. (2007). *Implementation handbook for the Convention on the Rights of the Child* (3rd ed.) UNICEF. Retrieved April 19, 2020, from https://www.unicef.org/publications/index_43110.html

United Nations. (2006). *Compilation of General Comments and General Recommendations adopted by human rights treaty bodies, HRI/GEN/1/Rev. 8*. UN. Retrieved April 19, 2020, from http://digitallibrary.un.org/record/576098

van Bueren, G. (2007). *Child rights in Europe: Convergence and divergence in judicial protection*. Council of Europe Pub.

Vučković-Šahović, N., Doek, J. E., & Zermatten, J. (2012). *The rights of the child in international law: Rights of the child in a nutshell and in context: All about children's rights*. Stämpfli.

Open Access This chapter is licensed under the terms of the Creative Commons Attribution 4.0 International License (http://creativecommons.org/licenses/by/4.0/), which permits use, sharing, adaptation, distribution and reproduction in any medium or format, as long as you give appropriate credit to the original author(s) and the source, provide a link to the Creative Commons license and indicate if changes were made.

The images or other third party material in this chapter are included in the chapter's Creative Commons license, unless indicated otherwise in a credit line to the material. If material is not included in the chapter's Creative Commons license and your intended use is not permitted by statutory regulation or exceeds the permitted use, you will need to obtain permission directly from the copyright holder.

Chapter 16
Article 11: The Right to Protection from Illicit Transfer and Non-return of Children Abroad

Ziba Vaghri and Gavin Kotze

1. States Parties shall take measures to combat the illicit transfer and non-return of children abroad.
2. To this end, States Parties shall promote the conclusion of bilateral or multilateral agreements or accession to existing agreements.

What Did Children Say?
'When questioned about what the State should do, they consider "that today much time is lost in bureaucracies and that the process should be faster" and that for this "the state should apply more rules to change this."' (*Western Europe/Other*)

At airports and embassies, authorities should be trained to detect when children are uncomfortable or in possible danger and individual or one-on-one interview sessions (where parents are not present) should be conducted with all children. (*Latin America/Caribbean*)

Professionals who are working in the area against child trafficking should receive training. (*Asia-Pacific*)

Z. Vaghri (✉)
University of New Brunswick Saint John, Saint John, NB, Canada
e-mail: ziba.vaghri@unb.ca

G. Kotze
The New Brunswick Child, Youth and Seniors' Advocate Office, Fredericton, NB, Canada
e-mail: Gavin.Kotze@gnb.ca

Overview

Article 11 places obligations on States Parties to provide mechanisms to protect children from being wrongfully or illegally taken from their home country, and to provide mechanisms to prevent children from being held outside their home country in breach of custodial rights. Ratifying states have a duty to take measures, including legislative and administrative action (as per Article 4), to protect against abduction and to recover and return children who have been abducted. Implementation of Article 11 therefore requires States Parties to institute effective measures that are restorative and rehabilitative including police and legal assistance, targeted border security practices and protocols, assuring the necessary care and protection of the child with a view to planned reunification, ongoing training of officials, financial and diplomatic supports for the return of children, and international co-operation mechanisms.

This Article overlaps with Article 35, which is also meant to prevent abduction of children for any purpose or in any form it might occur. However, the focus of Article 11 is distinct from that of Article 35 in two ways. First, Article 11 focuses only on international abduction, whereas trafficking and other forms of exploitation may occur within a state. Second, even though it does not refer to the identity of the abductor, encompassing as a consequence both parental and non-parental abductions, based on its drafting history it is clear that Article 11 relates primarily to parental abduction of children for personal rather than monetary or exploitative reasons (Tobin et al., 2019, p. 370).

Paragraph 2 of Article 11 specifically requires that States Parties have an absolute obligation (using the imperative term 'shall') to promote the conclusion of international agreements to combat illicit transfer and non-return. States Parties must therefore seek to create and join binding legal instruments that promote international co-operation to counter child abduction. These include regional instruments such as the Inter-American Convention on the International Return of Children. The principal international private law instrument in relation to Article 11 implementation is the 1980 *Hague Convention on the Civil Aspects of International Child Abduction* (the Hague Abduction Convention). The Committee has recommended ratification of this 'key international human rights instrument' as a general measure of implementation of the Convention on the Rights of the Child (2003a). The Hague Abduction Convention establishes a process whereby children may return to their home country. This process is facilitated by the mandatory establishment of Central Authorities in Contracting States.

General Principles

Article 2 Children may face discrimination based on ethnicity or parental country of origin in situations where a State Party to the Convention does not recognise or adhere to custody and visitation rights for a child when one parent lives outside of the State Party (UN Committee on the Rights of the Child, 2005a, para. 48).

Article 3 The best interests principle must take into account the views of the child and the role of both parents in the development of the child. This principle encompasses substantive, interpretative, and procedural rights. The timely resolution of child abduction cases is a procedural right in accordance with best interests.

Article 6 The potential impact of parental abduction on the well-being and development of the child strongly connects Article 11 with Article 6. Article 11 protects children from the harmful consequences that are associated with abduction, including the uprooting of the child and the consequent removal from the family context, and the losses of contacts with the other parent, relatives, and friends (Tobin et al., 2019, p. 372). Moreover, pursuant to article 13 of the *Hague Convention on the Civil Aspects of International Child Abduction*, a court may refuse to order the return of a child if there is 'a grave risk that his or her return would expose the child to physical or psychological harm or otherwise place the child in an intolerable situation' (UN Committee on the Rights of the Child, 2005b, para. 84). Survival and development of the child to the maximum extent possible, as per Article 6 of the Convention, should be taken into account.

Article 12 States Parties to the Convention must consider the opinions of children of ages up to 18 when determining return to home country or other matters. The child's participation rights require that the child's views are both heard and taken seriously in decisions relating to abduction. The child's views would need to be balanced against those facts or concerns such as where the child habitually resided before removal or retention (The Supreme Court—United Kingdom, 2014), whether the child has settled in the new environment after a year (House of Lords (UK), 2007), and whether there is a grave risk that a return would expose the child to physical or psychological harm or otherwise place the child in an intolerable situation. The child's views must also inform the ultimate decision as to whether the child should be returned (House of Lords (UK), 2007). The right for 'the views of the child being given due weight in accordance with the age and maturity of the child' have led courts to find that children 10 years old and younger can have the necessary maturity and capacity to have their views taken into account (Ontario Court of Justice, 2013; Re B (Abduction: views of the child), 1983; Superior Court—Quebec, Canada, 1997).

The child's rights to participation may also be dependent upon the provision of legal representation. Article 12 adherence includes the right of the child to be informed generally about their rights, and how they can participate at all stages of the proceedings, including settlement discussions, in a child-friendly manner. The right of the child to have their views heard and afforded due weight is reflected in Article 13 of the *Hague Convention on the Civil Aspects of International Child Abduction*, which states that the 'judicial or administrative authority may also refuse to order the return of the child if it finds that the child objects to being returned and has attained an age and degree of maturity at which it is appropriate to take account of its views.' The *Hague Convention on the Civil Aspects of International Child Abduction* does not apply to children over the age of 16, due to presumed autonomy.

Articles Related to or Linked to Article 11

Article 4 places an obligation on States Parties to undertake all appropriate legislative, administrative, and other measures for implementation. Article 11(2) specifically requires States Parties to take measures to ratify relevant treaties to prevent and/or remedy child abduction. States Parties must also institute administrative measures and institute domestic legislative protections (see 'Measures to combat the illicit transfer and non-return of children abroad' below).

Article 5 ensures that States Parties institute respect for the responsibilities, rights, and duties of parents to provide guidance to children. The Convention is supportive of parents' primary role in the upbringing of children (UNICEF, 2007).

Article 7 enshrines the right to birth registration and nationality, and to know and be cared for by one's parents. Birth registration is a recognition of the child's status in law and is imperative for identification after abduction. This right is arguably connected to parental abduction, especially when one parent is not recognised in the birth record (United Nations, 2006).

Article 8 enshrines the child's right to preservation of identity, nationality, and family relations. Deprivation of aspects of identity must be remedied speedily.

Article 10 ensures the right of the child or parent to enter or leave a country for reunification. States Parties' immigration laws must allow for entry of a parent who has been separated from a child due to abduction, as well as allowing for the child to leave a country for reunification.

Article 16 enshrines the right to protection against interference with privacy, family, or home. The child's privacy must be protected in any administrative or judicial proceedings relating to abduction and reunification.

Article 18 recognises that both parents have common responsibilities for the development of the child. States Parties have obligations to support parents in their responsibilities, but also to provide the legal structure to ensure that parents act in the best interests of the child. States Parties must also ensure general legal equality between mothers and fathers.

Article 19 provides protection against all forms of abuse and neglect. States Parties must institute administrative, legislative, and judicial measures for prevention of abuse or neglect, and for identification, reporting, referral, investigation, treatment, and follow-up.

Article 20 concerns appropriate alternative care (temporary basis), with a view to reunification.

Article 35 is closely linked with Article 11 but addresses the obligation on States Parties to undertake measures to protect children who are abducted, sold or trafficked either nationally or internationally.

Article 39 enshrines the obligation of States Parties to take all appropriate measures for psychological recovery and social reintegration of a child victim of abuse or neglect. Article 11 obligates States Parties to ensure the return of children who have been illicitly transferred. Article 39 requires that a returned child be provided all necessary means of psychological recovery and social reintegration.

Optional Protocol to the Convention on the Rights of the Child on the Sale of Children, Child Prostitution and Child Pornography.

Relevant Instruments

International Covenant on Civil and Political Rights (1966), Articles 2, 12, 16, 17, 23, 24, 26, 27

International Covenant on Economic, Social and Cultural Rights (1966), Articles 2, 10

Hague Convention on the Civil Aspects of International Child Abduction (1980)

Hague Convention on Jurisdiction, Applicable Law, Recognition, Enforcement and Co-operation in Respect of Parental Responsibility and Measures for the Protection of Children (1996)

Inter-American Convention on the International Return of Children (1989)

European Convention on Recognition and Enforcement of Decisions concerning Custody of Children and on Restoration of Custody of Children (1980)

European Convention on Nationality (1997)

European Convention on the Exercise of Children's Rights (1996)

Attributes

Attribute One: Measures to Combat the Illicit Transfer and Non-return of Children Abroad

Article 11(1) states the obligation to take all needed preventive, rehabilitative and restorative measures to combat international abduction and non-return of children abroad (Tobin et al., 2019, pp. 372, 374–379). With reference to the preventive measures, an essential aspect of combatting the illicit transfer and non-return of children abroad is the promotion of a legal and social environment that reduces the risk of abduction. This is crucial, as when 'international instruments concerning child abduction have been implemented successfully, are operating effectively and are well-publicized, they may deter abductions' (Hague Conference on Private International Law, 2005).

With reference to rehabilitative and restorative measures, the Committee has recommended that States Parties ratify the Hague Abduction Convention,[1] and formally recognise all other countries as parties to that Convention in order for protections to have full effect.[2] Furthermore, the Committee has recommended that all professionals working in areas related to international child abduction receive adequate and ongoing training.[3] The Committee has favourably noted practices such as providing financial assistance for recovering illicitly transferred or non-returned children.[4]

Attribute Two: Measures to Promote the Conclusion of Bilateral or Multilateral Agreements or Accession to Existing Agreements

Article 11(2) advises States Parties to conclude bilateral agreements with countries that are not party to the Hague Abduction Convention[5] and encourage other countries to become parties to the Hague Abduction Convention.[6] With the inclusion of this obligation, the drafters of the Convention hoped to overcome the absence of a common definition of illegal abduction. The *Travaux Préparatoires* show that the issue of what constitutes illegal abduction in various states was, in fact, raised as problematic, although a suggestion to include a definition of when removal and non-return should be deemed unlawful was rejected (Detrick et al., 1992, p. 217). As a consequence, such a definition does not exist in Article 11, and States Parties must turn to instruments such as the Hague Abduction Convention for further clarity. The ways domestic courts recognise and apply conflict of law (private international law) matters vary from country to country. Therefore, there was strong support for the emphasis on the need for bilateral and multilateral agreements.

However, it needs to be underlined that the existence of the Hague Abduction Convention and other regional treaties creates some inconsistency between instruments of international private law and the provision of the Convention on the Rights of the Child (Tobin et al., 2019, p. 373). For example, the Hague Abduction Convention only applies to children under the age of 16, in contrast to the age of 18 for the Convention on the Rights of the Child. Moreover, an application for return of a child under the Hague Abduction Convention may only be made if that Convention is in force between the two countries involved. Bilateral agreements

---

[1] See, for example, concluding observations for Philippines (2009, para. 79).
[2] See, for example, concluding observations for Mauritius (2006, paras. 39, 40).
[3] See, for example, concluding observations for Croatia (2004, para. 46).
[4] See, for example, concluding observations for Sweden (2005c, para. 27).
[5] See, for example, concluding observations for Sweden (1999, para. 15).
[6] See, for example, concluding observations for Canada (2003b, paras. 28, 29).

can be in place to provide similar protections between countries where the Hague Abduction Convention is not in force (e.g., the Australia-Egypt agreement[7]).

References

Detrick, S., Doek, J. E., & Cantwell, N. (1992). *The United Nations Convention on the Rights of the Child: A guide to the "Travaux Préparatoires."* Martinus Nijhoff Publishers.

Hague Conference on Private International Law. (2005). *Guide to good practice child abduction convention: Part III—Preventive measures.* https://www.hcch.net/en/publications-and-studies/publications2/guides-to-good-practice

House of Lords (UK). re M (FC) and another (FC) (Children) (FC), House of Lords, [2007] UKHL 55, No. [2007] UKHL 55 (House of Lords (UK) 5 December 2007). Retrieved November 6, 2020, from https://publications.parliament.uk/pa/ld200708/ldjudgmt/jd071205/inrem%20-1.htm

Ontario Court of Justice. Borisovs v. Kubiles, No. FO-11-10032-00 (Ontario Court of Justice 26 February 2013). Retrieved November 6, 2020, from http://canlii.ca/t/fwbtj

Re B (Abduction: Views of the child), No. 3 FCR 260 (1983).

Superior Court—Quebec, Canada. C. (M.L.L.) c. R. (J.L.R.), No. 500-04-010132-976 (Superior Court—Quebec, Canada 17 September 1997). Retrieved November 6, 2020, from http://canlii.ca/t/gnwtq

The Supreme Court—United Kingdom. In the matter of LC (Children)—The Supreme Court, [2014] UKSC 1, No. UKSC 2013/0221 (The Supreme Court—United Kingdom 15 January 2014). Retrieved November 6, 2020, from https://www.supremecourt.uk/cases/uksc-2013-0221.html

Tobin, J., Lowe, N., & Luke, E. (2019). Article 11: Protection against the illicit transfer and non-return of children abroad. In J. Tobin (Ed.), *The UN Convention on the Rights of the Child: A commentary* (pp. 370–396). Oxford University Press.

UN Committee on the Rights of the Child. (1999). *Concluding observations: Sweden, May 10, 1999, CRC/C/15/Add.101*. UN. Retrieved November 6, 2020, from http://digitallibrary.un.org/record/275206

UN Committee on the Rights of the Child. (2003a). *General Comment No. 5 (2003) General measures of implementation of the Convention on the Rights of the Child (arts. 4, 42 and 44, para. 6), November 27, 2003, CRC/GC/2003/5*. Retrieved October 12, 2020, from https://digitallibrary.un.org/record/513415?ln=en

UN Committee on the Rights of the Child. (2003b). *Concluding observations: Canada, October 27, 2003, CRC/C/15/Add.215*. Retrieved October 11, 2020, from https://digitallibrary.un.org/record/513561?ln=en

UN Committee on the Rights of the Child. (2004). *Concluding observations: Croatia, November 3, 2004, CRC/C/15/Add.243*. Retrieved October 11, 2020, from https://digitallibrary.un.org/record/557375?ln=en

UN Committee on the Rights of the Child. (2005a). *Concluding observations: Algeria, October 12, 2005, CRC/C/15/Add.269*. Retrieved October 24, 2020, from https://digitallibrary.un.org/record/570473?ln=en

UN Committee on the Rights of the Child. (2005b). *General Comment No. 6 (2005) Treatment of Unaccompanied and Separated Children Outside their Country of Origin, September 1, 2005,*

---

[7] Agreement Between The Government Of Australia And The Government Of The Arab Republic Of Egypt Regarding Cooperation On Protecting The Welfare Of Children, (Cairo, 22 October 2000), Australian Treaty Series [2002] ATS 3.

CRC/GC/2005/6. Retrieved October 12, 2020, from https://digitallibrary.un.org/record/566055?ln=en

UN Committee on the Rights of the Child. (2005c). *Concluding observations: Sweden, March 30, 2005, CRC/C/15/Add.248*. Retrieved October 11, 2020, from https://digitallibrary.un.org/record/557390?ln=en

UN Committee on the Rights of the Child. (2006). *Concluding observations: Mauritius, March 17, 2006, CRC/C/MUS/CO/2*. UN. , Retrieved November 6, 2020, from http://digitallibrary.un.org/record/575779

UN Committee on the Rights of the Child (UNCRC). (2009). *Concluding observations: Philippines, October 22, 2009, CRC/C/PHL/CO/3-4*. UN. Retrieved November 6, 2020, from http://digitallibrary.un.org/record/669130

UNICEF. (2007). *Implementation handbook for the Convention on the Rights of the Child* (3rd ed.) UNICEF. Retrieved April 19, 2020, from https://www.unicef.org/publications/index_43110.html

United Nations. (2006). *Compilation of General Comments and General Recommendations adopted by human rights treaty bodies, HRI/GEN/1/Rev. 8*. UN. Retrieved April 19, 2020, from http://digitallibrary.un.org/record/576098

Open Access This chapter is licensed under the terms of the Creative Commons Attribution 4.0 International License (http://creativecommons.org/licenses/by/4.0/), which permits use, sharing, adaptation, distribution and reproduction in any medium or format, as long as you give appropriate credit to the original author(s) and the source, provide a link to the Creative Commons license and indicate if changes were made.

The images or other third party material in this chapter are included in the chapter's Creative Commons license, unless indicated otherwise in a credit line to the material. If material is not included in the chapter's Creative Commons license and your intended use is not permitted by statutory regulation or exceeds the permitted use, you will need to obtain permission directly from the copyright holder.

Chapter 17
Article 18: Rights Concerning Parental Responsibility

Roberta Ruggiero

1. States Parties shall use their best efforts to ensure recognition of the principle that both parents have common responsibilities for the upbringing and development of the child. Parents or, as the case may be, legal guardians, have the primary responsibility for the upbringing and development of the child. The best interests of the child will be their basic concern.
2. For the purpose of guaranteeing and promoting the rights set forth in the present Convention, States Parties shall render appropriate assistance to parents and legal guardians in the performance of their child-rearing responsibilities and shall ensure the development of institutions, facilities and services for the care of children.
3. States Parties shall take all appropriate measures to ensure that children of working parents have the right to benefit from child-care services and facilities for which they are eligible.

What Did Children Say?
'Governments should help them to do so. For me, States should put in place means to help parents and their children. For example, suppose there are six children in a house with two bedrooms, we should help them move to a social

(continued)

R. Ruggiero (✉)
Centre for Children's Rights Studies, University of Geneva, Geneva, Switzerland
e-mail: roberta.ruggiero@unige.ch

> house with six bedrooms. We have to look at all this in relation to the situation of children.' (*Western Europe/Other*)
>
> 'The opportunity to have parental care (basic needs such as food, clothing, medicine, safety). In almost all areas children under 18 can only get help with adults.' (*Eastern Europe*)
>
> 'If this one is respected, we don't need the others anymore! Article 18 is the cornerstone.' (*Western Europe/Other*)

Overview

Article 18 concerns parents and other primary caregivers' equal responsibilities for the upbringing and the development of their children and the States Parties role in assisting them in the performing of their primary responsibility. The article strives to achieve a balance of responsibility between the child's parents, including other primary caregivers, and the States Parties (UNICEF, 2007, p. 231).

Article 18 supplements Article 3(2) and 5, directly bestowing on parents and other primary caregivers the primary responsibility for the rearing and development of the child, further underlining that parental decisions should always be taken with due consideration for the best interests of the child (Article 18(1)). Furthermore, it is complementary to Article 27(2), which charges parents with the responsibility to secure 'the conditions of living necessary for the child's development.'

It also reiterates States Parties' obligations to provide appropriate assistance to parents in the performance of their child-rearing responsibility (Article 18(2)). The combined reading of Articles 18(2) and 3(2) and (3) bestow on States Parties the responsibility to render appropriate assistance to parents in the performance of their child-rearing responsibility, namely through the creation of institutions, facilities, and services for the care of children and monitoring of the latter's compliance with the quality standards. Both provisions are therefore closely intertwined, even though Article 3(3) does not exclusively refer to institutions dedicated to child-rearing, but to those dedicated to child protection generally (de Detrick, 1999, p. 29; Freeman, 2007, pp. 71–72; Ruggiero et al., 2017).

In addition, Article 18 combined with 'Article 5 (parental and family duties and rights, the child's evolving capacities) and Articles 3(2) and 27 (the States Parties' responsibility to assist parents in securing that children have adequate protection and care and an adequate standard of living) affirms that (UNICEF, 2007, p. 231):

- both parents and other primary caregivers have common and equal responsibility for the upbringing and development of the child
- parents and other primary caregivers hold the primary responsibility for securing the child's best interest, but at the same time this responsibility on the basis of the circumstances of the child and in the respect of his/her rights may be shared with others such as members of the wider family

- the best interest of the child will be parents' basic concern in the fulfillment of their responsibility.

During the drafting of Article 18, the American delegate remarked that the wording of paragraph 1 was rather strange because an international treaty cannot create a responsibility on individuals but can only set binding obligations for ratifying governments (de Detrick, 1999, pp. 302–303; Detrick et al., 1992, p. 270; UN Commission on Human Rights, 1989, pp. 50–52; UNICEF, 2007, pp. 232–233). However, the imperative tense used remained in the final version of Article 18(1) because the principle implies a direct bearing on the actions of States Parties, which are obliged to translate all legislation on parents' rights into principles of 'parental responsibilities'—the legal responsibility of parents to act in the best interests of their children—as required by the Convention.

Following the wording of Article 18(2), States Parties have the obligation to support parents and other primary caregivers in the fulfillment of their responsibility and undertake all the appropriate measures to assist them in the accomplishment of their child-rearing responsibility.

With reference to Article 18 (3), States Parties must step in to secure the child's rights and needs, in all those cases where parents are not able to fulfil their responsibility,

The content of these two last paragraphs is in line with Article 10 of the International Covenant on Economic, Social and Cultural Rights, which accords to the family the 'widest possible protection and assistance' of States Parties in particular, while the family 'is responsible for the care and education of dependent children.' Articles 23 and 24 of the International Covenant on Civil and Political Rights reiterate these principles (UNICEF, 2007, p. 232).[1]

Article 18 does not juxtapose parents' rights to children's rights, but it rather asserts 'parents and other primary caregivers' primacy in relation to the state, not the child, and the article is about parental responsibilities rather than rights. In doing so, the Convention 'imposes on States parties the' *obligation to respect* the parent's role, by refraining from arbitrary interferences in the exercise of the parental responsibility and the *obligation to fulfil,* by taking all appropriate legislative and administrative measures to nurture parental resources—both in terms of personal skills and availability of support facilities (UN Committee on the Rights of the Child, 2006, para. 15, 2013a, para. 56). In this framework, parents enjoy a degree of discretion as holders of what have been defined as *limited* (Archard, 2014, pp. 149–152) and *functional* (Reynaert et al., 2009, p. 518) rights (Ruggiero et al., 2017, p. 75). The limitations of these rights are of a twofold nature. First, they are limited by the evolving capacity of the child. As the child matures, the rights will be automatically

---

[1] Here we do not unpack the definitions of 'family' and 'caregivers'. However, for information about these aspects see: General Comment no. 5, 1994, of the Committee on Economic, Social and Cultural Rights (United Nations, 2006, p. 31), Human Rights Committee, General Comment No. 17, 1989 (United Nations, 2006, p. 184), and Committee on the Rights of the Child General Comment no. 7 (2006, para. 15).

restricted or reshaped in their content and scope (Article 5). Secondly, the parents' right, including the rights of other primary caregivers, should be exercised in the full respect of the best interest of the child and their enjoyment of the full range of rights included in the Convention (Ruggiero et al., 2017, pp. 71–75).

General Principles

Article 2 Article 18 reaffirms that parents have the primary responsibility for promoting children's development and well-being, with the child's best interests as their basic concern (UN Committee on the Rights of the Child, 2006, para. 18). This applies equally to younger and older children, and to children belonging to all possible kind of families with no discrimination (UN Committee on the Rights of the Child, 2006, paras. 5, 18, 20), including children in the context of migration (UN Committee on the Protection of the Rights of All Migrant Workers and Members of Their Families and UN Committee on the Rights of the Child, 2017, para. 44).

Article 3 The best interests of the child is the parents 'basic concern' in the performing of their responsibilities for the upbringing and development of the child. In particular, General Comment no. 14 provides guidelines on how to determine the child best interests and leads the decisions by all those concerned with children, including parents and caregivers (UN Committee on the Rights of the Child, 2013b, para. 10).

Article 6 Based on Article 18, parents hold the primary responsibility for the child's development. Development is a wide concept that needs to be determined on the basis of Articles 6, 27 and 29. 'If a child's physical, psychological or intellectual development is being impaired by the avoidable actions of the parents, then the parents can be found to be failing in their responsibilities' (UNICEF, 2007, p. 232).

Article 12 Parenting support should be provided with the intention of strengthening parent's ability to enhance children's capacities to exercise their right to participation under Article 12. To express their opinion, children need to be informed about issues concerning them, possible decisions to be taken, and related consequences. Parents as primary caregivers should be able to provide their children with all the needed information (UN Committee on the Rights of the Child, 2009, para. 25).

States Parties need to introduce national legal provisions regulating the balance between parental consent and parental responsibility towards children's rights to express their opinion on matters that affect their lives. The Committee underlies that in all cases in which the child demonstrates sufficient understanding, they should be entitled to give or refuse consent and their voluntary and informed consent should be obtained, 'whether or not the consent of a parent … is required for any medical treatment or procedure' (2009, para. 101, 2016, para. 39). Moreover, the Committee also suggests the adoption of national legislation with the twofold aim of making a distinction between the right to give medical consent and to have access to health commodities, and introducing the 'legal presumption that adolescents are competent to seek and have access to preventive or time-sensitive sexual and reproductive health commodities and services' without the consent of a parent and irrespective of their age (2009, para. 101, 2016, para. 39).

Articles Related to or Linked to Article 18

Article 5 states that parents' role is to offer appropriate direction and guidance in the exercise by children of their rights in the respect of the child's evolving capacities.

Articles 3 imposes, in paragraph 2, the States Parties' responsibility to assist parents in performing their role. It also requires, in paragraph 3, States Parties to ensure that institutions, services, and facilities responsible for the care or protection of children, shall conform to the standards established by competent authorities.

Articles 6, 27 and 29: The combined reading of these three articles allow the outlining of the child's physical, psychological, and/or intellectual development. If the child's full development is being impaired by parents' behaviour, 'then the parents can be found to be failing in their responsibilities' (UNICEF, 2007, p. 232).

Article 7 is child's right to know and be cared for by parents.

Article 9 deals with separation from parents, which extends to the State obligation not to separate children from their parents unless it is in the child's best interests and it is not due to economic issues and poor parenting that could be improved with adequate parenting support by the State.

Article 10 concerns family reunification.

Articles 14 requires that parents should be supported in order to provide rights-based parenting, in a child-centred way, in respect of the child's right to freedom of religion.

Article 16 concerns protection from arbitrary interference, with family and home.

Article 26 deals with the right of the child to benefit from social security, including social insurance.

Article 27 states that parents or other caregivers have the primary responsibility to secure the conditions of living necessary for the full child's development and that States Parties have the obligation to assist them in the fulfilment of their role.

Article 31 protects the child's right to rest, leisure, play, recreational activities, cultural life, and art. States Parties are obliged 'to adopt specific measures aimed at achieving respect for the right of every child, individually or in association with others', including guidance and support for caregivers (UN Committee on the Rights of the Child, 2013a, para. 56).

Relevant Instruments

UN Universal Declaration of Human Rights (1948), Article 16
International Covenant on Economic, Social and Cultural Rights (1966), Article 10
International Covenant on Civil and Political Rights (1966), Articles 23 and 24
UN Convention on the Elimination of All Forms of Discrimination against Women (1979), Article 16, 11(2)(c) and Article 5(b)
International Convention on the Protection of the Rights of All Migrant Workers and Members of Their Families (1990), Article 12(4)
UN Convention on the Rights of Persons with Disabilities (2006), Article 23
African Charter on Human and Peoples' Rights (1981), Article 18(3)
American Convention on Human Rights 'Pact of San Jose, Costa Rica' (B-32) (1978), Article 17(4)

Attributes

Attribute One: Common Primary Responsibilities for the Upbringing Under the Primary Consideration of the Child Best Interest

Based on Article 18(1), the parents' responsibility for the upbringing of the child is composed of three provisions. First, it must be common and shared in equal measure between the parents. This reflects the provision of the Articles 5 and 16 of the Convention on the Elimination of All Forms of Discrimination against Women and invites States Parties to include this principle in their legislation, provisions of services and all the education measures dedicated to parents. Furthermore, it completes the provisions of Article 27 with reference to single-parent families, for what measures exist to ensure the recovery of maintenance, which goes beyond the financial responsibility and includes upbringing responsibilities, including those of fathers of children born out of wedlock (UNICEF, 2007, p. 235).

Second, responsibility is primarily attributed to parents or other caregivers. During the drafting of Article 18(1), it was underlined that the second sentence of the first paragraph was meant to balance States Parties and parents' position with the twofold intention to protect parents against excessive intervention by the States Parties, and 'to indicate that parents could not expect the state always to intervene because the upbringing and development of their children was primarily their responsibility' (de Detrick, 1999, pp. 301–303).

Third, it must be provided in a manner consistent with the child's best interests as a basic concern. The perceptions of the child's best interests vary from case to case. However, the requirement to ensure that they are guided by reference to respect for the child's rights under the Convention does serve to provide a framework. As a consequence, States Parties are required to monitor parents' compliance with the Convention and provide parent education on rights-based parenting (UN Committee on the Rights of the Child, 2003, 2006; UNICEF, 2007, p. 233).

Attribute Two: State's Appropriate Assistance to Parents

Article 18(2) imposes States Parties responsibility to provide appropriate assistance to parents. It reflects the provisions of Article 3(2),[2] Article 27(3), with reference to the child's right to an adequate standard of living,[3] and with Article 26 with reference to the right of the child to benefit from social security, including social insurance.[4]

The States Parties must set up an adequate legislative and policy framework able to secure the providing of a wide range of support, which may include, to name a few, financial assistance, social security benefits, initiatives of advice and education on positive parenting and positive child-parent relationships, adequate training to social workers, housing, day-care, home helps, equipment and so forth, as well as psychological and professional support. States Parties support should create the living conditions necessary to give parents and other primary caregivers the opportunity to fully exercise their primary responsibility (de Detrick, 1999, pp. 307–308). Therefore, this assistance, also defined as a tertiary approach (Cantwell et al., 2012), should be provided when appropriate and in particular when parents for whatever reason, whether or not it is their fault, are unable to carry out their child-rearing responsibility (UN Committee on the Rights of the Child, 2003, 2013a, 2016; UNICEF, 2007, p. 237). However, state support should be provided not exclusively in case of need, but also as a general form of assistance to all parents, as a manifestation of the States Parties' responsibility and interest in children as an investment in social well-being (UNICEF, 2007, pp. 234, 237–238).[5]

---

[2] Article 3(2): 'States Parties undertake to ensure the child such protection and care as is necessary for his or her well-being, taking into account the rights and duties of his or her parents, legal guardians, or other individuals legally responsible for him or her, and, to this end, shall take all appropriate legislative and administrative measures;'

[3] Article 27(3): 'States Parties, in accordance with national conditions and within their means, shall take appropriate measures to assist parents and others responsible for the child to implement this right.'

[4] Article 26: '1. States Parties shall recognize for every child the right to benefit from social security, including social insurance, and shall take the necessary measures to achieve the full realization of this right in accordance with their national law. 2. The benefits should, where appropriate, be granted, taking into account the resources and the circumstances of the child and persons having responsibility for the maintenance of the child, as well as any other consideration relevant to an application for benefits made by or on behalf of the child.' (de Detrick, 1999, p. 305; UNICEF, 2007, p. 237).

[5] United Nations Guidelines for the Prevention of Juvenile Delinquency (the Riyadh Guidelines) states: 'Measures should be taken and programmes developed to provide families with the

Attribute Three: Development of Institutions, Facilities, and Services for the Care of Children

Article 18(2) refers to a specific category of institutions, facilities, and services for the care of children. These could include community-based centres, for example, those dedicated to single parents with young children, play-groups, toys, libraries or youth clubs, and support centres for adolescent parents. These could also provide education to parents, including for those whose traditions and norms may differ from those in the society where they live (de Detrick, 1999, pp. 304–305; UN Committee on the Rights of the Child, 2003, para. 7, 2006, para. 16; UNICEF, 2007, p. 238). Under Article 18(2), States Parties are required to 'ensure the development' of all those institutions, facilities and services that are not already identified by:

- Article 20 for what is required to meet the state responsibility to provide for out-of-home-children
- Article 18(3), with reference to States Parties' obligation to provide services for children of working parents
- Articles 23, 24 and 28, in relation to facilities and services for children with disabilities, health and education (UNICEF, 2007, p. 238).

States Parties are in any case obliged to secure the compliance of these services and facilities with standards established by competent authorities, in terms of health, safety, and quality of their staff, in line with Article 3(3) (de Detrick, 1999, pp. 309–305).

Attribute Four: Appropriate Measures for the Care of Children of Working Parents

Based on several General Comments, the needs of children of working parents must be afforded a high priority. Therefore, as per Article 18(3), States Parties are obliged to secure the availability and accessibility of public and private child-day-care services and facilities. Access to these services is determined on the basis of eligibility criteria set by the States Parties. States Parties are required to set up these services in respect of the wording of the second sentence of Article 4 ('to the maximum extent of their available resources') and should ensure that these services and facilities conform with standards established by competent authorities, in terms of health, safety, and quality of their staff, in line with Article 3(3) (de Detrick, 1999, pp. 309–310).

---

opportunity to learn about parental roles and obligations as regards child development and childcare, promoting positive parent-child relationships, sensitizing parents to the problems of children and young persons and encouraging their involvement in family and community based activities' (UN General Assembly, 1991, para. 16).

References

Archard, D. (2014). *Children: Rights and childhood* (3rd ed.). Routledge.
Cantwell, N., Davidson, J., Elsley, S., Milligan, I., & Quinn, N. (2012). *Moving forward: Implementing the 'guidelines for the alternative care of children'*. The Centre for Excellence for Looked After Children in Scotland. https://www.alternativecareguidelines.org/MovingForward/tabid/2798/language/en-GB/Default.aspx
de Detrick, S. L. (1999). *A commentary on the United Nations Convention on the Rights of the Child*. Brill Nijhoff. Retrieved November 6, 2020, from https://brill.com/view/title/10630
Detrick, S., Doek, J. E., & Cantwell, N. (1992). *The United Nations Convention on the Rights of the Child: A guide to the "Travaux Préparatoires."* Martinus Nijhoff Publishers.
Freeman, M. (2007). *A commentary on the United Nations Convention on the Rights of the Child, Article 3: The best interests of the child*. Brill Nijhoff.
Reynaert, D., Bouverne-de-Bie, M., & Vandevelde, S. (2009). A review of children's rights literature since the adoption of the United Nations Convention on the Rights of the Child. *Childhood, 16*(4), 518–534. https://doi.org/10.1177/0907568209344270
Ruggiero, R., Volonakis, D., & Hanson, K. (2017). The inclusion of "third parties": The status of parenthood in the Convention on the Rights of the Child. In E. Brems, E. Desmet, & W. Vandenhole (Eds.), *Children's rights law in the global human rights landscape: Isolation, inspiration, integration?* (1st ed., pp. 71–75). Routledge.
UN Commission on Human Rights. (1989). *Report of the working group on a Draft Convention on the Rights of the Child, 1989, E/CN.4/1989/48*. Retrieved October 12, 2020, from https://digitallibrary.un.org/record/57437?ln=en
UN Committee on the Protection of the Rights of All Migrant Workers and Members of Their Families, & UN Committee on the Rights of the Child. (2017). *Joint General Comment No. 3 (2017) of the Committee on the Protection of the Rights of All Migrant Workers and Members of Their Families and No. 22 (2017) of the Committee on the Rights of the Child on the general principles regarding the human rights of children in the context of international migration, CMW/C/GC/3, CRC/C/GC/22*. UN. Retrieved November 6, 2020, from http://digitallibrary.un.org/record/1323014
UN Committee on the Rights of the Child. (2003). *General Comment No. 4 (2003) Adolescent health and development in the context of the Convention on the Rights of the Child, July 1, 2003, CRC/GC/2003/4*. Retrieved October 12, 2020, from https://digitallibrary.un.org/record/503074?ln=en
UN Committee on the Rights of the Child. (2006). *General Comment No. 7 (2005) Implementing child rights in early childhood, September 20, 2006, CRC/C/GC/7/Rev.1*. Retrieved October 12, 2020, from https://digitallibrary.un.org/record/584854?ln=en
UN Committee on the Rights of the Child. (2009). *General Comment No. 12 (2009) The right of the child to be heard, July 20, 2009, CRC/C/GC/12*. Retrieved October 12, 2020, from https://digitallibrary.un.org/record/671444?ln=en
UN Committee on the Rights of the Child. (2013a). *General Comment No. 17 (2013) on the right of the child to rest, leisure, play, recreational activities, cultural life and the arts (art. 31), April 17, 2013, CRC/C/GC/17*. Retrieved October 12, 2020, from https://digitallibrary.un.org/record/778539?ln=en
UN Committee on the Rights of the Child. (2013b). *General Comment No. 14 (2013) On the right of the child to have his or her best interests taken as a primary consideration (art. 3, para. 1), May 29, 2013, CRC/C/GC/14*. Retrieved October 12, 2020, from https://digitallibrary.un.org/record/778523?ln=en

UN Committee on the Rights of the Child. (2016). *General Comment No. 20 (2016) on the implementation of the rights of the child during adolescence, December 6, 2016, CRC/C/GC/20*. Retrieved October 12, 2020, from https://digitallibrary.un.org/record/855544?ln=en

UN General Assembly. (1991). *United Nations guidelines for the prevention of juvenile delinquency (The Riyadh Guidelines), 1990, A/RES/45/112*. UN. Retrieved November 6, 2020, from http://digitallibrary.un.org/record/105349

UNICEF. (2007). *Implementation handbook for the Convention on the Rights of the Child* (3rd ed.) UNICEF. Retrieved April 19, 2020, from https://www.unicef.org/publications/index_43110.html

United Nations. (2006). *Compilation of General Comments and General Recommendations adopted by human rights treaty bodies, HRI/GEN/1/Rev. 8*. UN. Retrieved April 19, 2020, from http://digitallibrary.un.org/record/576098

Open Access This chapter is licensed under the terms of the Creative Commons Attribution 4.0 International License (http://creativecommons.org/licenses/by/4.0/), which permits use, sharing, adaptation, distribution and reproduction in any medium or format, as long as you give appropriate credit to the original author(s) and the source, provide a link to the Creative Commons license and indicate if changes were made.

The images or other third party material in this chapter are included in the chapter's Creative Commons license, unless indicated otherwise in a credit line to the material. If material is not included in the chapter's Creative Commons license and your intended use is not permitted by statutory regulation or exceeds the permitted use, you will need to obtain permission directly from the copyright holder.

Chapter 18
Article 20: Rights Concerning Children Deprived of Their Family Environment

Adem Arkadas-Thibert and Gerison Lansdown

> 1. A child temporarily or permanently deprived of his or her family environment, or in whose own best interests cannot be allowed to remain in that environment, shall be entitled to special protection and assistance provided by the State.
> 2. States Parties shall in accordance with their national laws ensure alternative care for such a child.
> 3. Such care could include, inter alia, foster placement, kafalah of Islamic law, adoption or, if necessary, placement in suitable institutions for the care of children. When considering solutions, due regard shall be paid to the desirability of continuity in a child's upbringing and to the child's ethnic, religious, cultural and linguistic background.

> **What Did Children Say?**
> They should help children to return to their family home if possible. (*Eastern Europe*)
>
> Children that are living without parents should be given a special support. Governments should do as much as possible to avoid sending children to orphanages. (*Eastern Europe*)
>
> (continued)

A. Arkadas-Thibert (✉)
Marseille, France

G. Lansdown
Carleton University, Ottawa, ON, Canada

> They should be placed somewhere that helps them be healthy and develop their potential, for as short a time as possible and they should stay with their brothers and sisters. (*Eastern Europe*)

Overview

Article 20 provides protection for children, who, for whatever reasons, are deprived of a family environment. It applies to both temporary and permanent needs for alternative care, to situations where no extended family care is available, and to all possible reasons as to the causes for separation (Office of the United Nations High Commissioner for Human Rights and Rädda barnen (Society: Sweden), 2007, pp. 526–527). While other articles, including Articles 7, 8, 18, and 27, obligate States Parties to provide the necessary support to families to enable them to care for their children, Article 20 requires that if, despite those measures, children are unable to be cared for by their own families, they are entitled to special protection and assistance from the state.

International law has long recognised the importance of the family for children's healthy development and well-being. As stated in Article 16(3) of the Universal Declaration of Human Rights, 'the family is the natural and fundamental group unit of society and is entitled to protection by society and the State.' Article 23 of International Covenant on Civil and Political Rights and Article 10 of International Covenant on Economic, Social and Cultural Rights similarly underline the importance given to the family. The 1924 and 1959 Declarations on the Rights of the Child acknowledged the need for protection of children without parents or whose parents were unable to care for them. The preamble of the Convention on the Rights of the Child also states that the child 'should grow up in a family environment, in an atmosphere of happiness, love and understanding.' Unsurprisingly, therefore, the text of Article 20 was one of the first articles of the Convention that was discussed, and it was adopted without much disagreement by the Working Group.

There is a considerable body of jurisprudence in international law, including both the Convention on the Rights of the Child and the Convention on the Rights of Persons with Disabilities, regarding children deprived of a family environment.[1] The Committee has afforded significant attention to Article 20 through both its General Comments[2] and Concluding Observations. In addition, the United Nations Guidelines for the Alternative Care of Children (stemming from a recommendation from the Committee's Day of General Discussion on Children Without Parental Care in 2005), provide detailed interpretation and guidance for States Parties on the implementation of Article 20 (UN General Assembly, 2010).

---

[1] See Relevant Treaties section for additional examples.

[2] All General Comments have a section on children deprived of family environment.

General Principles

Article 2 The United Nations Guidelines for the Alternative Care of Children (paragraph 10) outlines a number of discrimination grounds that can give rise to relinquishment, abandonment, or removal of a child from their family such as poverty, ethnicity, religion, sex, mental and physical disability, HIV/AIDS or other serious physical or mental illnesses, migration status, birth out of wedlock, parents' marital status, criminal status, socio-economic status, and all forms of violence, among others. The Convention on the Rights of Persons with Disabilities, Article 23, paragraph 5 (alternative care in family environment), General Comment no. 11 on Indigenous Children, General Comment no. 6 on Unaccompanied and Separated Children, and the latest General Comments on migrant children and children in street situations, along with growing number of jurisprudences,[3] all outline linkages and state obligations with respect to Article 20 and prohibition of discrimination.

Article 3 Article 20 is one of the Convention articles where the best interests principle is explicitly referred to. However, in Article 20 best interests is 'the determining factor', not just 'a primary consideration' as in Article 3. Read with Article 9 of the Convention, it is clear that care outside of the family should be seen as a measure of last resort and should, whenever possible, be temporary and for the shortest possible duration. General Comment no. 14 provides non-exhaustive guidance for States Parties to enable the assessment and determination of best interests in situations such as the removal of a child from their family:

- The child's views—the 'best interests' of the child cannot be defined without consideration of the child's views
- The child's identity
- Preservation of the family environment and maintaining relations
- Care, protection, and safety of the child
- Situation of vulnerability
- The child's right to health
- The child's right to education.

Article 6 The Committee, in almost all its concluding observations to States Parties, underlines the importance of right to life and development of children in alternative care settings. It also urges countries to develop social policies to help families support their children by ensuring that adequate human, technical, and financial resources are allocated to relevant child protection services and alternative care centres in local and national agencies, in order to provide children with an adequate

---

[3] See for example, Concluding observations, Republic of Moldova (2017a); Concluding observations, Lebanon (2017b); Nencheva and Others v. Bulgaria, 18 June 2013, European Court of Human Rights; Chbihi Loudoudi and Others v. Belgium, 16 December 2014, European Court of Human Rights, among others.

standard of living, remove any barriers to their positive development, such as overcrowding, and facilitate their rehabilitation and social reintegration of children to the greatest extent possible.[4]

Article 12 General Comment no. 12 (paragraph 97) on child participation clearly outlines States Parties' obligations in terms of Article 20 and Article 12:

- Through legislation, regulation and policy directives, the child's views are solicited and considered, including decisions regarding placement in foster care or homes, development of care plans and their review, and visits with parents and family
- Legislation providing the child with the right to information about any placement, care and/or treatment plan and meaningful opportunities to express her or his views and for those views to be given due weight throughout the decision-making process
- Legislation ensuring the right of the child to be heard, and that her or his views be given due weight in the development and establishment of child-friendly care services
- Establishment of a competent monitoring institution, such as a children's ombudsperson, commissioner, or inspectorate, to monitor compliance with the rules and regulations governing the provision of care, protection or treatment of children in accordance with the obligations under Article 3. The monitoring body should be mandated to have unimpeded access to residential facilities (including those for children in conflict with the law), to hear the views and concerns of the child directly, and to monitor the extent to which his or her views are listened to and given due weight by the institution itself.

Effective mechanisms should also be established to enable representative councils of the children, of all genders, in residential care facilities, with the mandate to participate in the development and implementation of the policy and any rules of the institution.

Articles Related to or Linked to Article 20

Article 20 should be read with and linked to:

Combined reading of **Articles 7, 8, 9, 18, 26, and 27** require States Parties to provide guarantees and measures for children to facilitate staying with their families and placement as a matter of last resort only.

Article 21 provides for nature and conditions of adoption as an issue of the right of the child.

---

[4] See, for example, Concluding observations, Denmark (2017c).

Article 16 provide protection from arbitrary interference with privacy, family, and home for children deprived of family environment.

Combined reading of **Articles 22, 23, 30, 34, 35, 36, and 37(c)** provide for protection against discrimination in relation to deprivation of family environment.

Article 25 requires States Parties to set up legal and other measures to guarantee periodic review of placement of each and every child to avoid unnecessary placement and, potentially, facilitate speedy return to family environment.

Relevant Instruments

UN Convention Relating to the Status of Refugees (1951)

UN Declaration on Social and Legal Principles relating to the Protection and Welfare of Children, with special reference to Foster Placement and Adoption Nationally and Internationally (1987)

UN Convention on the Rights of Persons with Disabilities (2006), Article 23 (5) Respect for home and the family

Hague Convention on Jurisdiction, Applicable Law, Recognition, Enforcement and Co-operation in Respect of Parental Responsibility and Measures for the Protection of Children (1996)

European Convention on Human Rights (1950), Article 8 (respect for private and family life)

UN Guidelines for the Alternative Care of Children (2009)

Council of Europe Recommendation on the rights of children living in residential institutions (2005)

Council of Europe Recommendation on deinstitutionalisation and community living of children with disabilities (2010)

Attributes

Attribute One: Provision of Special Protection and Assistance

Article 20(1) addresses States Parties' express and comprehensive obligation to provide 'special protection and assistance' to any child temporarily or permanently deprived of their family environment, in order to protect their well-being.

Accordingly, States Parties' must establish a legal and administrative framework with competent bodies and qualified professionals for alternative care systems for such times when it is necessary for the child's best interest to be placed in an alternative care setting than their family environment. The Human Rights Committee's General Comment no. 17 on the rights of the child describes this system a set of 'measures of protection adopted to protect children who are abandoned or deprived of their family environment in order to enable them to develop in conditions that most closely resemble those characterising the family environment' (UN Office of the High Commissioner for Human Rights (OHCHR), 1989, para. 6). Such a system must have procedural safeguards for 'the child's full and harmonious development' (UN General Assembly, 1959). Fundamentals of alternative care systems are clearly outlined in the UN Guidelines for the Alternative Care of Children, which explicitly demand from the States Parties that all alternative care options should be supported with clear legislative and policy framework and adequate financial conditions as enshrined in Articles 3 and 4 of the Convention, as a part of the 'special care and protection.'

Attribute Two: Standards of Care

This attribute focuses on standards of care provision such as contact of the child with their parents, quality of care, continuity of care, quality of carers, and all other forms of legal, policy, and financial conditions made available for the quality-of-care provisions. States Parties are under international obligations to establish vigorous sets of standards of quality care regulated by law and policy, in order to ensure the well-being and protection of the child placed in alternative care, whatever the type or nature of this care placement, in accordance with the Article 3(3) of the Convention. Although such standards of care include systematic monitoring and inspection of care placement orders and settings, this component is dealt with under Article 25 of the Convention, later in this part.

Alternative care decisions should be temporary, made with the participation of the child, the parents, and the extended family, at a last resort, and for the shortest possible timeframe. States Parties are responsible for creating conditions for maintaining the child's contact with their parents, the wider family, and the community (UN Committee on the Rights of the Child, 2013, paras. 60, 65; UN General Assembly, 2010, para. 81).

Because separation from parents must be justified in terms of the best interest of the child, the standards of alternative care should be an improvement for the child from the situation the child was separated from, in terms of the quality of physical and emotional care (Sandberg, 2019, p. 204). These standards should include ensuring and maintaining the quality of care through rigorous training of staff and carers of residential care settings, foster carers, social workers, and others directly or indirectly involved in the care of the child (UN General Assembly, 2010, para. 71). It is also vital for the best interest of the child that the standards of care should include legal and policy frameworks to enable the best possible participatory transition out of alternative care, either back to their family environment or to an independent life (UN General Assembly, 2010, paras. 131–136).

Attribute Three: Nature of Care

This attribute deals with alternative care settings and nature of care placement. Although the Article specifically mentions 'foster placement, kafalah of Islamic law, adoption or, if necessary, placement in suitable institutions for the care of children', the list of care settings is open-ended, leaving States Parties a generous margin of appreciation to find the best possible care placement for the child according to their needs and to cultural, linguistic, and religious background, in order to 'develop in conditions that most closely resemble those characterising the family environment' (UN Office of the High Commissioner for Human Rights (OHCHR), 1989).

Although the placement decision must be made by a competent authority in accordance with national laws, it may be formal or informal, temporary or permanent, and public or private with the extended family, with community members previously known to the child, with foster placement, with family style or other forms of residential care, with kafalah of Islamic law, or adoption. Adoption is discussed in Article 21, as it represents the most permanent form where parental ties with the child are severed. The UN Guidelines for the Alternative Care of Children outline the nature of alternative care extensively in paragraph 29 (b and c), and exceptions to such care in paragraph 30, namely children in conflict with the law.

The UN Guidelines for the Alternative Care of Children also underline the obligation of the States Parties to prioritise family and community-based care amongst a wide range of best possible alternative care options (UN General Assembly, 2010, para. 53). The Guidelines also point out that the States Parties should have a 'deinstitutionalization strategy,' as they move away from large residential care options to foster care, 'individualised small group care' and other family-based and community-based care options (UN General Assembly, 2010, paras. 21, 23). Moreover, Article 20 stresses the obligation of States Parties to consider the child's ethnic, religious, cultural, and linguistic background so as to ensure the continuity of a child's upbringing, as also enshrined in Articles 5 and 29(1)(c).

Whatever the nature of care placement, 'the necessity and suitability' of care placement 'must be monitored and regularly reviewed, in consultation with the child and his or her family' (Cantwell and Holzscheiter, 2007, p. 64), against a clear set of legal standards in alternative care systems.

References

Cantwell, N., & Holzscheiter, A. (2007). A commentary on the United Nations Convention on the Rights of the Child, Article 20: Children Deprived of Their Family Environment. In *Leiden*. Brill-Nijhoff.

Office of the United Nations High Commissioner for Human Rights & Rädda barnen (Society). (2007). *Legislative history of the Convention on the Rights of the Child*. United Nations.

Sandberg, K. (2019). Alternative care and children's rights. In U. Kilkelly & T. Liefaard (Eds.), *International human rights of children* (pp. 187–213). Springer. https://doi.org/10.1007/978-981-10-4184-6_8

UN Committee on the Rights of the Child. (2013). *General Comment No. 14 (2013) On the right of the child to have his or her best interests taken as a primary consideration (art. 3, para. 1), May 29, 2013, CRC/C/GC/14*. Retrieved October 12, 2020, from https://digitallibrary.un.org/record/778523?ln=en

UN Committee on the Rights of the Child. (2017a). *Concluding observations: Moldova, October 20, 2017, CRC/C/MDA/CO/4-5*. UN. Retrieved November 6, 2020, from http://digitallibrary.un.org/record/1311387

UN Committee on the Rights of the Child. (2017b). *Concluding observations: Lebanon, June 22, 2017, CRC/C/LBN/CO/4-5*. UN. Retrieved November 6, 2020, from http://digitallibrary.un.org/record/1311380

UN Committee on the Rights of the Child. (2017c). *Concluding observations: Denmark, October 26, 2017, CRC/C/DNK/CO/5*. UN. Retrieved November 6, 2020, from http://digitallibrary.un.org/record/1311756

UN General Assembly. (1959). *Declaration of the rights of the child, 1959, A/RES/1386(XIV)*. https://digitallibrary.un.org/record/195831?ln=en

UN General Assembly. (2010). *Guidelines for the alternative care of children, 2010, A/RES/64/142*. https://digitallibrary.un.org/record/673583?ln=en

UN Office of the High Commissioner for Human Rights (OHCHR). (1989). *CCPR General Comment No. 17: (1989) Article 24 (Rights of the Child)*. Retrieved November 6 2020, from https://www.refworld.org/docid/45139b464.html

Open Access This chapter is licensed under the terms of the Creative Commons Attribution 4.0 International License (http://creativecommons.org/licenses/by/4.0/), which permits use, sharing, adaptation, distribution and reproduction in any medium or format, as long as you give appropriate credit to the original author(s) and the source, provide a link to the Creative Commons license and indicate if changes were made.

The images or other third party material in this chapter are included in the chapter's Creative Commons license, unless indicated otherwise in a credit line to the material. If material is not included in the chapter's Creative Commons license and your intended use is not permitted by statutory regulation or exceeds the permitted use, you will need to obtain permission directly from the copyright holder.

Chapter 19
Chapter 7: Article 21—Adoption

Gerison Lansdown

States Parties that recognize and/or permit the system of adoption shall ensure that the best interests of the child shall be the paramount consideration and they shall:

(a) Ensure that the adoption of a child is authorised only by competent authorities who determine, in accordance with applicable law and procedures and on the basis of all pertinent and reliable information, that the adoption is permissible in view of the child's status concerning parents, relatives and legal guardians and that, if required, the persons concerned have given their informed consent to the adoption on the basis of such counselling as may be necessary;

(b) Recognize that inter-country adoption may be considered as an alternative means of child's care, if the child cannot be placed in a foster or an adoptive family or cannot in any suitable manner be cared for in the child's country of origin;

(c) Ensure that the child concerned by inter-country adoption enjoys safeguards and standards equivalent to those existing in the case of national adoption;

(d) Take all appropriate measures to ensure that, in inter-country adoption, the placement does not result in improper financial gain for those involved in it;

(continued)

G. Lansdown (✉)
Carleton University, Ottawa, ON, Canada

(e) Promote, where appropriate, the objectives of the present article by concluding bilateral or multilateral arrangements or agreements, and endeavour, within this framework, to ensure that the placement of the child in another country is carried out by competent authorities or organs.

What Did Children Say?
'For me when a child is adopted, he should be able to know what his past is like, who his parents are, etc. And you can't adopt a child without his consent.' (*Eastern Europe*)

People who are involved in making decisions about adoption must be properly trained. (*Eastern Europe*)

Government should create a programme that would support parents to raise up their children. Adoption laws should be made to protect the interest of the children. (*Africa*)

Interests of children should be put over others. Only special professional services and organisations have to deal with the documents and support children in the process of adoption. (*Eastern Europe*)

Overview

Article 21 constitutes the first introduction into international human rights law of a provision relating to adoption, although a UN Declaration in 1986 made provision for its recognition and regulation (UN General Assembly, 1987) and influenced the drafting of Article 21 (Office of the United Nations High Commissioner for Human Rights & Rädda Barnen (Society: Sweden), 2007, pp. 537–538). The initial draft of the Convention from Poland contained no reference to adoption, but early proposals were submitted from Barbados on domestic adoption and Colombia on inter-country adoption, providing a framework for regulation and standards in respect of both (Office of the United Nations High Commissioner for Human Rights & Rädda Barnen (Society: Sweden), 2007, pp. 537–538). Building on the preamble that affirms the centrality of the family as the fundamental group of society, the drafting committee took the view that adoption should be recognised as a permanent solution for children unable to have their needs met within their birth families. However, a proposal that States Parties should actively facilitate adoption was rejected in favour of a position that it should be neither promoted nor advocated. Rather, the text defines the contexts in which it can be authorised and stipulates a regulatory framework must be present to avoid harm or exploitation (Hodgkin et al., 2007).

The Committee has subsequently encouraged States Parties to proactively recognise adoption as a means of providing alternative care where appropriate.[1] The best interests principle was recognised, not simply as a legal reference to prevail in all aspects of adoption, but as an overarching principle governing the issue (Vité & Boéchat, 2008, p. 22). Representations from Islamic countries, where adoption is not permitted, led to the introductory paragraph clarifying that Article 21 only applies to those countries where adoption is recognised or permitted (Office of the United Nations High Commissioner for Human Rights & Rädda Barnen (Society: Sweden), 2007, p. 547). The final text places emphasis on the imperative for adoption to be undertaken only through competent and authorised authorities with rigorous consent procedures involving birth parents, and where appropriate, the child. It demands equivalent safeguards and standards between national and inter-country adoption, with a prohibition on improper financial gain in respect of inter-country adoption. It embodies recognition of the principle of subsidiarity—inter-country adoption must only be pursued when all domestic options have been considered, consistent with the best interests of the child.[2] Finally, it encourages the development of bilateral and multilateral arrangements to ensure the effective protection of children.

General Principles

Article 2 Article 21 demands parity in the safeguards and standards provided between domestic and inter-country adoption, thereby prohibiting any unequal treatment of children between the two procedures, consistent with Article 2 (Vité & Boéchat, 2008, p. 48). The right to non-discrimination also imposes a requirement for equal treatment of children within domestic adoptions, whether placed within or outside their kinship networks (Vité & Boéchat, 2008, p. 49). The Committee has expressed concern about discriminatory practices towards certain groups of children, for example, Roma children, those with severe disabilities or, in certain cases, boys, being denied opportunities for adoption.[3] It has also criticised patterns of prioritising rich families as potential adopters (2006b). Disaggregated data on which children have been placed for adoption is necessary to identify and address any such patterns of discrimination (UN Committee on the Rights of the Child, 2009a).

Article 3 The Convention establishes a presumption that children's best interests are served by living with their parents whenever possible and requires States Parties to implement policies designed to support family preservation (UN Committee on

---

[1] See, for example concluding observations for Bosnia and Herzegovenia (2012a, para. 51(b)), China (1996, para. 38), and Eritrea (2003, para. 36).

[2] See, for example, concluding observations for the Russian Federation, (2005a, para. 42) and Commentary on the UNCRC Article 21, Adoption (Vité & Boéchat, 2008, p. 45).

[3] See, for example, Concluding observations for Grenada (2000a, para. 19), Hungary (2006a, paras. 34–35), and Serbia (2017a).

the Rights of the Child, 2005b). However, for those circumstances where adoption is required, the paramountcy of the best interests of the child must be embedded in all relevant legislation and explicitly frame every dimension of adoption processes, taking precedence over all other considerations. This represents the strongest formulation of the principle in the Convention.

Adoption cannot, therefore, be considered as a general approach to children without care, but rather, decisions must be made on a case-by-case basis. Furthermore, regulations such as rigid rules on age of adopters, or time limits before an adoption can take place, could serve to fetter, and thereby breach this principle (Hodgkin et al., 2007, p. 295; UN Committee on the Rights of the Child, 2002, para. 36, 2005c, para. 48). In respect of inter-country adoption, the paramountcy of the best interests of the child means proposals of adoptable children by country of origin take precedence over requests by receiving countries (Vité & Boéchat, 2008, p. 27). However, any assessment of the child's best interests must be determined with reference to the rights and principles of the Convention and not according to vague or subjective criteria (Hague Conference on Private International Law, 2008, para. 44).

Article 6 The overall aim of adoption is to promote the optimum development of a child consistent with the goal of Article 6 and the preamble of the Convention, which states that the child 'for the full and harmonious development of his or her personality, should grow up in a family environment in an atmosphere of happiness, love and understanding'.

Article 12 Although no reference is explicitly made to children's views in Article 21, the provision of Article 12, that children have the right to express views on all matters of concern to them, and to have them given due weight in accordance with age and maturity, clearly extends to adoption (UN Committee on the Rights of the Child, 2009b, para. 55). The Committee has consistently emphasised that the ascertainable views of children must be into account (1994, para. 18, 1995a, para. 29, 2016a, para. 29(c)). The first paragraph of Article 21 indicates that adoption can only take place where, if required, 'persons' concerned' have given their informed consent. The Committee has interpreted 'persons concerned' to include children, and, accordingly, has recommended that States Parties introduce age limits below the age of 18 years when children can give consent to an adoption (2016b). The Hague Convention makes specific reference to the requirement that children have given consent where such consent is required, and consideration given to their wishes and opinions (Hague Conference on Private International Law, 1995, para. 4(d)).

Articles Related to or Linked to Article 21

Article 7 provides for the right of children to know and be cared for by their biological parents, wherever possible.

Article 8 affirms the right of children to preserve their identity and to have their identity restored if illegally removed, with implications for access to information about birth parents in respect of adoption.

Article 9 affirms the principle of non-separation from parents unless it is in the best interests of the child.

Article 10 requires a positive approach to family reunification for refugees and asylum seekers. This mitigates against seeking early adoption as a solution for refugee and asylum-seeking children.

Article 11 demands measures to protect against illicit transfer and return of children.

Article 16, protection of privacy, includes prohibition of arbitrary or unlawful interference with one's family.

Article 18 recognises the joint responsibility of parents and rights of unmarried parents with regard to consent to adoption. The rights and responsibilities also extend to adoptive parents.

Article 20 recognises the right of children to alternative care, and also adoption, if unable to be cared for by parents.

Article 25 introduces the right of children placed by competent authorities to periodic review of their care.

Article 27 (3) obliges States Parties to provide assistance to parents to ensure that the child has an adequate standard of living for their proper development.

Article 35 requires states to introduce measures to prevent sale of or trafficking of children. It also requires States Parties to ensure all possible measures to ensure that adoption of children is compliant with applicable international instruments, including the Hague Convention on Protection of Children and Co-operation in respect of Inter-country Adoption.

Optional Protocol on the sale of children, child prostitution, and child pornography: Article 3 includes improperly inducing consent, as an intermediary, for the adoption of a child is prohibited. Article 3(5) requires States Parties to ensure all possible measures to ensure that adoption of children is compliant with applicable international instruments, including the Hague Convention on Protection of Children and Co-operation in respect of Inter-country Adoption.

Relevant Instruments

UN Declaration on Social and Legal Principles relating to the Protection and Welfare of Children, with special reference to Foster Placement and Adoption Nationally and Internationally (1987)

Hague Convention on Protection of Children and Co-operation in Respect of Intercountry Adoption (1993)

European Convention on the Adoption of Children (Revised) (2008)

Inter-American Convention on Conflict of Laws Concerning the Adoption of Minors (1984)

African Charter on the Rights and Welfare of the Child (1990), Article 24

Attributes

Attribute One: Authorisation and Regulation

All adoptions must be authorised by competent authorities, which includes judicial and professional authorities that are properly accredited, inspected by state authorities, and run by appropriately trained staff.[4] States Parties must also establish legislation and procedures to regulate adoption. Article 21 does not provide any provisions to guide potential eligibility of a person to adopt a child but the Committee,[5] as well as the Hague Convention (Article 15), recommends that States Parties draw up clear policies and procedures for determining both criteria and assessment of applicant parents to ensure that children are placed in appropriate environments consistent with their best interests. The Committee has emphasised the necessity for comprehensive policy, guidelines and collection of national statistics for adoption (2004a, para. 47, 2005d, para. 52), as well as mechanisms for reviewing, monitoring and following up on adoption procedures (2000b, paras. 31, 31, 2000c, para. 33). Inter-country adoption should always be undertaken by accredited adoption bodies, as defined in the Hague Convention,[6] and not through individual channels which can lead to risk of trafficking or sale of children, or to individual adopters being able to select the child they adopt.[7] The Committee has been critical of any use of informal adoption processes (2004c, para. 38, 2004d, para. 45). The more detailed Hague Convention can serve as an implementing instrument of Article 21 and the Committee consistently recommends its ratification by States Parties.[8]

Attribute Two: Permissibility of Adoption

Adoption must only be considered when parents are unwilling or unable to care for their child. The wording of paragraph 1, which refers to permissibility in respect of

---

[4] See, for example, concluding observations for Panama (1997, para. 31).

[5] See, for example, concluding observations for El Salvador (2010a, para. 50).

[6] Article 11 of the Hague Convention defines an accredited body as one pursuing only non-profit objectives, directed and staffed by competent authorities and subject to supervision by competent authorities of the State.

[7] See, for example, concluding observations for France (2004b, para. 33) and for the Russian Federation (2005a, para. 42).

[8] See, for example, concluding observations for Myanmar (2012b).

parents, relatives, and legal guardians, testifies to the fact that if the parents are unable, consideration must be given to the wider family and only if they too are unable to provide care, should adoption be considered. Consent to the adoption must be sought, if required by the state. In other words, the wording in Article 21 allows that individual states can determine whether to provide for this obligation. However, failure to make such provision, either in respect of parents or the child, could constitute a violation of other rights, for example, in respect of Articles 7, 9, or 12, and should therefore be seen to be the exception rather than the rule to accommodate situations where consent is not possible or its pursuit would run counter to the child's best interests (Alston et al., 2019, p. 792). States Parties should always provide parents with appropriate information and counselling prior to them giving consent to an adoption (Hague Conference on Private International Law, 1995, para. 4(c)). Furthermore, the Committee has stressed that parents should never be pressured to give consent before or immediately after a child is born (2004e, para. 41, 2006a, para. 34). In respect of unaccompanied and separated children, they should only be considered for adoption after all efforts at tracing and reunification, or safe, dignified, and voluntary repatriation, have been exhausted (UN Committee on the Rights of the Child, 2005e, para. 91; UN High Commissioner for Refugees, 1994).

With regard to inter-country adoption, both the Convention on the Rights of the Child (Article 21(b)) and the Hague Convention (preamble) affirm that states may only consider inter-country adoption if the child cannot be placed in a foster or adoptive family, or the child cannot be cared for in a suitable manner in the child's country of origin. The Committee consistently encourages states to invest in promoting domestic solutions to the provision of care (1994, para. 18, 2004a, para. 47, 2005a, para. 42, 2005f, para. 39). Inter-country adoption must not be viewed as a source of babies for would-be parents in rich countries.

Attribute Three: Safeguards for Inter-Country Adoption

Article 21 introduces specific safeguards for inter-country adoption. Both Article 21 paragraph (b) and the Hague Convention Article 4(b) embody a principle of subsidiarity. In other words, as indicated above, inter-country adoption should only be considered if the child cannot be cared for in their country of origin. The Committee has emphasised that both foster care and domestic adoption must be prioritised over inter-country adoption, bearing in mind the best interests of the child.[9] However, inter-country adoption can be prioritised if the alternative for the child is long-term institutional care in their country of birth.[10]

---

[9] See, for example, concluding observations for Belize (2005g, para. 47) and Lithuania (2001a).

[10] See, for example, concluding observations for Nicaragua (2010b, paras. 56–57).

In cases where it is considered appropriate, Article 21 requires that States Parties ensure that children affected by inter-country adoption are provided with equivalent standards and safeguards to those applicable in national adoption. In addition, the Optional Protocol on the sale of children, child prostitution and child pornography, in Articles 3 and 5, requires States Parties to take measures to criminalise any act of improperly inducing consent for adoption as well as making any sort of trafficking in children an extraditable offence. It also demands that States Parties undertake measures to combat illegal practices. The Committee has frequently raised grave concerns over the lack of normative frameworks and illegal practices placing children at risk of trafficking and exploitation, and demands that effective mechanisms are in place to prevent and combat such violations (1995b, para. 18, 2001b, para. 4). The requirement in Article 21 paragraph (d) that placement of a child must never result in improper financial gain for those involved is designed to protect against potential exploitation of the adoption process. Some concerns were expressed during the drafting process that this wording might imply that proper gain was permissible and thereby allow for a market in children (UN Commission on Human Rights, 1989, paras. 356, 729). However, the Hague Convention has since clarified (Article 32 (2) and (3)) that only costs and expenses including reasonable professional fees of persons involved in the adoption may be charged with no remuneration permitted that is unreasonably high in relation to the services rendered.

States are encouraged to promote bilateral or multilateral arrangements and to ensure that such arrangements guarantee that placement of a child in another country is always carried out by competent authorities or organs. To this end, the Committee recommends to all states that have not yet done so, that they ratify the Hague Convention, which provides for a co-operative system between states, through competent authorities and accredited adoption bodies, to promote the best interests and rights of children (2000b, para. 31, 2017b, 2017c).

References

Alston, P., Cantwell, N., & Tobin, J. (2019). Article 21: Adoption. In J. Tobin (Ed.), *The UN Convention on the Rights of the Child: A commentary* (pp. 759–817). Oxford University Press.

Hague Conference on Private International Law. (1995). *Convention of 29 May 1993 on Protection of children and co-operation in respect of intercountry adoption (HCCH 1993 Adoption Convention)*. https://www.hcch.net/en/instruments/conventions/specialised-sections/intercountry-adoption

Hague Conference on Private International Law. (2008). *The implementation and operation of the 1993 intercountry adoption convention: Guide to good practice*. https://www.hcch.net/en/publications-and-studies/publications2/guides-to-good-practice

Hodgkin, R., Newell, P., & UNICEF. (2007). *Implementation handbook for the Convention on the Rights of the Child* (t3rd ed.). UNICEF. Retrieved September 21, 2020, from https://digitallibrary.un.org/record/620060?ln=en

Office of the United Nations High Commissioner for Human Rights, & Rädda barnen (Society: Sweden). (2007). *Legislative history of the Convention on the Rights of the Child*. United Nations. https://digitallibrary.un.org/record/602462?ln=en

UN Commission on Human Rights. (1989). *Report of the working group on a Draft Convention on the Rights of the Child, 1989, E/CN.4/1989/48*. Retrieved October 12, 2020, from https://digitallibrary.un.org/record/57437?ln=en

UN Committee on the Rights of the Child. (1994). *Concluding Observations: Mexico, February 7, 1994, CRC/C/15/Add.13*. UN. Retrieved November 7, 2020, from http://digitallibrary.un.org/record/197661

UN Committee on the Rights of the Child. (1995a). *Concluding observations: Germany, November 27, 1995, CRC/C/15/Add.43*. UN. Retrieved November 7, 2020, from http://digitallibrary.un.org/record/210276

UN Committee on the Rights of the Child. (1995b). *Concluding observations: Nicaragua, June 20, 1995, CRC/C/15/Add.36*. Retrieved October 11, 2020, from https://digitallibrary.un.org/record/191818?ln=en

UN Committee on the Rights of the Child. (1996). *Concluding observations: China, June 7, 1996, CRC/C/15/Add.56*. UN. Retrieved November 7, 2020, from http://digitallibrary.un.org/record/219432

UN Committee on the Rights of the Child. (1997). *Concluding observations: Panama, January 24, 1997, CRC/C/15/Add.68*. UN. Retrieved November 7, 2020, from http://digitallibrary.un.org/record/231730

UN Committee on the Rights of the Child. (2000a). *Concluding observations: Grenada, February 28, 2000, CRC/C/15/Add.121*. UN. Retrieved November 7, 2020, from http://digitallibrary.un.org/record/415624

UN Committee on the Rights of the Child. (2000b). *Concluding observations: Armenia, February 24, 2000, CRC/C/15/Add.119*. UN. Retrieved November 7, 2020, from http://digitallibrary.un.org/record/415621

UN Committee on the Rights of the Child. (2000c). *Concluding observations: Tajikistan, October 23, 2000, CRC/C/15/Add.136*. UN. Retrieved November 7, 2020, from http://digitallibrary.un.org/record/429815

UN Committee on the Rights of the Child. (2001a). *Concluding observations: Lithuania. February 21, 2001, CRC/C/15/Add.146*. UN. Retrieved November 7, 2020, from http://digitallibrary.un.org/record/444358

UN Committee on the Rights of the Child. (2001b). *Concluding observations: Paraguay, November 6, 2001, CRC/C/15/Add.166*. UN. Retrieved November 7, 2020, from http://digitallibrary.un.org/record/458177

UN Committee on the Rights of the Child. (2002). *Concluding observations: Switzerland, June 13, 2002, CRC/C/15/Add.182*. UN. Retrieved November 7, 2020, from http://digitallibrary.un.org/record/473486

UN Committee on the Rights of the Child. (2003). *Concluding observations: Eritrea, July 2, 2003, CRC/C/15/Add.204*. UN. Retrieved November 7, 2020, from http://digitallibrary.un.org/record/503087

UN Committee on the Rights of the Child. (2004a). *Concluding observations: Brazil, November 3, 2004, CRC/C/15/Add.241*. UN. Retrieved November 7, 2020, from http://digitallibrary.un.org/record/557367

UN Committee on the Rights of the Child. (2004b). *Concluding observations: France, June 30, 2004, CRC/C/15/Add.240*. Retrieved October 12, 2020, from https://digitallibrary.un.org/record/536574?ln=en

UN Committee on the Rights of the Child. (2004c). *Concluding observations: Liberia, July 1, 2004, CRC/C/15/Add.236*. UN. Retrieved November 7, 2020, from http://digitallibrary.un.org/record/536566

UN Committee on the Rights of the Child. (2004d). *Concluding observations: Antigua and Barbuda, November 3, 2004, CRC/C/15/Add.247*. UN. Retrieved November 6, 2020, from http://digitallibrary.un.org/record/557388

UN Committee on the Rights of the Child. (2004e). *Concluding observations: Kyrgyzstan, November 3, 2004, CRC/C/15/Add.244*. UN. Retrieved November 7, 2020, from http://digitallibrary.un.org/record/557378

UN Committee on the Rights of the Child. (2005a). *Concluding observations: Russian Federation, November 23, 2005, CRC/C/RUS/CO/3*. UN. Retrieved November 7, 2020, from http://digitallibrary.un.org/record/570555

UN Committee on the Rights of the Child. (2005b). *Day of general discussion: Children without parental care*. UN. Retrieved November 6, 2020, from https://www.ohchr.org/EN/HRBodies/CRC/Pages/DiscussionDays.aspx

UN Committee on the Rights of the Child. (2005c). *Concluding observations: Philippines, September 21, 2005, CRC/C/15/Add.259*. Retrieved October 11, 2020, from https://digitallibrary.un.org/record/566067?ln=en

UN Committee on the Rights of the Child. (2005d). *Concluding observations: China, November 24, 2005, CRC/C/CHN/CO/2*. Retrieved October 24, 2020, from https://digitallibrary.un.org/record/575653?ln=en

UN Committee on the Rights of the Child. (2005e). *General Comment No. 6 (2005) Treatment of Unaccompanied and Separated Children Outside their Country of Origin, September 1, 2005, CRC/GC/2005/6*. Retrieved October 12, 2020, from https://digitallibrary.un.org/record/566055?ln=en

UN Committee on the Rights of the Child. (2005f). *Concluding observations: Nicaragua, September 21, 2005, CRC/C/15/Add.265*. Retrieved October 11, 2020, from https://digitallibrary.un.org/record/570466?ln=en

UN Committee on the Rights of the Child. (2005g). *Concluding observations: Belize, March 31, 2005, CRC/C/15/Add.252*. UN. Retrieved November 7, 2020, from http://digitallibrary.un.org/record/557398

UN Committee on the Rights of the Child. (2006a). *Concluding observations: Hungary, March 17, 2006, CRC/C/HUN/CO/2*. Retrieved October 11, 2020, from https://digitallibrary.un.org/record/575773?ln=en

UN Committee on the Rights of the Child. (2006b). *Concluding observations: Mexico, June 8, 2006, CRC/C/MEX/CO/3*. https://digitallibrary.un.org/record/582289?ln=en

UN Committee on the Rights of the Child. (2009a). *Concluding observations: Philippines, October 22, 2009, CRC/C/PHL/CO/3-4*. UN. Retrieved November 6, 2020, from http://digitallibrary.un.org/record/669130

UN Committee on the Rights of the Child. (2009b). *General Comment No. 12 (2009) The right of the child to be heard, July 20, 2009, CRC/C/GC/12*. Retrieved October 12, 2020, from https://digitallibrary.un.org/record/671444?ln=en

UN Committee on the Rights of the Child. (2010a). *Concluding observations: El Salvador, February 17, 2010, CRC/C/SLV/CO/3-4*. UN. Retrieved November 7, 2020, from http://digitallibrary.un.org/record/677081

UN Committee on the Rights of the Child. (2010b). *Concluding observations: Nicaragua, October 20, 2010, CRC/C/NIC/CO/4*. UN. Retrieved November 7, 2020, from http://digitallibrary.un.org/record/692406

UN Committee on the Rights of the Child. (2012a). *Concluding observations: Bosnia and Herzegovina, November 29, 2012, CRC/C/BIH/CO/2-4*. UN. Retrieved November 7, 2020, from http://digitallibrary.un.org/record/739168

UN Committee on the Rights of the Child. (2012b). *Concluding observations: Myanmar, March 14, 2012, CRC/C/MMR/CO/3-4*. UN. Retrieved November 7, 2020, from http://digitallibrary.un.org/record/723342

UN Committee on the Rights of the Child. (2016a). *Concluding observations: New Zealand, October 21, 2016, CRC/C/NZL/CO/5*. UN. Retrieved November 6, 2020, from http://digitallibrary.un.org/record/856035

UN Committee on the Rights of the Child. (2016b). *General Comment No. 20 (2016) on the implementation of the rights of the child during adolescence, December 6, 2016, CRC/C/GC/20*. Retrieved October 12, 2020, from https://digitallibrary.un.org/record/855544?ln=en

UN Committee on the Rights of the Child. (2017a). *Concluding observations: Serbia, March 7, 2017, CRC/C/SRB/CO/2-3*. Retrieved 12 October 2020, from https://www.refworld.org/pdfid/58e76fc14.pdf

UN Committee on the Rights of the Child. (2017b). *Concluding observations: Lebanon, June 22, 2017, CRC/C/LBN/CO/4-5*. UN. Retrieved November 6, 2020, from http://digitallibrary.un.org/record/1311380

UN Committee on the Rights of the Child. (2017c). *Concluding observations: Tajikistan, October 25, 2017, CRC/C/TJK/CO/3-5*. UN. Retrieved November 7, 2020, from http://digitallibrary.un.org/record/1311398

UN General Assembly. (1987). *Declaration on Social and Legal Principles relating to the Protection and Welfare of Children, with special reference to Foster Placement and Adoption Nationally and Internationally, 1986, A/RES/41/85*. UN. Retrieved November 7, 2020, from http://digitallibrary.un.org/record/126399

UN High Commissioner for Refugees. (1994). *Refugee children: guidelines on protection and care, 1994, ST/HCR(09)/C536*. UNHCR. Retrieved November 7, 2020, from http://digitallibrary.un.org/record/167226

Vité, S., & Boéchat, H. (2008). *A commentary on the United Nations Convention on the Rights of the Child, Article 21: Adoption. A Commentary on the United Nations Convention on the Rights of the Child, Article 21: Adoption*. Brill Nijhoff. Retrieved November 7, 2020, from https://brill.com/view/title/11637

Open Access This chapter is licensed under the terms of the Creative Commons Attribution 4.0 International License (http://creativecommons.org/licenses/by/4.0/), which permits use, sharing, adaptation, distribution and reproduction in any medium or format, as long as you give appropriate credit to the original author(s) and the source, provide a link to the Creative Commons license and indicate if changes were made.

The images or other third party material in this chapter are included in the chapter's Creative Commons license, unless indicated otherwise in a credit line to the material. If material is not included in the chapter's Creative Commons license and your intended use is not permitted by statutory regulation or exceeds the permitted use, you will need to obtain permission directly from the copyright holder.

Chapter 20
Article 25: The Right to Periodic Review of Treatment and All Other Circumstances of Placement

Gerison Lansdown and Ziba Vaghri

> States Parties recognize the right of a child who has been placed by the competent authorities for the purposes of care, protection or treatment of his or her physical or mental health to a periodic review of the treatment provided to the child and all other circumstances relevant to his or her placement.

What Did Children Say?
'More in-depth screening process for foster parents to ensure the housing placement will be safe before the follow-up.' (*Western Europe/Other*)

'The point in my life at which I became a drug addict was about a year after I got on my Youth Agreement. Looking back on it, I think the reason why was because my social worker hadn't checked in with me in over 6 months, and I didn't have any other responsible adults in my life—no outreach workers, advocates, nothing.' (*Western Europe/Other*)

'Social workers have regularly visit and provide both mental and physical care.' (*Asia-Pacific*)

They should be taken to the hospital when they are ill and they must be given proper/great care. E.g., going to school wearing proper uniform, be given all they need at school and proper (diet). (*Africa*)

G. Lansdown (✉)
Carleton University, Ottawa, ON, Canada

Z. Vaghri
University of New Brunswick Saint John, Saint John, NB, Canada
e-mail: ziba.vaghri@unb.ca

© The Author(s) 2022
Z. Vaghri et al. (eds.), *Monitoring State Compliance with the UN Convention on the Rights of the Child*, Children's Well-Being: Indicators and Research 25,
https://doi.org/10.1007/978-3-030-84647-3_20

Overview

Article 25 introduces a right for children, who have been placed by competent authorities for the purposes of care, protection, or treatment, to have treatment of their physical or mental health reviewed on a periodic basis. An earlier draft included reference to emotional health which was subsequently removed, although in practice, the term mental health is probably sufficiently broad to encompass emotional health (UN Commission on Human Rights, 1986, para. 60; Office of the United Nations High Commissioner for Human Rights & Rädda barnen (Society: Sweden), 2007, p. 605).

Article 25 was introduced into the Convention in recognition of the need for children, placed away from home, to be subject to independent oversight. The foresight of the drafters in anticipating the imperative for such protection has been highlighted since, in light of the widespread recent evidence that, without oversight and scrutiny, children placed away from home can be exposed to significant neglect and abuse, while individuals and institutions all too frequently fail to protect children's best interests.[1] The aim of Article 25 is to provide a mechanism to protect children and ensure oversight into their circumstances by requiring regular reviews to ascertain, for example, the appropriateness of placement, the quality of care, the goals for treatment and planning, and the progress of treatment plans (Hodgkin et al., 2007, p. 379; UN General Assembly, 2010).

Article 25 specifies that the obligation to undertake reviews applies to all forms of placement in private and public care and treatment facilities provided that they are undertaken by competent authorities. States Parties have overall responsibility for determining the standards necessary to be acknowledged as a competent authority. Beyond these parameters, Article 25 is not prescriptive as to the nature, form, content, or frequency of those reviews. They are within the discretion of States Parties. However, the Alternative Care Guidelines do provide more detailed recommendations as to how reviews should be implemented (UN General Assembly, 2010). In addition, the Committee has recommended that States Parties apply the obligation to interpret Article 25 to cover both formal and informal placements in the widest possible range of settings (1999a, para. 21, 1999b, para. 22).

---

[1] See, for example, the Final Report of the Australian Royal Commission into Institutional Responses to Child Sexual Abuse, https://www.childabuseroyalcommission.gov.au/; *Hidden Suffering: Romania's Segregation and Abuse of Infants and Children with Disabilities* (Ahern & Rosenthal, 2006), and *The Pindown Experience and the Protection of Children: Report of the Staffordshire Child Care Enquiry* (Levy & Kahan, 1991).

General Principles

Article 2 No differentiation in the quality or the frequency of the review process should be made on the basis of any of the prohibited grounds for discrimination. States Parties must ensure that they take all possible measures to identify and eliminate discrimination when assessing the appropriateness of placements and the ongoing need for care or treatment of any child who is the subject of a review (UN Committee on the Rights of the Child, 2003, para. 12, 2007, para. 8, 2013; UN Human Rights Committee, 1989; United Nations, 2003, p. 147).

Article 3 Periodic reviews, whether they be legislative, administrative or judicial, must be guided by, and ensure primary and explicit consideration to, the principle of the best interests of the child in respect of the care, protection, and treatment being provided. This principle must be applied in respect of all decisions and actions taken, directly or indirectly (UN Committee on the Rights of the Child, 2003, para. 12). Article 3 (3) complements Article 25 in that it ensures monitoring of institutions, systems, and staff, while Article 25 focuses on the individual circumstances of the child.

Article 6 Both the process and the ultimate aim of the review must be to respect and preserve the dignity of the child and their rights, while promoting outcomes that support their optimum health and development.

Article 12(2) The right of the child to be heard, either directly or through a representative, in any judicial or administrative proceeding affecting them, applies equally to periodic reviews. The Committee has emphasised that children should be provided with information about when, where, and how any review is to take place, and be afforded the opportunity to be present and to express their views. Children who are not able or willing to express a view are entitled have a representative to act on their behalf. The proceedings must be accessible and child friendly (UN Committee on the Rights of the Child, 2009a, paras. 65–66).

Articles Related to or Linked to Article 25

Article 5 requires that the evolving capacities of the child are taken into account within the review process.

Article 16 recognises the child's right to privacy and dignity throughout the review process.

Article 19 establishes the right to protection including for children placed for care, protection or treatment, as such children can be particularly vulnerable to abuse.

Article 20 is closely linked to Article 25 as all children who are provided with care by the State are entitled to periodic reviews of their placement.

Article 22 addresses the right of children seeking asylum or considered a refugee and such children, placed by state in care, are entitled to periodic reviews in the same way as any other child.

Article 23 (1) focuses on the rights of children with disabilities, who are entitled to reviews of their care and treatment to address the efficacy and impact any institutional or other forms of care.

Article 39 provides that if a review process finds that the child's rights have been violated or neglected, there should be appropriate reparation, including compensation, and, where needed, measures introduced to promote physical and psychological recovery, rehabilitation and reintegration (UN Committee on the Rights of the Child, 2003, para. 24).

Relevant Instruments

UN Universal Declaration of Human Rights (1948), Articles 8 and 10

International Covenant on Civil and Political Rights (1966), Article 9

International Convention on the Elimination of All Forms of Racial Discrimination (1966), Article 6

UN Convention on the Elimination of All Forms of Discrimination against Women (1979), Article 2

UN Convention against Torture and Other Cruel, Inhuman or Degrading Treatment or Punishment (1984), Article 13

UN Convention on the Rights of Persons with Disabilities (2006), Article 12

Attributes

Attribute One: Scope and Authorisation of Periodic Reviews

Despite the more restrictive wording of Article 25 as applying specifically to those children placed for purposes of care, protection, or treatment, the Committee, in its earlier reporting guidelines, interpreted the obligations under Article 25 to extend to the widest possible range of care environments for children, including, for example, those placed as a consequence of homelessness, abandonment, asylum or refugee status, children in institutional care, and those in conflict with the law (1996). Certainly, it imposes an obligation on States Parties to ensure that any child needing a placement, without which they would suffer from a lack of care, protection, or physical or mental health treatment, must have their situation reviewed on a periodical basis.

Furthermore, the wording of Article 25 states that it applies only to those placements that have been made by a competent authority. Both public and private bodies can be recognised as competent authorities for this purpose. During the drafting of the Convention, a decision was made to remove reference to placement 'with competent State authorities,' presumably in acknowledgement that the provision should apply more widely to include private bodies (UN Commission on Human Rights, 1986, para. 60; Office of the United Nations High Commissioner for Human Rights & Rädda barnen (Society: Sweden), 2007). However, the state should establish the legal standards for determining whether to grant an authority the legal competency to place a child, and the associated monitoring of compliance with those standards (UN General Assembly, 2010, paras. 23, 55). Despite the clear implication in the text of Article 25 that it applies only to children placed by competent authorities, the Committee has, at times, recommended to States Parties that they should introduce review mechanisms for children placed in informal forms of alternative care [2]

Attribute Two: Periodicity and Content of Reviews of the Placement

Article 25 does not define how frequently reviews should take place. The Alternative Care Guidelines suggest that a thorough review should be undertaken at least every 3 months (UN General Assembly, 2010, para. 67). However, the nature of the placement, its duration, and the needs of the children concerned will vary widely and will necessarily influence the periodicity with which they need to take place. The Committee has affirmed this approach arguing for decisions to be made on a case-by-case basis (2005, para. 667). Factors determining the frequency of reviews can include the individual circumstances of the child, and the importance of assessing both the necessity and the suitability of the placement (Cantwell et al., 2012).

No guidance is given by Article 25 about the content of the review process and by whom it should be undertaken. Tobin and Luke suggest that an effective system of review must ensure independent oversight of the institution, organisation, or individual with whom the child is placed, by individuals suitably qualified to perform the review (2019, p. 980). In terms of the content of the review, the wording of Article 25 makes clear that it needs to address not only the treatment of the child but also 'all other circumstances relevant to his or her placement.'

The Alternative Care Guidelines propose that reviews should address 'the appropriateness of his/her care and treatment, taking into account his or her family environment and the adequacy and necessity of the current placement' (UN General Assembly, 2010, para. 67). Persons undertaking the review must consider if the placement is reasonable, in terms of providing care, protection, or treatment, and whether there are other approaches that could avoid the need for alternative care. They must also consider the suitability of the placement in terms of

---

[2] See, for example, concluding observations for Guinea (1999a, para. 21) and Qatar (2009b, para. 46).

its capacity to ensure respect for the rights of the child being cared for. Thus, consideration should be given to the quality of the environment, the extent to which the child's needs are being met, the provision of education, access to medical treatment as necessary, opportunities for play and recreation, and respect for the child's religion, culture and language. The review should also give consideration to the long-term needs of the child, with consideration given to the reintegration with their family, where appropriate, or to permanent placements to avoid frequent changes of settings (UN Committee on the Rights of the Child, 2006, para. 39, 2012, para. 47(e)).

Attribute Three: Accountability and Transparency

The Committee has highlighted that 'children's special and dependent status creates difficulties for them in pursuing remedies for breaches of their rights' (2003, para. 24). This vulnerability lends significance to the value and necessity for periodic reviews, and the need for the review process to be transparent, inclusive, and accountable. The Alternative Care Guidelines recommend that children should be involved, as well as all persons involved in the child's life, including parents, legal guardians, and potential foster carers and other caregivers (UN General Assembly, 2010, para. 6). While Article 12 does not insist that the child's views are determinative, the Committee has strongly recommended that just listening to the child is insufficient: the views of the child have to be seriously considered in all cases where when the child is capable of forming her or his own views (2009a, para. 28). Equally, it must be recognised that the child's participation in the review process is a right, not an obligation. They should be provided with information about the review process, its purpose, who will be participating, location, and timing but they are entitled to choose to exclude themselves from the process, and should not be put under any pressure to take part against their wishes (UN Committee on the Rights of the Child, 2009a, para. 16). In all circumstances, they should be fully informed about the outcomes of the review.

Once a review has taken place, its findings must be fully implemented. However, if a child, or representative acting on the child's behalf, is dissatisfied with the outcome of the review, the failure to act on the findings, or, indeed, a failure to conduct a review, there should be a complaints mechanism in place through which the child can seek redress. Complaints mechanisms must be child friendly, expeditious with timely remedies, and offer a confidential process to encourage children to share their views and wishes and have their concerns appropriately resolved (UN Committee on the Rights of the Child, 2003, para. 24).

References

Ahern, I., & Rosenthal, E. (2006). *Hidden suffering: Romania's segregation and abuse of infants and children with disabilities*. Mental Disability Rights International. https://hsrc.himmelfarb.gwu.edu/books/196/

Cantwell, N., Davidson, J., Elsley, S., Milligan, I., & Quinn, N. (2012). *Moving Forward: Implementing the 'Guidelines for the Alternative Care of Children'*. The Centre for Excellence for Looked After Children in Scotland. https://www.alternativecareguidelines.org/MovingForward/tabid/2798/language/en-GB/Default.aspx

Hodgkin, R., Newell, P., & UNICEF. (2007). *Implementation handbook for the Convention on the Rights of the Child* (3rd ed.). UNICEF. Retrieved September 21, 2020, from https://digitallibrary.un.org/record/620060?ln=en

Levy, A., & Kahan, B. (1991). *The pindown experience and the protection of children: The report of the Staffordshire Child Care Inquiry 1990*. Staffordshire County Council.

Office of the United Nations High Commissioner for Human Rights, & Rädda barnen (Society: Sweden). (2007). *Legislative history of the Convention on the Rights of the Child*. United Nations. https://digitallibrary.un.org/record/602462?ln=en

Tobin, J., & Luke, E. (2019). Article 25: The right to periodic review. In J. Tobin (Ed.), *The UN Convention on the Rights of the Child: A commentary* (pp. 970–985). Oxford University Press.

UN Commission on Human Rights. (1986). *Report of the working group on a Draft Convention on the Rights of the Child, 1986, E/CN.4/1986/39*. UN. Retrieved October 23, 2020, from http://digitallibrary.un.org/record/121490

UN Committee on the Rights of the Child. (1996). *General Guidelines regarding the form and contents of periodic reports to be submitted by states parties under article 44, paragraph 1 (b) of the Convention, November 20, 1996, CRC/C/58*. Retrieved October 12, 2020, from https://digitallibrary.un.org/record/230051?ln=en

UN Committee on the Rights of the Child. (1999a). *Concluding observations: Guinea, May 10, 1999, CRC/C/15/Add.100*. UN. Retrieved November 8, 2020, from http://digitallibrary.un.org/record/275070

UN Committee on the Rights of the Child. (1999b). *Concluding observations: Chad, August 24, 1999, CRC/C/15/Add.107*. UN. Retrieved November 8, 2020, from http://digitallibrary.un.org/record/286863

UN Committee on the Rights of the Child. (2003). *General Comment No. 5 (2003) General measures of implementation of the Convention on the Rights of the Child (arts. 4, 42 and 44, para. 6), November 27, 2003, CRC/GC/2003/5*. Retrieved October 12, 2020, from https://digitallibrary.un.org/record/513415?ln=en

UN Committee on the Rights of the Child. (2005). *Day of General Discussion: Children Without Parental Care*. UN. Retrieved November 6, 2020, from https://www.ohchr.org/EN/HRBodies/CRC/Pages/DiscussionDays.aspx

UN Committee on the Rights of the Child. (2006). *Concluding observations: Azerbaijan, March 17, 2006, CRC/C/AZE/CO/2*. Retrieved October 11, 2020, from https://digitallibrary.un.org/record/575654?ln=en

UN Committee on the Rights of the Child. (2007). *General Comment No. 9 (2006) The rights of children with disabilities, November 13, 2007, CRC/C/GC/9*. Retrieved October 12, 2020, from https://digitallibrary.un.org/record/593891?ln=en

UN Committee on the Rights of the Child. (2009a). *General Comment No. 12 (2009) The right of the child to be heard, July 20, 2009, CRC/C/GC/12*. Retrieved October 12, 2020, from https://digitallibrary.un.org/record/671444?ln=en

UN Committee on the Rights of the Child. (2009b). *Concluding observations: Qatar, October 14, 2009, CRC/C/QAT/CO/2*. UN. Retrieved November 8, 2020, from http://digitallibrary.un.org/record/669131

UN Committee on the Rights of the Child. (2012). *Concluding observations: Viet Nam, August 22, 2012, CRC/C/VNM/CO/3-4*. UN. Retrieved November 8, 2020, from http://digitallibrary.un.org/record/732970

UN Committee on the Rights of the Child. (2013). *General Comment No. 14 (2013) On the right of the child to have his or her best interests taken as a primary consideration (art. 3, para. 1), May 29, 2013, CRC/C/GC/14*. Retrieved October 12, 2020, from https://digitallibrary.un.org/record/778523?ln=en

UN General Assembly. (2010). *Guidelines for the alternative care of children, 2010, A/RES/64/142*. https://digitallibrary.un.org/record/673583?ln=en

UN Human Rights Committee. (1989). *CCPR General Comment No. 18 (1989) Non-discrimination, November 21, 1989, CCPR/C/21/Rev.1/Add.1*. https://digitallibrary.un.org/record/84170?ln=en

United Nations. (2003). *Compilation of General Comments and General Recommendations adopted by human rights treaty bodies, HRI/GEN/1/Rev. 6*. UN. Retrieved April 19, 2020, from https://digitallibrary.un.org/record/502688?ln=en

Open Access This chapter is licensed under the terms of the Creative Commons Attribution 4.0 International License (http://creativecommons.org/licenses/by/4.0/), which permits use, sharing, adaptation, distribution and reproduction in any medium or format, as long as you give appropriate credit to the original author(s) and the source, provide a link to the Creative Commons license and indicate if changes were made.

The images or other third party material in this chapter are included in the chapter's Creative Commons license, unless indicated otherwise in a credit line to the material. If material is not included in the chapter's Creative Commons license and your intended use is not permitted by statutory regulation or exceeds the permitted use, you will need to obtain permission directly from the copyright holder.

Part IV
Disability, Health, and Welfare Rights

Articles 23, 24, 26, 27 and 33

Introduction

This part addresses a core set of the economic and social rights relating to health and welfare, including disability, health, incorporating protection from drug misuse, an adequate standard of living, and social security.

Article 23 represented a breakthrough in recognition of the rights of children with disabilities. It was a unique provision in a human rights treaty and its inclusion in the Convention on the Rights of the Child (the Convention) establishes emphatically that children with disabilities are rights holders, challenging the traditional welfare model that constructs them as objects of pity or passive recipients of care and protection. Its focus on the goals of ensuring dignity, self-reliance, and participation in the community for children with disabilities affords them visibility and inclusion. Coupled with the explicit demand in Article 2 that disability is a ground for protection against discrimination, Article 23 provides recognition of children with disabilities as entitled to equal rights and treatment with all other children. It also elaborates a broad range of measures required by States Parties to give effect to those goals, including a commitment to international cooperation.

Article 24, the right to health, builds on earlier provisions in the International Covenant on Economic, Social and Cultural Rights. It asserts that every child has the right to the highest attainable standard of health and access to appropriate health services. The consequent obligations on States Parties reiterate those in the Covenant but include an additional focus on addressing disease and malnutrition, through provision of food and clean drinking water, emphasise the importance of health education and family planning services, and add an obligation to adopt measures that abolish harmful traditional practices. Moreover, by introducing a further health perspective, Article 33 represents an innovative provision introducing obligations to protect children from illicit use of narcotic drugs. Overall, the Committee on the Rights of the Child (the Committee) has provided significant guidance to States

Parties on the implementation of health rights, through its Concluding Observations and General Comments, including on Article 24 itself and on migration, adolescence, HIV/AIDs, and harmful practices.

Finally, Articles 26 and 27 address issues relating to children's living standards and social security. Both articles recognise the child as a subject of rights who cannot simply be subsumed within the family. Specific recognition must be afforded to their right of an adequate standard of living for their full development and to any necessary social security benefits to support that goal. While the parents or other caregivers are recognised as having primary responsibility for the provision of care of their children, Articles 26 and 27 place explicit obligations on States Parties to support parents in that role.

Together these articles provide a framework of provision for children to secure and protect their best interests and optimum development. The obligations on States Parties in respect of economic and social rights is that they undertake measures to the 'maximum extent of their available resources, and where needed, within the framework of international co-operation.' This wording mirrors that used by the International Covenant and is included in recognition of the resource constraints faced by some States Parties in guaranteeing certain rights. However, the Committee has made clear that this wording does not imply that these rights are merely aspirational and that their implementation can be deferred. Rather, it affirms that they do impose an immediate obligation and that States Parties must introduce targeted measures as expeditiously and effectively as possible towards the full realisation of these rights (UN Committee on the Rights of the Child 2007).

Regardless of progressive realisation, States Parties have minimum core obligations that must be met at all times. The Committee also emphasises that when States Parties ratify the Convention, they undertake obligations not only to implement it within their jurisdiction, but also to support global implementation through development cooperation (2003, para. 7).

References

UN Committee on the Rights of the Child. (2003). General Comment No. 5 (2003) General measures of implementation of the Convention on the Rights of the Child (arts. 4, 42 and 44, para. 6), November 27, 2003, CRC/GC/2003/5. https://digitallibrary.un.org/record/513415?ln=en. Accessed 12 October 2020

UN Committee on the Rights of the Child. (2007). Day of General Discussion: Resources for the Rights of the Child - Responsibility of States. UN. https://www.ohchr.org/EN/HRBodies/CRC/Pages/DiscussionDays.aspx. Accessed 19 December 2020

Chapter 21
Article 23: The Rights of Children with Disabilities

Gerison Lansdown

1. States Parties recognize that a mentally or physically disabled child should enjoy a full and decent life, in conditions which ensure dignity, promote self-reliance and facilitate the child's active participation in the community.
2. States Parties recognize the right of the disabled child to special care and shall encourage and ensure the extension, subject to available resources, to the eligible child and those responsible for his or her care, of assistance for which application is made and which is appropriate to the child's condition and to the circumstances of the parents or others caring for the child.
3. Recognizing the special needs of a disabled child, assistance extended in accordance with paragraph 2 of the present article shall be provided free of charge, whenever possible, taking into account the financial resources of the parents or others caring for the child, and shall be designed to ensure that the disabled child has effective access to and receives education, training, health care services, rehabilitation services, preparation for employment and recreation opportunities in a manner conducive to the child's achieving the fullest possible social integration and individual development, including his or her cultural and spiritual development
4. States Parties shall promote, in the spirit of international cooperation, the exchange of appropriate information in the field of preventive health care and of medical, psychological and functional treatment of disabled children, including dissemination of and access to information concerning methods of rehabilitation, education and vocational services, with the aim

(continued)

G. Lansdown (✉)
Carleton University, Ottawa, ON, Canada

© The Author(s) 2022
Z. Vaghri et al. (eds.), *Monitoring State Compliance with the UN Convention on the Rights of the Child*, Children's Well-Being: Indicators and Research 25, https://doi.org/10.1007/978-3-030-84647-3_21

of enabling States Parties to improve their capabilities and skills and to widen their experience in these areas. In this regard, particular account shall be taken of the needs of developing countries.

What Did Children Say?
'Existence of laws such as anti-discrimination law would protect children with disabilities from discrimination. Some children with disabilities have been abused by other people.' (Asia-Pacific)

'Government should give free assistive devices. Our [district] sometimes gives away assistive devices during medical missions only and upon request from the Department of Health. Sometimes patients in public hospitals have to pay for these assistive devices.' (Asia-Pacific)

'Provision of free equipment and services e.g., Braille textbooks, wheelchairs, hearing aids, cane and glasses.' (Latin America/Caribbean)

Overview

The struggle for recognition of the equal rights of persons with disabilities, including children, dates back many decades. Although United Nations declarations in the 1970s affirmed equal civil and political rights, [1] it was not until the adoption of the Convention, in 1989, that a reference to disability rights was formally embodied in a human rights treaty. Article 2 of the Convention includes reference to disability as a ground for protection from discrimination, and Article 23 provides a dedicated focus on the rights of children with disabilities.

The initial draft presented to the Working Group in 1979 comprised a brief text simply affording special treatment, education, and care to children who are 'physically, mentally or socially handicapped' (Office of the United Nations High Commissioner for Human Rights & Rädda Barnen (Society: Sweden), 2007, p. 564). Subsequent discussion highlighted the importance of affirming the equal rights of children with disabilities, and thereby the right to the services and provisions necessary for them to ensure the enjoyment of those rights. The Working Group also debated the balance of responsibility for care of children with disabilities between the parents and the state. It concluded that, although parents continue to have primary responsibilities, the state carries the primary obligation for the financial

---

[1] See, for example, the 1971 Declaration on the Rights of Mentally Retarded Persons and the 1974 Declaration on the Rights of Disabled Persons. The 1948 Universal Declaration of Human Rights, in article 25, included reference to the right to security in the context of unemployment, sickness, or disability.

burden of services, which must be made available for children with disabilities free of charge wherever possible.

The final text of Article 23 seeks to achieve several objectives:

- to afford recognition that children with disabilities should be able to enjoy a decent life with full participation in the community
- to recognise their right to special services necessitated by virtue of their disability
- to ensure that children with disabilities have access to education, health care, rehabilitation, preparation for employment and recreation, free of charge subject to the financial resources of parents, to enable them to achieve the fullest possible integration and development
- to promote international cooperation.

It is important, however, when addressing the rights of children with disabilities, that States Parties consider their rights in respect of the Convention in its entirety, and not simply in respect of Article 23 (UN Committee on the Rights of the Child, 2007a, para. 5).

Since the adoption of the Convention, the rights of persons with disabilities, including children, have subsequently been significantly enhanced beyond the provisions of the Convention, with the elaboration of the Standard Rules for the Equalisation of Opportunities for Persons with Disabilities in 1993, and, most importantly, with the adoption by the United Nations General Assembly in 2006 of the Convention on the Rights of Persons with Disabilities (CRPD).

This comprehensive treaty, which includes a dedicated article on children with disabilities, does apply equally and in its entirety to children, and represents a paradigm shift in the attitudes and treatment of persons with disabilities, from seeing them as objects of charity to subjects of rights. It recognises that persons with disabilities include those 'who have long-term physical, mental, intellectual or sensory impairments which in interaction with various barriers may hinder their full and effective participation in society on an equal basis with others' (UN General Assembly, 2006, Article 1). Accordingly, whereas Article 23 identifies the obligation to provide services to address and help mitigate exclusion as a consequence of children's disabilities, the CRPD addresses the need to remove the barriers that serve to deny those with disabilities from equal and inclusive participation without discrimination. This human rights-based approach has been adopted and reinforced by the Committee, which has also consistently recommended ratification and implementation of the CRPD (2007a, para. 5, 2009, para. 54, 2010, para. 51). However, the continued inclusion of Article 23 within the health and welfare cluster of the reporting guidelines maintains its characterisation as a medical or welfare issue rather than an issue of discrimination (UN Committee on the Rights of the Child, 2005a).

It is worth noting that language has changed between the drafting of the two treaties. For example, the Convention uses the term 'special care' which has been the subject of much subsequent criticism in that it perpetuates a welfare or individualised approach to disability. The CRPD, in contrast, speaks of 'specialist or support services,' language that has now been widely adopted by the Committee (Byrne,

2019, p. 871). The Convention also refers to 'integration' whereas the CRPD demands 'inclusion.' While the former can simply mean placing children with disabilities within a mainstream environment, with the onus on them to adapt, the latter demands that the environment itself is adapted to become meaningfully inclusive (UN Committee on the Rights of Persons with Disabilities, 2016, para. 11), and accordingly, is now generally the preferred term employed by the Committee.

General Principles

Article 2 Article 2 represents the first ever inclusion of disability as a ground for protection against disability in a human rights treaty. The Committee highlights the vulnerability of children with disabilities to direct and indirect discrimination and urges States Parties to legislate disability as a forbidden ground for discrimination in their constitutions or within wider non-discrimination legislation. The Committee also presses for effective and accessible remedies for violations, and campaigns to raise awareness of discrimination (2005b, para. 53, 2007b, para. 9). It is important to recognise that the obligation to promote the dignity of children with disabilities demands that they are not subjected to discrimination (Byrne, 2019, p. 865).

Article 3 The obligation to ensure that the best interests of children are taken as a primary consideration extends to public or private welfare institutions, including those that provide services for children with disabilities (UN Committee on the Rights of the Child, 2013a). All decisions concerning children with disabilities must be guided by this principle, in line with the interpretation provided by the Committee in its General Comment on best interests.

Article 6 Children with disabilities have an equal right to life and optimum development with all other children, but discrimination can serve to reduce survival prospects and quality of life (UN Committee on the Rights of the Child, 2006, para. 11 (b) (ii)). Accordingly, practices that serve to deny them these rights, for example abandonment, infanticide, and discrimination in the provision of medical treatment, need to be addressed (UN Committee on the Rights of the Child, 2007a, para. 31; UN General Assembly, 2006 Article 25, para (f)). In addition, the UN Study on Violence has identified children with disabilities as a group of children especially vulnerable to violence (Pinheiro, 2006), which will necessarily impede their optimum development. And, also relevant to the right to life and optimum development, the Committee has expressed deep concern about the prevailing practice of forced sterilisation of girls with disabilities and urged States Parties to prohibit this practice. Early assessment and identification are imperative if children with disabilities are to achieve their optimum development (UN Committee on the Rights of the Child, 2007a, paras. 56–57; UN General Assembly, 2006 Article 23, para 3).

Article 12 Children with disabilities are commonly excluded from opportunities to contribute to decisions that affect their lives. The Committee emphasises the obligation on States Parties to provide the necessary support to children with disabilities to enable them to express their views, and to provide training for parents and professionals on promoting and respecting the evolving capacities of children with disabilities to take increasing responsibilities for decision-making in their lives (2007a, para. 32). The Committee encourages advocacy at the national and local levels to promote the effective participation of children with disabilities in matters that affect them.[2] The CRPD re-asserts Article 12 of the Convention with regard to children with disabilities and demands that this is ensured on an equal basis with other children and that they are provided with disability and age-appropriate assistance to realise that right (UN General Assembly, 2006 Article 7, para 3). It also demands that children with disabilities, through their representative organisations, are consulted when legislation and policies affecting them are being developed and implemented (UN General Assembly, 2006, Article 4, para 3).

Articles Related or Linked to Article 23

As children with disabilities have the same rights as other children, all the articles in the Convention are of potential relevance but of particular significance are:

- **Article 5**, as the evolving capacities of children with disabilities are commonly disregarded and they are denied opportunities to take increasing responsibility for decision-making in their own lives (Byrne, 2012, p. 419).
- **Article 7**, since children with disabilities are more likely than other children not to be registered at birth.
- **Article 8**, as institutionalisation, a practice more common for children with disabilities, can result in loss of family relations and identity.
- **Article 9**, as children with disabilities are more likely to be separated from their parents and placed in institutions.
- **Article 18**, since the requirement on States Parties to provide support for families to facilitate community-based care has added significance for children with disabilities to reduce vulnerability to institutional placement.
- **Articles 19 and 34**, as children with disabilities are disproportionately vulnerable to physical, sexual and emotional violence, and when they do experience violence, it is more likely to go unreported and unchallenged (UN Secretary General, 2011, paras. 45–49).
- **Article 20**, since disproportionate numbers of children with disabilities are deprived of a family environment and placed in the care of the state.

---

[2] See, for example, concluding observations for Chile (2015, para. 56).

- **Article 21**, as although children with disabilities are more likely to be placed in care, they are less likely than other children to be placed for adoption and thereby have the opportunity for family-based care.
- **Article 24**, since many children with disabilities are denied equal rights to health care treatments, as a result of discriminatory quality of life assessments, lack of resources, information, transport, or appropriately targeted programmes (UN Committee on the Rights of the Child, 2007b, para. 51).
- **Article 25**, as it is of particular importance that periodic reviews are undertaken for children with disabilities placed in the care of the state, and that these reviews are made accessible and safe through the provision of disability-appropriate information and communication.
- **Articles 26 and 27**, since multiple factors contribute to families of children with disabilities being particularly likely to be living in poverty, including additional costs associated with the disability, and discrimination in the provision of health insurance schemes (UN General Assembly, 2006, Article 28; UN Secretary General, 2011, paras. 41–43).
- **Articles 28 and 29**, as children with disabilities are entitled to education based on equality of opportunity.
- **Article 31**, since the Committee draws attention to the significant barriers impeding the right to play and recreation for children with disabilities, and welcomes Article 30 of the CRPD, requiring States Parties to ensure that children with disabilities have equal access with other children to participate in play, recreation, sporting and leisure activities including in the mainstream system (UN Committee on the Rights of the Child, 2013b, para. 50).
- **Articles 37 and 40**, as children with disabilities, in particular those with psychosocial and intellectual impairments, may be particularly vulnerable within the juvenile justice system, with a lack of appropriate provision for their needs (UN Committee on the Rights of the Child, 2007b, para. 4 (a), 2019).

Relevant Instruments

UN Universal Declaration of Human Rights (1948), Article 25
  UN Declaration on the Rights of Mentally Retarded persons (1971)
  UN Declaration on the Rights of Disabled Persons (1975)
  UN World Programme of Action Concerning Disabled Persons (1982)
  UN Standard Rules on the Equalization of Opportunities for Persons with Disabilities (1993)
  UN Convention on the Rights of Persons with Disabilities (2006), with particular reference to Article 7 although the Convention as a whole extends to children with disabilities

Attributes

Attribute One: Inclusive Environments to Promote Dignity, Independence, and Participation

Paragraph 1 of Article 23 demands that States Parties recognise that children with disabilities should have full and decent lives in conditions that ensure dignity, promote self-reliance, and facilitate participation. The Committee emphasises that measures taken by States Parties, in respect of realising the rights of children with disabilities, must be directed to this goal (2007a, para. 11). Accordingly, it consistently affirms the need for States Parties to adopt a human rights-based model of disability with comprehensive, cross-departmental strategies to ensure legislation, policies, services, and funding are directed towards the fullest possible inclusion. This would apply, for example, in respect of the rights to health, education, play and recreation, protection from violence, family-based alternative care, and an adequate standard of living.[3]

The CRPD also affirms that any social protection measure must be provided based on equality of opportunity and without discrimination. Priority investment, in particular, is required to introduce inclusive educational environments and bring an end to the practice of institutionalisation of children with disabilities (UN Committee on the Rights of Persons with Disabilities, 2016, paras. 64, 67–68). Such developments should be coordinated across government and supported at the highest level. Significantly, in the children's consultation for General Comment no. 19 on public expenditure, the Committee highlighted the need for sufficient funding for all children and demanded that 'children with special needs' should not be forgotten (2016, para. 8).

Action by States Parties is also needed to address the wider economic, cultural, social, legal, attitudinal, physical, and communication barriers elaborated in the CRPD that must be removed in order to achieve effective inclusion, participation, and respect for the dignity of the child. Such action includes measures in respect of non-discrimination, awareness-raising, accessibility, equal recognition before the law, access to justice, liberty and security, respect for personal and mental integrity, mobility, privacy, respect for home and the family, and participation in political, public and cultural life.[4]

---

[3] Convention on the Rights of the Child, Article 23, paragraph 3. See also, for example, concluding observations for Spain (2018, para. 31) and Guatemala (2017, para. 30), CRC/C/GTM/CO/5-6, 2018, para 30.

[4] See CRPD Articles 8, 9, 12, 13, 17, 20, 22, 23, 29 and 30 (UN General Assembly, 2006); and also Convention on the Rights of the Child General Comment no. 9, The rights of children with disabilities (UN Committee on the Rights of the Child, 2007a, para. 5).

Attribute Two: Access to Targeted Assistance and Services

In addition to the removal of barriers to ensure the creation of inclusive environments, Article 23 requires, in paragraph 2, that States Parties recognise the right of children with disabilities to targeted care and services appropriate to their condition and to the circumstances of the parents or other carers. Such services should be designed to ensure the realisation of the children's rights and optimum inclusion, and can include, for example, early assessment, identification and treatment programmes, alternative family care provision for children unable to be cared for at home, respite care, social security allowances, targeted measures to ensure birth registration, aids and adaptation, and access to assistive technologies (UN Committee on the Rights of the Child, 2007a, paras. 35–36, 45–46, 51–52, 56–57, 2014, para. 45). The Committee has stressed that, in accordance with paragraph 3 of Article 23, provision of these services and assistance should be provided free of charge whenever possible and should be recognised as a matter of high priority (2007a, para. 14). The CRPD insists that within an inclusive education system, from which children with disabilities must not be excluded due to disability, they must also be provided with reasonable accommodation and individualised support measures to enable them to maximise their educational opportunities (UN General Assembly, 2006, Article 28, para 1 and 2 (a), (c), and (d)).

Attribute Three: International Cooperation

States Parties have an obligation to cooperate with one another in the promotion of respect for human rights, including the rights of the child (UN Committee on the Rights of the Child, 2016, para. 39). Article 23, paragraph 4, requires that States Parties promote international cooperation and information exchange in respect of children with disabilities, obligations that, the Committee notes, have generally been poorly implemented (2007a, para. 15). The CRPD also affirms the importance of international cooperation between relevant international and national organisations and civil society, in particular organisations of persons with disabilities to support capacity-building research and scientific knowledge, and technical assistance (UN General Assembly, 2006, Article 32).

International cooperation in respect of disability has two core priorities. First, it needs to support measures to address the causes of disability, for example, diseases, poverty, malnutrition, accidents, child labour, hazardous environments, and armed conflict. In this regard, States Parties need to seek technical and financial assistance, including from UN agencies, as well as, for example, promoting cooperation in the removal of landmines and unexploded ordnance (UN Committee on the Rights of the Child, 2007a, paras. 23, 53–55). Second, it must be directed to the realisation of the rights of children with disabilities. The Committee encourages States Parties to ensure that in the framework of bilateral or multilateral assistance, particular attention is paid to children with disabilities. Such assistance should facilitate the exchange and support of best possible knowledge and involve development and implementation of special programmes to promote inclusion, with dedicated budgets attached. It recommends that the international community adopt innovative approaches to raising funds, including resources from governments and the private sector (UN Committee on the Rights of the Child, 2007a, paras. 22–23). It also encourages knowledge exchange, particularly in respect of medical knowledge and good practice, early assessment and identification, and support for families. International assistance providing financial support for all forms of segregated residential mental health institutions and services should be ended (UN Human Rights Council, 2017, para. 94(a)).

References

Byrne, B. (2012). Minding the Gap? Children with Disabilities and the United Nations Convention on the Rights of Persons with Disabilities. In M. Freeman (Ed.), *Law and childhood studies: Current legal issues volume 14*. Oxford University Press. Retrieved November 12, 2020, from https://oxford.universitypressscholarship.com/view/10.1093/acprof:oso/9780199652501.001.0001/acprof-9780199652501

Byrne, B. (2019). Article 23: Children with Disabilities. In J. Tobin (Ed.), *The UN Convention on the Rights of the Child: A commentary* (pp. 856–901). Oxford University Press.

de M. S. Pinheiro, P. S. (2006). *Report of the Independent Expert for the United Nations Study on Violence against Children, A/61/299*. UN. Retrieved November 12, 2020, from http://digitallibrary.un.org/record/584299

Office of the United Nations High Commissioner for Human Rights & Rädda Barnen (Society: Sweden). (2007). *Legislative history of the Convention on the Rights of the Child*. United Nations. https://digitallibrary.un.org/record/602462?ln=en

UN Committee on the Rights of Persons with Disabilities. (2016). *CRPD General Comment No. 4 (2016) on the right to inclusive education, CRPD/C/GC/4*. UN. Retrieved November 12, 2020, from http://digitallibrary.un.org/record/1313836

UN Committee on the Rights of the Child. (2005a). *General Guidelines regarding the form and content of periodic reports to be submitted by States parties under article 44, paragraph 1 (b) of the Convention, June 3, 2005, CRC/C/58/Rev.1*. Retrieved October 12, 2020, from https://digitallibrary.un.org/record/575788?ln=en

UN Committee on the Rights of the Child. (2005b). *Concluding observations: Algeria, October 12, 2005, CRC/C/15/Add.269*. Retrieved October 24, 2020, from https://digitallibrary.un.org/record/570473?ln=en

UN Committee on the Rights of the Child. (2006). *General Comment No. 7 (2005) Implementing child rights in early childhood, September 20, 2006, CRC/C/GC/7/Rev.1*. Retrieved October 12, 2020, from https://digitallibrary.un.org/record/584854?ln=en

UN Committee on the Rights of the Child. (2007a). *General Comment No. 9 (2006) The rights of children with disabilities, November 13, 2007, CRC/C/GC/9*. Retrieved October 12, 2020, from https://digitallibrary.un.org/record/593891?ln=en

UN Committee on the Rights of the Child. (2007b). *General Comment No. 10 (2007) Children's rights in juvenile justice, April 25, 2007, CRC/C/GC/10*. Retrieved October 12, 2020, from https://digitallibrary.un.org/record/599395?ln=en

UN Committee on the Rights of the Child. (2009). *Concluding observations: Philippines, October 22, 2009, CRC/C/PHL/CO/3-4*. UN. Retrieved November 6, 2020, from http://digitallibrary.un.org/record/669130

UN Committee on the Rights of the Child. (2010). *Concluding observations: Tajikistan, February 5, 2010, CRC/C/TJK/CO/2*. UN. Retrieved November, 12 2020, from http://digitallibrary.un.org/record/676495

UN Committee on the Rights of the Child. (2013a). *General Comment No. 14 (2013) On the right of the child to have his or her best interests taken as a primary consideration (art. 3, para. 1), May 29, 2013, CRC/C/GC/14*. Retrieved October 12, 2020, from https://digitallibrary.un.org/record/778523?ln=en

UN Committee on the Rights of the Child. (2013b). *General Comment No. 17 (2013) on the right of the child to rest, leisure, play, recreational activities, cultural life and the arts (art. 31), April 17, 2013, CRC/C/GC/17*. Retrieved October 12, 2020, from https://digitallibrary.un.org/record/778539?ln=en

UN Committee on the Rights of the Child. (2014). *Concluding observations: Hungary, October 14, 2014, CRC/C/HUN/CO/3-5*. Retrieved October 11, 2020, from https://digitallibrary.un.org/record/793888?ln=en

UN Committee on the Rights of the Child. (2015). *Concluding observations: Chile, October 30, 2015, CRC/C/CHL/CO/4-5*. UN. Retrieved November 12, 2020, from http://digitallibrary.un.org/record/814421

UN Committee on the Rights of the Child. (2016). *General Comment No. 19 (2016) on public budgeting for the realization of children's rights (art.4), CRC/C/GC/19*. UN. Retrieved November 12, 2020, from http://digitallibrary.un.org/record/838730

UN Committee on the Rights of the Child. (2017). *Concluding observations: Guatemala, February 28, 2017, CRC/C/GTM/5-6*. Retrieved October 12, 2020, from https://digitallibrary.un.org/record/536574?ln=en

UN Committee on the Rights of the Child. (2018). *Concluding observations: Spain, March 5, 2018, CRC/C/ESP/CO/5-6*. Retrieved October 11, 2020, from https://digitallibrary.un.org/record/1476613?ln=en

UN Committee on the Rights of the Child. (2019). *General comment No. 24 (2019) on children's rights in the child justice system, CRC/C/GC/24*. Retrieved November 29, 2020, from https://tbinternet.ohchr.org/_layouts/15/treatybodyexternal/Download.aspx?symbolno=CRC%2fC%2fGC%2f24&Lang=en

UN General Assembly. (2006). *Convention on the rights of persons with disabilities, 2006, A/RES/61/106*. Retrieved May 3, 2020, from https://digitallibrary.un.org/record/588742?ln=en

UN Human Rights Council. (2017). *Report of the special rapporteur on the right of everyone to the enjoyment of the highest attainable standard of physical and mental health, A/HRC/35/21*. UN. Retrieved November 12, 2020, from http://digitallibrary.un.org/record/1298436

UN Secretary General. (2011). *Status of the Convention on the Rights of the Child: Report of the Secretary-General, A/66/230*. UN. Retrieved November 12, 2020, from http://digitallibrary.un.org/record/709902

Open Access This chapter is licensed under the terms of the Creative Commons Attribution 4.0 International License (http://creativecommons.org/licenses/by/4.0/), which permits use, sharing, adaptation, distribution and reproduction in any medium or format, as long as you give appropriate credit to the original author(s) and the source, provide a link to the Creative Commons license and indicate if changes were made.

The images or other third party material in this chapter are included in the chapter's Creative Commons license, unless indicated otherwise in a credit line to the material. If material is not included in the chapter's Creative Commons license and your intended use is not permitted by statutory regulation or exceeds the permitted use, you will need to obtain permission directly from the copyright holder.

Chapter 22
Article 24: The Right to Health

Christian Whalen

Article 24
1. States Parties recognize the right of the child to the enjoyment of the highest attainable standard of health and to facilities for the treatment of illness and rehabilitation of health. States Parties shall strive to ensure that no child is deprived of his or her right of access to such health care services.
2. States Parties shall pursue full implementation of this right and, in particular, shall take appropriate measures:

    (a) To diminish infant and child mortality;
    (b) To ensure the provision of necessary medical assistance and health care to all children with emphasis on the development of primary health care;
    (c) To combat disease and malnutrition, including within the framework of primary health care, through, inter alia, the application of readily available technology and through the provision of adequate nutritious foods and clean drinking water, taking into consideration the dangers and risks of environmental pollution;
    (d) To ensure appropriate pre-natal and post-natal health care for mothers;
    (e) To ensure that all segments of society, in particular parents and children, are informed, have access to education and are supported in the use of basic knowledge of child health and nutrition, the advantages of

(continued)

C. Whalen (✉)
Office of the Child, Youth and Seniors Advocate, Fredericton, NB, Canada
e-mail: Christian.Whalen@gnb.ca

breastfeeding, hygiene and environmental sanitation and the prevention of accidents;
(f) To develop preventive health care, guidance for parents and family planning education and services.

3. States Parties shall take all effective and appropriate measures with a view to abolishing traditional practices prejudicial to the health of children.
4. States Parties undertake to promote and encourage international cooperation with a view to achieving progressively the full realization of the right recognized in the present article. In this regard, particular account shall be taken of the needs of developing countries.

What Did Children Say?
'Parents—instead of making additions like—I know that this is beliefs that stems with it, but they should use logical decisions. They shouldn't like put their child in risk. Again the vaccination thing. They should think twice before saying no, we are going to do it because even if that autism thing is an actual thing, we rather have a child living in autism than not living at all.' (Asia-Pacific)

'Providing free vaccines and vaccinations in schools, colony and societies.' (Asia-Pacific)

'Don't give children only information, but give them pictures, do some activity or play as a way of spreading awareness.' (Asia-Pacific)

To ensure this right, every child, especially those isolated/living in reserves, or small communities, should have access to health care with hospital that have enough staff. (Western Europe/Other)

Overview

Article 24 sets out a fundamental right to the maximum attainable standard of health. This language is consistent with the human rights standards embodied in the International Covenant on Economic Social and Cultural Rights, but also with Article 6 and its insistence that States Parties ensure 'to the maximum extent possible the survival and development of the child.' The basic economy of this provision reflects the first draft of the Polish delegation of 1989 (S. Detrick et al., 1992, p. 344).

Following non-governmental organisation submissions, paragraph 3 was inserted to abolish traditional practices harmful to children. Express reference to female circumcision was left out in favour of the broader language adopted, on the understanding that these terms were well established and defined in the 1986 report of the

Working Group on Traditional Practices affecting the Health of Women and Children (S. Detrick et al., 1992, p. 352).

Paragraph 4 was added later to address the concerns of some states that the vast majority of premature infant death resulting from disease occurs in developing countries (S. Detrick et al., 1992, p. 353).[1] A further paragraph prohibiting medical experimentation, investigation, or treatment harmful to children was dropped from the final text due to the lack of consensus on language.

In its final form, Article 24 reflects the perspective of the drafters that the right to health cannot be understood in narrow bio-medical terms or limited to the delivery of health services. Rather, in its reference, for example, to food, water, sanitation, and environmental dangers, it recognises the wider social and economic factors that influence and impact on the child's state of health (Tobin, 2019, p. 909). Thus, the text of Article 24 sets out:

- a broad right to health for all children combined with a right of access to health services
- a priority focus on measures to address infant and child mortality, the provision of primary health care, nutritious food and clean drinking water, pre-natal and post-natal care, and preventive health care, including family planning
- the need for effective measures to abolish traditional practices harmful to children's health
- a specific obligation on States Parties to cooperate internationally towards the realisation of the child's right to health everywhere, having particular regard to the needs of developing countries (Kilkelly, 2015).

While the provision is framed in relation to pressing priorities at the time of drafting, like all human rights provisions in the Convention, Article 24 is part of a living tree; recent General Comments and Concluding Observations have emphasised the significance of Article 24 not just for physical health but also, for example, for 'new morbidities' (2013, para. 5)[2] related to mental and emotional well-being (2013, paras. 5, 38, 39, 109), and for rights to sexual and reproductive health (2013, para. 24). Furthermore, the Committee has endorsed the respect, protect, and fulfil, typology, adopted by the Committee on Economic, Social and Cultural Rights, that the right to health imposes obligations to ensure that States Parties do not violate the child's right to health, take measures to prevent third parties violating the right to health, and take appropriate measures to fulfil health rights through provision of services (2013, para. 71).

---

[1] Regrettably, the problem remains pervasive since 1989, as WHO estimated in 2017 that children in sub-Saharan Africa are 15 times more likely to die before 5 years of age than children in the developed world (World Health Organization, 2017). See also, current Facts Sheets (World Health Organization, 2020).

[2] See also, Leading the realization of human rights to health and through health: report of the High-Level Working Group on the Health and Human Rights of Women, Children and Adolescents (High-Level Working Group on the Health and Human Rights of Women, Children and Adolescents, 2017).

General Principles

Article 2 Children's right to health is often compromised by their minority status or by other discrimination in health services, whether overt or unintentional. The obligation to ensure equal access to health services requires that specific measures be taken to reach children in vulnerable sectors, such as infants, children with disabilities, children in remote or rural areas, living in poverty, or in institutionalised care, as well as children with minority gender identities or sexual orientations. Providing health services in multilinguistic and multi-ethnic states requires accommodations to ensure that health services, including proper instructions to consent to care and for post discharge care, can be properly administered. The Convention itself and the Committee in its General Comment draw particular attention to gender-based discrimination, in relation to sex selection practices in reproductive health, harmful traditional practices, feeding practices, etc. (UN Committee on the Rights of the Child, 2013, para. 9; UN General Assembly, 1990, Article 24, (3)).

Article 3 Determining a child's best interests in a health care setting requires a holistic rights-based approach that goes beyond a purely medical framework (Kilkelly, 2015, p. 219). The Committee has stated that the determination of a child's best interests needs to be based upon 'their physical, emotional, social and educational needs, age, sex, relationship with parents and caregivers, and their family and social background, and after having heard their views according to Article 12 of the Convention' (2013, para. 12). This principle must guide decision-making in policy matters as well as in individual case plans (UN Committee on the Rights of the Child, 2013, para. 12). It should be a primary consideration and supersede economic considerations (UN Committee on the Rights of the Child, 2013, para. 12). The integrity of the family and parent child bonds are important best interests' considerations and should not lightly be disrupted (UN Committee on the Rights of the Child, 2013, para. 15).

Article 6 This General Principle requires States Parties to ensure the child's right to survival and development to the maximum extent possible and serves as a capstone right to the health rights set out in Articles 23, 24 and 25. As Kilkelly has observed, it 'makes it clear that children are entitled to a standard of health that is commensurate with their healthy development' (2015, p. 218). This requires a commitment to child rights, together with a public health and social determinants approach. In the Committee's view, this includes 'individual factors such as age, sex, educational attainment, socio-economic status and domicile; determinants at work in the immediate environment of families, peers, teachers and service providers, notably the violence that threatens the life and survival of children as part of their immediate environment; and structural determinants, including policies, administrative structures and systems, social and cultural values and norms' (2013, para. 17).[3] Specifically, Article 6 supports health policy in relation to all matters addressing infant

---

[3] See also, General Comment no. 3 on HIV/AIDS (UN Committee on the Rights of the Child, 2003).

mortality, including maternal health in the perinatal period and parental health behaviours (UN Committee on the Rights of the Child, 2013, para. 18). The *2018 Nurturing Care Framework* reinforces, with the lens of economic impacts, the benefits of this holistic approach to development, which extends well beyond survival interests and requires a much higher level of commitment from States Parties in terms of resources and political will (Puras, 2015, paras. 14–23; World Health Organization et al., 2018).

Article 12 The child's right to express their views and to have them considered is important in informing health service provision in individual cases, but equally important in informing the development of health policy (Kilkelly, 2015, p. 19). The Committee insists that the child's voice needs to be considered on the broadest range of health policy matters: 'including, for example, what services are needed, how and where they are best provided, barriers to accessing or using services, the quality of the services and the attitudes of health professionals, how to strengthen children's capacities to take increasing levels of responsibility for their own health and development, and how to involve them more effectively in the provision of services, as peer educators' (2013, para. 19). The age of consent to medical treatment in each state is not determinative of the duty health care providers have to consult young patients, in respect of information or understanding about their treatment (Kilkelly, 2015, p. 19).[4] The Committee recognises that children's evolving capacities have a bearing on their independent decision-making on their health issues but invites States Parties to recognise that some children may be provided fewer opportunities to exercise autonomy in various health care decisions (2013, para. 21).

Articles Related or Linked to Article 24

Article 5, recognises the parents' rights and obligations to provide guidance and direction to their children, including in health matters

Article 7 affirms the child's right to be registered at birth, without which some children may denied access to health care

Article 9, the right to not be separated from one's parents, has implications for hospitals and health care providers

Articles 13 and 17, the child's right to receive information, both in care settings and more generally aimed at the promotion of their well-being and physical and mental health

Article 14, the child's freedom of conscience, thought and religion often intersects with health care provision

Article 16, the child's right to privacy and the inviolability of his or her family life in relation to health records and health care services is of universal concern

---

[4] See also, *Child Friendly Health care: The Views and Experiences of Children and Young People in the Council of Europe* (Kilkelly, 2011)

Article 19 and the several specific protection rights of children, protecting them from all forms of violence and abuse including drug endangerment (Article 33), sexual abuse (Article 34), trafficking (Article 35), or other exploitation (Article 36), have significant intersection and implications for the child's right to health

Article 23 sets out the specific rights of inclusion of children with physical and mental disabilities

Article 25 guarantees the right of children in any form of state care, including in health services care, to periodic review of their treatment and all aspects of their placement

Article 26, child's right to social security provides for children to access benefits that will contribute to their health and well-being

Article 27, the child's right to a standard of living adequate for the child's physical, mental, spiritual, moral, and social development

Articles 28 and 29, the child's right to education directed to the development of the child's mental and physical abilities to the fullest potential as determinants of health

Article 31, the child's right to rest, play, physical activity, and cultural and artistic activities contributes to the child's state of health

Article 39, the child's right to recovery and reintegration as a victim of neglect, abuse, exploitation, torture or any other form of cruel treatment or armed conflicts, in an environment that fosters the health, self-respect and dignity of the child

Relevant Instruments

UN Declaration of the Rights of the Child (1959), Principles 2, 4, 5, and 8

International Covenant on Civil and Political Rights (1966), Articles 6, 9, and 17

International Covenant on Economic, Social and Cultural Rights (1966), Article 12

International Convention on the Elimination of All Forms of Racial Discrimination (1966), Article 5

UN Convention on the Elimination of All Forms of Discrimination against Women (1979), Article 12

UN Convention on the Rights of Persons with Disabilities (2006), Article 25

European Convention on Human Rights (1950), Article 8

European Social Charter (1961), Articles 11 and 13

American Convention on Human Rights 'Pact of San Jose, Costa Rica' (B-32) (1978), Articles 11, 17 through 20

African Charter on Human and Peoples' Rights (1981), Article 16

Social Charter of the Americas (2012), Article 17

Attributes

Attribute One: A Right to the Enjoyment of the Highest Attainable Standard of Health

Article 24 outlines the essence of the right to health, expressed as a right to the enjoyment of the highest attainable standard of health. It is an exacting standard which reflects the language of the right to health guaranteed under Article 12 of the International Covenant on Social Economic and Cultural Rights and affirms that these rights are programmatic in nature and require progressive implementation. It includes the right of access to facilities for treatment and rehabilitation as well as the freedom to make fundamental choices with respect to one's own health and body (UN Committee on the Rights of the Child, 2013, para. 24).

Under the Convention, health is understood as 'a state of complete physical, mental and social well-being and not merely the absence of disease or infirmity' (Preamble to the Constitution of the World Health Organization, qtd. in UN Committee on the Rights of the Child, 2013, para. 4)'. The highest attainable standard of health for any child takes into account the child's own biological, social, cultural, and economic preconditions as well as the state's available resources, supplemented by all available sources (UN Committee on the Rights of the Child, 2013, para. 23). The Committee has argued that this must be achieved by programmes that address the underlying determinants of health (2013, para. 2). These include:

- road and environmental safety
- racial prejudice
- access to education
- persistence of forced and early marriage
- corporal punishment
- social, economic, political, cultural, and legal barriers to health services, including sexual and reproductive health services
- inadequate social protection
- institutionalisation
- punitive drug laws
- absence of comprehensive sexuality education
- criminalisation of exposure, non-disclosure of HIV status and transmission of HIV
- criminalisation of same-sex relationships
- lax legal frameworks governing the sale of tobacco, alcohol and fast foods (UN Human Rights Council, 2016, para. 36).

The Committee has drawn particular attention to the challenges faced by adolescents in respect of the right to health, highlighting that health services are rarely designed to accommodate their needs and that their 'health outcomes are predominantly a consequence of social and economic determinants and structural inequalities, mediated by behaviour and activity, at the individual, peer, family, school, community and societal levels.' Accordingly, they call on States Parties to invest in a collaborative approach to analysis of their needs to inform health policies, strategies and services (2016, paras. 56–57).

Health services include prevention, promotion, treatment, rehabilitation, and palliative care services. These should be available to every child at the primary care level, while secondary and tertiary care services should be available to the extent possible, consistent with progressive realisation (UN Committee on the Rights of the Child, 2013, para. 26). This entails substantial investment in the development of professional staff to support services at all levels of care. Recourse must be available to challenge any denial of access to such services, together with educational and administrative efforts to ensure access to remedies. Ensuring the right to access to health care entails working with parents and communities to create an environment and knowledge base around how to seek appropriate care. It also requires adequate consent-based management systems for parents and competent children, and the removal of financial, cultural, and institutional barriers to care (UN Committee on the Rights of the Child, 2013, paras. 23–31). For adolescents, specific guidance is also available from the World Health Organization's *Global Health Standards for Quality Health Care Services for Adolescents* (World Health Organization, 2015).

Attribute Two: A Right to the Basic Minimum Standards of Child Health

The core aspect of the right to health set out in the first attribute is developed further in paragraph 2 of Article 24, which has been analysed as establishing basic minimum standards in relation to the child's right to health (Kilkelly, 2015, p. 218). Universal access to primary health care requires robust financial investment and professionalisation of practice within well-administered facilities with strong quality assurance. States Parties can be assessed in relation to their ability to make progress in implementing each of the goals to:

- diminish infant and child mortality
- provide primary health care to all children
- combat disease and malnutrition by proper means including adequate nutritious food supply and clean drinking water
- ensure peri-natal maternal health care
- provide child and infant public health education and promotion
- develop preventive child health care, including family planning.

Through its Concluding Observations and General Comments, the Committee has provided detailed guidance in relation to the requirements of each of these areas of focus. For example, the goal of diminishing infant and child mortality requires a host of interventions to address pre-term birth complications and low birth weight, mother to child transmission of HIV, diarrhoea, malaria and measles, and traffic accidents and suicide. Neonatal deaths and adolescent morbidity are identified by the Committee as priority areas of focus. The Committee has also underscored the importance of efforts to address the mental health needs of adolescents and the health care needs of child victims displaced by natural disasters or conflict as crucial concerns in the provision of universal access to primary care. Efforts to eradicate disease and malnutrition must make use of innovative but proven treatments and technologies. They must ensure access to nutritious food, clean drinking water and sanitation while supporting public health education around all these subjects.

Article 24 (2) (c) outlines critical environmental rights of children and the Committee has called upon States Parties to ensure that efforts to mitigate environmental impacts on child health look beyond controls on environmental pollution to broader impacts, including efforts to put children's health concerns at the centre of climate change adaptation and mitigation strategies. General Comment no. 15 provides equally detailed advice in relation to the implementation of Article 24 (2)'s priority focus on perinatal care, for both mothers and children, from pre-natal education classes for parents and child health public education efforts in general to preventive health measures particularly in providing guidance for parents and family planning. As stated above, all of the basic minimal criteria enumerated in paragraph 2 needs to be interpreted in light of emerging concerns with social and emotional learning and resilience as pathways to well-being and a more holistic understanding of child health (Puras, 2015, paras. 14–23).

Finally, while the obligation to take all effective measures to abolish traditional practices harmful to child health is set out separately in paragraph 3, its inclusion there only augments the global consensus on this priority area of focus for child health implementation efforts. Much work has been done to advance the consensus on the definition of the term 'harmful traditional practices' (Connors, 2011), but clear priorities for the Committee in this area are female genital mutilation and early marriages (UN Committee on the Elimination of Discrimination against Women and UN Committee on the Rights of the Child, 2014).[5]

Attribute Three: Child Health Accountability Mechanisms

A third attribute of Article 24's guarantee of the child's right to health is what the Committee refers to as a framework for implementation and accountability (2013, paras. 90–120). Inherent in broad programmatic rights like the right to health or education, or social security, is an obligation on governments to develop robust frameworks for implementation. States Parties must have a plan of action that

---

[5]In many countries in central Africa, rates of FGM are estimated to be as high as 75% and the problem is therefore one of making a lasting cultural change that goes well beyond mere law reform (Vučković-Šahović et al., 2012, p. 197).

addresses the many general measures of implementation specific to the right as elaborated under Article 4. The plan must involve a cyclical system of evaluation of programmes leading to improved policy and new investment and new programmes that in turn require further evaluation in what the Committee terms an action cycle of rights enforcement. In the health sector, following the example of the Committee on Economic, Social and Cultural Rights, the Committee of the Rights of the Child has adopted the Availability, Accessibility, Acceptability, and Quality approach to accountability which establishes the goals against which child health policies and programmes should be assessed (UN Committee on the Rights of the Child, 2013, paras. 112–116):

- Availability in ensuring sufficient quantity of health services to ensure that every child has access to the services they need, including measures to address underlying social determinants of health (UN Committee on Economic, Social and Cultural Rights, 2000, para. 12(a))
- Accessibility in terms of non-discrimination, as well as physical, informational and financial accessibility
- Acceptability in ensuring that services are respectful of every child's health needs
- Quality in ensuring that services are based on the best possible science and medical practice standards.

The above accountability measures must be accompanied by broad public education efforts and accessible remedies for violations of the child's right to health (UN Committee on Economic, Social and Cultural Rights, 2000, paras. 119–120).

Attribute Four: International Cooperation for Child Health in Developing Countries

Finally, Article 24 closes with a call for international cooperation to respect, protect, and fulfil the child's right to health, with specific regard to the needs of developing countries. More than half of the world's early child deaths are due to preventable conditions that could be easily treated (World Health Organization, 2017). The Committee has not elaborated the implications of this obligation in detail but regularly recommends that States Parties seek the assistance of UN bodies such as UNICEF, WHO, and UNAIDS. International cooperation is critically important and guidance in this area can be found in global commitment documents such as *A World fit for Children*, the *Sustainable Development Goals* and the *WHO Global Strategy for Women's, Children and Adolescent Health* (Vučković-Šahović et al., 2012, p. 195).[6]

---

[6] See also, *Leading the realization of human rights to health and through health: report of the High-Level Working Group on the Health and Human Rights of Women, Children and Adolescents* (High-Level Working Group on the Health and Human Rights of Women, Children and Adolescents, 2017).

References

Connors, J. (2011). Evolution and definition of harmful traditional practices. *IDE Harmful Practices and Human Rights, (13)*.

Detrick, S., Doek, J. E., & Cantwell, N. (1992). *The United Nations Convention on the Rights of the Child: A Guide to the "Travaux Préparatoires."* Martinus Nijhoff Publishers.

High-Level Working Group on the Health and Human Rights of Women, Children and Adolescents. (2017). *Leading the realization of human rights to health and through health: report of the High-Level Working Group on the Health and Human Rights of Women, Children and Adolescents.* : World Health Organization. Accessed November 12, 2020, from https://www.who.int/life-course/publications/hhr-of-women-children-adolescents-report/en/

Kilkelly, U. (2011). *Child-friendly health care: the views and experiences of children and young people in Council of Europe member States*. Council of Europe. http://www.each-for-sick-children.org/images/2015/EU_Council_Child_Friendly_Healthcare_Final_Report__English_version__1.pdf

Kilkelly, U. (2015). Health and children's rights. In *Routledge international handbook of children's rights studies* (pp. 216–233). Routledge.

Puras, D. (2015). *Right of everyone to the enjoyment of the highest attainable standard of physical and mental health, A/70/213*. UN. Accessed November 12, 2020, from http://digitallibrary.un.org/record/801865

Tobin, J. (2019). Article 24: The Right to health. In J. Tobin (Ed.), *The UN convention on the rights of the child: A commentary* (pp. 902–969). Oxford University Press.

UN Committee on Economic, Social and Cultural Rights. (2000). *General comment No. 14 (2000), The right to the highest attainable standard of health (article 12 of the International Covenant on Economic, Social and Cultural Rights), E/C.12/2000/4*. UN. Accessed November 13, 2020, from http://digitallibrary.un.org/record/425041

UN Committee on the Elimination of Discrimination against Women & UN Committee on the Rights of the Child. (2014). *Joint General Recommendation No. 31 of the Committee on the Elimination of Discrimination against Women/general comment No. 18 of the Committee on the Rights of the Child on harmful practices, CEDAW/C/GC/31, CRC/C/GC/18*. UN. Accessed November 13, 2020, from http://digitallibrary.un.org/record/807256

UN Committee on the Rights of the Child. (2003). *General Comment No. 3 (2003) HIV/AIDS and the rights of the child, March 17, 2003, CRC/GC/2003/3*. Accessed October 12, 2020, from https://digitallibrary.un.org/record/501529?ln=en

UN Committee on the Rights of the Child. (2013). *General Comment No. 15 (2013) on the right of the child to the enjoyment of the highest attainable standard of health (art. 24), April 17, 2013, CRC/C/GC/15*. UN. Accessed October 26, 2020, from http://digitallibrary.un.org/record/778524

UN Committee on the Rights of the Child. (2016). *General Comment No. 20 (2016) on the implementation of the rights of the child during adolescence, December 6, 2016, CRC/C/GC/20*. Accessed October 12 2020, from https://digitallibrary.un.org/record/855544?ln=en

UN General Assembly. (1990). *Convention on the Rights of the Child, 1990, A/RES/45/104*. Accessed April 19, 2020, from https://digitallibrary.un.org/record/105613?ln=en

UN Human Rights Council. (2016). *Report of the Special Rapporteur on the right of everyone to the enjoyment of the highest attainable standard of physical and mental health A/HRC/32/32*. http://digitallibrary.un.org/record/842322

Vučković-Šahović, N., Doek, J. E., & Zermatten, J. (2012). *The rights of the child in international law: rights of the child in a nutshell and in context: All about children's rights*. Stämpfli.

World Health Organization. (2015). WHO | Global standards for quality health care services for adolescents. World Health Organization. Accessed November 13, 2020, from http://www.who.int/maternal_child_adolescent/documents/global-standards-adolescent-care/en/

World Health Organization. (2017, October). Children: Reducing mortality. *Internet Archive Wayback Machine/WHO Fact Sheets*. Accessed December 19, 2020, from http://web.archive.org/web/20180209220023/http://www.who.int/mediacentre/factsheets/fs178/en/

World Health Organization. (2020, September 8). Children: Improving survival and well-being. *WHO Fact Sheets*. Accessed December 19, 2020, from https://www.who.int/news-room/fact-sheets/detail/children-reducing-mortality

World Health Organization, United Nations Children's Fund, & World Bank Group. (2018). *Nurturing care for early childhood development: a framework for helping children survive and thrive to transform health and human potential*. World Health Organization. https://apps.who.int/iris/bitstream/handle/10665/272603/9789241514064-eng.pdf?ua=1&ua=1

Open Access This chapter is licensed under the terms of the Creative Commons Attribution 4.0 International License (http://creativecommons.org/licenses/by/4.0/), which permits use, sharing, adaptation, distribution and reproduction in any medium or format, as long as you give appropriate credit to the original author(s) and the source, provide a link to the Creative Commons license and indicate if changes were made.

The images or other third party material in this chapter are included in the chapter's Creative Commons license, unless indicated otherwise in a credit line to the material. If material is not included in the chapter's Creative Commons license and your intended use is not permitted by statutory regulation or exceeds the permitted use, you will need to obtain permission directly from the copyright holder.

Chapter 23
Article 26: The Right to Benefit from Social Security

Roberta Ruggiero

1. States Parties shall recognize for every child the right to benefit from social security, including social insurance, and shall take the necessary measures to achieve the full realisation of this right in accordance with their national law.
2. The benefits should, where appropriate, be granted, taking into account the resources and the circumstances of the child and persons having responsibility for the maintenance of the child, as well as any other consideration relevant to an application for benefits made by or on behalf of the child.

What Did Children Say?
'When deciding how much help and money is needed, governments should consider the particular situation of the child and family. Government should provide families with some support and money to help bring up their children. Some families will need more support and money than others. Everybody gets what they need rather than everybody gets the same.' *(Asia-Pacific)*

'Government should not take heavy taxes. Because of the heavy taxes, the poor people get more poor and poor.' *(Asia-Pacific)*

To ensure money is spent on the child, government assistance should only be spent in certain places e.g., government to partner with businesses to accept government vouchers. *(Latin America/Caribbean)*

R. Ruggiero (✉)
Centre for Children's Rights Studies, University of Geneva, Geneva, Switzerland
e-mail: roberta.ruggiero@unige.ch

Overview

Article 26 deals with the right of the child to benefit from social security and social insurance.[1] As underlined by the Committee, this right is important in itself and plays a key instrumental role in the realisation of other Convention rights (UN Committee on the Rights of the Child, 2003a, para. 6, 2006a, paras. 10, 26, 2007, para. 20; Vandenhole, 2007, pp. 1, 11–13). It guarantees financial and other support of the child provided by the state in all cases where the adult(s) responsible for the child are not in the position to provide for the child, because they are unemployed or for other reasons, such as illness, disability, childbearing, old age, widowhood, being a single parent and in total absence of both parent (orphanhood) and so on. These are all circumstances that might prevent the adult(s) from securing work and an income.

Contrary to other international legal provisions dealing with the issue of social security, Article 26 does not guarantee the right to social security, but the right to 'benefit from' social security. The use of this expression is due to a proposal of the International Labour Organization (ILO) delegation during the drafting of the Convention, which underlined that the recognition to children of the 'right to social security' would not mirror the real position of the child in relation to their entitlement to social security benefits. Parents and/or legal guardians hold the rights to receive benefits 'by the reason of their responsibility for the maintenance of the child' (S. L. de Detrick, 1999, p. 447; S. Detrick et al., 1992, pp. 364–370) based on Article 18. Therefore, the position of dependency of the child towards their parents or legal guardians and their entitlement to social security had been more adequately reflected by recognising to the child right to 'benefit from' social security and not the right to social security.

Nevertheless, Article 26(2) ensures that applications for benefits can be 'made by or on behalf of the child.' Furthermore, in the general guidelines for the periodic reports, the Committee asks States Parties to describe in their reports the circumstances and the conditions under which children are authorised to apply themselves directly or through a legal representative for social security benefits (S. L. de Detrick, 1999, p. 447; UN Committee on the Rights of the Child, 1996a, para. 100).

With reference to the implementation of Article 26, it is worth underlining that it is subject to the provision of Article 4, which provides that States Parties are obliged to 'undertake all appropriate, legislative, administrative, and other measures to the maximum of the available resources and where applicable within the framework of the international cooperation' (Hodgkin et al., 2007, p. 385). Therefore, the right of the child to benefit from 'social security is not an immediate States Parties' obligation, but one of progressive achievement' (S. L. de Detrick, 1999, p. 447; Vandenhole, 2007, pp. 24–30). So far, the Committee has not provided yet a comprehensive clarification of Article 26 by way of General Comments, nor through the Concluding Observations on reports of States Parties (Vandenhole, 2007,

---

[1] Social security and social insurance are used as corresponding concepts.

pp. 1, 15). Therefore, the specific and technical meaning of 'social security' needs to be identified in many universal and regional treaties dedicated to the right to social security. In these treaties, 'social security' is composed of the nine traditional branches identified by the ILO Convention 102 on Minimum Standards, namely health, care, sickness, unemployment, employment injury, family, maternity, invalidity and survivor's benefits; and a social security system should comply with the following four principles identified by the (Revised) European Social Charter (1996):

- The social security system should be set up or maintained
- A minimum level should be defined for each social security system
- The principle of progressive improvement of the system should apply
- Equality of treatment should be ensured for nationals of other contracting states, along with 'granting, maintenance and resumption of social security rights' (Vandenhole, 2007, p. 7).

General Principles

Article 2 The setting up of a social security system should be intended to support those most in need on an equal basis. Therefore, States Parties' implementation of Article 26 should be fulfilled with no discrimination. In this respect, the Committee, in its concluding observations to various States Parties' reports, has raised concerns in relation to discrimination related to sex, age, ethnicity, disability, the geographical location of potential beneficiaries, nationality, and so on (2003b, para. 20, 2003c, para. 52, 2003d, paras. 49, 50, 2006b, paras. 45, 46, 2006c, para. 54, 2007, para. 20, 2012a, para. 60, 2012b, para. 62, 2016a, para. 56, 2017a, para. 69, 2017b, para. 51, 2017c, para. 55). With reference to children with disabilities, the *Report of the Secretary General on Status of the Convention on the Rights of the Child* highlights that some social protection mechanisms discriminate against this group of children. For example, conditional cash transfers may be dependent on attending school when places are not available, and additional costs associated with disability are not taken into consideration (2011, para. 57 (ii), (iii)).

Article 3(2) The creation of a social security system is an integrative part of the overarching States Parties' obligations to undertake all appropriate legislative and administrative measures needed 'to ensure the child such protection and care as is necessary for his or her well-being, taking into account the rights and duties of his or her parents, legal guardians, or other individuals legally responsible for him or her.'

Article 6 Article 26 is instrumental to the fulfilment of Article 6 with reference to the inherent right to life and the States Parties' obligation to ensure 'to the maximum extent possible the survival and development of the child' (UN Committee on the Rights of the Child, 2003a, para. 6, 2006a, paras. 10, 26). The creation of a quality social security service could contribute to the eradication of poverty, hunger, exclusion, inequality, low level of schooling and health care (Hodgkin et al., 2007, pp. 386–387). There are all factors that dramatically influence the survival and full development of the child.

Article 12 Children's perspectives on their experience of poverty, and the measures needed to address the problems, should be solicited by States Parties. The Committee has highlighted the imperative for children's views on budgetary decisions to be heard and taken seriously, and for States Parties to take all necessary measures to facilitate this process (2016b, paras. 52–53).

Articles Related or Linked to Article 26

Based on the interpretation of Article 26 provided by the Committee, this Article is instrumental to the realisation of all the other rights listed in the Convention. In particular, it is instrumental to the fulfilment of:

- **Article 3(2)**, in relation the States Parties' obligation to ensure to children the necessary protection and care.
- **Article 17**, with reference to the right to be informed about the available social security benefits available and the procedure meant to obtain them. This could be achieved through the setting up of large public information campaigns on benefit entitlements and through more specific information procedure related to detailed vulnerable groups. Furthermore, the dissemination of information could be addressed to children as well as parents, caregivers and legal representatives (Hodgkin et al., 2007, pp. 387–388; UN Committee on the Rights of the Child, 1999a, para. 18, 2005, paras. 71–74).
- **Article 18(2) and Article 18(3)**, respectively, with reference to the States Parties' obligation to support parents in the exercise of their child-rearing responsibilities and 'to ensure that children of working parents have the right to benefit from childcare services and facilities for which they are eligible' (UN Committee on the Rights of the Child, 1996a, para. 101). Furthermore, often social security is limited to financial benefits for families with children. This is important part of social security. However, preventive services, such as services to support parents in the fulfilment of their role, for example to improve their parenting skills or to educate them in non-violent child-rearing techniques, are often absent. There is a need of a better balance.
- **Article 23,** with reference to the right to benefit from social security entitled to children with disabilities meant to avoid further marginalisation.
- **Article 24,** for the fulfilment of the right to health care services and their connection with medical social benefits.
- **Article 27** deals with the children's right to an adequate standard of living meant to guarantee the child's physical, mental, spiritual, moral and social development and to provide material and support programmes, with reference to nutrition, clothing and housing maintenance. Article 27(1) represents a general guarantee to

an adequate standard of living, which is specified in Article 26 social security (which covers allowances related to certain risks—sickness, maternity, unemployment, etc.) and Article 27(3) social assistance (in which the individual need is the main criterion for eligibility and the allowances are intended to compensate for a state of need) (Vandenhole, 2007, pp. 16–17).

- **Article 28**, again, an instrumental approach to social security benefits helps free the child from needing to work to protect the economic security of the family. Less economically active children will be better equipped to realise their right to education.
- **Article 32,** since social security benefits providing the child with adequate maintenance (allowances) may make the economic activity of the child unnecessary. This makes the child also less vulnerable and strength his/her ability to fulfil the right to education (van Bueren, 1998, p. 268; Vandenhole, 2007, p. 13).

Relevant Instruments

UN Universal Declaration of Human Rights (1948). Article 25(1). In one single paragraph it refers to both social welfare (adequate standard of living) and social security. With reference to the latter, it enumerates risks, such as unemployment, illness, disability, widowhood, and old age. Thus, compared with the Convention on the Rights of the Child, it provides a more specific provision of social security.

International Covenant on Economic, Social and Cultural Rights (1966).

- Article 9 provides a short and general reference on the right of social security, thereby leaving to the UN specialised agencies (in particular the ILO) to identify the details of this clause (UN Commission on Human Rights, 1951, p. 13; Vandenhole, 2007, p. 4).
- Article 10(2) accords special protection to mothers during a reasonable period before and after childbirth. To working mothers it offers, during such a period, paid leave or leave with adequate social security benefits.

UN Convention on the Elimination of All Forms of Discrimination against Women (1979).

- Article 11(1) is in line with the scope of the treaty, as it focuses on the equal right to social security for women in a number of specific situations such as retirement, unemployment, sickness, invalidity and old age (like the Universal Declaration of Human Rights).
- Article 14(2) deals with the discrimination against women in rural areas and aims to ensure the right to 'benefit directly from social security programmes.'

International Convention on the Protection of the Rights of All Migrant Workers and Members of Their Families (1990):

- Article 27 deals with the equal treatment of migrant workers and members of their families to benefit from social security on the same bases as it is granted to nationals.
- Article 61(3) enable project-tied workers to 'remain adequately protected by the social security system of their Sates of origin or habitual residence'.

Even though they are not *stricto sensus* human rights treaties, International Labour Organization conventions are the main international treaties setting and implementing social security standards. Therefore, they are the main source of interpretation of human rights provision on social security (Lamarche, 2002, p. 9; Scheinin, 2001, pp. 214–215; Vandenhole, 2007, pp. 4–7).

Primarily, ILO Convention 102, Social Security (Minimum Standards) (1952)[2] covers the nine main branches of any social security system: medical care benefits, sickness benefits, unemployment benefits, old-age benefits, employment injury benefits, family benefits, maternity benefits, invalidity benefits and survivors' benefits. Based on Article 2, States Parties are requested to comply with at least three out of the nine mentioned benefits and among these, one of the following benefits should be included: unemployment, old age, employment injury, invalidity, or survivor's benefits. Articles 71 and 72 of this same Convention state that:

- The cost of the social security system is mainly the responsibility of the States Parties and the cost on the employees should not be excessive
- Participation of beneficiaries in the administration of the system should be provided
- A right to appeal should be available in cases of refusal of a benefit and in case of poor quality and quantity of the benefits provided.

European Social Charter (Revised) (1996), Article 12, guarantees the right to social security and identifies four principles to which the system should comply (Vandenhole, 2007, p. 7). Article 12 also refers to the European Code of Social Security of the Council of Europe (1964). This latter is similar to ILO Convention 102, but the minimum requirements of acceptance for ratification are twice as high for the Code. Thus, it requires a higher standard of social security than provided by the ILO Convention (Nickless, 2002).

American Declaration of the Rights and Duties of Man (1948), Article 16, includes the right to social security in specific areas.

Additional Protocol to the American Convention on Human Rights in the Area of Economic, Social, and Cultural Rights 'Protocol of San Salvador' (1988), Article 9 refers to provisions related to old age and disability and to social security benefits for employees in the field of healthcare, work-related injuries, diseases and maternity.

---

[2] Others ILO Conventions in this field are the Employment Injury Benefits Convention No. 121 (1964), the Invalidity, Old-age and Survivors' Benefits Convention No. 128 (1967), the Medical Care and Sickness Benefits Convention No. 130 (1969), and the Employment Promotion and Protection against Unemployment Convention No. 168 (1988).

Attributes

Attribute One: States Parties' Obligations to Undertake All Necessary Measures

As seen in the main concerns of the Committee, many national social security systems, laws, and policies contain shortfalls (Hodgkin et al., 2007, p. 388). The most recurrent one pertains to the inability of ensuring resources to the children most in need of social security benefits (Vandenhole, 2007, pp. 20–21). Therefore, it remains essential to the renovation and the strengthening of a comprehensive system of social security to:

- Cover all the nine traditional branches of social security: medical care, cash sickness benefits, maternity benefits, old-age benefits, survivors' benefits, employment injury benefits, unemployment benefits, and family benefits
- Follow up on the living reality of the children that benefit from social security
- Set up policy measures meant to facilitate the access to social security benefits by the most disadvantaged groups.

Furthermore, following the provisions of the (Revised) European Social Charter (1996) (Article 12), to ensure the child right to benefit from social security, the system should comply with the following criteria:

- Availability (social security should be set up or maintained)
- The system should be progressively improved in terms of quality and quantity of benefits (risks covered)
- Accessibility should be ensured also to children directly and indirectly in a non-discriminatory manner.

With reference to the last point, for the Committee, medical care, medical insurance, and family benefits are particularly relevant to children and the quality of social security systems (Vandenhole, 2007, pp. 22, 40–41).

Attribute Two: Focus on the Personal Resources and Circumstances of the Child and Caregivers

Article 26 further underlines that the child's economic stability and social security is generally intertwined with that of their adult caregivers. Thus, States Parties are required to set up tools meant to test the social security of the child and as consequence reinforce the attention for the social security of adults.

The process through which the benefits granted take into account the resources and the circumstances of the child and of the persons having responsibility for the child's maintenance should be particularly keen to detect any other considerations relevant to an application for benefits made by or on behalf of the child.

In relation to this aspect, it should be acknowledged that the Committee invites States Parties to provide a certain financial support to all children regardless of their parents' circumstances as a form of investment on the future stability of the society, strengthening children's ability to exercise their rights, break poverty cycles, and bring high economic returns (Lundy et al., 2015; UN Committee on the Rights of the Child, 2016b, paras. 7, 50; UN High Commissioner for Human Rights, 2014).

Attribute Three: Children's Direct Accessibility to the Application Process to Secure Social Security Benefits

Article 26(2) emphasises that 'it is equally important to ensure that children are directly eligible in their own right where necessary' (Hodgkin et al., 2007, p. 389). As a consequence, even though the right of the child to social security derives from that of their parents, there are cases in which the child might need to lodge an application for social security benefits when parents or other caregivers are for some reason disqualified or unable to claim them (UN Committee on the Rights of the Child, 1996b, para. 34, 1999b, para. 7, 2002, paras. 48, 49, 2004, paras. 10, 11). Children's access to benefits should not be dependent only on their adult caregivers, for example, in cases where children are the heads of households or parents. Therefore, a support system should be put into place in order to facilitate the possibility to submit a claim for social security benefits in a child-friendly manner and to involve in it all those actors supporting the child in this process, including 'persons in public offices or public services' (UN Committee on the Rights of the Child, 1993, para. 50). The child should be provided with all the necessary information to facilitate the procedure, and applications should be dealt with in a timely fashion.

References

Detrick, S. L. de. (1999). *A commentary on the United Nations convention on the rights of the child*. Brill Nijhoff. Accessed November 6, 2020, from https://brill.com/view/title/10630

Detrick, S., Doek, J. E., & Cantwell, N. (1992). *The United Nations convention on the rights of the child: A guide to the "Travaux Préparatoires."* Martinus Nijhoff Publishers.

Hodgkin, R., Newell, P., & UNICEF. (2007). Implementation handbook for the convention on the rights of the child (3rd ed.). : UNICEF. Accessed September 21, 2020, from https://digitallibrary.un.org/record/620060?ln=en

Lamarche, L. (2002). The right to social security in the international covenant on economic, social and cultural rights. In A. R. Chapman & S. Russell (Eds.), *Core obligations: Building a framework for economic, social and cultural rights*. Intersentia.

Lundy, L., Orr, K., & Marshall, C. (2015). *Towards better investment in the rights of the child: The views of children* (p. 33). Queen's University. https://pure.qub.ac.uk/en/publications/towards-better-investment-in-the-rights-of-the-child-the-views-of

Nickless, J. (2002). *European code of social security: Short guide.* Council of Europe Publishing. https://www.coe.int/t/dg3/sscssr/Source/short%20guide_Code%20E.pdf

Scheinin, M. (2001). The right to social security. In A. Eide, C. Krause, & A. Rosas (Eds.), Economic, social and cultural rights: A textbook. Leiden: . Accessed 14 November 2020, from https://brill.com/view/title/9432?language=en

UN Commission on Human Rights. (1951). *Commission on Human Rights, 7th session: Summary record of the 220th meeting held at the Palais des Nations*, Geneva, on Monday, 30 April 1951. UN. Accessed November 14, 2020, from http://digitallibrary.un.org/record/1490391

UN Committee on the Rights of the Child. (1993). *Initial reports: Denmark, October 12, 1993, CRC/C/8/Add.8*. UN. Accessed November 14, 2020, http://digitallibrary.un.org/record/193803

UN Committee on the Rights of the Child. (1996a). *General guidelines regarding the form and contents of periodic reports to be submitted by states parties under article 44, paragraph 1 (b) of the Convention, November 20, 1996, CRC/C/58*. Accessed October 12, 2020, from https://digitallibrary.un.org/record/230051?ln=en

UN Committee on the Rights of the Child. (1996b). *Concluding observations: Lebanon, June 7, 1996, CRC/C/15/Add.54*. UN. Accessed November 14, 2020, from http://digitallibrary.un.org/record/219126

UN Committee on the Rights of the Child. (1999a). *Concluding observations: Sweden, May 10, 1999, CRC/C/15/Add.101*. UN. Accessed November 6, 2020, from http://digitallibrary.un.org/record/275206

UN Committee on the Rights of the Child. (1999b). *Concluding observations: Netherlands, October 26, 1999, CRC/C/15/Add.114*. UN. Accessed November 14, 2020, from http://digitallibrary.un.org/record/391709

UN Committee on the Rights of the Child. (2002). *Concluding observations: Greece, April 2, 2002, CRC/C/15/Add.170*. UN. Accessed October 26, 2020, from http://digitallibrary.un.org/record/473476

UN Committee on the Rights of the Child. (2003a). *General Comment No. 3 (2003) HIV/AIDS and the rights of the child, March 17, 2003, CRC/GC/2003/3*. Accessed October 12, 2020, from https://digitallibrary.un.org/record/501529?ln=en

UN Committee on the Rights of the Child. (2003b). *Concluding observations: Iceland, January 31, 2003, CRC/C/15/Add.203*. Accessed October 12, 2020, from https://digitallibrary.un.org/record/497804?ln=en

UN Committee on the Rights of the Child. (2003c). *Concluding observations: Georgia, October 27, 2003, CRC/C/15/Add.222*. Accessed October 23, 2020, from https://digitallibrary.un.org/record/513575?ln=en

UN Committee on the Rights of the Child. (2003d). *Concluding observations: Cyprus, July 2, 2003, CRC/C/15/Add.205*. UN. Accessed November 14, 2020, from http://digitallibrary.un.org/record/503088

UN Committee on the Rights of the Child. (2004). *Concluding observations: Netherlands, February 26, 2004, CRC/C/15/Add.227*. UN. Accessed November 14, 2020, from http://digitallibrary.un.org/record/528936

UN Committee on the Rights of the Child. (2005). *Concluding observations: Nepal, September 1, 2005, CRC/C/15/Add.261*. Accessed October 11, 2020, from https://digitallibrary.un.org/record/569886?ln=en

UN Committee on the Rights of the Child. (2006a). *General Comment No. 7 (2005) Implementing child rights in early childhood, September 20, 2006, CRC/C/GC/7/Rev.1*. Accessed October 12, 2020, from https://digitallibrary.un.org/record/584854?ln=en

UN Committee on the Rights of the Child. (2006b). *Concluding observations: Hungary, March 17, 2006, CRC/C/HUN/CO/2*. Accessed October 11, 2020, from https://digitallibrary.un.org/record/575773?ln=en

UN Committee on the Rights of the Child. (2006c). *Concluding observations: Mexico, June 8, 2006, CRC/C/MEX/CO/3*. https://digitallibrary.un.org/record/582289?ln=en

UN Committee on the Rights of the Child. (2007). *General Comment No. 9 (2006) The rights of children with disabilities, November 13, 2007, CRC/C/GC/9*. Accessed October 12, 2020, from https://digitallibrary.un.org/record/593891?ln=en

UN Committee on the Rights of the Child. (2012a). *Concluding observations: Bosnia and Herzegovina, November 29, 2012, CRC/C/BIH/CO/2-4*. UN. Accessed November 7, 2020, from http://digitallibrary.un.org/record/739168

UN Committee on the Rights of the Child. (2012b). Concluding observations: Algeria, July 18, 2012, CRC/C/DZA/CO/3-4. UN. Accessed November 14, 2020, from http://digitallibrary.un.org/record/731358

UN Committee on the Rights of the Child. (2016a). *Concluding observations: Kenya, March 21, 2016, CRC/C/KEN/CO/3-5*. UN. Accessed November 14, 2020, from http://digitallibrary.un.org/record/834997

UN Committee on the Rights of the Child. (2016b). *General Comment No. 19 (2016) on public budgeting for the realization of children's rights (art.4), CRC/C/GC/19*. UN. Accessed November 12, 2020, from http://digitallibrary.un.org/record/838730

UN Committee on the Rights of the Child. (2017a). *Concluding observations: Serbia, March 7, 2017, CRC/C/SRB/CO/2-3*. Accessed October 12, 2020, from https://www.refworld.org/pdfid/58e76fc14.pdf

UN Committee on the Rights of the Child. (2017b). *General Comment No. 21 (2017) on children in street situations, June 21, 2017, CRC/C/GC/21*. Accessed October 12, 2020, from https://digitallibrary.un.org/record/1304490?ln=en

UN Committee on the Rights of the Child. (2017c). *Concluding observations: Central African Republic, March 8, 2017, CRC/C/CAF/CO/2*. UN. Accessed November 14, 2020, from http://digitallibrary.un.org/record/1311376

UN High Commissioner for Human Rights. (2014). *Towards better investment in the rights of the child: Report of the United Nations High Commissioner for Human Rights, A/HRC/28/33*. UN. Accessed November 14, 2020, from http://digitallibrary.un.org/record/792330

UN Secretary General. (2011). *Status of the Convention on the Rights of the Child: Report of the Secretary-General, A/66/230*. UN. Accessed November 12, 2020, from http://digitallibrary.un.org/record/709902

van Bueren, G. (1998). *The international law on the rights of the child*. Brill Nijhoff. Accessed September 22, 2020, from https://brill.com/view/title/10563

Vandenhole, W. (2007). *A commentary on the United Nations convention on the rights of the child, Article 26: The right to benefit from social security*. Brill Nijhoff. Accessed November 13, 2020, from https://brill.com/view/title/11639

Open Access This chapter is licensed under the terms of the Creative Commons Attribution 4.0 International License (http://creativecommons.org/licenses/by/4.0/), which permits use, sharing, adaptation, distribution and reproduction in any medium or format, as long as you give appropriate credit to the original author(s) and the source, provide a link to the Creative Commons license and indicate if changes were made.

The images or other third party material in this chapter are included in the chapter's Creative Commons license, unless indicated otherwise in a credit line to the material. If material is not included in the chapter's Creative Commons license and your intended use is not permitted by statutory regulation or exceeds the permitted use, you will need to obtain permission directly from the copyright holder.

Chapter 24
Article 27: The Right to a Standard of Living Adequate for Physical, Mental, Spiritual, Moral, and Social Development

Adem Arkadas-Thibert and Gerison Lansdown

1. States Parties recognize the right of every child to a standard of living adequate for the child's physical, mental, spiritual, moral and social development.
2. The parent(s) or others responsible for the child have the primary responsibility to secure, within their abilities and financial capacities, the conditions of living necessary for the child's development.
3. States Parties, in accordance with national conditions and within their means, shall take appropriate measures to assist parents and others responsible for the child to implement this right and shall in case of need provide material assistance and support programmes, particularly with regard to nutrition, clothing and housing.
4. States Parties shall take all appropriate measures to secure the recovery of maintenance for the child from the parents or other persons having financial responsibility for the child, both within the State Party and from abroad. In particular, where the person having financial responsibility for the child lives in a state different from that of the child, States Parties shall promote the accession to international agreements or the conclusion of such agreements, as well as the making of other appropriate arrangements.

A. Arkadas-Thibert (✉)
Marseille, France

G. Lansdown
Carleton University, Ottawa, Canada

> **What Did Children Say?**
> 'Government should help provide housing and clothing facilities to the children that will help us realise our potentials.' *(Africa)*
> 'Adults would understand that what defines' good standard of living' can be different depending on the youth. Success is different for everybody.' *(Western Europe/Other)*
> Outreach workers would have lower caseloads so they can spend more time caring for youth and ensuring their standard of living is adequate. *(Western Europe/Other)*
> 'Government and schools are helping to boost self-esteem in children.' *(Latin America/Caribbean)*

Overview

The right to an adequate standard of living is established in international law in the Universal Declaration of Human Rights, Article 25, and the International Covenant on Economic Social and Cultural Rights, Article 11. However, unlike Article 11, which requires that States Parties undertake 'appropriate steps to ensure the realization' and 'to the maximum of their available resources,' the text of the Convention on the Rights of the Child, in Article 27, formulates the obligation as requiring States Parties to adopt appropriate measures 'in accordance with national conditions and within their means.' This weakened formulation provides for the child's right to a minimal, not optimal, standard of living, that supports their holistic development, and reflects the drafters' concerns to limit states' legal obligations (Office of the United Nations High Commissioner for Human Rights and Rädda barnen (Society: Sweden), 2007, p. 629).

Article 27 asserts the right of the child to their holistic and optimal development: not only physical and mental, but also spiritual, moral, and social development. Again, it differs from the formulation in Article 11 of the Covenant on Economic, Social and Economic Rights, in constructing the right to an adequate standard of living instrumentally, as a means through which to promote the optimum development of the child, rather than an end in itself (Nolan, 2019, pp. 1023–1024). In so doing, it clearly affirms that the child is entitled to a standard of living that provides more than poverty alleviation but is consistent with respect for the human dignity of the child (Pais, 1997). The Article recognises the child as the holder of their own right to development with support from parents and other caretakers through provision of adequate and necessary living conditions including but not limited to nutrition, clothing, and housing to children (Eide, 2006, pp. 1–9).

In line with the spirit of the Convention, as asserted in the preamble and Articles 5 and 18, Article 27, paragraph 2, assigns primary responsibility of care for living conditions to the family and other caretakers within their abilities and financial capacities. Together with paragraph 3, this defines the family and other caretakers as both duty-bearers towards the child, and rights holders. It imposes obligations on States Parties within their means to provide material assistance when needed, and to support families and caretakers in the performance of their parental care responsibilities. Article 27, paragraph 4, recognises the child's right to recovery of maintenance from the parents even when that parent is living in another state. It obliges States Parties to negotiate and accede to international agreements for recovery of maintenance of the child in the same country or in another country so that they enjoy family care.

Hence, it is imperative to stress that, according to Article 27, both the family and other caretakers have responsibilities, but the States Parties are duty-bearers with obligations to respect, protect, and fulfil the rights of the child. If the child's best interest calls for it, States Parties have obligations to provide alternative care to the child with a standard of living adequate for holistic development, to protect the child from harm to their holistic development within the family and other care environments including in care and education settings, and to develop an enabling social and economic environment for the caretakers to provide for the child's right to a standard of living (Andrews, 1999, p. 5).

General Principles

Article 2 Along with prohibited grounds for discrimination as articulated in Article 2, the Convention affirms special circumstances which expose children to discrimination and inequality-based harm, for example, poverty-based exclusion, family separation, penal system involvement, minority or indigenous group status, traumatisation, exposure to armed conflict, and refugee status. Assuring a standard of living adequate for the holistic development of the child threatened by such risk of discrimination requires special protection measures by the States Parties. The Committee emphasises the 'interrelation between Articles 2, 6 and 27 (1) of the Convention on the Rights of the Child' such that, regardless of the child's status or that of their parents, States Parties have an obligation to fulfil the child's right to a standard of living adequate for their holistic development (UN Committee on the Protection of the Rights of All Migrant Workers and Members of Their Families and UN Committee on the Rights of the Child, 2017, para. 43).

Article 3 Many legal and policy decisions affect how children experience their standard of living. The impact of poverty is different for children than it is for adults. The deprivation of basic material needs has permanent effects on children, with even short periods of deprivation able to affect long-term development. Therefore, the Committee repeatedly reminds States Parties of their obligation to uphold the child's best interests in the allocation of national resources for programmes and measures in fulfilling their right to optimal and holistic development, and when necessary with international assistance or development aid (2013a, p. 15(d)).

Article 6 States Parties must create an environment that respects human dignity and ensures the holistic development of every child (UN Committee on the Rights of the Child, 2013a, para. 42). Article 6 gives States Parties the responsibility to 'ensure to the maximum extent possible the survival and development of the child.' In the assessment and determination of the child's best interests, States Parties must ensure full respect for the child's inherent right to life, survival, and development (UN Committee on the Rights of the Child, 2013a, para. 42). Article 27 is about a child's physical, mental, spiritual, moral, and social development. Each element of child development is equally important. Protection of the right to an adequate standard of living must be directed to the realisation of the holistic development of the child.

Article 12 The child's right to be heard has two main implications in respect of Article 27. First, children have a right to be heard in any administrative proceedings affecting the child, including decisions that affect their standard of living and living conditions, as well as in the development of broader policy developments that impact on this right. Second, States Parties are required to provide appropriate support, in the form of legal and administrative information and redress mechanisms to assist children to claim their rights, and to provide support to parents and caregivers in fulfilling their responsibilities towards the children (UN Committee on the Rights of the Child, 2009, para. 32).

Articles Related or Linked to Article 27

Articles 5, 7 and 18, like Article 27, address the balance of responsibility between parents and the state for providing care for children.

Article 20 addresses the right to alternative care for children deprived of their family environment. The Committee has emphasised that States Parties should address the adequacy of the standard of living of a child rather than remove a child into care in response to family poverty.

Article 22, 23, and 30 focus respectively on the rights of refugee and asylum-seeking children, children with disabilities, and those belonging to minorities or indigenous groups. These children are at high risk of exclusion and poverty and States Parties need to adopt all appropriate measures to protect their standard of living consistent with their optimum development

Article 24 is closely linked with the right to an adequate standard of living without which it is not possible for children to achieve the best possible health.

Article 26 provides for the child's right to benefit from social security as an assurance to their right to a standard of living adequate for holistic development.

Articles 28, 29, and 31 cannot be realised if children do not have an adequate standard of living to enable them to learn effectively or the time, space, and opportunities to play as a consequence of poverty.

Article 32, 34, 35, and 36 address forms of exploitation of the child, which is widely associated with poverty and an inadequate standard of living

Relevant Instruments

UN Universal Declaration of Human Rights (1948), Article 25
International Covenant on Economic, Social and Cultural Rights (1966), Article 11

Attributes

Attribute One: Securing an Adequate Standard of Living for Each Child's Holistic Development

As Article 27 asserts that children are entitled to a standard of living adequate for their physical, mental, spiritual, moral and social development, and not merely their material welfare, it is clear that it demands more than an exclusive focus on economic measures. The concept of adequacy is not explicitly defined but the Committee has referred to a standard of living that allows for optimal, healthy or holistic development (Nolan, 2019, p. 1036). Thus, although, it does not, unlike the International Covenant on Economic Social and Cultural Rights, Article 11, elaborate the elements necessary for an adequate standard of living, the Committee has urged States Parties to introduce measures that would ensure access to nutrition, shelter, clothing, water and sanitation (2007, para. 3, 2010, para. 61, 2012a, para. 55, 2012b, para. 61, 2013b, para. 61). Such measures are necessary to provide children with the basic security to allow for adequate nourishment and growth, educational attainment, health, as well as emotional, social and psychological development as a whole, basic security in infancy and childhood, and an environment in which families and alternative care settings can provide basic material needs for children under their care (Vaghri et al., 2010, pp. 73–74).

The obligations on States Parties in respect of Article 27 demand that States Parties recognise the child's realization of adequate living standards, rather than 'simply access to opportunities through a family's or a community's living standards' (Andrews and Kaufman, 1999, p. 4), and adjust policies accordingly to develop a comprehensive policy beyond supporting parental roles.

States Parties are therefore obliged to take into account the child's right to a standard of living adequate for the child's holistic development through all fiscal, monetary, and exchange rate policies as well as development, health, education, food security, and business regulations that support a dignified life for the child and their family or other caretakers (Eide, 2006, pp. 34–35; UN Committee on the Rights of the Child, 2006a, para. 26, 2006b, paras. 65, 66, 2012c, para. 68, 2016a, para. 71, 2018a, para. 9).

Attribute Two: Obligation to Take Measures to Assist Parents and Other Caretakers

The Convention obliges States Parties, in accordance with national conditions and within their means, to take appropriate measures to assist parents and others responsible for the child to ensure their optimal physical, mental, spiritual, moral, and social development. They must 'in case of need provide material assistance and support programmes, particularly with regard to nutrition, clothing and housing.'

Therefore, measures to assist parents and other caretakers can take many forms including

- Simplified procedures for families with children in vulnerable situations and children living below the poverty line to have quick and adequate access to social protection in diverse forms, such as tax advantages, financial aid, services, and counselling[1]
- Improving the provision of housing and basic services and strengthening support for families facing eviction as a result of financial difficulties[2]
- Holding targeted consultations with families, children, children's rights organisations, and civil society organisations on the issue of child poverty, with a view to strengthening the strategies and measures for fulfilling children's rights in poverty reduction strategies[3]
- Creating employment conditions which assist working parents and caregivers in fulfilling their responsibilities to children in their care, such as the introduction of family-friendly workplace policies, including parental leave, support for breastfeeding, and access to quality childcare services; as well as payment of wages sufficient for an adequate standard of living, protection from discrimination and violence in the workplace, and ensuring security and safety in the workplace.[4]

---

[1] See, for example, concluding observations for Canada (2012c, para. 33(e)), Serbia (2017a, para. 51 (c), 52 (d)–(e)), and Ireland (2016b, para. 70 (c)).

[2] See, for example, concluding observations for Serbia (2017a, para. 52 (c)) and Georgia (2017b, para. 35 (a)). See also, General Comment no. 7 regarding Implementation of the International Covenant on Economic, Social and Cultural Rights (UN Committee on Economic, Social and Cultural Rights, 1997, paras. 9, 10), and UN Special Rapporteur on the right to adequate housing (Farha, 2019, paras. 55–58).

[3] See, for example, concluding observations for Ecuador (2017c), Denmark (2017d), and Spain (2018b).

[4] See, for example, concluding observations for Croatia (2014, para. 38b)

Attribute Three: Recovery of Maintenance for the Child

The Committee has consistently asked States Parties to set up accessible and timely maintenance systems with clear legislation, definitions, and duties, as well as information campaigns, to manage national and international recovery of maintenance for the child from the parents or other persons having financial responsibility for the child. This might include cases of the separation or divorce of the parents, unmarried parents, adolescent parents, and children in second families.[5] However, States Parties should not use this to shift their care and protection obligations to the parents or other caretakers as a means of reducing their public expenditure bill (Hodgkin et al., 2007, p. 401).

Measures should also be in place to avoid instances of one of the parents using financial leverage to secure unwanted access to the child, to assert a greater right to determine the child's future, or to retain custody of children to secure financial support or accommodation for themselves (Hodgkin et al., 2007, p. 401).

When international recovery is required, States Parties are urged to enter into bilateral and international agreements that secure recovery of maintenance for the child, guided by the best interests principle of Article 3 (Hague Conference on Private International Law, 1976; Hodgkin et al., 2007, p. 402; UN General Assembly, 1957).

References

Andrews, A. B. (1999). Securing adequate living conditions for each child's development. In A. B. Andrews & N. H. Kaufman (Eds.), *Implementing the U.N. convention on the rights of the child: A standard of living adequate for development* (pp. 3–16). Praeger. Accessed November 14, 2020, from http://ebooks.abc-clio.com/?isbn=9780313003615

Andrews, A. B., & Kaufman, N. H. (Eds.). (1999). *Implementing the U.N. Convention on the rights of the child: A standard of living adequate for development*. Praeger. Accessed November 14, 2020, from http://ebooks.abc-clio.com/?isbn=9780313003615

Eide, A. (2006). *A commentary on the United Nations convention on the rights of the child, Article 27: The right to an adequate standard of living*. Brill Nijhoff. Accessed November 14, 2020, from https://brill.com/view/title/11640

Farha, L. (2019). *Guidelines for the implementation of the right to adequate housing: Report of the special rapporteur on adequate housing as a component of the right to an adequate standard of living, and on the right to non-discrimination in this context, A/HRC/43/43*. UN. Accessed November 15, 2020, from http://digitallibrary.un.org/record/3872412

Hague Conference on Private International Law. (1976). *Convention of 2 October 1973 on the recognition and enforcement of decisions relating to maintenance obligations*. Accessed November 14, 2020, from https://www.hcch.net/en/instruments/conventions/full-text/?cid=85

---

[5] See, for example, concluding observations for Ukraine (2002, para. 42), Belize (2005, paras. 44, 45) and Ecuador (2017c).

Hodgkin, R., Newell, P., & UNICEF. (2007). *Implementation handbook for the convention on the rights of the child* (3rd ed.). UNICEF. Accessed September 21, 2020, from https://digitallibrary.un.org/record/620060?ln=en

Nolan, A. (2019). Article 27: The right to a standard of living adequate for the child's development. In J. Tobin (Ed.), *The UN convention on the rights of the child: A commentary* (pp. 1021–1055). Oxford University Press.

Office of the United Nations High Commissioner for Human Rights & Rädda barnen (Society: Sweden). (2007). *Legislative history of the Convention on the Rights of the Child*. United Nations. https://digitallibrary.un.org/record/602462?ln=en

Pais, M. S. (1997). The convention on the rights of the child. In *Manual on human rights reporting under six major international human rights instruments HR/PUB/91/1 (Rev.1)* (pp. 393–505). OHCHR. Accessed May 16, 2020, from https://www.refworld.org/docid/428085252.html

UN Committee on Economic, Social and Cultural Rights. (1997). *Implementation of the international covenant on economic, social and cultural rights: general comment no. 7 (1997), The right to adequate housing (art.11.1 of the Covenant): forced evictions*. UN. Accessed 15 November 2020, from http://digitallibrary.un.org/record/240198

UN Committee on the Protection of the Rights of All Migrant Workers and Members of Their Families & UN Committee on the Rights of the Child. (2017). *Joint General Comment No. 3 (2017) of the Committee on the Protection of the Rights of All Migrant Workers and Members of Their Families and No. 22 (2017) of the Committee on the Rights of the Child on the general principles regarding the human rights of children in the context of international migration, CMW/C/GC/3, CRC/C/GC/22*. UN. Accessed November 6, 2020, from http://digitallibrary.un.org/record/1323014

UN Committee on the Rights of the Child. (2002). *Concluding observations: Ukraine, October 9, 2002, CRC/C/15/Add.191*. UN. Accessed November 14, 2020, from http://digitallibrary.un.org/record/481013.

UN Committee on the Rights of the Child. (2005). *Concluding observations: Belize, March 31, 2005, CRC/C/15/Add.252*. UN. Accessed November 7, 2020, from http://digitallibrary.un.org/record/557398

UN Committee on the Rights of the Child. (2006a). *General Comment No. 7 (2005) Implementing child rights in early childhood, September 20, 2006, CRC/C/GC/7/Rev.1*. Accessed October 12, 2020, from https://digitallibrary.un.org/record/584854?ln=en

UN Committee on the Rights of the Child. (2006b). *Concluding observations: Colombia, June 8, 2006, CRC/C/COL/CO/3*. UN. Accessed November 15, 2020, from http://digitallibrary.un.org/record/582283

UN Committee on the Rights of the Child. (2007). *General Comment No. 9 (2006) The rights of children with disabilities, November 13, 2007, CRC/C/GC/9*. https://digitallibrary.un.org/record/593891?ln=en. Accessed October 12, 2020

UN Committee on the Rights of the Child. (2009). *General Comment No. 12 (2009) The right of the child to be heard, July 20, 2009, CRC/C/GC/12*. Accessed October 12, 2020, from https://digitallibrary.un.org/record/671444?ln=en

UN Committee on the Rights of the Child. (2010). *Concluding observations: Burundi, October 19, 2010, CRC/C/BDI/CO/2*. UN. Accessed November 14, 2020, from http://digitallibrary.un.org/record/692497

UN Committee on the Rights of the Child. (2012a). *Concluding observations: Madagascar, March 8, 2012, CRC/C/MDG/CO/3-4*. UN. Accessed November 14, 2020, from http://digitallibrary.un.org/record/723341

UN Committee on the Rights of the Child. (2012b). *Concluding observations: Togo, March 8, 2012, CRC/C/TGO/CO/3-4*. UN. Accessed November 14, 2020, from http://digitallibrary.un.org/record/723343

UN Committee on the Rights of the Child. (2012c). *Concluding observations: Canada, December 6, 2012, CRC/C/CAN/CO/3-4*. Accessed October 11, 2020, from https://digitallibrary.un.org/record/739319?ln=en

UN Committee on the Rights of the Child. (2013a). *General Comment No. 14 (2013) On the right of the child to have his or her best interests taken as a primary consideration (art. 3, para. 1), May 29, 2013, CRC/C/GC/14*. Accessed October 12, 2020, from https://digitallibrary.un.org/record/778523?ln=en

UN Committee on the Rights of the Child. (2013b). *Concluding observations: Guinea-Bissau, July 8, 2013, CRC/C/GNB/CO/2-4*. Accessed October 12, 2020, from https://digitallibrary.un.org/record/756269?ln=en

UN Committee on the Rights of the Child. (2014). *Concluding observations: Croatia, October 13, 2014, CRC/C/HRV/CO/3-4*. UN. Accessed November 15, 2020, from http://digitallibrary.un.org/record/785292

UN Committee on the Rights of the Child. (2016a). *Concluding observations: United Kingdom, July 12, 2016, CRC/C/GBR/CO/5*. UN. Accessed November 15, 2020, from http://digitallibrary.un.org/record/835015

UN Committee on the Rights of the Child. (2016b). *Concluding observations: Ireland, March 1, 2016, CRC/C/IRL/CO/3-4*. UN. Accessed November 15, 2020, from http://digitallibrary.un.org/record/834930

UN Committee on the Rights of the Child. (2017a). *Concluding observations: Serbia, March 7, 2017, CRC/C/SRB/CO/2-3*. Accessed October 12, 2020, from https://www.refworld.org/pdfid/58e76fc14.pdf

UN Committee on the Rights of the Child. (2017b). *Concluding observations: Georgia, March 9, 2017, CRC/C/GEO/CO/4*. UN. http://digitallibrary.un.org/record/1311377. Accessed November 15, 2020

UN Committee on the Rights of the Child. (2017c). *Concluding observations: Ecuador, October 26, 2017, CRC/C/ECU/CO/5-6*. UN. Accessed November 14, 2020, from http://digitallibrary.un.org/record/1311757

UN Committee on the Rights of the Child. (2017d). *Concluding observations: Denmark, October 26, 2017, CRC/C/DNK/CO/5*. UN. Accessed November 6, 2020, from http://digitallibrary.un.org/record/1311756

UN Committee on the Rights of the Child. (2018a). *Concluding observations: Panama, February 28, 2018, CRC/C/PAN/CO/5-6*. UN. Accessed November 15, 2020, from http://digitallibrary.un.org/record/1476615

UN Committee on the Rights of the Child. (2018b). *Concluding observations: Spain, March 5, 2018, CRC/C/ESP/CO/5-6*. Accessed October 11, 2020, from https://digitallibrary.un.org/record/1476613?ln=en

UN General Assembly. (1957). *Convention on the recovery abroad of maintenance, 1957*.

Vaghri, Z., Arkadas, A., Hertzman, C., Krappmann, L., Gertsch, L., Cabral, M., et al. (2010). *Manual for early childhood rights indicators (manual of the indicators of general comment 7*)* (p. 229). UNICEF. https://resourcecentre.savethechildren.net/library/manual-early-childhood-rights-indicators-manual-indicators-general-comment-7

Open Access This chapter is licensed under the terms of the Creative Commons Attribution 4.0 International License (http://creativecommons.org/licenses/by/4.0/), which permits use, sharing, adaptation, distribution and reproduction in any medium or format, as long as you give appropriate credit to the original author(s) and the source, provide a link to the Creative Commons license and indicate if changes were made.

The images or other third party material in this chapter are included in the chapter's Creative Commons license, unless indicated otherwise in a credit line to the material. If material is not included in the chapter's Creative Commons license and your intended use is not permitted by statutory regulation or exceeds the permitted use, you will need to obtain permission directly from the copyright holder.

Chapter 25
Article 33: The Right to Protection from Illicit Use of Narcotic Drugs and Psychotropic Substances

Damon Barrett and Ziba Vaghri

States Parties shall take all appropriate measures, including legislative, administrative, social and educational measures, to protect children from the illicit use of narcotic drugs and psychotropic substances as defined in the relevant international treaties, and to prevent the use of children in the illicit production and trafficking of such substances

What Did Children Say?
Schools have courses for students and communities to understand well the consequences of harmful drug and know how to deal with the activities of drug trading. *(Asia-Pacific)*

Governments should follow international treaties to determine which substances should be legal or illegal. *(Eastern Europe)*

Governments should allow substances to be supplied in a safe way. *(Eastern Europe)*

Control over pharmaceutical companies. *(Eastern Europe)*

D. Barrett
University of Gothenburg, Göteborg, Sweden
e-mail: damon.barrett@gu.se

Z. Vaghri (✉)
University of New Brunswick, Saint John, Canada
e-mail: ziba.vaghri@unb.ca

Overview

Article 33 enshrines the right to protection from narcotic drugs and psychotropic substances. It has no equivalent in earlier human rights treaties (Barrett, 2020, pp. 19–59). The later ILO Convention 182, in Article 3(c), and the African Charter on the Rights and Welfare of the Child, in Article 28, complement the provision. While originally discussed as part of the draft provision on the right to health, the Article was ultimately placed between provisions on economic and sexual exploitation, though there was little discussion in drafting as to what the provision required (Barrett, 2020, pp. 50–59; Office of the United Nations High Commissioner for Human Rights and Rädda barnen (Society: Sweden), 2007).

There are two related but separate clauses in Article 33: the protection of children from illicit use, and the prevention of the use of children in illicit production and trafficking. Thus, the former is placed by the Committee (since 2010) within basic health and welfare cluster, while the latter is assessed as a special protection measure (UN Committee on the Rights of the Child, 2010). The phrase 'shall take' indicates a strong formulation that, commensurate with other provisions in the Convention, requires positive obligations on the part of States Parties.

While protecting children from drugs is self-evidently important, the means to do so are a constant political and social debate. Article 33 is very generally framed and finds itself within a contested area of law and policy. Protecting children from drugs and the drug trade could cover all drug policy. The added value of the Convention provision is in bringing the question of drug use and the drug trade into the normative child rights framework.[1] Thus, rather than merely providing a child rights rationale for existing drug laws and policies, the periodic reporting process is an opportunity for critical child rights reflection on them. What, in other words, are the appropriate legislative, administrative, social, and educational measures for the achievement of the aims of Article 33? This approach requires unpacking the normative content of appropriate measures.

It is also important to note that this provision clearly links Article 33 to the UN drug control conventions listed in the Relevant Instruments section. The drafting history demonstrates, however, that the reference to the 'relevant international treaties' was intended to demarcate the substances in question rather than to indicate which measures are appropriate to take (Barrett, 2017). There are good reasons for this, including that there are parties to the Convention on the Rights of the Child that are not parties to drug control conventions (Barrett, 2019).

However, as the scope of Article 33 is defined by reference to substances 'defined in the relevant international treaties,' when the UN Commission on Narcotic Drugs places a new substance under international control, that decision engages the obligations of all parties to the Convention on the Rights of the Child (Barrett and Lohman, 2020). Alcohol and tobacco are, strictly speaking, omitted as they are not

---

[1] For a discussion, see 'Article 33: Protection from Narcotic Drugs and Psychotropic Substances' (Barrett and Tobin, 2019).

captured by these treaties, though these have been addressed by the Committee under the broader umbrella of 'adolescent health' (Barrett, 2020, pp. 132–135).

The provision does not relate to licit uses of controlled substances. These include opiates for the control of pain, such as morphine. Instead, children have the right to access such essential medicines under Article 24 (discussed earlier in this part). However, controlled medicines are lacking for about two-thirds of the world's population, according to the WHO. It is an area the Committee has yet to address in the light of this connection between Articles 24 and 33.

Similarly, Article 33 does not cover licit production, such as licenced opium poppy production. Instead, any such work is covered by Article 32. The difference is that Article 32 entails a qualitative assessment of working conditions based on child labour standards, whereas Article 33 is an absolute prohibition as a worst form of child labour (see also, ILO Convention 182) (Barrett and Lohman, 2020).

General Principles

Article 2 Understood in a negative sense, there are various ways in which children and young people may be discriminated against in drug policy, for example, through legal age restrictions on access to services without a medical or ethical basis. In a more positive sense, States Parties have obligations to ensure the collection of adequately disaggregated data on drug use to uncover patterns of vulnerability and target those in need. However, drug use data are poor outside of high-income countries, where there are significant difficulties collecting such information.

Article 3 In general, the best interests principle leads to a similar dilemma as that posed by Article 33 itself. It is not agreed which legal and policy approaches are in children's best interests. It is likely more fruitful to apply the test to specific context than to attempt to link it to broad policy prescriptions, e.g., replacing the kinds of legal age restrictions noted above with best interests assessments.

Article 6 Problematic drug use is a mix of personal and environmental factors. Article 6 speaks to the necessity of viewing the drugs issue holistically, rather than to focus on enforcement, where most drug policy budgets are directed. Contemporary epidemiological and prevention evidence suggests a need to focus on social and economic determinants, and on resilience and empowerment instead of 'just say no' messaging.

Article 12 In practice, children are rarely consulted in the development of drug policies. Article 12 would require that their views and experiences are gathered and applied to inform legislation and policy governing drug use, including issues such as random school drug testing and compulsory drug treatment.

Articles Related or Linked to Article 33

Given the widespread influence of the drug issue on many spheres of children's lives, there are few Convention articles to which Article 33 is not connected. Specifically, however:

- **Article 13,** children have the right to receive 'accurate and objective' information about drugs and related harms (Barrett and Tobin, 2019).
- **Article 17**, children should be protected from misinformation about drugs and from material injurious to their well-being.[2]
- **Article 18(2)**, children of parents with drug dependence are at risk of later drug use themselves. Assistance to such parents is an important form of protection.
- **Article 19**, children who use drugs, with parents who are drug dependent, and those involved in the drug trade are at risk of various forms of neglect and abuse.
- **Article 24**, children and young people who use drugs do not forfeit their right to health, and require programmes targeted for their health needs (UN Committee on the Rights of the Child, 2003, 2013, Article 24, 2016).
- **Article 27**, children involved in the drug trade are often from poor socio-economic backgrounds.
- **Article 28**, as education plays a protective role with regard to delaying drug use initiation and protecting children from exploitation. However, some school-based interventions may violate the right to education, including random testing, sniffer dogs, and strip searches.
- **Article 30**, as the rights of indigenous children or children from minority groups to enjoy their culture may clash with Article 33. For example, chewing coca leaf is an indigenous practice in the Andean region, but banned under the UN drugs conventions ('the relevant international treaties' for Article 33).
- **Article 31**, as many young people initiate drug use out of boredom and a lack of other activities.
- **Article 37**, as children and young people who use drugs and that have been involved in the drug trade have been subjected to cruel, inhuman, and degrading treatment, both at the hands of police and in drug treatment facilities.
- **Article 40**, since children and young people who use drugs and who are involved in the drugs trade are involved in criminality, therefore requiring attention to juvenile justice standards.

Relevant Instruments

UN Single Convention on Narcotic Drugs (1961)

---

[2]This arose in *Handyside v UK*, App No 5493/72, [1976] ECHR 5.

International Covenant on Economic, Social and Cultural Rights (1966), Articles 10(3) and 12
International Covenant on Civil and Political Rights (1966), Article 24(1)
UN Convention on Psychotropic Substances (1971)
UN Convention against Illicit Traffic in Narcotic Drugs and Psychotropic Substances (1988)
WHO Framework Convention on Tobacco Control (2005)
ILO Convention 182, Worst forms of child labour (1999)
African Charter on the Rights and Welfare of the Child (1990), Article 28

Attributes

Attribute One: Protection from the Illicit Use of Narcotic Drugs and Psychotropic Substances

The Committee has issued hundreds of concluding observations raising drugs issues. Several General Comments are also relevant. Clearly, States Parties have prevention and treatment obligations relating to drug use, and this has been the overwhelming focus of the Committee's recommendations (Barrett, 2020, pp. 125–137).[3] More recently, the Committee has recommended harm reduction measures for children and young people who use drugs. It has recommended accurate and objective drugs information, schools-based programmes, healthy lifestyles and life skills education, access to services without parental consent, and youth-friendly services. Children who use drugs, moreover, should be treated as victims and not criminals according to the Committee, though the victim label may also be problematised from a child rights perspective. The Committee has also recommended the development of national actions plans and legislative frameworks (Barrett, 2020, pp. 125–137).

Complications arise, however, when questions are asked of what such laws, policies, and interventions entail. It is an area of law and policy that is rife with human rights problems. Random school drug testing as a form of prevention, for example, raises important child rights concerns in terms of consent and the consequences of positives tests for the right to education. Some prevention interventions are not only ineffective but counterproductive. Children have experienced serious abuses in drug treatment centres, which the Committee has strongly condemned (Barrett, 2020, pp. 168–171).

---

[3] See also, UN Commission on Narcotic Drugs, Resolution 58/2 'Supporting the availability, accessibility and diversity of scientific evidence-based treatment and care for children and young people with substance use disorders', 2015; Resolution 60/7 Promoting scientific evidence-based community, family and school programmes and strategies for the purpose of preventing drug use among children and adolescents', 2017.

Accordingly, with regard to protection from illicit use of drugs, States Parties should:

- ensure that state actors do not encourage, expose or facilitate the illicit use of controlled substances by children and do not block or impede prevention, harm reduction and treatment interventions for children who have used such substances (*the obligation to respect*)
- ensure that non-state actors do not encourage, expose, or facilitate the illicit use of controlled substances by children and do not block or impede effective prevention, harm reduction and treatment interventions (*the obligation to protect*); create an effective enabling environment for the prevention of drug use by children and the reduction of any health and social harms associated with drug use (*the obligation to fulfil*) (Barrett and Tobin, 2019)

Attribute Two: Prevention of the Use of Children in Illicit Production and Trafficking

The balance of concluding observations has been overwhelmingly towards the first clause of Article 33, with very few considering involvement in the drug trade (Barrett, 2020, pp. 125–137). Standards from juvenile justice and economic exploitation (see Part 9), and other areas may, however, be applied. As with protection from illicit use, it may be helpful to again begin with basic standards in order to:

- ensure that state actors do not encourage, expose, or facilitate the use of children in the illicit production and trafficking of the substances controlled by the relevant international instruments (*the obligation to respect*)
- ensure that non-state actors do not encourage, expose, or facilitate the use of children in the illicit production and trafficking of the substances controlled by the relevant international instruments (*the obligation to protect*)
- ensure that the underlying reasons for children's involvement in the illicit drug trade are addressed and that those children involved in the drug trade are removed and provided with appropriate measures to address any harm they may have suffered (*the obligation to fulfil*) (Barrett and Tobin, 2019)

Attribute Three: Appropriate Measures—Rights Compliance and Effectiveness as a Normative Test

The added value of Article 33 and the periodic reporting process should be as a critical review of what States Parties are doing, based on child rights standards. No other international mechanism has a direct mandate to do this. By and large, however, the periodic reporting process demonstrates that this has not been the focus. General Comments and Concluding Observations, and imbalances in focus, tend to reaffirm state actions, whatever these might be, while failing to challenge legal and policy structures for either compliance with child rights or their progress towards the goals enshrined in Article 33 (Barrett, 2020, pp. 148–149).

For a more evaluative lens, Barrett and Tobin have developed a test of appropriate measures based on two complementary top line principles. As with other areas of the Convention, 'appropriate measures' for the purposes of Article 33 must be human rights compliant and evidence-based (Barrett, 2020, pp. 148–189). The test is general so as to be universally applicable, but its key feature is that it leans towards a rights-based analysis of the quality and content of the laws, policies, and practices States Parties have put in place.

There is an ever-increasing volume of literature around interventions for children and young people in the context of drug use. However, what might be considered human rights compliant measures has been less clear. The UN system, via the Chief Executives Board for Coordination, has also issued a 'common position' on drug policies, which places considerable weight upon the human rights aspects of national responses (UN System Chief Executives Board for Coordination, 2019). Providing even more detail, the International Centre on Human Rights and Drug Policy has developed the International Guidelines on Human Rights and Drug Policy, endorsed by the UN Development Program, the WHO, UNAIDS, and the Office of the High Commissioner for Human Rights.[4] These includes a dedicated section on children, producing specific guidelines rooted in the work of the Committee on the Rights of the Child and other human rights mechanisms, as well as international standards on drug prevention and other issues.

References

Barrett, D. (2017). The Child's right to protection from drugs: Understanding history to move forward. *Health and Human Rights Journal, 19*(1), 263–268.

Barrett, D. (2019). Canada, cannabis and the relationship between UN child rights and drug control treaties. *International Journal of Drug Policy, 71*, 29–35. https://doi.org/10.1016/j.drugpo.2019.02.010

Barrett, D. (2020). *Child rights and drug control in international law*. Brill Nijhoff. Accessed November 15, 2020, from https://brill.com/view/title/55876

Barrett, D., & Lohman, D. (2020). Incorporating child rights into scheduling decisions at the UN commission on narcotic drugs. *International Development Policy | Revue internationale de politique de développement*, (12). doi:https://doi.org/10.4000/poldev.3972

Barrett, D., & Tobin, J. (2019). Article 33: Protection from narcotic drugs and psychotropic substances. In J. Tobin (Ed.), *The UN convention on the rights of the child: A commentary* (pp. 1273–1309). Oxford University Press.

---

[4]For more information, refer to the interactive website International Guidelines on Human Rights and Drug Policy, https://www.humanrights-drugpolicy.org/

Office of the United Nations High Commissioner for Human Rights & Rädda barnen (Society: Sweden). (2007). *Legislative history of the convention on the rights of the child*. United Nations. https://digitallibrary.un.org/record/602462?ln=en

UN Committee on the Rights of the Child. (2003). *General comment no. 3 (2003) HIV/AIDS and the rights of the child, March 17, 2003, CRC/GC/2003/3*. Accessed October 12, 2020, from https://digitallibrary.un.org/record/501529?ln=en

UN Committee on the Rights of the Child. (2010). *Treaty-specific guidelines regarding the form and content of periodic reports to be submitted by States parties under article 44, paragraph 1 (b), of the Convention on the Rights of the Child, November 23, 2010, CRC/C/58/Rev.2*. Accessed October 12, 2020, from https://digitallibrary.un.org/record/709813?ln=en

UN Committee on the Rights of the Child. (2013). *General comment no. 15 (2013) on the right of the child to the enjoyment of the highest attainable standard of health (art. 24), April 17, 2013, CRC/C/GC/15*. UN. Accessed October 26, 2020, from http://digitallibrary.un.org/record/778524.

UN Committee on the Rights of the Child. (2016). *General comment no. 20 (2016) on the implementation of the rights of the child during adolescence, December 6, 2016, CRC/C/GC/20*. Accessed October 12, 2020, from https://digitallibrary.un.org/record/855544?ln=en

UN System Chief Executives Board for Coordination. (2019). *Summary of deliberations: Chief Executives Board for Coordination, 2nd regular session of 2018, New York, 7 and 8 November 2018, CEB/2018/2*. Accessed November 15, 2020, from http://digitallibrary.un.org/record/3792232

Open Access This chapter is licensed under the terms of the Creative Commons Attribution 4.0 International License (http://creativecommons.org/licenses/by/4.0/), which permits use, sharing, adaptation, distribution and reproduction in any medium or format, as long as you give appropriate credit to the original author(s) and the source, provide a link to the Creative Commons license and indicate if changes were made.

The images or other third party material in this chapter are included in the chapter's Creative Commons license, unless indicated otherwise in a credit line to the material. If material is not included in the chapter's Creative Commons license and your intended use is not permitted by statutory regulation or exceeds the permitted use, you will need to obtain permission directly from the copyright holder.

Part V
Education, Leisure, and Cultural Activities Rights

Articles 28, 29, 30, and 31

Introduction

The cluster of articles relating to education, leisure, and culture speak powerfully to the Convention on the Rights of the Child's (the Convention) focus on the child's right to optimum development. Together they affirm not only the right of every child to learn and play in a safe and stimulating environment, respectful of their own culture and language, but also insist on the importance of respecting the child's own agency and contribution to their own development.

Article 28, the right to education, sets out in some detail the right to access education, which has been defined by the Committee on the Rights of the Child (the Committee) as taking place from birth and not restricted to the formal school environment (2001, para. 2). It emphasises that it should be provided with equality of opportunity at all levels. Article 28 introduces new obligations on States Parties, beyond those included in the Covenant on Economic, Social and Cultural Rights, to ensure that action is taken to reduce school drop-out rates, and to ensure that school discipline is administered in a manner consistent with the child's dignity. In these ways, Article 28 embodies a requirement not only that education is provided for every child but also that the nature of that education is designed to treat children with respect and to encourage and support their active participation and engagement in it. Thus, it is not sufficient for States Parties to provide education to every child: they must ensure that it is available, accessible, acceptable and adaptable without discrimination on any grounds.

Article 29 was created as a separate article elaborating the aims of education. Its overriding goal is the development of the child's fullest potential, but it acknowledges the wider aims of promoting respect for human rights, recognition and respect for the child's own cultural identity, preparation for life in a free society, and respect for the natural environment. The Committee has highlighted that implementation of these aims demands a participatory pedagogy in schools and for the school environment to be one where children experience respect for their human rights within the classroom as well as the wider school environment – learning through their lived experience.

Article 30 reiterates the provision in the Covenant on Civil and Political Rights recognising the child' right to enjoy their culture and practice their own religion and language. It differs only in that it adds recognition of indigenous rights. Although it is Article 30 that provides the key focus on the rights of minorities, these rights are reinforced by provisions throughout the Convention. The right to respect for the child's own culture is affirmed in relation to the child's identity, to family life, to freedom of expression, and to arts and culture. Moreover, in conjunction with Article 29, it necessitates that both the formal and informal school curriculum reflects this culture of respect.

Finally, Article 31 amalgamates separate provisions from the Covenant on Economic, Social and Cultural Rights that provide for rest and leisure and to cultural life, and brings them together with the important addition of play in the life of a child. Although Article 31 has often been taken less seriously than other rights, in fact it represents the very essence of childhood - with profound importance both for the enjoyment of childhood itself and for the child's future life.

This part explores how the Convention has adapted these rights from their iteration in previous treaties to reflect the particular circumstances, status, and developmental needs of children, and consequent obligations of States Parties in their implementation.

Reference

UN Committee on the Rights of the Child. (2001). *General Comment No. 1 (2001) Article 29 (1): The Aims of Education, April 17, 2001, CRC/GC/2001/1*. https://digitallibrary.un.org/record/447223?ln=en. Accessed 10 October 2020

Chapter 26
Article 28: The Right to Education

Gerison Lansdown and Ziba Vaghri

1. States Parties recognize the right of the child to education and with a view to achieving this right progressively and on the basis of equal opportunity, they shall, in particular:
   (a) Make primary education compulsory and available free to all;
   (b) Encourage the development of different forms of secondary education, including general and vocational education, make them available and accessible to every child, and take appropriate measures such as the introduction of free education and offering financial assistance in case of need;
   (c) Make higher education accessible to all on the basis of capacity by every appropriate means;
   (d) Make educational and vocational information and guidance available and accessible to all children;
   (e) Take measures to encourage regular attendance at schools and the reduction of drop-out rates.
2. States Parties shall take all appropriate measures to ensure that school discipline is administered in a manner consistent with the child's human dignity and in conformity with the present Convention.

(continued)

G. Lansdown (✉)
Carleton University, Ottawa, Canada

Z. Vaghri
University of New Brunswick, Saint John, Canada
e-mail: ziba.vaghri@unb.ca

> 3. States Parties shall promote and encourage international cooperation in matters relating to education, in particular with a view to contributing to the elimination of ignorance and illiteracy throughout the world and facilitating access to scientific and technical knowledge and modern teaching methods. In this regard, particular account shall be taken of the needs of developing countries.

> **What Did Children Say?**
> 'I would tell him to fix the lower income places where these schools are ... because some of the schools the cafeteria do not serve proper food for the children at lunch time and stuff.' *(Latin America/Caribbean)*
> 'Public call should be announced for students to give their views and proposal what should they learn in particular educational programmes or educational profiles.' *(Eastern Europe)*
> 'Inspections should be more frequent and spontaneous (unannounced). When inspectors announce the inspection, then teachers know in advance and they instruct students what are they going to teach, which questions will they ask students and what should students say.' *(Eastern Europe)*

Overview

Article 28 echoes the International Covenant on Economic and Social Rights, Article 13, in enshrining the right to education for all (Pinheiro, 2006; UN Secretary General, 2020, paras. 41–48). It has been described as a 'multiplier right,' epitomising the indivisibility of rights as it contributes to the realisation of many other rights (Courtis and Tobin, 2019, p. 1058; Tomaševski, 2006, p. 7). However, Article 28 differs from Article 13 in several significant ways. It expands the scope of the right to education to include obligations on States Parties to encourage school attendance and reduce drop-out rates, to ensure that school discipline is administered in a manner consistent with the child's dignity, and to promote and encourage international cooperation in matters relating to education. It lacks any reference to the right of parents to choose an education for their children in conformity with their moral or religious convictions, although this issue is addressed in Article 29, the aims of education.

The provision of education for all has significant resource implications and, accordingly, Article 28 is subject to progressive realisation. The text affirms that States Parties must, with a view to achieving the right progressively, make primary education compulsory and free to all. The obligations on secondary education are lower, requiring that States Parties encourage its development, and accessibility and availability to all, including through provision of free education and financial support. Higher education must be made available by every appropriate means, and education and vocational guidance available to all children. However, the Committee on Economic, Social and Cultural Rights has proposed that minimum core requirements must be introduced irrespective of available resources. These include non-discrimination in access to education, consistency of the curricula with international human rights standards, and compulsory and free primary education to all (1999, para. 57).

Non-discrimination and free and compulsory primary education for all have also been re-affirmed as core obligations by the Committee on the Rights of Persons with Disabilities (2016, para. 41). The Committee on the Rights of the Child has not explicitly articulated any core obligations. However, it consistently recommends that States Parties endorse these measures as an immediate core obligation, not subject to progressive realisation, particularly in respect of its demands that budget allocations are sufficiently directed to the implementation of the right to education (UN Committee on the Rights of the Child, 2000a, para. 18, 2003, para. 60 (a), 2005a, para. 59, 2010a, para. 59).

The Convention does not define the word education. However, the Committee makes clear that education extends 'beyond formal schooling to embrace the broad range of life experiences and learning processes which enable children … to develop their personalities, talents and abilities and to live a full and satisfying life within society' (2001, para. 2). Accordingly, education is not confined to those levels elaborated in Article 28. It is interpreted as beginning at birth, and extends to the provision of preschool education (UN Committee on the Rights of the Child, 2006a, para. 28). Although silent on ages for starting or finishing school, the Committee has asked States Parties to establish minimum and maximum ages for compulsory education (Verheyde, 2005), encouraged the inclusion of early childhood education and care (UN Committee on the Rights of the Child, 2004a, 2006a, 2016a, para. 69 (g)), and suggested that the end of compulsory education should coincide with the minimum age for employment (1995a, b, 1996). Furthermore, the Committee has interpreted the article to apply to regular and non-formal education (2000b, para. 90) and has recommended non-formal education for children who have difficulty attending schools (2002a, para. 306, 2004b, para. 58).

General Principles

Article 2 Article 28 requires that education be provided on the basis of equal opportunity to all children. The obligation to ensure non-discrimination in respect of the right to education is an immediate obligation and applies to all aspects of education (UN Committee on Economic, Social and Cultural Rights, 1999, para. 13). No child can be discriminated against in respect of their right to education on any of the prohibited grounds elaborated in Article 2. The Committee has repeatedly highlighted many groups of children who are vulnerable to discrimination in education and demanded that States Parties take action to secure their equal right to education. These groups include, among many others, children with disabilities (2004c, para. 48), girls (2005b, para. 75), indigenous children (2005c, para. 59), Roma children (2002b, para. 42 (a)), children in detention (2005d, para. 53), rural, immigrant, refugee and asylum-seeking children, children affected by armed combat, working children, children in conflict with the law, and those living with HIV/AIDs (UN Committee on the Protection of the Rights of All Migrant Workers and Members of Their Families and UN Committee on the Rights of the Child, 2017, paras. 59–63; UN Committee on the Rights of the Child, 2007a, paras. 62–72, 2007b, para. 89, 2009a, paras. 56–63, 2017a, para. 19; Verheyde, 2005).

Article 3 Education is the individual right of every child and it is in their best interests that they receive a quality education. In developing an education system, States Parties must ensure that the best interests of the child are its primary focus, and that it is not subordinated to broader economic or instrumental societal goals, such as conformity with specific religious or political views (Courtis and Tobin, 2019, p. 1062).

Article 6 The realisation of the right to education is an integral dimension in contributing towards the child's optimum development. The breadth of the education curriculum, as well as the means through which is it delivered, must be designed to promote children's optimum development.

Article 12 The right of the child to be heard is fundamental to the right to education. The Committee have affirmed that children should be listened to and engaged through a participatory pedagogy within the classroom, and schools should adopt a culture of respect for the right of the child to be heard (2009b, para. 107). In addition, States Parties must ensure that children have opportunities to influence decisions from their individual education to the way their school is run, through class and school councils, and representation on school boards, and also in the development of broader education legislation and policy (UN Committee on the Rights of the Child, 2009b, paras. 109–111). Finally, children must have the opportunity to be heard in any disciplinary proceedings (UN Committee on the Rights of the Child, 2009b, para. 113).

Articles Related or Linked to Article 28

Article 4 obliges States Parties to take all appropriate measures to implement education as described in Article 28 (1), and to assist those with inadequate resources to do so.

Articles 13–17 contain provisions on access to information and participation the two essential pillars of education.

Article 19 (1) provides protection to the child from maltreatment from teachers and others.

Article 23 (3) ensures that children with disabilities have access to education.

Article 24 (e) requires children receive health education.

Article 29 describes the appropriate content and aims of education.

Article 30 requires provision of conditions for children of indigenous or minority groups to be educated on and enjoy their own culture, religion, and use their own language.

Article 31, consistent with current knowledge of the important role of art-based and play-based learning, also requires that rest, play, leisure, and recreation are provided for in education.

Article 32 obliges States Parties to ensure labour does not compromise the child's enjoyment of their right to education (Verheyde, 2005).

Relevant Instruments

UN Universal Declaration of Human Rights (1948), Article 26
  UN Declaration of the Rights of the Child (1959), Principle 7
  UN Convention Against Discrimination in Education (1960)
  International Covenant on Economic, Social and Cultural Rights (1966), Article 13
  UN Convention on Technical and Vocational Education (1989)
  Treaties which address the education rights of vulnerable groups:

- UN Convention Relating to the Status of Refugees (1951), Article 22
- International Convention on the Elimination of All Forms of Racial Discrimination (1966), Article 5
- UN Declaration on the Rights of Disabled Persons (1975), Principle 6
- UN Convention on the Elimination of All Forms of Discrimination against Women (1979), Article 10
- International Convention on the Protection of the Rights of all Migrant Workers and their Families (1990), Article 30
- UN Declaration on the Rights of Persons Belonging to National or Ethnic Religious and Linguistic Minorities (1992), Article 4 (3)
- UN Convention on the Rights of Persons with Disabilities (2006), Articles 7 and 24.

Attributes

Attribute One: Access to Primary, Secondary, and Higher Education

States Parties must make primary education compulsory and available free to all. Although no age range is prescribed, it would typically be for 6 years up to the age of

12 (UNESCO Institute for Statistics, 2012, para. 122). The compulsory provision exists in recognition of essential nature of primary education for development of the child and their effective functioning in society. It is intended to ensure that neither the state nor the parent (or indeed the child) can prioritise other options potentially harmful for the child's development (Courtis and Tobin, 2019, p. 1083).

The Committee has consistently demanded of States Parties that they provide sufficient funding to ensure free compulsory primary education, including by abolishing fees (2010b, para. 72 (a), (b)). The Committee is also highly critical of the imposition of indirect costs such as obligatory school uniforms, textbooks and other materials, meals, transport, fees for participation in certain activities, or exam fees, and has recommended their abolition.[1]

States Parties must also encourage the development of secondary education, which is commonly between the ages of 12 and 17 years, and must be provided in different forms to allow flexible curricula and systems to accommodate both academic and vocational opportunities. Notably, Article 28 does not impose the requirements that it is either free or compulsory. However, the Committee has welcomed the introduction of measures by States Parties to extend mandatory education to secondary level (2012c, para. 63). It also recommends measures to render secondary education free to every child (2011, para. 62 (b)). Finally, States Parties must make higher education accessible to all on the basis of capacity. Although the Committee has afforded minimal attention to this provision, it has drawn attention to potential discrimination in access and recommended that States Parties take action to ensure equal opportunities for higher education for marginalised groups of children (2012d, para. 63 (b)).

The overarching requirements in implementing the right to education have been conceptualised as the 4As: education must be available, accessible, acceptable, and adaptable (Tomaševski, 1999). Availability requires that the requisite resources have been allocated to enable sufficient school places, trained teachers, equipment, books, and other materials, as well as, for example, adequate sanitation facilities, to enable every child to attend school. Accessibility necessitates that no barriers to education exist for any child whether as a consequence of discrimination, physical access, or affordability (UN Committee on Economic, Social and Cultural Rights, 1999, para. 69 (b)). Acceptability demands that education is relevant, culturally appropriate, and of good quality (UN Committee on Economic, Social and Cultural Rights, 1999, para. 69 (c)). Finally, adaptability requires a flexible education system that is capable of responding to the needs of a diverse range of students in a variety of different and potentially changing contexts (UN Committee on Economic, Social and Cultural Rights, 1999, para. 69 (d)).

States Parties are encouraged to adopt a range of measures to achieve these objectives. They must ensure the ongoing collection of adequate disaggregated data to identify gaps, needs, and violations of education rights, and plan future or

---

[1] See, for example, concluding observations for Vietnam (2012a, para. 67 (b)) and Turkey (2012b, para. 59 (e)).

remedial action. Data should include, for example, primary enrolment rates and ratios by target groups, drop-out rates (including reasons for drop-out), proportion of children who are covered under publicly supported programmes and those required to pay fees, and proportion of children who attend preschool (United Nations OHCHR, 2012, p. 93),[2] the share of household expenditure on education at the secondary or tertiary level, and the proportion of fully qualified teachers (United Nations OHCHR, 2012, p. 93). In addition, States Parties are advised to formulate and implement national plans of action that address all elements of Article 28 and establish goals, timetables, and benchmarks. Plans should include appropriate legislative and administrative measures, for example, establishing the right to compulsory education, ensuring school leaving age consistent with the minimum age of employment (Verheyde, 2005), and complaints mechanisms to address, for example, school exclusions, corporal punishment, and violence in schools.

Attribute Two: Education on the Basis of Equality of Opportunity

The principle of non-discrimination and equal opportunity relating to the right to education is well-established in international human rights law and is affirmed in Article 28 of the Convention. States Parties must ensure that no child is discriminated against directly or indirectly in either the public or private sphere of education on any of the prohibited grounds elaborated in Article 2 (UN Committee on Economic, Social and Cultural Rights, 2009). However, it is not only permitted but also required that States Parties adopt special measures to ensure equality of access to groups of children vulnerable to unequal access to and opportunity in education (Courtis and Tobin, 2019, p. 1077). Such measures must not result in unequal standards for different groups or continue after the objectives for which they were established have been achieved. The Committee on the Rights of Persons with Disabilities has insisted that the right to non-discrimination and education on the basis of equality includes the right not to be segregated and to be provided with reasonable accommodation and accessible learning environments (2016, para. 13). The Committee on the Rights of the Child has consistently affirmed this approach (2019, para. 43 (c)).

In order to monitor compliance with this obligation, States Parties must monitor relevant policies, institutions, programmes, and spending patterns to identify evidence of discrimination (UN Committee on Economic, Social and Cultural Rights, 1999, para. 37). Data should be collected to identify any differences in access to primary or secondary education on the basis of race, colour, sex, language, religion, national, ethnic or social origin, disability, birth or other analogous status including

---

[2]The UN Statistical Services Branch survey summarized in *Leaving No One Behind* (United Nations OHCHR, 2018) may serve as a useful guide for the collection of disaggregated data.

parental circumstances, maltreatment, and cultural resistance (UN Committee on the Rights of the Child, 2006b, para. 77 (g), 2013a, para. 52 (d), 53 (f); Verheyde, 2005).

Where discrimination is identified, measures are required to combat the problem and prevent recurrence. Article 28 demands measures to address inequalities leading to poor attendance and early drop-out rates among some groups of children, including those in nomadic and migrant families, as a consequence of poverty, or those supporting the family through paid work or taking care of siblings and household chores (UN Committee on the Rights of the Child, 2012e). The Committee has suggested a range of potential measures to be adopted by States Parties to promote greater equality of access and improved attendance, including:

- scholarships
- financial subsidies
- flexible educational arrangements
- enhanced provision in rural areas
- affirmative action programmes
- provision of free early childhood education (2013b)[3]
- transportation, health and nutrition services, to facilitate attendance for children living in poverty (Verheyde, 2005)[4]
- alternative education programmes for children having difficulty in regular systems (including those living in remote communities) (Verheyde, 2005)
- providing educational and vocational information and guidance (Verheyde, 2005).

Attribute Three: School Discipline Consistent with Human Dignity

Article 28, paragraph 2, constitutes an important innovation in respect of the right to education. It demands that any school discipline must be administered in a manner consistent with the child's dignity and in conformity with all other rights in the Convention. This requires that discipline must never violate the child's best interests, the right to non-discrimination, or the right to be heard. Furthermore, it must not violate, for example, the right to protection from all forms of violence or cruel, inhuman, degrading treatment, or, indeed, the rights to play and recreation, to health, cultural expression or freedom of religion.

The Committee has elaborated some specific forms of punishment that can never be justified as legitimate. These include any form of corporal punishment in which 'physical force is used and intended to cause some degree of pain or discomfort'

---

[3] For additional recommendations, see 'The Right to education' (Courtis and Tobin, 2019, p. 1079).

[4] The Committee has also suggested the development of national strategies to address the high dropout rate of minority children. See, for example, concluding observations to Canada (2012f, para. 70 (b)) and Ecuador (2017b, para. 37 (a)).

(UN Committee on the Rights of the Child, 2007c, para. 11). The Committee has also been uncompromising on the suggestion that some forms of corporal punishment can be tolerated if 'reasonable' or 'moderate,' asserting that such practices can never be justified as they conflict with the child's dignity and right to physical integrity (2007c, para. 26). In addition, the Committee insists that punishments that serve to humiliate, denigrate, frighten or ridicule the child must never be used (2007c, para. 11).

Paragraph 2, which requires that States Parties take all appropriate measures, demands immediate and comprehensive action to address school discipline. The Committee has emphasised that States Parties must undertake legislative, administrative, social, and educational measures to eliminate degrading forms of punishment in both public and private schools. Furthermore, it has stressed that this is an immediate and unqualified obligation, not subject to progressive realisation (2007c, para. 22). It has suggested a range of practical measures to support positive discipline in schools including awareness raising campaigns, training of teachers, and the participation of children in the design and development of school discipline policies.[5]

Attribute Four: International Cooperation

Paragraph 3 of Article 28 recognises the positive value of cooperation and information sharing between States Parties. Although Article 4 imposes a general obligation with respect to international cooperation, its inclusion in Article 28 highlights its specific importance in the context of education, a priority also reflected in the Jomtien Declaration on Education for All (Courtis and Tobin, 2019, p. 1110; World Conference on Education for All, 1990, para. 10 (1) (2)).

No specific form of assistance is mandated by paragraph 3. The obligation is to promote and encourage cooperation, which implies that all reasonable efforts are undertaken within the scope of available resources (Tobin, 2012, pp. 330–331). It is assumed that developed states must carry a greater burden in seeking global implementation of children's right to education (UN Committee on Economic, Social and Cultural Rights, 1991 General Comment no. 3, pp. 83-87). However, the Committee on the Rights of the Child has emphasised that states that are recipients of international aid also have an obligation to use such support effectively and efficiently (2002d, paras. 15–16, 2003, para. 60 (b)).

The focus of aid elaborated in paragraph 3 is to eliminate ignorance and illiteracy and to facilitate access to scientific and technical knowledge and modern teaching methods. However, in any programme of assistance, it is imperative that account is

---

[5] See, for example, General Comment no. 8 (UN Committee on the Rights of the Child, 2007c, paras. 45–46); concluding observations for Turkey (2012b, para. 59 (d)), Hungary (2006c, para. 55), and United Kingdom and Northern Ireland (2002c, para. 48 (a)).

taken of the 'needs of developing countries' and to ensure that it is developed in consultation with and is sensitive to social and cultural characteristics or context of any given state (Courtis and Tobin, 2019, p. 1114). For example, children affected by emergencies including natural disasters and conflicts, commonly experience disrupted access to education, or no education at all (UN Committee on the Rights of the Child, 2007d). When needed, States Parties must request and be provided with assistance from wealthier countries to ensure the right to education (UN Committee on the Rights of the Child, 2016b). Its provision should be seen as a humanitarian relief measure with sufficient resources allocated to assure that education continues for children in such emergency situations (UN Committee on the Rights of the Child, 2007d).

References

Courtis, C., & Tobin, J. (2019). Article 28: The right to education. In J. Tobin (Ed.), *The UN convention on the rights of the child: A commentary* (pp. 1056–1115). Oxford University Press.

Pinheiro, P. S. de M. S. (2006). *Report of the independent expert for the United Nations study on violence against children, A/61/299*. UN. Accessed November 12, 2020, from http://digitallibrary.un.org/record/584299

Tobin, J. (2012). *The right to health in international law*. Oxford University Press.

Tomaševski, K. (1999). *Preliminary report of the special rapporteur on the right to education, Katarina Tomasevski, submitted in accordance with commission on human rights resolution 1998/33. E/CN.4/1999/49*. UN. Accessed November 17, 2020, from http://digitallibrary.un.org/record/1487535

Tomaševski, K. (2006). *Human rights obligations in education: The 4-A scheme*. Wolf Legal Publishers.

UN Committee on Economic, Social and Cultural Rights. (1991). *Committee on economic, social and cultural rights: Report on the 5th session, 26 November–14 December 1990, E/1991/23*. UN. http://digitallibrary.un.org/record/114868. Accessed 17 November 2020

UN Committee on Economic, Social and Cultural Rights. (1999). *ICESCR general comment no. 13: the right to education, E/C.12/1999/10*. UN. Accessed November 16, 2020, from http://digitallibrary.un.org/record/407275

UN Committee on Economic, Social and Cultural Rights. (2009). *ICESCR general comment no. 20: Non-discrimination in economic, social and cultural rights (art. 2, para. 2, E/C.12/GC/20*. UN. Accessed November 17, 2020, from http://digitallibrary.un.org/record/659980

UN Committee on the Protection of the Rights of All Migrant Workers and Members of Their Families & UN Committee on the Rights of the Child. (2017). *Joint general comment no. 23 (2017) on State obligations regarding the human rights of children in the context of international migration in countries of origin, transit, destination and return, November 16, 2017, CMW/C/GC/4, CRC/C/GC/23*. Accessed October 12, 2020, from https://digitallibrary.un.org/record/1323015?ln=en

UN Committee on the Rights of Persons with Disabilities. (2016). *CRPD general comment no. 4 (2016) on the right to inclusive education, CRPD/C/GC/4*. UN. Accessed November 12, 2020, from http://digitallibrary.un.org/record/1313836

UN Committee on the Rights of the Child. (1995a). *Concluding observations: Nicaragua, June 20, 1995, CRC/C/15/Add.36*. Accessed October 11, 2020, from https://digitallibrary.un.org/record/191818?ln=en.

UN Committee on the Rights of the Child. (1995b). *Concluding observations: Tunisia, June 21, 1995, CRC/C/15/Add.39*. UN. Accessed November 16, 2020, from http://digitallibrary.un.org/record/200967.
UN Committee on the Rights of the Child. (1996). *Concluding observations: Korea, February 13, 1996, CRC/C/15/Add.51*. UN. Accessed November 16, 2020, from http://digitallibrary.un.org/record/210140
UN Committee on the Rights of the Child. (2000a). *Concluding observations: Burundi, October 16, 2000, CRC/C/15/Add.133*. Accessed October 11, 2020, from https://digitallibrary.un.org/record/429241?ln=en
UN Committee on the Rights of the Child. (2000b). *Concluding observations: India, February 23, 2000, CRC/C/15/Add.115*. Accessed October 11, 2020, from https://digitallibrary.un.org/record/412551?ln=en
UN Committee on the Rights of the Child. (2001). *General comment no. 1 (2001) Article 29 (1): The Aims of Education, April 17, 2001, CRC/GC/2001/1*. Accessed October 10, 2020, from https://digitallibrary.un.org/record/447223?ln=en
UN Committee on the Rights of the Child. (2002a). *Concluding observations: Mozambique, April 3, 2002, CRC/C/15/Add.172*. UN. Accessed November 16, 2020, from http://digitallibrary.un.org/record/467261
UN Committee on the Rights of the Child. (2002b). *Concluding observations: Spain, June 13, 2002, CRC/C/15/Add.185*. UN. Accessed November 6, 2020, from http://digitallibrary.un.org/record/473490.
UN Committee on the Rights of the Child. (2002c). *Concluding observations: United Kingdom, October 9, 2002, CRC/C/15/Add.188*. UN. Accessed November 17, 2020, from http://digitallibrary.un.org/record/481009
UN Committee on the Rights of the Child. (2002d). *Concluding observations: Burkina Faso, October 9, 2002, CRC/C/15/Add.193*. UN. Accessed November 17, 2020, from http://digitallibrary.un.org/record/481016
UN Committee on the Rights of the Child. (2003). *Concluding observations: Pakistan, October 27, 2003, CRC/C/15/Add.217*. UN. http://digitallibrary.un.org/record/513564. Accessed 16 November 2020
UN Committee on the Rights of the Child. (2004a). *Day of general discussion: Implementing child rights in early childhood*. UN. Accessed 16 November 2020, from https://www.ohchr.org/EN/HRBodies/CRC/Pages/DiscussionDays.aspx
UN Committee on the Rights of the Child. (2004b). *Concluding observations: El Salvador, June 30, 2004, CRC/C/15/Add.232*. UN. Accessed November 16, 2020, from http://digitallibrary.un.org/record/536551
UN Committee on the Rights of the Child. (2004c). *Concluding observations: France, June 30, 2004, CRC/C/15/Add.240*. Accessed October 12, 2020, from https://digitallibrary.un.org/record/536574?ln=en
UN Committee on the Rights of the Child. (2005a). *Concluding observations: Ecuador, September 13, 2005, CRC/C/15/Add.262*. UN. Accessed November 16, 2020, from http://digitallibrary.un.org/record/570463
UN Committee on the Rights of the Child. (2005b). *Concluding observations: China, November 24, 2005, CRC/C/CHN/CO/2*. Accessed October 24, 2020, from https://digitallibrary.un.org/record/575653?ln=en
UN Committee on the Rights of the Child. (2005c). *Concluding observations: Australia, October 20, 2005, CRC/C/15/Add.268*. UN. Accessed October 26, 2020, from http://digitallibrary.un.org/record/569889
UN Committee on the Rights of the Child. (2005d). *Concluding observations: Bolivia, February 11, 2005, CRC/C/15/Add.256*. UN. Accessed 16 November 2020, from http://digitallibrary.un.org/record/557402

UN Committee on the Rights of the Child. (2006a). *General comment no. 7 (2005) Implementing child rights in early childhood, September 20, 2006, CRC/C/GC/7/Rev.1*. Accessed October 2020, 12, from https://digitallibrary.un.org/record/584854?ln=en

UN Committee on the Rights of the Child. (2006b). *Concluding observations: Colombia, June 8, 2006, CRC/C/COL/CO/3*. UN. Accessed November 15, 2020, from http://digitallibrary.un.org/record/582283

UN Committee on the Rights of the Child. (2006c). *Concluding observations: Hungary, March 17, 2006, CRC/C/HUN/CO/2*. Accessed October 11, 2020, from https://digitallibrary.un.org/record/575773?ln=en

UN Committee on the Rights of the Child. (2007a). *General comment no. 9 (2006) The rights of children with disabilities, November 13, 2007, CRC/C/GC/9*. Accessed October 12, 2020, from https://digitallibrary.un.org/record/593891?ln=en

UN Committee on the Rights of the Child. (2007b). *General comment no. 10 (2007) Children's rights in juvenile justice, April 25, 2007, CRC/C/GC/10*. Accessed October 12, 2020, from https://digitallibrary.un.org/record/599395?ln=en

UN Committee on the Rights of the Child. (2007c). *General comment no. 8 (2006) The right of the child to protection from corporal punishment and other cruel or degrading forms of punishment (arts. 19; 28, para. 2; and 37, inter alia), March 2, 2007, CRC/C/GC/8*. Accessed October 12, 2020, from https://digitallibrary.un.org/record/583961?ln=en

UN Committee on the Rights of the Child. (2007d). *Day of general discussion: Resources for the rights of the child - Responsibility of states*. UN. Accessed December 19, 2020, from https://www.ohchr.org/EN/HRBodies/CRC/Pages/DiscussionDays.aspx

UN Committee on the Rights of the Child. (2009a). *General comment no. 11 (2009), Indigenous children and their rights under the convention, February 12, 2009, CRC/C/GC/11*. Accessed October 24, 2020, from https://digitallibrary.un.org/record/648790?ln=en

UN Committee on the Rights of the Child. (2009b). *General comment no. 12 (2009) The right of the child to be heard, July 20, 2009, CRC/C/GC/12*. Accessed October 12, 2020, from https://digitallibrary.un.org/record/671444?ln=en

UN Committee on the Rights of the Child. (2010a). *Concluding observations: Angola, October 19, 2010, CRC/C/AGO/CO/2-4*. UN. Accessed November 16, 2020, from http://digitallibrary.un.org/record/692405

UN Committee on the Rights of the Child. (2010b). *Concluding observations: Nigeria, June 21, 2010, CRC/C/NGA/CO/3-4*. Accessed October 11, 2020, from https://digitallibrary.un.org/record/685180?ln=en

UN Committee on the Rights of the Child. (2011). *Concluding observations: Bahrain, August 3, 2011, CRC/C/BHR/CO/2-3*. https://digitallibrary.un.org/record/708488?ln=en

UN Committee on the Rights of the Child. (2012a). *Concluding observations: Viet Nam, August 22, 2012, CRC/C/VNM/CO/3-4*. UN. Accessed November 8, 2020, from http://digitallibrary.un.org/record/732970

UN Committee on the Rights of the Child. (2012b). *Concluding observations: Turkey, July 20, 2012, CRC/C/TUR/CO/2-3*. UN. Accessed November 17, 2020, from http://digitallibrary.un.org/record/731354

UN Committee on the Rights of the Child. (2012c). *Concluding observations: Algeria, July 18, 2012, CRC/C/DZA/CO/3-4*. UN. Accessed November 14, 2020, from http://digitallibrary.un.org/record/731358

UN Committee on the Rights of the Child. (2012d). *Concluding observations: Korea, February 2, 2012, CRC/C/KOR/CO/3-4*. UN. Accessed November 17, 2020, from http://digitallibrary.un.org/record/720645

UN Committee on the Rights of the Child. (2012e). *Day of general discussion: The rights of all children in the context of international migration*. UN. Accessed December 19, 2020, from https://www.ohchr.org/EN/HRBodies/CRC/Pages/Discussion2012.aspx

UN Committee on the Rights of the Child. (2012f). *Concluding observations: Canada, December 6, 2012, CRC/C/CAN/CO/3-4*. Accessed October 11, 2020, from https://digitallibrary.un.org/record/739319?ln=en

UN Committee on the Rights of the Child. (2013a). *Concluding observations: Rwanda, July 8, 2013, CRC/C/RWA/CO/3-4*. UN. Accessed November 17, 2020, http://digitallibrary.un.org/record/756221

UN Committee on the Rights of the Child. (2013b). *General comment no. 14 (2013) On the right of the child to have his or her best interests taken as a primary consideration (art. 3, para. 1), May 29, 2013, CRC/C/GC/14*. Accessed October 12, 2020, from https://digitallibrary.un.org/record/778523?ln=en

UN Committee on the Rights of the Child. (2016a). *Concluding observations: Zimbabwe, March 7, 2016, CRC/C/ZWE/CO/2*. UN. Accessed November 16, 2020, from http://digitallibrary.un.org/record/834986

UN Committee on the Rights of the Child. (2016b). *General comment no. 19 (2016) on public budgeting for the realization of children's rights (art.4), CRC/C/GC/19*. UN. Accessed November 12, 2020, http://digitallibrary.un.org/record/838730

UN Committee on the Rights of the Child. (2017a). *General comment no. 21 (2017) On children in street situations, June 21, 2017, CRC/C/GC/21*. Accessed October 12, 2020, from https://digitallibrary.un.org/record/1304490?ln=en

UN Committee on the Rights of the Child. (2017b). *Concluding observations: Ecuador, October 26, 2017, CRC/C/ECU/CO/5-6*. UN. Accessed November 14, 2020, from http://digitallibrary.un.org/record/1311757

UN Committee on the Rights of the Child. (2019). *Concluding observations: Australia, November 1, 2019, CRC/C/AUS/CO/5-6*. UN. Accessed November 17, 2020, from http://digitallibrary.un.org/record/3863406

UN Secretary General. (2020). *Progress towards the sustainable development goals: Report of the Secretary-General, E/2020/57*. UN. Accessed November 16, 2020, from http://digitallibrary.un.org/record/3865828

UNESCO Institute for Statistics. (2012). *International standard classification of education: ISCED 2011*. UNESCO Institute for Statistics.

United Nations OHCHR. (2012). *Human rights indicators: A guide to measurement and implementation, HR/PUB/12/5*. United Nations. https://www.ohchr.org/Documents/Publications/Human_rights_indicators_en.pdf

United Nations OHCHR. (2018). *A human rights based approach to data - Leaving no one behind in the 2030 agenda for sustainable development: Guidance note to data collection and disaggregation*. United Nations OHCHR. Accessed December 19, 2020, from https://www.ohchr.org/Documents/Issues/HRIndicators/GuidanceNoteonApproachtoData.pdf

Verheyde, M. (2005). *A commentary on the United Nations convention on the rights of the child, Article 28: The right to education*. Brill Nijhoff. Accessed November 16, 2020, from https://brill.com/view/title/11618

World Conference on Education for All. (1990). *World declaration on education for all and framework for action to meet basic learning needs* (p. 21). Inter-Agency Commission (UNDP, Unesco, UNICEF, World Bank) for the World Conference on Education for All.

Open Access This chapter is licensed under the terms of the Creative Commons Attribution 4.0 International License (http://creativecommons.org/licenses/by/4.0/), which permits use, sharing, adaptation, distribution and reproduction in any medium or format, as long as you give appropriate credit to the original author(s) and the source, provide a link to the Creative Commons license and indicate if changes were made.

The images or other third party material in this chapter are included in the chapter's Creative Commons license, unless indicated otherwise in a credit line to the material. If material is not included in the chapter's Creative Commons license and your intended use is not permitted by statutory regulation or exceeds the permitted use, you will need to obtain permission directly from the copyright holder.

Chapter 27
Article 29: The Aims of Education

Gerison Lansdown, Katherine Covell, and Ziba Vaghri

1. States Parties agree that the education of the child shall be directed to:
   (a) The development of the child's personality, talents and mental and physical abilities to their fullest potential;
   (b) The development of respect for human rights and fundamental freedoms, and for the principles enshrined in the Charter of the United Nations;
   (c) The development of respect for the child's parents, his or her own cultural identity, language and values, for the national values of the country in which the child is living, the country from which he or she may originate, and for civilizations different from his or her own;
   (d) The preparation of the child for responsible life in a free society, in the spirit of understanding, peace, tolerance, equality of sexes, and friendship among all peoples, ethnic, national and religious groups and persons of indigenous origin;
   (e) The development of respect for the natural environment.

(continued)

G. Lansdown (✉)
Carleton University, Ottawa, Canada

K. Covell
Cape Breton University, Richmon, BC, Canada
e-mail: Katherine_Covell@cbu.ca

Z. Vaghri
University of New Brunswick, Saint John, Canada
e-mail: ziba.vaghri@unb.ca

2. No part of the present article or article 28 shall be construed so as to interfere with the liberty of individuals and bodies to establish and direct educational institutions, subject always to the observance of the principle set forth in paragraph 1 of the present article and to the requirements that the education given in such institutions shall conform to such minimum standards as may be laid down by the State.

What Did Children Say?
'The Ministry of Education organises trainings for teachers, to educate them how to treat children. Teachers should have exams about that.' *(Africa)*

'In some schools, the discipline that students receive is biased against students of colour. For instance, some schools have higher rates of discipline actions and suspensions among Hispanic and Black students, compared to white students in the same schools. Government should do more to monitor the different discipline actions.' *(Western Europe/Other)*

'Every schoolbook has video and audio material (with) additional explanation of lectures and additional information.' *(Africa)*

Overview

Recognition that education should be directed towards the full development of the personality and respect for human rights was first addressed in Article 26 (2) of the Universal Declaration of Human Rights, and strengthened in the International Covenant of Economic, Social and Cultural Rights through the provision, in Article 13, that education must also be directed to the sense of dignity and to enable all persons to participate in a free society. Article 29 affirms these aims and expands them, for both state and private schools, to require that education addresses respect for the child's family, for tolerance and diversity, and for the natural environment. It is closely linked with Article 28, but whereas Article 28 focuses primarily on access to and provision of education, Article 29 is directed to the content and style of the education provided. In neither article does the Convention define education, but the Committee has made clear that it endorses an approach that understands education to go 'beyond formal schooling to embrace the broad range of life experiences and learning which enables children ... to develop their personalities, talents and abilities and to live a full and satisfying life within society' (2001, para. 2). The Committee also affirms that, although Article 29 does not remove the freedom of individuals or bodies to establish their own schools, in doing so they must comply with the article's aims.

Article 29 elaborates an approach to education which promotes, supports, and protects the core values of the Convention, and requires that the provision of education is grounded in the principles on which it is based. In other words, education must be 'child-centred, child friendly and empowering' (UN Committee on the Rights of the Child, 2001, para. 2). The drafters of the Convention recognised that the vision of education elaborated in Article 29 does have significant resource implications and it is therefore subject to progressive realisation. However, the Committee has emphasised that resources must be available to the maximum extent possible and cannot be a justification for failing to adopt any of the measures required (2001, para. 28). In this regard, it urges States Parties providing development cooperation to design programmes consistent with the implementation of Article 29 (2001, para. 28).

General Principles

Article 2 To comply with Article 2, all aspects of the education system and school provision must be free from all forms of discrimination. Thus, for example, the curriculum should be consistent with principles of gender, disability, and race equality. Teachers must demonstrate equal respect for all students and not discriminate in the treatment of different groups of children in schools. An active focus within the curriculum on respect for human rights should also give explicit attention to the importance of challenging all forms of discrimination, xenophobia, and prejudice.

Article 3 The best interests of the child demand educational services that are child friendly and child-centred such that each child can develop to their potential.

Article 6 The aims of education explicitly speak to the development of the child's personality, talents, mental and physical abilities to their fullest potential.

Article 12 Children's participation in school communities and school councils, peer education, peer counselling and disciplinary proceedings are integral to the process of learning about and experiencing the realisation of rights (UN Committee on the Rights of the Child, 2001, para. 8). In addition, children should be enabled to contribute to the development of education legislation and policy, the design of the curriculum, teaching methods, schools' structures, standards, budgeting, and child protection systems (UN Committee on the Rights of the Child, 2001, paras. 105–114). Their participation in all these aspects of education will contribute towards the overall aims of education as elaborated in Article 29.

Articles Related or Linked to Article 29

Article 5 requires that children's evolving capacities are reflected in the nature of the education that they receive

Article 18 recognises that both parents have common responsibilities for the upbringing and development of the child and that the state cannot interfere with the liberty of parents to choose the education they wish for their child, as long as it complies with the principles outlined in paragraph 1 of Article 29

Article 13 provides children with the right to freedom of expression in education, and to seek, receive, and impart information through a variety of media

Article 14 allows the child freedom of thought and conscience in education settings, and to manifest their beliefs or religion. Children cannot be compelled to follow any particular religion in an educational setting

Article 17 encourages the provision of sources of information to children through appropriate mass media dissemination, international cooperation in production of educational materials and children's books, and the development of guidelines to protect children from potentially injurious information

Article 23 requires the provision of quality education to children living with disabilities

Article 24 obligates educational settings to provide health information

Article 28 requires children to have access to schools that are child friendly, safe, and respect the child's dignity

Article 30 provides linguistic and cultural rights to children belonging to minority groups, that should be respected in schools

Article 31 protects the child's right to rest, leisure, play, recreation activities, and to participate in artistic and cultural life, all of which must inform educational services, hours of study, and rest and play times during the school day

Article 40 protects the right to education of children detained as a measure of criminal justice enforcement

Article 42 obligates States Parties to take active measures to ensure children and adults are educated about the principles and provisions of the Convention.

Relevant Instruments

International Covenant on Economic, Social and Cultural Rights (1966), Article 13

International Covenant on Civil and Political Rights (1966), Article 2

International Convention on the Elimination of All Forms of Racial Discrimination (1966), Articles 2 and 7

UN Convention on the Elimination of All Forms of Discrimination against Women (1979), Article 10

UN Convention against Torture and Other Cruel, Inhuman, or Degrading Treatment or Punishment (1984), Article 2

UN Convention on the Rights of Persons with Disabilities (2006), Article 24

UN Convention Against Discrimination in Education (1960)

UNESCO Recommendation concerning Education for International Understanding, Co-operation and Peace and Education relating to Human Rights and Fundamental Freedoms (1974)

UN Convention on Technical and Vocational Education (1989)
UNESCO Declaration of Principles on Tolerance (1995)
UNESCO Convention on the Protection and Promotion of the Diversity of Cultural Expressions (2005)

Attributes

Attribute One: Ensuring that Aims and Objectives of Education Are in Conformity with the Convention

Article 29, paragraph 1(a) establishes that the overarching objective of education is the fullest possible development of the child's personality, talents, and physical and mental abilities. In its entirety, Article 29 provides for a framework of education for the realisation of the child's human dignity and rights. This requires a curriculum far broader than the traditional focus on literacy and numeracy, and necessitates teaching on developing respect for human rights, for the child's parents, and for cultural identity as for well as the values of the country in which the child is living, for life in a free society, and for the natural environment. To realise this goal, it is imperative that the principles in Article 29 inform all aspects of education, and that they are explicitly addressed in all States Parties' education laws, policies, and programmes (UN Committee on the Rights of the Child, 2001, para. 17).

The Committee has urged cooperation among internal bodies concerned with education and human rights, and has called on States Parties to develop comprehensive national plans of action to promote and monitor implementation of the Article 29 objectives (2001, para. 23). In order to strengthen accountability, the Committee recommends that States Parties establish review procedures to allow for complaints or practices that are in breach of or inconsistent with Article 29 (2001, para. 25). National level monitoring is also strongly recommended to ensure that children, teachers, and parents have input into decisions relevant to education (UN Committee on the Rights of the Child, 2001, para. 22). Where an educational institution is established privately, it must comply with the aims of education as elaborated in Article 29, as well as with the Convention as a whole. The state must provide minimum standards for such schools and create systems for monitoring compliance.[1]

---

[1] See, for example, concluding observations for Senegal (2016a, para. 38 (b)) and Guinea (2013a, para. 73 (e)).

Attribute Two: Rights-Consistent Curricula

The aims elaborated in Article 29 have significant implications for the curriculum delivered in schools. In respect of the formal curriculum, the Committee has stressed that it requires ensuring that school curricula, textbooks, and other teaching materials address the full scope of the aims elaborated in Article 29 (2001, para. 18), and at all levels of the education system.[2] The curriculum needs to go beyond the basic areas of knowledge such as literacy, numeracy, and science, to provide a 'holistic approach to education that ensures that the educational opportunities made available reflect an appropriate balance between promoting the physical, mental, spiritual and emotional aspects of education, the intellectual, social and practical dimensions and the childhood and lifelong aspects' (UN Committee on the Rights of the Child, 2001, para. 12). The skills needed include critical thinking and decision-making, social relationships, citizenship, and healthy lifestyles (UN Committee on the Rights of the Child, 2001, para. 9). The Committee also has underscored the importance of curricula relevant to the child's daily life and context. The Committee has called for peace and conflict-resolution education for children and, in light of climate change, for education that empowers children to become agents of change and defenders of the environment.[3] The curricula should include the life skills needed for 'responsible life in a free society' (Verheyde, 2005, pp. 26–28).

The Committee has consistently called for human rights education in schools and expressed concern over its absence from the curriculum. Moreover, where it is provided, it often fails to include a specific focus on the rights of the child (Jerome et al., 2015). The Committee recommends non-formal educational tools such as outdoor activities and field trips, as well as direct involvement of children in environmental protection, as a crucial component of their learning process and an exercise in social practices that constitute civic participation (2016c). The Committee also places considerable emphasis on the importance of health education (2003a, para. 17), and in line with the child's evolving capacities and development, the school curriculum should provide children with age-appropriate, comprehensive, and inclusive sexual and reproductive health education, including gender equality, sexual diversity, sexual and reproductive rights, responsible parenthood and sexual behaviour, and violence prevention (2016d, para. 61). It should also address tobacco, alcohol, and drug use, and diet (UN Committee on the Rights of the Child, 2003b).

---

[2] See, for example, concluding observations for Canada (2012a, para. 24), Antigua and Barbuda (2017a, para. 17 (b)), Congo (2014, para. 23), and Benin (2016b, para. 21).

[3] See *Day of General Discussion: Children's Rights and the Environment* (UN Committee on the Rights of the Child, 2016c). Particular concerns were expressed about children's exposure to environmental toxins, the impact of climate change, and the loss of biodiversity.

Participation of children in curriculum development is identified by the Committee as a strategy to achieve relevance,[4] to increase children's engagement in learning (2006a, para. 22), and to ensure respect for the principles of the Convention (2001).

Attribute Three: Rights-Respecting Pedagogy

Article 29 challenges educators to restructure education from a child rights perspective (UN Committee on the Rights of the Child, 2001), recognising that traditional teaching styles may stifle individuality and promote conformity, and result in education lacking a global and human rights perspective (UN Secretary General, 1978).[5] The Committee has emphasised that pedagogy focused on knowledge accumulation and competition can compromise the development of children's abilities (2001). It has criticised States Parties for priority given to rote-learning (2003c, para. 46), the competitive nature of schooling (2004, para. 49, 2006b, para. 63), and for the lack of human rights education in schools (2012a, paras. 24–25, 2014, para. 23, 2016b, para. 21, 2017b, para. 37).

Consistency with the aims of education and the principles of the Convention therefore requires a participatory pedagogy through which children learn about human rights through experiencing them in practice. Education must be designed to enable children to participate actively in their own learning (UN Committee on the Rights of the Child, 2001, para. 12). Achieving such education requires training for both pre-service and in-service teachers, to equip them with competency in participatory methodologies, as well as the provisions and principles of the Convention (UN Committee on the Rights of the Child, 2006d, para. 24; Verheyde, 2005, p. 28), The lack of appropriate teacher training and child rights awareness among educators continue to be of serious concern and criticism in assessments of States Parties' reports.[6] Meaningful implementation can only be achieved with supportive school management, awareness raising and participation of communities and parents, and the necessary materials and infrastructure.

---

[4]See, for example, concluding observations to Costa Rica (2000, para. 24) and Italy (1995, para. 21).

[5]See, in particular, the comments expressed by UNESCO, Norway, and Greece.

[6]Recent examples include concluding observations to Antigua and Barbuda (2017a, para. 17), Benin (2016b, para. 21), Canada (2012a, para. 27), Congo (2014, para. 23), Haiti (2016e, para. 17 (b)), and Zimbabwe (2016f, para. 22 (b)).

Attribute Four: Rights-Reflecting School Environment

Children learn much from the environment in which their education takes place. The school environment, which includes all policies and practices including the behaviour of school staff and administrators, must be infused with and reflect the values of the Convention—respect for rights, peace, tolerance, understanding, and equality— and allow children to exercise rights such as the right to participation under Article 12 (Office of the United Nations High Commissioner for Human Rights and Rädda barnen (Society: Sweden), 2007). A rights-respecting school environment will promote and teach the values and behaviours associated with human rights by allowing children to experience them (UN Committee on the Rights of the Child, 2001).

The Committee has identified bullying in schools to be a serious impediment to an appropriate school environment.[7] States Parties have been urged to adopt programmes and activities that create a culture in schools which rejects bullying behaviours and all forms of discrimination.[8]

To promote the exercise of rights and citizenship, it is important that schools have policies and practices that systematically provide for children's participation in non-discriminatory ways. Children should be represented by peers on all committees including disciplinary proceedings, and be provided opportunities for participation in student councils, peer education, and peer counselling (UN Committee on the Rights of the Child, 2006a, para. 20). Data should be collected to enable monitoring and evaluation of how human rights values are reflected in the daily experiences of children and how children are empowered to defend their rights when these are not respected.

References

Jerome, L., Emerson, L., Lundy, L., & Orr, K. (2015). *Teaching and learning about child rights: A study of implementation in 26 countries.* UNICEF. Accessed November 18, 2020, from https://pure.qub.ac.uk/en/publications/teaching-and-learning-about-child-rights-a-study-of-implementatio

Office of the United Nations High Commissioner for Human Rights & Rädda barnen (Society: Sweden). (2007). *Legislative history of the convention on the rights of the child.* United Nations. https://digitallibrary.un.org/record/602462?ln=en

UN Committee on the Rights of the Child. (1995). *Concluding observations: Italy, November 27, 1995, CRC/C/15/Add.41.* UN. Accessed 18 November 2020, from http://digitallibrary.un.org/record/208045

---

[7] See, for example, concerns about high rates of bullying in schools in Hong Kong (2013b, para. 77), Iceland (2012b, para. 46 (b)), and Sweden (2015, para. 31).

[8] See, for example, concluding observations to Canada (2012a), and to Lithuania (2006c, para. 27).

UN Committee on the Rights of the Child. (2000). *Concluding observations: Costa Rica, February 24, 2000, CRC/C/15/Add.117*. UN. Accessed 18 November 2020, from http://digitallibrary.un.org/record/415617

UN Committee on the Rights of the Child. (2001). *General Comment No. 1 (2001) Article 29 (1): The Aims of Education, April 17, 2001, CRC/GC/2001/1*. Accessed October 10, 2020, from https://digitallibrary.un.org/record/447223?ln=en

UN Committee on the Rights of the Child. (2003a). *General Comment No. 3 (2003) HIV/AIDS and the rights of the child, March 17, 2003, CRC/GC/2003/3*. Accessed 12 October 2020, from https://digitallibrary.un.org/record/501529?ln=en

UN Committee on the Rights of the Child. (2003b). *General Comment No. 4 (2003) Adolescent health and development in the context of the Convention on the Rights of the Child, July 1, 2003, CRC/GC/2003/4*. Accessed October 12, 2020, from https://digitallibrary.un.org/record/503074?ln=en

UN Committee on the Rights of the Child. (2003c). *Concluding observations: Syria, July 10, 2003, CRC/C/15/Add.212*. UN. Accessed November 18, 2020, from http://digitallibrary.un.org/record/503095

UN Committee on the Rights of the Child. (2004). *Concluding observations: Japan, February 26, 2004, CRC/C/15/Add.231*. Accessed October 24, 2020, from https://digitallibrary.un.org/record/530812?ln=en

UN Committee on the Rights of the Child. (2006a). *Day of general discussion: The right of the child to be heard*. Accessed October 12, 2020, from https://www.ohchr.org/EN/HRBodies/CRC/Pages/DiscussionDays.aspx

UN Committee on the Rights of the Child. (2006b). *Concluding observations: Thailand, March 17, 2006, CRC/C/THA/CO/2*. UN. Accessed 18 November 2020, Accessed November 18, 2020, from http://digitallibrary.un.org/record/575783

UN Committee on the Rights of the Child. (2006c). *Concluding observations: Lithuania, March 17, 2006, CRC/C/LTU/CO/2*. UN. Accessed November 18, 2020, http://digitallibrary.un.org/record/575775

UN Committee on the Rights of the Child. (2006d). *Day of general discussion: The right of the child to be heard*. UN

UN Committee on the Rights of the Child. (2012a). *Concluding observations: Canada, December 6, 2012, CRC/C/CAN/CO/3-4*. Accessed 11 October 2020, from https://digitallibrary.un.org/record/739319?ln=en

UN Committee on the Rights of the Child. (2012b). *Concluding observations: Iceland, January 23, 2012, CRC/C/ISL/CO/3-4*. UN. Accessed November 18, 2020, from http://digitallibrary.un.org/record/720863

UN Committee on the Rights of the Child. (2013a). *Concluding observations: Guinea, June 13, 2013, CRC/C/GIN/CO/2*. UN. Accessed November 18, 2020, from http://digitallibrary.un.org/record/751394

UN Committee on the Rights of the Child. (2013b). *Concluding observations: China, October 29, 2013, CRC/C/CHN/CO/3-4*. UN. Accessed November 18, 2020, from http://digitallibrary.un.org/record/767367

UN Committee on the Rights of the Child. (2014). *Concluding observations: Congo, February 25, 2014, CRC/C/COG/CO/2-4*. UN. Accessed November 18, 2020, from http://digitallibrary.un.org/record/778842

UN Committee on the Rights of the Child. (2015). *Concluding observations: Sweden, March 6, 2015, CRC/C/SWE/CO/5*. UN. Accessed November 18, 2020, from http://digitallibrary.un.org/record/789728

UN Committee on the Rights of the Child. (2016a). *Concluding observations: Senegal, March 7, 2016, CRC/C/SEN/CO/3-5*. UN. Accessed November 18, 2020, from http://digitallibrary.un.org/record/834989

UN Committee on the Rights of the Child. (2016b). *Concluding observations: Benin, February 25, 2016, CRC/C/BEN/CO/3-5*. UN. Accessed November 18, 2020, from http://digitallibrary.un.org/record/834979

UN Committee on the Rights of the Child. (2016c). *Day of general discussion: Children's rights and the environment*. UN. Accessed November 18, 2020, from https://www.ohchr.org/EN/HRBodies/CRC/Pages/Discussion2016.aspx

UN Committee on the Rights of the Child. (2016d). *General Comment No. 20 (2016) on the implementation of the rights of the child during adolescence, December 6, 2016, CRC/C/GC/20*. Accessed October 12, 2020, from https://digitallibrary.un.org/record/855544?ln=en

UN Committee on the Rights of the Child. (2016e). *Concluding observations: Haiti, February 24, 2016, CRC/C/HTI/CO/2-3*. UN. Accessed November 18, 2020, http://digitallibrary.un.org/record/834934

UN Committee on the Rights of the Child. (2016f). *Concluding observations: Zimbabwe, March 7, 2016, CRC/C/ZWE/CO/2*. UN. Accessed November 16, 2020, from http://digitallibrary.un.org/record/834986

UN Committee on the Rights of the Child. (2017a). *Concluding observations: Antigua and Barbuda, June 30, 2017, CRC/C/ATG/CO/2-4*. UN. Accessed November 18, 2020, from http://digitallibrary.un.org/record/1311381

UN Committee on the Rights of the Child. (2017b). *Concluding observations: Denmark, October 26, 2017, CRC/C/DNK/CO/5*. UN. Accessed November 6, 2020, from http://digitallibrary.un.org/record/1311756

UN Secretary General. (1978). *Question of a convention on the rights of the child: Report of the Secretary-General, E/CN.4/1324*. UN. Accessed November 18, 2020, from http://digitallibrary.un.org/record/6629

Verheyde, M. (2005). *A commentary on the United Nations convention on the rights of the child, Article 28: The right to education*. Brill Nijhoff. Accessed November 16, 2020, from https://brill.com/view/title/11618

Open Access This chapter is licensed under the terms of the Creative Commons Attribution 4.0 International License (http://creativecommons.org/licenses/by/4.0/), which permits use, sharing, adaptation, distribution and reproduction in any medium or format, as long as you give appropriate credit to the original author(s) and the source, provide a link to the Creative Commons license and indicate if changes were made.

The images or other third party material in this chapter are included in the chapter's Creative Commons license, unless indicated otherwise in a credit line to the material. If material is not included in the chapter's Creative Commons license and your intended use is not permitted by statutory regulation or exceeds the permitted use, you will need to obtain permission directly from the copyright holder.

Chapter 28
Article 30: Cultural, Religious, and Linguistic Rights of Minority or Indigenous Children

Adem Arkadas-Thibert and Roberta Ruggiero

In those states in which ethnic, religious or linguistic minorities or persons of indigenous origin exist, a child belonging to such a minority or who is indigenous shall not be denied the right, in community with other members of his or her group, to enjoy his or her own culture, to profess and practice his or her own religion, or to use his or her own language.

What Did Children Say?
'By promoting the differences through accepting their holidays, respecting their important days, celebrating important days connected with their tradition and culture.' *(Eastern Europe)*

'Governments should help to support local museums and cultural activities.' *(Western Europe/Other)*

In the US now, there is a lot of tension about immigration and it seems like a lot of minority children are very anxious and ashamed of their culture, rather than it being celebrated, it is often held against them. *(Western Europe/Other)*

'Other children are informed about other cultures: through curricula and through classes.' *(Eastern Europe)*

(continued)

A. Arkadas-Thibert (✉)
Marseille, France

R. Ruggiero
Centre for Children's Rights Studies, University of Geneva, Geneva, Switzerland
e-mail: roberta.ruggiero@unige.ch

> 'Through schooling they should learn more about their culture and knowledge. One of the children expressed her concern that children make fun when she speaks in her local dialect.' *(Asia-Pacific)*

Overview

Article 30 of the Convention confers the right of the child who belongs to a minority or indigenous community or group to claim, enjoy, and practice their language, culture, and religion. Integral concepts that must be considered are protection for, measures to support and enable retention of, and the ability of the child to choose, have, adopt, and learn their culture, religion, and language (Office of the United Nations High Commissioner for Human Rights and Rädda barnen (Society: Sweden), 2007, pp. 675–682).

The particular rights of minorities and indigenous groups are not addressed within the Convention. However, to properly consider, protect, and respect those rights requires appreciation of the circumstances and conditions of children belonging to these groups or communities, for example, the connection of indigenous communities with their territory and their way of life (United Nations, 2006, pp. 198–200). The right to exercise cultural rights can be regarded as intimately connected to the use of traditional territory and its resources (UN Committee on the Rights of the Child, 2009, para. 16). From this perspective, considerable importance is attributed to traditions and cultural values and they are essential to the individual's development and enjoyment of culture (UN Committee on the Rights of the Child, 2009, para. 35).

Article 30, while fostering specific protection to minority and indigenous children, also points out the complex relationships behind the protection of cultural, religious, and linguistic rights. In consequence, it raises three main interpretation issues under Article 30:

1. When is the child considered an indigenous person or recognised as belonging to an ethnic, religious, or linguistic minority?
2. What are the States Parties' obligations to fulfil the rights under Article 30?
3. What are the implications on the child in the exercise of Article 30 as individual and/or collective rights (Harris-Short and Tobin, 2019, p. 1159)?

Unfortunately, the Committee's own jurisprudence, Concluding Observations to States Parties' reports, responds only in part to these interpretation issues, but it provides a more detailed, although not exhaustive interpretation, in its General Comment no. 11 on the rights of indigenous children.

Although reference is made throughout the Convention, particularly in articles such as 6, 8, 14, 17(d), 20 (3), 21, 29(c), and 31, for the protection of language, culture, and religion, Article 30 reinforces and underscores that these rights and protections apply to children of minorities and indigenous peoples (Hodgkin et al., 2007, p. 455).

While affirming the right to the enjoyment and practices of diverse cultures, the Convention safeguards children from possible harm from traditional practices and beliefs that conflict or are not in accordance with human rights. Moreover, 'the Committee underlines that cultural practices provided by Article 30 of the Convention must be exercised in accordance with other provisions of the Convention and under no circumstances may be justified if deemed prejudicial to the child's dignity, health, and development' (2009, para. 22).

With reference to the nature of the obligation of States Parties, the statement 'shall not be denied' underlines that it does not bestow the mere negative obligation of non-interference, but also the positive obligation of undertaking measures that respect, protect, and ensure the fulfilment of the rights identified in Article 30. This positive obligation imposed upon States Parties includes the duty to protect the child from state and non-state actors that might threaten the effective exercise of these rights (Harris-Short and Tobin, 2019, pp. 1159, 1173–1177). This includes actively addressing oppression and discrimination from which vulnerable communities or groups experience disproportionate effects or disadvantages as a result of diminished religious, cultural, or linguistic rights.

While political and economic entitlements are not the focus of this right, recognition of how these circumstances impinge on the enjoyment of this right is important (Hodgkin et al., 2007). States Parties are recognised as playing an instrumental role in safeguarding the rights of all children in their jurisdictions and ensuring equality before, and protection of, the law (UN General Assembly, 1966, Article 26; United Nations, 2006, p. 198). Harris-Short and Tobin assert that these positive States Parties' obligations to respect, protect and fulfil, as indicated by the Committee in General Comment no. 11, paragraph 19, are justified by the intention to ensure the survival of minority and indigenous groups through the empowerment of indigenous children and their effective exercise of the rights to culture, religion and language (2019, p. 1159). With the same intention, Article 29 (1), among the aims of education lists respect for human rights, cultural identity, language and values.

On this aspect, Article 28 of ILO Convention 169 on Indigenous and Tribal Peoples, and Article 14 of United Nations Declaration on the Rights of Indigenous Peoples, significantly call upon states to take effective measures to ensure indigenous children have access to education in their own language and culture. There is recognition for the group or the communities' role in establishing and controlling education and institutions but also regarding the need for state support to enable children's access to such programmes. Compulsory education, therefore, cannot prohibit a child from learning to adopt or have the culture of their parent, community, or group to which they belong (Office of the United Nations High Commissioner for Human Rights and Rädda barnen (Society: Sweden), 2007, pp. 675–682).

Article 45 of the International Convention on the Protection of the Rights of All Migrant Workers and Members of Their Families supports facilitating integration of migrant workers' children into local education, emphasising teaching local language, teaching about the respective workers' language and culture, and making teaching available in their mother tongue. Here again, the state is necessary to provide support and resources.

In relation to the issue pertaining to the individual or collective nature of the rights enshrined by Article 30, the content of Article 30 remains true to the text of Article 27 of the International Covenant on Civil and Political Rights (ICCPR) with one noteworthy exception, which is the addition of indigenous rights (Hodgkin et al., 2007, p. 456; Office of the United Nations High Commissioner for Human Rights and Rädda barnen (Society: Sweden), 2007, pp. 679–680). Particular reference to the 'child' differing from the language of 'persons' contained in Article 27 of ICCPR signals recognition of both the individual and collective nature of rights, which may or may not happen in community with other members of their group (UN Office of the High Commissioner for Human Rights (OHCHR), 1997, p. 489). The Committee has made clear that the best interests of the individual child cannot be diminished or neglected by giving preference to the best interests of the group. As a consequence, 'the rights under Article 30 belong to the individual child,' to underline once more that the child is an autonomous right holder, 'rather than a mere instrument of parental, community, cultural, or state preferences' (Harris-Short and Tobin, 2019, p. 1160).

Again, with reference to Article 27 of the ICCPR, it is worth noting the need to distinguish the right to freedom of expression from the right to use minority language (United Nations, 2006, pp. 198–200). The right to minority language is a separate right. It connotes a cultural right of children of minority groups who must not be denied the freedom to speak their language in community with members of their group. As a cultural right, it should be distinguished clearly from the freedom of expression and other civil-political rights.

General Principles

Article 2 This article secures the right to be free from any kind of discrimination irrespective of a child's parent or guardian's, 'race, colour, . . . language, religion, . . . national, ethnic or social origin . . . or other status.' The prohibition of discrimination must be enshrined in domestic legislation. This should be strengthened with legislative and administrative measures to guarantee the freedom to exercise rights based on children's respective origins and identities. States Parties should develop initiatives that ensure greater access to culturally relevant services that foster respect and understanding amongst indigenous and minority peoples, as well as promoting positive regard for their contributions by society at large (UN Committee on the Rights of the Child, 2009, paras. 23–27).

Article 3 In determining the best interests of the child with regards to Article 30, consideration must be given to the child's choice and evolving capacity, as well as their well-being and development. This should be assessed in a broadly participatory way that includes the child and their views, leaders and members of the community, parents, professionals, and other relevant stakeholders, to better understand the living reality of the child or the group of children (UN General Assembly, 2010, para. 62). The need to provide distinct consideration of the collective cultural right is important in the application of these rights of indigenous children. Care must be taken to ensure individual rights are not neglected in favour of group rights (UN Committee on the Rights of the Child, 2009, paras. 30–32).

Article 6 There is a relationship between the right to survival and the right to culture that requires appreciation and protections for the collective traditions and values that sustain and preserve communities of minorities and indigenous groups (UN Committee on the Rights of the Child, 2009, para. 16). Article 30 is contingent on the ability to claim religious, cultural, and linguistic rights. It has implications for the preservation of identity, history, values, familial, and communal ties, which bond an individual to the group to which they belong. States Parties are responsible for the provision of culturally appropriate material supports and assistance programmes that ensure an adequate standard of living, encompassing economic, social, and cultural rights. Significantly, the United Nations Sustainable Development Goals will be advanced with States Parties' active engagement of indigenous individuals, including children and communities (UN Committee on the Rights of the Child, 2009, paras. 34–36).

Article 12 The need for qualified representatives, interpretative services, and materials in the language of the child's choosing facilitates the child's right to choose and participate in their communities and associated activities and broader society (UN General Assembly, 2010, paras. 6, 88). This assures continuity in socialisation and development (UN General Assembly, 2010, para. 158). For example, this will include efforts meant to support the participation and inclusion of indigenous and minority children at all levels of education, including preschool education, and the promotion of cultural awareness (UN Committee on the Rights of the Child, 2016, 2017, para. 55 (e)).

Articles Related or Linked to Article 30

Articles 7 and 9 prevent the unnecessary or unreasonable separation of indigenous and/or minority children from their parents.

Article 8 secures the child's right to preserve their indigenous and/or minority identity.

Article 14 safeguards freedom of religion recognising the parents' role in this respect. It should be noted that Article 14 brings focus to the individuality of the child in relation to the community or group to which they belong, whereas Article 30 sees the child as a member of the broader community and group to which they are a part of, therefore impressing the right of the child in a community context and representing the child as a representative of it (Harris-Short and Tobin, 2019, p. 1160)

Article 16 prevents arbitrary or unlawful interference of the indigenous and/or minority child's family.

Article 17 prompts States Parties to encourage mass media regard linguistic needs of children from minority and/or indigenous groups.

Article 20 ensures that where children are removed from their families, consideration is given to continuity of the child's upbringing and to their ethnic, religious, cultural, and linguistic background.

Article 21 recognises the circumstances of inter-country adoption reaffirm the need for due regard to the child's indigenous and/or minority background.

Article 28 requires education to be provided on the basis of equal opportunity and to enable participation of indigenous and/or minority child in greater society.

Article 29 ensures the aims of education instil respect for the child's language, culture, and values, the promotion of a culture of human rights, and affirms the right to be educated outside the state system in a manner that promotes individual empowerment and self-determination

Article 40 requires the use of interpreters when an indigenous and/or minority child is unable to understand the proceedings within the context of the administration of juvenile justice.

Relevant Instruments

International Covenant on Civil and Political Rights (1966), Article 27, guarantees the rights of ethnic, religious, or linguistic minorities to enjoy their own culture, to profess and practise their own religion, and to use their own language.

International Convention on the Protection of the Rights of All Migrant Workers and Members of Their Families (1990), Article 45, supports facilitating integration of migrant workers' children into local education emphasising teaching local language and teaching about the respective workers' language and culture.

UN Declaration on the Rights of Indigenous Peoples (2007), Article 11, addresses the right to practice and revitalise cultural traditions and customs and have access to education in their own language and culture, Article 14. Significantly, the community takes the lead, self-determining the preservation of culture and community from a historical perspective and as its shape evolves. The state is a supportive actor in this process.

ILO Convention 169, Indigenous and Tribal Peoples (1989), Article 2, mentions not only protection of rights but also guarantees respect for their integrity.

Attributes

Attribute One: The Right of the Child Who Belongs to an Ethnic, Religious, or Linguistic Minority or Indigenous Group to Enjoy Their Own Culture

This attribute focuses on how children from an early age are made aware of and induced to appreciate cultural rights and prepared for participation in cultural life in society. It also deals with how textbooks and educational materials kindle in children the spirit of learning to live together, respecting diverse cultures and cultural identities, especially cultural rights of children who belong to ethnic, religious, or linguistic minorities or indigenous groups. To that end, school environments should foster cultural pluralism, intercultural dialogue, and rapprochement of cultures with the overarching framework of human rights.

This attribute is also linked to freedom in education. Compulsory education should not prohibit a child from learning, adopting, or having the culture of their parent or community or group to which they belong.

The Committee, in its General Comment no. 11 on indigenous children, asserts that:

- Indigenous children and minority children are to effectively enjoy their rights on an equal level with non-indigenous children (2009, para. 1)
- There must be reflection of indigenous and minority groups and communities in pedagogy and curricula, that situates the experiences, contributions, and legacies of the groups in building the social fabric of society (2009, para. 27)
- Experiences, circumstances, and conditions of disadvantage and discrimination that disproportionately affect or cause de- facto discrimination based on religion, cultural and language must be identified and addressed. This includes educational and awareness initiatives countering negative attitudes towards individuals and groups (2009, paras. 23–29)
- Resources, training, and staff to sufficiently enact programmes and policies that promote and protect these rights must be allocated. This includes trained teachers capable of delivering the national education curriculum as well as education specific to communities or groups, in the desired language and in a culturally appropriate manner (2009, para. 71)
- There must be accessible health, social welfare services, and education that sustains respect for language, culture, and practices of the community or group (2009, paras. 49–55)
- The quality of education should enable the participation, contribution, and enjoyment of economic, social, and cultural aspects of life and community, achieving individual empowerment and self-determination. Particular efforts are required to improve access to education for indigenous children, recruit teachers from within the communities, and support the development of culturally relevant curricula in partnership with communities that promote instruction in the respective language

and consistent with culture and traditions (2009, paras. 56–63). Policy and program development, including monitoring and evaluation efforts, in all areas should be done in direct cooperation with indigenous communities and in consultation with indigenous children (2009, paras. 80–82).

In line with the rationale of Article 30, it is worth recalling that in adopting the 2030 Agenda for Sustainable Development, governments pledged themselves 'to foster inter-cultural understanding, tolerance, mutual respect and an ethic of global citizenship and shared responsibility,' and acknowledged 'the natural and cultural diversity of the world' and recognised that 'all cultures and civilizations can contribute to, and are crucial enablers of, sustainable development' (UN General Assembly, 2015).

Attribute Two: The Right of the Child Who Belong to an Ethnic, Religious, or Linguistic Minorities or Indigenous Groups to Profess and Practice Their Own Religion

Freedom of religion or belief is a universal human right. Any expression or manifestation of disrespect or hatred towards others because of their religion or belief, and incitement to discrimination, hostility, or acts of violence, constitutes an affront to the principle of freedom of religion or belief. Special consideration must be given to ethnic, religious, or linguistic minorities or indigenous groups to profess and practice their own religion or beliefs. Article 30 has its raison d'etre in that perspective, bearing in mind Article 14 of the Convention as regards a child's freedom of thought and conscience in education settings, and of manifesting their beliefs or religion.

Hence, it is important to teach children to respect everyone's right to exercise their religion or belief freely and to offer the opportunity to access faith-based education. This would make the school environment conducive to pluralism and promote interreligious and intercultural dialogue so that children belonging to ethnic, religious, or linguistic minorities or indigenous groups can profess and practice their religion with due respect and in a spirit which is respectful of human rights.

The key role of education is underlined as to be particularly relevant in a large array of United Nations Resolutions on freedom of religion or belief, for example, Resolution 72/177 on the Freedom of religion or belief adopted by the General Assembly on 19 December 2017. The resolution stipulates that governments should 'promote, through education and other means, mutual understanding, tolerance, non-discrimination and respect in all matters relating to freedom of religion or belief by encouraging, in society at large, a wider knowledge of the diversity of religions and beliefs and of the history, traditions, languages and cultures of the various religious minorities existing within their jurisdiction' (UN General Assembly, 2018, para. 13 (1)). Accordingly, the fulfilment of the right of the child who belongs to an ethnic, religious, or linguistic minority or indigenous group to profess and practice their religion also requires:

- Health and education delivered in a manner that does not infringe on or prohibit choice of learning or adopting the culture, religion, or language of the community or group to which the child belongs
- Protection from traditional practices that pose risks or are prejudicial to ones' health and well-being
- Investment in and developing resources for the protection and promotion of religious, linguistic, and cultural rights as well as measures that enable the equal participation in broader society
- Limiting recognition of groups can create and entrench discrimination and inequality
- Organisations, professionals, and individuals working with children, particularly those responsible for their direct care, should be properly sensitised to cultural, social, gender, and religious issues that impact children belonging to minority and indigenous communities and groups (UN Committee on the Rights of the Child, 2009).

Attribute Three: The Right of the Child Who Belong to an Ethnic, Religious, or Linguistic Minorities or Indigenous Groups to Use Their Own Language

A growing body of evidence points to the fact that children learn better in their first language (Bühmann and Trudell, 2008). Therefore, it is important for children to receive early education in their first language. This raises a number of issues regarding facilities for the use of their language, such as availability of textbooks, qualified teachers, and other resources, in the language(s) of ethnic, religious, or linguistic minorities or indigenous groups, particularly considering the large number of vernacular languages and dialects among minority communities in some regions. Reasonableness and feasibility are other criteria for the steps taken in this direction.

Accessibility to media and communication that enable participation in public life in their respective communities and broader society need to be ensured by States Parties. This includes translation and dissemination of the Convention and other human rights instruments and documents in a format that is child friendly and in the minority and indigenous languages, in order to develop, respect, and promote a culture of human rights.

States Parties should ensure the exposure to and instruction in one's own language as an important tool towards the preservation of identity and psychological integrity, and to the academic achievement of marginalised, vulnerable, disadvantaged, and disproportionately represented groups, including children who have been displaced.

References

Bühmann, D., & Trudell, B. (2008). *Mother tongue matters: Local language as a key to effective learning, ED.2007/WS/56 REV*. Paris: UNESCO. Accessed November 18, 2020, from https://unesdoc.unesco.org/ark:/48223/pf0000161121

Harris-Short, S., & Tobin, J. (2019). Article 30: Cultural, linguistic and religious rights of minorities and indigenous children. In J. Tobin (Ed.), *The UN convention on the rights of the child: A commentary* (pp. 1153–1194). Oxford University Press.

Hodgkin, R., Newell, P., & UNICEF. (2007). *Implementation handbook for the convention on the rights of the child* (3rd ed.). UNICEF. Accessed 21 September 2020, from https://digitallibrary.un.org/record/620060?ln=en

Office of the United Nations High Commissioner for Human Rights & Rädda barnen (Society: Sweden). (2007). *Legislative history of the convention on the rights of the child*. United Nations. https://digitallibrary.un.org/record/602462?ln=en

UN Committee on the Rights of the Child. (2009). *General comment No. 11 (2009), Indigenous children and their rights under the Convention, February 12, 2009, CRC/C/GC/11*. Accessed October 24, 2020, from https://digitallibrary.un.org/record/648790?ln=en

UN Committee on the Rights of the Child. (2016). *Concluding observations: Bulgaria, November 21, 2016, CRC/C/BGR/CO/3-5*. UN. Accessed November 6, 2020, from http://digitallibrary.un.org/record/856034.

UN Committee on the Rights of the Child. (2017). *Concluding observations: Serbia, March 7, 2017, CRC/C/SRB/CO/2-3*. Accessed October 12, 2020, from https://www.refworld.org/pdfid/58e76fc14.pdf

UN General Assembly. (1966). *International covenant on civil and political rights, 1966, A/RES/2200(XXI)*. Accessed May 3, 2020, from https://digitallibrary.un.org/record/660192?ln=en

UN General Assembly. (2010). *Guidelines for the alternative care of children, 2010, A/RES/64/142*. https://digitallibrary.un.org/record/673583?ln=en

UN General Assembly. (2015). *Transforming our world: The 2030 agenda for sustainable development: Resolution/adopted by the general assembly, A/RES/70/1*. UN. Accessed November 18, 2020, from http://digitallibrary.un.org/record/808134

UN General Assembly. (2018). *Freedom of religion or belief: Resolution adopted by the general assembly, A/RES/72/177*. UN. Accessed November 18, 2020, from http://digitallibrary.un.org/record/1467023

UN Office of the High Commissioner for Human Rights (OHCHR). (1997). *Manual on human rights reporting under six major international human rights instruments, 1997, HR/PUB/91/1 (rev.1)*. Accessed May 16, 2020, from https://digitallibrary.un.org/record/254708?ln=en

United Nations. (2006). *Compilation of general comments and general recommendations adopted by human rights treaty bodies, HRI/GEN/1/Rev. 8*. UN. Accessed April 19, 2020, from http://digitallibrary.un.org/record/576098

Open Access This chapter is licensed under the terms of the Creative Commons Attribution 4.0 International License (http://creativecommons.org/licenses/by/4.0/), which permits use, sharing, adaptation, distribution and reproduction in any medium or format, as long as you give appropriate credit to the original author(s) and the source, provide a link to the Creative Commons license and indicate if changes were made.

The images or other third party material in this chapter are included in the chapter's Creative Commons license, unless indicated otherwise in a credit line to the material. If material is not included in the chapter's Creative Commons license and your intended use is not permitted by statutory regulation or exceeds the permitted use, you will need to obtain permission directly from the copyright holder.

Chapter 29
Article 31: The Rights to Rest, Play, Recreation, and Cultural and Artistic Activities

Gerison Lansdown

1. States Parties recognize the right of the child to rest and leisure, to engage in play and recreational activities appropriate to the age of the child and to participate freely in cultural life and the arts.
2. States Parties shall respect and promote the right of the child to participate fully in cultural and artistic life and shall encourage the provision of appropriate and equal opportunities for cultural, artistic, recreational and leisure activity.

What Did Children Say?
'We have to make sure that school establishment organise artistic and cultural competition.' *(Africa)*

'Inclusion of traditions in school subjects and student clubs (Glee club, different native instruments, arts club, Flores de Mayo/Santacruzan, Language Month).' *(Asia-Pacific)*

The playing areas outside the camp are very far where parents should accompany their children so at the end the parents will stop doing that because of having more priority duties for living. *(Asia-Pacific)*

G. Lansdown (✉)
Carleton University, Ottawa, Canada

© The Author(s) 2022
Z. Vaghri et al. (eds.), *Monitoring State Compliance with the UN Convention on the Rights of the Child*, Children's Well-Being: Indicators and Research 25, https://doi.org/10.1007/978-3-030-84647-3_29

Overview

The initial proposal for recognition of the right to play, during the Convention drafting process, was based on an earlier principle in the Declaration of the Rights of the Child. Both were included as a provision within education and described as having common purposes: to develop abilities, individual judgement, a sense of moral and social responsibility, and to become a useful member of society (Office of the United Nations High Commissioner for Human Rights and Rädda barnen (Society: Sweden), 2007, p. 683). Subsequent debate highlighted the need to understand play as having a different and broader meaning for children that could not be limited to educational pursuits. Concern was also raised that the initial draft contained no recognition of the role of cultural life and the arts in the lives of children. Accordingly, the drafters moved towards the development of a discrete article encompassing rest, leisure, play, recreation, cultural life, and the arts. In its reporting guidelines, the Committee includes Article 31 within the cluster containing education, not with the intention of limiting its scope, but to indicate the strong links to this area (David, 2006, p. 15).

Initially, the Committee paid scant attention to Article 31. Analysis of 98 concluding observations from 2000 to 2004 revealed that the Committee only addressed its provisions in 15 cases (David, 2006, p. 17). It has been described as the forgotten right and for many years there was limited jurisprudence in respect of its implementation (Hodgkin et al., 2007). The Committee now recognises that it has been one of the most neglected rights in the reporting process, with States Parties rarely seeking to reference measures undertaken to ensure its realisation (2006, para. 34, 2013, para. 2).

The Committee notes that failure to prioritise Article 31 has led to lack of investment and weak or non-existent protective legislation, and that when investment is made it tends to be orientated towards structured and organised activities rather than ensuring the time and space for children to engage in spontaneous play, recreation, and creativity. Multiple barriers have been identified as impeding the implementation of Article 31, many of which are attitudinal rather than resource based and indicate the need for a commitment to building social norms that value Article 31 rights. They highlight that challenges exist in countries at all income levels and include lack of recognition of play's importance, unsafe and hazardous environments, resistance to children's use of public spaces, pressure for educational achievement, overly structured and programmed schedules, neglect of Article 31 in development programmes, lack of investment in cultural and artistic opportunities, growing role of digital media, and commercialisation of children's play (UN Committee on the Rights of the Child, 2006, para. 34, 2013, paras. 33–47, 2016, para. 75).

In response to earlier neglect, and in recognition of the significance it now attaches to Article 31, the Committee prepared General Comment no. 17, which details the obligations to respect, protect, and fulfil the rights Article 31 embodies. The Committee emphasises that the constituent parts of Article 31 must be understood holistically and that they have implications for the Convention in its entirety. Play, recreation, rest, leisure, and cultural life are not optional extras. They serve 'to enrich the lives of children, ... (and) describe conditions necessary to protect the unique and evolving nature of childhood' and 'their realisation is fundamental to ... children's entitlement to optimum development ... (and) the promotion of resilience and to the realisation of other rights' (UN Committee on the Rights of the Child, 2013, para. 8).

General Principles

Article 2 Some groups of children are disproportionately excluded from exercising their Article 31 rights (UN Committee on the Rights of the Child, 2013, paras. 48–53). The Committee emphasises the imperative for attention to be paid to all children, regardless of gender, including children from the most marginalised communities, as well as those in more affluent environments where, for example, academic pressures or over-protection can serve to exclude children from realising these rights. It also welcomes the explicit obligation in the United Nations Convention on the Rights of Persons with Disabilities, Article 30 (d), to ensure that children with disabilities have equal access with other children to participation in play, recreation, leisure, and sporting activities, including those activities within school.

Article 3 Article 31 requires that States Parties take into consideration children's best interests in respect of resource allocation, planning, environmental policies, residential and transport policies, provision of parks and leisure facilities, labour and education legislation, and protections in the digital environment.

Article 6 Realisation of all the Article 31 rights is necessary for children's optimum development. Any measures provided must take into account children's evolving capacities and developmental needs (UN Committee on the Rights of the Child, 2006, para. 17). To achieve this goal, efforts need to be made to raise awareness and understanding of the centrality and importance of Article 31 rights in the lives of children.

Article 12 Children must be enabled to exercise choice and autonomy in their play as well as in participation in cultural and artistic activities, consistent with their evolving capacities. They must have opportunities to contribute to legislation, policies, and design of services affecting their Article 31 rights, as well as contributing feedback on their experiences of how their Article 31 rights are respected in schools and the wider community.

Articles Related or Linked to Article 31

Article 5: All Article 31 rights must be implemented with regard to children's evolving capacities

Article 13: Freedom of expression is necessary for children to realise their rights to artistic and cultural life as well as play and recreation

Article 15: Play and recreation require opportunities for freedom of assembly and association

Article 17: Access to mass media is integral to cultural and artistic life

Article 19: Children are entitled to protection in the exercise of their Article 31 rights

Article 23: Appropriate measures must be implemented to ensure that children with disabilities are able to exercise their Article 31 rights on an equal basis with other children

Article 24: The realisation of Article 31 rights promotes health and development of children

Article 27: Poverty and poor housing serve to limit the opportunity to participate fully in Article 31 rights

Articles 28 and 29: Rest, play, and leisure need to be built into the school structures, and the curriculum must reflect the right of children to participation in the arts and cultural life. Play is an important means through which children learn

Article 30: Children from minority communities must be enabled to enjoy and participate in their own cultures

Article 32: Children must be protected from work that denies them adequate rest and leisure

Articles 37 and 40: Provision must be made to ensure that children who are detained in the juvenile justice system are equally able to exercise their Article 31 rights

Article 39: Children who have experienced violence, abuse, or exploitation can be supported to make sense of their past and cope with the future through opportunities for play or artistic expression

Relevant Instruments

UN Universal Declaration of Human Rights (1948), Article 24

UN Declaration of the Rights of the Child (1959), Article 7

International Covenant on Economic, Social and Cultural Rights (1966), Article 15

UN Convention on the Elimination of All Forms of Discrimination against Women (1979), Article 13

UNESCO Mexico City Declaration on Cultural Policies (1982)

ILO Convention 79, Night Work of Young Persons (Non-Industrial Occupations) (1946), Article 2, prohibiting children under 14 from working at night.

ILO Convention 90, Night Work of Young Persons (Industry) (Revised) (1948), Article 2, mandating a rest period of at least seven hours for workers between 16 and 18 years of age.

ILO Convention 138, Minimum Age (1973), Article 2, requiring states to regulate the minimum age for work.

ILO Convention 182, Worst Forms of Child Labour (1999), Article 3, prohibiting children from carrying out work which is likely to harm their health.

Attributes

Attribute One: Rest and Leisure

Rest and leisure are closely linked and affirm the importance of space in children's lives when there is no expectation of activity or responsibility. Leisure is free or unobligated time that does not involve formal education, work, home responsibilities, performing other life-sustaining functions, or engaging in activity directed from outside the individual (UN Committee on the Rights of the Child, 2013, para. 14). It can be defined as the time in which play or recreation can take place. The Committee argues that children are entitled to, and need opportunity for leisure, which they can choose to fill as actively or inactively as they wish.

The right to rest originated in the Universal Declaration on Human Rights and focused on the need for employees regain their strength *and* to enjoy leisure activities (Melander, 1993, pp. 379, 380). This meaning also extends to children whose working lives are protected under Article 32, and accordingly the Committee encourages States Parties to ratify and implement ILO Conventions Nos. 79, 90, 138, and 182, and introduce legislation and regulations for child employees to guarantee appropriate limits on the nature, hours and days of work, rest periods and recreational facilities, in accordance with their evolving capacities (2013, para. 56 (b)).

The text of Article 31 does not restrict the concept of rest to time apart from work. Indeed, proposals to define it in those terms were rejected in the drafting stages of the CRC (Office of the United Nations High Commissioner for Human Rights and Rädda barnen (Society: Sweden), 2007, p. 689). The Committee has argued that the right to rest requires that children are afforded sufficient respite from work, education or exertion of any kind, to ensure their optimum health and well-being. It also requires that they are provided with the opportunity for adequate sleep. In fulfilling the right to both respite from activity and adequate sleep, regard must be afforded to children's evolving capacities and their developmental needs (UN Committee on the Rights of the Child, 2013, para. 14 (a)). The Committee has expressed concern, for example, that in many states, children are subjected to pressures for educational achievement that lack recognition of the necessity of appropriate rest (2013, para. 41). It has pointed out 'that children are exposed to developmental disorders due to the stress of a highly competitive educational system and the consequent lack of time for leisure' (1998, para. 22, 2012, paras. 62–63). It has also emphasised that States Parties must ensure that school days guarantee sufficient opportunities for rest, in accordance with children's age and developmental needs (2013, para. 58 (g)). However, it does not seek to prescribe the appropriate levels of either rest or leisure for children.

Attribute Two: *Play and Recreation*

The Committee takes the view that play and recreation are fundamental and vital dimensions of childhood. Both can take place when children are on their own but also together with peers and supportive adults. Play and recreation have an instrumental role in promoting and advancing children's development and agency, as well as an intrinsic value in terms of the pleasure and enjoyment they afford. However, the Committee does point to a difference between the two.

There is a surprising lack of consensus regarding the definition of play.[1] The Committee has defined play as 'any behaviour, activity, or processes initiated, controlled and structured by children themselves; it takes place whenever and wherever opportunities arise' (2013, para. 14 (c)). It is characterised by being self-directed and undertaken for its own sake rather than as a means to an end. It has the potential to take infinite forms and is characterised by being fun, uncertain, challenging, flexible and non-productive. Although it is often dismissed as non-essential or unproductive time, the Committee argues that play contributes to children's health and well-being as well as 'the development of creativity, imagination, self-confidence, self-efficacy, as well as physical, social, cognitive and emotional strength and skills' (2013, para. 9). In many cases, children's right to play requires no specific resources but rather recognition of the need for time and space to pursue their imaginations and interests (Lansdown and Tobin, 2019, p. 1216).

On the other hand, recreation is an umbrella term used to describe a broad range of activities, including participation in music, arts, clubs, sports, games, online gaming, hobbies, and community engagement. It applies to online and offline activities freely chosen by children because they perceive value in pursuing them. The Committee makes clear that compulsory or enforced games, sports or other activities do not constitute recreation.

---

[1] For discussions on the definitions of play, see, Doris Bergen, 'Play as the Learning Medium for Future Scientists, Mathematicians, and Engineers' (2009, n. 55, p. 416); Stuart Lester and Wendy Russell, Children's Right to Play (2010, n. 5, pp. 7–14); Albert Solnit, 'A Psychoanalytic view of play (1987, p. 205); Jerry Lewis, 'Childhood Play in Normality, Pathology and Therapy' (1993, pp. 6–7); Peter Neubauer, 'The Many Meanings of Play' (1987, p. 3); Anthea Holme and Peter Massie, *Children's Play: A Study of Needs and Opportunities* (1970, p. 39); and James Johnson, James Christie, and Thomas Yawkey, *Play and Early Childhood Development* (1987, pp. 10–11).

In order to create environments where children are able to exercise their rights to play and recreation, States Parties need to invest in measures to raise awareness of their importance in the lives of children and introduce support for parents in the creation of environments that facilitate children's play in accordance with their evolving capacities. Investment is also required in the provision of sports and games facilities, including in schools and school playgrounds, access to parks and green spaces, safe and affordable transport, safe living environments for free play, and traffic safety measures, as well as safe access to the digital environment (UN Committee on the Rights of the Child, 2013, para. 58).

Attribute Three: Cultural Life and the Arts

Article 31, paragraph 1, requires that children are able to participate freely in cultural life. The Committee on Economic, Social and Cultural Rights has argued that it is through the expression of these rights that children and their communities express their identity and the meaning they give to their existence, a view endorsed by the Committee on the Rights of the Child (UN Committee on Economic, Social and Cultural Rights, 2009, para. 13). In its General Comment on Article 31, the Committee clarifies that it focuses on the creative or artistic aspects of cultural life, rather than the broader definition embraced in Article 30 on the right of the child to enjoy their own culture (UN Committee on Economic, Social and Cultural Rights, 2009, para. 6).

Recognition must be afforded to the extent to which children are not merely passive recipients of an inherited culture, but play a significant role in maintaining and transforming cultural life through imaginative play, songs, and stories, and increasingly in the online environment. They contribute to a culture of childhood (Lansdown and Tobin, 2019). Cultural and artistic expression take place in the home, school, streets, and public spaces and through many media, including dance, festivals, theatre, music, cinema, and digital platforms. The role of States Parties is to facilitate this expression, not supply or provide it (World Conference on Cultural Policies, 1982). Accordingly, its implementation for all children necessitates measures to ensure the availability of dedicated and affordable cultural activities for children, which also allow children to produce and create their own cultural forms, and a review of cultural policies, programmes, and institutions, to ensure their accessibility and relevance for all children. The school curriculum needs to allow time for children to learn about and participate in cultural activities including music, drama, literature, poetry, and art (UN Committee on the Rights of the Child, 2013, para. 58 (f), (g)).

Attribute Four: Creating Appropriate and Equal Opportunities for Enjoyment of Article 31 Rights

Article 31, paragraph 2, imposes an obligation to respect and promote the right to participate fully in cultural and artistic life as well as encouraging provision of appropriate and equal opportunities for cultural, artistic, recreational, and leisure activity. Interestingly, play is excluded from this explicit obligation. However, the Committee has interpreted paragraph 2 as extending also to play (2013, para. 15 (b)). In order to strengthen commitment to the realisation of Article 31 rights, the Committee has argued for the introduction of a broad range of strategic measures including legislation and cross-departmental planning, data collection, allocation of budgets, training, and capacity building (2013, para. 58).

With specific reference to the need for 'appropriate' opportunities for enjoying Article 31 rights, provision is needed that is age-appropriate, taking into account changing needs of children as they grow older, including amounts of time afforded, nature of spaces and environments, forms of stimulation, and degrees of adult oversight (UN Committee on the Rights of the Child, 2013, para. 14 (e)). In addition, the Committee has recognised the need to balance Article 31 rights with the right to protection from injury and harm. In this respect, it has called for regulations to ensure the safety of toys and games, limit advertising, and establish child protection policies and codes of practice for all professionals working with children in the fields of play, sports, culture, and the arts (UN Committee on the Rights of the Child, 2013, para. 57 (b), (c)). While acknowledging the positive role of the digital environment, the Committee emphasises the need for action to empower children to act safely online, as well as measures to reduce impunity of abusive adults, limit access to harmful material, and improve information for parents, professionals, and adults (2013, para. 57 (d), 2014).

The obligation to ensure equal opportunities for all children requires the introduction of universal design, legislation to ensure non-discrimination to guarantee access for every child, and reviews of cultural policies, programmes, and institutions to ensure they reflect the differing needs and aspirations of all children (UN Committee on the Rights of the Child, 2013, para. 57 (a), 58 (f)). It also requires ending the imposition of curfews and other restrictions on children's access to public spaces, and the erosion of traditional play spaces.

References

Bergen, D. (2009). Play as the learning medium for future scientists, mathematicians, and engineers. *American Journal of Play, 1*(4), 413–428.

David, P. (2006). *A commentary on the United Nations convention on the rights of the child, Article 31: The right to leisure, play and culture*. Brill Nijhoff. Accessed November 18, 2020, from https://brill.com/view/title/11643

Hodgkin, R., Newell, P., & UNICEF. (2007). *Implementation handbook for the convention on the rights of the child* (3rd ed.). UNICEF. Accessed September 21, 2020, from https://digitallibrary.un.org/record/620060?ln=en

Holme, A., Massie, P., & Council for Children's Welfare. (1970). *Children's play: A study of needs and opportunities: A study for the council for children's welfare*. Joseph.

Johnson, J. E., Christie, J. F., & Yawkey, T. D. (1987). *Play and early childhood development*. Scott, Foresman.

Lansdown, G., & Tobin, J. (2019). Article 31: The right to rest, leisure, play, recreation and participation in cultural life and the arts. In J. Tobin (Ed.), *The UN convention on the rights of the child: A commentary* (pp. 1195–1224). Oxford University Press.

Lester, S., & Russell, W. (2010). *Children's right to play: An examination of the importance of play in the lives of children worldwide. Working papers in early childhood development, no. 57. Bernard van Leer Foundation (NJ1)*. Bernard van Leer Foundation. Accessed December 19, 2020, https://eric.ed.gov/?id=ED522537

Lewis, J. M. (1993). Childhood play in normality, pathology, and therapy. *American Journal of Orthopsychiatry, 63*(1), 6–15. https://doi.org/10.1037/h0079403

Melander, G. (1993). Article 24. In A. Eide, G. Alfredsson, G. Melander, L. A. Rehof, & A. Rosas (Eds.), *The universal declaration of human rights: A commentary* (1st ed.). Oxford University Press.

Neubauer, P. B. (1987). The many meanings of play: introduction. In A. J. Solnit & P. B. Neubauer (Eds.), *The psychoanalytic study of the child* (Vol. 42). Yale University Press.

Office of the United Nations High Commissioner for Human Rights & Rädda barnen (Society: Sweden). (2007). *Legislative history of the convention on the rights of the child*. United Nations. https://digitallibrary.un.org/record/602462?ln=en

Solnit, A. J. (1987). A psychoanalytic view of play. In A. J. Solnit & P. B. Neubauer (Eds.), *The Psychoanalytic study of the child: Volume 42* Yale University Press.

UN Committee on Economic, Social and Cultural Rights. (2009). *General comment no. 21, Right of everyone to take part in cultural life (art. 15, para. 1a of the Covenant on Economic, Social and Cultural Rights), E/C.12/GC/21*. UN. Accessed November 18, 2020, from http://digitallibrary.un.org/record/679354

UN Committee on the Rights of the Child. (1998). *Concluding observations: Japan, June 24, 1998, CRC/C/15/Add.90*. UN. Accessed November 18, 2020, from http://digitallibrary.un.org/record/259749.

UN Committee on the Rights of the Child. (2006). *General comment no. 7 (2005) Implementing child rights in early childhood, September 20, 2006, CRC/C/GC/7/Rev.1*. Accessed October 12, 2020, from https://digitallibrary.un.org/record/584854?ln=en

UN Committee on the Rights of the Child. (2012). *Concluding observations: Korea, February 2, 2012, CRC/C/KOR/CO/3-4*. UN. Accessed November 17, 2020, from http://digitallibrary.un.org/record/720645

UN Committee on the Rights of the Child. (2013). *General comment no. 17 (2013) on the right of the child to rest, leisure, play, recreational activities, cultural life and the arts (art. 31), April 17, 2013, CRC/C/GC/17*. Accessed October 12, 2020, from https://digitallibrary.un.org/record/778539?ln=en

UN Committee on the Rights of the Child. (2014). *Day of general discussion: digital media and children's rights*. UN. Accessed October 24, 2020, from https://www.ohchr.org/EN/HRBodies/CRC/Pages/Discussion2014.aspx

UN Committee on the Rights of the Child. (2016). *General comment no. 20 (2016) on the implementation of the rights of the child during adolescence, December 6, 2016, CRC/C/GC/20*. Accessed October 12, 2020, from https://digitallibrary.un.org/record/855544?ln=en

World Conference on Cultural Policies. (1982). *Mexico City declaration on cultural policies* (No. CLT/MD/1). UNESCO. Accessed November 18, 2020, from https://unesdoc.unesco.org/ark:/48223/pf0000052505

Open Access This chapter is licensed under the terms of the Creative Commons Attribution 4.0 International License (http://creativecommons.org/licenses/by/4.0/), which permits use, sharing, adaptation, distribution and reproduction in any medium or format, as long as you give appropriate credit to the original author(s) and the source, provide a link to the Creative Commons license and indicate if changes were made.

The images or other third party material in this chapter are included in the chapter's Creative Commons license, unless indicated otherwise in a credit line to the material. If material is not included in the chapter's Creative Commons license and your intended use is not permitted by statutory regulation or exceeds the permitted use, you will need to obtain permission directly from the copyright holder.

Part VI
Protection Measures from Violence

Articles 19, 37 and 39

Introduction

Articles 19, 37, and 39 represent a cluster of provisions that address the right of children to protection from all forms of violence and abuse, and to rehabilitative help if those rights are violated or neglected. Their inclusion and specific formulation with the Convention on the Rights of the Child (the Convention) achieves a dual purpose.

First, in recognising that no form of violence against a child is acceptable, and asserting their fundamental human right to protection, these protection rights acknowledge the imperative for respecting the human dignity and integrity of the child. In so doing, they represent a profound change in the prevailing approaches that have characterised children primarily as objects of protection rather than subjects of rights. The Committee on the Rights of the Child (the Committee) have argued that this requires a paradigm shift in how children are treated (2011, para. 3 (b)). Prior to the Convention, many forms of violence against children were widely sanctioned and endorsed – within the family, schools, residential institutions, and the penal system. However, the broad interpretation by the Committee, particularly of Article 19, has contributed to a profound reconceptualisation of what constitutes violence, recognition of the wide range of potential perpetrators, and consistent recommendations to achieve a total prohibition in all settings.

At the same time, these articles recognise that although children, like adults, are subjects of rights and entitled to protection from violence, they are also entitled to additional protections because of their age. Accordingly, Article 37 goes beyond comparable provisions in earlier treaties and prohibits capital punishment or life imprisonment without possibility of parole. The Committee demands additionally that life imprisonment under any circumstances is an unacceptable punishment for a child. Article 37 insists on imprisonment of children only as a measure of last resort and for the shortest possible time. In addition, Article 39, an innovative provision in international human rights law, introduces the right of children who have experienced any form of violence, abuse, neglect, exploitation, torture, or armed conflict to help with physical and psychological recovery and rehabilitation. While the principle of reparation and compensation for human rights violations is well established, Article 39 goes further, in imposing a child-centred and proactive responsibility on States Parties to promote children's positive recovery even where the State Party itself is not responsible for harm that has been experienced (Tobin and Marshall 2019, p. 1562).

This part elaborates the implications of these three articles and the contribution they make to defining violence and abuse of children, and transforming societal understanding of, and responses to, that violence.

References

Tobin, J., & Marshall, C. (2019). Article 39: The Right to Reintegration and Recovery. In J. Tobin (Ed.), *The UN Convention on the Rights of the Child: A Commentary* (pp. 1561–1595). Oxford, New York: Oxford University Press.

UN Committee on the Rights of the Child. (2011). *General Comment No. 13 (2011) The right of the child to freedom from all forms of violence, April 18, 2011, CRC/C/GC/13*. https://digitallibrary.un.org/record/711722?ln=en. Accessed 12 October 2020.

Chapter 30
Article 19: The Right to Protection from All Forms of Violence

Christian Whalen

Article 19
1. States Parties shall take all appropriate legislative, administrative, social and educational measures to protect the child from all forms of physical or mental violence, injury or abuse, neglect or negligent treatment, maltreatment or exploitation, including sexual abuse, while in the care of parent(s), legal guardian(s) or any other person who has the care of the child.
2. Such protective measures should, as appropriate, include effective procedures for the establishment of social programmes to provide necessary support for the child and for those who have the care of the child, as well as for other forms of prevention and for identification, reporting, referral, investigation, treatment and follow-up of instances of child maltreatment described heretofore, and, as appropriate, for judicial involvement.

C. Whalen (✉)
Office of the Child and Youth Advocate, Fredericton, NB, Canada
e-mail: Christian.Whalen@gnb.ca

> **What Did Children Say?**
> 'There are laws prohibiting violence.' *(Eastern Europe)*
> 'It is important to have training on how to be good parents (parenthood) and that this training be extended to the whole community because all people in the community are responsible for the education of children.' *(Western Europe/Other)*
> The state must make an annual report on child rights violations. *(Africa)*
> 'Policies to stop children from physical punishment should be introduced.' *(Africa)*

Overview

Article 19 is the core provision in the Convention in relation to efforts to address and eliminate all forms of harm to children (UN Committee on the Rights of the Child, 2011, para. 7 (a)). As a principle, it is closely linked to the child's right to life and maximum survival and development and informs the many protection rights set out in the Convention. However, it also is linked to many of the child's provision and participation rights, such as those touching upon abolishing harmful traditional practices, or protecting children from harmful information, while introducing the child's rights in relation to alternative family care settings when removed from their parents' care.[1]

It asserts, as a broad principle, the child's right to be free from all forms of harm, well beyond Article 37 and the comparable human rights standard of protection from cruel or unusual punishment afforded adults in other global human rights instruments (UNICEF, 2007, p. 249). It includes a specific requirement to protect children in the care of their parents, guardians, or any person who has care of the child.

Violence is broadly defined to include all forms of harm (UN Committee on the Rights of the Child, 2011, para. 4), and encompasses mental violence, sexual and other forms of exploitation, as well as non-intentional forms of harm, such as neglect. The Committee has been careful to guard against restrictive interpretations of the term violence. The World Health Organization has a similarly expansive interpretation of the term (UN Committee on the Rights of the Child, 2011, para. 4).[2] As such, Article 19 articulates full respect for the human dignity and physical and personal integrity of children as rights-bearing individuals. The Committee stresses that this requires a paradigm shift of caregiving and protection away from the perception of children primarily as victims (2011, para. 3 (b)). Article 19 does not

---

[1] Convention Articles 20, 21, 22, and 25.
[2] WHO defines violence to children to include 'the intentional use of physical force or power, threatened or actual, against a child, by an individual or group that either results in or has a high likelihood of resulting in an actual or potential harm to the child's health, survival, development or dignity' (Krug et al., 2002, p. 5).

have any direct precedent in global human rights treaties, as they did not specifically address concerns in relation to violence to children (Vučković-Šahović et al., 2012, p. 185).

Following the publication of the 1996 Report on the *Impact of Armed Conflict on Children* (Machel, 1996), the United Nations developed and ratified two additional protocols to the Convention, the Optional Protocol on the Involvement of Children in Armed Conflict (A/RES/54/263) and the Optional Protocol on the sale of children, child prostitution and child pornography (A/RES/54/263), that further extend the protections of Article 19. In addition, *General Comment No. 13 (2011), The right of the child to freedom from all forms of violence*, the 2006 *World Report on Violence Against Children* (Pinheiro, 2006), and the 2015 Global Survey on Violence Against Children (UN Special Representative of the Secretary-General on Violence against Children, 2015) constitute key reference documents in understanding the scope and purpose of Article 19.

General Principles

Article 2 While children of marginalised sectors of the population may in principle be at no greater risk of harm within their own families than others, the marginalisation of these families by society as a whole may expose them to greater risks of harm, both at home and from public sector service providers. Disabled children, for example, are at significantly greater risk of sexual harm than their able-bodied peers (UN Committee on the Rights of the Child, 2007a, para. 42). Children in early childhood, children affected by HIV/AIDS, indigenous children, and unaccompanied or separated children are also particularly at risk and the Committee has frequently underlined the importance of special measures of protection for these populations (2003a, paras. 37, 38, 2005, paras. 50–53, 2006, para. 36, 2009, paras. 22, 64–65, 70, 72).

The gender dimensions of violence must also be considered by States Parties in developing and implementing violence prevention strategies (UN Committee on the Rights of the Child, 2011, paras. 19, 72 (b)). An intersectional analysis of children in such populations reveals that the discriminatory impacts experienced by children with a double or triple disadvantage are among the most vulnerable (Ravnbøl, 2009). The solutions to ensure equal access to the child's right to be free from violence need to address these complexities.

Article 3 The Committee emphasises that the interpretation of a child's best interests cannot be used to justify practices, including corporal punishment, which conflict with a child's human dignity and right to physical integrity. Moreover, the Committee maintains that the best interests of the child in relation to Article 19 are best served by prevention of all forms of violence and the promotion of positive child-rearing through a national coordinating framework and adequate investment of resources in a child rights based and integrated child protection and support system

(2011, para. 61). Articles 3 (2) and (3) require legislative and administrative measures to ensure such protection and care as is necessary for the child's well-being, and that state institutions, services, and facilities responsible for the care and protection of children conform with necessary standards and supervision.

Article 6 The child's inherent right to life, and to maximum survival and development, expresses positively, as a guiding principle, many of the goals set out in Article 19's promise of a life free from violence. Development is to be interpreted in the broadest possible sense, encompassing not simply protection from violence and exploitation but implementation measures which ensure the optimal physical, mental, spiritual, moral, psychological, and social development of the child (UN Committee on the Rights of the Child, 2011, para. 62). Articles 19 and 6 are also closely linked because of their common connection to the core human rights value of preserving the child's human dignity which underpins both articles (Lenzer, 2015, p. 278).

Article 12 The child's right to be heard and to have their opinions considered is critically important in all matters related to the application of Article 19, particularly in the identification, reporting, and investigation of child maltreatment, decisions regarding disruption of the family environment and the possibility of alternative care, and in health sector interventions addressing injuries or harms suffered by children. The Committee makes clear that children's views must be invited and given due weight as a mandatory step at every point in a child protection process, and that barriers to participation, particularly for marginalised children, must be addressed (2011, para. 63).

States Parties are invited to involve children in the development of prevention strategies and protective responses to violence in general, and in school (UN Committee on the Rights of the Child, 2003a, para. 63, 2016, para. 49). Initiatives and programmes aimed at strengthening children's own capacities to eliminate violence should be supported (UN Committee on the Rights of the Child, 2011, para. 63).

The Committee has made a strong case to respect child participation in child protection matters (2011, para. 63), and many encouraging best practices are emerging globally in this field. Article 12 includes the child's right to complaint mechanisms within institutions and the right to be informed of all institutional rules to which they may be subject and of existing procedures for redress (UNICEF, 2007, p. 566; UN Committee on the Rights of the Child, 2007b, para. 28).

Articles Related or Linked to Article 19

Article 5 proclaims the child's right to guidance and protection from their parents and family in the exercise of their rights, including the child's right to be protected from all forms of violence within and without the parental home.

Article 9 guarantees the child's right to not be separated from their parents unless it is necessary and in their best interests, such as in a case of abuse or neglect by their parents.

Article 11 protects children from illicit transfer and non-return from other countries including international child abduction, which is a specific form of violence falling implicitly within the ambit of Article 19.

Article 16 concerns the child's right to privacy, the inviolability of their family life, and right to protection from unlawful attacks on their honour and reputation, such as bullying and cyber-bullying that will often infringe both Article 16 and Article 19.

Article 17 states the child's right to information and the States Parties' obligation to encourage guidelines for the protection of children from information and material injurious to their well-being. For example, latent and overt violence in the pornography industry points to the common obligations under Article 17 and 19.

Article 18 is the child's right to have both parents as primary caregivers and appropriate assistance to parents. Parents without appropriate state supports may be at greater risk of perpetrating violence towards their children hence the clear connection between Articles 18 and 19 of the Convention, as their juxtaposition suggests.

Article 20, the child's right to special protection, assistance, and alternative care if deprived of their family follows logically and sequentially from the guarantees in Article 19.

Article 21 proclaims the best interests of the child as the paramount consideration in relation to adoption and it must be applied judiciously where permanent removal of the child from a violent parent is the cause for the adoption placement.

Article 22 protects the rights of refugee children who are at increased risk of many forms of institutional violence and may be in great need of recovery supports for the violence from which they are fleeing.

Article 23 protects the rights of disabled children who are also at much greater risk of violence than their able-bodied peers.

Article 24, the child's right to the highest attainable standard of health, includes protections to combat child mortality, infectious diseases, harmful traditional practices, and environmental hazards.

Article 25, the right to periodic review of placement and treatment of children in care, includes those placed in care as a protection measure in response to their experience of violence at home.

Article 27 proclaims the child's right to an adequate standard of living, a key social determinant in preventing violence to children.

Article 28 (3) requires school discipline to be consistent with child's human dignity.

Article 32 requires protection from economic exploitation.

Article 33 requires protection from drug endangerment.

Article 34 requires protection from sexual exploitation.

Article 35 addresses the child's right to be protected from abduction, sale, or trafficking.

Article 36 addresses protection from all other forms of exploitation.

Article 37 proclaims the child's right to be protected from torture or other cruel, inhuman, or degrading treatment or punishment.

Article 38 prohibits forced enrolment in armed conflict.

Article 39 provides the right to recovery and reintegration for child victims of neglect, exploitation, abuse, torture, cruel treatment, or armed conflict.

Article 40, the right to a separate system of youth criminal justice, which when read with Article 19 must be one that guards against institutional violence to children.

Optional Protocol on the involvement of children in armed conflict.

Optional Protocol on the sale of children, child prostitution and child pornography.

Relevant Instruments

International Covenant on Civil and Political Rights (1966), Articles 6, 7, 8, 9 and 10

UN Convention against Torture and Other Cruel, Inhuman or Degrading Treatment or Punishment (1984)

UN Standard Minimum Rules for the Administration of Juvenile Justice (Beijing Rules) (1985)

UN Rules for the Protection of Juveniles Deprived of their Liberty (Havana Rules) (1990)

UN Guidelines for the Prevention of Juvenile Delinquency (Riyadh Guidelines) (1990)

UN Guidelines on Justice in Matters involving Child Victims and Witnesses of Crime (2005)

UN Declaration on the Rights of Indigenous Peoples (2007), Articles 7(2), 17 (2) and 22(2)

UN Guidelines for the Alternative Care of Children (2009), paras 96-97

European Convention on Human Rights (1950), Articles 2, 3, 4 and 8

African Charter on the Rights and Welfare of the Child (1990)

Inter-American Convention on the International Return of Children (1989)

Inter-American Convention on International Traffic in Minors (1994)

Attributes

Attribute One: Protection from All Forms of Violence

No violence against children is justifiable, all violence against children is preventable (UN Committee on the Rights of the Child, 2011, para. 3). Article 19 leaves no room for any level of legalised violence to children. Frequency or severity of harm, or intent to harm, are not relevant factors in the application of this right.

Physical and mental violence include belittling, spurning, rejecting children or conveying that they are worthless, unwanted, or unloved, and also physical and psychological hazing or bullying. Neglect includes failing to protect children from preventable harm, and failure to provide the basic necessities, including lack of emotional supports, withholding of essential medical care or educational services, and abandonment. Prohibited violence outlined by the Committee includes corporal punishment in any setting, sexual abuse or exploitation, torture or degrading treatment, self-harm, violence between children, harmful practices (such as forced marriage and genital mutilation), violence in mass media and through social media, and institutional or systemic violations due to poor policy, poor evaluation, poor delivery, or underinvestment regarding child protection practices (UN Committee on the Elimination of Discrimination against Women and UN Committee on the Rights of the Child, 2014, paras. 10–30; UN Committee on the Rights of the Child, 2011, paras. 17–32, 2016, para. 49).

States Parties need to have comprehensive national coordinating frameworks in compliance with Article 4 to ensure that all forms of violence against children are adequately addressed and combatted, providing specific safeguards for children in vulnerable situations, such as children in residential care and children separated from family or kin.

Attribute Two: Protection While in the Care of Parents, Legal Guardians, or Any Other Person

The Committee has adopted a position whereby it assumes that all children under the age of 18 years are or should be in the care of someone. Accordingly, Article 19 applies to every child, despite the apparently restrictive language that protection applies while in the care of parents, legal guardian, or any other person (UN Committee on the Rights of the Child, 2011, para. 33). Article 19 extends to arrangements where the state may be the caregiver when parents cannot fulfil this responsibility, and to other caregivers including legal guardians or any other person who has care of the child: foster parents, adoptive parents, extended family and community members, school and day-care personnel, caregivers employed by parents (e.g. coaches and youth group supervisors), and institutional personnel (such as residential, health care and juvenile justice staff) (UN Committee on the Rights of the Child, 2011, para. 33).

Article 19 also applies to children without a primary or proxy caregiver, such as children in street situations and unaccompanied minors (UN Committee on the Rights of the Child, 2011, para. 35). Children may be subject to violence by primary or proxy caregivers, and others against whom the caregiver is expected to provide protection (for example, neighbours, peers, and strangers), as well as by state actors who misuse their authority in various settings. All these situations are captured by Article 19, which is not limited to violence perpetrated by caregivers in a personal context only (UN Committee on the Rights of the Child, 2011, para. 36).

Attribute Three: All Appropriate Measures

States Parties must not only address all forms of violence, but Article 19 (1) requires that they do so through all appropriate measures: 'legislative, administrative, social and educational.' These include the general measures of implementation of child rights set out by the Committee in its General Comment no. 5 (2003b). Moreover, the Committee calls for 'an integrated, cohesive, interdisciplinary and coordinated system,' including all the measures enumerated in Article 19 (1) and all the interventions identified in Article 19 (2), for all children inclusively (2011, para. 39). For instance, 'legislative measures,' including budgets, means both laws and sub-regulatory instruments of enforcement at national, sub-national, and local levels. General Comment no. 13 elaborates a broad and comprehensive range of measures that must be undertaken as the national, regional, and local levels including obligations to (UN Committee on the Rights of the Child, 2011, paras. 41–44):

- ratify relevant instruments and international and regional instruments
- review and lift reservations and declarations
- strengthen cooperation with treaty bodies
- ensure conformity with all domestic legislation
- provide effective redress mechanisms for rights violations domestically
- establish social programmes to support positive parenting
- establish a national institution for children's rights, as well as sub-national independent human rights institutions with specific child rights mandates

Attribute Four: Effective Identification, Reporting, Investigation, and Treatment of Harm

Article 19 (2) completes the call for comprehensiveness in relation to measures to combat all violence by enumerating the range of interventions to be addressed. States Parties must take measures to intervene effectively in relation to proactive prevention and prohibition of all forms of violence and also with respect to its identification, reporting, referral, investigation, treatment, and follow-up, including appropriate processes for judicial intervention (UN Committee on the Rights of the Child, 2011, paras. 45–57).

The Committee has emphasised that child protection must begin with proactive measures to prevent and prohibit all forms of violence (2011, para. 46). In this regard, it has identified the importance of awareness raising and training as a key preventive strategy, along with the adoption of national policy statements on violence against children and comprehensive studies on the extent, nature, causes and impact of such violence (2001, para. 723). Children must be provided with as many opportunities as possible to signal emerging problems before they reach a state of crisis, and for adults to recognise and effectively act on such problems in a manner that gives due weight to the child's views (UN Committee on the Rights of the Child, 2011, paras. 48, 50). The importance of child participation at every stage of the child protection system must be recognised.

References

Krug, E. G., Dahlberg, L. L., Mercy, J. A., Zwi, A. B., & Lozano, R. (Eds.). (2002). *World report on violence and health*. World Health Organization. Accessed November 21, 2020, from https://www.who.int/violence_injury_prevention/violence/world_report/chapters/en/

Lenzer, G. (2015). Violence against children. In *Routledge international handbook of children's rights studies*. Routledge.

Machel, G. (1996). *Impact of armed conflict on children: Note by the Secretary-General, A/51/306*. UN. Accessed November 21, 2020, from http://digitallibrary.un.org/record/223213

Pinheiro, P. S. de M. S. (2006). *Report of the independent expert for the United Nations Study on violence against children, A/61/299*. UN. Accessed November 12, 2020, from http://digitallibrary.un.org/record/584299

Ravnbøl, C. I. (2009). Intersectional discrimination against children: Discrimination against Romani children and anti-discrimination measures to address child trafficking. *Innocenti Working Papers, 2009*(11). https://doi.org/10.18356/7e89512e-en

UN Committee on the Elimination of Discrimination against Women & UN Committee on the Rights of the Child. (2014). *Joint general recommendation no. 31 of the committee on the elimination of discrimination against women/general comment no. 18 of the committee on the rights of the child on harmful practices, CEDAW/C/GC/31, CRC/C/GC/18*. UN. Accessed November 13, 2020, from http://digitallibrary.un.org/record/807256

UN Committee on the Rights of the Child. (2001). *Day of general discussion: Violence against children within the family and in school*. UN. Accessed November 22, 2020, from https://www.ohchr.org/EN/HRBodies/CRC/Pages/DiscussionDays.aspx

UN Committee on the Rights of the Child. (2003a). *General comment no. 3 (2003) HIV/AIDS and the rights of the child, March 17, 2003, CRC/GC/2003/3*. Accessed October 12, 2020, from https://digitallibrary.un.org/record/501529?ln=en

UN Committee on the Rights of the Child. (2003b). *General comment no. 5 (2003) General measures of implementation of the convention on the rights of the child (arts. 4, 42 and 44, para. 6), November 27, 2003, CRC/GC/2003/5*. Accessed October 12, 2020, from https://digitallibrary.un.org/record/513415?ln=en

UN Committee on the Rights of the Child. (2005). *General comment no. 6 (2005) treatment of unaccompanied and separated children outside their country of origin, September 1, 2005, CRC/GC/2005/6*. Accessed October 12, 2020, from https://digitallibrary.un.org/record/566055?ln=en

UN Committee on the Rights of the Child. (2006). *General Comment No. 7 (2005) Implementing child rights in early childhood, September 20, 2006, CRC/C/GC/7/Rev.1*. Accessed October 12, 2020, from https://digitallibrary.un.org/record/584854?ln=en

UN Committee on the Rights of the Child. (2007a). *General Comment No. 9 (2006) The rights of children with disabilities, November 13, 2007, CRC/C/GC/9*. Accessed October 12, 2020, from https://digitallibrary.un.org/record/593891?ln=en

UN Committee on the Rights of the Child. (2007b). *General Comment No. 10 (2007) Children's rights in juvenile justice, April 25, 2007, CRC/C/GC/10*. Accessed October 12, 2020, https://digitallibrary.un.org/record/599395?ln=en

UN Committee on the Rights of the Child. (2009). *General comment No. 11 (2009), Indigenous children and their rights under the Convention, February 12, 2009, CRC/C/GC/11*. Accessed October 24, 2020, from https://digitallibrary.un.org/record/648790?ln=en

UN Committee on the Rights of the Child. (2011). *General comment No. 13 (2011) The right of the child to freedom from all forms of violence, April 18, 2011, CRC/C/GC/13*. Accessed October 12, 2020, from https://digitallibrary.un.org/record/711722?ln=en

UN Committee on the Rights of the Child. (2016). *General comment no. 20 (2016) on the implementation of the rights of the child during adolescence, December 6, 2016, CRC/C/GC/20*. Accessed October 12, 2020, from https://digitallibrary.un.org/record/855544?ln=en

UN Special Representative of the Secretary-General on Violence Against Children. (2015). *Toward a world free from violence: Global survey on violence against children*. UN. Accessed November 21, 2020, from http://digitallibrary.un.org/record/3846479

UNICEF. (2007). *Implementation handbook for the convention on the rights of the child* (3rd ed.). UNICEF. Accessed September 21, 2020, from https://digitallibrary.un.org/record/620060?ln=en

Vučković-Šahović, N., Doek, J. E., & Zermatten, J. (2012). *The rights of the child in international law: Rights of the child in a nutshell and in context: All about children's rights*. Stämpfli.

Open Access This chapter is licensed under the terms of the Creative Commons Attribution 4.0 International License (http://creativecommons.org/licenses/by/4.0/), which permits use, sharing, adaptation, distribution and reproduction in any medium or format, as long as you give appropriate credit to the original author(s) and the source, provide a link to the Creative Commons license and indicate if changes were made.

The images or other third party material in this chapter are included in the chapter's Creative Commons license, unless indicated otherwise in a credit line to the material. If material is not included in the chapter's Creative Commons license and your intended use is not permitted by statutory regulation or exceeds the permitted use, you will need to obtain permission directly from the copyright holder.

Chapter 31
Article 37: Prohibition of Torture, Capital Punishment, and Arbitrary Deprivation of Liberty

Christian Whalen

> States Parties shall ensure that:
>
> (a) No child shall be subjected to torture or other cruel, inhuman or degrading treatment or punishment. Neither capital punishment nor life imprisonment without possibility of release shall be imposed for offences committed by persons below 18 years of age;
> (b) No child shall be deprived of his or her liberty unlawfully or arbitrarily. The arrest, detention or imprisonment of a child shall be in conformity with the law and shall be used only as a measure of last resort and for the shortest appropriate period of time;
> (c) Every child deprived of liberty shall be treated with humanity and respect for the inherent dignity of the human person, and in a manner which takes into account the needs of persons of his or her age. In particular, every child deprived of liberty shall be separated from adults unless it is considered in the child's best interest not to do so and shall have the right to maintain contact with his or her family through correspondence and visits, save in exceptional circumstances;
>
> (continued)

C. Whalen (✉)
Office of the Child, Youth and Seniors Advocate, Fredericton, NB, Canada
e-mail: Christian.Whalen@gnb.ca

(d) Every child deprived of his or her liberty shall have the right to prompt access to legal and other appropriate assistance, as well as the right to challenge the legality of the deprivation of his or her liberty before a court or other competent, independent and impartial authority, and to a prompt decision on any such action.

What Did Children Say?
Does anyone go where accused or convicted children stay to 'ask questions and verify the truth?' The person would work in the prison. *(Western Europe/ Other)*
  Government should build places where not only children can be imprisoned but also an institution where they can learn trade and educate them about the negativity of committing crimes at an early age. *(Africa)*
  Train enough guards, police officers, chiefdom officers, more youths, and school authorities and bordering community people to make sure that any child labour, illegal movement of persons, and criminal issues against girls should be reported. *(Africa)*

Overview

Articles 37 and 40 share a common genesis in the several rounds of working sessions leading to the adoption of the Convention. The debate and work on these articles was sustained and intense. It occurred at a time when international norms for juvenile justice were rapidly evolving. States Parties were significantly divided on the wording of the juvenile justice provision, and after several drafts, suggested edits by the UN Office's Centre for Social Development and Humanitarian Affairs gave a new direction (S. Detrick et al., 1992, pp. 458–478). Following much debate, the provision was divided into two separate articles. The first one, which became Article 37, dealt with the prohibition of torture and cruel treatment, capital punishment and deprivation of liberty. The second article, which became Article 40, set out the minimum standards of fairness for criminal trials involving minors.

In both instances, emphasis on the child's human dignity, and the rehabilitation and reintegration of youth, are paramount concerns. The articles were drafted with close attention to emerging global standards in the area and with existing human rights treaty provisions (S. Detrick et al., 1992, pp. 458–478).[1] In its final wording, it is evident that a large part of the text of Article 37 is inspired by Articles 6 (5), 7, 9, and 10 of the International Covenant on Civil and Political Rights (ICCPR).

---

[1] See also Ton Liefaard, *Juvenile Justice and Children's Rights* (Liefaard, 2015, pp. 252–254).

However, without duplicating the wording of the ICCPR, Article 37 extends the ICCPR's provisions to the protection of the children by:

- Imposing the prohibition of life imprisonment for children without the possibility of release
- Demanding that detention of a child shall be used as a measure of last resort and be imposed for the shortest period of time
- Providing to children deprived of their liberty the rights to maintain contacts with their family members (Tobin and Hobbs, 2019, p. 1421).

As underlined by the Committee, Article 37 imposes a child-centred understanding of its provisions and rights (Tobin and Hobbs, 2019, p. 1422). This clarified that the rights recognised by Article 37 extend beyond the ambit of child justice administration to all situations where children may be deprived of liberty, including, for example, child protection settings, health care settings, and immigration settings.

Article 37 can be analysed succinctly in accordance with its four constituent paragraphs:

- The prohibition in paragraph (a) on torture or ill-treatment, specifically ruling out capital punishment and life imprisonment without parole for minors
- The prohibition in paragraph (b) of unlawful and arbitrary deprivations of liberty, insisting that such sanctions are a measure of last resort that must only be imposed for the shortest appropriate period
- Limitations on the deprivation of liberty, including the core commitment in paragraph (c) to upholding the child's inherent dignity and right to be treated with humanity in such circumstances
- The Article establishes, in paragraph (d), the minimal due process guarantees which must accompany any child's deprivation of liberty.

While youth criminal justice practice varies greatly from state to state, Articles 37 and 40 have emerged as a codification of global standards set out in the Beijing Rules and a summary prompt to the adoption of guidelines and minimum rules for the protection of children deprived of liberty and the prevention of youth crime (Vučković-Šahović et al., 2012, p. 298). Article 37 should therefore be applied consistently with the recent General Comment no. 24 (2019) on Children's Rights in the Child Justice System.

General Principles

Article 2 Children deprived of liberty are a vulnerable sector of the youth population, much in need of non-discrimination and equality protections, within the meaning of 'other status' in Article 2. At the same time minority, indigenous, disabled, LBGTQ+ youth, and other vulnerable youth populations are particularly at risk of marginalisation and criminalisation. They are also more likely to be deprived of liberty in non-correctional settings, including health care, immigration detention, and child protection settings (Nowak, 2019, paras. 30–34).

Article 3 There is an inherent contradiction between the best interests principle and the cautioning of child imprisonment in Article 37 (Liefaard, 2015, para. 252). Goldson and Kilkelly maintain that the practical realities of child imprisonment are so pervasively detrimental to human development that even the best efforts at penal reform cannot escape the categorisation that child imprisonment results in the deliberate imposition of 'organized hurt' (Goldson and Kilkelly, 2013, p. 370). State interests will bend understandably towards a minimum threshold of repressive penal sanction, even regarding children in exigent circumstances, but the best interest principles will invariably support Article 37's insistence on recourse to imprisonment as a last resort and for the shortest reasonable time. Best interests analysis will also support Article 37's emphasis on separation of youth and adult prisoners, maintenance of family contact, prohibition of solitary confinement, and of certain measures of restraint; it will support access to education, sanitary conditions, clothing, healthy nutrition, rest, and physical activity during detention.

Article 6 Article 6 is the General Principle most closely linked with Article 37, since the guarantee of the right to life is echoed in Article 37's prohibition on imposition of the death penalty. Survival and maximum development of the child provide a counterpoint to the prohibition of life imprisonment, torture, or cruel or degrading punishment. Moreover, the guarantee of the right to life in human rights instruments is typically combined with the right to liberty and security of the person,[2] foundational rights that lie at the heart of the child's evolving path towards autonomy and their right to survival and development. This stands as a positive formulation of the child's liberty interests, as protected in the prohibition against unlawful and arbitrary detention of children. There are very few situations of possible Article 37 infringements where Article 6 would not also be in play.

Article 12 The child's right to be heard and to have their opinions considered is never so clearly manifest as when a deprivation of liberty may be imposed, and yet child participation rights in detention proceedings are often compromised. Article 12 includes the child's right to complaint mechanisms within institutions and the right to be informed of all institutional rules to which they may be subject and of existing procedures for redress (UNICEF, 2007, p. 566; UN Committee on the Rights of the Child, 2007a, para. 28).

---

[2] See, for example, Article 3 of the UDHR's proclamation 'Everyone has the right to life, liberty and security of the person', a formulation repeated verbatim as section 7 of the Canadian Charter of Rights and Freedoms and inspired by the American Declaration of Independence's assertion of the rights to 'life, liberty and the pursuit of happiness'.

Articles Related or Linked to Article 37

Article 9 provides for the child's right to not be separated from their parents unless it is necessary in the child's best interests, as determined by competent authorities, which may occur where cruel and degrading treatment of children occurs within the family home.

Article 16 addresses the child's right to privacy and the inviolability of their family life and against affronts to honour and reputation. Cases of egregious bullying may infringe both Articles 16 and 37.

Article 19 establishes the child's right to be free from all forms of violence, abuse, neglect, and maltreatment and thus intersects closely with the protections in Article 37.

Article 20 provides for the child's right to alternative care if deprived of his or her family, as may occur if the child was a victim of cruelty at home.

Article 22 notes the rights of refugee children to special protection and access to their rights, and intersects with Article 37 when children are deprived of liberty in immigration detention centres or treated cruelly or in a degrading manner through the immigration process.

Article 24 addresses the child's right to the highest attainable standard of health and to access health care services, and these rights are vitally in play for every child victim of a violation of Article 37 rights.

Article 25 provides the right to periodic review of placement or treatment, notably with a view to guard against cruel or inhuman treatment in such placements.

Article 34 states the child's right to be protected from sexual exploitation, which may occur while in detention and which invariably may raise questions regarding possible violations of Article 37.

Article 35 addresses the child's right to be protected from abduction, sale, or trafficking, any one which may be characterised as cruel, degrading, or inhuman.

Article 38 covers prohibition of forced enrolment in armed conflicts, another express form of cruel and degrading treatment of children.

Article 39 provides for the right to recovery and reintegration for child victims of neglect, exploitation, abuse, torture, cruel treatment, or armed conflict, such that all violations of Article 37 should be scrutinised for applicable Article 39 rights.

Article 40 provides for the right to a separate system of youth criminal justice.

Optional Protocol on the sale of children, child prostitution and child pornography.

Optional Protocol on the involvement of children in armed conflict.

Relevant Instruments

UN Convention Relating to the Status of Refugees (1951)

International Covenant on Civil and Political Rights (1966), Articles 6, 7, 9, and 10

UN Convention against Torture and Other Cruel, Inhuman or Degrading Treatment or Punishment (1984)

UN Standard Minimum Rules for the Administration of Juvenile Justice (Beijing Rules) (1985)

UN Rules for the Protection of Juveniles Deprived of their Liberty (Havana Rules) (1990)

UN Guidelines for the Prevention of Juvenile Delinquency (Riyadh Guidelines) (1990)

Geneva convention for the amelioration of the condition of the wounded and sick in armed forces in the field (1949), and their Protocols I and II

European Convention on Human Rights (1950), Articles 3 and 5

African Charter on Human and Peoples' Rights (1981), Articles 4, 5, and 6

African Charter on the Rights and Welfare of the Child (1990), Articles 16 and 17

Attributes

Attribute One: Prohibition of Capital Punishment, Life Imprisonment, Torture or Degrading Treatment

The first attribute repeats for children the general human right provision on the prohibition of torture or other cruel or inhuman or degrading treatment or punishment, but it immediately expands this right with explicit prohibitions of capital punishment and life imprisonment without parole for offences committed by children. While the Convention contemplates the possibility of life imprisonment for a child, the Committee does not, arguing that life imprisonment, even with the possibility of parole, would defeat the rehabilitative aims of juvenile justice (2007a, para. 77). The Committee recommends that all States Parties abandon recourse to life imprisonment for any offence by minors (2007a, para. 77).

With reference to the prohibition of cruel, inhuman, or degrading treatment or punishment, the Committee has never provided a list of prohibited acts or clarification of the distinction between the different kind of punishments or treatments. Therefore, a case by case assessment is required to determine the nature, purpose and severity of the treatment imposed (Tobin and Hobbs, 2019, p. 1439). The prohibition imposed by Article 37 is absolute and non-derogable. Furthermore, based on the General Comment no. 8, it extends to encompass any use of corporal punishment as a penal or administrative sanction (UN Committee on the Rights of the Child, 2007a, para. 71, 2007b, paras. 2, 16, 18). In addition, the Committee, in its concluding observation to States Parties' reports, has categorised as torture, amputations and mutilations against children (2000, paras. 44, 45), sexual assaults in conflict zones (2006a, paras. 50, 51) and solitary confinement of children (2005, para. 59, 2007a, para. 89).

Attribute Two: Principle of Non-detention of Children, and If Necessary, Only as Last Resort and for the Shortest Appropriate Time

Paragraph 37 (b) sets out the principle of non-detention of children. It repeats the general human rights criterion that there can be no arbitrary or unlawful deprivation of liberty but illustrates it with the new rule that children under 18 can only be deprived of liberty as a measure of last resort and for the shortest appropriate time. In practice, this requires use of alternative sanction measures, such as probation, community service, and suspended sentences (UN Committee on the Rights of the Child, 2006b, para. 62 (d)). In General Comment no. 24, the Committee recommends that pre-trial detention must be limited to the greatest extent possible from the moment of arrest forward and that its duration should also be limited in law and subject to regular review (2019, paras. 8, 82–95).

Attribute Three: Humane Treatment and Respect for Human Dignity at All Times

General Comment no. 24 reinforces the language of Article 37 (c) and sets out human dignity as the foundational human rights value underpinning the protection of liberty in Article 37. This attribute serves to remind all duty-bearers that young persons accused of crimes are children first. The purpose of youth criminal justice is to rehabilitate and reintegrate the youth offender. Owing to their stage of development, youth have not the moral blameworthiness or the mental capacity to be held to account for their behaviour the way adults should be. Separation from adults and contact with family are two indicators that will exemplify this criterion of humanity and human dignity. But the requirements are far-reaching. Detained children are not deprived of their other rights under the Convention, and their educational, social, psychological, and spiritual development must continue, and centres of detention must provide this in an adapted child-friendly setting (Liefaard, 2015, p. 254; UN Committee on the Rights of the Child, 2007a, paras. 88–89; UN General Assembly, 1985, Rule 10.3).

Attribute Four: No Deprivation of Liberty Without Due Process

Most of the fairness requirements upon arrest are set out in Article 40, but Article 37 (d) sets out minimal requirements that are applicable in all deprivations of liberty, whether in the penal law context or in health, immigration, or other administrative contexts. Prompt access to legal and other assistance, including interpretation and counselling services as required, must be provided. The mechanisms for review must be explained and made promptly available as well, normally within 24 h (UNICEF, 2007, p. 565; UN Committee on the Rights of the Child, 2007a, para. 28 (a)).

Prompt and easy access to child sensitive complaints mechanisms must be provided to children, who should be informed of the response without delay (UN Committee on the Rights of the Child, 2007a, para. 28 (c)). Training in child rights principles should be provided to all court officials, policing and correctional officials, and other institutional staff involved with children under detention (UNICEF, 2007, pp. 566–567).

References

Detrick, S., Doek, J. E., & Cantwell, N. (1992). *The United Nations convention on the rights of the child: A guide to the "Travaux Préparatoires."* Martinus Nijhoff Publishers.

Goldson, B., & Kilkelly, U. (2013). International human rights standards and child imprisonment: Potentialities and limitations. *The International Journal of Children's Rights, 21*(2), 345–371. https://doi.org/10.1163/15718182-55680011

Liefaard, T. (2015). Juvenile justice and children's rights. In *Routledge international handbook of children's rights studies* (pp. 234–256). Routledge.

Nowak, M. (2019). *Global study on children deprived of liberty, A/74/136*. UN. Accessed November 22, 2020, from http://digitallibrary.un.org/record/3813850

Tobin, J., & Hobbs, H. (2019). Article 37: Protection against torture, capital punishment, and arbitrary deprivation of liberty. In J. Tobin (Ed.), *The UN convention on the rights of the child: A commentary* (pp. 1420–1502). Oxford University Press.

UN Committee on the Rights of the Child. (2000). *Concluding observations: Sierra Leone, February 24, 2000, CRC/C/15/Add.116*. UN. Accessed November 22, 2020, from http://digitallibrary.un.org/record/414185

UN Committee on the Rights of the Child. (2005). *Concluding observations: Denmark, November 23, 2005, CRC/C/DNK/CO/3*. UN. Accessed November 22, 2020, from http://digitallibrary.un.org/record/569980

UN Committee on the Rights of the Child. (2006a). *Concluding observations: Colombia, June 8, 2006, CRC/C/COL/CO/3*. UN. Accessed November 15, 2020, from http://digitallibrary.un.org/record/582283

UN Committee on the Rights of the Child. (2006b). *Concluding observations: Latvia, June 28, 2006, CRC/C/LVA/CO/2*. UN. Accessed November 22, 2020, from http://digitallibrary.un.org/record/580091

UN Committee on the Rights of the Child. (2007a). *General comment no. 10 (2007) Children's rights in juvenile justice, April 25, 2007, CRC/C/GC/10*. Accessed October 12, 2020, from https://digitallibrary.un.org/record/599395?ln=en

UN Committee on the Rights of the Child. (2007b). *General comment no. 8 (2006) The right of the child to protection from corporal punishment and other cruel or degrading forms of punishment (arts. 19; 28, para. 2; and 37, inter alia), March 2, 2007, CRC/C/GC/8.* Accessed October 12, 2020, from https://digitallibrary.un.org/record/583961?ln=en

UN Committee on the Rights of the Child. (2019). *General comment no. 24 (2019) on children's rights in the child justice system, CRC/C/GC/24.* Accessed November 29, 2020, from https://tbinternet.ohchr.org/_layouts/15/treatybodyexternal/Download.aspx?symbolno=CRC%2fC%2fGC%2f24&Lang=en

UN General Assembly. (1985). United Nations standard minimum rules for the administration of Juvenile Justice ("The Beijing Rules"), 1985, A/RES/40/33. Accessed November 6, 2020, from http://digitallibrary.un.org/record/120958

UNICEF. (2007). *Implementation handbook for the convention on the rights of the child* (3rd ed.). UNICEF. Accessed September 21, 2020, from https://digitallibrary.un.org/record/620060?ln=en

Vučković-Šahović, N., Doek, J. E., & Zermatten, J. (2012). *The rights of the child in international law: Rights of the child in a nutshell and in context: All about children's rights.* Stämpfli.

Open Access This chapter is licensed under the terms of the Creative Commons Attribution 4.0 International License (http://creativecommons.org/licenses/by/4.0/), which permits use, sharing, adaptation, distribution and reproduction in any medium or format, as long as you give appropriate credit to the original author(s) and the source, provide a link to the Creative Commons license and indicate if changes were made.

The images or other third party material in this chapter are included in the chapter's Creative Commons license, unless indicated otherwise in a credit line to the material. If material is not included in the chapter's Creative Commons license and your intended use is not permitted by statutory regulation or exceeds the permitted use, you will need to obtain permission directly from the copyright holder.

Chapter 32
Article 39: The Right to Physical and Psychological Recovery of Child Victims

Ziba Vaghri, Katherine Covell, and Gerison Lansdown

> States parties shall take all appropriate measures to promote physical and psychological recovery and social reintegration of a child victim of: any form of neglect, exploitation, or abuse; torture or any other form of cruel, inhuman or degrading treatment or punishment; or armed conflicts. Such recovery and reintegration shall take place in an environment which fosters the health, self-respect and dignity of the child.

What Did Children Say?
'All youth protection services should be free.' *(Western Europe/Other)*
    'Through UNICEF, an NGO, other people, there to make sure children's rights are respected.' *(Western Europe/Other)*
    'Are the abused children in a safe space?' *(Western Europe/Other)*

(continued)

Z. Vaghri (✉)
University of New Brunswick, Saint John, Canada
e-mail: ziba.vaghri@unb.ca

K. Covell
Cape Breton University, Richmon, BC, Canada
e-mail: Katherine_Covell@cbu.ca

G. Lansdown
Carleton University, Ottawa, Canada

> There should be a forum or office which is readily available to channel their issue when they need funding and who are very serious in handling the affairs of child victims. *(Africa)*
>
> Victims of such nature needs constant frequent counselling for them to return to normalcy. *(Africa)*

Overview

Article 39 was drafted to ensure that all children who have experienced any of the harmful treatments noted, as well as armed conflict, have the right to reintegration and recovery, regardless of whether the State Party is in any way responsible for that harm (Tobin and Marshall, 2019, p. 1562). The Committee has interpreted the scope of Article 39 broadly, to include harm as a result of human rights violations, child labour or forced labour, being a refugee, institutionalisation, being a victim of crime, or involved in judicial proceedings.[1]

It is important to understand Article 39 in the context of the Convention's wider protective provisions. It serves to provide remedial interventions when any of those protective rights have been neglected or violated (Tobin and Marshall, 2019, p. 1562). However, neither the drafting history, nor the subsequent work of the Committee, provide any detailed guidance as to the definition of recovery or reintegration. The wording of Article 39 requires promotion rather than attainment of recovery, thus placing a lower burden on States Parties, and arguably a more reasonable one. Nevertheless, States Parties must take all appropriate measures within the scope of their available resources to promote the recovery of a child who has faced any of the listed harms. It therefore requires a broad range of services—medical, legal, educational, vocational, and psychological. Services must be provided in accordance with the Convention in its entirety and must therefore be gender and culturally sensitive, scientifically and medically supported, private and confidential, and non-discriminatory (UN Committee on the Rights of the Child, 2003, para. 37 (c)).

Article 39 was reinforced by the Optional Protocol to the Convention on the Rights of the Child on the sale of children, child prostitution and child pornography and the Optional Protocol to the Convention on the Rights of the Child on the involvement of children in armed conflict. Commitment to these protocols requires States Parties to have a clear focus on rehabilitation, giving children appropriate assistance, by provision of high-quality programmes of recovery and reintegration, which are available and accessible on a non-discriminatory basis.

---

[1] See, for example, concluding observations for Congo (2014a, para. 43 (b)), Russian Federation (2014b, para. 66), Cameroon (2010a, para. 68 (d)), Ecuador (2010b, para. 80), and Afghanistan (2011a, paras. 36–36).

General Principles

Article 2 Respecting Article 2 obliges States Parties to ensure that all children are offered recovery and rehabilitation services, regardless of age, gender identity, sexual orientation, ethnic or national origin, disability, religion, health, or economic status.[2] Services must be extended to children who are not nationals of a state, including asylum-seeking, refugee, and migrant children (UN Committee on the Rights of the Child, 2005, para. 12). Recovery programmes of equal quality must be provided for all children who need them, with no discrimination based on parental or child circumstances or characteristics, document status, or location. Some groups of children are more vulnerable to the likelihood of experiencing harms, for example, girls or very young children. The Committee has emphasised the importance of States Parties' ensuring that all such vulnerable children are provided with the appropriate recovery and reintegration services that reflect the nature of harms experienced.

Article 3 When determining the needs of a child who has experienced abuse or harm, and the most appropriate means to address it, the best interests of the child must be a primary consideration. In so doing, a broad range of considerations must be addressed, including the child's views, identity, preservation of family, the necessity for care, protection and safety, and degree of vulnerability (UN Committee on the Rights of the Child, 2013, paras. 53–76).

Article 6 Efforts to promote recovery and reintegration must focus on the child's survival, and on the child's optimal physical, psychological, and social development. To this end, interventions must occur in an environment that fosters the child's health, dignity, and self-respect.

Article 12 States Parties must ensure that children fully understand any options available to them, in terms of their recovery programme, and have their views taken into account and given due weight in decision-making, in accord with their age and maturity.

---

[2] See, for example, the Committee concerns expressed to the Central African Republic regarding the persistent discrimination against girls, and other groups of children including albinos, orphans, children with disabilities, and children accused of witchcraft (2017a, para. 24), and to Qatar where they note there continues to be pervasive discrimination against girls due to the persistence of traditional attitudes (2017b, para. 13). See also Joint General Comment No. 3 (UN Committee on the Protection of the Rights of All Migrant Workers and Members of Their Families and UN Committee on the Rights of the Child, 2017) and the Legislative History (Office of the United Nations High Commissioner for Human Rights and Rädda barnen (Society: Sweden), 2007, pp. 314–334).

Articles Related or Linked to Article 39

Article 19 reinforces the provisions of Article 4 and specifies the establishment of programmes of support for child maltreatment victims and for those who care for the child, in addition to programmes of prevention.

Article 20 requires that children who are temporarily or permanently deprived of their family environment are provided with special care and assistance as needed to promote recovery and reintegration.

Article 24 provides for the right to the highest attainable standard of health and to access health care services. This provision is key to recovery and reintegration.

Article 25 provides children who have been placed for care, protection, or treatment—including for purposes of rehabilitation—with a right to a periodic review.

Article 27 describes the right of all children to an adequate standard of living, and the responsibilities of their caregivers to secure, within their abilities, living conditions that promote healthy development.

Article 28 provides for the availability and accessibility of education, a crucial component of recovery and fostering health, dignity, and self-respect.

Article 31 describes children's rights to play, recreation, rest, and leisure. The realisation of these rights can be an effective intervention that helps children make sense of their past and facilitates healing.

Articles 32–38 describe the child's right to protection from economic exploitation, illicit and psychotropic drugs, sexual exploitation and abuse, abduction or trafficking, torture, degrading or cruel punishment, and armed conflict. The enjoyment of these rights is fundamental to effective reintegration and recovery, and to the child's capacity to develop to potential.

Article 40 requires that all children who come within the scope of the juvenile justice system must be treated in a manner consistent with 'promoting the child's reintegration and the child's assuming a constructive role in society.'

The Optional Protocol to the Convention on the Rights of the Child on the sale of children, child prostitution and child pornography. In Article 8, this protocol requires States Parties to take appropriate measures to protect the rights and interests of child victims of the practices prohibited under the Protocol, including for their rehabilitation.

The Optional Protocol to the Convention on the Rights of the Child on the involvement of children in armed conflict. Ratifying states are required to give children appropriate assistance, where necessary, for their recovery and social integration.

Relevant Instruments

UN Protocol to Prevent, Suppress and Punish Trafficking in Persons Especially Women and Children, supplementing the United Nations Convention against Transnational Organized Crime (2000)

International Convention on the Protection of the Rights of All Migrant Workers and Members of Their Families (1990), which affirms the importance of respecting the rights of children of migrant workers, including those described in Article 39.

Attributes

Attribute One: Quality and Comprehensiveness of the Programmes of Recovery and Reintegration

For programmes to be of appropriate quality, they require four components. First, services must be scientifically and medically evidence-based, with mechanisms in place for regular review procedures (UN Committee on the Rights of the Child, 2003, para. 41 (d)). Second, programmes or services must be based on a child's holistic developmental needs. Specific vulnerabilities and needs should be assessed in relation to the Convention and other relevant human rights standards.[3] Third, children must be afforded opportunities for participation in all aspects of recovery and reintegration programmes, and be provided with information about options available, possible decisions, and their consequences.[4] Conditions that support and encourage children to express their views are essential (UN Committee on the Rights of the Child, 2009, para. 49). Finally, service and programme providers should be well-qualified professionals with knowledge of children's rights.[5]

Recovery and reintegration programmes should be comprehensive and go beyond treatment for survival to include the child's holistic and optimal development (United Nations High Commissioner for Refugees, 1993). In particular, it is essential that any measures provided take into account the specific age and circumstances of the individual child, as well as the nature of any harm experienced including, for example, medical treatment, physical rehabilitation, family therapy or counselling for trauma (Tobin and Marshall, 2019, pp. 1574–1575). In addition, early responses and treatments are important to mitigate the effects of the violence or neglect experienced (Pinheiro, 2006a), as well as ongoing services and support, such as

---

[3] For example, the *Convention Relating to the Status of Refugees* would also be considered in assessing the needs of a refugee child (UN Committee on the Rights of the Child, 2013).

[4] See, for example, concluding observations Qatar, (2017b, para. 23 (a)), 2012 Day of General Discussion (2012, paras. 23, 24), General Comment no. 13 (2011b, para. 56).

[5] See, for example, concluding observations for Cameroon (2017c, para. 25 (b)) and Vanuatu (2017d, para. 27 (f)), and General Comment no. 12 (2009, para. 49).

ensuring access to education, to provide a sense of normalcy, structure, and stability that can serve to promote healthy development (UN Committee on the Rights of the Child, 2008, para. 29). Longer-term follow-up services should be provided as necessary in order to promote continued physical and psychological recovery, and to provide protection against potential further maltreatment for all child victims of violence.[6]

Attribute Two: Availability, Accessibility, and Acceptability of the Programmes of Recovery and Reintegration

States Parties should take all reasonable measures ensure that programmes of recovery and reintegration are available to all child victims of violence, abuse, and exploitation who require them (Nowak, 2005, pp. 36–37) with sufficient resources allocated to ensure that measures taken are adequately funded and sustainable.[7] Helplines, for example, must be widely available and accessible to maintain effectiveness.[8]

Programmes and services for child victims must also be accessible to them.[9] Accessibility comprises a number of dimensions (Tobin and Marshall, 2019, p. 1579):

- All relevant services must be affordable to all children requiring help
- Services must be accessible to children in the remotest regions, as well as to children with disabilities
- Children, and where relevant, their families, must be aware of the nature of restorative services and how to access them.

Accordingly, States Parties should undertake information campaigns identifying what constitute abusive and exploitative behaviours, together with provision of

---

[6] See, for example, concluding observations for Republic of Moldovia (2017e, para. 21 (e), 23 (d)), Lebanon (2017f, para. 20 (e)), and Estonia (2017g, para. 29 (b)) and General Comment no. 13 (2011b).

[7] For example, the Committee asked Guinea to allocate the necessary resources to implement a comprehensive policy of recovery and reintegration (2017h, para. 30 (a)). See also, concluding observations for Moldovia (2017e, para. 221 (b)), Central African Republic (2017a, para. 12 (a)), General Comment no. 13 (2011b) and General comment No. 19 (2016).

[8] The Committee has noted the lack of resourcing or widespread availability of child Helplines. See, for example, concluding observations for Bhutan (2017i, para. 27), Lebanon (2017f, para. 20 (e)), and Vanuatu (2017d, para. 29 (a)).

[9] For example, the Committee has recommended to Bhutan, Ecuador, and Tajikistan that they ensure children have access to adequate services for recovery and reintegration (2017i, para. 24 (e), 2017j, para. 25 (f), 2017k, para. 21 (d)). See also the Report of the Independent Expert for the United Nations study on violence against children (Pinheiro, 2006a) and the related World Report on Violence against Children (Pinheiro, 2006b).

information on how to report and to access help and information.[10] All such information must be provided to children in child-friendly, age-appropriate language, and be distributed to parents and caregivers (UN Committee on the Rights of the Child, 2017c, para. 25 (c)). Information campaigns to promote accessibility are important in conflict and disaster-affected regions, where children are especially vulnerable to physical, emotional, and sexual abuse, exploitation, trafficking, and the worst forms of child labour (UN Committee on the Rights of the Child, 2003).[11]

Finally, services provided under Article 39 must be accessible to every child without discrimination on any of the prohibited grounds in Article 2. Children who have experienced trafficking, sexual exploitation and abuse should always be assumed to be victims and not offenders.[12] In addition, as specifically referenced in Article 39, and reinforced by the Committee, children involved in any aspect of armed conflict must be considered as victims, and entitled to priority participation in rehabilitation programmes (2005, paras. 56–57). To achieve this end, the adoption of measures to combat racism and xenophobia, and to prevent, reduce, and eliminate attitudes causing or perpetuating discrimination is recommended.[13] Discriminatory attitudes include misperceptions and negative perceptions of children involved in armed combat,[14] juvenile justice, or the sex trade, and stigmatisation of unaccompanied or separated migrant or refugee children (UN Committee on the Protection of the Rights of All, Migrant Workers and Members of Their Families and UN Committee on the Rights of the Child, 2017; UN Committee on the Rights of the Child, 2005). It is recommended that States Parties adopt legislative and policy measures to ensure that non-discrimination is an explicit principle in all laws and policies affecting children (UN Committee on the Rights of the Child, 2012).

Programmes must also be acceptable to the child, and States Parties must take all reasonable measures to ensure that they are sensitive to the different needs of different ages or groups of children, according to the harm they have experienced. Particular attention should be made to the specific cultural characteristics of the child's community that may be of relevance in helping them recover, for example,

---

[10] See, for example, concluding observations for Antigua and Barbuda (2017l, para. 34), Cameroon (2017c, para. 29), Estonia (2017g, para. 29 (a)), and Vanuatu (2017d, para. 27 (b)).

[11] See also Concluding Observations: Central African Republic (2017a, para. 40 (b), 41 (f)).

[12] For example, as described in the 2012 Day of Discussion (UN Committee on the Rights of the Child, 2012), the criminalization of migration poses a serious challenge to the enjoyment of rights, and punitive approaches to child victims of violence are highly destructive as noted in General Comment no. 13. See also concluding observations for Afghanistan, (2011a, para. 39), in which the Committee points out that child victims of abuse and violence are treated as criminals whereas their abusers enjoy impunity, and Qatar (2017b, para. 23 (d)).

[13] See, for example, concluding observations to Estonia (2017g, para. 29 (a)) and Vanuatu (2017d, para. 27 (d)), General Comment no.6 (2005), and the Joint Comment on Migration (UN Committee on the Protection of the Rights of All Migrant Workers and Members of Their Families and UN Committee on the Rights of the Child, 2017).

[14] See, for example, Concluding Observations on the Optional Protocol: Guinea (2017h, para. 28 (a)).

community-based approaches or traditional healing rituals (Machel, 1996, paras. 174–175).

References

Machel, G. (1996). *Impact of armed conflict on children: Note by the Secretary-General, A/51/306*. UN. Accessed November 21, 2020, from http://digitallibrary.un.org/record/223213

Nowak, M. (2005). *A commentary on the United Nations convention on the rights of the child, Article 6: The right to life, survival and development*. Brill Nijhoff. Accessed September 22, 2020, from https://brill.com/view/title/11606

Pinheiro, P. S. de M. S. (2006a). *Report of the independent expert for the United Nations study on violence against children, A/61/299*. UN. Accessed November 12, 2020, from http://digitallibrary.un.org/record/584299

Pinheiro, P. S. de M. S. (2006b). *World report on violence against children*. UN. Accessed November 22, 2020, from http://digitallibrary.un.org/record/587334

Tobin, J., & Marshall, C. (2019). Article 39: The right to reintegration and recovery. In J. Tobin (Ed.), *The UN convention on the rights of the child: A commentary* (pp. 1561–1595). Oxford University Press.

UN Committee on the Protection of the Rights of All Migrant Workers and Members of Their Families & UN Committee on the Rights of the Child. (2017). *Joint General Comment No. 3 (2017) of the Committee on the Protection of the Rights of All Migrant Workers and Members of Their Families and No. 22 (2017) of the Committee on the Rights of the Child on the general principles regarding the human rights of children in the context of international migration, CMW/C/GC/3, CRC/C/GC/22*. UN. Accessed November 6, 2020, from http://digitallibrary.un.org/record/1323014

UN Committee on the Rights of the Child. (2003). *General comment no. 4 (2003) Adolescent health and development in the context of the Convention on the rights of the child, July 1, 2003, CRC/GC/2003/4*. Accessed October 12, 2020, from https://digitallibrary.un.org/record/503074?ln=en

UN Committee on the Rights of the Child. (2005). *General comment No. 6 (2005) Treatment of unaccompanied and separated children outside their country of origin, September 1, 2005, CRC/GC/2005/6*. Accessed October 12, 2020, from https://digitallibrary.un.org/record/566055?ln=en

UN Committee on the Rights of the Child. (2008). *Day of general discussion: The right of the child to education in emergency situations*. UN. Accessed December 20, 2020, from https://www.ohchr.org/EN/HRBodies/CRC/Pages/DiscussionDays.aspx

UN Committee on the Rights of the Child. (2009). *General comment no. 12 (2009) The right of the child to be heard, July 20, 2009, CRC/C/GC/12*. Accessed October 12, 2020, from https://digitallibrary.un.org/record/671444?ln=en

UN Committee on the Rights of the Child. (2010a). *Concluding observations: Cameroon, February 18, 2010, CRC/C/CMR/CO/2*. UN. Accessed November 22, 2020, from http://digitallibrary.un.org/record/678065

UN Committee on the Rights of the Child. (2010b). *Concluding observations: Ecuador, March 2, 2010, CRC/C/ECU/CO/4*. UN. Accessed November 22, 2020, from http://digitallibrary.un.org/record/678501

UN Committee on the Rights of the Child. (2011a). *Concluding observations: Afghanistan, April 8, 2011, CRC/C/AFG/CO/1*. UN. Accessed November 22, 2020, from http://digitallibrary.un.org/record/702362

UN Committee on the Rights of the Child. (2011b). *General comment No. 13 (2011) The right of the child to freedom from all forms of violence, April 18, 2011, CRC/C/GC/13*. Accessed October 12, 2020, from https://digitallibrary.un.org/record/711722?ln=en

UN Committee on the Rights of the Child. (2012). *Day of general discussion: The rights of all children in the context of international migration*. UN. Accessed December 19, 2020, from https://www.ohchr.org/EN/HRBodies/CRC/Pages/Discussion2012.aspx

UN Committee on the Rights of the Child. (2013). *General comment No. 14 (2013) On the right of the child to have his or her best interests taken as a primary consideration (art. 3, para. 1), May 29, 2013, CRC/C/GC/14*. Accessed October 12, 2020, from https://digitallibrary.un.org/record/778523?ln=en

UN Committee on the Rights of the Child. (2014a). *Concluding observations: Congo, February 25, 2014, CRC/C/COG/CO/2-4*. UN. Accessed November 18, 2020, from http://digitallibrary.un.org/record/778842

UN Committee on the Rights of the Child. (2014b). *Concluding observations: Russian Federation, February 25, 2014, CRC/C/RUS/CO/4-5*. UN. Accessed November 22, 2020, from http://digitallibrary.un.org/record/778843

UN Committee on the Rights of the Child. (2016). *General comment No. 19 (2016) on public budgeting for the realization of children's rights (art.4), CRC/C/GC/19*. UN. Accessed November 12, 2020, from http://digitallibrary.un.org/record/838730

UN Committee on the Rights of the Child. (2017a). *Concluding observations: Central African Republic, March 8, 2017, CRC/C/CAF/CO/2*. UN. Accessed November 14, 2020, from http://digitallibrary.un.org/record/1311376

UN Committee on the Rights of the Child. (2017b). *Concluding observations: Qatar, June 22, 2017, CRC/C/QAT/CO/3-4*. UN. Accessed November 22, 2020, from http://digitallibrary.un.org/record/1311379

UN Committee on the Rights of the Child. (2017c). *Concluding observations: Cameroon, July 6, 2017, CRC/C/CMR/CO/3-5*. UN. Accessed November 22, 2020, from http://digitallibrary.un.org/record/1311383

UN Committee on the Rights of the Child. (2017d). *Concluding observations: Vanuatu, October 25, 2017, CRC/C/VUT/CO/2-4*. UN. Accessed November 22, 2020, from http://digitallibrary.un.org/record/1311399

UN Committee on the Rights of the Child. (2017e). *Concluding observations: Moldova, October 20, 2017, CRC/C/MDA/CO/4-5*. UN. http://digitallibrary.un.org/record/1311387. Accessed November 6, 2020

UN Committee on the Rights of the Child. (2017f). *Concluding observations: Lebanon, June 22, 2017, CRC/C/LBN/CO/4-5*. UN. Accessed November 6, 2020, from http://digitallibrary.un.org/record/1311380

UN Committee on the Rights of the Child. (2017g). *Concluding observations: Estonia, March 8, 2017, CRC/C/EST/CO/2-4*. UN. Accessed November 22, 2020, from http://digitallibrary.un.org/record/1311375

UN Committee on the Rights of the Child. (2017h). *Concluding observations: Guinea, under article 8 (1) of the Optional Protocol to the Convention on the Rights of the Child on the Involvement of Children in Armed Conflict, October 25, 2017, CRC/C/OPAC/GIN/CO/1*. UN. Accessed November 22, 2020, from http://digitallibrary.un.org/record/1311405

UN Committee on the Rights of the Child. (2017i). *Concluding observations: Bhutan, July 5, 2017, CRC/C/BTN/CO/3-5*. UN. Accessed November 22, 2020, from http://digitallibrary.un.org/record/1311382

UN Committee on the Rights of the Child. (2017j). *Concluding observations: Ecuador, October 26, 2017, CRC/C/ECU/CO/5-6*. UN. Accessed November 14, 2020, from http://digitallibrary.un.org/record/1311757

UN Committee on the Rights of the Child. (2017k). *Concluding observations: Tajikistan, October 25, 2017, CRC/C/TJK/CO/3-5*. UN. Accessed November 7, 2020, from http://digitallibrary.un.org/record/1311398

UN Committee on the Rights of the Child. (2017l). *Concluding observations: Antigua and Barbuda, June 30, 2017, CRC/C/ATG/CO/2-4*. UN. Accessed November 18, 2020, from http://digitallibrary.un.org/record/1311381

United Nations High Commissioner for Refugees. (1993). *UNHCR policy on refugee children*. Accessed November 22, 2020, from https://www.unhcr.org/excom/scip/3ae68ccc4/unhcr-policy-refugee-children.html

United Nations Office of the High Commissioner for Human Rights & Rädda Barnen (Society: Sweden). (2007). *Legislative history of the convention on the rights of the child*. United Nations. https://digitallibrary.un.org/record/602462?ln=en

Open Access This chapter is licensed under the terms of the Creative Commons Attribution 4.0 International License (http://creativecommons.org/licenses/by/4.0/), which permits use, sharing, adaptation, distribution and reproduction in any medium or format, as long as you give appropriate credit to the original author(s) and the source, provide a link to the Creative Commons license and indicate if changes were made.

The images or other third party material in this chapter are included in the chapter's Creative Commons license, unless indicated otherwise in a credit line to the material. If material is not included in the chapter's Creative Commons license and your intended use is not permitted by statutory regulation or exceeds the permitted use, you will need to obtain permission directly from the copyright holder.

Part VII
Protection Measures from Exploitation

Articles 32, 34, 36

Introduction

During the drafting of the Convention on the Rights of the Child (the Convention), there was a strong call for inclusion of the right of the child to protection from abuse and exploitation. Although the concepts of abuse and exploitation are sometimes used interchangeably, it is easiest to differentiate them by defining abuse as actions which cause a child harm, whereas exploitation can broadly be defined as any harmful action that involves an exchange, often commercial, for the benefit of a person other than the child, and which takes advantage of the child.[1] The initial proposal from the Polish delegation included a generic article protecting children from all forms of exploitation, trafficking or harmful employment (Office of the United Nations High Commissioner for Human Rights and Rädda barnen (Society: Sweden) 2007, p. 693). However subsequent debate resulted in recognition of the need for the issues of abuse and exploitation to be addressed in separate articles in light of the range and complexity of the issues. Three of those articles are explored in this part.

Article 32 addresses the child's right to protection from economic exploitation and work that causes them harm. It does not prohibit children from all forms of work but seeks to reconcile the right to education with participation in the labour market and to ensure that the child does not engage in any form of work detrimental to their health and physical, mental, spiritual, or moral development. The Convention does not sit alone in seeking to address the scale and severity of the problem of exploitative child labour. It needs to be understood in the context of a broad range of international instruments including:

---

[1] For a further discussion of the relationship between abuse and exploitation, see Soew and Tobin, 'Protection from Sexual Exploitation and Sexual Abuse,' in The Convention on the Rights of the Child (2019, pp. 1314–1319).

- numerous International Labour Organization (ILO) Conventions
- findings from the Committee on Economic, Social and Cultural Rights
- the two Optional Protocols to the Convention
- the World Fit for Children
- the Sustainable Development Goals
- multiple reports by Special Rapporteurs on Sale of Children, and of Contemporary Forms of Slavery.

It is important to note that the Committee on the Rights of the Child (the Committee) has adopted a broad interpretation of States Parties obligations in respect of Article 32, insisting that enforcement of protective age limits alone is an insufficient approach. Measures are also needed to remove the drivers of exploitative child labour, including poverty, poor education, discrimination and social exclusion, and lack of knowledge and awareness.

Article 34 emphasises the child's right to protection from sexual abuse and exploitation, an issue that was largely hidden from view, denied, or ignored prior to the Convention. The specific practices from which children must be protected include coercion into unwanted sexual activity, prostitution, use in pornographic activities, and child sex tourism. It is now widely recognised that huge numbers of children are subjected to sexual abuse and exploitation, and that the opportunities for such practices have grown exponentially in recent years. Migration, conflict, and advances in online technology, for example, have exposed more and more children to additional and new forms of exploitation, while rendering it harder to provide appropriate protection. In this context, the provisions in Article 34 that explicitly demand that States Parties undertake bilateral and multilateral measures to protect children from sexual abuse and exploitation take on a higher significance. Like Article 32, this right is reinforced by other instruments including the Optional Protocols to the Convention and the outcome documents of the World Congresses against Commercial Sexual Exploitation.

Article 36 was included in the Convention as an umbrella provision to protect children from any form of exploitation that might be prejudicial to the child's welfare and that is not explicitly addressed in other articles. It serves to ensure that any new or emerging forms of exploitation can be adequately addressed and places an obligation on States Parties to take proactive measures to respond to all forms of exploitation.

In respect of all three articles, the Committee has stressed consistently that protection from exploitation is strengthened through effective participation of children. It is essential to acknowledge children as agents who must be actively engaged in any discussion about, for example, their involvement in work, their perspectives on exploitation and what is needed to keep them safe, and their views must be given due weight in accordance with Article 12.

References

Office of the United Nations High Commissioner for Human Rights & Rädda barnen (Society: Sweden). (2007). *Legislative history of the Convention on the Rights of the Child*. New York: United Nations. https://digitallibrary.un.org/record/602462?ln=en

Tobin, J., & Seow, F. (2019). Article 34: Protection from Sexual Exploitation and Sexual Abuse. In J. Tobin (Ed.), *The UN Convention on the Rights of the Child: A Commentary* (pp. 1310–1355). Oxford, New York: Oxford University Press.

Chapter 33
Article 32: The Right to Protection from Economic Exploitation and Hazardous Activities

Gerison Lansdown

1. States Parties recognize the right of the child to be protected from economic exploitation and from performing any work that is likely to be hazardous or to interfere with the child's education, or to be harmful to the child's health or physical, mental, spiritual, moral or social development.
2. States Parties shall take legislative, administrative, social and educational measures to ensure the implementation of the present article. To this end, and having regard to the relevant provisions of other international instruments, States Parties shall in particular:
   (a) Provide for a minimum age or minimum ages for admission to employment;
   (b) Provide for appropriate regulation of the hours and conditions of employment;
   (c) Provide for appropriate penalties or other sanctions to ensure the effective enforcement of the present article.

> **What Did Children Say?**
> 'Governments should advertise more about children rights as well as make regular check-ups on homes and workplaces to ensure children are not doing child labour or unfairly paid.' *(Latin America/Caribbean).*

(continued)

G. Lansdown (✉)
Carleton University, Ottawa, ON, Canada

> 'Schools holding public education initiatives by talking to parents about harmful work.' *(Latin America/Caribbean).*
> We have to make sure that they are reliable statistics on working children. *(Africa).*
> 'Having an enforced documented minimum age where children can start working.' *(Latin America/Caribbean).*

Overview

Article 32 establishes the right of children to protection from economic exploitation, and from work deemed to be harmful to their health or detrimental to any dimension of their development, or which interferes with their education. It also identifies, in broad terms, the measures required by States Parties to achieve this protection. The development of the text during the drafting process moved from a focus on protection of the child towards an understanding of the right to protection in this context (Swepston, 2012, pp. 14–15).

However, after much debate, and influence from the ILO, the drafters agreed to rely on a general formulation of the standards necessary to provide appropriate protection. For example, prescribed minimum ages for work were removed in favour of a general requirement that States Parties introduce legislative age limits (Office of the United Nations High Commissioner for Human Rights and Rädda barnen (Society: Sweden), 2007, pp. 693–708). This approach was adopted in acknowledgement of the different levels of development between States Parties, as well as the importance of differentiating between the protections needed for different types of work. It was left to the Committee to provide subsequent interpretation, drawing on the more detailed provisions in ILO Conventions, 138 and 182 in particular, on the definitions of work, the nature of the regulatory environment needed, recommended age limits, and the nature of hazardous or harmful work.

The drafting process involved a gradual consensus that the purpose of Article 32 was to incorporate the issue within the Convention in the context of existing international law, notably standards established by the ILO, rather than seeking to adopt new protections (Swepston, 2012, p. 17). This approach is clearly envisioned in the reference in paragraph 2 to the need to have 'regard to the relevant provisions of other national instruments'.

General Principles

Article 2 Some groups of children are particularly vulnerable to economic exploitation. The Committee has repeatedly highlighted concerns, for example, over the abuse of girls in domestic labour (2016a, paras. 84–86),[1] the exploitation of children with disabilities in begging and drug trafficking (2007a, para. 75), and the criminalisation of children in street situations leading to commercial sexual exploitation (2017b, para. 59). It urges States Parties to take appropriate actions to address these discriminatory vulnerabilities. Furthermore, children who do work should not suffer wage discrimination, for example, being forced to accept low wages that do not reflect their skills (UN Committee on Economic, Social and Cultural Rights, 2016, para. 47 (b)).

Article 3 While harmful or hazardous work is clearly not in the best interests of the child, the Committee has recognised that work can play a positive role, particularly in the lives of older children. It highlights the importance of a transitional approach towards balancing the role of work in the lives of adolescents while ensuring their other rights.

Article 6 Article 32 focuses on the right of the child to protection from any work that is harmful to their health or physical, mental, spiritual, moral, or social development, a broader requirement than that included in the ILO Conventions, which only address morals and health. States Parties are required to introduce all necessary measures to ensure that protection. However, the Committee recognises the positive developmental role of appropriate work, highlighting its potential for equipping them to learn skills, take responsibility, contribute to their families' well-being, and support their access to education (2003, paras. 18, 39 (e), 2016a, para. 85).

Article 12 The Committee emphasises that States Parties must ensure children are involved in the development of all relevant legislation and policies that affect their lives, a prescription that includes measures relating to child labour (2016a, para. 23). It specifically affirms that children, and where they exist, representatives of working children's organisations, should be heard when labour laws are drafted or when enforcement of laws is considered and evaluated (2009a, para. 117).

Although Article 15, the right to freedom of association and assembly, does not reference the right to join a trades union, the restrictions outlined in its paragraph 2 do not justify any prohibition on children from either forming their own or joining existing unions (UN Committee on the Rights of the Child, 2001, para. 38; Office of the United Nations High Commissioner for Human Rights and Rädda barnen (Society: Sweden), 2007, p. 469). Article 41, which stipulates that the standards of other international instruments should not be lowered by any provision in the Convention on the Rights of the Child, lends further weight to the argument that Article 15 should be interpreted to include the right of working children to trade union rights, to the same standard as that provided by the International Covenant on Civil and Political Rights (Daly, 2016, p. 35).

---

[1] See also, for example, concluding observations for Senegal (2006a, paras. 60–63), and Qatar (2017a, para. 35).

Articles Related or Linked to Article 32

Article 11 deals with illicit transfer of children and includes the right to protection from trafficking.

Article 15 establishes the right of children to freedom of association, which includes the right to join and form trade unions or associations.

Article 19 asserts the right to protection from all forms of violence including within environments where children are working.

Article 24 addresses the right to the best possible health, and accordingly, children must not be exposed to work that is detrimental to their health and well-being.

Article 27 asserts that children have the right to a standard of living that is good enough to meet their physical and social needs and support their development.

Article 28 recognises the right to education, and children must not be involved in child labour that deprives them of that right.

Article 31 recognises rights to rest, play, leisure, and recreation and the arts, and these must not be compromised by the demands of children's involvement in work.

Article 33 recognises that children must not be used in the illicit production or trafficking of narcotic drugs.

Article 34 asserts that children must be protected from all forms of sexual exploitation and abuse.

Article 35 provides that children are entitled to protection from being sold, abducted or trafficked.

Article 38 provides protection for children affected by war and states that children under 15 must not be recruited into hostilities.

Article 39 requires that children who are exposed to harmful work must be entitled to recovery and reintegration.

Optional Protocol on sale of children, elaborates prohibitions on the sexual exploitation of children, and their use in any form of sexual activity for purposes of remuneration.

Optional Protocol on involvement of children in armed conflict, prohibits compulsory recruitment of children under 18 into armed forces and no recruitment into armed groups is acceptable under 18 years.

Relevant Instruments

Child labour has been addressed in many international treaties, dating back to the 1919 ILO Convention. Although many of the early ILO treaties remain in force, they have been largely superseded by later ILO Conventions, which are those most frequently referenced by the Committee on the Rights of the Child. ILO Conventions and other instruments most frequently referenced by the Committee include:

- ILO Convention 138, Minimum Age (1973), consolidates earlier ILO Conventions dating back to 1919
- ILO Convention 182, Worst Forms of Child Labour (1999)
- ILO Declaration on Fundamental Principles and Rights at Work (1998), which includes the elimination of child labour as one of its four fundamental rights guaranteed to all as an immediate consequence of membership in ILO
- ILO Recommendation 146, Minimum Age (1973)
- ILO Recommendation 190, Worst Forms of Child Labour (1999)

In addition, the ILO Global Report 2002, *A future without child labour*, clarifies the boundaries of term child labour. It does not apply to all work but only that which violates international standards. It elaborates three categories of work to be abolished:

- Labour by a child under the minimum age prescribed in national legislation and in line with international standards
- Labour that jeopardises the physical, mental or moral well-being of child – defined as hazardous work
- Worst forms of child labour which, are defined as slavery, trafficking, debt bondage, and other forced labour, forced recruitment for armed conflict, prostitution and pornography, and illicit activities.

Other Relevant Instruments:

- UN Universal Declaration of Human Rights (1948), Articles 4, 23, which state no one shall be held in slavery; everyone has the right to work, fair remuneration, and join a trades union.
- International Covenant on Civil and Political Rights (1966), Article 8, which requires no forced labour or servitude.
- International Covenant on Economic, Social and Cultural Rights (1966), Article 7, which elaborates the right to work and just and favourable conditions. It requires special measures of protection and assistance for children including from economic and social exploitation. Work harmful to morals or health or likely to damage their development should be punishable in law. It also recommends minimum age limits.
- African Charter on the Rights and Welfare of the Child (1990), Article 15, which spells out that provisions on economic exploitation apply to both formal and informal work, and explicitly refers to ILO Conventions.
- European Social Charter (Revised) (1996), Article 7, establishes detailed rights to protection at work for children.
- Additional Protocol to the American Convention on Human Rights in the Area of Economic, Social, and Cultural Rights 'Protocol of San Salvador' (1988), Article 7, which prohibits night work or dangerous work for those under 18, and for all under 16, asserts that work must not impede full time education.
- Charter of Fundamental Rights of the European Union (2000), Article 32, which states that employment of children is prohibited, that minimum working age must

correspond to school leaving age. And children must be protected from exploitation and harmful work or any work interfering with education.

Attributes

Attribute One: Protection from Economic Exploitation and Harmful Work

Article 32 establishes the right to protection from economic exploitation. It does not imply that all work is unacceptable. Rather, it sets out in general terms the nature of exploitative work from which children must be protected, including that which is hazardous (relating to an immediate or imminent danger), harmful to their development (applying to longer-term risks), or interferes with education. Such work has been defined as child labour by the ILO (n.d.), and has been described by the ILO as including (International Labour Organization, 2002):

- any work under the minimum age prescribed in national legislation or which fails to comply with the relevant protective standards
- hazardous work that jeopardises the physical, mental or moral well-being of a child
- the worst forms of child labour including slavery, trafficking, debt bondage, or other forced labour, forced recruitment for armed conflict, child sexual abuse and illicit activities (International Labour Organization, 1999, p. 182).

The Committee has emphasised the importance of adopting a holistic approach to child labour, addressing it in the context of the four General Principles (as above). It has made clear that work must be defined to cover both formal and informal activities, including, for example, domestic labour, agricultural work for the family, and street activities (International Labour Organization, 2006, p. 11; UN Committee on the Rights of the Child, 2000a, paras. 65–71).[2]

Building on ILO Convention 182 on the worst forms of child labour, the Committee has outlined in more detail the types of work that are prohibited and must be legislated against, including that which is contrary to the child's human dignity, cruel, inhuman or degrading, dangerous or harmful, discriminatory, below the minimum age, and that which involves legally punishable criminal activities (1994a, pp. 38–43). The Committee has highlighted a number of specific forms of child labour needing abolition including, for example, cotton-picking, mining, working on sugar cane plantations, working as a child jockey, and domestic labour for girls, the latter sometimes defined as a worst form of child labour under ILO

---

[2]See also, for example, concluding observations for Iran (2005a, para. 69) and Kenya (2016b, para. 71 (b)).

182.[3] Since ILO 182 was adopted in 1999, the Committee has consistently referred States Parties to its standards and encouraged ratification and implementation.[4]

Attribute Two: Regulatory Framework to Provide Protection

Article 32 imposes on States Parties a requirement to introduce a regulatory framework prescribing ages and conditions of employment for children. In this regard, the Committee consistently recommends that States Parties ratify and implement ILO Convention 138 which elaborates the need to progressively raise the minimum age for work to a level consistent with physical and mental development, to define the work activities permitted, and prescribe the number of hours and conditions of work.[5] The Committee, in line with ILO 138, regularly recommends the age of 15 years as the appropriate minimum age for full time work, and also presses for consistency between the minimum school leaving age and entry into full time employment as an added level of protection.[6] However, the Committee emphasises that it is not the intention of Article 32 to prevent, for example, flexible engagement of children in seasonal work, nor to prohibit domestic chores, as long as these activities are consistent with receiving an education (1993, para. 44).

Consistent with its focus on a holistic approach to Article 32, the Committee has drawn States Parties attention to the need for legislation and regulation to protect other rights in the context of work. In addition to the importance of applying the General Principles, and the need to ensure the right to education and healthy development, it highlights reports from children of exposure to violence in the workplace as a means of coercion, punishment or control, and the imperative for explicit prohibition of corporal punishment in all work environments (2007b, paras. 35–36). The Committee also emphasises the need for legal standards that afford children the opportunity to exercise their rights to rest, leisure, play and recreation under Article 31 (2013, para. 29).

---

[3] See, for example, concluding observations for Mongolia (2005b, paras. 60, 61), Uzbekistan (2006b, paras. 64, 65), Bolivia (2009b, para. 74), and Senegal (2006a, paras. 60–63), and Preliminary Observations: Colombia (1994b, para. 9).

[4] See, for example Concluding Observations: Korea (2017c).

[5] See, for example, Concluding Observations: Mongolia (2017d, para. 41).

[6] See, for example, concluding observations for Belarus (1994c) and Sri Lanka (1994d, para. 41).

Attribute Three: Administrative, Social, and Educational Measures for Protection

Article 32 requires States Parties to go beyond the introduction of an appropriate legislative framework and to adopt administrative, social, and educational measures for protecting children from exploitative or harmful work. The introduction of age limits and prohibited forms of work will not address the problem of child labour without being undertaken in the context of wider measures. The Committee has recommended a range of approaches necessary to contribute to such protection:

- Disaggregated data collection to understand the dynamics of child labour and support recommendations that will address its root causes and dangers[7]
- Investment in social and economic development and poverty eradication (2016a, para. 85)
- Universal free access to quality, inclusive primary and secondary education (2016a, para. 85)
- Coordination of schooling and introduction to decent work, with support for school-to-work transitions (2016a, para. 85)
- Family support programmes to eliminate child labour (2016c, para. 66 (e))
- Establishing and strengthening monitoring capacity at government and local levels to identify children engaged in the worst forms of child labour and ensure their removal, rehabilitation and reintegration (2017e, para. 43 (a))
- Awareness-raising programmes, including campaigns, targeting children and their parents on the rights of working children (2016d, para. 44 (d))
- Co-operation with the International Programme on the Elimination of Child Labour ILO/IPEC (2006c, paras. 67–68).

Attribute Four: Penalties and Enforcement for Effective Protection

States Parties are required to introduce mechanisms for effective enforcement of measures to protect children under their Article 32 rights. This includes a regulatory framework establishing responsibilities for compliance in both the formal and non-formal sectors which must be reinforced by a trained labour inspectorate, backed up with the necessary support and appropriate penalties in cases of non-compliance (UN Committee on the Rights of the Child, 2006d, para. 89).

The Committee encourages awareness raising among the public of the legal protections against exploitation of child labour with a view to encouraging the reporting of violations and ensuring these are thoroughly investigated and

---

[7] See, for example, concluding observations for South Africa (2000b, para. 14) and Peru (2016c, para. 66 (g)).

perpetrators are sanctioned (2017f, para. 43 (c)). However, it is imperative that interventions designed to protect children are not undertaken in a manner that undermines protection, for example, criminalising children and resulting in engagement in more harmful and less regulated work. Dialogue with children on the most appropriate means of providing protection, together with community engagement, is essential.[8]

References

Daly, A. (2016). *A commentary on the United Nations convention on the rights of the child, article 15: The right to freedom of association and to freedom of peaceful assembly. A commentary on the United Nations Convention on the Rights of the Child, Article 15: The right to freedom of association and to freedom of peaceful assembly.* Brill Nijhoff. Retrieved October 24, 2020, from https://brill.com/view/title/11631

International Labour Organization. (1999). *Convention C182 - worst forms of child labour convention, 1999 (no. 182).* Geneva: ILO. Retrieved November 26, 2020, from https://www.ilo.org/dyn/normlex/en/f?p=NORMLEXPUB:12100:0::NO::P12100_ILO_CODE:C182

International Labour Organization. (2002). *A future without child labour. Global report under the follow-up to the ILO Declaration on Fundamental Principles and Rights at Work. Report of the Director-General, 2002 (Report).* Retrieved November 26, 2020, from http://www.ilo.org/global/publications/ilo-bookstore/order-online/books/WCMS_PUBL_9221124169_EN/lang%2D%2Den/index.htm

International Labour Organization. (2006). *The end of child labour: Within reach.* Geneva. Retrieved December 20, 2020, from https://www.ilo.org/ipec/Informationresources/WCMS_IPEC_PUB_2419/lang%2D%2Den/index.htm

International Labour Organization. (n.d.). *IPEC - What is child labour.* International Programme on the Elimination of Child Labour. Retrieved November 26, 2020, from https://www.ilo.org/ipec/facts/lang%2D%2Den/index.htm

Office of the United Nations High Commissioner for Human Rights & Rädda barnen (Society: Sweden). (2007). *Legislative history of the convention on the rights of the child.* New York: United Nations. Retrieved from https://digitallibrary.un.org/record/602462?ln=en

Swepston, L. (2012). *A commentary on the United Nations convention on the rights of the child, article 32: Protection from economic exploitation. A commentary on the United Nations convention on the rights of the child, article 32: Protection from economic exploitation.* Brill Nijhoff. Retrieved November 26, 2020, from https://brill.com/view/title/11644

The Concerned for Working Children. (n.d.). *Child work and child labour. The concerned for working children.* Retrieved November 26, 2020, from http://www.concernedforworkingchildren.org/empowering-children/child-work-and-child-labour/

UN Committee on Economic, Social and Cultural Rights. (2016). *ICESCR General Comment No. 23 (2016) on the right to just and favourable conditions of work, E/C.12/GC/23.* UN. Retrieved November 26, 2020, from http://digitallibrary.un.org/record/1312521

UN Committee on the Rights of the Child. (1993). *Summary record of the 68th meeting, held at the Palais des Nations, Geneva, on Tuesday, 26 January 1993 (Concluding observations: Egypt).* UN. Retrieved November 26, 2020, from http://digitallibrary.un.org/record/164601

UN Committee on the Rights of the Child. (1994a). *Report on the 5th session, 10–28 January 1994, CRC/C/24.* Retrieved October 12, 2020, from https://digitallibrary.un.org/record/193291?ln=en

---

[8] See, for example, 'Child work and child' (The Concerned for Working Children, n.d.)

UN Committee on the Rights of the Child. (1994b). *Preliminary observations: Colombia, February 7, 1994, CRC/C/15/Add.15*. UN. Retrieved November 26, 2020, from http://digitallibrary.un.org/record/197663

UN Committee on the Rights of the Child. (1994c). *Concluding observations: Belarus, February 7, 1994, CRC/C/15/Add.17*. UN. Retrieved November 26, 2020, from http://digitallibrary.un.org/record/197665

UN Committee on the Rights of the Child. (1994d). *Concluding observations: Sri Lanka, June 21, 1994, CRC/C/15/Add.40*. Retrieved November 6, 2020, from https://digitallibrary.un.org/record/191817?ln=en

UN Committee on the Rights of the Child. (2000a). *Concluding observations: India, February 23, 2000, CRC/C/15/Add.115*. Retrieved October 11, 2020, from https://digitallibrary.un.org/record/412551?ln=en

UN Committee on the Rights of the Child. (2000b). *Concluding observations: South Africa, February 22, 2000, CRC/C/15/Add.122*. UN. Retrieved November 26, 2020, from http://digitallibrary.un.org/record/414198

UN Committee on the Rights of the Child. (2001). *Concluding observations: Turkey, July 9, 2001, CRC/C/15/Add.152*. Retrieved October 23, 2020, from https://digitallibrary.un.org/record/451935?ln=en

UN Committee on the Rights of the Child. (2003). *General Comment No. 4 (2003) Adolescent health and development in the context of the Convention on the Rights of the Child, July 1, 2003, CRC/GC/2003/4*. Retrieved October 12, 2020, from https://digitallibrary.un.org/record/503074?ln=en

UN Committee on the Rights of the Child. (2005a). *Concluding observations: Iran, March 31, 2005, CRC/C/15/Add.254*. Retrieved October 12, 2020, from https://digitallibrary.un.org/record/557400?ln=en

UN Committee on the Rights of the Child. (2005b). *Concluding observations: Mongolia, September 21, 2005, CRC/C/15/Add.264*. UN. Retrieved November 26, 2020, from http://digitallibrary.un.org/record/570464

UN Committee on the Rights of the Child. (2006a). *Concluding observations: Senegal, October 20, 2006, CRC/C/SEN/CO/2*. UN. Retrieved November 26, 2020, from http://digitallibrary.un.org/record/589674

UN Committee on the Rights of the Child. (2006b). *Concluding observations: Uzbekistan, June 2, 2006, CRC/C/UZB/CO/2*. UN. Retrieved November 26, 2020, from http://digitallibrary.un.org/record/594828

UN Committee on the Rights of the Child. (2006c). *Concluding observations: Benin, October 20, 2006, CRC/C/BEN/CO/2*. UN. Retrieved November 26, 2020, from http://digitallibrary.un.org/record/589640

UN Committee on the Rights of the Child. (2006d). *Concluding observations: Jordan, November 1, 2006, CRC/C/JOR/CO/3*. UN. Retrieved November 26, 2020, from http://digitallibrary.un.org/record/589751

UN Committee on the Rights of the Child. (2007a). *General Comment No. 9 (2006) The rights of children with disabilities, November 13, 2007, CRC/C/GC/9*. Retrieved October 12, 2020, from https://digitallibrary.un.org/record/593891?ln=en

UN Committee on the Rights of the Child. (2007b). *General Comment No. 8 (2006) The right of the child to protection from corporal punishment and other cruel or degrading forms of punishment (arts. 19; 28, para. 2; and 37, inter alia), March 2, 2007, CRC/C/GC/8*. Retrieved October 12, 2020, from https://digitallibrary.un.org/record/583961?ln=en

UN Committee on the Rights of the Child. (2009a). *General Comment No. 12 (2009) The right of the child to be heard, July 20, 2009, CRC/C/GC/12*. Retrieved October 12, 2020, from https://digitallibrary.un.org/record/671444?ln=en

UN Committee on the Rights of the Child. (2009b). *Concluding observations: Bolivia, October 16, 2009, CRC/C/BOL/CO/4*. UN. Retrieved December 20, 2020, from http://digitallibrary.un.org/record/668535

UN Committee on the Rights of the Child. (2013). *General Comment No. 17 (2013) on the right of the child to rest, leisure, play, recreational activities, cultural life and the arts (art. 31)*, April 17, 2013, CRC/C/GC/17. Retrieved October 12, 2020, from https://digitallibrary.un.org/record/778539?ln=en

UN Committee on the Rights of the Child. (2016a). *General Comment No. 20 (2016) on the implementation of the rights of the child during adolescence*, December 6, 2016, CRC/C/GC/20. Retrieved October 12, 2020, from https://digitallibrary.un.org/record/855544?ln=en

UN Committee on the Rights of the Child. (2016b). *Concluding observations: Kenya*, March 21, 2016, CRC/C/KEN/CO/3-5. UN. Retrieved November 14, 2020, from http://digitallibrary.un.org/record/834997

UN Committee on the Rights of the Child. (2016c). *Concluding observations: Peru*, March 2, 2016, CRC/C/PER/CO/4-5. UN. Retrieved November 26, 2020, from http://digitallibrary.un.org/record/834928

UN Committee on the Rights of the Child. (2016d). *Concluding observations: New Zealand*, October 21, 2016, CRC/C/NZL/CO/5. UN. Retrieved November 6, 2020, from http://digitallibrary.un.org/record/856035

UN Committee on the Rights of the Child. (2017a). *Concluding observations: Qatar*, June 22, 2017, CRC/C/QAT/CO/3-4. UN. Retrieved November 22, 2020, from http://digitallibrary.un.org/record/1311379

UN Committee on the Rights of the Child. (2017b). *General Comment No. 21 (2017) on children in street situations*, June 21, 2017, CRC/C/GC/21. Retrieved October 12, 2020, from https://digitallibrary.un.org/record/1304490?ln=en

UN Committee on the Rights of the Child. (2017c). *Concluding observations: Korea*, October 23, 2017, CRC/C/PRK/CO/5. UN. Retrieved November 26, 2020, from http://digitallibrary.un.org/record/1311397

UN Committee on the Rights of the Child. (2017d). *Concluding observations: Mongolia*, July 12, 2017, CRC/C/MNG/CO/5. UN. Retrieved November 26, 2020, from http://digitallibrary.un.org/record/1311385

UN Committee on the Rights of the Child. (2017e). *Concluding observations: Tajikistan*, October 25, 2017, CRC/C/TJK/CO/3-5. UN. Retrieved November 7, 2020, from http://digitallibrary.un.org/record/1311398

UN Committee on the Rights of the Child. (2017f). *Concluding observations: Cameroon*, July 6, 2017, CRC/C/CMR/CO/3-5. UN. Retrieved November 22, 2020, from http://digitallibrary.un.org/record/1311383

Open Access This chapter is licensed under the terms of the Creative Commons Attribution 4.0 International License (http://creativecommons.org/licenses/by/4.0/), which permits use, sharing, adaptation, distribution and reproduction in any medium or format, as long as you give appropriate credit to the original author(s) and the source, provide a link to the Creative Commons license and indicate if changes were made.

The images or other third party material in this chapter are included in the chapter's Creative Commons license, unless indicated otherwise in a credit line to the material. If material is not included in the chapter's Creative Commons license and your intended use is not permitted by statutory regulation or exceeds the permitted use, you will need to obtain permission directly from the copyright holder.

Chapter 34
Article 34: The Right to Protection from All Forms of Sexual Exploitation and Sexual Abuse

Adem Arkadas-Thibert

> States Parties undertake to protect the child from all forms of sexual exploitation and sexual abuse. For these purposes, States Parties shall in particular take all appropriate national, bilateral and multilateral measures to prevent:
>
> (a) The inducement or coercion of a child to engage in any unlawful sexual activity;
> (b) The exploitative use of children in prostitution or other unlawful sexual practices;
> (c) The exploitative use of children in pornographic performances and materials.

> **What Did Children Say?**
> 'There should be more information/training about the dangers of personal exposure on dating sites and apps, but this information should be transmitted according to the child's level of maturity. Ex: When giving information in schools to younger students, this often causes more curiosity than protection.' (Western Europe/Other).
>
> Government and schools have communication activities to raise awareness on preventing sexual abuse against children. (Asia-Pacific).

(continued)

A. Arkadas-Thibert (✉)
Marseille, France

> School—Provide knowledge, life skills, self-protection from danger. (Asia-Pacific).
> The government has serious measures to law enforcement of child protection. (Asia-Pacific).

Overview

Although protection from sexual abuse of children is mentioned in Article 19 of the Convention, Article 34 provides preventive and reactive measures that States Parties must take to tackle child sexual abuse and exploitation. The proposal in the first draft of the Convention was to offer one article combining Articles 34 (sexual exploitation of children), 35 (abduction, sale and trafficking of children) and 36 (all other forms of exploitation of children), to cover sexual and other related forms of exploitation. However, drafting delegates ultimately opted for separate articles in order to provide stronger protection for different forms of exploitation of children (Office of the United Nations High Commissioner for Human Rights and Rädda barnen (Society: Sweden), 2007, pp. 723–737).

Article 34 has been further elaborated in the Optional Protocol to the Convention on the Rights of the Child on the sale of children, child prostitution and child pornography which imposes additional specific obligations on States Parties, and in the associated Committee Guidelines (UN Committee on the Rights of the Child, 2019). Article 34 must also be understood in the context of the many international instruments that have been developed to provide and extend protection in the field of sexual abuse and exploitation (see below).

The Convention does not provide a comprehensive definition of sexual abuse or sexual exploitation, but the Committee has defined sexual abuse as 'any sexual activity imposed by an adult on a child, against which the child is entitled to protection by criminal law. Sexual activities are also considered as abuse when committed against a child by another child, if the child offender is significantly older than the child victim or uses power, threat or other means of pressure. Sexual activities between children are not considered as sexual abuse if the children are older than the age limit defined by the State Party for consensual sexual activities.' (2011, n. 9). Sexual exploitation is interpreted as sexual abuse that involves an exchange, whether financial or otherwise, between a third party, a perpetrator, or the child (Greijer et al., 2016, para. 19). In its General Comment on Article 19, the Committee elaborated its interpretation of sexual abuse and exploitation to include:

- The inducement or coercion of a child to engage in any unlawful or psychologically harmful sexual activity
- The use of children in commercial sexual exploitation
- The use of children in audio or visual images of child sexual abuse
- Child prostitution, sexual slavery, sexual exploitation in travel and tourism, trafficking (within and between countries) and sale of children for sexual

purposes and forced marriage. Many children experience sexual victimisation which is not accompanied by physical force or restraint, but which is nonetheless psychologically intrusive, exploitive and traumatic (2011, paras. 25, 31).

The Committee has subsequently recognised that the digital environment opens up new ways for sexual offenders to solicit children for sexual purposes, participate in online child sexual abuse via live video streaming, distribute child sexual abuse material, and commit the sexual extortion of children (Livingstone et al., 2016, p. 23; UN Committee on the Rights of the Child, 2019, para. 2, 2020). Furthermore, forms of digitally mediated sexual exploitation may be perpetrated within the child's circle of trust, for instance by family and friends or, for adolescents, by intimate partners (UN Committee on the Rights of the Child, 2019, para. 97 (e), 2020).

With its focus on the physical and bodily integrity of the child, Article 34 is best understood as a civil right and thereby subject to immediate implementation (Tobin & Seow, 2019, p. 1330). Indeed, the Committee has argued explicitly that resource constraints are not a justification for failure on the part of the State Party to adopt any or sufficient measures required for child protection (2011, para. 73). Implementation therefore requires States Parties to introduce a comprehensive protection strategy, which includes preventive and reactive measures, such as laws and policies, effective actions fostering awareness through education, socialisation, and mobilisation at the national, bilateral, and multilateral levels (UN Committee on the Rights of the Child, 2011, paras. 61–69).

General Principles

Article 2 All children are equally entitled to protection from sexual abuse and exploitation. However, the Committee has identified many risk factors, or groups of children who are at particular risk, including girls, internally displaced children, street children, orphans, children from rural areas, refugee children and children belonging to more vulnerable castes, LGBTQ children, aboriginal children, children with disabilities, and children in armed conflict (2011, para. 65 (g)). Accordingly, States Parties must introduce specific measures to identify, prevent, and protect such children from sexual abuse and exploitation.

Article 3 The child's safety is one of the fundamental tenets of the child's best interests. Effective protective interventions for children must be introduced to guarantee the best interests of the child. The Committee has emphasised that the child's best interests require States Parties to make 'adequate investment in human, financial and technical resources dedicated to the implementation of a child rights-based and integrated child protection and support system' (2011, para. 54).

Article 6 Sexual abuse and exploitation severely impede children's optimum development, resulting in profound and long-term negative consequences for physical, emotional and psychological well-being.[1] States Parties therefore have an obligation to provide comprehensive protection from sexual violence and exploitation, which are a threat to the fulfilment of the child's right to life, survival and development, and 'implementation measures should be aimed at achieving the optimal development for all children (UN Committee on the Rights of the Child, 2011, para. 62).'

Article 12 The right of children to be heard is integral to their right to protection (UN Committee on the Rights of the Child, 2009, para. 120). Violence perpetrated against children often goes unchallenged because certain types of abusive behaviour are seen by children as accepted practices, and due to the lack of child-friendly reporting mechanisms. Therefore, children must be provided with information about their right to be heard and to grow up free from all forms of violence as well as given the life skills and the knowledge to protect themselves from sexual abuse and exploitation, and how to seek assistance and justice when needed (UN Committee on the Rights of the Child, 2009, para. 120).

Children must be recognised not merely as victims and objects of protection but also as agents in their own lives with a right to contribute to the development, implementation, and evaluation of protection programmes (UN Committee on the Rights of the Child, 2009, para. 121). Accordingly, their views must be invited and given due weight as a mandatory step at every point in a child protection process (UN Committee on the Rights of the Child, 2009, para. 118, 2011, para. 56).

Articles Related or Linked to Article 34

Article 5 proclaims the child's right to guidance from their parents and family in the exercise of their rights to protection from any form of sexual exploitation.

Article 9 guarantees the child's right to not be separated from one's parents unless it is necessary in one's best interests, such as in the case of sexual exploitation, abuse, or neglect by one's parents.

Article 11 protects children from illicit transfer and non-return from abroad for any purposes of sexual exploitation.

Article 19 guarantees a child's right to protection from all forms of violence including any form of sexual exploitation in all settings.

Article 35 ensures the prevention of abduction, sale, and trafficking for sexual purposes.

Article 39 provides for physical and psychological recovery and social reintegration of survivors of sexual exploitation of children.

---

[1] See, for example, *Report of the Special Rapporteur on Sale of children, child prostitution and child pornography* (Calcetas-Santos, 1996, paras. 24–28), 'Stockholm Declaration and Agenda for Action' (World Congress Against Commercial Sexual Exploitation, 1996).

Article 32 protects children against economic exploitation, such as trafficking, forced labour, and slavery-like sexual exploitation.

Article 36 provides for protection from all other forms of exploitation that are not fully defined or understood, especially ones involving information and communication technologies involving sexual exploitation.

Article 17(e) provides that States Parties are under obligation to provide information, education, and guidelines for the protection of the child from injurious information and material, including new and emerging forms of sexual exploitation of children, such as online.

Article 24 (3) requires that States Parties must take measures to effectively abolish traditional practices, such as genital mutilation and child marriage which may be treated as sexual abuse and sexual exploitation of children, which are detrimental to the rights and well-being of children.

Article 26 requires that States Parties provide the child with available, accessible, and quality social security in accordance with their circumstances, taking into account the resources of their care providers, with a view to minimising the risk of sexual exploitation of children.

Article 27 provides that States Parties must provide the child with adequate living conditions, and assistance to parents and care providers, for the child's physical, mental, spiritual, moral, and social development as a preventive and protective measure from all forms of sexual exploitation of children.

Optional Protocol on the involvement of children in armed conflict, Article 4 (prohibition of use of children in armed conflict by non-state actors) and Article 7 (rehabilitation, reintegration, international cooperation).

Optional Protocol on the sale of children, child prostitution, and child pornography, Article 2(b) and (c).

Relevant Instruments

UN Universal Declaration of Human Rights (1948), Article 4, requires generally that: 'No one shall be held in slavery or servitude; slavery and the slave trade shall be prohibited in all their forms'.

International Covenant on Civil and Political Rights (1966), Article 8, prohibits 'forced and compulsory labour.' The Human Rights Committee, in the General Comment on Article 24 of the International Covenant (which recognises children's right to protection), notes the need to protect children 'from being exploited by means of forced labour or prostitution' (Committee on the Rights of the Child, 2007, p. 184).

International Covenant on Economic, Social and Cultural Rights (1966), Article 10(3), states 'Children and young persons should be protected from economic and social exploitation. Their employment in work harmful to their morals or health or dangerous to life or likely to hamper their normal development should be punishable by law'.

UN Convention on the Elimination of All Forms of Discrimination against Women (1979), Article 6, requires States Parties to 'take all appropriate measures, including legislation, to suppress all forms of traffic in women and exploitation of prostitution of women'.

UN Protocol to Prevent, Suppress and Punish Trafficking in Persons Especially Women and Children, supplementing the United Nations Convention against Transnational Organized Crime (2000), Article 3(a), which provides a definition of 'trafficking of children for sexual purposes'.

Hague Convention on Protection of Children and Co-operation in Respect of Intercountry Adoption (1993), definition in Article 1 (b).

ILO Convention 182, Worst Forms of Child Labour (1999), definition in Article 3 (b).

Rome Statute of International Criminal Court (1998), Articles 2 (c), 6, 8 (b).

American Convention on Human Rights 'Pact of San Jose, Costa Rica' (B-32) (1978), Article 6, freedom from slavery.

African Charter on the Rights and Welfare of the Child (1990), Articles 27, sexual exploitation, 29, trafficking, and 16, abuse and torture.

Inter-American Convention on International Traffic in Minors (1994), definition in Article 2 (c).

Council of Europe Convention on Cybercrime (Budapest Convention) (2001), Article 9.

Council of Europe Convention on Action against Trafficking in Human Beings (2005).

Council of Europe Convention on the Protection of Children against Sexual Exploitation and Sexual Abuse (2007).

Council of Europe Convention on preventing and combating violence against women and domestic violence (2011), especially Articles 25, support to victims of sexual violence, 36, sexual violence, and 37, forced marriage.

Attributes

Attribute One: Legislative Protection from Sexual Exploitation and Abuse

The obligation to protect children from all forms of sexual exploitation and abuse requires adequate national legal frameworks to address unlawful sexual activity and practices. Both the Convention and subsequent legal and policy documents emphasise law reform in the criminal and penal law contexts to protect children from sexual abuse and exploitation. Effective protection requires that the measures introduced by States Parties address the following three broad areas.

First, while there is discretion as to the particular legislative framework States Parties can adopt, they must introduce comprehensive provisions to criminalise all sexual abuse and exploitation of children (UN Committee on the Rights of the Child, 2013a, para. 30 (a), 2015a, para. 34 (a)), including the potential to penalise those committing offences domestically and transnationally, and by individuals or groups (UN Committee on the Rights of the Child, 2019, Article 3). Bilateral and multilateral measures are essential given the extent to which sexual abuse and exploitation is increasingly transnational. Such legislation must take account of the increasing potential for the sexual abuse and exploitation of children in the digital environment (Buquicchio-de Boer, 2014, para. 87 (a)). It needs to address a commitment to international cooperation involving information sharing, learning from good practice, joint prevention networks and harmonisation of legislation (Maalla M'jid, 2013, para. 109). The necessary legislation measures are elaborated in the Optional Protocol and other international instruments (noted above).

However, it is important that children who are survivors of such exploitation are not subjected to criminal procedures or sanctions for offences related to their situation.[2] In addition, the Committee has expressed concern that many legal frameworks fail to provide protection for boys and has therefore stressed that frameworks must be gender neutral (2014a, para. 32, 2014b, para. 33).

Secondly, States Parties must ensure that legislation is adequately enforced and that sufficient investment is made to ensure effective investigations, prosecution, and punishment of offenders (UN Committee on the Rights of the Child, 2013b, paras. 52–53, 2014c, paras. 43–44). In this regard, the Committee has stressed the importance of measures such as mandatory reporting and civil remedies for children who have been victims of sexual abuse and exploitation (2001a, para. 52, 2015b, para. 35 (a)). The Committee and other agencies also emphasise the importance of confidential, safe, and accessible complaints mechanisms for children to report cases of abuse and exploitation, and for the criminal justice system at all stages to respond to any complaints in a child and gender sensitive and timely manner (Council of Europe, 2012; UN Committee on the Rights of the Child, 2019, Article 8.1 (a)).[3] Children must be provided with appropriate support services, protection, and privacy throughout the legal process (UN Committee on the Rights of the Child, 2019, Article 8.1).

Finally, States Parties must introduce measures to address the physical, psychological and social recovery, rehabilitation and reintegration of survivors of sexual abuse and exploitation, including compensation for damage suffered, livelihood, housing, counselling and information, and education (Council of Europe, 2012, Article 14; UN Committee on the Rights of the Child, 2019, Article 8.5, 9.3; World Congress Against Commercial Sexual Exploitation, 1996).

---

[2] See, for example, Concluding Observations: India (2000, para. 75) and CRC Guidelines regarding the implementation of the Optional Protocol to the Convention on the Rights of the Child on the sale of children, child prostitution and child pornography (UN Committee on the Rights of the Child, 2019, para. 18).

[3] See also Concluding Observations: Czech Republic (2003, para. 62 (b)).

Attribute Two: All Other Measures to Prevent Sexual Abuse and Exploitation

Article 34 also requires that administrative, economic, social and educational measures are introduced to prevent sexual abuse and exploitation of children, consistent with Article 4 of the Convention, General Comment no. 5 on the General Measures of Implementation, and the Stockholm Declaration and Agenda for Action. Such measures include national strategies for gender-sensitive national social and economic policies and programmes to assist vulnerable children (Hodgkin et al., 2007, p. 525), together with coordination and monitoring mechanisms, which must all be accompanied by the necessary budgetary and human resources (Council of Europe, 2012, Articles 10.2 (a) and 45.1; World Congress Against Commercial Sexual Exploitation, 1996).

Education is consistently identified as a vital dimension of prevention. States Parties must invest in programmes of public awareness raising (UN Committee on the Rights of the Child, 2001b, para. 73, 2015c, para. 34 (d)), and training for all professionals working with children (UN Committee on the Rights of the Child, 2002, para. 67 (c), 2014d, para. 47 (a)). Education and information must be provided for children themselves, not only on their rights under the Convention but also, for example, on identifying abuse, negotiating skills, self-confidence, resisting peer pressure, and navigating the digital environment safely (Council of Europe, 2012, Articles 5, 6, 8, 9; UN Committee on the Rights of the Child, 2019, Article 9.2; World Congress Against Commercial Sexual Exploitation, 1996).

The root causes of sexual abuse and exploitation of children are complex. While poverty can be a key factor, multiple other factors serve to facilitate the abuse, including gender bias, racial and social discrimination, lack of education, migration, harmful traditional practices and armed conflict (World Congress Against Commercial Sexual Exploitation, 1996, para. 6). A broad range of measures in response to all these factors is required if States Parties are to successfully prevent sexual abuse and exploitation (World Congress Against Commercial Sexual Exploitation, 1996, para. 3 (a)-(l)). In addition, States Parties must engage and regulate the private sector, including the media, the travel and tourism industry, and online technology businesses in order to fulfil their obligations under Article 34.[4]

References

Buquicchio-de Boer, M. (2014). *Report of the Special Rapporteur on the sale of children, child prostitution and child pornography, Maud de Boer-Buquicchio, A/HRC/28/56*. UN. Retrieved November 27, 2020, from http://digitallibrary.un.org/record/792635

---

[4] For a detailed elaboration of the necessary measures, see 'Protection from sexual exploitation and sexual abuse' (Tobin & Seow, 2019, pp. 1347–1350).

Calcetas-Santos, O. (1996). *Sale of children, child prostitution and child pornography: note by the Secretary-General, A/51/456*. UN. Retrieved November 26, 2020, from http://digitallibrary.un.org/record/223096

Committee on the Rights of the Child. (2007). *Compilation of general comments and general recommendations adopted by human rights treaty bodies: addendum HRI/GEN/1/Rev.8/Add.1* (p. 88). Geneva: 2007-06-11: UN. Retrieved from http://digitallibrary.un.org/record/601793

Council of Europe. (2012). *Council of Europe Convention: Protection of children against sexual exploitation and sexual abuse (Lanzarote convention)*. Strasbourg: Council of Europe Publishing. Retrieved November 27, 2020, from https://rm.coe.int/protection-of-children-against-sexual-exploitation-and-sexual-abuse/1680794e97

Greijer, S., Doek, J., & Interagency Working Group. (2016, 28 January). *Terminology guidelines for the protection of children from sexual exploitation and sexual abuse: Adopted by the Interagency Working Group in Luxembourg*. Bangkok: ECPAT International. Retrieved from https://www.ecpat.org/wp-content/uploads/2016/12/Terminology-guidelines_ENG.pdf

Hodgkin, R., Newell, P., & UNICEF. (2007). *Implementation handbook for the convention on the rights of the child* (3rd ed.). New York: UNICEF. Retrieved September 21, 2020, from https://digitallibrary.un.org/record/620060?ln=en

Livingstone, S., Byrne, J., & Carr, J. (2016). *One in three: Internet governance and Children's rights*. Innocenti Discussion Papers, 2016(1), 37.

Maalla M'jid, N. (2013). *Report of the Special Rapporteur on the sale of children, child prostitution and child pornography, A/HRC/25/48*. UN. Retrieved November 27, 2020, from http://digitallibrary.un.org/record/766858

Office of the United Nations High Commissioner for Human Rights & Rädda barnen (Society: Sweden). (2007). *Legislative history of the convention on the rights of the child*. New York: United Nations. Retrieved from https://digitallibrary.un.org/record/602462?ln=en

Tobin, J., & Seow, F. (2019). Article 34: Protection from sexual exploitation and sexual abuse. In J. Tobin (Ed.), *The UN convention on the rights of the child: A commentary* (pp. 1310–1355). Oxford University Press.

UN Committee on the Rights of the Child. (2000). *Concluding observations: India, February 23, 2000, CRC/C/15/Add.115*. Retrieved October 11, 2020, from https://digitallibrary.un.org/record/412551?ln=en

UN Committee on the Rights of the Child. (2001a). *Concluding observations: Egypt, February 21, 2001, CRC/C/15/Add.145*. UN. Retrieved November 27, 2020, from http://digitallibrary.un.org/record/444357

UN Committee on the Rights of the Child. (2001b). *Concluding observations: Ethiopia, February 21, 2001, CRC/C/15/Add.144*. UN. Retrieved November 27, 2020, from http://digitallibrary.un.org/record/444356

UN Committee on the Rights of the Child. (2002). *Concluding observations: Mozambique, April 3, 2002, CRC/C/15/Add.172*. UN. Retrieved November 16, 2020, from http://digitallibrary.un.org/record/467261

UN Committee on the Rights of the Child. (2003). *Concluding observations: Czech Republic, March 18, 2003, CRC/C/15/Add.201*. UN. Retrieved November 27, 2020, from http://digitallibrary.un.org/record/497801

UN Committee on the Rights of the Child. (2009). *General Comment No. 12 (2009) The right of the child to be heard, July 20, 2009, CRC/C/GC/12*. Retrieved October 12, 2020, from https://digitallibrary.un.org/record/671444?ln=en

UN Committee on the Rights of the Child. (2011). *General Comment No. 13 (2011) The right of the child to freedom from all forms of violence, April 18, 2011, CRC/C/GC/13*. Retrieved October 12, 2020, from https://digitallibrary.un.org/record/711722?ln=en

UN Committee on the Rights of the Child. (2013a). *Concluding observations: Rwanda, July 8, 2013, CRC/C/RWA/CO/3-4*. UN. Retrieved November 17, 2020, from http://digitallibrary.un.org/record/756221

UN Committee on the Rights of the Child. (2013b). *Concluding observations: Guinea, June 13, 2013, CRC/C/GIN/CO/2*. UN. Retrieved November 18, 2020, from http://digitallibrary.un.org/record/751394

UN Committee on the Rights of the Child. (2014a). *Concluding observations: Jordan, July 8, 2014, CRC/C/JOR/CO/4-5*. UN. Retrieved November 27, 2020, from http://digitallibrary.un.org/record/778713

UN Committee on the Rights of the Child. (2014b). *Concluding observations: Saint Lucia, July 8, 2014, CRC/C/LCA/CO/2-4*. UN. Retrieved November 27, 2020, from http://digitallibrary.un.org/record/778719

UN Committee on the Rights of the Child. (2014c). *Concluding observations: Holy See, February 25, 2014, CRC/C/VAT/CO/2*. UN. Retrieved November 27, 2020, from http://digitallibrary.un.org/record/778845

UN Committee on the Rights of the Child. (2014d). *Concluding observations: Congo, February 25, 2014, CRC/C/COG/CO/2-4*. UN. Retrieved November 18, 2020, from http://digitallibrary.un.org/record/778842

UN Committee on the Rights of the Child. (2015a). *Concluding observations: Dominican Republic, March 6, 2015, CRC/C/DOM/CO/3-5*. UN. Retrieved November 27, 2020, from http://digitallibrary.un.org/record/789732

UN Committee on the Rights of the Child. (2015b). *Concluding observations: Jamaica, March 10, 2015, CRC/C/JAM/CO/3-4*. Retrieved October 12, 2020, from https://digitallibrary.un.org/record/789759?ln=en

UN Committee on the Rights of the Child. (2015c). *Concluding observations: Uruguay, March 5, 2015, CRC/C/URY/CO/3-5*. UN. Retrieved November 27, 2020, from http://digitallibrary.un.org/record/789741

UN Committee on the Rights of the Child. (2019). *Guidelines regarding the implementation of the Optional Protocol to the Convention on the Rights of the Child on the sale of children, child prostitution and child pornography, CRC/C/156*. Retrieved November 26, 2020, from https://undocs.org/en/CRC/C/156

UN Committee on the Rights of the Child. (2020). *Draft General comment No. 25 (202x): Children's rights in relation to the digital environment*. Retrieved December 20, 2020, from https://tbinternet.ohchr.org/_layouts/15/treatybodyexternal/Download.aspx?symbolno=CRC%2fC%2fGC%2f25&Lang=en

World Congress Against Commercial Sexual Exploitation. (1996). *Stockholm declaration and agenda for action*. Retrieved November 26, 2020, from https://www.ecpat.org/wp-content/uploads/legacy/stockholm_declaration_1996.pdf

Open Access This chapter is licensed under the terms of the Creative Commons Attribution 4.0 International License (http://creativecommons.org/licenses/by/4.0/), which permits use, sharing, adaptation, distribution and reproduction in any medium or format, as long as you give appropriate credit to the original author(s) and the source, provide a link to the Creative Commons license and indicate if changes were made.

The images or other third party material in this chapter are included in the chapter's Creative Commons license, unless indicated otherwise in a credit line to the material. If material is not included in the chapter's Creative Commons license and your intended use is not permitted by statutory regulation or exceeds the permitted use, you will need to obtain permission directly from the copyright holder.

Chapter 35
Article 36: The Right to Protection from Other Forms of Exploitation

Adem Arkadas-Thibert

> States Parties shall protect the child against all other forms of exploitation prejudicial to any aspects of the child's welfare.

What Did Children Say?
'There should be awareness raising and campaigns through different mediums such as radio, TV, newspapers, forums and blogging on trafficking, abductions, child labour, child marriage and all forms of violation and discrimination against children and youths.' (Africa).

Governments should have a public campaign on child rights and ways persons often harm children. (Latin America/Caribbean).

Children learn where to make reports or seek refuge when these things happen. (Africa).

Government should create a forum where children especially girls and women have a voice to stand strong and say 'No' to violence and abuses against their rights. (Africa).

A. Arkadas-Thibert (✉)
Marseille, France

Overview

Children should be protected from any activity that takes advantage of them or could harm their welfare and development. Article 36 of the Convention provides for all encompassing fail-safe preventive and protective safeguards against all forms of exploitation and slavery-like conditions everywhere that are not covered by other articles of the Convention.

Initially designed as part of one article combining commercial sexual exploitation of children (Article 34), and abduction of, sale of, and traffic in children (Article 35), to cover sexual and other related forms of exploitation (Office of the United Nations High Commissioner for Human Rights and Rädda barnen (Society: Sweden), 2007, pp. 723–737), drafters of the Convention designed a wider and a fail-safe protection for children. Article 36 was introduced to ensure that the 'social' exploitation of children was recognised, along with their sexual and economic exploitation, though examples of social exploitation were not provided (Hodgkin et al., 2007, p. 543). It integrates the other articles of the Convention concerned with the exploitation of children taking place in specific context, namely:

- Article 19 against all forms of violence taking place when in care of parents or other caregivers
- Article 32 against economic exploitation
- Article 33 against the use of children in illicit production and trafficking of drug
- Article 34 against sexual exploitation
- Article 35 against abduction of, sale of, traffic in children (Tobin, 2019, p. 1403)

With increasingly globalised criminal activities and introductions of new technologies, new forms of exploitation are emerging, in addition to traditional forms of trafficking (within and between countries) and sale of children for sexual purposes and forced marriage. Children are exposed to forms of exploitation which are 'not accompanied by physical force or restraint but which are nonetheless psychologically intrusive, exploitive and traumatic' (UN Committee on the Rights of the Child, 2011, para. 25). As Tobin clarifies, those 'new' forms of exploitation of children will be generally dealt by the above-mentioned provisions of the Convention focused on exploitative practices in combination with Articles 3 and 6 of the Convention, respectively meant to ensure the respect of the best interests principle and the right to survival and development of the child (2019, p. 1403).

However, as a safety net, Article 36 is designed to fill any eventual gap of the Convention in relation to the exploitation of children and, as a consequence, it extends the protection over a variety of forms of exploitations such as exploiting gifted children, media exploitation, commercial and advertising exploitation, medical experimentation, and research activities concerning children in different capacities. For example, as discussed in relation to Articles 16 and 17, children can be exploited by the media by identifying child victims or child offenders, or by securing performances by children without their informed consent, which are potentially harmful to their development (Hodgkin et al., 2007). Children with talents in competitive sports, games, performing arts, and other fields may have these talents developed by families, the media, businesses, and state authorities at the expense of their overall physical and mental development. With reference to the medical research and experimentation, even though Article 7 of the International Covenant on Civil and Political Rights expressly prohibits medical or scientific experimentation without free consent, children can be exposed to breaches of their privacy, or be required to undertake tasks that breach their rights or are disrespectful of their human dignity (Hodgkin et al., 2007).

At the same time, the wording 'shall protect' in Article 36 constitutes a mandatory obligation on States Parties. It demands that they adopt measures to protect children from all other forms of exploitation by setting in place 'all the appropriate measures to respect, protect and fulfil the right of all children to be protected against exploitation' including among them preventive measures (Tobin, 2019, pp. 1404–1408).

General Principles

Article 2 Every child is entitled to protection from all forms of exploitation, but certain groups of children are more at risk of exploitation than adults and other children (UN Committee on the Rights of the Child, 2011, para. 72 (g)). States Parties must introduce measures to identify, prevent and protect such children from exploitation.

Article 3 The child's safety is one of the fundamental tenets of the child's best interests. Effective preventive and protective measures for children must be taken to guarantee the best interest of the child.

Article 6 All forms of exploitation of children are a threat to the fulfilment of their right to life, survival, and development (UN Committee on the Rights of the Child, 2011, para. 15).

Article 12 Children have rights to access information, including life skills and knowledge to protect themselves from exploitation, and to seek assistance and justice whenever needed.

Articles Related or Linked to Article 36

Article 17 provides that States should encourage and support the provision of information to children from the mass media, and to encourage the development of guidelines to provide children from harmful information that might be exploitative or lead to potential exploitation.

Article 24(3) which requires measures to effectively abolish traditional practices, such as child marriage, which are detrimental to the rights and well-being of children.

Article 26 ensures the child's right to available, accessible, and quality social security in accordance with their circumstances and their care providers' resources, so that the child is less at risk of exploitation (van Bueren, 1998, p. 268).

Article 27 provides for adequate living conditions for the child's physical, mental, spiritual, moral, and social development, as a preventive and protective measure from all forms of exploitation.

Article 32 protects children against trafficking forced labour and slavery-like working conditions.

Article 33 protects from use of children in crimes of illicit substance trafficking.

Article 34 protects children from their use in the sex trade, including prostitution or the production pornography, or through forced marriages.

Article 35 protects against the abduction, sale, and trafficking of children.

Article 39 requires that States Parties provide the child who is exposed to any form of exploitation with physical and psychological recovery and social reintegration.

Optional Protocol on the involvement of children in armed conflict, Article 4, provides that non-state armed forced are barred from using children in armed conflict which extends to exploitation of children for any purposes.

Optional Protocol on the sale of children, child prostitution, and child pornography. The protocol is 'meant to achieve the purposes of the CRC and the implementation of its provisions' including Article 36 (Greijer et al., 2019, p. 21).

Relevant Instruments

UN Protocol to Prevent, Suppress and Punish Trafficking in Persons Especially Women and Children, supplementing the United Nations Convention against Transnational Organized Crime (2000).

Hague Convention on the Civil Aspects of International Child Abduction (1980).

Hague Convention on Protection of Children and Co-operation in Respect of Intercountry Adoption (1993).

ILO Convention 182, Worst Forms of Child Labour (1999).

African Charter on the Rights and Welfare of the Child (1990), Articles 27, 28 and 29.

Inter-American Convention on International Traffic in Minors (1994).

Attributes

Attribute One: Monitoring and Identification of All Other Forms of Exploitation Prejudicial to Any Aspects of the Child's Welfare

In fulfilling their preventive role and to develop consistent evidence-based policies, Articles 36 requires that States Parties must actively monitor and identify existing, new, and unknown forms of exploitation of children as a preventive and protective measure. This requires regularly reviewing children's well-being in general, children at risk as defined in General Comment no. 13 on violence against children (Office of the United Nations High Commissioner for Human Rights and Rädda barnen (Society: Sweden), 2007) in particular, and also survivors and victims who are exposed to exploitation. These reviews should provide data or support research on new and emerging forms of exploitation. States Parties must work with children, respecting their right to be heard, and undertake monitoring of their well-being and forms of exploitation with children (UN Committee on the Rights of the Child, 2009, paras. 118–122).

Attribute Two: Protection from All Other Forms of Exploitation Prejudicial to Any Aspects of the Child's Welfare

Article 36 asserts that States Parties shall introduce protection measures for children against all other forms of exploitation already identified and addressed. It is a fail-safe protective net for children to eradicate all known forms of exploitation of children and to proactively address unknown forms of exploitation of children. This should include introduction of strict regulatory environments for businesses, including media and other local, national, and international commercial enterprises. In accordance with Article 19 and General Comment no. 13, violence against children, protection measures shall include 'all appropriate legislative, administrative, social and educational measures' (2011, paras. 38–44).

References

Greijer, S., Doek, J., & Interagency Working Group. (2019). *Explanatory report to the guidelines regarding the implementation of the optional protocol to the convention on the rights of the child on the sale of children, child prostitution and child pornography.* Bangkok: ECPAT International. Retrieved from https://www.ecpat.org/wp-content/uploads/2019/09/OPSC-Guidelines-Explanatory-Report-ECPAT-International-2019.pdf

Hodgkin, R., Newell, P., & UNICEF. (2007). *Implementation handbook for the convention on the rights of the child* (3rd ed.). New York: UNICEF. Retrieved September 21, 2020, from https://digitallibrary.un.org/record/620060?ln=en

Office of the United Nations High Commissioner for Human Rights & Rädda barnen (Society: Sweden). (2007). *Legislative history of the convention on the rights of the child*. New York: United Nations. Retrieved from https://digitallibrary.un.org/record/602462?ln=en

Tobin, J. (2019). Article 36: Protection against all other forms of exploitation. In J. Tobin (Ed.), *The UN convention on the rights of the child: A commentary* (pp. 1420–1502). Oxford University Press.

UN Committee on the Rights of the Child. (2009). *General Comment No. 12 (2009) The right of the child to be heard, July 20, 2009, CRC/C/GC/12*. Retrieved October 12, 2020, from https://digitallibrary.un.org/record/671444?ln=en

UN Committee on the Rights of the Child. (2011). *General Comment No. 13 (2011) The right of the child to freedom from all forms of violence, April 18, 2011, CRC/C/GC/13*. Retrieved October 12, 2020, from https://digitallibrary.un.org/record/711722?ln=en

van Bueren, G. (1998). *The international law on the rights of the child*. Brill Nijhoff. Retrieved September 22, 2020, from https://brill.com/view/title/10563

Open Access This chapter is licensed under the terms of the Creative Commons Attribution 4.0 International License (http://creativecommons.org/licenses/by/4.0/), which permits use, sharing, adaptation, distribution and reproduction in any medium or format, as long as you give appropriate credit to the original author(s) and the source, provide a link to the Creative Commons license and indicate if changes were made.

The images or other third party material in this chapter are included in the chapter's Creative Commons license, unless indicated otherwise in a credit line to the material. If material is not included in the chapter's Creative Commons license and your intended use is not permitted by statutory regulation or exceeds the permitted use, you will need to obtain permission directly from the copyright holder.

Part VIII
Protection Measures for Children in Vulnerable Situations

Articles 22, 35, 38 and 40

Introduction

Children can encounter a range of challenging situations that expose them to particular risk of rights violations and which, accordingly, demand additional forms of protection. This part addresses the rights relating to four of those situations: children who are refugees or asylum seekers; children who are abducted, trafficked, or sold; children in situations of armed conflict as civilians or combatants; and children in conflict with the law. In each case, the provisions in the Convention on the Rights of the Child (the Convention) build on multiple international instruments that have been developed, since the middle of the twentieth century, to strengthen the commitment to appropriate protection for children caught in these circumstances.

Each article in this part affirms that the situation in which a child is placed does not, and cannot be used to, undermine or minimise States Parties' obligations to uphold all the rights of that child. On the contrary, their vulnerability entitles them to additional protections to guarantee their rights. Furthermore, each of these rights must be implemented within the broader context of the Convention as a whole, with particular reference to the four General Principles.

Article 22 affirms a longstanding recognition in international law that refugee children are entitled to special care and protection, building on the 1949 *Geneva Conventions* and *Refugee Convention* but providing a new, explicit human rights focus on refugee children. It captures the broad international consensus, comprising four key dimensions including protection and assistance, respect for rights, co-operation and family reunification.

Article 35, initially drafted as a generic provision to address exploitation of children, was subsequently refined to focus specifically on abduction, trafficking, and sale of children. Other forms of exploitation are addressed in Articles 34 and 36 (see Part VII). Article 35 builds on a series of previous instruments, including the 1949 Convention on the Suppression of Traffic in Persons and the Exploitation of the Prostitution of Others as well as the Convention on the Elimination of all Forms of Discrimination against Women, and has been strengthened through the Optional Protocol on Sexual Exploitation, and the 2000 Trafficking Protocol. These elaborations of the necessary protections reflect the significant increase in the scale and nature of abduction, trafficking, and sale of children since the Convention was first drafted, aided primarily by the digital environment and rapid globalisation. Article 35 introduces obligations to adopt all possible political, social, economic, and cultural measures to prevent such exploitation, as well as legislative and policy measures to criminalise, investigate, and prosecute all perpetrators of crimes of exploitation against children, nationally, regionally, and internationally.

Children and armed conflict are addressed in Article 38, which integrates both human rights and international humanitarian law. It was the provision that, during the drafting stage, generated the greatest challenge in finding a consensus. The final text reflects a compromise that afforded lower levels of protection than many members of the Working Group were seeking, particularly in its commitment only to prohibit recruitment of children into the armed forces below the age of 15 years. Overall, Article 38 requires of States Parties that they ensure compliance with international humanitarian law, protect children under the age of 15 from direct participation in hostilities, refrain from recruiting children under 15 into armed forces, and take measures to protect civilian children affected by armed conflict. The *Optional Protocol on children and armed conflict*, adopted in 2000, strengthens these provisions and, furthermore, the Committee consistently argues that States Parties should extend the age of protection for all children, including those recruited or used as combatants, to 18 years, as elaborated below.

Article 40 introduces a child rights-based approach to youth justice policy, grounded in respect for dignity, best interests, due process, minimum ages of criminal responsibility, diversion from the criminal justice system, and reintegration. It requires that States Parties establish specialised youth justice systems with a focus on rehabilitation and restorative justice rather than retribution and repression.

Chapter 36
Article 22: The Right to Protection for Refugee and Asylum-Seeking Children

Christian Whalen

1. State Parties shall take appropriate measures to ensure that a child who is seeking refugee status or who is considered a refugee in accordance with applicable international or domestic law and procedures shall, whether unaccompanied or accompanied by his or her parents or by any other person, receive appropriate protection and humanitarian assistance in the enjoyment of applicable rights set forth in the present Convention and in other international human rights or humanitarian instruments to which the said States are Parties.
2. For this purpose, States Parties shall provide, as they consider appropriate, co-operation in any efforts by the United Nations and other competent intergovernmental organizations or non-governmental organizations co-operating with the United Nations to protect and assist such a child and to trace the parents or other members of the family of any refugee child in order to obtain information necessary for reunification with his or her family. In cases where no parents or other members of the family can be found, the child shall be accorded the same protection as any other child permanently or temporarily deprived of his or her family environment for any reason, as set forth in the present Convention.

C. Whalen (✉)
Office of the Child, Youth and Seniors Advocate, Fredericton, NB, Canada
e-mail: Christian.Whalen@gnb.ca

What Did Children Say?
'Provide good nutrition for refugees especially children to ensure their growth.' *(Africa)*.

'Government should provide shelters or housing for refugees' and 'Equal education, health care, etc., for refugees as for other children.' *(Latin America/Caribbean)*.

Give assistance to refugees' parents so that they can improve their financial situation to take care of their children. *(Africa)*.

'Government should have support for children and their families affected by displacement or during migration as refugees, to provide them all necessaries as required by the UN Code of conduct.' *Africa)*.

Overview

Article 22 came about in the drafting of the Convention at a time when international law started to distinguish between refugee children and adult refugees (UNHCR, Notification to Executive Committee on Refugee Children, cited in Vučković-Šahović et al., 2012, pp. 231–232). Consensus on the text of Article 22 was found relatively rapidly following Denmark's initial proposal in 1981, and the provision was reworked into its final form in the 1989 Working Group (Detrick et al. 1992, pp. 319–329). The provision captures the broad international consensus that:

- refugee children are owed appropriate protection and humanitarian assistance
- all their rights under the Convention as well as under other international human rights treaties and humanitarian law must be upheld
- States Parties must cooperate with the UN and related agencies to protect and assist such children
- family reunification is a priority obligation of governments serving the best interests of refugee children, having particular regard for unaccompanied and separated children.

Article 22 therefore guarantees the substantive application of all Convention rights to the particular situation of asylum seeking and refugee children, and also guarantees them protection and assistance in advancing their immigration and residency status claims and in overcoming the hurdles posed by international migration channels, including guarantees of due process (Ceriani Cerandas, 2015, p. 342). The particular concern for unaccompanied migrants and tracing and reuniting them with their parents is reinforced by Articles 9 and 10, and other provisions of the Convention and its protocols, including Articles 38 and 39 and the Optional Protocol on children and armed conflict.

Further to General Comment no. 6, on the Treatment of Unaccompanied and Separated Children Outside their Country of Origin, the Committee on the Rights of the Child (the Committee) revisited this topic in a Day of General Discussion in 2012, which informed two joint General Comments with the Committee of the International Convention on the Protection of the Rights of All Migrant Workers and Members of Their Families. General Comment no. 22 deals with the General Principles regarding the human rights of children in the context of international migration (UN Committee on the Protection of the Rights of All Migrant Workers and Members of Their Families and UN Committee on the Rights of the Child, 2017a) and General Comment no. 23 deals with States Parties obligations regarding the human rights of children in the context of international migration in countries of origin, transit, destination and return (UN Committee on the Protection of the Rights of All Migrant Workers and Members of Their Families and UN Committee on the Rights of the Child, 2017b). These new statements of the law reinforce how all the rights of the child must be upheld for migrant children at every stage of the migration journeys and that all decisions affecting them must be informed by the child's voice and determined in accordance with their best interests.

Article 22's focus on appropriate protection and humanitarian assistance to refugee children and children seeking refugee status is inherently tied to respect for children's rights both in the country of origin and in the country of refuge. It is often a violation of the core principles of child rights that may force children and their parents to flee persecution and it is all too often the denial of these same rights in the country of refuge that inform child rights claims in relation to Article 22 (Ceriani Cerandas, 2015, p. 338).

While the framing of Article 22 limits its application to the context of international migration by asylum seeking and refugee children (UNICEF, 2007, p. 311), the Committee has urged States Parties to provide assistance and protection to internally displaced children (2000, paras. 57, 68, 2006a, paras. 78, 79), consistent with the particular needs of these children as outlined by the UN in its *Guiding Principles on Internal Displacement* (Deng et al., 2004). Similarly, the Committee has expressed concern regarding States Parties' failures to take account of the particular needs of children as economic migrants (2006b, paras. 68, 69), even though they may have no particular claim to protection as refugees fleeing persecution within the meaning of the 1951 Refugee Convention or Article 22.

General Principles

Article 2 Refugee children or their parents are often forced into migration by patterns of discrimination, for example on the basis of ethnic or religious affiliation, language, or sexual orientation. All asylum seeking and refugee children are already at a disadvantage in relation to their peers and that very status attracts the protection of Article 2's non-discrimination principle (UN Committee on the Rights of the Child, 2005a, para. 18). Certain classes of marginalised children are at particular risk in migration contexts, for example disabled children, children of minorities, indigenous children, LBGTQ youth, and current and former child soldiers. States Parties must take positive measures to ensure de facto equality of migrant children in host societies as well as in the case of children returned to their country of origin (UN Committee on the Protection of the Rights of All Migrant Workers and Members of Their Families and UN Committee on the Rights of the Child, 2017a, paras. 21–26).

Article 3 The overarching consideration in implementation of child refugee claims under Article 22 will always be the best interests of the individual child or children in the case (Ceriani Cerandas, 2015, p. 339; Vučković-Šahović et al., 2012, p. 332). This basic principle must be respected during all stages of the displacement cycle, and decisions at any of these stages must be appropriately documented through a formal and rigorous best interests determination (UN Committee on the Protection of the Rights of All Migrant Workers and Members of Their Families and UN Committee on the Rights of the Child, 2017a, paras. 27–33; UN Committee on the Rights of the Child, 2005a, paras. 19–22). The Committee has emphasised in particular that 'the best interests of the child should be ensured explicitly through individual procedures as an integral part of any administrative or judicial decision concerning the entry, residence or return of a child, placement or care of a child, or the detention or expulsion of a parent associated with their own migration status' (UN Committee on the Protection of the Rights of All Migrant Workers and Members of Their Families and UN Committee on the Rights of the Child, 2017a, paras. 27–33; UN Committee on the Rights of the Child, 2005a, paras. 19–22).

Article 6 The protection of child rights in many states is at its weakest in immigration contexts (Harris et al., 2009; van Bueren, 2007, p. 123; Vučković-Šahović et al., 2012, pp. 165–170), and it is often the denial of the child's right to maximum survival and development that is the major root cause of migration (legal and illegal) of children, adolescents, and their parents (Ceriani Cerandas, 2015, p. 338) This underscores the importance of appropriate safeguarding of Article 6 rights in addressing the root causes of mass migrations of children and families the world over. At the same time, children in transit engage in threatening and extremely dangerous migration journeys and States Parties have obligations to take special measures to protect and assist children. Immigration policies should focus on facilitating and regulating mobility rights rather than on repressive detention and deportation practices, so as to advance Article 6 rights and not violate them (UN Committee on the Protection of the Rights of All Migrant Workers and Members of Their Families and UN Committee on the Rights of the Child, 2017a, paras. 40–44). The child's right to optimum development also must inform Article 22 rights in relation to immigration policy affecting the deportation or detention of a child's parent (UN Committee on the Protection of the Rights of All Migrant Workers and Members of Their Families and UN Committee on the Rights of the Child, 2017a, para. 44).

Article 12 Children in migration contexts are vulnerable in relation to their participation rights. They are regularly denied standing and treated as mere dependents of adult asylum seekers. The Committee, in its Joint General Comment no. 22, strongly reinforces the States Parties' obligation to ensure child participation in immigration matters affecting both children and their parents, as their best interests will be in play in both instances and children often have 'their own migration projects and migration-driving factors' (UN Committee on the Protection of the Rights of All Migrant Workers and Members of Their Families and UN Committee on the Rights of the Child, 2017a, paras. 34–39).

Articles Related or Linked to Article 22

Article 7 proclaims the child's right to a name and nationality and to be cared for by his or her parents, both aspects of which come into play in every child migration journey.

Article 8 protects children's right to preserve their name, nationality, identity, and family relations and to be reconnected with family if these relations are disrupted, as may happen during migration.

Article 9 establishes the right to not be separated from one's parents unless it is necessary in one's best interests as determined by competent authorities and therefore intersects with the family reunification principle in Article 22.

Article 10 establishes the child's right to family reunification, to be dealt with in a positive, humane, and expeditious manner, a right which will almost invariably be read jointly with Article 22.

Article 11 establishes the child's right to be protected from international abduction, another situation which will attract scrutiny in relation to Article 22.

Article 16 affirms the child's right to privacy and the inviolability of his or her family life, rights which are often jeopardised during child migration journeys.

Article 20 establishes the child's right to alternative care if deprived of his or her family, as may happen as a result of immigration detention practices.

Article 21 elaborates the child's rights in relation to adoption, rights which are not diminished by a child's migrant status.

Article 35 establishes the child's right to be protected from abduction, sale, or trafficking which may intersect with Article 22 rights in relation to international trafficking.

Article 37 establishes protection of children from deprivation of liberty, except as a measure of last resort, including in relation to immigration processes where detention of children should be strictly avoided.

Article 38 asserts the child's right to protection from early enlistment, and these rights may intersect with Article 22 rights of children whose migration journeys cross conflict zones.

Article 39 establishes the right to recovery and reintegration for child victims of neglect, exploitation, abuse, torture, cruel treatment, or armed conflict, and migrant children may be at higher risk of abuse and their rights to recovery and rehabilitation should not be overlooked.

Optional Protocol on the involvement of children in armed conflict.

Optional Protocol on the sale of children, child prostitution and child pornography.

Relevant Instruments

UN Convention Relating to the Status of Refugees (1951).
   UN Convention relating to the Status of Stateless Persons (1954).
   UN Convention on the Reduction of Statelessness (1961).
   International Covenant on Civil and Political Rights (1966), Articles 12 and 13.
   UN Protocol Relating to the Status of Refugees (1967).
   UN Convention against Torture and Other Cruel, Inhuman or Degrading Treatment or Punishment (1984).
   UNHCR Refugee Children: Guidelines on Protection and Care (1994).
   UN Protocol to Prevent, Suppress and Punish Trafficking in Persons Especially Women and Children, supplementing the United Nations Convention against Transnational Organized Crime (2000).
   UNHCR Inter-agency Guiding Principles on Unaccompanied and Separated Children (2004).
   UNHCR Guidelines on International Protection No. 8: Child Asylum Claims under Articles 1(A)2 and 1(F) of the 1951 Convention and/or 1967 Protocol relating to the Status of Refugees (2009).
   The Geneva convention for the amelioration of the condition of the wounded and sick in armed forces in the field (1949), and their Protocols I and II.
   Hague Convention on Protection of Children and Co-operation in Respect of Intercountry Adoption (1993).
   European Convention on Human Rights (1950), Protocols 4 and 7 on non-expulsion of nationals and foreigners.
   American Convention on Human Rights 'Pact of San Jose, Costa Rica' (B-32) (1978), Article 22, Freedom of Movement and Residence.
   African Charter on Human and Peoples' Rights (1981), Article 12, Freedom of Movement and Residence.
   African Charter on the Rights and Welfare of the Child (1990), Article 23, appropriate protection and humanitarian assistance for Refugee Children.

Attributes

Attribute One: Appropriate Protection and Humanitarian Assistance

The first attribute guarantees to asylum seeking and refugee children the same substantive rights as are guaranteed to all children. This is the meaning of 'appropriate protection' as opposed to 'special protection' as first proposed in the *Travaux Préparatoires* (UNICEF, 2007, p. 306). Refugee children are not granted a special status under the Convention, but they are not given any lesser status. They are to be treated as children first and foremost and not as migrants per se (Ceriani Cerandas, 2015, p. 339), in the sense that national immigration policy cannot trump child rights. The basic rights to education, health, and child welfare of these children needs to be protected to the same extent, and as much as possible, as children who are nationals of the host country (Ceriani Cerandas, 2015, p. 339). The criterion of humanitarian assistance amplifies the concept of appropriate protection. For example, in addition to mainstreaming refugee children in regular school classrooms, they may need therapy to assist with their recovery from traumatic journeys and successful integration into a new host culture (UNICEF, 2007, p. 306; UN Committee on the Rights of the Child, 2005b, para. 42). Humanitarian assistance should avoid discriminatory consequences as between categories of entrants in family reunification cases (UN Committee on the Rights of the Child, 2005c, paras. 63, 64); it should avoid detention of children for immigration purposes (UN Committee on the Rights of the Child, 2005a, paras. 61–63) and possibly also of their parents (Ceriani Cerandas, 2015, pp. 347–348); it should help defend the principle of non-deportation of children (Ceriani Cerandas, 2015, pp. 342–343); and reinforce the child's right to preserve his or her family life (Ceriani Cerandas, 2015, pp. 348–349; UN Committee on the Rights of the Child, 2005a, paras. 82, 83).

Attribute Two: Preservation of Rights

The second attribute preserves the rights of refugee children not only under the Convention but under all other international human right treaties and humanitarian instruments binding on the relevant States Party. These may include, for many governments, the 1951 *Refugee Convention*, the *Convention on the Reduction of Statelessness*, the *Geneva Conventions* and the *Hague Convention for the Protection of Minors*, 1961, among others. Careful consideration must be given in interpreting and determining claims in relation to Article 22 to the many other public and private international law provisions that may bear on the child's status.

The United Nations High Commissioner for Refugees has published guidelines in relation to child asylum claims that adapt the fear of persecution standard under the 1951 *Refugee Convention* and/or its 1967 Protocol to:

- the specific rights of children, for instance under Articles 9, 19, 24, 27, 37, or 38
- the manner in which children experience persecution differently than adults and may be more susceptible due to their level of maturity, vulnerability, dependency or limited coping mechanisms
- child-specific forms of persecution which must be considered separately from forms of persecution to which adults may or may not also be open, and which include underage recruitment into armed forces, child trafficking, female genital

mutilation, forced or underage marriage, hazardous child labour, forced prostitution, family and domestic violence, and child pornography (UN High Commissioner for Refugees, 2009, paras. 13–18).[1]

With respect to unaccompanied and separated children, the Inter-agency Guiding Principles on Unaccompanied and Separated Children are especially helpful in clarifying priority focus areas for intervening effectively with these vulnerable youth, but they should not be interpreted as minimum standards or used to read down any of the rights of unaccompanied minors under the Convention. More recently, the Office of the High Commissioner for Human Rights developed *The Principles and practical guidance on the protection of the human rights of migrants in vulnerable situations*. It provides specific child protection measures for unaccompanied and separated children who do not qualify for international protection as refugees and who may need assistance, regardless of their status, and giving primary consideration at all times to the best interests of the child (UN High Commissioner for Human Rights and Global Migration Group, 2018).

Attribute Three: Duty to Protect and Assist at National and International Level

The obligation to protect and assist contains a clear duty to provide children with appropriate due process rights throughout the several stages of their asylum and refugee claims procedures. These would include the child's right to be heard and participate in all the processes determining the child's residence or immigration status, including border admission, deportation, repatriation, detention, alternative measures, or placement, including best interest determination processes. It would also include the child's right to an interpreter, a legal representative, and to a guardian. Interviews and hearings should be conducted in a child-friendly manner and should include similarly child-friendly appeal mechanisms (Vučković-Šahović et al., 2012, p. 233). Legal aid should be provided freely to child asylum seekers by lawyers trained in child rights and accustomed to working in culturally sensitive multidisciplinary teams involving psychologists, social workers and trauma-informed care providers (Ceriani Cerandas, 2015, p. 347).

States Parties' also have obligations to protect and assist asylum seeking and refugee children in cooperation with UN agencies and other international organisations. From the outset, the framers of the Convention recognised the pivotal role played in this field by the High Commissioner for Refugees, as well as by the several organisations involved in the development of the *Inter-agency Guiding Principles*, such as the Red Cross, Save the Children, UNICEF, and World Vision. This

---

[1] With reference to the relationship between the Convention and the larger system of provisions on refugee protection, see also 'Article 22: Refugee Children' (Pobjoy, 2019, pp. 822–824).

cooperation, including with the International Organization for Migration, is particularly important in tracing family members, promoting family reunification, and monitoring child migration patterns.

Attribute Four: Best Interests and Family Reunification Principles

Finally, two basic principles should guide each activity with the refugee child: the best interests of the child and the principle of family unity (Vučković-Šahović et al., 2012, p. 232). After extensive field testing, the Commissioner for Refugees adopted, in May 2008, its *Guidelines on Determining the Best Interests of the Child* (United Nations High Commissioner for Refugees, 2008). While they are only one reference tool in the practitioners' toolkit, they have helped standardise and provide practical guidance in operationalising the best interests principle in child refugee determination processes in many states (Ceriani Cerandas, 2015, p. 342). Best interests procedures require a holistic child rights-based approach child refugee determination processes that factors in human and budget resources, training in children's rights and inter-institutional coordination, drawing upon the cooperation and evidence available from countries of origin, transit, and destination (Ceriani Cerandas, 2015, p. 342).

Family reunification has to comply with the principle of non-refoulement: a child cannot be returned to a country where there are substantial grounds for believing that there is a real risk of irreparable harm to the child, either in the country to which removal is to be effected or in any country to which the child may subsequently be removed (UN Committee on the Rights of the Child, 2005a, para. 27). Family reunification should be based on a robust assessment of upholding the child's best interests as a primary consideration and should not be delayed because of a best interests procedure, considering family reunification as one aspect, not the sole aspect, and with a sustainable reintegration plan and after guaranteeing the child's right to participate in the process (UN Committee on the Rights of the Child, 2005a, paras. 79–83).

References

Ceriani Cerandas, P. (2015). The human rights of children in the context of international migration. In *Routledge international handbook of Children's rights studies* (pp. 331–356). Routledge.

Deng, F. M., UN Representative of the Secretary-General on Internally Displaced Persons, & UN Office for the Coordination of Humanitarian Affairs (OCHA). (2004). *Guiding Principles on Internal Displacement, [ST/]OCHA/IDP/2004/1 (E/CN.4/1998/53/Add.2)*. UN, OCHA. Retrieved November 29, 2020, from https://www.unhcr.org/protection/idps/43ce1cff2/guiding-principles-internal-displacement.html

Detrick, S., Doek, J. E., & Cantwell, N. (1992). *The United Nations convention on the rights of the child: A guide to the "Travaux Préparatoires"*. Martinus Nijhoff Publishers.

Harris, D., O'Boyle, M., Bates, E., & Buckley, C. (2009). *Harris, O'Boyle & Warbrick: Law of the European convention on human rights* (2nd ed.). OUP Oxford.

Pobjoy, J. M. (2019). Article 22: Refugee children. In J. Tobin (Ed.), *The UN convention on the rights of the child: A commentary* (pp. 818–855). Oxford University Press.

UN Committee on the Protection of the Rights of All Migrant Workers and Members of Their Families & UN Committee on the Rights of the Child. (2017a). *Joint General Comment No. 3 (2017) of the Committee on the Protection of the Rights of All Migrant Workers and Members of Their Families and No. 22 (2017) of the Committee on the Rights of the Child on the general principles regarding the human rights of children in the context of international migration, CMW/C/GC/3, CRC/C/GC/22*. UN. Retrieved November 6, 2020, from http://digitallibrary.un.org/record/1323014

UN Committee on the Protection of the Rights of All Migrant Workers and Members of Their Families & UN Committee on the Rights of the Child. (2017b). *Joint General Comment No. 23 (2017) on State obligations regarding the human rights of children in the context of international migration in countries of origin, transit, destination and return, November 16, 2017, CMW/C/GC/4, CRC/C/GC/23*. Retrieved October 12, 2020, from https://digitallibrary.un.org/record/1323015?ln=en

UN Committee on the Rights of the Child. (2000). *Concluding observations: Burundi, October 16, 2000, CRC/C/15/Add.133*. Retrieved October 11, 2020, from https://digitallibrary.un.org/record/429241?ln=en

UN Committee on the Rights of the Child. (2005a). *General Comment No. 6 (2005) Treatment of Unaccompanied and Separated Children Outside their Country of Origin, September 1, 2005, CRC/GC/2005/6*. Retrieved October 12, 2020, from https://digitallibrary.un.org/record/566055?ln=en

UN Committee on the Rights of the Child. (2005b). *Concluding observations: Norway, September 21, 2005, CRC/C/15/Add.263*. Retrieved October 23, 2020, from https://digitallibrary.un.org/record/569887?ln=en

UN Committee on the Rights of the Child. (2005c). *Concluding observations: Australia, October 20, 2005, CRC/C/15/Add.268*. UN. Retrieve October 26, 2020, from http://digitallibrary.un.org/record/569889

UN Committee on the Rights of the Child. (2006a). *Concluding observations: Colombia, June 8, 2006, CRC/C/COL/CO/3*. UN. http://digitallibrary.un.org/record/582283. Accessed 15 November 2020.

UN Committee on the Rights of the Child. (2006b, March 17). *Concluding observations: Thailand, CRC/C/THA/CO/2*. UN. Retrieved November 18, 2020, from http://digitallibrary.un.org/record/575783

UN High Commissioner for Human Rights & Global Migration Group. (2018). *Principles and practical guidance on the protection of the human rights of migrants in vulnerable situations, A/HRC/37/34/Add.1*. UN. Retrieved November 29, 2020, from http://digitallibrary.un.org/record/1472491

UN High Commissioner for Refugees. (2009). *UNHCR Guidelines on International Protection No. 8: Child Asylum Claims under Articles 1(A)2 and 1(F) of the 1951 Convention and/or 1967 Protocol relating to the Status of Refugees, 22 December 2009*. Retrieved November 29, 2020, from https://www.unhcr.org/publications/legal/50ae46309/guidelines-international-protection-8-child-asylum-claims-under-articles.html

UNICEF. (2007). *Implementation handbook for the convention on the rights of the child* (3rd ed.). New York: UNICEF. Retrieved September 21, 2020, from https://digitallibrary.un.org/record/620060?ln=en

United Nations High Commissioner for Refugees. (2008). *UNHCR guidelines on determining the best interests of the child*. Geneva. Retrieved November 29, 2020, from https://www.unhcr.org/protection/children/4566b16b2/unhcr-guidelines-determining-best-interests-child.html

van Bueren, G. (2007). *Child rights in Europe: Convergence and divergence in judicial protection*. Council of Europe Pub.

Vučković-Šahović, N., Doek, J. E., & Zermatten, J. (2012). *The rights of the child in international law: Rights of the child in a nutshell and in context: All about children's rights*. Stämpfli.

Open Access This chapter is licensed under the terms of the Creative Commons Attribution 4.0 International License (http://creativecommons.org/licenses/by/4.0/), which permits use, sharing, adaptation, distribution and reproduction in any medium or format, as long as you give appropriate credit to the original author(s) and the source, provide a link to the Creative Commons license and indicate if changes were made.

The images or other third party material in this chapter are included in the chapter's Creative Commons license, unless indicated otherwise in a credit line to the material. If material is not included in the chapter's Creative Commons license and your intended use is not permitted by statutory regulation or exceeds the permitted use, you will need to obtain permission directly from the copyright holder.

Chapter 37
Article 35: Prevention of Abduction, Sale, and Trafficking

Adem Arkadas-Thibert and Gerison Lansdown

> States Parties shall take all appropriate national, bilateral and multilateral measures to prevent the abduction of, the sale of or traffic in children for any purpose or in any form.

> **What Did Children Say?**
> 'There should be strong laws against child abduction and trafficking made by the government to protect the interest of children.' (Africa).
> For every child crossing the border, the state must create an administrative document for the consent of the child and his or her parents and caregivers. (Africa).
> Governments should train special formidable force in executing duties in rescuing and rehabilitation of victims and prosecuting perpetrator. (Africa).
> 'Is government encouraging children to speak up about issues?' (Latin America/Caribbean).

A. Arkadas-Thibert (✉)
Marseille, France

G. Lansdown
Carleton University, Ottawa, ON, Canada

Overview

Protection from many forms of exploitation of children, such as intercountry parental abduction, adoption for profit, forced labour, sexual exploitation, and military recruitment, are covered under the Convention. Article 35 adds an extra layer of protection, reinforcing States Parties' obligation to have preventive measures against acts of abduction, traffic, or sale of children, not only across borders but also within their jurisdiction. It recognises that States Parties have wide-ranging national, bilateral, and multilateral obligations of prevention of all acts that render the child into some form of commodity. Therefore, it serves as a supplementary layer of protection for children from commercial exploitation.

Since the Convention was drafted, awareness of all forms of trafficking has become much better understood, while the emergence of the digital environment has exposed children to significantly greater risks in this regard. The Committee, for example, has noted that the globalised online and increasingly mobile world opens up new ways to connect with, solicit, and groom children, as well as viewing online child sexual abuse via live video streaming, distributing child sexual abuse material, and engaging in the sale and sexual exploitation of children in the context of travel and tourism (2019, paras. 2–3). In recognition of the need to strengthen protection of children, in 2000, the Committee published the *Optional Protocol to the Convention on the Rights of the Child on the sale of children, child prostitution and child pornography*, and in 2019, developed guidelines to enable more effective implementation (2019).

The *Travaux Préparatoires* of the Convention reveal that it was first suggested to have one composite article combining Articles 34 (commercial sexual exploitation of children), 35, and 36 (all other forms of exploitation) to cover sexual and other related forms of exploitation. However, drafting delegates opted for separate articles to provide a wider and fail-safe protection for children as the sale or traffic of children was wider in scope than that of sexual exploitation (Office of the United Nations High Commissioner for Human Rights and Rädda barnen (Society: Sweden), 2007, pp. 723–737). Neither the *Travaux Préparatoires* nor Article 35 provide definitions for abduction of, sale of, or trafficking in children. It has, however, been addressed in multiple subsequent international instruments and it is to these other instruments that one can turn for more specific definitions.

Abduction means the removal or the retention of a child in breach of rights of custody internationally and within the borders of the States Party.[1] In the context of Article 35, this means any non-familial abductions, as abductions between family members would fall under Article 11 (Gallagher, 2019, p. 1362).

Sale of children means 'any act or transaction whereby a child is transferred by any person or group of persons to another for remuneration or any other consideration.' This definition, from the Optional Protocol on the sale of children, child

---

[1] See the full definition in the *Convention on the Civil Aspects of International Child Abduction*, Article 3.

prostitution and child pornography, Article 2, clearly interprets sale of children as being a form of exploitation. The Committee has recognised that the sale of children can be not only for sexual exploitation, but also, for example, for the purposes of transfer of organs, engagement in forced labour, and situations in which adoption constitutes the sale of children (UN Committee on the Rights of the Child, 2019, para. 14).

Trafficking in persons means the recruitment, transportation, transfer, harbouring, or receipt of persons, by means of the threat or use of force or other forms of coercion, of abduction, of fraud, of deception, of the abuse of power or of a position of vulnerability, or of the giving or receiving of payments or benefits to achieve the consent of a person having control over another person, for the purpose of exploitation. 'Exploitation shall include, at a minimum, the exploitation of the prostitution of others or other forms of sexual exploitation, forced labour or services, slavery or practices similar to slavery, servitude or the removal of organs.' This definition, from the *Protocol to Prevent, Suppress and Punish Trafficking in Persons, Especially Women and Children, supplementing the United Nations Convention against Transnational Organized Crime, Article 3*, has been recognised by the Committee and it has acknowledged a number of practices as falling within the scope of Article 35, including sexual exploitation, forced and exploitative labour, begging, forced and temporary marriage, and domestic servitude. Three aspects (action, means, and purpose) must be involved to constitute trafficking (Gallagher, 2019, p. 1364).

In addition, the United Nations Working Group on Contemporary Forms of Slavery has recognised forced marriage as a form of contemporary slavery, trafficking, and sexual exploitation (UN Working Group on Contemporary Forms of Slavery, 2003). The *African Charter on the Rights and Welfare of the Child* includes the use of children in all forms of begging in Article 29(b). This is a form of exploitation not mentioned in other human rights treaties.

The Committee has noted that abduction, trafficking, and sale of children are linked yet distinct phenomena, but States Parties largely concentrate on trafficking in children to deal with these three different forms of commercial exploitation. This creates a gap in collection of data and subsequent knowledge for States Parties to introduce relevant and targeted measures of prevention (Giammarinaro et al., 2017, para. 16).

General Principles

Article 2 Every child has the right to be protected from abduction, trafficking, or sale. Certain groups of children are more at risk than adults and/or other children, for example, children of minority gender or sex identities and orientations, children with disabilities, children in institutions, migrant children, children in street situations, and children in other vulnerable or marginalised situations (UN Committee on the Rights of the Child, 2019, para. 13). The Committee has highlighted the gender dimension of such offences against children and noted that although most victims are girls, boys are also vulnerable. Despite this, very few support structures for boys are in place (2019, para. 4). States Parties must introduce measures to identify, prevent and protect all such children from abduction, sale, or trafficking.

Article 3 Children's current and future safety is one of the fundamental tenets of the child's best interests (UN Committee on the Rights of the Child, 2013). Effective preventive and protective measures for children must be taken to guarantee the best interest of the child. In particular, in criminal justice systems, the best interests of the child who is a victim of crimes of abduction, sale, or trafficking must be the primary consideration (UN General Assembly, 2001, Article 8, para. 3). This includes decriminalisation of children involved as victims or used as instruments in such crimes.

Article 6 All forms of exploitation of children constitute a threat to the fulfilment of their right to life, survival, and development (UN Committee on the Rights of the Child, 2011, para. 15).

Article 12 Children, including 'child victims of physical or psychological violence, sexual abuse or other crimes,' have the right to be heard in any judicial proceedings, as victims or subjects, and administrative proceedings, as agents to shape policies and actions (UN Committee on the Rights of the Child, 2009, paras. 32, 118–121). Children have rights to access information, including life skills and the knowledge to protect themselves from exploitation, and seek assistance and justice whenever needed. States Parties should seek to include children in the processes of both drafting and implementing legislative and policy measures. Consultations with children must be carried out in an age-appropriate and gender-sensitive manner by adults with the necessary training and resources (UN Committee on the Rights of the Child, 2019, para. 12).

Articles Related or Linked to Article 35

Article 11 addresses measures to deal with international abductions between family members.

Article 21 protects children from sale in the form of international adoption for the purposes of financial gain.

Article 24(3) requires States Parties to take measures to effectively abolish traditional practices, such as child marriage, as a form of sale of or traffic in children, which are detrimental to the rights and well-being of children.

Article 26 requires States Parties to provide children with available, accessible, and quality social security in accordance with their circumstances and their care providers' resources, and in so doing reduces the child's risk of being in a position of exploitation.

Article 27 requires States Parties to provide the child with adequate living conditions for their physical, mental, spiritual, moral, and social development. This serves as a preventive and protective measure from abduction, sale, or traffic in children.

Article 32 protects children against trafficking, forced labour, and slavery-like working conditions.

Article 33 protects from the use of children in crimes of illicit substance trafficking.

Article 34 protects from children's use in the sex trade, in prostitution, in the production of pornography, or through forced marriages.

Article 36 protects from all other forms of exploitation, including those involving information and communication technologies.

Article 38 protects children in conditions of war, where children can be forced to become soldiers or servants to armed forces.

Article 39 requires States Parties to provide the child who is exposed to abduction, sale, or trafficking with physical and psychological recovery and social reintegration.

Optional Protocol to the Convention on the Rights of the Child on the involvement of children in armed conflict, esp. Article 3 (2000).

Optional Protocol to the Convention on the Rights of the Child on the sale of children, child prostitution and child pornography (2000).

Relevant Instruments

UN Protocol to Prevent, Suppress and Punish Trafficking in Persons Especially Women and Children, supplementing the United Nations Convention against Transnational Organized Crime (2000).

Hague Convention on the Civil Aspects of International Child Abduction (1980).

Hague Convention on Protection of Children and Co-operation in Respect of Intercountry Adoption (1993), especially Article 1.

ILO Convention 182, Worst Forms of Child Labour (1999), especially Article 3.

American Convention on Human Rights 'Pact of San Jose, Costa Rica' (B-32) (1978), Articles 6 and 19.

African Charter on Human and Peoples' Rights (1981), especially Article 5.

African Charter on the Rights and Welfare of the Child (1990), Article 29.

Inter-American Convention on International Traffic in Minors (1994).

Attributes

Attribute One: National, Bilateral, and Multilateral Measures to Prevent Abduction, Traffic, and Sale of Children

Article 35 provides that States Parties must set up preventive measures to remove risk factors of abduction, traffic, and sale of children, including through national, bilateral, and multilateral level agreements, in order to address the phenomenon both within and beyond the states' borders. Such agreements should involve state agencies, law enforcement actors, judicial authorities, and other relevant stakeholders.

The obligation to prevent abduction, traffic, and sale of children requires that measures are undertaken to identify those groups of children likely to be vulnerable, as well as addressing the political, social, economic, and cultural root causes of that vulnerability. States Parties should provide information and awareness raising of the risks for parents, teachers, and other professionals, mandatory education in schools on how children can keep safe and protect themselves, including online, and effective measures for safe reporting and effective and prompt responses to any reports of such harm (UN Committee on the Rights of the Child, 2019, paras. 37–40).

Access to legal documentation such as birth certificates, to equality education, and strategies to address the particular vulnerabilities of some groups can also serve to protect children. States Parties must adopt measures to address both employer and consumer demand for cheap labour and goods (Gallagher, 2019, p. 1394). Finally, they must undertake regular monitoring and sharing of information about the state of children who are exposed to abduction, sale, or trafficking locally, nationally, and regionally, together with provision of data or supporting research on the issues concerned, and introduce international and national strategies and plans of action to eradicate them.

Attribute Two: Establishing a Protective Legal and Policy Framework

Article 35 requires States Parties to introduce deterrent, preventive, and reactive legislation and policies, including criminalising trafficking and related offences, together with appropriate sanctions, as well as establishing effective mechanisms of investigation and prosecution for the abduction, traffic, or sale of children. The Committee has emphasised the importance of appropriately trained law enforcement officials for dealing with trafficking in children (2012a, para. 82, 2012b, para. 64). The rules for criminal jurisdiction must ensure that perpetrators can be punished wherever the offences take place, as required in the *Optional Protocol on the sale of children, child prostitution and child pornography* (UN Committee on the Rights of the Child, 2019, pp. 80–89).

Prevention efforts, including legislation, must recognise that children exposed to abduction, sale, and trafficking are victims, not criminals. The Committee, for example, has emphasised that victims of trafficking must not be criminalised solely for reasons of their illegal entry or presence in the country' (2005, para. 62, 2010, para. 75, 2016, para. 64 (c)). Where children who are victims of trafficking are subsequently detained for the purposes of safeguarding and protection of their rights, the conditions under which they are cared for must be governed by their best interests and take account of their vulnerability to abuse, victimisation, and further violation of their rights (Gallagher, 2019, p. 1383).

In any criminal proceedings, child victims must be provided with legal representation and counselling, interviews must be held without delay and in a child-friendly environment, and the child's privacy and safety must be protected at all times. Any decision concerning repatriation should take account of the child's safety, availability of care, the child's views, duration of absence from the home country, and the child's right to preservation of identity (UN Committee on the Rights of the Child, 2005, para. 84).

Attribute Three: Protection of Survivors/Victims of Abduction, Sale and Trafficking

The priority in respect of Article 35 must be to protect children's human dignity and their rights. As enshrined in Article 39 of the Convention, States Parties must take all appropriate measures to promote the recovery and social reintegration of child victims (Hodgkin et al., 2007, p. 538). Article 35 also implies that States Parties must ensure that survivors or victims of the abduction, traffic, or sale are identified, protected, and supported. A comprehensive range of measures are recommended in Article 8 of the *Optional Protocol on the sale of children, child prostitution and child pornography*, as well as Articles 6 through 8 of the *Protocol to Prevent, Suppress and Punish Trafficking in Persons, Especially Women and Children*, and further elaborated in the Committee Guidelines to the Optional Protocol. The articles include measures to ensure privacy and confidentiality, physical safety and protection from further harm, access to information, access to justice, being heard effectively, support for recovery, medical, physical and psychological assistance, compensation, and opportunities for repatriation where appropriate.

References

Gallagher, A. (2019). Article 35: Protection against the abduction, traffic and Sale of children. In J. Tobin (Ed.), *The UN convention on the rights of the child: A commentary* (pp. 1356–1401). Oxford University Press.

Giammarinaro, M. G., Buquicchio-de Boer, M., & UN Secretary General. (2017). *Joint report of the Special Rapporteur on the Sale and sexual exploitation of children, including child prostitution, child pornography and other child sexual abuse material; and trafficking in persons, especially women and children. A/72/164*. UN. Retrieved November 29, 2020, from http://digitallibrary.un.org/record/1300900

Hodgkin, R., Newell, P., & UNICEF. (2007). *Implementation handbook for the convention on the rights of the child* (3rd ed.). New York: UNICEF. Retrieved September 21, 2020, from https://digitallibrary.un.org/record/620060?ln=en

Office of the United Nations High Commissioner for Human Rights & Rädda barnen (Society: Sweden). (2007). *Legislative history of the convention on the rights of the child*. New York: United Nations. Retrieved from https://digitallibrary.un.org/record/602462?ln=en

UN Committee on the Rights of the Child. (2005). *General Comment No. 6 (2005) Treatment of Unaccompanied and Separated Children Outside their Country of Origin, September 1, 2005, CRC/GC/2005/6*. Retrieved October 12, 2020, from https://digitallibrary.un.org/record/566055?ln=en

UN Committee on the Rights of the Child. (2009). *General Comment No. 12 (2009) The right of the child to be heard, July 20, 2009, CRC/C/GC/12*. Retrieved October 12, 2020 from https://digitallibrary.un.org/record/671444?ln=en

UN Committee on the Rights of the Child. (2010). *Concluding observations: Argentina, June 21, 2010, CRC/C/ARG/CO/3-4. UN*. Retrieved November 29, 2020, from http://digitallibrary.un.org/record/684966

UN Committee on the Rights of the Child. (2011). *General Comment No. 13 (2011) The right of the child to freedom from all forms of violence, April 18, 2011, CRC/C/GC/13*. Retrieved October 12, 2020, from https://digitallibrary.un.org/record/711722?ln=en

UN Committee on the Rights of the Child. (2012a). *Concluding observations: Canada, December 6, 2012, CRC/C/CAN/CO/3-4*. Retrieved October 11, 2020, from https://digitallibrary.un.org/record/739319?ln=en

UN Committee on the Rights of the Child. (2012b). *Concluding observations: Madagascar, March 8, 2012, CRC/C/MDG/CO/3-4. UN*. Retrieved November 14, 2020, from http://digitallibrary.un.org/record/723341

UN Committee on the Rights of the Child. (2013). *General Comment No. 14 (2013) On the right of the child to have his or her best interests taken as a primary consideration (art. 3, para. 1), May 29, 2013, CRC/C/GC/14*. Retrieved October 12, 2020, from https://digitallibrary.un.org/record/778523?ln=en

UN Committee on the Rights of the Child. (2016). *Concluding observations: Oman, March 14, 2016, CRC/C/OMN/CO/3-4. UN*. Retrieved November 29, 2020, from http://digitallibrary.un.org/record/835003

UN Committee on the Rights of the Child. (2019). *Guidelines regarding the implementation of the Optional Protocol to the Convention on the Rights of the Child on the sale of children, child prostitution and child pornography, CRC/C/156*. Retrieved November 26, 2020, from https://undocs.org/en/CRC/C/156

UN General Assembly. (2001). *Optional protocols to the Convention on the Rights of the Child on the involvement of children in armed conflict and on the sale of children, child prostitution and child pornography, A/RES/54/263. UN*. Retrieved November 29, 2020, from http://digitallibrary.un.org/record/416571

UN Working Group on Contemporary Forms of Slavery. (2003). *Report of the Working Group on Contemporary Forms of Slavery on its 28th session, E/CN.4/Sub.2/2003/31. UN*. Retrieved November 29, 2020, from http://digitallibrary.un.org/record/500172

Open Access This chapter is licensed under the terms of the Creative Commons Attribution 4.0 International License (http://creativecommons.org/licenses/by/4.0/), which permits use, sharing, adaptation, distribution and reproduction in any medium or format, as long as you give appropriate credit to the original author(s) and the source, provide a link to the Creative Commons license and indicate if changes were made.

The images or other third party material in this chapter are included in the chapter's Creative Commons license, unless indicated otherwise in a credit line to the material. If material is not included in the chapter's Creative Commons license and your intended use is not permitted by statutory regulation or exceeds the permitted use, you will need to obtain permission directly from the copyright holder.

Chapter 38
Article 38: The Right to Protection from Armed Conflict

Gerison Lansdown

1. States Parties undertake to respect and to ensure respect for rules of international humanitarian law applicable to them in armed conflicts which are relevant to the child.
2. States Parties shall take all feasible measures to ensure that persons who have not attained the age of 15 years do not take a direct part in hostilities.
3. States Parties shall refrain from recruiting any person who has not attained the age of 15 years into their armed forces. In recruiting among those persons who have attained the age of 15 years but who have not attained the age of 18 years, States Parties shall endeavour to give priority to those who are oldest.
4. In accordance with their obligations under international humanitarian law to protect the civilian population in armed conflicts, States Parties shall take all feasible measures to ensure protection and care of children who are affected by an armed conflict.

What Did Children Say?
'Children have to be educated on the dangers of armed conflict. A law has to be there that would protect children from participating in armed conflict.' *(Africa).*

(continued)

G. Lansdown (✉)
Carleton University, Ottawa, ON, Canada

> Children should never be forced to fight in the armed or militia forces, go to war or engaged in any conflict. *(Africa)*.
> Useful activities to engage children with rather than having free time to engage in those military parties. *(Asia-Pacific)*.
> Awareness workshops for children against recruitment to the armed conflicts and to be a child soldier. *(Asia-Pacific)*.

Overview

Article 38 introduces a framework for the protection of children in situations of armed conflict, both as civilians and as combatants or recruits to state armed forces or non-state armed groups. When drafted, it was unique in introducing international humanitarian law into a human rights treaty, thus affording it universal application, rather than being applicable only in times of armed conflict (Ang, 2005, p. 10). During the drafting process, Article 38 was probably the most contentious of all the Convention provisions, with strongly divided opinions on the proposed minimum age of recruitment into armed forces, differentiation between recruitment into state and non-state forces, age and level of protection from participation in conflicts, and the extent of measures demanded of States Parties in providing protection (Office of the United Nations High Commissioner for Human Rights and Rädda barnen (Society: Sweden), 2007, pp. 775–799). Disagreement arose as to whether the Working Group charged with drafting the text of the Convention had the mandate to review existing standards for protection in international humanitarian law, while fears were also expressed that the text might undermine or weaken those existing standards (Office of the United Nations High Commissioner for Human Rights and Rädda barnen (Society: Sweden), 2007, p. 794). Faced with the risk of no provision at all, the result was a compromise text affording much lower levels of protection than many members of the Working Group were seeking. In response, the Optional Protocol on children in armed conflict was later developed to strengthen the standards, although it, too, falls short of the protections sought by many working in this field. In response, the Paris Principles, published by UNICEF in 2007, affirm that most child protection actors will continue to press for the raising of the age of recruitment or use of children to 18 years in all cases (UNICEF, 2007).

In summary, Article 38 requires of States Parties that they ensure compliance with international humanitarian law, protect children under the age of 15 from direct participation in hostilities, refrain from recruiting children under 15 into armed forces, and take measures to protect civilian children affected by armed conflict. The Optional Protocol on armed conflict strengthens these provisions by raising the voluntary recruitment age to 16 years, and encouraging further raising of that age, prohibiting compulsory recruitment under 18 years, as well as any recruitment under 18 years by armed groups, and imposing obligations on States Parties to ensure that children under 18 do not directly participate in hostilities (UN General Assembly,

2001, paras. 1–4). It is important to note that the Committee highlights the complexity of addressing children's rights in situations of conflict and insists that States Parties have obligations to take measures to secure all the rights of children within their jurisdiction during such times, with no differentiation between child civilians or combatants, thus affirming the human rights principle of universality (Ang, 2005, p. 29; UN Committee on the Rights of the Child, 1992, para. 62 (d)).[1] Furthermore, the Convention is not subject to derogation in time of public emergency (Ang, 2005, p. 59; Hodgkin et al., 2007, p. 573; UN Committee on the Rights of the Child, 1992, para. 67).

General Principles

Article 2 All children suffer from exposure to armed conflict, but the Committee has highlighted the vulnerability of girls to systemic and serious sexual violence and sexual slavery in this context and urges States Parties to take measures to address the specific needs of formerly recruited girls in programmes of recovery and reintegration.[2] In this regard, no differentiation must be made between children who have been recruited or used and those who have not (UNICEF, 2007, para. 3.3). Discrimination and exclusion also result in children with disabilities being disproportionately vulnerable to violence, exploitation, and sexual abuse (UN High Commissioner for Refugees, 2003). The severity of the problems faced by children with disabilities led to the development of guidelines by the UNHCR to highlight the risks, strengthen protection and encourage States Parties to provide appropriate support (UN Executive Committee of the UNHCR Programme, 2010, Chap. III A).

Article 3 All measures to protect children from participation in or exposure to the consequences of armed conflict are premised on the recognition that so doing is in their best interests and must be determined by those best interests (UNICEF, 2007, para. 3.4).

Article 6 Children's exposure to armed conflict either as a civilian or combatant intensifies risk to optimum development, as well as loss of life. It potentially places at risk the realisation of all rights. Article 38 and the OPAC are drafted, although arguably inadequately, to seek to provide the maximum possible protection to enable children to live and thrive even in situations of armed conflict. Programmes and policies intended to benefit children associated with armed forces or armed groups should be informed by a child development perspective. Furthermore, in accordance with Article 37, capital punishment or imprisonment for life without possibility of release shall never be used against any person who is proved to have committed an

---

[1] See also, for example, Concluding observations: Cambodia (2000a, para. 48).
[2] See, for example, concluding observations for Colombia, (2015, para. 65) and Democratic Republic of Congo (2017a, para. 48).

offence against international or domestic criminal law while under 18 years of age (UNICEF, 2007, para. 3.9, 3.10).

Article 12 The Committee has consistently recommended that children must be involved in the development of all legislation, policies, and programmes that affect them (2009, para. 27, 2016a, para. 23). It has stressed the imperative to involve children in peace movements, programmes of non-violent conflict resolution, resilience building, and peace processes (2015, para. 65, 2016a, para. 82).

Articles Related or Linked to Article 38

Article 7, as children who are not registered at birth or subsequently are more vulnerable to underage recruitment into state armed forces or armed groups.

Article 8, as children caught up in armed conflict are at risk of loss of identity through loss of relevant papers.

Article 10 provides for the right to reunification in context of separation from families during or following armed conflict.

Article 11, as armed conflict can increase the risk of illicit transfer of children.

Article 13, since rights to freedom of expression may be curtailed in situations of armed conflict.

Article 15, as the right to peaceful of assembly may be curtailed in situations of armed conflict.

Article 19, as children affected and/or involved in armed conflicts are more at risk of experiencing neglect, violence, and abuse.

Article 22 applies as children may need to seek refugee status in situations of conflict.

Article 23, since armed conflict both places children at risk of experiencing disabling injuries and those who have a disability are at greater risk.

Article 24, as the right to health is potentially jeopardised in situations of conflict.

Article 28, since protecting the right to education needs to be prioritised in situations of armed conflict.

Article 29, since preparation for life in spirit of peace takes on added significance in both mitigating risk of conflict and promoting peace post-conflict.

Article 31, as exercising the right to play and leisure affords children opportunities to escape and heal in the context of the traumatic experiences of armed conflict.

Article 32, as forcible recruitment into armed forces or groups constitutes a prohibited form of worst child labour.

Article 34, since children, especially girls, can be exposed to sexual violence and exploitation in situations of armed conflict, both as civilians and as conscripts into armed forces or groups.

Article 35, since, in armed conflict, children are more at risk to be abducted, trafficked, or sold for various purposes including recruitment into armed groups.

Article 36, as armed conflict renders children vulnerable to all forms of exploitation.

Article 37, as children can be subjected to torture, and other forms of cruel, inhuman and degrading treatment in situations of conflict, both as civilians and as conscripts into armed forces or groups.

Article 39, as children must be provided with opportunities to achieve physical and psychological recovery and reintegration, both after release from recruitment into armed forces and direct experience of conflict as a civilian.

Article 40, since there is no consensus at the international level as to the appropriate minimum age for prosecution of child soldiers.

Optional Protocol to the Convention on the Rights of the Child on the involvement of children in armed conflict (OPAC), 2000

Relevant Instruments

A significant number of instruments contribute to the body of international and regional humanitarian and human rights law, and impact on the rights of children in the context of armed conflict. The following are the most relevant.

UN Declaration of the Rights of the Child (1959) Principle 8.

International Covenant on Civil and Political Rights (1966), Article 24.

UN Declaration on the Protection of Women and Children in Emergency and Armed Conflict (1974).

UN Convention on the Prohibition of the Use, Stockpiling, Production and Transfer of Anti-Personnel Mines and on their Destruction (Ottawa Convention or the Anti-Personnel Mine Ban Treaty) (1997).

UNICEF Principles and guidelines on children associated with armed forces or armed groups (Paris principles) (2007).

The Geneva Convention for the amelioration of the condition of the wounded and sick in armed forces in the field (1949), the Fourth Convention, the later (1977) Additional Protocol One to Geneva Conventions, dealing with international conflicts and in particular Article 77 and 78 that introduce specific protection to children, and the later (1977) Additional Protocol Two to the Geneva convention, dealing with non-international conflicts, and in particular Article 4 on special measures for children.

ILO Convention 182, Worst Forms of Child Labour (1999), forced recruitment of children is defined as a worst form of child labour.

African Charter on the Rights and Welfare of the Child (1990), Article 22 establishes age 18 as minimum for all compulsory recruitment and participation in hostilities.

Rome Statute of International Criminal Court (1998) establishes as war crimes: enlistment and use of persons under age 15 a war crime, attacks on schools and hospitals, rape and other forms of violence against children.

Attributes

Attribute One: Respect for International Humanitarian Law Applicable to the Child

It is important to note that humanitarian law, which comprises Hague law, dealing broadly with use of weapons, and Geneva law that serves to protect those affected by conflict, only applies during the period of an armed conflict.[3] Furthermore, the Geneva Conventions and protocols only extend protection to those who do not take part in hostilities and therefore provide no protection for children recruited or used as combatants. It therefore contrasts, and is, to some extent, in tension with Article 38, paragraph 1 (and indeed, the Convention in its entirety), which applies to all children under 18 years, consistent with Article 1, whether civilian or combatants. This is a complex arena of law, but the Committee has sought to address it, by arguing that Article 41 of the Convention asserts that States Parties must always apply the norms most conducive to the rights of the child, whether in applicable international law or national legislation (1992, para. 75 (e)).[4]

Article 38 applies to both internal and external conflicts. It requires States Parties to both respect and ensure respect for international humanitarian law applicable to children and provides the framework for effective monitoring of compliance with Article 38, together with relevant provisions of international humanitarian law. Paragraph 1 imposes an obligation on States Parties to *respect* the law, including in contexts where other parties to a conflict are not signatories to it (*Kupreškić* et al. *(IT-95-16)*, 2000), and the obligation to *ensure respect* includes the regulation of behaviour of non-state actors such as armed groups, or rebel forces (de Detrick, 1999, p. 651). The Committee has also argued that the obligation extends to paramilitary groups and private companies (2001a, para. 6, 2004a, para. 71 (d)). Together they have been interpreted to require establishment of minimum ages for recruitment, dissemination of information on humanitarian law, provision of training programmes on the rights of the child, and implementation of penal obligations under international humanitarian law for breaches of the Geneva Conventions (1998, para. 14, 2017b, para. 67). The Committee has given a high priority to challenging impunity, recommending establishment of judicial mechanisms to deal with gross violations, and making sanctions widely known (2000b, para. 45). It has also called for States Parties to amend their penal law in order to provide for the exercise of extraterritorial jurisdiction for the offences committed by or against a citizen of the States Party (2010, para. 26). In its guidelines for OPAC, the Committee seeks detailed information on sanctions in force, their scope and the extent of their

---

[3] See 'The Geneva Conventions of 1949 and their Additional Protocols' (International Committee of the Red Cross, 2010).

[4] See also 'The Rights of Children in Armed Conflict' (Tobin & Drumbl, 2019, pp. 1511–1514) for a fuller discussion of the relationship between international humanitarian law and human rights law.

application and implementation (2007a, paras. 20–26). It also calls for states to become parties to all relevant instruments (2007a, para. 22).

Attribute Two: Age Limits on Participation in Hostilities

Article 38 must be applied with regard to international humanitarian law, as well as the provisions of OPAC. However, the protected age for participation in hostilities and the nature and scope of protection varies significantly in the different instruments.

Article 38 paragraph 2 introduces 15 years as the minimum age for direct participation in hostilities. This is amended by OPAC which demands 'all feasible measures' to ensure that children under age 18 in the armed forces do not take a direct part in hostilities but provides stronger protection in respect of armed groups which are prohibited from allowing any participation of children under 18 years. 'All feasible measures' is a weak requirement that does not appear elsewhere in international human rights language and there is no clear definition of its meaning. However, despite the limitations of Article 38 and OPAC, the Committee has consistently pressed States Parties to employ 18 years as the minimum age for any participation in hostilities (2017a, para. 48). Their focus is on determining outcomes (whether any actual participation has taken place) rather than processes (what feasible measures have been adopted to preclude participation of persons under age 18).

Further complexities arise in respect of defining direct participation in hostilities. There is consistency in the interpretation of the concept of hostilities, which are commonly understood to describe acts of war intended to hit personnel and facilities of an opposing armed force, including preparations for and return from combat (International Committee of the Red Cross, 1987). In addition, a consensus exists that any participation is understood to be judged objectively and not in relation to the will or choice of the child in question (Ang, 2005, p. 36). However, the definition of 'direct participation' in hostilities is less clear. A higher standard applies in the Additional Protocols, which prohibit any participation by children in hostilities. The associated commentaries make clear that the intention was to keep all children away from all hostilities in every way (Ang, 2005, p. 38). The International Criminal Court appears to limit the definition to actual fighting, which narrows the scope and thereby allows for a far wider range of permitted activities on the part of children. Many types of indirect participation can expose children to significant risk, for example, engagement as messengers, spies, or porters. Again, the position of the Committee has been unambiguous, as it presses States Parties to ensure neither direct or indirect participation of any children under 18 years, and welcomes commitments from States Parties to adopt such policies (2004b, paras. 81–82, 2005a, paras. 69–70, 2005b, para. 82, 2005c, paras. 65–66).

Attribute Three: Age of Recruitment

As noted above, different standards prevail in different relevant instruments regarding age of recruitment. Article 38 prohibits recruitment of children under the age of 15 years and this prohibition applies to compulsory, forced, and voluntary recruitment (Ang, 2005, p. 50). Under International Labour Organization 182 and OPAC, compulsory or forced recruitment under age 18 is prohibited, and OPAC requires States Parties to raise the minimum age for voluntary recruitment to 16 years, and further urges States Parties to raise it to 18 years, taking into account that the Convention affords special protection for all children (UN General Assembly, 2001, Annex I, Article 3, para 1). It also prohibits any recruitment of persons under 18 by armed groups.

In respect of recruiting children aged between 15 and 18 years, Article 38 requires States Parties to endeavour to give priority to those who are oldest. This relatively weak formulation imposes an obligation merely of conduct, not of result. However, the commentaries to the Additional Protocols argue that the concept of 'endeavour' points to a duty, which can be extended by implication to the implementation of Article 38, to establish a system guaranteeing the obligation to apply the priority rule (Ang, 2005, p. 57). In any case, the Committee has made clear that it seeks an end to all recruitment of persons under 18 years old in all contexts, and consistently presses States Parties to take measures to achieve that objective (1992, para. 61 et seq, 2016b, para. 85, 2017a, para. 48, 2017c, para. 9). It also presses States Parties to take measures to de-mobilise children already recruited and to facilitate their recovery and reintegration (2017d, para. 38).

Attribute Four: All Feasible Measures of Care and Protection

Article 38, paragraph 4, requires States Parties to take all feasible measures to ensure protection and care for civilian children in accordance with obligations under international humanitarian law. Notably child combatants are excluded. General protection measures elaborated in international humanitarian law, such as the *Geneva Conventions* and their *Additional Protocols*, require humane treatment, including respect for life and physical and moral integrity, and they forbid coercion, corporal punishments, torture, collective penalties, and reprisals. Additional specific protections are afforded to children including, for example, the right to care and aid, family unity, special care for orphans or separated children, education, special treatment for children deprived of their liberty, and a prohibition on the death penalty. These provisions represent a considerable overlap with rights embodied in the Convention and the approach of the Committee is to identify violations in terms of all the applicable Convention articles, including the right to education. In relation to Article 38 paragraph 4, the Committee asserts education to be a core obligation in situations of emergency in light of its significance as a measure of physical, psychological, and cognitive protection (2008, para. 29), and also regularly raises States Parties' compliance with the Ottawa Convention on Landmines, urging action on de-mining, prevention, and rehabilitation for victims, as well as advocating ratification (2006, para. 69, 2007b, paras. 23, 78).

The formulation of 'all feasible measures' represents a considerable weakening of the provisions in the Geneva Conventions and Additional Protocols, which employ unambiguous language such as 'shall take all necessary steps' (Ang, 2005, p. 62). The Committee has taken a clear position on this, consistently employing stronger terms with which to press States Parties into action and demanding more than the strict letter of Article 38, paragraph 4, would indicate. For example, a formulation has been used stating that States Parties should 'at all times ensure respect for human rights and humanitarian law aimed at the protection and care of children in armed conflict' (UN Committee on the Rights of the Child, 2000c, para. 49, 2000d, para. 64, 2001b, para. 57 (a)).

With regards to the rights of children who are alleged to have committed offences, Articles 37 and 40, taken together with the United Nations rules and guidelines on juvenile justice and the Committee's General Comments no. 6 and no. 10, make clear that, although such children may be held accountable for crimes, any hearings to determine responsibility must be fair and entirely separate from the adult justice system and that the subsequent treatment of the child must be focused on achieving their rehabilitation, with deprivation of liberty used only as a last resort for the shortest appropriate time.

References

Ang, F. (2005). *A Commentary on the United Nations Convention on the Rights of the Child, Article 38: Children in Armed Conflicts. A Commentary on the United Nations Convention on the Rights of the Child, Article 38: Children in Armed Conflicts*. Brill Nijhoff. Retrieved November 29, 2020, from https://brill.com/view/title/11620

de Detrick, S. L. (1999). *A Commentary on the United Nations Convention on the Rights of the Child*. Brill Nijhoff. Retrieved November 6, 2020, from https://brill.com/view/title/10630

Hodgkin, R., Newell, P., & UNICEF. (2007). *Implementation handbook for the convention on the rights of the child* (3rd ed.). : UNICEF. Retrieved September 21, 2020, from https://digitallibrary.un.org/record/620060?ln=en

International Committee of the Red Cross. (1987). *Commentary on the Additional Protocols of 8 June 1977 to the Geneva Conventions of 12 August 1949*. International Committee of the Red Cross. Retrieved November 29, 2020, from https://www.icrc.org/en/publication/0421-commentary-additional-protocols-8-june-1977-geneva-conventions-12-august-1949

International Committee of the Red Cross. (2010, October 29). The Geneva conventions of 1949 and their additional protocols. *International Committee of the Red Cross*. Retrieved November 29, 2020, from https://www.icrc.org/en/war-and-law/treaties-customary-law/geneva-conventions

Kupreškić, M., et al. (2000). (IT-95-16) (International Criminal Tribunal for the former Yugoslavia (ICTY) 14 January 2000). Retrieved November 29, 2020, from https://www.icty.org/case/kupreskic

Office of the United Nations High Commissioner for Human Rights & Rädda barnen (Society: Sweden). (2007). *Legislative history of the convention on the rights of the child*. New York: United Nations. Retrieved from https://digitallibrary.un.org/record/602462?ln=en

Tobin, J., & Drumbl, M. A. (2019). Article 38: The rights of children in armed conflict. In J. Tobin (Ed.), *The UN convention on the rights of the child: A commentary* (pp. 1503–1560). Oxford University Press.

UN Committee on the Rights of the Child. (1992). *Report adopted by the Committee at its 46th Meeting on 9 October 1992, CRC/C/10*. UN. Retrieved November 29, 2020, from http://digitallibrary.un.org/record/197134

UN Committee on the Rights of the Child. (1998). *Concluding observations: Iraq, October 26, 1998, CRC/C/15/Add.94*. UN. Retrieved November 29, 2020, from http://digitallibrary.un.org/record/265317

UN Committee on the Rights of the Child. (2000a). *Concluding observations: Cambodia, June 28, 2000, CRC/C/15/Add.128*. UN. Retrieved November 29, 2020, from http://digitallibrary.un.org/record/424986

UN Committee on the Rights of the Child. (2000b). *Concluding observations: Sierra Leone, February 24, 2000, CRC/C/15/Add.116*. UN. Retrieved November 29, 2020, from http://digitallibrary.un.org/record/414185

UN Committee on the Rights of the Child. (2000c). *Concluding observations: Armenia, February 24, 2000, CRC/C/15/Add.119*. UN. Retrieved November 7, 2020, from http://digitallibrary.un.org/record/415621

UN Committee on the Rights of the Child. (2000d). *Concluding observations: India, February 23, 2000, CRC/C/15/Add.115*. Retrieved October 11, 2020, from https://digitallibrary.un.org/record/412551?ln=en

UN Committee on the Rights of the Child. (2001a). *Concluding observations: Democratic Republic of the Congo, July 9, 2001, CRC/C/15/Add.153*. UN. Retrieved November 29, 2020, from http://digitallibrary.un.org/record/451937

UN Committee on the Rights of the Child. (2001b). *Concluding observations: Bhutan, July 9, 2001, CRC/C/15/Add.157*. UN. Retrieved November 29, 2020, from http://digitallibrary.un.org/record/451942

UN Committee on the Rights of the Child. (2004a). *Concluding observations: Indonesia, February 26, 2004, CRC/C/15/Add.223*. UN. Retrieved November 29, 2020, from http://digitallibrary.un.org/record/530584

UN Committee on the Rights of the Child. (2004b). *Concluding observations: Myanmar, June 30, 2004, CRC/C/15/Add.237*. UN. Retrieved Occtober 26, 2020, from http://digitallibrary.un.org/record/536569

UN Committee on the Rights of the Child. (2005a). *Concluding observations: Algeria, October 12, 2005, CRC/C/15/Add.269*. Retrieved October 24, 2020, from https://digitallibrary.un.org/record/570473?ln=en

UN Committee on the Rights of the Child. (2005b). *Concluding observations: Nepal, September 1, 2005, CRC/C/15/Add.261*. Retrieved Octobber 11, 2020, from https://digitallibrary.un.org/record/569886?ln=en

UN Committee on the Rights of the Child. (2005c). *Concluding observations: Uganda, November 23, 2005, CRC/C/UGA/CO/2*. UN. Retrieved November 6, 2020, from http://digitallibrary.un.org/record/570558

UN Committee on the Rights of the Child. (2006). *Concluding observations: Lebanon, June 8, 2006, CRC/C/LBN/CO/3*. Retrieved October 11, 2020, from https://digitallibrary.un.org/record/580379?ln=en

UN Committee on the Rights of the Child. (2007a). *Revised guidelines regarding initial reports to be submitted by States Parties under Article 8, para. 1, of the Optional Protocol to the Convention on the Rights of the Child on Involvement of Children in Armed Conflict*, September 2007, *CRC/C/OPAC/2*. UN. Retrieved November 29, 2020, from http://digitallibrary.un.org/record/635885

UN Committee on the Rights of the Child. (2007b). *General Comment No. 9 (2006) The rights of children with disabilities, November 13, 2007, CRC/C/GC/9*. Retrieved October 12, 2020, from https://digitallibrary.un.org/record/593891?ln=en

UN Committee on the Rights of the Child. (2008). *Day of general discussion: The right of the child to education in emergency situations*. UN. Retrieved December 20, 2020, from https://www.ohchr.org/EN/HRBodies/CRC/Pages/DiscussionDays.aspx

UN Committee on the Rights of the Child. (2009). *General Comment No. 12 (2009) The right of the child to be heard, July 20, 2009, CRC/C/GC/12*. Retrieved October 12, 2020, from https://digitallibrary.un.org/record/671444?ln=en

UN Committee on the Rights of the Child. (2010). *Concluding observations: Sierra Leone, under article 8 of the Optional Protocol to the Convention on the Rights of the Child on the Involvement of Children in Armed Conflict, Cotber 14, 2010, CRC/C/OPAC/SLE/CO/1*. UN. Retrieved November 29, 2020, from http://digitallibrary.un.org/record/692399

UN Committee on the Rights of the Child. (2015). *Concluding observations: Colombia, March 6, 2015, CRC/C/COL/CO/4-5*. UN. Retrieved November 29, 2020, from http://digitallibrary.un.org/record/789737

UN Committee on the Rights of the Child. (2016a). *General Comment No. 20 (2016) on the implementation of the rights of the child during adolescence, December 6, 2016, CRC/C/GC/20*. Retrieved October 12, 2020, from https://digitallibrary.un.org/record/855544?ln=en

UN Committee on the Rights of the Child. (2016b). *Concluding observations: United Kingdom, July 12, 2016, CRC/C/GBR/CO/5*. UN. Retrieved November 15, 2020, from http://digitallibrary.un.org/record/835015

UN Committee on the Rights of the Child. (2017a). *Concluding observations: Democratic Republic of the Congo, February 28, 2017, CRC/C/COD/CO/3-5*. UN. Retrieved November 29, 2020, from http://digitallibrary.un.org/record/1311372

UN Committee on the Rights of the Child. (2017b). *Concluding observations: Central African Republic, March 8, 2017, CRC/C/CAF/CO/2*. UN. Retrieved November 14, 2020, from http://digitallibrary.un.org/record/1311376

UN Committee on the Rights of the Child. (2017c). *Concluding observations: United States of America, under article 8 (1) of the Optional Protocol to the Convention on the Rights of the Child on the Involvement of Children in Armed Conflict, July 11, 2017, CRC/C/OPAC/USA/CO/3-4*. UN. Retrieved November 29, 2020, from http://digitallibrary.un.org/record/1311404

UN Committee on the Rights of the Child. (2017d). *Concluding observations: Lebanon, June 22, 2017, CRC/C/LBN/CO/4-5*. UN. Retrieved November 6, 2020, from http://digitallibrary.un.org/record/1311380

UN Executive Committee of the UNHCR Programme. (2010). *Report of the 61st session of the Executive Committee of the High Commissioner's Programme, A/AC.96/1095*. UN. Retrieved November 29, 2020, from http://digitallibrary.un.org/record/697102

UN General Assembly. (2001). *Optional protocols to the Convention on the Rights of the Child on the involvement of children in armed conflict and on the sale of children, child prostitution and child pornography, A/RES/54/263*. UN. Retrieved November 29, 2020, from http://digitallibrary.un.org/record/416571

UN High Commissioner for Refugees. (2003). *Sexual and gender-based violence against refugees, returnees and internally displaced persons: Guidelines for prevention and response*. UN High Commissioner for Refugees. Retrieved November 29, 2020, from http://digitallibrary.un.org/record/532805

UNICEF. (2007). *Principles and guidelines on children associated with armed forces or armed groups (Paris principles)*. Retrieved November 29, 2020, from https://www.unicef.org/mali/en/reports/paris-principles

Open Access This chapter is licensed under the terms of the Creative Commons Attribution 4.0 International License (http://creativecommons.org/licenses/by/4.0/), which permits use, sharing, adaptation, distribution and reproduction in any medium or format, as long as you give appropriate credit to the original author(s) and the source, provide a link to the Creative Commons license and indicate if changes were made.

The images or other third party material in this chapter are included in the chapter's Creative Commons license, unless indicated otherwise in a credit line to the material. If material is not included in the chapter's Creative Commons license and your intended use is not permitted by statutory regulation or exceeds the permitted use, you will need to obtain permission directly from the copyright holder.

Chapter 39
Article 40: The Rights in the Juvenile Justice Setting

Roberta Ruggiero

> 1. States Parties recognize the right of every child alleged as, accused of, or recognized as having infringed the penal law to be treated in a manner consistent with the promotion of the child's sense of dignity and worth, which reinforces the child's respect for the human rights and fundamental freedoms of others and which takes into account the child's age and the desirability of promoting the child's reintegration and the child's assuming a constructive role in society.
> 2. To this end, and having regard to the relevant provisions of international instruments, States Parties shall, in particular, ensure that:
>
>   (a) No child shall be alleged as, be accused of, or recognized as having infringed the penal law by reason of acts or omissions that were not prohibited by national or international law at the time they were committed;
>
>   (b) Every child alleged as or accused of having infringed the penal law has at least the following guarantees:
>
>   (i) To be presumed innocent until proven guilty according to law;
>   (ii) To be informed promptly and directly of the charges against him or her, and, if appropriate, through his or her parents or legal guardians, and to have legal or other appropriate assistance in the preparation and presentation of his or her defence;
>
> (continued)

R. Ruggiero (✉)
Centre for Children's Rights Studies, University of Geneva, Geneva, Switzerland
e-mail: roberta.ruggiero@unige.ch

(iii) To have the matter determined without delay by a competent, independent and impartial authority or judicial body in a fair hearing according to law, in the presence of legal or other appropriate assistance and, unless it is considered not to be in the best interest of the child, in particular, taking into account his or her age or situation, his or her parents or legal guardians;

(iv) Not to be compelled to give testimony or to confess guilt; to examine or have examined adverse witnesses and to obtain the participation and examination of witnesses on his or her behalf under conditions of equality;

(v) If considered to have infringed the penal law, to have this decision and any measures imposed in consequence thereof reviewed by a higher competent, independent and impartial authority or judicial body according to law;

(vi) To have the free assistance of an interpreter if the child cannot understand or speak the language used;

(vii) To have his or her privacy fully respected at all stages of the proceedings.

3. States Parties shall seek to promote the establishment of laws, procedures, authorities and institutions specifically applicable to children alleged as, accused of, or recognized as having infringed the penal law, and, in particular:

(a) The establishment of a minimum age below which children shall be presumed not to have the capacity to infringe the penal law;

(b) Whenever appropriate and desirable, measures for dealing with such children without resorting to judicial proceedings, providing that human rights and legal safeguards are fully respected.

4. A variety of dispositions, such as care, guidance and supervision orders; counselling; probation; foster care; education and vocational training programmes and other alternatives to institutional care shall be available to ensure that children are dealt with in a manner appropriate to their well-being and proportionate both to their circumstances and the offence.

What Did Children Say?
'There should be visits in cells, do activities to know the rights because the children there are already stressed. A real human that walks around the cells.' (Western Europe/Other).

(continued)

Government to build a training camp where child who may be convicted, sentenced for short time will do their time in prison and by the end of their jail term, and they will come out as a changed person. They need government to provide them with trained and qualify lawyers that will be looking into the case of juvenile. (Africa).

Overview

Article 40 imposes a child rights-based approach to juvenile criminal justice, with the objective of setting up a comprehensive and autonomous juvenile justice policy. Based on the General Comment no. 24, this policy should establish the minimum age of criminal responsibility and include measures to prevent children's offending behaviour. It should also focus upon the rehabilitation and reintegration of children in conflict with the law into society (UN Committee on the Rights of the Child, 2007a, paras. 2, 3, 10, 2019, paras. 17, 22,28; van Bueren, 2005, pp. 1–3). With the adoption of Article 40, the concept of the child's well-being and best interests become aspects of basic concern in the administration of juvenile justice. The specific physical, psychological, development, and educational needs of the child justify this requirement for a specialised juvenile justice system and the replacement of the traditional objectives of criminal justice repression and retribution, with 'rehabilitation and restorative justice objectives' (UN Committee on the Rights of the Child, 2007a, paras. 2–3, 10, 2019, paras. 22, 28).

Article 40 concerns the rights of all children alleged as, accused of, or recognised as having infringed the penal law, from the moment a complaint is made, through the investigation phase, the arrest, and the accusation, to the pre-trial period, the trial, and the sentence (Hodgkin et al., 2007, p. 601). Based on its experience in reviewing the States Parties' performance, the Committee has indicated that even though detailed attention is paid to the rights of children and many efforts are undertaken to establish juvenile justice systems in compliance with the Convention, there is still a long way to go. Progress is needed in relation to:

- respect and enforcement of procedural rights
- development and implementation of measures for dealing with children in conflict with the law without resorting to judicial proceedings (diversion)
- use of deprivation of liberty only as a measure of last resort
- setting up of comprehensive juvenile justice policy and the undertaking of measures meant to prevent children from coming into conflict with the law
- systemic gathering of comprehensive statistical data in this field (UN Committee on the Rights of the Child, 2007a, paras. 2–3; van Bueren, 2005, pp. 1–3).

Article 40 provides a list of minimum guarantees for the child and identifies a series of States Parties' obligations meant to ensure the fulfilment of these guarantees. Even though the Convention is a holistic treaty, there are two other Articles dedicated to children in contact with the criminal justice system: Article 37 and Article 39, which extend the protection enshrined by Article 40. Article 37 bans the death penalty and life imprisonment 'without the possibility of release' and requires that any deprivation of liberty must be used as a last resort and for the shortest appropriate time. Article 39 requires States Parties to adopt 'measures to promote physical and psychological recovery and reintegration of child victims' (Hodgkin et al., 2007, p. 601).

The final version of Article 40 codifies the core elements of the United Nations Standard Minimum Rules for the Administration of Juvenile Justice (The Beijing Rules). The initial draft of the article was less ambitious and merely reproduced the texts of the pre-existing international standards dealing with the administration of justice. However, the drafters of the Convention realised they had the opportunity of strengthening the attention on children's rights in justice administration and of raising the status of The Beijing Rules (soft-law provisions) (van Bueren, 2005, p. 5).[1]

In comparison with related international human rights treaties, many of the provisions contained in Article 40 are *de novo*. In other words, they mirror the content of other treaties, but with a stronger child rights approach. This is particularly evident for the following issues as main principles of the juvenile justice system. (van Bueren, 2005, p. 7):

- Minimum age of criminal responsibility
- Use of diversion
- Promotion of the child's sense of dignity and worth.

General Principles

Article 2 Based on the General Comment no. 10, States Parties must 'take all appropriate measures to ensure that all children in conflict with the law are treated equally' and special attention should be dedicated to vulnerable groups. Therefore, States Parties are requested to establish rules, regulations, and protocols to enhance equal treatment of child offenders and provide redress, remedies, and compensation.

Many children in conflict with the law are also victims of discrimination. Further discriminatory victimisation can affect former child offenders, trying to get education or work. States should intervene in order to prevent such discrimination and

---

[1] The United Nations Standard Minimum Rules for the Administration of Juvenile Justice (The Beijing Rules) were adopted by the General Assembly in 1985, while the Convention on the Rights of the Child was being drafted. The Beijing Rules provide relevant standards for the implementation of the Convention.

provide former child offenders with appropriate support and assistance in their reintegration process into society, as required by Article 40 (1) (UN Committee on the Rights of the Child, 2007a, paras. 6–9). Moreover, criminal codes often contain provisions criminalising behavioural problems of children such as vagrancy, truancy, runaways, and other acts, which often are the outcome of psychological or socio-economic problems. These acts, 'also known as Status Offences, are not considered to be such if committed by adults' (UN Committee on the Rights of the Child, 2007a, para. 8). This is a form of discrimination that negatively impacts on children, particularly those belonging to vulnerable groups and poor households.[2]

Article 3 The principle of the best interests of the child is the basic concern of the juvenile justice system and it receives primary consideration in all decisions in this field. Furthermore, the specific physical, psychological, developmental, and educational needs of the child justify the necessity for a specialised juvenile justice system and a lesser culpability approach in the administration of justice for those in conflict with the law. Therefore, the protection of the best interests of the child implies the replacement of the traditional objectives of criminal justice, repression, and retribution, with the objectives of rehabilitation and restorative justice (UN Committee on the Rights of the Child, 2007a, para. 10, 2013, para. 28).

Article 6 Because of the negative impact of delinquency on child's development, States Parties should develop national programmes and undertake preventive measures meant to ensure the right to life, survival, and development of all children. Furthermore, this basic right should result in the state's policy responding to juvenile delinquency in ways from supporting the child's development to prohibiting the death penalty and a life sentence without parole (Article 37), and in which the deprivation of liberty, including arrest and detention, is used only as a measure of last resort and for the shortest appropriate period of time needed, as per Article 37 (b)) (UN Committee on the Rights of the Child, 2007a, para. 11).

Article 12 Throughout the juvenile justice process, the child must have the opportunity to express their views freely, and to those views should be given due weight in accordance with the age and maturity of the child (Article 12 (1)). 'He/she can be heard directly and not only through a representative or an appropriate body if it is in her/his best interests.' This applies to all stages of the process, such as the pre-trial 'when the child has the right to remain silent, as well as the right to be heard by the police, the prosecutor and the investigating judge', and also to the phases of adjudication, implementation of the sentence and imposition of measures (UN Committee on the Rights of the Child, 2007a, paras. 12, 43–45). For a comprehensive juvenile justice policy, based on the '*Riyadh Guidelines*,' child participation should be furthered in governmental and non-governmental delinquency prevention programmes (paragraphs 3 and 9(h)) (Hodgkin et al., 2007, p. 609; UN Committee on the Rights of the Child, 2009, paras. 57–61).

---

[2] See Article 56 of the Riyadh Guidelines.

Articles Related or Linked to Article 40

Article 13, since in order to fully participate during the different phases of the proceedings the child must be informed not only of the charges, 'but also of the juvenile justice process as such and of the possible measures' (UN Committee on the Rights of the Child, 2007a, paras. 47–48).

Article 16, right to privacy in connection with Article 40(2)(vii) (see below).

Articles 19, 32 and 34, as protection from all forms of violence and from economic or sexual exploitation during all the judicial and non-judicial process and the undertaking of the related measures.

Article 18 and Article 27, with reference to the importance of setting up a holistic policy on juvenile justice meant to

- promote the child's sense of dignity and worth
- to reinforce 'the child's respect for the human rights and fundamental freedoms of others' and
- to facilitate 'the child's reintegration and the child's assuming a constructive role in society' (Article 40(1)) and in the undertaking of some diversion measures (Article 40(4)).

Both these articles refer to the importance of the educational role of parents from prevention on to the reintegration, in line with the United Nations Guidelines for the Prevention of Juvenile Delinquency (the Riyadh Guidelines).[3] General Comment no. 10 reiterates the importance of the responsibility of parents for the upbringing of their children, but at the same time, it asks States Parties to provide the necessary assistance to parents (or other caretakers) in the performance of their parental responsibilities and confirm the States Parties' duty to promote the social potential of parents also for the prevention of juvenile delinquency (2007a, paras. 15–20).

Article 20 and Article 25, in relation to alternative care measures and the periodic review of placement or treatment. The principles of these provisions apply to all forms of placement of the child outside the family context. This implies the undertaking of constant monitoring of children placement for the purpose of care, protection, or treatment, to assess the quality of the child's life and their harmonious and full development. In particular, in relation to Article 25, the Committee underlines that it applies to all sentences imposed upon children, for which 'the possibility of release should be realistic and regularly considered' (UN Committee on the Rights of the Child, 2007a, para. 77).

---

[3] United Nations Guidelines for the Prevention of Juvenile Delinquency (the Riyadh Guidelines) states: 'Measures should be taken and programmes developed to provide families with the opportunity to learn about parental roles and obligations as regards child development and childcare, promoting positive parent-child relationships, sensitizing parents to the problems of children and young persons and encouraging their involvement in family and community-based activities.' (UN General Assembly, 1991a, para. 16).

Article 24, with reference to the access to health care and the highest attainable standards, in particular in relation to all the forms of institutional placement and the deprivation of the liberty of the child.

Article 28, with reference to the fact that often penal sanctions interrupt education, proper juvenile justice systems should avoid this by following the standard set by Article 40 (UN Committee on the Rights of the Child, 2007a, paras. 18, 23, 89).

Article 29, in relation to the most important goal of the administration of juvenile justice: the promotion of the full and harmonious development 'of the child's personality, talents and mental and physical abilities.' As also indicated in the Preamble and in Article 6 of the Convention, the child should be prepared to live a responsible life, assuming a 'constructive role with respect for human rights and fundamental freedoms' of others (UN Committee on the Rights of the Child, 2007a, para. 16).

Article 37 bans the death penalty and life imprisonment 'without possibility of release' and requires that any restriction of liberty must be used as a last resort and for the shortest appropriate period. It integrates, together with Article 39, the protection enshrined in Article 40.

Article 39 requires States Parties to adopt 'measures to promote physical and psychological recovery and reintegration of child victims', particularly important also in the reintegration of the child perpetrator of a crime. It also integrates, together with Article 37, the protection enshrined in Article 40.

Relevant Instruments

International Covenant on Civil and Political Rights (1966):

- Article 7(4), in case of detention, the 'detained shall be informed of the reasons for his detention and shall be promptly notified of the charge or charges against him'
- Article 10(2)(b), with reference to the necessity to determine the case 'without delay'
- Article 14(2)(b), in relation to the right of adults and children to defence and to a qualified legal assistance
- Article 14(3), with reference to the following rights:
  - to be informed promptly and in detail about the nature and cause of the charges
  - to have adequate time and facilities for the preparation of his defence
  - to be tried without undue delay
  - defence through legal assistance of his own choosing or if needed to have legal assistance assigned, and without payment in any such case where sufficient means are missing
  - to have the free assistance of an interpreter if he cannot understand or speak the language used in court
  - not to be compelled to testify against himself or to confess guilt.

- Article 14(4) with reference to the necessity that the procedures concerning children should 'take into account their age and the desirability of promoting rehabilitation'
- Article 15(1) principle of non-retroactivity of the penal law

UN Standard Minimum Rules for the Administration of Juvenile Justice (Beijing Rules) (1985).

UN Standard Minimum Rules for Non-custodial Measures (The Tokyo Rules) (1990), are relevant to the implementation of Article 40(3)(b) and provide minimum safeguards for persons subject to alternatives to imprisonment.

UN Guidelines for the Prevention of Juvenile Delinquency (Riyadh Guidelines) (1990).

UN Rules for the Protection of Juveniles Deprived of their Liberty (Havana Rules) (1990).

American Convention on Human Rights 'Pact of San Jose, Costa Rica' (B-32) (1978), Article 5(5), states: 'Minors while subject to criminal proceedings shall be separated from adults and brought before specialised tribunals, as speedily as possible, so that they may be treated in accordance with their status as minors'. This Article imposes a stricter States Parties' obligation to bring accused children before of a specialised tribunal, whereas Article 40(3) asks States Parties 'to seek to promote the establishment of laws, procedures, authorities, and institutions specifically applicable to children' (van Bueren, 2005, p. 8).

African Charter on Human and Peoples' Rights (1981), Articles 17 and 30, do not incorporate the States Parties' obligation to set up specialised juvenile justice institutions.

Guidelines of the Committee of Ministers of the Council of Europe on child friendly justice (2010).

Attributes

Attribute One: Specialised Juvenile Justice System and the Related Comprehensive Policy (Article 40(1) and (3))

Article 40 (1) introduces the main innovative aspect of this article as the 'principle of children's rights approach to the administration of juvenile justice.' It sets the fundamental principles guiding the treatment of children in conflict with the law and, as explained in General Comment no. 24, suggests that the treatment is consistent with the age of the child and with the child's sense of dignity and worth. Furthermore, it should have an educative aim, meant to reinforce 'the child's respect for the human rights and fundamental freedoms of others' and to facilitate 'the child's reintegration and the child's assuming a constructive role in society' (UN General Assembly, 1991b), which is consistent with Article 29 of the Convention (UN Committee on the Rights of the Child, 2019, para. 15).

Article 40(3) requires States Parties to promote the setting up of a specialised juvenile justice policy and systems to be applied to children alleged as, accused of, or recognised as having infringed the penal law. This requires the establishment of dedicated laws, procedures, authorities and institutions such as specialised police units, judiciary, courts system, prosecutors' office and the provision of specialised defenders or other representatives for children and specialised services such as probation, counselling or supervision along specialised facilities, for example day treatment centres, facilities for residential care and treatment of child offenders (Hodgkin et al., 2007, p. 616; UN Committee on the Rights of the Child, 2007a, paras. 30–31, 90–95).[4]

Attribute Two: Fair Trial Principles for Children (Article 40 (2))

Article 40(2) identifies the main States Parties' obligations to ensure to the child the benefit of the principle of non-retroactivity of the penal law. This principle is as also mentioned in Article 15(1) of the International Covenant on Civil and Political Rights and from which no derogation is permitted (van Bueren, 2005, pp. 13–14).

Article 40(2)(a)) lists the legal rights of children alleged or accused of having committed a crime. Those include the following:

- Respect for the principle of the presumption of innocence. This equally applies to adults and implies that according to the law a child is innocent until proven guilty (Article 40(2)(b)(i)) (van Bueren, 2005, p. 14)
- The right be informed promptly and directly of their charges and to have appropriate assistance in the preparation and presentation of their defence (Article 40(2)(b)(ii)) (van Bueren, 2005, pp. 14–15)
- If the case has not been diverted away from the juvenile justice system, the right to benefit from the 'principle of equality' before the law (Article 40(2)(b)(iii)). This implies:
  - The right to see their case determined by a competent 'independent and impartial authority or judicial body', including administrative bodies. The broad formulation is meant to reflect the diversity of juvenile proceeding available throughout the world.
  - The right to 'have the matter determined without delay, in a fair hearing according to the law.' This is also emphasised in Article 10(2)(b) of the International Covenant on Civil and Political Rights.
  - The right to benefit from the presence of legal or other appropriate assistance 'unless it is not considered to be in the interest of the child', through a

---

[4] See also *Beijing Rules*, Rule 2 (3) and *A Commentary on the United Nations Convention on the Rights of the Child, Article 40: Child Criminal Justice* (van Bueren, 2005, pp. 25–26).

well-trained, informed, and independent body whom the child can rely on and feel confident with.[5] This should allow the child to participate directly or indirectly in the procedure, in the full exercise of Article 12(2) of the Convention on the Rights of the Child and Article 14(2)(b) of the International Covenant on Civil and Political Rights (van Bueren, 2005, pp. 15–20).

- The right to remain silent and to not be obliged to give testimony or to confess guilt (Article 40(2)(b)(iv)). This mirrors Article 13(4)(g) of the International Covenant on Civil and Political Rights and Article 11 of the Universal Declaration of Human Rights. However, to be precise, the right to silence as a basic procedural safeguard is found only in the Beijing Rules and in General Comment no. 10. It is foreseen because children are more vulnerable to pressures to confess and the right to silence might help them to limit or prevent such pressure. Therefore, this silence should not be interpreted as supporting the finding of guilt (Hodgkin et al., 2007, p. 613; UN Committee on the Rights of the Child, 1995, paras. 20, 34).
- In case the child is convicted, they have the right to appeal and to see their conviction and sentence reviewed by a higher tribunal in line with Article 14 (5) International Covenant on Civil and Political Rights (Article 40(2)(b)(v)) (UN Committee on the Rights of the Child, 2007a, paras. 23–24, 2019, para. 57).
- In circumstances where the child cannot understand the language used, they have the right to have the free assistance of an interpreter. This applies to a court trial as well as to all stages of the juvenile justice process and implies that the 'interpreter has been trained to work with children.' The child's use and understanding of their birth language might be different from that of an adult. In line with Article 40(2)(vi), and in accordance with the special protection measures attributed to children with disabilities by Article 23, the inability to understand the language must also be recognised in relation to children with speech impairment or other disabilities (UN Committee on the Rights of the Child, 2007a, paras. 62–63, 2007b).
- The right to full respect for the child's privacy. This reflects the right to protection of privacy enshrined in Article 16 of the Convention and it covers all stages of the proceedings from the 'initial contact with law enforcement (e.g., a request for information and identification) up until the final decision by a competent authority, or release from supervision, custody, or deprivation of liberty'. The provision mirrors the wording of Article 14(1) of the *International Covenant on Civil and Political Rights* and is expanded by the *Beijing Rules* (Rule 8(1) and (2)), with the intention to avoid harm caused by undue publicity, for example through press releases or a public hearing, because of its effect of stigmatisation, and possible impact on the child's ability to have access to education, work, housing, or to be safe (Hodgkin et al., 2007, pp. 615–616; UN Committee on the Rights of the Child, 2007a, paras. 64–65).

---

[5] The qualification of the child's representative as legal or non-legal is meant to underline that the juvenile's representative ought to be a well-trained, informed, and independent professional.

Attribute Three: The Establishment of the Minimum Age of Criminal Responsibility (Article 40(3)(a))

Article 40(3)(a) asks States Parties to establish a minimum age of criminal responsibility (MACR). Based on the interpretation provided in its General Comment no. 24, the Committee has clarified that:

- Children who commit an offence under the specified MACR cannot be formally charged or held responsible in a penal law procedure (2019, para. 20).
- A MACR below 14 is not internationally acceptable. Therefore, the Committee recommends that States Parties should regard 14 as the absolute minimum and once a MACR is set no exception should apply, not even when serious offences are committed (2019, para. 21).
- If there is no reliable proof of age and it cannot be established, the child shall not be held criminally responsible (2019).[6]

Attribute Four: The Diversion Process and Alternatives Measures to Institutionalisation (Article 40(3)(b) and (4))

Article 40(3)(b) incorporates the principle of diverting children away from formal trial procedure whenever appropriate and desirable, 'providing that human rights and legal safeguards are fully respected.' The Committee's General Comment no. *24* clarifies that (2019)[7]:

- Diversion can be implemented when the States Parties have a variety of dispositions available such as care, guidance and supervision orders, counselling, probation, foster care, educational and training programmes, and other alternatives to institutional care.
- It should be proposed only where there is convincing evidence that the child has committed the alleged offence and voluntarily acknowledges responsibility without intimidation or pressure.[8]
- The child must freely and willingly consent in writing to the diversion.
- The completion of the diversion should result in a definite and final closure of the case (2019, paras. 16–18).[9]

---

[6] See also the *Beijing Rules* Rule 4 and its interpretation, General Comment no. 7 (2006, para. 36 (i)) and the *Implementation Handbook* (Hodgkin et al., 2007, pp. 616–617).

[7] See also the *Beijing Rules* Rule 4 and its interpretation, General Comment no. 7 (2006, para. 36 (i)) and the *Implementation Handbook* (Hodgkin et al., 2007, pp. 616–617).

[8] This acknowledgement must not be used against the child in any subsequent legal proceedings.

[9] The *Beijing Rules* expand on the use of diversion from judicial proceedings in rules 11, 14(1). See their official commentary (Hodgkin et al., 2007, p. 618).

The *United Nations Standard Minimum Rules for Non-custodial Measures (The Tokyo Rules)* are relevant to the implementation of Article 40(3)(b). The rules provide minimum safeguards for all persons subject to alternatives to imprisonment. They do not include any specific reference to children, but state that they should be applied with no discrimination based on age. Article 40(3)(b) also provides a connection with Article 37(b) and the provisions of alternatives to arrest, detention, and imprisonment (van Bueren, 2005, p. 28).

Article 40(4) identifies the duty of States Parties to provide a variegated range of measures as alternatives to institutional care, in order to not give the impression that diversion is a cheap solution or that States Parties follow a one size fits all solution. Based on the Convention, the diversion procedures need to suit the personal needs of each child and they should be proportionate to the child's circumstances and the offence committed (van Bueren, 2005, pp. 22–23, 30–31). Article 37 completes the protection enshrined in Article 40(4) and emphasises that depriving children of liberty must only be used as a last resort and for the shortest appropriate period' and it also bans capital punishment, life imprisonment without possibility of release, and any cruel, inhuman or degrading treatment or punishment' (Pinheiro, 2006, pp. 216, 217).

References

de Pinheiro, P. S. (2006). *Report of the independent expert for the United Nations Study on violence against children, A/61/299*. UN. Retrieved November 12, 2020, from http://digitallibrary.un.org/record/584299

Hodgkin, R., Newell, P., & UNICEF. (2007). *Implementation handbook for the convention on the rights of the child* (3rd ed.). New York: UNICEF. Retrieved September 21, 2020, from https://digitallibrary.un.org/record/620060?ln=en

UN Committee on the Rights of the Child. (1995). *Concluding observations: United Kingdom, February 15, 1995, CRC/C/15/Add.34*. UN. Retrieved November 6, 2020, from http://digitallibrary.un.org/record/198509

UN Committee on the Rights of the Child. (2006). *General Comment No. 7 (2005) Implementing child rights in early childhood, September 20, 2006, CRC/C/GC/7/Rev.1*. Retrieved October 12, 2020, from https://digitallibrary.un.org/record/584854?ln=en

UN Committee on the Rights of the Child. (2007a). *General Comment No. 10 (2007) Children's rights in juvenile justice, April 25, 2007, CRC/C/GC/10*. Retrieved October 12, 2020, from https://digitallibrary.un.org/record/599395?ln=en

UN Committee on the Rights of the Child. (2007b). *General Comment No. 9 (2006) The rights of children with disabilities, November 13, 2007, CRC/C/GC/9*. Retrieved October 12, 2020, from https://digitallibrary.un.org/record/593891?ln=en

UN Committee on the Rights of the Child. (2009). *General Comment No. 12 (2009) The right of the child to be heard, July 20, 2009, CRC/C/GC/12*. Retrieved October 12, 2020, from https://digitallibrary.un.org/record/671444?ln=en

UN Committee on the Rights of the Child. (2013). *General Comment No. 14 (2013) On the right of the child to have his or her best interests taken as a primary consideration (art. 3, para. 1), May 29, 2013, CRC/C/GC/14*. Retrieved October 12, 2020, from https://digitallibrary.un.org/record/778523?ln=en

UN Committee on the Rights of the Child. (2019). *General comment No. 24 (2019) on children's rights in the child justice system, CRC/C/GC/24*. Retrieved November 29, 2020, from https://tbinternet.ohchr.org/_layouts/15/treatybodyexternal/Download.aspx?symbolno=CRC%2fC%2fGC%2f24&Lang=en

UN General Assembly. (1991a). *United Nations Guidelines for the Prevention of Juvenile Delinquency (The Riyadh Guidelines), 1990, A/RES/45/112*. UN. Retrieved November 6, 2020, from http://digitallibrary.un.org/record/105349

UN General Assembly. (1991b). *United Nations Rules for the Protection of Juveniles Deprived of Their Liberty, 1990, A/RES/45/113 (The Havana Rules)*. UN. Retrieved October 26, 2020, from http://digitallibrary.un.org/record/105555

van Bueren, G. (2005). *A Commentary on the United Nations Convention on the Rights of the Child, Article 40: Child Criminal Justice. A Commentary on the United Nations Convention on the Rights of the Child, Article 40: Child Criminal Justice*. Brill Nijhoff. Retrieved November 29, 2020, from https://brill.com/view/title/11607

Open Access This chapter is licensed under the terms of the Creative Commons Attribution 4.0 International License (http://creativecommons.org/licenses/by/4.0/), which permits use, sharing, adaptation, distribution and reproduction in any medium or format, as long as you give appropriate credit to the original author(s) and the source, provide a link to the Creative Commons license and indicate if changes were made.

The images or other third party material in this chapter are included in the chapter's Creative Commons license, unless indicated otherwise in a credit line to the material. If material is not included in the chapter's Creative Commons license and your intended use is not permitted by statutory regulation or exceeds the permitted use, you will need to obtain permission directly from the copyright holder.

Part IX
General Measures of Implementation

Articles 1, 4, 42 and 44(6)

Introduction

The articles covered in this part, unlike the articles in the previous parts, do not introduce rights. Rather, they provide the architecture within which and through which all the rights in the Convention on the Rights of the Child (the Convention) must be understood. They provide guidance to States Parties on the measures States Parties must adopt to support the implementation of children's rights.

Article 1 provides the definition as to who is a child under the terms of the Convention. This part elaborates how, after much debate, and a failure to reach a consensus by the original Working Group charged with drafting the Convention, the text avoids any prescription as to whether childhood commences at conception or birth. States Parties make that determination for themselves. However, it does affirm that all the rights it embodies apply to every child up to their eighteenth birthday.

Article 4 builds on earlier iterations of general implementation measures developed in the International Covenant on Economic, Social and Cultural Rights (ICESCR) and the International Covenant on Civil and Political Rights (ICCPR). It provides a comprehensive and overarching framework of all the measures that States Parties must undertake to give effect to the Convention rights and must be read and understood alongside each of those individual rights. Thus, while many articles in the Convention outline specific measures needed to ensure compliance, States Parties must also consider their implementation in accordance with the provisions of Article 4, as elaborated in the Committee's General Comment no. 5. This includes reconsideration of any reservations and ratification of relevant treaties, comprehensive reviews of legislation, and remedies for violations. It involves a broad range of administrative measures including national strategies, cross-departmental coordination, transparency of budgets, the nature of engagement with the private sector and civil society, training and capacity building, monitoring, data collection, and establishment of national human rights institutions.

Article 4 also affirms that, again in accordance with the ICESCR and the ICCPR, implementation of economic, social and cultural rights in the Convention is subject to progressive realisation, in recognition of their significant resource implications. However, this accommodation does not provide an excuse for States Parties to avoid the responsibilities they undertook on ratification. On the contrary, States Parties are obliged to 'move as expeditiously and effectively as possible towards full realisation of economic, social and cultural rights' (Committee on Economic, Social and Cultural Rights (CESCR) 1990, para. 9). The Committee on the Rights of the Child (the Committee) has stressed that 'States Parties are expected to demonstrate that they have made every effort to mobilize, allocate and spend budget resources to fulfil the economic, social and cultural rights of all children' (2016, para. 30).

Finally, this part considers Articles 42 and 44(6), which impose obligations, respectively, to make the provisions of the Convention widely known to children and adults alike and to disseminate their reports to the Committee on the Rights of the Child to the public. These articles testify to the importance afforded to knowledge and awareness of what rights children have, understanding of how to exercise them, and information on the measures States Parties have undertaken to translate them into reality.

Overall, these articles provide the mechanisms to guide States Parties' implementation of the Convention and enable children and their families and advocates to hold those States Parties to account in meeting the obligations they have committed to respect, protect, and fulfil.

References

Committee on Economic, Social and Cultural Rights (CESCR). (1990). *ICESCR General Comment No. 3: The Nature of States Parties' Obligations (Art. 2, Para. 1, of the Covenant)*. https://www.refworld.org/pdfid/4538838e10.pdf

UN Committee on the Rights of the Child. (2016). *General Comment No. 19 (2016) on public budgeting for the realization of children's rights (art.4), CRC/C/GC/19*. UN. http://digitallibrary.un.org/record/838730. Accessed 12 November 2020

Chapter 40
Article 1: Definition of a Child

Gerison Lansdown and Ziba Vaghri

> 1. For the purposes of the present Convention, a child means every human being below the age of 18 years unless under the law applicable to the child, majority is attained earlier.

Overview

While all international human rights treaties apply to children, only the Convention explicitly elaborates who is defined as a child. Article 1 defines the child as a human being who is below the age of 18 years.[1] Majority is set at age 18 unless, under domestic law, it is attained earlier. During the negotiations of the text of the Convention, there was significant debate regarding definitions of both the commencement and the ending of childhood. The initial text, proposed by the Polish Government, drawing on Principle 1 of the UN Declaration of the Rights of the Child, 1959, provided no definition of childhood at all (Office of the United Nations High Commissioner for Human Rights and Rädda barnen (Society: Sweden), 2007,

---

[1] Article 1 is 'the first definition of the child in international law' (de Detrick, 1999, p. 52; Vučković-Šahović et al., 2012, p. 85).

G. Lansdown (✉)
Carleton University, Ottawa, ON, Canada

Z. Vaghri
University of New Brunswick, Saint John, Canada
e-mail: ziba.vaghri@unb.ca

© The Author(s) 2022
Z. Vaghri et al. (eds.), *Monitoring State Compliance with the UN Convention on the Rights of the Child*, Children's Well-Being: Indicators and Research 25,
https://doi.org/10.1007/978-3-030-84647-3_40

p. 301). However, government delegates on the Working Group immediately highlighted the need for clarification. The first revision of the text therefore proposed that a child is a human being from birth to the age of 18 years unless majority is attained earlier. However, with regard to the beginning of childhood, the Working Group were unable to come to a consensus. An unresolvable division persisted on whether childhood, in respect of the Convention, commenced from the point of conception, or from birth (Office of the United Nations High Commissioner for Human Rights and Rädda barnen (Society: Sweden), 2007, pp. 301–313). The conflict was ultimately resolved by removing any reference to the start of childhood.

On the termination of childhood, an upper age had to be defined. Because childhood is a social construct, there is no shared legal definition (Vučković-Šahović et al., 2012, pp. 1–18). Account needs to be taken of the cultural differences in definitions of childhood, with majority being obtained much earlier in some states, the increasingly early development of children, the heterogeneity of children, and the potentially excessive burden for developing states in providing the protections afforded by the Convention to everyone under the age of 18 years. After some debate by the Working Group, a consensus was forged over a definition that a human being is a child until the age of 18 years. However, the opportunity for attaining majority earlier was retained in the text of Article 1, and in this way, the text seeks to accommodate existing cultural and religious diversities reflected in national age limits (Van Bueren, 1998, p. 37). The Convention therefore is prescriptive, but not inflexible in defining childhood.

In summary, Article 1 establishes the framework of childhood within which to apply the Convention in its entirety. Every person under the age of 18 years, as a consequence of their greater vulnerability, will always be entitled to the overarching special protections foreseen in the Convention (Vučković-Šahović et al., 2012, pp. 85–87). However, Article 1 does not preclude the introduction by States Parties of lower age limits in respect of the exercise of certain rights, in recognition of the evolving capacities of the child.

General Principles

Article 2 Every human being under the age of 18 years must be recognised as a child, without discrimination based on any attribute of the child or parent. Importantly, the definition of childhood must extend equally to all genders without discrimination.

Article 3 The best interests principle must be applied to every child up to the age of 18 years.

Article 6 The right to life, survival, and development must be recognised for every child under the age of 18 years.

Article 12 Childhood status as defined under Article 1 does not preclude recognition of the right of the child to express views and have them given due weight in accordance with age and maturity.

Articles Related or Linked to Article 1

Article 1 is relevant and has application to every article in the Convention, and the Optional Protocols.

Relevant Instruments

All human rights treaties apply to children but, at the international level, only the Convention defines the child. An exception at the regional level is provided by Article 2 of the African Charter on the Rights and Welfare of the Child (1990) which states that for its purposes, 'a child means every human being below the age of 18 years.'

Attributes

Attribute One: Ages of Majority

Article 1 explicitly sets a benchmark of 18 years as the end of childhood. This age limit needs to be applied by States Parties as both a rule and a reference point, for the establishment of any other age for any specific purpose or activity (Pais, 1997, p. 414). The Convention, therefore, needs to be respected, protected, and fulfilled for every child under that age. States Parties are required to review all relevant legislation to achieve that goal in all spheres of the child's life. The Committee has emphasised, for example, that the definition of a child under customary law must be consistent with Article 1 (2002, paras. 23, 24). The only explicit exception in the Convention arises in Article 38, which provides that the minimum age for participation in hostilities is 15 years.

States Parties can aim for a higher standard of protection by raising the ages defined in the Convention, in accordance with Article 41 which clarifies that nothing in the Convention precludes the retention or introduction by any state of provisions that are more conducive to the rights of the child. Thus, many States Parties have determined that the age of 15 years is too low for participation in hostilities and have raised the age accordingly (Pais, 1997, p. 414). The Optional Protocol on children in armed conflict was drafted to seek to strengthen the provisions in Article 38, by raising the age limits for protection, although it does still contain significant weaknesses, as discussed in Part 8.

Article 1 does allow for the age of majority to be attained earlier than 18 years. This provision should not be interpreted as a general escape clause from the obligations under the Convention, nor to allow for ages to be established which are inconsistent with its principles and provisions (Pais, 1997, pp. 414–415). The Committee has stressed that where the age of majority is below the age of eighteen years, States Parties are expected to indicate how all children benefit from protection and enjoy their rights under the Convention up to the age of 18 years. The Committee has demanded justification of any diminution in protection of children and urged States Parties to reconsider in order to ensure that all children up to 18 years continue to receive the full protections of the Convention (2009, para. 27, 2010, para. 27, 2012, para. 26). The Human Rights Committee has also emphasised that States Parties cannot absolve themselves from obligations to children under 18 years even where they have reached the age of majority under domestic law (UN Office of the High Commissioner for Human Rights (OHCHR), 1989, para. 4).

Attribute Two: Accommodation of Differential Ages

It is not possible to establish a uniform age for all aspects of the lives of children applicable in every country in the world. The Committee seeks to promote recognition that all children are subjects of the rights under the Convention until the age of 18, and thereby entitled to special protection measures, while simultaneously acknowledging their right to progressively exercise their rights in accordance with their evolving capacities (2003, para. 1). Article 1 therefore does also allow for flexibility in setting up minimum ages for certain purposes.

Some articles specifically recognise the need for States Parties to provide a minimum age, for example, in relation to admission to employment, Article 32, and the establishment of an age of criminal responsibility, Article 40, paragraph 3(a). In other cases, the Convention leaves it open to States Parties to determine, for example, the age for the end of compulsory education, Article 28, and access to medical and legal counselling without parental consent, Article 24. However, the Committee does require that States Parties address these areas of legislation, and that in so doing must have regard to the entire Convention and in particular, the General Principles (Hodgkin et al., 2007, p. 5). The Human Rights Committee has also emphasised that in setting ages below 18 years, such ages must not be set too low (UN Office of the High Commissioner for Human Rights (OHCHR), 1989, para. 4).

In the Committee's periodic guidelines, States Parties are asked to provide relevant and up-to-date information with respect to Article 1 of the Convention concerning the definition of the child in its domestic laws and regulations (2015, para. 2). The only specific requirement demanded by the Committee is for States Parties to indicate the minimum age for marriage for girls and boys in its legislation.

The Committee has strongly argued that this should be 18 years for both girls and boys (2016, para. 40).

References

Bueren, G. V. (1998). *The international law on the rights of the child*. Martinus Nijhoff Publishers.

de Detrick, S. L. (1999). *A commentary on the United Nations convention on the rights of the child*. Brill Nijhoff. Retrieved November 6, 2020, from https://brill.com/view/title/10630

Hodgkin, R., Newell, P., & UNICEF. (2007). *Implementation handbook for the convention on the rights of the child* (3rd ed.). New York: UNICEF. Retrieved September 21, 2020, from https://digitallibrary.un.org/record/620060?ln=en

Office of the United Nations High Commissioner for Human Rights & Rädda barnen (Society: Sweden). (2007). *Legislative history of the convention on the rights of the child*. United Nations. Retrieved from https://digitallibrary.un.org/record/602462?ln=en

Pais, M. S. (1997). The convention on the rights of the child. In *manual on human rights reporting under six major international human rights instruments HR/PUB/91/1 (rev.1)* (pp. 393–505). OHCHR. Retrieved May 16, 2020, from https://www.refworld.org/docid/428085252.html

UN Committee on the Rights of the Child. (2002). *Concluding observations: Mozambique, April 3, 2002, CRC/C/15/Add.172*. UN. Retrieved November 16, 2020, from http://digitallibrary.un.org/record/467261

UN Committee on the Rights of the Child. (2003). *General Comment No. 4 (2003) Adolescent health and development in the context of the Convention on the Rights of the Child, July 1, 2003, CRC/GC/2003/4*. Retrieved October 12, 2020, from https://digitallibrary.un.org/record/503074?ln=en

UN Committee on the Rights of the Child. (2009). *Concluding observations: Pakistan. October 15, 2009, CRC/C/PAK/CO/3-4.* . Retrieved from https://digitallibrary.un.org/record/669129?ln=en

UN Committee on the Rights of the Child. (2010). *Concluding observations: Nigeria, June 21, 2010, CRC/C/NGA/CO/3-4*. Retrieved October 11, 2020, from https://digitallibrary.un.org/record/685180?ln=en

UN Committee on the Rights of the Child. (2012). *Concluding observations: Albania, December 7, 2012, CRC/C/ALB/CO/2-4*. UN. Retrieved October 26, 2020, from http://digitallibrary.un.org/record/739974

UN Committee on the Rights of the Child. (2015). *Treaty-specific guidelines regarding the form and content of periodic reports to be submitted by States parties under Article 44, paragraph 1 (b), of the Convention on the Rights of the Child, March 3, 2015, CRC/C/58/Rev.3*. UN. Retrieved December 1, 2020, from http://digitallibrary.un.org/record/789762

UN Committee on the Rights of the Child. (2016). *General Comment No. 20 (2016) on the implementation of the rights of the child during adolescence, December 6, 2016, CRC/C/GC/20*. Retrieved October 12, 2020, from https://digitallibrary.un.org/record/855544?ln=en

UN Office of the High Commissioner for Human Rights (OHCHR). (1989). *CCPR General Comment No. 17: (1989) Article 24 (Rights of the Child)*. Retrieved November 6, 2020, from https://www.refworld.org/docid/45139b464.html

Vučković-Šahović, N., Doek, J. E., & Zermatten, J. (2012). *The rights of the child in international law: Rights of the child in a nutshell and in context: All about children's rights*. Stämpfli.

Open Access This chapter is licensed under the terms of the Creative Commons Attribution 4.0 International License (http://creativecommons.org/licenses/by/4.0/), which permits use, sharing, adaptation, distribution and reproduction in any medium or format, as long as you give appropriate credit to the original author(s) and the source, provide a link to the Creative Commons license and indicate if changes were made.

The images or other third party material in this chapter are included in the chapter's Creative Commons license, unless indicated otherwise in a credit line to the material. If material is not included in the chapter's Creative Commons license and your intended use is not permitted by statutory regulation or exceeds the permitted use, you will need to obtain permission directly from the copyright holder.

Chapter 41
Article 4: States Parties' Obligations

Roberta Ruggiero

> States Parties shall undertake all appropriate legislative, administrative, and other measures for the implementation of the rights recognized in the present Convention. With regard to economic, social and cultural rights, States Parties shall undertake such measures to the maximum extent of their available resources and, where needed, within the framework of international cooperation.

Overview

Article 4 deals with the nature of the States Parties' obligations and it therefore relates 'to all the substantive articles of the Convention' (Rishmawi, 2006, pp. 22, 57). Together with Articles 42 and 44(6), it comprises the heading 'General Measures of Implementation' in the States Parties' periodic reports (Hodgkin et al., 2007, p. 47; Rishmawi, 2006, p. 22; UN Committee on the Rights of the Child, 1991, paras. 9–11, 1996, paras. 11–24, 2002a, p. 58, 2015, paras. 18–21).

It imposes on States Parties the obligation to 'undertake all appropriate legislative, administrative, and other measures' necessary for the implementation of the rights enshrined in the Convention and in its Optional Protocols. It qualifies the nature of States Parties' obligations related to the economic, social, and cultural

R. Ruggiero (✉)
Centre for Children's Rights Studies, University of Geneva, Geneva, Switzerland
e-mail: roberta.ruggiero@unige.ch

rights internally to the limit of 'the maximum extent of their available resources' and if needed through international cooperation.

The initial wording of Article 4 did not contain any reference to the two categories of rights (civil and political rights, and economic, social, and cultural rights), but observations were raised by States Parties about the necessity of adjusting the wording in accordance with Article 2 (1) of the ICESCR (Office of the United Nations High Commissioner for Human Rights and Rädda barnen (Society: Sweden), 2007, p. 349). After several amendments and proposals, a new version of the provision was made. It introduced the phrase 'in accordance with their available resources', but without specifying that this applied only to economic, social, and cultural rights.[1]

Thus, after several proposals, it was decided that only economic, social, and cultural rights should be connected to the availability of resources. This compromise brought about the current text of Article 4, which was adopted unanimously, and its interpretation can be elucidated by the interpretation provided respectively by the ICCPR Committee and the Committee on Economic, Social and Cultural Rights.

However, the distinction of the nature of the States Parties' obligations in relation to the implementation of the two categories of rights have several practical

---

[1] Text of Article 4 adopted at first reading: 'The States Parties to the present Convention shall undertake all appropriate administrative and legislative measures, in accordance with their available resources and, where needed, within the framework of international cooperation, for the implementation of the rights recognized in this Convention' (Rishmawi, 2006, p. 19; UN Commission on Human Rights and Working Group on a Draft Convention on the Rights of the Child, 1988; Office of the United Nations High Commissioner for Human Rights and Rädda barnen (Society: Sweden), 2007, p. 352).

The UN Secretary-General asked for a technical review of this 'first reading' and requested comments from a number of UN bodies and agencies, UNICEF included. UNICEF introduced a major shift in the discussion. It underlined that Article 4 of the Convention was essentially based on three aspects:

The obligation to implement
In 'accordance with their available resources'
'where needed within the framework of international cooperation.'

With reference to the second point, UNICEF underlined that none of the States Parties' obligations related to the implementation of the ICCPR and CEDAW are limited in accordance with the 'available resources.' UNICEF requested the deletion of the reference to available resources, on the grounds that the draft of Article 4 'would achieve a radical diminution of the standards contained in existing instruments and would run counter to all of the assumptions that have hitherto governed the recognition of civil and political rights in international law.'

After the UNICEF observation, several delegations expressed their concerns. Some underlined that the Convention should not weaken civil and political rights, which in the ICCPR are not subject to the availability of resources. Others were against the deletion, on the grounds that economic difficulties indeed justify the constraints faced by developing countries. This was the first time during the drafting of the Convention that the nature of the States parties' obligations in relation to the availability of resources was addressed, along with its implication in relation to the two categories of human rights (Rishmawi, 2006, p. 20; Office of the United Nations High Commissioner for Human Rights and Rädda barnen (Society: Sweden), 2007, pp. 352–354).

implications. In fact, during the drafting, it was decided that the Convention should consist of concrete provisions, supplementary to those already existing in the other international treaties, in particular the ICCPR and the ICESCR (de Detrick, 1999, p. 6). Therefore, the Convention not only combines both categories of rights, but it also adds new rights, many of which encapsulate different aspects of both categories. This implies that many rights of the Convention cannot be classified in a straightforward manner as civil, political, or economic, social, or cultural rights (Rishmawi, 2006, pp. 13–18). Examples include the States Parties obligation to respect the rights and duties of parents to provide direction to the child in the exercise of their rights (Article 14(2) and Article 5) and the right of the child to express their views freely in all matters affecting them (Article 12(1)).

In the Convention, there are rights which are not included in the ICCPR and the ICESR. These include those enshrined in Articles 31 (right to rest and leisure), 35 (right to be protected against abduction and sale), 36 (right to be protected from all forms of exploitation) and 39 (right to integration and social recovery for victims). Based on General Comment no. 5, 'there is no simple or authoritative division of human rights in general or of Convention rights into the two categories' and this reflects the indivisibility of all human rights and the 'enjoyment of economic, social and cultural rights is inextricably intertwined with enjoyment of civil and political rights' (Rishmawi, 2006, pp. 14–15; UN Committee on the Rights of the Child, 2003a, para. 6).

General Principles

The link between Article 4 and the General Principles is well documented in the reporting guidelines and General Comment no. 5, in which the Committee clarifies that the 'development of a children's rights perspective throughout government, parliament and the judiciary' is a precondition for the effective implementation of the whole Convention, in particular, in the light of its General Principles.

Article 2 The non-discrimination principle requires States Parties to implement the rights in the Convention to each child without discrimination. This also requires States Parties to undertake all the 'special measures' necessary for the implementation of the right of an individual child and/or groups of children in accordance with their specific condition. In those cases, the special measures are justified by the necessity to diminish or eliminate conditions that cause discrimination, with the intention of facilitating equal access to rights (the latter does not always imply identical treatment) (UN Human Rights Committee, 1989). For this reason, the Committee highlights 'the need for data collection to be disaggregated to enable discrimination or potential discrimination to be identified'. Furthermore, to overcome discrimination, changes in legislation, administration and resource allocation, as well as attitudes and practices, may be required (2003a, para. 12).

Article 3(1) Every 'legislative, administrative and judicial body or institution is required to apply the best interests principle, by systematically considering how children's rights and interests are or will be affected by their decisions and actions'. This principle also applies in those cases in which children would only indirectly be affected, by a proposed or existing law or policy or administrative action or court decision (UN Committee on the Rights of the Child, 2003a, para. 12).

Article 6 Based on the Committee's interpretation, the concept of 'development' is a holistic concept, embracing the child's physical, mental, spiritual, moral, psychological, and social development. Under Article 4, States Parties are requested to undertake all adequate implementation measures with the aim of achieving 'the optimal development for all children' (2003a, para. 12).

Article 12 With reference to the role of the child as an active participant in the implementation and monitoring of their rights, States Parties are requested to apply this principle equally to all measures adopted to implement the Convention. This can include, for example, involving children in the government decision-making processes, parliamentary procedures, providing them access to documents, adequate information, and giving due weight to their views. The Committee underlines that 'Article 12 requires consistent and ongoing arrangements' (2003a, para. 12). The consultation of children should be a constant part of the decision and discussion processes, and the emphasis on 'matters that affect them' entails the assessment of the opinions of particular groups confronted with the issue under discussion. Therefore, both Governments and children should have their direct appropriate channel of contact.

Articles Related or Linked to Article 4

Based on the interpretation of Article 4 provided by the Committee, this Article is instrumental to the implementation of all the other substantive rights listed in the Convention. Therefore, it is worth underlining that the wording of Article 4 is similar to that used in other provisions of the Convention, in particular with reference to the two notions of 'maximum available resources' and of 'progressive realization.' These two notions compose the essence of the progressive nature of implementation of some Convention rights. For example:

Article 23 identifies the States Parties' obligation to encourage and ensure assistance to children with disabilities in the limit of 'the available resources.'

Article 24(4), with reference to the progressive full realisation of the right to 'the highest attainable standard of health.'

Article 27, in relation to the right to an adequate standard of living and the obligation of the States Parties to assist parents and other caregivers in the fulfilment of this right 'in accordance with national conditions and within their means.'

Article 28 (1), in which the implementation of the right to education implies 'achieving this right progressively' (Rishmawi, 2006, pp. 22, 23).

Relevant Instruments

The following are the main international human rights treaties with particular relevance to children's rights, that, like Article 4 of the Convention on the Rights of the Child, contain provisions defining the nature of States Parties' obligations.

International Covenant on Civil and Political Rights (1966), Article 2(2).

International Covenant on Economic, Social and Cultural Rights (1966), Article 2 (1).

International Convention on the Elimination of All Forms of Racial Discrimination (1966), Article 2(1)(c).

UN Convention on the Elimination of All Forms of Discrimination against Women (1979), Article 2 (2) and Article 3.

UN Convention against Torture and Other Cruel, Inhuman or Degrading Treatment or Punishment (1984), Article 2(1).

International Convention on the Protection of the Rights of All Migrant Workers and Members of Their Families (1990), Article 73(1).

UN Convention on the Rights of Persons with Disabilities (2006), Article 4(2).

European Convention on Human Rights (1950), does not deal with nature of the States Parties' obligations. These latter have been clarified by judgements of the European Court of Human Rights.

American Convention on Human Rights 'Pact of San Jose, Costa Rica' (B-32) (1978), Article 2 and Article 26.

African Charter on the Rights and Welfare of the Child (1990), defines the nature of States Parties obligation in Article 1(1), however it does not qualify the nature of the States Parties obligations in relation to economic, social and cultural rights (Rishmawi, 2006, pp. 3, 14).

Attributes

Attribute One: States Parties' Obligations to 'Undertake All Appropriate, Legislative, Administrative and Other Measures'

Both the ICECR and the ICCPR have articles similar to Article 4 of the Convention on the Rights of the Child, but they provide different levels of detail in the identification of the 'appropriate measures of implementation'. For example, while Article 2(2) of the ICCPR refers to legislative and others measures 'necessary to give effect to the rights,' Article 4 of the Convention on the Rights of the Child states that those measures should be taken in accordance with the national constitutional processes and does not refer to administrative measures. On the other hand, Article 2(1) of the ICESCR also states the use of all 'appropriate means,' but it particularly emphasises the adoption of legislative measures for the fulfilment of the rights recognised in the ICESCR.

Article 4 presents the most comprehensive list of possible measures of implementation and the Committee, in its General Comment no. 5, provides a more detailed description of these measures, building on the General Comments issued by treaty bodies responsible for the ICCPR and the ICESCR (Rishmawi, 2006, pp. 26–27).

Considering the wide range of systems of government among states in the General Comment no. 5, the Committee groups those measures into four categories:

1. **Review of reservations:** Based on Article 2 of the Vienna Convention on the Law of Treaties, a 'reservation' is a unilateral statement 'made by a State, when signing, ratifying, accepting, approving or acceding to a Treaty, whereby it purports to exclude or to modify the legal effect of certain provisions of the Treaty in their application to that State.' States Parties are entitled at the time of ratification to make a reservation unless it is 'incompatible with the object and purpose of the treaty' (Article 19). Similarly, Article 51(2) of the Convention states that 'A reservation incompatible with the object and purpose of the present Convention shall not be permitted.' Therefore, States Parties that have made reservations which plainly breach Article 51 (2), for example, by suggesting that 'respect for the Convention is limited by the state's existing Constitution or legislation, including in some cases religious law,' are requested to withdraw their reservation. In any case, Article 27 of the Vienna Convention on the Law of Treaties provides: 'A party may not invoke the provisions of its internal law as justification for its failure to perform a treaty' (Rishmawi, 2006, pp. 44–48; UN Committee on the Rights of the Child, 2003a, paras. 13–16).
2. **Ratification of other international human rights instruments:** The Committee consistently encourages States Parties to consider signing and ratifying all the Optional Protocols to the Convention, and other international human rights instruments, 'in the light of the principles of indivisibility and interdependence of human rights.' In General Comment no. 5 it provides a non-exhaustive list of them (2003a, para. 17, Annex).
3. **Legislative measures**. This includes the following:

   - Harmonisation of the national legislation, to ensure the full compatibility of national legislation with the Convention provisions. This should be addressed through a comprehensive and constant ongoing review of all national legislation (UN Committee on the Rights of the Child, 1994, para. 15, 1997, paras. 12, 29, 2002b, para. 9), to ensure compatibility of implementation with no discrimination, in particular within federal states.

     This process also applies to customary and religious laws. In this case, States Parties are requested to ensure the harmonisation of customary law, and the interpretation of religious laws should be reconciled with fundamental human rights (UN Committee on the Rights of the Child, 2003b, para. 8) and should not be used as an excuse for failure in implementation of the Convention (Rishmawi, 2006, pp. 25–26). The harmonisation process equally applies to civil and political rights, and to economic, social, and cultural rights regarding 'immediate obligations.' In particular, the ICESCR Committee has clarified that even though the obligation related to the ICESCR implies a progressive implementation, there are always 'obligations of immediate effect.'[2]

- Giving legal effect to all rights, by considering the Convention status in domestic legislation. The harmonisation of national legislation in compliance with the Convention does not ensure the 'direct applicability' of its provisions, which is related to the status of the Convention within national legal systems. Therefore, in order to ensure the legal effect of all Convention rights, States Parties are requested to clarify the 'extent of applicability of the Convention in States where the principle of self-execution' applies and others where it is claimed that the Convention 'has constitutional status or has been incorporated into domestic law' (UN Committee on the Rights of the Child, 2003a, para. 19). In particular, with reference to Convention incorporation into domestic legislation, this should imply that the Convention can be 'directly invoked before the courts and applied by national authorities and that the Convention will prevail where there is a conflict with domestic legislation or common practice' (Hodgkin et al., 2007, p. 54; UN Committee on the Rights of the Child, 2003a, paras. 20, 21).[3]
- Ensuring justiciability of rights. In cases of violations, effective legal remedies must be available to redress violations. 'Children's special and dependent status' poses additional challenges 'in pursuing remedies for breaches of their rights.' Therefore, States Parties are requested to set up effective, child-sensitive procedures available to children and their representatives. Furthermore, in cases of confirmed breach of rights, 'appropriate reparation, including compensation, and, where needed, measures to promote physical and psychological recovery, rehabilitation and reintegration' should be provided (Article 39) (UN Committee on the Rights of the Child, 2003a, para. 24). This applies to all Convention rights on an equal basis. Domestic law needs to set out detailed entitlements able to allow effective remedies for non-compliance and violation (Committee on Economic, Social and Cultural Rights (CESCR), 1998). These measures are a combination of legislative and administrative actions that provide a comprehensive system of remedies (UN Committee on the Rights of the Child, 2003a, paras. 24–25).

4. **Administrative and other measures.** In recognition of the significant differences between national systems, the Committee in the General Comment no. 5 provides some key advice:

---

[2] For example, the inclusion within the national legislation of provisions related to economic, social, and cultural rights, such as the right to education, or the right to non-discrimination (immediate obligations) (Rishmawi, 2006, p. 27; UN Committee on Economic, Social and Cultural Rights, 1991, pp. 83–87).

[3] See also 'A Commentary on the United Nations Convention on the Rights of the Child, Article 4: The Nature of States Parties' Obligations' (Rishmawi, 2006, pp. 23–24).

- National comprehensive strategy or national plan of action: This should cover all the provisions of the Convention and be related to the situation of all children, while giving specific attention to identifying and giving priority to marginalised and disadvantaged groups.

  It could be elaborated in sectoral national plans of action, for example, for education, health, trafficking and so on, but coherence and coordination should be ensured. The development of a national strategy is not a one-off task, and thus it should include arrangements for monitoring and continuous review of its outcomes (UN Committee on the Rights of the Child, 2003a, para. 26).
- Coordination: The Committee has underlined that the effective implementation of the Convention requires visible cross-sectoral coordination, in order to recognise and realise children's rights at the government and society level (2003a, para. 27). Many, if not all, government departments and other governmental or quasi-governmental bodies have a regular direct or indirect effect on children's lives' (2003a, para. 27). Thus, the Committee asks for a permanent governmental coordination mechanism to further the coordination between central government and local departments, and between government and civil society, children included. The concept of coordination has a horizontal and vertical connotation. The latter refers to coordination among different governmental levels (central and local entities). It is particularly relevant to delegation and decentralisation of competencies from the central government to local entities. This evidently characterises federalised states, but centralised states are also confronted with high devolution or delegation of power to the local authority. The Committee reiterates that this administrative organisation does not reduce the direct responsibility of the State Party, but on the contrary imposes more responsibility in terms of vertical coordination and budgetary allocation (2003a, paras. 40–41).
- Privatisation: Many States Parties hand over public services to private entities, which includes businesses, NGOs, and other private associations, both for-profit and not-for-profit (UN Committee on the Rights of the Child, 2002c). Enabling the private sector to provide services does not reduce 'the State's obligation to ensure for all children within its jurisdiction the full recognition and realization' of all Convention rights. Thus, privatisation includes the responsibility 'to ensure that non-state service providers operate in accordance with the CRC provision' and it creates an indirect obligation on private entities, on which a permanent monitoring mechanism could be imposed to ensure that non-state service providers respect the Convention (UN Committee on the Rights of the Child, 2003a, paras. 42–44).
- Monitoring implementation: Effective respect for and implementation of the Convention and the respect of the best interests of the child in legislation and policy development, and delivery at all levels of government, demands a

continuous process of child impact assessment[4] and child impact evaluation.[5] In terms of self-monitoring and evaluation, this constant ongoing process needs to be built into government at all levels and for all policy. However, the Committee also emphasises the necessity of an external and independent monitoring of the implementation process, 'by, for example, parliamentary committees, NGOs, academic institutions, professional associations, youth groups and independent human rights institutions' (Rishmawi, 2006, pp. 48–49; UN Committee on the Rights of the Child, 2003a, paras. 47–48).

- Data collection and development of indicators: The Committee always requires detailed statistical data, which is disaggregated in terms of not just gender and age, but also in terms of geography, ethnicity, and religion, with the aim of building up a longitudinal understanding of children's condition over time. This allows understanding of whether there is any kind of discrimination in relation to one of these sectors in policies or practices. Furthermore, the data collection needs to extend over the whole period of childhood, up to the age of 18 years, and it needs to be coordinated through the jurisdiction, ensuring nationally applicable indicators (Rishmawi, 2006, pp. 51–55; UN Committee on the Rights of the Child, 2003a, paras. 47–48).
- Budget allocation: Lack of resources cannot be used as a reason not to establish social security programmes and a social safety net.[6] The Committee dedicates increasing attention to the identification and analysis of resources for children in national and other budgets. It argues that 'no State can tell whether it is fulfilling children's economic, social and cultural rights 'to the maximum extent of... available resources', as it is required to do under Article 4, unless it can identify the proportion of national and other budgets allocated to the social sector and, within that, to children, both directly and indirectly.' In its General Comment no. 19, the Committee provides guidelines and recommendations on how to realise children's rights in relation to each of the four stages of the public budget process: planning, enacting, executing, and follow up (2016, paras. 61–111, 57–63).
- Training and capacity building: Like all the other general measures of implementation, this is a transversal one that requires States Parties to 'develop training and capacity building for all those involved in the implementation process' including all those working with and for children.[7] This training must

---

[4] Predicting the impact of any proposed law, policy or budgetary allocation which affects children and the enjoyment of their rights.

[5] Evaluating the actual impact of implementation.

[6] For children belonging to vulnerable or financially disadvantage groups including children with disabilities, children affected or/and infected by HIV/AIDS, street children and children living in poverty (UN Committee on the Rights of the Child, 2002d, paras. 14, 15, 2006a, paras. 17, 18, 2006b, paras. 20, 2, 2016, para. 21).

[7] These include, for example, government officials at all level, parliamentarians, members of the judiciary, community and religious leaders, teachers, social workers and other professionals, including those working with children in institutions and places of detention, the police and

be included in professional training curricula, codes of conduct, and educational curricula at all levels, included among children themselves (Article 42) (Rishmawi, 2006, pp. 50–51; UN Committee on the Rights of the Child, 2001, 2003a, paras. 66–70). Within this measure is included the obligation of States Parties to make their reports widely available to the public (adults and children) (Article 44(6)) (UN Committee on the Rights of the Child, 2003a, paras. 71–73).

- Cooperation with civil society: Even though States Parties hold the main responsibility for the implementation of the Convention, this extends 'in practice beyond the State and State-controlled services and institutions to include children, parents and wider families, other adults, and non-State services and organizations' (UN Committee on the Rights of the Child, 2003a, paras. 56–69), as stated in the General Comment no. 14 of the Committee on Economic, Social and Cultural Rights on the right to the highest attainable standard of health (2000). In addition, the Committee on the Rights of the Child has emphasised that 'It is important that governments develop a direct relationship with children, not simply one mediated through non-governmental organizations (NGOs) or human rights institutions' (2003a, para. 12).

- International cooperation: Articles 55 and 56 of the Charter of the United Nations identify the overall purposes of international economic and social cooperation. Drawing on these provisions, the Committee advises States Parties to establish a rights-based framework for international development assistance and to increase the percentage of gross domestic product invested in this sector, in compliance with the international standards. It also encourages States Parties that receive international financial and technical aid and assistance to allocate a substantive part of that aid specifically to children (Rishmawi, 2006, pp. 35–54; UN Committee on the Rights of the Child, 2003a, paras. 60–64).

- Independent human rights institutions: The setting up of these entities falls within the ratification commitment of States Parties (UN Committee on the Rights of the Child, 2002e, para. 1). These independent institutions are complementary to governmental structures and their role is to 'monitor independently the State's compliance and progress towards implementation' of the Convention. Their main characteristic is independence and thus government cannot delegate to them its monitoring obligations on child impact assessment of their strategies and policy-outcomes evaluation. Furthermore, they need to remain 'entirely free to set their own agenda and determine their own activities' (UN Committee on the Rights of the Child, 2002e, para. 25, 2003b, para. 65).

---

armed forces, including peacekeeping forces, those working in the media, parents/caregivers and many others.

References

Committee on Economic, Social and Cultural Rights (CESCR). (1998). *Draft General Comment No. 9: The domestic application of the Covenant E/C.12/1998/24 (No. E/C.12/1998/24)*. Geneva: 1998-12-03: UN. Retrieved from http://digitallibrary.un.org/record/1490423

de Detrick, S. L.. (1999). *A commentary on the United Nations convention on the rights of the child. A commentary on the United Nations Convention on the Rights of the Child*. Brill Nijhoff. Retrieved November 6, 2020, from https://brill.com/view/title/10630

Hodgkin, R., Newell, P., & UNICEF. (2007). *Implementation handbook for the convention on the rights of the child* (3rd ed.). : UNICEF. Retrieved September 21, 2020, from https://digitallibrary.un.org/record/620060?ln=en

Office of the United Nations High Commissioner for Human Rights & Rädda barnen (Society: Sweden). (2007). *Legislative history of the convention on the rights of the child*. : United Nations. Retrieved from https://digitallibrary.un.org/record/602462?ln=en

Rishmawi, M. (2006). *A commentary on the United Nations convention on the rights of the child, Article 4: The nature of states parties' obligations*. Leiden, The Netherlands: Brill Nijhoff. https://doi.org/10.1163/ej.9789004147089.i-57

UN Commission on Human Rights & Working Group on a Draft Convention on the Rights of the Child. (1988). *Draft Convention on the Rights of the Child: text of the draft Convention / E/CN.4/1988/WG.1/WP.1/Rev.1*. Geneva: 1988-02-24: UN. Retrieved from http://digitallibrary.un.org/record/157295

UN Committee on Economic, Social and Cultural Rights. (1991). *Committee on Economic, Social and Cultural Rights: report on the 5th session, 26 November-14 December 1990, E/1991/23*. UN. Retrieved November 17, 2020, from http://digitallibrary.un.org/record/114868

UN Committee on Economic, Social and Cultural Rights. (2000). *General comment No. 14 (2000), The right to the highest attainable standard of health (article 12 of the International Covenant on Economic, Social and Cultural Rights), E/C.12/2000/4*. UN. Retrieved November 13, 2020, from http://digitallibrary.un.org/record/425041

UN Committee on the Rights of the Child. (1991). *General guidelines regarding the form and content of initial reports to be submitted by States Parties under article 44, paragraph 1(a), of the Convention, October 30, 1991, CRC/C/5*. Retrieved October 12, 2020, from https://digitallibrary.un.org/record/137523?ln=en

UN Committee on the Rights of the Child. (1994). *Concluding observations: Burkina Faso, April 25, 1994, CRC/C/15/Add.19* (p. 4). Geneva: UN. Retrieved from http://digitallibrary.un.org/record/197675

UN Committee on the Rights of the Child. (1996). *General guidelines regarding the form and contents of periodic reports to be submitted by states parties under article 44, paragraph 1 (b) of the Convention, November 20, 1996, CRC/C/58*. Retrieved October 12, 2020, from https://digitallibrary.un.org/record/230051?ln=en

UN Committee on the Rights of the Child. (1997). *Concluding observations: Algeria, June 18, 1997, CRC/C/15/Add.76* (p. 7). Geneva: UN. Retrieved from http://digitallibrary.un.org/record/241621

UN Committee on the Rights of the Child. (2001). *General Comment No. 1 (2001) Article 29 (1): The Aims of Education, April 17, 2001, CRC/GC/2001/1*. Retrieved October 10, 2020, from https://digitallibrary.un.org/record/447223?ln=en

UN Committee on the Rights of the Child. (2002a). *Concluding observations: Mozambique, April 3, 2002, CRC/C/15/Add.172*. UN. Retrieved November 16, 2020, from http://digitallibrary.un.org/record/467261

UN Committee on the Rights of the Child. (2002b). *Concluding observations: Belgium, June 13, 2002, CRC/C/15/Add.178* (p. 10). Geneva. Retrieved from http://digitallibrary.un.org/record/473481

UN Committee on the Rights of the Child. (2002c). *Day of general discussion: The private sector as a service provider*. UN. Retrieved December 1, 2020, from https://www.ohchr.org/EN/HRBodies/CRC/Pages/DiscussionDays.aspx

UN Committee on the Rights of the Child. (2002d). *Concluding observations: Republic of Moldova, October 31, 2002, CRC/C/15/Add.192*. Geneva: 2002-10-31: UN. Retrieved from http://digitallibrary.un.org/record/481015

UN Committee on the Rights of the Child. (2002e). *General Comment No. 2 (2002) The role of independent national human rights institutions in the promotion and protection of the rights of the child, November 15, 2002, CRC/GC/2002/2*. Retrieved October 12, 2020, from https://digitallibrary.un.org/record/490983?ln=en

UN Committee on the Rights of the Child. (2003a). *General Comment No. 5 (2003) General measures of implementation of the Convention on the Rights of the Child (arts. 4, 42 and 44, para. 6), November 27, 2003, CRC/GC/2003/5*. Retrieved October 12, 2020, from https://digitallibrary.un.org/record/513415?ln=en

UN Committee on the Rights of the Child. (2003b). *Concluding observations: Libya, July 3 2003, CRC/C/15/Add.209* (p. 12). Geneva: 2003-07-04: UN. Retrieved from http://digitallibrary.un.org/record/503092

UN Committee on the Rights of the Child. (2006a). *Concluding observations: Ghana, March 17, 2006, CRC/C/GHA/CO/2*. Geneva: 2006-03-17: UN. Retrieved from http://digitallibrary.un.org/record/575770

UN Committee on the Rights of the Child. (2006b). *Concluding observations: Colombia, June 8, 2006, CRC/C/COL/CO/3*. UN. Retrieved November 15, 2020, from http://digitallibrary.un.org/record/582283

UN Committee on the Rights of the Child. (2015). *Treaty-specific guidelines regarding the form and content of periodic reports to be submitted by States parties under Article 44, paragraph 1 (b), of the Convention on the Rights of the Child, March 3, 2015, CRC/C/58/Rev.3*. UN. Retrieved December 1, 2020, from http://digitallibrary.un.org/record/789762

UN Committee on the Rights of the Child. (2016). *General Comment No. 19 (2016) on public budgeting for the realization of children's rights (art.4), CRC/C/GC/19*. UN. Retrieved November 12, 2020, from http://digitallibrary.un.org/record/838730

UN Human Rights Committee. (1989). *CCPR General Comment No. 18 (1989) Non-discrimination, November 21, 1989, CCPR/C/21/Rev.1/Add.1*. Retrieved from https://digitallibrary.un.org/record/84170?ln=en

Open Access This chapter is licensed under the terms of the Creative Commons Attribution 4.0 International License (http://creativecommons.org/licenses/by/4.0/), which permits use, sharing, adaptation, distribution and reproduction in any medium or format, as long as you give appropriate credit to the original author(s) and the source, provide a link to the Creative Commons license and indicate if changes were made.

The images or other third party material in this chapter are included in the chapter's Creative Commons license, unless indicated otherwise in a credit line to the material. If material is not included in the chapter's Creative Commons license and your intended use is not permitted by statutory regulation or exceeds the permitted use, you will need to obtain permission directly from the copyright holder.

Chapter 42
Articles 42 and 44(6): Making the Convention and States Parties' Compliance Widely Known

Christian Whalen and Gerison Lansdown

> **Article 42**
> States Parties undertake to make the principles and provisions of the Convention widely known, by appropriate and active means, to adults and children alike.
>
> **Article 44(6)**
> States Parties shall make their reports widely available to the public in their own countries.

Overview

These two articles place obligations on States Parties regarding dissemination of information about the Convention. Article 42 demands that both adults and children must be informed about the rights in the Convention and its protocols. Rights holders must have knowledge of their rights and knowledge of how to exercise them if those rights are to be meaningful. Article 44(6) addresses the initial and periodic reports to the Committee on the Rights of the Child (the Committee) that States Parties are required to produce on progress in implementing the Convention and imposes an

C. Whalen (✉)
Office of the Child, Youth and Seniors Advocate, Fredericton, NB, Canada
e-mail: Christian.Whalen@gnb.ca

G. Lansdown
Carleton University, Ottawa, ON, Canada

obligation on States Parties to disseminate the reports widely. The Committee insists that its Concluding Observations be broadly disseminated by States Parties, to inform the public of the responses given by governments and ensure accountability in this regard (2003, para. 73).

In General Comment no. 5, the Committee sets out the principal requirements of States Parties in meeting their obligations under Article 42 and 44(6), together with its rationale. These include ensuring the visibility of children, enhancing respect for them and for democratic institutions, reaffirming the value of their rights, strengthening awareness among adults about children's rights, building accountability, and opening opportunity for debate (2003, paras. 66–73).

General Principles

Article 2 States Parties must make diligent efforts in their dissemination and educational programmes to reach all children (Sedletzki, 2013, p. 67), including marginalised children and youth. Every child, without discrimination on any grounds, has an equal right to knowledge about their rights (UN Committee on the Rights of the Child, 2001, para. 15). States Parties must adopt the necessary measures to ensure that children, including, for example, those who are out of school, street affected children, migrant, refugee, and asylum-seeking children as well as those living in conflict zones, are provided with accessible information on the Convention, including through non-formal and street education (UN Committee on the Rights of the Child, 2017, para. 55). Efforts to advance equality will be seriously diminished if Article 2 is not assiduously respected in the implementation of Article 42. Children cannot challenge discrimination without knowledge and understanding that they have the right to be treated equally and have knowledge of the actions states have taken in this regard.

Article 3 It is in the best interests of every child to know about their rights. States Parties must ensure that their dissemination and educational programmes are designed and delivered in a manner consistent with children's best interests and have their best interests as a primary concern. In addition, children's best interests need to inform the States Parties reports. Dissemination of the reports serves as a powerful accountability mechanism for child rights enforcement.

Article 6 Children are entitled to be informed about their right to life, survival, and development and this overarching principle needs to inform the approach taken to dissemination of the Convention and subsequent reports.

Article 12 The child's right to be heard and to have their opinions considered is critically important in the development of dissemination and educational programmes concerning children's rights. Furthermore, any education or awareness raising, both for children and adults, must include an explicit focus on children's participation rights and how this can be exercised. Children should be actively engaged in every aspect of child rights education programming from the ideation to the design stage right through to program delivery.

The Committee has developed *Working Methods for the Participation of Children in the Reporting Process of the Committee on the Rights of the Child* (2014a). The *Treaty Specific Guidelines* on States Parties reports also invites States Parties to take appropriate measures to consult and include opportunities for child participation both in the preparation of States Parties reports and the dissemination of the Committee's concluding observations.

Articles Related or Linked to Articles 42 and 44(6)

All the other substantive rights set out in the Convention are necessarily linked to Articles 42 and 44(6) because the obligation to educate others about child rights applies specifically with respect to each of those rights. For ease of reference however, only the other procedural rights from part II and the substantive rights in part I having a strong procedural connection to Articles 42 are identified here.[1]

Article 4 establishes the States Parties obligations to take all appropriate measures for full implementation of the rights guaranteed under the Convention.

Article 41 addresses the preservation of other rights guaranteed in other treaties or under domestic law.

Article 43 sets out the composition, role, and functions of the UN Committee on the Rights of the Child.

Article 44 sets out States Parties' obligation to make reports to the Committee on the Rights of the Child regarding the treaty's implementation.

Article 45 provides for international cooperation and establishes the role of UNICEF, UN organs, and others as technical experts in relation to child rights.

Relevant Instruments

International Covenant on Civil and Political Rights (1966), Article 2.

International Covenant on Economic, Social and Cultural Rights (1966), Article 2.

---

[1] For a more complete list of educational priorities related to child rights pursuant to Article 42 please refer to the original guidelines for periodic reports (UN Committee on the Rights of the Child, 1991). A helpful summary is provided in the *Implementation Handbook* (UNICEF, 2007, pp. 630–631).

Attributes

Attribute One: Making the Convention Widely Known

Making both the principles and provisions of the Convention widely known, by appropriate and active means, requires dedicated resources by governments through coordinating mechanisms across government, educational systems, and the work of independent national human rights institutions and specialised institutions for children's rights. It requires cooperation and partnership between all these organizations and with civil society and the private sector (Sedletzki, 2013, p. 70). The Committee has consistently encouraged such measures in its General Comments and its Days of General Discussion (UN Committee on the Protection of the Rights of All Migrant Workers and Members of Their Families and UN Committee on the Rights of the Child, 2017, paras. 52–54; UN Committee on the Rights of the Child, 2016, para. 90, 2017, para. 62).[2] However, the Committee has expressed concern over the continued lack of awareness of rights in many countries around the world.[3] In a global survey of 1600 children on their civil and political rights, a strong message emerged of their demand for better information about their rights (Orr et al., 2016). Without knowledge of rights, it is not possible to exercise them. Accordingly, the Committee has placed special emphasis on incorporating learning about the Convention and human rights in general into the school curriculum at all stages (2003, para. 68).[4]

States Parties should engage the support of local and national media in disseminating information and news related to child rights awareness and education (UN Committee on the Rights of the Child, 2003, para. 70). The dissemination of States Parties reports reinforces education and understanding of children's rights. Furthermore, by learning what measures states have undertaken through the dissemination of their States Parties reports, children and adults will gain an enhanced understanding of their rights and implementation.

Attribute Two: Educating Adults and Children Alike

Child rights efforts will fail if the adults who nurture and care for children are not cognizant of their rights and familiar with their obligations as duty-bearers to children. Therefore, the Convention emphasises the need to educate both children

---

[2] Concluding observations to States Parties regularly reinforce this message on the need for dissemination of child rights information, including the Committee's concluding observations for Hungary (2020a, para. 48) and Austria (2020b, para. 48).

[3] See, for example, concluding observations for Hungary (2014b, paras. 15–16) and Rwanda (2020c, para. 12).

[4] See also Article 29.

and adults about child rights (UN Committee on the Rights of the Child, 2003, para. 66). This education requires knowledge of rights and the extent to which they have or have not been implemented. States Parties need a comprehensive strategy to educate all of society about children's rights, but they need to adapt public education efforts to the distinct audiences based upon age. Child-friendly and youth-friendly versions of the Convention should be widely available in all national languages, in schools and in social media, libraries and online resources (UN Committee on the Rights of the Child, 2003, para. 67).

Pre- and post-training of professionals working with children needs to include the Convention, its implementation, and its implications for their work at all levels. Such training needs to 'emphasize the status of the child as a holder of human rights, to increase knowledge and understanding of the Convention and to encourage active respect for all its provisions' (UN Committee on the Rights of the Child, 2003, para. 53). Training on children's rights should include reference to States Parties reports and Concluding Observations. Specialised child rights training modules should be developed as orientation tools upon recruitment of all staff working directly with children or for children (UNICEF, 2007, pp. 629–630).

References

Orr, K., Emerson, L., Lundy, L., Royal-Dawson, L., & Jimenez, E. (2016). *Enabling the exercise of civil and political rights: The views of children*. Save the Children. Retrieved from https://resourcecentre.savethechildren.net/library/enabling-exercise-civil-and-political-rights-views-children

Sedletzki, V. (2013). *Championing Children's rights: A global study of independent human rights institutions for children*. Innocenti Publications. Retrieved from https://www.unicef-irc.org/publications/701-championing-childrens-rights-a-global-study-of-independent-human-rights-institutions.html

UN Committee on the Protection of the Rights of All Migrant Workers and Members of Their Families & UN Committee on the Rights of the Child. (2017). *Joint General Comment No. 3 (2017) of the Committee on the Protection of the Rights of All Migrant Workers and Members of Their Families and No. 22 (2017) of the Committee on the Rights of the Child on the general principles regarding the human rights of children in the context of international migration, CMW/C/GC/3, CRC/C/GC/22*. UN. Retrieved November 6, 2020, from http://digitallibrary.un.org/record/1323014

UN Committee on the Rights of the Child. (1991). *General guidelines regarding the form and content of initial reports to be submitted by States Parties under article 44, paragraph 1(a), of the Convention, October 30, 1991, CRC/C/5*. Retrieved October 12, 2020, from https://digitallibrary.un.org/record/137523?ln=en

UN Committee on the Rights of the Child. (2001). *General Comment No. 1 (2001) Article 29 (1): The Aims of Education, April 17, 2001, CRC/GC/2001/1*. Retrieved October 10, 2020, from https://digitallibrary.un.org/record/447223?ln=en

UN Committee on the Rights of the Child. (2003). *General Comment No. 5 (2003) General measures of implementation of the Convention on the Rights of the Child (arts. 4, 42 and 44, para. 6), November 27, 2003, CRC/GC/2003/5*. Retrieved October 12, 2020, from https://digitallibrary.un.org/record/513415?ln=en

UN Committee on the Rights of the Child. (2014a). *Working methods for the participation of children in the reporting process of the Committee on the Rights of the Child, CRC/C/66/2*. UN. Retrieved December 1, 2020, from http://digitallibrary.un.org/record/785298

UN Committee on the Rights of the Child. (2014b). *Concluding observations: Hungary, October 14, 2014, CRC/C/HUN/CO/3-5*. Retrieved October 11, 2020, from https://digitallibrary.un.org/record/793888?ln=en

UN Committee on the Rights of the Child. (2016). *General Comment No. 20 (2016) on the implementation of the rights of the child during adolescence, December 6, 2016, CRC/C/GC/20*. Retrieved October 12, 2020, from https://digitallibrary.un.org/record/855544?ln=en

UN Committee on the Rights of the Child. (2017). *General Comment No. 21 (2017) on children in street situations, June 21, 2017, CRC/C/GC/21*. Retrieved October 12, 2020, from https://digitallibrary.un.org/record/1304490?ln=en

UN Committee on the Rights of the Child. (2020a). *Concluding observations: Hungary, March 3, 2020, CRC/C/HUN/CO/6*. Geneva: 2020-03-03: UN. Retrieved from http://digitallibrary.un.org/record/3862647

UN Committee on the Rights of the Child. (2020b). *Concluding observations: Austria, March 6, 2020, CRC/C/AUT/CO/5-6* (p. 12). Geneva: 2020-03-06: UN. Retrieved from http://digitallibrary.un.org/record/3862649

UN Committee on the Rights of the Child. (2020c). *Concluding observations: Rwanda, February 28, 2020, CRC/C/RWA/CO/5-6* (p. 16). Geneva: 2020-02-28: UN. Retrieved from http://digitallibrary.un.org/record/3862645

UNICEF. (2007). *Implementation handbook for the convention on the rights of the child* (3rd ed.). : UNICEF. Retrieved September 21, 2020, from https://digitallibrary.un.org/record/620060?ln=en

Open Access This chapter is licensed under the terms of the Creative Commons Attribution 4.0 International License (http://creativecommons.org/licenses/by/4.0/), which permits use, sharing, adaptation, distribution and reproduction in any medium or format, as long as you give appropriate credit to the original author(s) and the source, provide a link to the Creative Commons license and indicate if changes were made.

The images or other third party material in this chapter are included in the chapter's Creative Commons license, unless indicated otherwise in a credit line to the material. If material is not included in the chapter's Creative Commons license and your intended use is not permitted by statutory regulation or exceeds the permitted use, you will need to obtain permission directly from the copyright holder.

Appendix

Relevant Instruments to the Convention on the Rights of the Child, by Article

Additional Protocol to the American Convention on Human Rights in the area of Economic, Social, and Cultural Rights 'Protocol of San Salvador' (1988)	26, 32
African Charter on Human and Peoples' Rights (1981)	14, 9, 10, 18, 24, 37, 22, 35, 40
African Charter on the Rights and Welfare of the Child (1990)	2, 3, 12, 7, 14, 15, 16, 9, 21, 33, 19, 37, 32, 34, 36, 22, 35, 38, 1, 4
American Convention on Human Rights 'Pact of San Jose, Costa Rica' (B-32) (1978)	2, 7, 14, 15, 16, 17, 9, 10, 18, 24, 26, 34, 36, 22, 35, 40, 7, 4
American Declaration of the Rights and Duties of Man (1948)	26
Charter of Fundamental Rights of the European Union (2000)	14, 32
Council of Europe Convention on Action against Trafficking in Human Beings (2005)	34
Council of Europe Convention on Cybercrime (Budapest Convention) (2001)	34
Council of Europe Convention on preventing and combating violence against women and domestic violence (2011)	34
Council of Europe Convention on the Protection of Children against Sexual Exploitation and Sexual Abuse (2007)	34
Council of Europe Recommendation on deinstitutionalisation and community living of children with disabilities (2010)	20

(continued)

Council of Europe Recommendation on the rights of children living in residential institutions (2005)	20
European Convention on Human Rights (1950)	2, 14, 15, 16, 17, 9, 10, 20, 24, 19, 37, 22, 4
European Convention on Nationality (1997)	11
European Convention on Recognition and Enforcement of Decisions concerning Custody of Children and on Restoration of Custody of Children (1980)	3, 11
European Convention on the Adoption of Children (Revised) (2008)	21
European Convention on the Exercise of Children's Rights (1996)	3, 11
European Social Charter (1961)	24
European Social Charter (Revised) (1996)	26, 32
Guidelines of the Committee of Ministers of the Council of Europe on child friendly justice (2010)	12, 40
Hague Convention on Jurisdiction, Applicable Law, Recognition, Enforcement and Co-operation in Respect of Parental Responsibility and Measures for the Protection of Children (1996)	10, 11, 20
Hague Convention on Protection of Children and Co-operation in Respect of Intercountry Adoption (1993)	3, 10, 21, 34, 36, 22, 35
Hague Convention on the Civil Aspects of International Child Abduction (1980)	11, 36, 35
ILO Convention 102, Social Security (Minimum Standards) (1952)	26
ILO Convention 111, Discrimination (Employment and Occupation) (1958)	2
ILO Convention 138, Minimum Age (1973)	31, 32
ILO Convention 169, Indigenous and Tribal Peoples (1989)	30
ILO Convention 182, Worst Forms of Child Labour (1999)	33, 31, 32, 34, 36, 35, 38
ILO Convention 79, Night Work of Young Persons (Non-Industrial Occupations) (1946)	31
ILO Convention 87, Freedom of Association and Protection of the Right to Organise Convention (1948)	15
ILO Convention 90, Night Work of Young Persons (Industry) (Revised) (1948)	31
ILO Convention 98, Right to Organise and Collective Bargaining Convention (1949)	15
ILO Declaration on Fundamental Principles and Rights at Work (1998)	32

(continued)

ILO Recommendation 146, Minimum Age (1973)	32
ILO Recommendation 190, Worst Forms of Child Labour (1999)	32
Inter-American Convention on Conflict of Laws Concerning the Adoption of Minors (1984)	21
Inter-American Convention on International Traffic in Minors (1994)	19, 34, 36, 35
Inter-American Convention on the International Return of Children (1989)	11, 19
Protocol to the African Charter on Human and Peoples' Rights on the Rights of Women in Africa (2003)	7
Recommendation of the Committee of Ministers of the Council of Europe on the participation of children and young people under the age of 18 (2012)	12
Rome Statute of International Criminal Court (1998)	34, 38
Social Charter of the Americas (2012)	24
Geneva convention for the amelioration of the condition of the wounded and sick in armed forces in the field (1949)	10, 37, 22, 38
UN Convention against Discrimination in Education (1960)	2, 14, 28, 29
UN Convention against Illicit Traffic in Narcotic Drugs and Psychotropic Substances (1988)	33
UN Convention against Torture and Other Cruel, Inhuman or Degrading Treatment or Punishment (1984)	22, 25, 29, 19, 37, 4
UN Convention on Psychotropic Substances (1971)	33
UN Convention on Technical and Vocational Education (1989)	28, 29
UN Convention on the Elimination of All Forms of Discrimination against Women (1979)	2, 3, 7, 15, 5, 18, 25, 24, 26, 28, 29, 31, 34, 4
International Convention on the Elimination of All Forms of Racial Discrimination (1966)	2, 7, 13, 14, 25, 24, 28, 29, 4
UN Convention on the Prohibition of the Use, Stockpiling, Production and Transfer of Anti-Personnel Mines and on their Destruction (Ottawa Convention or the Anti-Personnel Mine Ban Treaty) (1997)	38
UN Convention on the Reduction of Statelessness (1961)	10, 22

(continued)

UN Convention on the Rights of Persons with Disabilities (2006)	2, 3, 6, 7, 12, 13, 15, 17, 5, 9, 18, 20, 25, 23, 24, 28, 29, 4
UN Convention Relating to the Status of Refugees (1951)	10, 20, 28, 19, 22
UN Convention relating to the Status of Stateless Persons (1954)	10, 22
UN Declaration of the Rights of the Child (1959)	3, 9, 10, 24, 28, 31, 38,
UN Declaration on Social and Legal Principles relating to the Protection and Welfare of Children, with special reference to Foster Placement and Adoption Nationally and Internationally (1987)	20, 21
UN Declaration on the Protection of Women and Children in Emergency and Armed Conflict (1974)	38
UN Declaration on the Rights of Disabled Persons (1975)	23, 28
UN Declaration on the Rights of Indigenous Peoples (2007)	30, 19
UN Declaration on the Rights of Mentally Retarded Persons (1971)	23
UN Declaration on the Rights of Persons Belonging to National or Ethnic Religious and Linguistic Minorities (1992)	28
UN Guidelines for the Alternative Care of Children (2009)	9, 20, 19
UN Guidelines for the Prevention of Juvenile Delinquency (Riyadh Guidelines) (1990)	19, 37, 40
UN Guidelines on Justice in Matters involving Child Victims and Witnesses of Crime (2005)	19
UN International Convention for the Protection of All Persons from Enforced Disappearance (2007)	7, 8
International Convention on the Protection of the Rights of All Migrant Workers and Members of Their Families (1990)	7, 14, 18, 25, 26, 28, 30, 39, 4
International Covenant on Civil and Political Rights (1966)	2, 6, 7, 12, 13, 14, 15, 16, 17, 5, 9, 10, 11, 18, 25, 24, 33, 29, 30, 19, 37, 32, 34, 22, 38, 40, 1, 4, 42/46
International Covenant on Economic, Social and Cultural Rights (1966)	2, 14, 5, 9, 10, 11, 18, 20, 24, 26, 27, 33, 28, 29, 31, 32, 34, 4, 42/46
UN Protocol Relating to the Status of Refugees (1967)	10, 22
UN Protocol to Prevent, Suppress and Punish Trafficking in Persons Especially Women and Children, supplementing the United Nations Convention against Transnational Organized Crime (2000)	39, 34, 36, 22, 35

(continued)

UN Rules for the Protection of Juveniles Deprived of their Liberty (Havana Rules) (1990)	19, 37, 40
UN Single Convention on Narcotic Drugs (1961)	33
UN Standard Minimum Rules for Non-custodial Measures (The Tokyo Rules) (1990)	40
UN Standard Minimum Rules for the Administration of Juvenile Justice (Beijing Rules) (1985)	19, 37, 40
UN Standard Rules on the Equalization of Opportunities for Persons with Disabilities (1993)	23
UN Universal Declaration of Human Rights (1948)	2, 6, 7, 13, 14, 15, 16, 17, 5, 9, 18, 25, 23, 26, 27, 28, 31, 32, 34
UN World Programme of Action concerning Disabled Persons (1982)	23
UNESCO Convention on the Protection and Promotion of the Diversity of Cultural Expressions (2005)	29
UNESCO Declaration of Principles on Tolerance (1995)	29
UNESCO Mexico City Declaration on Cultural Policies (1982)	31
UNESCO Recommendation concerning Education for International Understanding, Co-operation and Peace and Education relating to Human Rights and Fundamental Freedoms (1974)	29
UNHCR Guidelines on International Protection No. 8: Child Asylum Claims under Articles 1(A)2 and 1(F) of the 1951 Convention and/or 1967 Protocol relating to the Status of Refugees (2009)	22
UNHCR Inter-agency Guiding Principles on Unaccompanied and Separated Children (2004)	22
UNHCR Refugee Children: Guidelines on Protection and Care (1994)	22
UNICEF Principles and guidelines on children associated with armed forces or armed groups (Paris principles) (2007)	38
WHO Framework Convention on Tobacco Control (2005)	33

Ingram Content Group UK Ltd.
Milton Keynes UK
UKHW020135050723
424579UK00003B/231